wrestling with the

BARBARA FOLEY

Duke University Press · Durham and London 2010

WRESTLING WITH THE LEFT

The Making of

Ralph Ellison's

Invisible Man

© 2010 Duke University Press

All rights reserved

Printed in the United States

of America on acid-free paper ∞

Designed by Amy Ruth Buchanan

Typeset in Iowan Oldstyle

by Tseng Information Systems, Inc.

Library of Congress Cataloging-

in-Publication Data appear on the

last printed page of this book.

To the two Peters

contents

acknowledgments

This book has been in the making for many years during which I have accrued debts to many friends, colleagues, and comrades. Apologizing for the impersonality of this alphabetical listing, I wish to thank the following people: Jonathan Auerbach; Sterling Bland; Patricia Carter; Neil Chesanow; Brian Dolinar; Kathy Fischer; Peter Foley; H. Bruce Franklin; Grover Furr; Peter Gardner; Donald Gibson; Laura Gray-Rosendale; Rodney Green; Gerald Horne; David Hoddeson; Lawrence Jackson; David Laibman; William Maxwell; Gregory Meyerson; Bill Mullen; Joseph Ramsey; Dick Reavis; Brian Roberts; James Smethurst; Adam Stevens; Houston Stevens; Margaret Stevens; Virginia Tiger; Alan Wald; Fengzhen Wang; Mary Helen Washington.

Various groups of people have stimulated my thinking about Ellison in particular and twentieth-century culture, politics and history in general: fellow-members of the Marxist Literary Group; colleagues on the manuscript collective at *Science & Society*; the students in my classes at Rutgers University-Newark.

I am especially grateful to two scholars who helped bring this study to fruition. John F. Callahan, literary executor of the Ellison estate, gave me access to a number of restricted texts as well as permission to quote extensively from the Ellison papers. Without his generous consent, this book would not have been possible. Arnold Rampersad allowed me to see a pre-publication copy of his *Ralph Ellison: A Biography*, thereby eliminating the nine months I would have had to wait to read his invaluable biography.

Reynolds Smith of the Duke University Press has been kind and patient during the long gestation of this study; Sharon Torian and Neal McTighe have been consistently affable, competent, and efficient throughout the production process.

Various forms of prose texts by Ralph Ellison are cited in this work, some transcribed from handwritten drafts, others from typescripts at various stages of completion. The misspellings that occur in these texts have been for the most part retained; "[*sic*]" has been used sparingly. In cases where meaning is hard to discern at first glance, but unambiguous, entire words have been replaced by bracketed corrections. In cases where Ellison's intention is not entirely clear, the misspelled word has been reproduced, along with a bracketed respelling followed by a question mark.

Reading Forward to *Invisible Man*

The Promethean instinct
will reappear in Negro life.
—Ralph Ellison,
unpublished correspondence,
Negro Quarterly, c. 1942

With its unsympathetic treatment of the left, caricature of black nationalism, embrace of existential ambivalence, and closing assertion of vital center patriotism—characteristics that contributed to its winning the National Book Award—Ralph Ellison's *Invisible Man* (1952) bears many traces of its early cold war origins. Although most critics and teachers, acting on Ellison's frequent warnings that *Invisible Man* is neither political allegory nor autobiography, have viewed the novel as only loosely aligned with twentieth-century historical and political movements, they have for the most part accepted the premise that the invisible man's negative experiences with the Brotherhood faithfully replicate typical features of U.S. Communism. Even critics otherwise opposed to doctrines of literary reflection routinely assume that Ellison got it right about the left. Especially when read in conjunction with other cold war–era African American texts—novels like Chester Himes's *Lonely Crusade* (1947), autobiographies like Richard Wright's *Black Boy (American Hunger)* (1993), and political histories like Harold Cruse's *The Crisis of the Negro Intellectual: A Historical Analysis of the Failure of Black Leadership* (1967)—Ellison's novel has functioned over the years as Exhibit A for the case that Communism is antithetical to the interests of Americans in general and African Americans in particular. Widely taught in both high schools and colleges, adjudged one of the most important novels of the twentieth century, and situated at the hub of a veritable critical industry in the twenty-first, *Invisible Man* is routinely read through critical and historical lenses that the novel itself played no small role in creating. I aim to befog those lenses by demonstrating that Ellison's masterwork emerged only after a protracted, and torturous, wrestling down of his former political radicalism.[1]

Ellison's publishers did their best, when *Invisible Man* first appeared, to efface traces of the author's earlier connections with radical publications and organizations. The dust-jacket biography of the Random House edition featured Ellison's early studies in music and sculpture; his work experience in a factory, for a psychologist, and as a freelance photographer; his service in the merchant marine during the Second World War; and his lectures on American literature at New York University and Bennington College. Nothing was said, however, of the approximately three dozen pieces of left-wing fiction and reportage he had produced before 1946. In a *New York Times* profile published in 1952, the columnist Harvey Breit made no mention of Ellison's publications in *New Challenge, New Masses, Direction, Tomorrow, Negro Quarterly, Negro Story, Common Ground,* or other left or left-affiliated organs, listing only a small handful of appearances in safer venues like *American Writing* and *Cross-Section.* The biographical sketch accompanying the *Saturday Review*'s greeting of *Invisible Man* effaced Richard Wright from Ellison's background, claiming—in a trend that Ellison would encourage over the years—T. S. Eliot as the dominant influence on the young novelist. The flurry of second-round reviews accompanying Ellison's reception of the National Book Award compounded the portrait of the artist as political innocent. The handful of angry and dismissive reviews of *Invisible Man* appearing in leftist publications, revealing the bile of not just antagonists but former associates, was buried in the historical cellar of the early cold war.[2]

In the years following the publication of *Invisible Man* Ellison customarily disparaged the left but remained evasive regarding the novel's relationship to his own political history. In an interchange with Irving Howe about Negro writers and politics in 1963 he remarked that it was "awful" that Wright had "found the facile answers of Marxism before he learned to use literature as a means for discovering the forms of American Negro humanity." In the preface to *Shadow and Act* Ellison claimed that he had himself "soon rejected . . . Marxist political theory." He had been, he claimed in 1971, a "true outsider" of the left. In his introduction to the thirtieth-anniversary reissue of the novel he acknowledged his youthful participation in the Scottsboro and Angelo Herndon defenses, support for the Loyalists during the Spanish Civil War, and protests against discriminatory hiring along 125th Street, but implied that he had been situated at the periphery rather than the core of these left-led mass activities. Writing to the Wright biographer Michel Fabre in 1982, Ellison claimed that his political outlook had always been "a product

of [his] own grappling" and had "emphasized the Negroes' rather than the
workers' point of view. . . . There was no way for me to accept the Communist notion that workers and Negroes were unite[d] without a large dose of
salts."[3]

On rare occasions Ellison implied a somewhat fuller past involvement
in left politics. In a 1965 interview he admitted to having "gone through the
political madness that marked the intellectual experience of the thirties" and
articulated a critique of the Communist Party (CP) that corresponds quite
closely with the depiction of Brotherhood perfidy in *Invisible Man*:

> If I were to write an account of the swings and twitches of the U.S. Com-
> munist line during the thirties and forties, it would be a very revealing ac-
> count, but I wouldn't attempt to do this in terms of fiction. It would have
> to be done in terms of political science, reportage. You would have to look
> up their positions, chart their moves, look at the directives handed down
> by the Communist International—whatever the overall body was called.
> And you would be in a muck and a mire of dead and futile activity—
> much of which had little to do with their ultimate goals or with American
> reality. They fostered the myth that communism was twentieth-century
> Americanism, but to be a twentieth-century American meant, in their
> thinking, that you had to be more Russian than American and less Negro
> than either. That's how they lost the Negroes. The communists recog-
> nized no plurality of interests and were really responding to the necessi-
> ties of Soviet foreign policy, and when the war came, Negroes got caught
> and were made expedient in the shifting of policy.

Ellison's claim not to know the precise name of the Communist International implies only a vague acquaintance with leftist centers of power, while
his demurral—"I wouldn't attempt to do this in fiction"—signals that *Invisible Man* is not to be read as a historically grounded account of the Communist myth- and policymaking he pejoratively describes. Yet his assertion
that all the same he could write a "very revealing account" of the "swings
and twitches of the U.S. Communist line during the thirties and forties" suggests that he had hardly been an outsider to the left. Ellison purports to have
studied leftist politics from a safe distance, close enough to have felt the heat
but not so close as to have been burned.[4]

While Ellison was welcomed with open arms by the mainstream white literary establishment, for more than two decades he and his novel were viewed
with considerable skepticism in the black literary world, where he was frequently scorned for his depoliticized existentialism, Eurocentric notion of

universality, and elitist detachment from the struggle in the streets. Even though a number of Ellison's African American critics were familiar with his earlier association with the left, however, they tended to omit this information from their polemics. Before Ellison's death in 1994 critical commentary on *Invisible Man* across the spectrum was almost completely silent about his former political radicalism, even though his early writings had been in the public domain and his correspondence with Wright—documenting both men's intimate and complex relationship with the Communist Party—had long been available to researchers at Yale University's Beinecke Library.[5]

Since 1994 it has been more difficult to accept at face value Ellison's claim to marginality in his former relation to the left. The publication in 1996 of *Flying Home and Other Stories*, which included a number of short stories unpublished in Ellison's lifetime, revealed him to have been a committed (and skilled) writer of proletarian fiction in his apprentice years. In 1999 there appeared in *The New Republic* some tantalizing excerpts from letters written in 1937 by Ellison to his mother in which the young man declared his fervent hope that Soviet-style socialism would be instituted in the United States. Lawrence Jackson's *Ralph Ellison: The Emergence of Genius* (2002), which ends with the publication of *Invisible Man*, thoroughly documents the young Ellison's several years of intense involvement with left-wing politics and political organization. Arnold Rampersad, in his definitive *Ralph Ellison: A Biography* (2007), demonstrates that Ellison was a figure of considerable significance in leftist literary circles before he repudiated his radical connections and, after the publication of *Invisible Man*, joined the Congress for Cultural Freedom and became a solid member of the cold war–era New York literary establishment.[6]

The record of Ellison's early leftism as a writer remains largely incomplete, however, because the vast archive of his unpublished short stories, novel outlines, journalism, and drafts and notes to *Invisible Man* to this point remains unexamined, both as a body of material of interest in its own right and as the vital back story to the novel. As a result most critical commentary on Ellison's oeuvre, with a few notable exceptions, remains premised on the same old narrative. To the extent that it matters at all, the story goes, Ellison's leftist commitment was an early one, reflecting the idealistic enthusiasm of youth, the urgency of the Depression and wartime years, and the appeal of the Communist-led cultural movement before it revealed its political and artistic limitations (or, in harsher assessments, its Stalinist essence). *Invisible Man* is read as testimony to Ellison's maturation; the novel's repudia-

tion of leftist authoritarianism and scientism and its embrace of democratic
pluralism and epistemological ambivalence exhibit not just its protagonist's
development from ranter to writer, but the increasing sophistication of the
text's creator as well. Even as revisionary accounts of the cold war era have
reconfigured, at least to a degree, the history of U.S. Communism in relation to antiracist and workers' movements, literary critics continue to read
Invisible Man backward from the standpoint of an abidingly anticommunist
discourse that is all the more difficult to track for its having invisibly entered
the groundwater of U.S. cultural history. That this discourse is invoked in
otherwise incompatible approaches to the novel—ranging from performa-
tive readings of its deconstructive indeterminacy to foundationalist readings
of its celebratory democratic individualism—tells a good deal about the ideologies shaping the political unconscious of much contemporary criticism
and theory.[7]

To no small degree Ellison assisted his critics' proclivity to read the novel
from the perspective of cold war ideology by developing in his own post–
Invisible Man oeuvre a lexicon for analyzing not only American culture and
society at large but also, and perhaps especially, his own novel. The avail-
ability of this body of "god-terms" (Kenneth Burke's designation of analytical categories possessing unquestionable authority) has enabled, indeed
pressured, critics to examine the novel from the vantage point that the author fully codified only after its publication. Starting with his acceptance
speech at the National Book Award ceremony in 1953, Ellison proposed that
the "experimental form" of his novel, departing from the "final and unre-
lieved despair" of "narrow naturalism," reflected the "rich diversity and
. . . almost magical fluidity . . . [of] America." Following in the tradition of
nineteenth-century forebears who had been "willing to confront the broad
complexities of American life" and to view "the Negro . . . [as] the gauge of
the human condition as it waxed and waned in our democracy," *Invisible Man*
sought to "[confront] the inequalities and brutalities of our society forth-
rightly," while still "thrusting forth its images of hope, human fraternity, and
individual self-realization." The task of the American novelist, Ellison concluded, was to grapple, as had Odysseus, with the shape-changing god Proteus, who "stands for both America and the inheritance of illusion through
which all men must fight to achieve reality." Only by extracting the "truth"
from the "mad, vari-implicated chaos" of American life, asserted the exuber-
ant Ellison, can the writer complete his odyssey toward "that condition of
being at home in the world, which is called love, and which we term democ-

racy." Melding artistic experimentalism with political pluralism, Ellison situated his novel as an exemplary modernist extension of the grand tradition of American letters.[8]

Ellison subsequently expanded on a number of key terms in his National Book Award speech and added others. "Complexity," his favorite term, would come to signify the binary opposite of reductionism, whether leftism in politics, naturalism in writing, or sociology in the study of human beings. Implying a root connection between epistemology and politics, "fluidity" would describe not only the imperviousness of reality to logical categorization but also the fundamental classlessness of American society. "Chaos" would denote the existential void threatening to engulf those courageous enough to explore complexity and fluidity. "Democracy" would designate the "rock" of "sacred principles," the "articles of faith" binding the nation and enabling the writer to steer clear of the abyss of chaos. "Diversity" would signify both the premise and the achievement of American democracy, "frequently burdensome and always a source of conflict, but in it . . . our fate and our hope." "Discipline" would point to both African American stoicism in the face of slavery and Jim Crow and, along with "technique," the careful craft required of the writer confronting the "mysterious possibilities generated by our unity within diversity and our freedom within unfreedom." "Ritual," with its cognates "sacrifice" and "scapegoat," would allude to the means by which societies achieve consensus. "Underground," often coupled with "consciousness, subconsciousness and conscience," would designate the peculiar status of the Negro as both the repressed other of the national psyche and the means to national redemption. Often cited in conjunction with the epilogue of *Invisible Man*, where early variants of several of these words and phrases direct the narrator's backward glance over his life, this handy tool kit of "god-terms" has routinely been deployed by critics parsing the novel. Despite the stated commitment to pluralism informing the lexicon, it has often functioned in a highly "discipline-ary" manner, enforcing multiple rules and restrictions on readers' engagement with Ellison's oeuvre, especially the novel.[9]

I depart from the circular practice of reading *Invisible Man* through the palimpsest supplied by Ellison's writings after 1952 and, more generally, by the cold war narrative that abidingly shapes most discussion of American writers—especially African American writers—and the left. Drawing upon an examination of the multiple drafts, outlines, and notes for the novel, as well as Ellison's early journalism and fiction, I read forward to *Invisible Man*. I view that novel not as a well-wrought urn awaiting exegesis through the

critical categories that presumably guided Ellison's shaping hand, but as a
conflicted and contradictory text bearing multiple traces of his struggle to repress and then abolish the ghost of his leftist consciousness and conscience.
Ellison might retrospectively describe the composition of *Invisible Man* as a
struggle with Proteus, the shape-changing god of the sea who challenges
Odysseus as he seeks to find his way home. But before Proteus Ellison's
favored mythological figure was the rebellious titan Prometheus, designated
the "patron saint of the proletariat" in the discourse of the Popular Frontist cultural left, who stole fire from the Olympian gods to enable humanity
to conquer nature on its own. Ellison's early writings, both published and
unpublished, testify not just to his radical political beliefs, in particular his
attraction to the figure of the African American Communist as Promethean
hero, but also to his reliance on Marxist categories of historical and political
analysis. In the published novel the invisible man refers to history as a boomerang (or, alternatively, a gambler) and warns off his readers from those
who claim that history is a spiral. But Ellison's early writings view freedom
as the recognition of necessity, ask continually "What is to be done?," and
endorse the dialectical view of history illustrated by Engels's famous spiral
analogy. In abandoning Marxism Ellison abandoned both a passion and a
paradigm.

I treat *Invisible Man* from the standpoint of the many decisions that went
into its making rather than as the product that resulted from those decisions, seemingly inevitable once enclosed between covers. The novel's narrator asserts that "the end is in the beginning," and the text's apparently
seamless symbolic patterning suggests that the major rhetorical strategies
deployed in *Invisible Man* were from the outset neatly ordered in the novelist's mind. The homologous character structures of the text's antagonists —
showing Jim Crow racists, Uncle Tom apologists, Wall Street capitalists,
blood-thinking black nationalists, and authoritarian Communists all enacting the governing ritual of the battle royal — were largely imposed a posteriori. Indeed Ellison contemplated organizing his novel around clustered
symbols and character systems possessing substantially different ideological inflections than those informing the text. Moreover the movement from
purpose through *passion* to *perception* — the Burkean patterning that famously
underlies the invisible man's blundering toward insight, within individual
episodes as well as in the arc of the narrative as a whole — was by no means
mapped out in advance. The political revelations that constituted *perception*
would undergo particular reformulation. The familiar ending of *Invisible Man*
was in fact nowhere in view when, in July 1945, Ellison sat in the doorway

of a barn in Waitsfield, Vermont, and penned the words, "I am an invisible man." During the next seven years of writing, rewriting, and re-rewriting Ellison expunged multiple characters and incidents conveying a radical, even in places pro-Communist politics.

This process of anticommunist-ization entailed far more, however, than canceling, supplementing, and reconfiguring the portraits of characters associated with the Brotherhood. While retaining the atmosphere of the Great Depression, Ellison effaced from the published text all references to international and domestic fascism, left-led union organizing, and, above all, the Second World War, gradually replacing these with materials that would depoliticize the novel's historical context and facilitate its critique of the left. Even though he had distanced himself from Communist organizations and publications by mid-1943, and by mid-1945 was expressing vehemently anti-Communist views, it would take Ellison several years to relinquish the analytical categories through which he had previously understood the world and to substitute new ones in their place. Although he would write to his friend Albert Murray that his main problem in finishing the novel was a formal one—handling "transitions"—his multiple rewritings of the novel testify above all to his struggle to tame his radical materials and bring them into alignment with a far more conservative worldview. Prometheus was not to be easily wrestled down.[10]

The paradigm shift taking place within Ellison's text was accompanied, at once enabled and driven, by the paradigm shift taking place in the novel's audience: both the implied and the historical readers to whom, and above all *for* whom, the invisible man offers to speak on the lower frequencies in the novel's ringing finale. When Ellison began work on his novel in 1945, sympathy with leftist causes was fairly widespread. Joseph Stalin had been *Time* magazine's Man of the Year twice during the war, and memories of the Grand Alliance remained strong even after Winston Churchill proclaimed the lowering of the Iron Curtain. Postwar rebellions against colonial regimes all around the globe indicated that the antifascist war had generated irreversible changes; a "better world" for many of the world's inhabitants of color was in the making. Throughout the United States a massive wave of postwar strikes, deferred by the wartime no-strike pledge, strengthened the hand of organized labor. In New York City, where Ellison would write almost all of *Invisible Man*, Harlem's Communist councilman Benjamin J. Davis Jr. was reelected in 1945 with the second largest percentage of votes in the city's history. In 1946 the city saw its largest May Day march ever, and the wartime antiracist agitation for jobs and justice turned into a vigorous postwar

movement for civil rights. As late as April 1949 some twenty-eight hundred
prominent artists and intellectuals, including a delegation from the USSR,
participated in the Cultural and Scientific Conference for World Peace at the
Waldorf-Astoria, suggesting the continuing vitality of the left-led cultural
front. In the postwar years many potential and actual readers of novels, radicalized during the 1930s and 1940s, were not readily inclined to exclude leftists from the rubric of universal humanity; they could not be interpellated,
that is, hailed and recognized, as anti-Communist, much less anticommunist.[11]

By 1952, however, there had come into being a substantial anticommunist readership, one able and willing to take part in cold war fictional rites
of consensus. Not only had the U.S. government witch hunt of leftists entailed a massive campaign of repression and intimidation, including the assault on Paul Robeson and other antiracists at a peaceful picnic at Peekskill,
New York; the handcuffing and arrest of the eighty-three-year-old W. E. B.
Du Bois as an "unregistered foreign agent"; the deportation of the National
Maritime Union leader Ferdinand Smith; and the expulsion of Ben Davis
from New York's City Council (and his eventual imprisonment under the
Smith Act). The peacetime trial and conviction of Ethel and Julius Rosen-
berg for alleged wartime treason reminded the population at large of the
need for continuing vigilance against the enemy within, usefully coded as
Jewish and Communist. Ex-Communist memoirs such as Louis Budenz's
Men without Faces: The Communist Conspiracy in the U.S.A. (1950) and the recan-
tations gathered in Richard Crossman's *The God That Failed* (1950) testified
to the psychic self-betrayal entailed by commitment to red organizations.
Arthur Schlesinger Jr.'s *The Vital Center: The Politics of Freedom* (1949) and Eric
Hoffer's *The True Believer: Thoughts on the Nature of Mass Movements* (1951) represented Communists as dogmatists fearful of doubt and ambiguity; the thesis
that Communists shared these features with their fascist counterparts was
argued by Hannah Arendt in *The Origins of Totalitarianism* (1951). *Red Channels*, with its signature icon of a red-gloved hand brandishing a microphone,
warned Americans of the omnipresence of Russian spy faces and voices in
the mass media; the movie *I Was a Communist for the FBI*, nominated for an
Oscar as best feature-length documentary in 1951, displayed the inhumanity
of reds, even as husbands and lovers, and urged viewers to hand over the
subversives in their midst.[12]

That this barrage of propaganda was directed as much toward its working-
class listeners and viewers as toward its targeted victims went largely unnoticed. Even as thousands of reds, disproportionately immigrants and

workers of color, lost their jobs and in some cases their lives in the postwar attack on the CIO unions, social scientists were proclaiming the class
struggle a chimera. As David Riesman asserted, "[The] distribution of power
in America [is] . . . amorphous . . . situational and mercurial. . . . Ruling-class
theories, applied to contemporary America, seem to be spectral survivals
of [an] earlier time." As the long boom got under way the new rites of consensus required the expulsion of those members of the tribe still embracing
such spectral survivals and identifying with their dispossessed counterparts
around the globe. The universalism experienced by the cultural audience
emerging in the early years of the cold war was largely premised upon the
scapegoating of Communists, now recognized, through the logic of guilt by
association, as foreign agents invading the body politic. Just as Ben Davis
would no longer stand for the people of Harlem, leftist characters in fiction
would no longer stand for shared human values. *Invisible Man* both emerged
from and contributed to this discursive ejection of reds from the circle of
humanity.[13]

John Callahan, the executor of the Ellison literary estate, compiler of *Juneteenth*, and editor of various editions of Ellison's works, has written, "Before going through [Ellison's] papers, I would never have guessed that they
would provide enough clues for someone to write a biography tracking the
making of *Invisible Man*." *Wrestling with the Left* is — at least aspires to be — that
biography. As a biography of a text it draws primarily on other texts, many
of them unpublished; while Ellison's experiences supply a necessary context,
my principal focus here is not on the life but on the oeuvre: the early journalism, literary criticism, short stories, and especially the drafts and notes
of *Invisible Man*. The present-participle formulation of each of the chapter
titles emphasizes process: Ellison is viewed in a continuing present as he
grapples with his developing project, rather than from a retrospective standpoint from which the end of his odyssey is always already known.[14]

Part I comprises three chapters focusing on Ellison's pre-*Invisible Man*
writings. Chapter 1, "Forming a Politics," examines journalistic and nonfic-
tional texts, published and unpublished, including work that Ellison produced for the Federal Writers Project, articles and reviews published in the
New Masses and other journals of the left, writings composed at his desk at
Negro Quarterly, fragments and meditations from his notebooks, and correspondence with a range of friends, most notably Richard Wright. In these
documents Ellison addressed such matters as capitalism and socialism; fas-

cism and antifascism; Negro nationalism, American nationalism, and proletarian internationalism; Negro migration; democracy; the meaning of victory in the Second World War; and, directly or indirectly, the Communist
Party. As he worked out his views he initially attached distinct meanings to
various concepts, including "discipline," "fluidity," and "sacrifice," that would
later receive very different inflection as "god-terms." Ellison for several years
adhered to Party positions on "the Negro question," the nature of fascism,
the relationship of democracy to socialism, and the changing character of
the war between 1939–41 and 1941–45. During the war, however, he became
increasingly critical, in some respects from the left, of the Party's subordination of antiracist and working-class demands to the need for national unity;
by mid-1945 he was expressing disgust with the Party for its wartime opportunism. All the same, as late as 1948, when he was halfway through the writing of *Invisible Man*, Ellison asserted the necessity to reject red-baiting and
continued to adhere to key aspects of Marxism; it would take him some time
to assume the mantle of a cold warrior. Throughout this chapter I situate
Ellison's relationship with the left, in both its conjunctive and its conflicted
phases, within a critical analysis of the contradictions informing the theory
and practice of the CP-led movement between the late 1930s and the beginnings of the cold war.

Chapter 2, "Developing an Aesthetic," focuses on the theory of representation that guided Ellison's maturing ideas about what literature could and
should be and do. Starting with his first book review in 1938, the young Ellison, a rigorous Marxist strongly influenced by the example of Wright as both
critic and creative writer, initially evaluated literature primarily in terms of
the adequacy of its realism and the partisanship of its politics. Increasingly
interested in the role of universals in effecting literary communication but
seeking heroes embodying class consciousness, he explored Negro American folklore, especially broad figures like the mythic worker-hero John
Henry, in relation to transcultural archetypes of the Promethean hero found
in the comparative folklore of Stanley Edgar Hyman and in the myth and
ritual doctrines of the Cambridge School of Classical Anthropology. Preoccupied, like other radicals of his time, with the phenomenon of fascism,
both Hitlerism and its Jim Crow variant, Ellison explored the connections
between Marx and Freud; aware that language and ideology were inextri-
cably intertwined, he examined the rhetorical theory of the leftist cultural
critic Kenneth Burke, who posited that "equations," "associational clusters,"
and other devices function to impose ideologically saturated systems of assumptions upon the readers of texts. While Ellison's engagement with myth,

folklore, psychology, and Burkean symbolic action are generally viewed as manifestations of a retreat from politics and history, embrace of formalism, and absorption of African American experience into Eurocentric mythology, this interest was originally fostered in contexts supplied by the *New Masses* and the League of American Writers. Here, in his words, "myth, ritual, and revolution were slammed around" and Negro folklore was viewed as the expression of an oppositional, at times revolutionary political consciousness. The hegemony of New Criticism, involving formalist close reading without attention to historical and ideological context, and of myth-and-symbol archetypalism, entailing the assimilation of literary works to transhistorical psychological and aesthetic universals, was yet to come.[15]

In chapter 3, "Writing from the Left," I examine Ellison's substantial body of early fiction, much of it unpublished to this day. The same movement from proletarian realism to a more experimental method that is perceptible in his analytical writings is visible in his short stories as well. A good deal of this material is unabashedly revolutionary, featuring class struggle north and south, linking class exploitation with racial oppression, and invoking the international movement against fascism as surrounding ethical context. Partial drafts of stories with African American Communist protagonists show Ellison assessing reds very differently than he does in the published text of *Invisible Man*. The chapter ends with a glance at several character sketches and plot outlines for novels that relate suggestively to that novel. These early fictional works reveal that a number of symbolic motifs and dramatic structures prominent in *Invisible Man*—the figure of the sacrificial scapegoat, patterns of initiation and rebirth, the movement through *agon* to *peripeteia*—guided Ellison's imagination in his Marxist days. He did not need to abandon the left in order to explore the relevance of Greek tragedy and comparative anthropology to the experiences of African American workers and radicals. Indeed the figure of Prometheus was his preferred embodiment of revolutionary energies linking radicals of the present with the red line of history.

Part II reads forward through the drafts and plot outlines of *Invisible Man*. Featured in the scrutiny of these materials are fully dramatized episodes and chapters that went through several drafts but were dropped from the final version; narrative segments that were retained but revised, often substantially, in the published text; and notes and jottings sketching out possible plot developments that Ellison never fleshed out in narration or dialogue. Taken together these scattered unpublished materials indicate the very different novel that Ellison might have written, indeed started to write.

In chapters 4 and 5 I examine the portions of the novel treating the protagonist's pre-Brotherhood days. Chapter 4, "Living Jim Crow," introduces Ellison's early outlines for the entire novel and focuses on the section of the novel set in the South. Featured here is Ellison's original inclusion of materials relating to lynch violence and sharecropper union organizing, which significantly reconfigure the portrayal of the college, the Norton-Trueblood encounter, and the maddened vets in the Golden Day. Featuring issues relating to class struggle and political economy, the early drafts of the southern section also emphasize motifs relating to ritual and myth; Eliot's hanged man, in fact, makes a startling appearance in the figure of a lynched sharecropper. Notable too in these draft versions of the novel's opening chapters is a considerably more daring treatment of sex and sexuality, including homosexuality as a reaction to Jim Crow, than appears in the published text. Ellison's drawing more fully upon Marx did not preclude, indeed if anything encouraged, a more intense engagement with Freud.

In chapter 5, "Becoming Proletarian," I examine Ellison's changing representation of the invisible man's migrant odyssey from neofeudalism to modernity. Emphasized here are various episodes, omitted from the novel, that expand upon the protagonist's experiences as a worker; his invisibility in no small part derives from his absorption into the market for abstract labor in the industrial North. Also at work in the draft chapters delineating his migrant experiences is a pronounced antipatriotic trope that would be significantly etiolated, although not entirely expunged, in the final draft. Of greatest interest is the early text's portrayal of the class-conscious inhabitants of Mary Rambo's Harlem boardinghouse, in particular the figure of LeRoy, a young organic intellectual and maritime union activist, recently murdered at sea, who has left behind a journal full of radical meditations. He is the source of the phrases "more human" and "dedicated and set aside" whose provenance the invisible man ponders in the published text. Figuring as the novel's embodiment of the proletarian hanged god, a politicized avatar of the cross-cultural mythic hero-king described by the Cambridge School, LeRoy, "the king," functions as both benchmark and double in relation to the invisible man. He also supplies Ellison with a voice with which to express, if obliquely, certain aspects of the left critique of Communist theory and practice that he had developed during the wartime years; LeRoy's elimination from the novel signals Ellison's final suppression of his own abiding Marxist affinities. Relegated to the cellar of the published text, sending out signals that can be heard only by readers familiar with the early drafts, LeRoy is the invisible man within *Invisible Man*.

The next two chapters treat the sections of *Invisible Man* depicting the protagonist's relationship with the Brotherhood. In chapter 6, "Finding Brotherhood," I chart Ellison's changing representation of his protagonist's experiences with the multiracial organized left. The description of his halcyon days as a political organizer, which receives highly compressed treatment in the novel, originally encompassed several dramatized episodes and chapters displaying the Brotherhood's Depression-era popularity in Harlem. While the novel restricts its portrayal of Harlem's residents to folkish characters who appear impervious to the historical forces shaping their world, earlier drafts depict a range of class-conscious Harlemites capable of historical agency. Moreover by depicting some individual Brotherhood members sympathetically—Hambro, humble and wise, is a former concentration camp inmate; the invisible man enters into a love affair with a young white woman named Louise—these excised episodes dramatically recast the text's representation of the left, which in the published novel focuses on the cartoonish characters of Jack, Tobitt, and Wrestrum. The original episodes are of sufficient number and impact to reshape the novel's overall tripartite arc. "Purpose" having consisted in the college and early New York chapters, the text's "passion" section comprises both the LeRoy material and the extended Brotherhood narrative; "perception," the protagonist's eventual discovery of Brotherhood perfidy, is substantially delayed. Ellison's drafts and notes for this section indicate that he considered complicating the text's unifying trope of vision and blindness by adding the metaphor of Marxism as magnifying lens, a symbolism that obviously had to be expunged from the final draft.

Chapter 7, "Recognizing Necessity," investigates Ellison's revisions of the portion of the novel depicting the period of crisis and betrayal, personal and public, which culminates in the Harlem riot. Displaying Ellison's gradual demonization of the Brotherhood—at first there is no Tod Clifton manipulating Sambo dolls; Brother Jack neither loses his eye nor writes the note warning the invisible man to stay in his place; Ras is identified with a black fascist notorious in wartime Harlem—these chapter drafts show Ellison deploying a dense patterning of antagonists, rituals, and symbols in a formal equivalent to the anticommunist doctrine of guilt by association. Of particular importance here is the published text's elimination of all references to fascism and the Second World War. This move enables Ellison to accuse the Brotherhood of treachery without considering the difficult political choices that faced leftists, himself included, during the wartime years. Through this obliteration of context the narrative's initially class-conscious representation of the historical situation facing Harlem's workers and radicals devolves into an epistemologically grounded critique of Marxist scientism.

In chapter 8, "Beginning and Ending," I map and analyze the process by which Ellison reconfigured the arc of his narrative as a boomerang, enabling the invisible man to declare that "the end is in the beginning." I pay particular attention to the further occlusion of elements in the prologue that would have brought in the war. In the epilogue LeRoy's journal is pillaged for conclusions quite different from those the radical mariner would have reached; the invisible man's trickster grandfather is invoked as a key source of his newfound faith in American democracy. The invisible man's final positioning of himself as "speaking for you" is premised upon an exclusion of "Brother Jack and the boys," whose attempt at castrating the American eagle has placed them beyond the ethical pale: universalism is premised on anticommunism.

A few points on methodology. Since my focus here is primarily on Ellison's process of revision, especially of *Invisible Man*, the devil will be in the details. Readers are free to take up this book wherever they wish, but they are strongly urged to peruse it from beginning to end. The benefits of reading forward from Ellison's earliest works to the published text of *Invisible Man* are cumulative and cannot be readily encapsulated in nuggets of information or insight. I do not, however, devote equal time to all features of *Invisible Man*; since I am concerned primarily with Ellison's creative process, portions that were not extensively rewritten receive less attention. The purpose here is not a new reading of *Invisible Man* (or of any other work by Ellison), although I hope my findings will challenge existing readings premised upon uninterrogated assumptions about Ellison's political outlook. This study's relevance to the large body of commentary on Ellison's oeuvre is thus relegated to footnotes; disputes over interpretation do not occupy the main text.

More crucially some comments are in order regarding the way I approach the question that has probably by this point arisen for the reader: Why? Why? has two components. The first is, Why did Ellison relinquish his former leftist commitments and become a fixture in the cold war literary establishment? Was it inevitable that he would become an anticommunist, or were choices involved? If so, what were these, and at what level of determination did they operate? The second is, Why bother to write such a long book about the making of *Invisible Man*? What is at stake in this project?

Regarding Why? number one. While much of this study will be devoted to untangling the webs of specific positions and values that constituted Ellison's consciousness at specific moments, the question warrants a methodological response since it directs attention to the model of causality upon which this biography of *Invisible Man* is premised. In Ellison's life, as in all lives, the forces producing change and development occurred on multiple levels, all interpenetrating at any given moment. On the individual level, signifying the site where Ellison was uniquely inserted into the matrix of historical forces shaping his time and place, his two biographers have both ably described the features of an immensely talented man at once hemmed in by the constraints of American racism and beset by various personal demons. Jackson emphasizes the anger and insecurity resulting from the early death of his father and the ensuing poverty of his family that drove the young Ellison to seek temporary fulfillment in leftist politics and, by the time he undertook *Invisible Man*, to explore greener pastures. Rampersad, elaborating on this depiction of the early pressures on Ellison, stresses his development of a self-protective emotional shell which, coupled with a streak of ruthlessness, enabled him, when the occasion arose, readily to replace his proletarian aesthetic with mythic archetypes, his challenge to capitalism with an affirmation of American nationalism. Rampersad's compelling delineation of Ellison's deepening isolation behind increasingly elitist and conservative barriers, as well as his defensiveness about not publishing a second novel, is steeped in irony and pathos; for all its distance from its subject the biography is profoundly moving. While *Ralph Ellison: The Emergence of Genius* and *Ralph Ellison: A Biography* delineate with scholarly precision Ellison's participation in leftist cultural circles over a few years, both biographies depict a man who was ambitious to transcend the limitations of his early life at practically any cost. The Ellison who takes shape in both portraits was never passionate in his attraction to the literary left; that he would relinquish his radicalism well before the arrival of McCarthyism—both biographers date his detachment from the left to 1943—comes as no great surprise.

Despite their acute portrayal of Ellison's psychology and scrupulous narration of his activities, both biographies considerably narrow the domain of causality in Ellison's life by insufficiently appreciating the impact of the radical movement, both cultural and more broadly political, to which he was drawn as a young man in the late 1930s and which continued to influence his feeling and thinking for several years after he had presumably cut his ties with the left. This truncation of causality is traceable in part to the fact that neither Jackson nor Rampersad examines Ellison's unpublished early fiction and novel outlines or more than cursorily the drafts of *Invisible Man*, an omission that is understandable since the life alone is sufficiently complicated to divert attention from these hard-to-access materials.[16] Yet it is these unpublished texts which contain the clearest evidence that Ellison not only took his Marxism seriously but also continued to think like a Marxist well past 1943. These texts supply the basis for hypothesizing that, despite Ellison's severing of his connections with leftist magazines after 1943 and his stated antipathy toward CP members and CP policies from 1945 onward, the programmatic anticommunism shaping the published text of *Invisible Man* took definitive form only in the late 1940s, and not before.

Neither Jackson nor Rampersad, moreover, has much regard for the project of the Depression-era and wartime cultural left; this low estimate necessarily colors their representations of Ellison's connection with literary radicalism. Jackson characterizes the Communist-led literary movement in such consistently derogatory terms, and freely attributes to his biographical subject such consistently hostile reactions to his leftist associates after the bloom was presumably off the revolutionary rose, that Ellison's decision to distance himself from his early radicalism emerges as a well-advised (if also opportunist) course of action. Even though Jackson peruses LeRoy's journal, perceives its leftism, and recognizes that Ellison eliminated it from *Invisible Man* only late in the day, his insistence upon Ellison's negativism toward the Communist movement from 1940 onward makes it hard for the reader to understand why such politically defiant, indeed deviant materials would have been allowed to remain in the manuscript for so long. Rampersad simply views Ellison's relinquishment of his Communist aesthetic as a precondition to his emergence as a writer of genius. While hardly admiring of Ellison's ability to cut himself off from people who no longer served his interests, Rampersad evidently views Ellison's abandonment of his leftist affiliations as just one among his many self-advancing acts, and perhaps, when all is said and done, the wisest. For both Jackson and Rampersad, then, character, formed in the crucible of early familial dynamics amid the overarching constraints of Jim Crow, is, in a sense, fate.[17]

To return to the matter of levels of causality. This study is premised upon a different view of Ellison's insertion within the Communist movement, that is, of causality operating at the level of the larger historical matrix. Careful scrutiny of Ellison's published early journalism and fiction, unpublished proletarian fiction and novel outlines, and above all the drafts and notes for *Invisible Man* reveals a man who took his left politics, as a source of both radical joy and existential doubt, very seriously indeed. I argue that the contradictions within Ellison, as both a man and a writer, cannot be understood apart from the contradictions informing his historical moment, which means, given his particular convictions, the contradictions informing the American left between the late 1930s and late 1940s. There is, in other words, no inside of Ellison that can be sealed off from the outside of that history. To answer the question Why? in relation to *Invisible Man* it is necessary to steer away from using the terms in which Communist movements routinely are at once described and dismissed—"dogmatic," "rigid," "Stalinist," or whatever—not only because such labels falsify, but also because, in their reductiveness, they answer the question of causality before it is asked: given the nature of leftists and leftist movements certain results are purportedly inevitable.

I try instead to re-create the vantage point from which Ellison engaged with his moment. I originally considering titling this study *Wrestling with Prometheus*, not only to indicate the proletarian origin of Ellison's fascination with classical mythology but also to suggest the titanic dimension of his grappling with the political and historical forces that shaped both his environment and his own sense of what it means to be a human being. While this literary reference proved too arcane for the title of a book aspiring to wide readership, I have retained the term *wrestling* in my title to indicate the centrality of struggle—with a "left" both internal and external—in Ellison's compositional process. My account of the novel's preparation, conception, and composition will be closely interwoven with, rather than placed at a distance from, the history of the CP-led left. I view the choices that Ellison made as an individual in his capacities as both man and artist in the context of various strategic options taken by the left movement with which he identified for a significant period of time. To propose that this movement made choices, both monumental and misguided, may sound odd to some readers, particularly those predisposed to associate Marxism with mechanistic determinism, the relentless "storm" of "necessity" in which, as Brother Jack famously says in *Invisible Man*, "individuals . . . don't count" (291). To be sure, what is meant by "choice" in this study as regards both Ellison and the larger Communist movement is not based on a notion of autonomous selfhood or free will. All the actors involved in this narrative were making their decisions in situations that were, to say the least—Marx's famous opening of *The Eighteenth Brumaire of Louis Bonaparte* comes to mind—not of their choosing. But to *read forward*, through both a historical movement and a life, is to view both as products of a series of roads taken and not taken. It is, in a sense, far more deterministic to view the fate of the Depression-era and wartime American left as molded by certain invariable features of the character of Communism or, for that matter to view the fate of Ellison himself as set in advance by a character molded in the crucible of his youth. This study seeks to construct the history of Ellison's text, American Communism, and *Invisible Man*'s re-

lationship with American Communism in as fully dialectical a manner as
possible.[18]

In future chapters I outline and discuss in greater detail the three strategic decisions by the CP-led left that bear particular relevance to the genesis and production of *Invisible Man*; I briefly summarize those decisions here so that the roads taken and not taken by Ellison can at least be glimpsed in their larger historical context. The first is the decision of the American Communist movement in 1928 to address what was called "the Negro question" by adopting the so-called Black Belt thesis, which held that African Americans in the rural South constituted a "nation within a nation," positioned to compensate for the "lag" produced by the neofeudalism of Jim Crow by fighting for self-determination and completing the "unfinished tasks" of the bourgeois democratic revolution. At the same time, African American migrants to urban areas were seen to constitute part of the multiracial proletariat, positioned to join with the rest of the working class to build a union- and community-based movement that would become powerful enough to overthrow capitalist rule and set up a society run by and for the masses of the dispossessed. This dual thrust, while moving the Communist movement ahead from its previous near-exclusive focus on class over racial oppression, generated a new set of potential problems. What was to be the relationship between national and class consciousness? Were African Americans a vanguard force that, by virtue of their sharper awareness of capitalist exploitation, could lead the revolutionary movement for a Soviet America? Or were they instead the "carriers of the widest democracy," a "people" whose struggle for democratic rights constituted them as a metonymy of fulfilled nationalist promise? Ellison's attempts to work out the relationship between the proletarian and the national features of Negro experience in his early journalism and fiction cannot be understood apart from the left's often contradictory analysis of this issue.[19]

The second important strategic option of the Depression-era left that would dramatically shape the course of subsequent events was the endorsement by the Seventh World Congress of the Third International of the view that fascism entailed not the brutal class rule of capitalism in crisis, but the domination of society by an especially reactionary sector of finance capital. The strategic implications of this analysis, which resulted in the Popular Front against Fascism, were far-reaching. While the possibility for building a broad-based movement was, from the standpoint of the left, greatly increased, so too was the risk of class collaboration. Were various sectors of the capitalist class, and the state apparatus itself, now allies of the masses of the dispossessed? Was democracy now coterminous with a populist-inflected patriotism? Could Communism, without irony, be described as "twentieth-century Americanism"? From the late 1930s to the mid-1940s Ellison found himself both embracing and querying Popular Frontist Americanism. And while his eventual codification of American patriotism would have precious little in common with Popular Front ideology, it is an irony worth contemplating that Ellison would turn against the left much of the political artillery that he had acquired during his youthful days in its ranks.

The third strategic decision of the Communist movement that shaped its fortunes, and not just in the eyes of Ralph Ellison, was its call for wartime unity in the antifascist "people's war" after the Nazi invasion of the USSR. Workers were enjoined to forgo strikes in order to keep war production at full throttle; African Americans were urged to join the segregated armed forces and channel demands for equality into fights to eliminate the poll tax and end discrimination in wartime industries. The CP went so far as to dissolve itself into the Communist Political Association (CPA) for nearly a year toward the end of the war, on the grounds that revolution was no longer on the agenda. Ellison's disappointment, indeed distress at these developments was palpable. By the time the CP reversed direction in the wake of the war he had jumped ship and would never get back on board. The fact that he would subsequently lambaste the left from the right should not obscure the fact that it was initially the left's failure to stay the course to the left that helped shift him to the right. Choices made all along the way, by both Communism the movement and Ellison the individual, resulted in the outlook encoded in *Invisible Man*.

Given, however, the canonical status of Ellison's novel—which endows the text's portraiture of politics and history with the stamp of academic approval, indeed the aura of holy writ—it bears noting that there was no inevitability to Ellison's migration to the right after the war. Just as it had not been foreordained that he would for a time embrace communism as the antidote to alienation and inequality, neither was it foreordained that he would become a cold warrior; various choices remained available. In the aftermath of the war, even as it suffered from internal demoralization and came under increasing repression, the CP continued its campaigns against police brutality, segregated housing, employment discrimination, and resurgent southern violence. As Washington sent its temporizing ambassadors, formal and informal, to what would soon be called the Third World, Paul Robeson sacrificed a celebrated career to become a full-time civil rights activist and advocate for colonial independence. W. E. B. Du Bois, rethinking his decades-long skepticism toward Communism, chose in this difficult period to move to the left, for which he was rewarded in 1948 by expulsion from the NAACP, which he had helped to found some four decades before, and by indictment in 1951 for being something close to a spy; he would decide to join the Communist Party in the decidedly unfashionable year of 1961.[20]

While it might be argued that writers were compelled to abandon their radicalism as the cold war heated up—and Ellison's Random House editors did indeed suggest revisions to *Invisible Man* that helped to strip away its residual connections with revolutionary politics—not all writers and artists followed the same course as Ellison, nor did they heed the advice of mainstream publishers. With the hearings of writers and artists by the House Un-American Activities Committee in full view and the jailing of the Hollywood Ten soon to come, Langston Hughes publicly condemned the Smith Act trials. Opting to go down a road very different from that traveled by Ellison, a number of African American writers and artists—including Louise Meriwether, Frank Marshall Davis, John Oliver Killens, Lorraine Hansberry, Lloyd Brown, Alice Childress, and the cartoonist Ollie Harrington—aligned themselves with the left, furthering its causes and publishing in its organs. A much larger number of Communists and fellow travelers, of all racial and ethnic backgrounds, quietly relinquished their former affiliations but refused to join the red-baiting chorus. Although much of the critical commentary on *Invisible Man* celebrates the narrator's closing rejection of Brotherhood scientism and affirmation of democratic individualism as manifestations of his hard-won wisdom, other historical actors had very different notions of what constituted hard-won wisdom in the world of 1952. Ellison did not have to take the road more traveled by, which became even more worn by his passing there.[21]

This reference to Ellison's critical fortunes raises the second Why? posed earlier, namely, Why write this book? Particularly for teachers of English, this question may comprise several interrelated queries. Why trace the genesis of Ellison's masterwork in such painstaking detail, when what matters is the final product, with its careful aesthetic patterning and well-honed irony? Why load so much analysis of history and politics, especially the politics of Communism and anticommunism, onto what is, after all, an investigation into a literary text? Doesn't this practice simply reduce literature to nonliterature, removing its ability to invest reality with what Ellison himself called "the bright magic of a fairy tale"?

One answer to this cluster of questions is that, when read as the product of the multiple rewritings that display Ellison's deliberate refashioning of multiple characters, events, and tropes, *Invisible Man* demonstrates that anticommunism is not in some way inherent in historical actuality, but is instead a discourse, selectively shaped and articulated in conjunction with and opposition to alternative discourses. The relationship between ideology and reference in mimesis, in other words, is brought to the fore: to study Ellison's novel as a literary arti-fact, that is, an artfully made product, requires defamiliarizing its relation to the reality it purports to represent. While this observation is often made in relation to fictional representation, it is especially relevant in the case of a novel that has played no small role in bringing into being the familiar portrait of Communism that its drafts help to deconstruct. This study thus asks teachers of literature to rethink what they are doing when they teach *Invisible Man* as an instance of the modernist well-wrought urn. To interpret the novel's patterning on its own terms, and not to query what is being equated with what and why, is to reproduce uncritically the ideological premises undergirding that patterning. An awareness that the symbolistic roundedness of Ellison's novel is the formal correlative of a politics of guilt by association makes it far more difficult simply to teach *Invisible Man* as a novel. It is necessary to confront the embeddedness of the political in the aesthetic.[22]

Another answer to the query Why write this book? calls for confronting the relationship of *Invisible Man* to the realm of historical possibility—past, present, and future. The examination of Ellison's many cuts and substitutions from early versions of *Invisible Man* conveys the cost of anticommunism, that is, what is sacrificed when a leftist vision is expunged. For just as the ultimate target of the McCarthy-era witch hunts was, arguably, not so much Communists themselves as the millions who might heed their message, what is lost from *Invisible Man* through Ellison's revisions is a full and rich sense of the potential for conscious and radical historical engagement on the part of Harlem's working class. Ellison wrote in 1944 that American literature had lacked "images of black and white fraternity" since the time of Mark Twain; in 1952 the invisible man asks whether politics might ever be "an expression of love" (452). But the published text conveys precious little of either fraternity or love. In the drafts, by contrast, where Ellison was motivated by residual memories of the revolutionary movement, he portrayed a range of characters, central and marginal, black and white, who embody the possibility for multiracial proletarian solidarity and interpersonal love in the struggle to bring a "better world" into being. The novel's anticommunism consists in far more than its creation of cartoonish stereotypes of commissars and bootlickers. By eliminating the novel's class-conscious characters and substituting for them folkish migrants whose consciousness is confined to vernacular culture, Ellison not only deprived Harlem's working class of historical agency. He also withheld from the novel's readers—past, present, and future—those images of fraternity and activism so badly needed to help them confront the crying issues of their times. While many teachers of literature are not accustomed to discussing capitalism, Communism, and anticommunism, they are generally comfortable with categories of literary analysis stemming from a valuation of humanism. This study intends to demonstrate that, because of the political standpoint from which its published version is composed, *Invisible Man* is a far less humane and antiracist novel than it might otherwise have been.[23]

The final answer to Why write this book? relates to literary history, in particular the history of African American literature. It is perhaps one of the best-kept secrets of American literary history that substantial numbers of black writers have had a significant relationship with the left. Through its prominent place in the canon of both African American literature and American literature generally, Ellison's novel has played no small role in defining the political and aesthetic criteria for what constitutes greatness in a work of literature, as well as what counts as the significant trends in African American literature between the Second World War and the present. Seen in the context of its own turbulent coming-into-being, *Invisible Man* will invite reconsideration of the many radical black writers who to this day remain the scapegoats of cold war rites of consensus. To readjust the lenses through which one can peer back at this past may aid the imagining of future possibilities for transforming the historical landscape, literary and otherwise.

PART I

Forming a Politics one

A leader while leading the ruled
is still controlled by the laws
which rule the group. A revolutionary transcends both the
group and the laws. He is under
the spell of another picture of
reality. He breaks the laws of
the status quo emotionally and
intellectually under the influence
of his will to create the new. . . .
Spartacus will come.
—Ralph Ellison, *Negro Quarterly*,
notes, 1942–43

[History consists] . . .
not . . . in repetition
but . . . in a spiral.
—Ralph Ellison,
undated notebook, c. 1941

Over the decade and more during which Ellison affirmed, queried, and finally rejected the theory and practice of the Communist-led left, his writings reflecting these shifts in political outlook. The process of reading forward through his oeuvre, both published and unpublished, will enable us to examine his changing stances as a series of choices among available courses rather than an odyssey whose homecoming is known in advance. Despite his later denials of having taken leftist politics seriously, Ellison was anything but naïve: the Marxism of the CPUSA supplied the analytical paradigm that for many years guided his understanding of the world, continuing to exercise significant influence even after he cut his organizational ties to the left. Ellison came of age thinking of the relationship of past to present to future as a spiral; it would take a major reordering of his thinking to reconfigure history as a boomerang.[1]

"Everybody'll be equal, in God's time":

Urban Folklore and the Federal Writers Project

Within two days of his arrival in New York in the summer of 1936, Ellison had made contact with Langston Hughes in the lobby of the Harlem YMCA ("Men's House" in *Invisible Man*). Hughes opened the doors to Harlem's leftist artistic community, including such figures as the writer and activist Louise Thompson and the sculptors Augusta Savage and Richmond Barthé, and Ellison was soon helping to edit the *Champion*, a radical youth journal. He wrote to his mother, Ida Ellison, of his "[disgust] with the whole system in which we live" and, in an early statement of his preoccupation with rebirth, of his desire that "the whole thing would explode so the world could start again from scratch." In mid-1937 Ellison met Richard Wright, then head of the Harlem Bureau at the *Daily Worker*, where Ellison would visit and peruse the drafts of the stories that would soon be published as *Uncle Tom's Children*. Although following the sudden death of his mother in the fall of 1937 Ellison spent several months in Dayton, Ohio, he was already hooked on radical politics and beginning to pen his first works of proletarian fiction. He founded the Dayton Youth Movement and wrote to his new mentor, "Workers of the world must write!!!" Soon after returning to New York in March 1938 Ellison, with Wright's assistance, obtained work as a writer for the Harlem branch of the Federal Writers Project.[2]

Part of Ellison's job for the FWP entailed digging up the history of the Negro in New York. Revealing his early attraction to Marxist categories of historical analysis, he summarized Carter Woodson's *The Beginning of Miscegenation of the Whites and Blacks*, stressing the class-based multiracial solidarity in early colonial life. "The slaves and white indentured servants having a community of interests frequently intermingled," Ellison writes, "but when class lines were drawn in a locality and laborers were largely of one class or other intermixture was not so prevelent." A piece about the New York slave rebellion in 1741 draws explicit parallels between the insurgents' trials and the *Scottsboro* case. In these writings of 1938 Ellison evidently sought out historical instances of black and white unity and viewed present-day Communist organizing as part of the red line of antiracist history.[3]

During most of his time with the FWP Ellison worked as an interviewer for the Project's Living Lore Unit. In this capacity he collected the songs and chants of Harlem's children and conducted numerous interviews that exposed him to the urban folklore of its recent migrant population. The Pullman porter and former Floridian Lloyd Green, a precursor of Mary Rambo, claims to have been in the city for a quarter-century but continually maintains, "I'm in New York, but New York ain't in me." The storyteller Leo Gurley remembers a legendary trickster down South named "Sweet-the-Monkey," who had the power to "make hisself invisible. . . . He was one sucker who didn't give a damn bout the crackers. . . . The white folks would wake up in the morning and find their stuff gone. He cleaned out the stores. He cleaned out the houses. Hell, he even cleaned out the damn bank! . . . [But] couldn't nobody do nothing about him. Because they couldn't never see im when he done it." For this class-conscious folk hero invisibility was evidently a means to reappropriating wealth extracted through Jim Crow economic practices.[4]

Other interviewees evinced bitterness toward continuing manifestations of Jim Crow in the North. The musician Jim Barber describes his rebuff of a white patron who has made clumsy overtures of friendship: "You ain't got nothing and I sho ain't got nothing. What's a poor colored cat and a poor white cat gonna do together? . . . Hell, that skin ain't no more good to you than mine is to me. You cain't marry one a Du Pont's daughters, and I know damn well I cain't. So what the hell you gon do up to my place?" Barber cynically anticipates, "Hitler's gonna reach in a few months and grab and then things'll start. All the white folks'll be killing off one another. And I hope they do a good job!" But, he bitterly jokes, even Hitler's triumph will not solve the problem of domination: "When Negroes start running things, I think I'll have to get off the earth before it's too late!"[5]

The religious zealot Eli Luster combines a prediction of biblical apocalypse with a call for social revolution. Claiming that God "step[ped] in" to sink the *Titanic* because it carried "all big rich folks: John Jacob Astor—all the big aristocrats," Luster prophesies that "God's time is coming":

Money won't be worth no more'n that dust blowing on the ground. Won't be no men down in Washington making fifty thousand dollars a week and folks cain't hardly make eighteen dollars a month. Everybody'll be equal, in God's time. Won't be no old man Rockefeller, no suh! . . . Them what done took advantage of everything'll be floating down the river. You'll go over to the North River, and over to the East River, and you'll see em all floating along, and the river'll be full and they won't know what struck em. The Lawd's gonna have his day.

Like Barber, Luster prophesies, "They'll be a war." He tells Ellison, "[But] it won't bother me and you. . . . It'll be the wicked killing the wicked!" More class-conscious than Barber, Luster too views the coming war as a conflict in which Harlemites have no stake.[6]

Most likely drawn from Ellison's FWP interviews are several fragments of conversations, filed among Ellison's short stories at the Library of Congress, that sound more like transcriptions from interviews than fictional narratives. One piece, supplied with the thematic title "Their Arms Are Strong," transmits the voices of women laundry workers. Their songs develop from a traditional spiritual, "Rock of Ages," to a rebellious one, "Dare to be Daniel," to a chant related to the pressures of their workplace, "I Lift My Iron." Through this sequence Ellison traces the women's movement from South to North, spirituals to urban blues, folk religiosity to proletarian class consciousness. The women move into a discussion of the brutishness of their boss, their attempts to form a union called Equity, and the causes and results of the riot in 1935, which is evidently in recent memory. One woman concludes, "We need to have some more riots. We ought to have one every six months to keep things straightened out."[7]

Another sketch, titled "No Discrimination," records the voice of the leader of an unnamed organization of the unemployed. Having called upon "Brother Finance" and "Brother Membership" to be ready to report, the speaker opens the meeting with a prayer:

> O, Lord, we are here gathered to say a prayer unto You for help and inspiration. . . . We are gathered here, all of us, black and white folks, in this here organization because we are going to do something to get ourselves and our children food and clothes and decent lodging. We're all of us poor folks, Lord. We ain't never had much and now this here relief don't give us much. . . . We're going to decide at this meeting what's going to be done, and whatever we decides we knows we're in the right, for we're fighting hard for our rights. . . . We ain't used to be gathered here like this before, for we were separated before—the whites from the blacks, and we didn't have no respect for each other. It's different now. This here's a united front because we're all suffering alike. . . . They ain't no discrimination in Your eyes, Lord, and they ain't none in this here organization.

Like Wright's Reverend Taylor in "Fire and Cloud," this preacher views multiracial solidarity as a necessity for those who are "suffering alike" and must "decide what's going to be done." As the Alabama Communist organizer Hosea Hudson recalled, it was commonplace for red-led working-class gatherings, especially those involving African Americans, to open with prayers. Whether or not Ellison added the Leninist embellishment, the speaker's "what's to be done" echoes the title of Lenin's famous pamphlet *What Is to Be Done?*, which in 1902 called for the emergence of revolutionary leadership from the ranks of the working class. This question would crop up frequently in Ellison's notes and writings over the next few years.[8]

In 1978 Ellison would fondly recall his FWP-era contacts with Harlem's rich oral lore; hearing several strapping African American men debating the relative merits of various sopranos at the Metropolitan Opera, he learned that their sophistication derived from their moonlighting as silent extras on the opera stage. Forty years after the encounter he viewed the men's anomalous expertise "in the clear, pluralistic melting-pot light of American cultural possibility"; from the "smoke" of the melting pot he watched "the phoenix's vernacular, but transcendent, rising." His younger self was apparently more fascinated by the wry commentaries on social inequality embedded in the vernacular of urban folklore.[9]

"A well organized Fascist offensive in Harlem":
Popular Front-Era Journalism

While working for the FWP Ellison began writing book reviews for leftist publications. In his first *New Masses* contribution in 1938, a review of *God's Faithful Pilgrim*, a biography of Sojourner Truth by the anthropologist Arthur Huff Fauset, Ellison stresses Truth's emergence from the crucible of religious mysticism, emerging as a "fight[er] for Negro freedom," the "Mother Bloor of the anti-slavery movement." But Fauset failed to "[allow] . . . scope for development and change of the individual through dynamic contact with the social and economic factors constituting environment," complains Ellison; instead he substituted "static philosophy" based in racialized notions of the Negro's "healthy paganism." Ellison's comparison of Truth with Ella Reeve "Mother" Bloor, in the late 1930s the leftist godmother of unionization struggles, suggests that Fauset would have avoided racial essentialism if he had grasped the continuity between the abolitionist movement of Truth's day and current red activity.[10]

Ellison's notebooks from this period further display his interest in the parallels between past and present radical movements. Among his notes on an article published in 1939 by the historian Benjamin Quarles on the relationship between Frederick Douglass and William Lloyd Garrison, Ellison writes, "Douglass / Vesey / Washington / Dubois / Ford / Patterson." Another entry, titled "Notes for Essay on Negro Personality, Intellectuals, or what have you," contains a longer list, starting with the fugitive slave and abolitionist orator and activist "WW Brown" (William Wells Brown) and ending with "the Marxists." Already preoccupied with the issue of Negro leadership, Ellison evidently viewed Communists as culminating the past century's development. Still another entry contained the observation, "The South from slavery and secession has captured . . . the government and are pushing the country toward fascism; slavery has once again become international. . . . [History consists] . . . not . . . in repetition but . . . in a spiral." The growth of fascism both international and domestic, here paralleling chattel slavery, leads the young radical to discern in history movement that is simultaneously forward and backward. The Marxist-Hegelian spiral of history— which the invisible man will ruthlessly lampoon in the epilogue to *Invisible Man*—here serves a vital explanatory function.[11]

Departing from the format of the book review, Ellison explored the international dimensions of racism in a commentary on "anti-Semitism among Negroes" that appeared in the *Jewish People's Voice* in April 1939. In the ecumenical spirit of the Popular Front, Ellison praises "Negro leaders" such as the NAACP's secretary Walter White, the president of the Brotherhood of Sleeping Car Porters, A. Philip Randolph, and the pastor of the Abyssinian Baptist Church, Adam Clayton Powell Sr., for helping raise funds for Jewish refugees from Nazism, urging their constituencies to reject anti-Semitism, and "cooperating . . . on the broad front . . . for Democratic rights." He condemns the "Tory capitalists" who have created a "well organized . . . Fascist offensive in Harlem," such as the pro-Franco *Concha Espana*, the *Pittsburgh Courier*, the New York *Amsterdam News*, and the *Harlem Bulletin*. This last, warns Ellison, carries the program of anti-Semitic black nationalists Sufi Abdul Hamid and Arthur Reid, who "advises Negroes to follow Hitler." African Americans are more fortunate than Jews in Hitler's Germany, Ellison states, because "the Government of the South is but a reactionary segment of a constitutional Democracy." But "the question is not whether or not Negro and Jewish discriminations can be linked," he concludes; "the question is whether discrimination toward any group can be tolerated in this, the greatest of Democracies."[12]

The continuity between racial violence in the South and in the North is the subject of Ellison's article "Judge Lynch in New York," published in August 1939 in the *New Masses*. Describing the brutal mob beating of three young Negro college students who had come to the city in search of summer jobs, Ellison notes the increasing frequency of such attacks, comparing this incident with another in which a Negro youth was beaten, thrown into the Hudson River, and "missed drowning only because a white longshoreman who happened to be passing did not share the feeling of the mob and rescued him." Ellison connects these incidents with overcrowding and rent gouging: "An attempt is being made to bottle Negroes up in the narrow confines of Harlem to the advantage of those landlords who charge exorbitant rents." Ellison charges police complicity, remarks on the mob's association with the Christian Front, organized by the notorious fascist "radio priest," Father Coughlin, and notes that downtown earlier that day the young Negro men had witnessed Christian Front members attacking a Jew.[13]

Ellison's original conclusion to "Judge Lynch in New York" dwells on the parallels between northern and southern fascisms. Echoing the conversation among the African American youths in Wright's "Big Boy Leaves Home," Ellison writes, "If there's a section where you are not supposed to go you know it; even if you're not told by a sign that says 'No Dogs and niggers allowed.' The only difference between the North and South . . . is that [in the North] they're beating the Jews as well as the Negroes." Ellison more optimistically concludes the published version with the observation that Negroes "*are* fighting back but in a democratic way." Community leaders of different religions and races are "making every effort . . . to curb these incidents, which, if allowed to continue, are sure to precipitate the sort of emotional reaction that made for the riots of 1935." Less sanguine than the laundry workers in "The Arms Are Strong" about the beneficial effects of urban rioting, Ellison refocuses his anger against "Judge Lynch" toward "democratic" resistance.[14]

Ellison's early political journalism demonstrates not only his rising star but also his endorsement of cardinal principles of Popular Front–era CP politics. His view that democracy has been withheld from African Americans because of the "lag" exerted by the backward South was central to the CP's Black Belt thesis, which proposed that Negro self-determination in the South would "complete the unfinished tasks of the bourgeois-democratic revolution," now long "delayed" and "overdue." In viewing present-day Communists as heirs of the abolitionist movement, he demonstrates his agreement with the CP's view of the struggle to extend democracy as a new Reconstruction. He links anti-Negro racism with anti-Semitism and domestic fascism with Hitlerism and warns of the dangerous appeal of fascism to Harlem's oppressed population. His designation of the fount of fascism not as the capitalist class as such, but as a sector of that class—the "Tory capitalists," the "reactionary segment of a constitutional Democracy"—draws upon the theorization of fascism as "the open terrorist dictatorship of the most reactionary, most chauvinistic and most imperialist elements of finance capital," in the words of the Bulgarian Communist Georgi Dimitrov, whose *The United Front against War and Fascism* set forth the Popular Front strategy settled upon at the Seventh World Congress of the Comintern in 1935. Ellison's naming the United States "the greatest of Democracies" echoes the CP's call in the late 1930s for the broadest possible coalition of liberal and progressive forces to stave off an American variant of Hitlerism, advance the interests of "the people," and prepare the way for the socialist transformation of society. For Ellison, as for many CP-affiliated radicals of the day, the term *democracy* signified far more than formalistic principles encoded in documents of state; it described at once a present aspiration and a future reality, enabling communism to dub itself "twentieth-century Americanism." At the same time, the term was bound to nationalism, evolutionism, and the notion that the state could be freed from its subservience to the capitalist class and appropriated by the dispossessed. Ellison's career, like that of many of his contemporaries, would play out this contradiction.[15]

"I said I was a black Yank and was not coming":
Writings in the Era of the Nonaggression Pact

During the period of the Russian-German Nonaggression Pact, September 1939 to June 1941, when the CP pledged, "The Yanks are not coming," Ellison's writings indicate his continued adherence to the Communist analysis of both international and domestic events. Hitting his stride as a politically engaged writer and deepening his involvement with both the League of American Writers and the *New Masses*, Ellison viewed the conflict between the Nazis and Italian fascists on the one hand and the European capitalist democracies on the other as a contestation between imperialist powers. France, Ellison concluded, was a "virulent fascist stronghold," and by undertaking Lend-Lease aid to Great Britain and proclaiming the United States the "arsenal of democracy," Roosevelt was betraying the New Deal. The working class had nothing to gain from taking sides in the war; African Americans in particular, engaged in their own battles with the "little Hitlers" of the South and used as strikebreaking "tools of fascism" in the North, had no stake in the war's outcome. "Liberalism because of its very structure," mulled Ellison, "is helpless. The historical answer to the ills of the Black masses is socialism." Although the Pact posed nearly insuperable contradictions to a number of writers and intellectuals in the orbit of the left—for example, Malcolm Cowley and Granville Hicks—for Ellison, as for many other African Americans, it entailed a left turn that would benefit African Americans, and the working class overall, by sharpening class contradictions, weakening the hold of imperialism on the world's subjugated peoples of color, and hasten the advent of socialist revolution.[16]

The Nonaggression Pact roughly coincided with the publication of *Native*

Son, which encountered a very mixed reception on the left, especially among black Communists. Notably neither Wright nor Ellison extended his anger and frustration at this reaction to a repudiation of the C P's international politics. Wright, despairing at the obtuseness manifested in the *Daily Worker* commentary on *Native Son* by the Harlem C P leader Ben Davis, nonetheless declared with delight, "Boy, the nazis are running wild. Before this year is out, England will not exist as she was before. It will mean a new day in this world. . . . Then we'll have to take care of herr Hitler. But not before. . . . Before this war is over, the red army will stand on the banks of the rhine!!!!" Ellison wrote in April 1940 to Wright, who was vacationing in Mexico after the publication of *Native Son*, that the novel "shook the Harlem section to its foundation and some of the rot it has brought up is painful to smell." Referring to the recent capitulation of the Netherlands to Hitler's armies, however, Ellison noted in May 1940, "The fat queen [Wilhelmina] jumped on her bicycle and took a runout powder, like the rulers of all the countries Hitlers pushed into. He's saving us a hell of a lot of trouble, only he doesnt know it." Right before the Nazi invasion of the USSR, Wright addressed the fourth American Writers Congress about the parallels between the Great War and the current conflict, declaring the latter "not my people's war." It may in fact have been the C P's harsh critique of the Second World War as a falling-out among imperialist thieves that anchored the two writers' commitment to the left between late 1939 and mid-1941, despite the sharp controversy over cultural matters.[17]

Ellison published a series of pieces deploring the Roosevelt administration's pretensions to democracy and its flirtation with intervention. In "Camp Lost Colony," a description of a movement among some seventeen hundred black and white Missouri sharecroppers and tenant farmers protesting eviction, Ellison targets the alliance of business and government as the campers' prime antagonist. Lambasting Roosevelt's Farm Security Agency for setting up local administrations and commissions consisting of "ginners, merchants, and large landowners with no representation of the agricultural workers," he declares that the New Deal agency supposedly set up to aid "dispossessed Americans" is in collusion with the landowners. But the domestic class struggle is not the sole subject of his acerbic critique: "[The sharecroppers] hope that the President will turn his attention from Mannerheim Finland long enough to save the measures which sent these American farming people to the polls for him in 1936." Alluding to Roosevelt's courting of the anti-Soviet Finnish government during the Winter War of 1939–40, Ellison evinces sympathy with the Soviet Union's need to strengthen defenses along its western borders. The fight to save the remnants of the New Deal from the depredations of elites, now seen as constituting a unitary Euro-American ruling class, is linked with a politics of left-wing isolationism.[18]

Ellison inserted comments about the current war into literary reviews, at times stretching his points about novels in order to express his views about imperialism. In a hostile commentary on J. B. Priestley's *Let the People Sing* Ellison criticizes the novel's cavalier attitude toward English class hierarchy. In order to offset "rebellion from 'the people,'" Ellison writes, Priestley "advises the ruling class to take unto itself a bit of wisdom and plenty of the Comic Spirit, to get good and drunk and give the workers, 'the people,' as he puts it, an opportunity to enjoy some of the 'good life.'" Ellison highlights the speciousness of all-class national unity, pointing up the falsity of the term *the people*, that now bygone Popular Front byword, as a synonym for *the workers*. Commenting sympathetically, by contrast, on Herbert Clyde Lewis's novel *Spring Offensive* Ellison writes of the plight of its hero, Peter Winston, an unemployed American newspaperman who has volunteered to join the Allied forces. Winston's "class [conscious] . . . identity with his fellows" leads him to realize that "the enemy lies at home, not in distant battlefields." As he lies dying of German-inflicted bayonet wounds, flashbacks to his unhappy youth in the "decayed democracy" in a midwestern town portray "the human nuances of the American class struggle." The nation's heartland is for Ellison the site of class conflict, not democratic amity; U.S. democracy is not "delayed" but "decayed."[19]

In a review in March 1940 of Conrad Richter's historical novel *The Trees*, set in the post–Revolutionary War frontier Midwest, Ellison relates the present world situation to the novel's treatment of "the trend toward civilization that was rising as a reaction against the long period of military domination necessary during a revolutionary period." Quoting the words of a character who is opposed to a possible U.S. invasion of Canada—"'God forbid! If our American eagle wants to scream, let it scream over the fields, forests, and workshops of its own white and red peoples for civil equality and justice!'"—Ellison remarks that these words "might well be said now to those who would place our frontiers across the Atlantic." He is not missing the opportunity to draw a lesson of contemporaneous relevance: the screaming eagle figures as a symbol not of democratic possibility, but of militaristic aggression.[20]

Ellison's *New Masses* review in November 1940 of *The Argonauts*, a collective memoir by American Youth Congress members who roamed the country to report on the state of the nation, highlights the youths' encounter with "the sources of American dignity and the forces which trample it down . . . unemployment, hunger, and threatening war." With its unremitting reminders of the class struggle at home, Ellison writes, "the book helps you to understand why, although President Roosevelt was re-elected, the people did not endorse his war policies." Yet *The Argonauts* "leaves you with the feeling that out there in the country are the forces that will someday, like Jason, seize the Golden Fleece and"—here he gestures toward Langston Hughes's poem—"make 'America America again.'" In this proletarian updating of the Greek myth of Jason and the Argonauts Ellison suggests that America will find its identity only when the Golden Fleece of capital is seized by those counterforces that, acting with "high consciousness and heroism," will reappropriate the wealth created by their class. Treading a fine line between embracing the nation and rejecting the state, he locates the antagonist to America's welfare in an increasingly decadent capitalism. Notably, however, the words "democracy" and "democratic" do not appear in the review, which speaks instead of "forces" ranged against one another in what is clearly a class war.[21]

"A Congress Jim Crow Didn't Attend," Ellison's most extended piece of Pact-era political journalism, was featured on the cover of *New Masses* in May 1940: the radical young writer had arrived. The article renders his excited, indeed impassioned response to the gathering in 1940 of the CP-affiliated Third National Negro Congress (NNC), a gathering of primarily African American union and community organizers. Ellison stresses the working-class makeup of the Congress—gathered, he points out, in the new building of the Department of Labor—and approvingly quotes the antiwar politics of the NNC's leader, John P. Davis: "The American people will refuse to follow American imperialism in any attack upon the Soviet Union, will refuse to fall victim to anti-Soviet adventures." By contrast, Ellison deplores the "unmistakable notes of Red-baiting" in the address by A. Philip Randolph, whom he adjudges a leader "in the act of killing his leadership."[22]

Ellison joyfully witnesses the presence of not just urban northerners, but also southerners for whose attendance at the meeting "someone has sacrificed." His account culminates with cameo portraits of the building trades CIO organizer Hank Johnson, an "urban hero," a man "transformed into a will to change a civilization"; an unnamed "tall black woman from Arkansas" who displays the worthless scrip in which she is paid; and Owen Whitfield, the preacher who had "sacrificed his home and farm" to lead the Missouri highway demonstration featured in "Camp Lost Colony." Ellison reflects:

Whitfield and Johnson and the people behind them are the answer to those who wonder why there is such a scramble to raise the Booker T. Washington symbol anew in Negro life. . . . A new pole of leadership has developed among the Negro people and the National Negro Congress is their organization. . . .

There in the faces of my people I saw strength. There with the whites in the audience I saw the positive forces of civilization and the best guarantee of America's future.

The abolitionist movement has been revived; the frequently invoked names of "Gabriel, Denmark Vesey, Harriet Tubman, Frederick Douglass" have assumed "a new meaning. . . . The age of the Negro hero had returned to American life." Ellison comes away from the Congress convinced that it has fulfilled "that yearning . . . [for] a sense of group unity that is the yearning of men for a flag: for a unity that cannot be compromised, that cannot be bought; that is conscious of itself, of its strength, that is militant. I had come to realize that such a unity is unity of a nation, and of a class." Describing the Congress to Wright, Ellison expressed his confidence in the African American masses: "I found in [the Congress] the first real basis for *faith* in our revolutionary potentialities. . . . I know now that we dont have to worry overmuch about the stupidities of black C P leaders. . . . Heres that something, that pent-up folk consciousness. Here's a fleeting glimpse of the heart of the Negro, the heart that beats and suffers and hopes—for freedom. . . . The *river* is harnessing itself! . . . The experience of the congress was almost mystical in its intensity."[23]

"A Congress Jim Crow Didn't Attend" clearly situates its author as a "black Yank" who, in "not coming," espouses current C P politics. The terms "sacrifice" and "hero," which in his writings after *Invisible Man* assume largely archetypal resonance, here signify militant class consciousness. When he conflates "nation" and "class" in his designation of the "unity that cannot be compromised," he is designating African Americans as at once members of a Negro "nation within a nation" and members of a multiracial working class; the "flag representing their yearning" is not, it would seem, the Stars and Stripes. At the same time Ellison's description of the Congress's attendees, black and white, as embodiments of the "best future of America," as well as his evident approval of the Department of Labor as its venue, suggest his continuing adherence to the notion that Communism is the real "twentieth-century Americanism"; even the term "black Yank" suggests a claim to a patriotism more authentic than that of the war-mongering ruling class. The heroes making sacrifices to and for this movement are at once the vanguard of class-based revolutionary change and the metonymy of an emergent national future where promises are kept and debts are paid. It is not apparent which definition will prevail.[24]

"The sacrifices necessary to participate in a total war":
New Masses Journalism in the "Win the War" Era

In the wake of the Nazi invasion of the USSR in June 1941, the CP's position on the war underwent an immediate and dramatic reversal: now the Yanks *were* coming, to defend both Soviet socialism and U.S. democracy. Workers were adjured to enter into a no-strike pledge; African Americans were asked to channel their grievances into demands that would aid the war effort. Frederick Douglass's Civil War–era call upon freedmen and fugitives alike to join the ranks of the segregated Union Army was regularly invoked in the CP press as a historical analogy urging present-day Negro participation in the Jim Crow armed forces. Insisting upon the priority of defeating the Axis powers, the Party largely boycotted not only the Double V campaign (simultaneous victory over fascism overseas and Jim Crow at home) spearheaded by the *Pittsburgh Courier* but also the March on Washington Movement, organized by Randolph to protest discrimination in the war industries and the armed forces. The Communists' call for "win the war" national unity, clearly a response to the imperatives of USSR foreign policy, situated the Party to the right of even some liberal organizations, occasioning the accusation that they were abandoning their earlier struggles for antiracist and working-class demands. These criticisms were exacerbated, especially in the armed forces, by the wave of racial confrontations that crested at 242 in forty-seven cities in the course of 1943. In December 1944 *Negro Digest* sponsored a symposium on the topic, "Have Communists Quit Fighting for Negro Rights?"; although most participants answered in the negative, the fact that the issue was raised at all speaks volumes. Since Ellison would later propose in both *Invisible Man* and subsequent essays and interviews that the Communists had betrayed African Americans during the war, his own wartime writings warrant close scrutiny.[25]

Although most of Ellison's wartime journalism would appear in *Negro Quarterly*, two pieces appeared in the *New Masses* in 1942. In a review of *Native Land*, the Frontier Films documentary about "the struggles of farmers and workers for civil liberties during the 1930's," narrated by Paul Robeson, Ellison stresses not so much the film's class struggle aspects as its relevance to the current moment. Focusing on the film's epilogue, which, added after *Native Land* was completed, proclaimed that "American labor and the American nation are stronger for having come through the fire," Ellison echoes Robeson's voice-over. The film portrays past struggles "not as an end, but as a beginning, a discipline for a broader struggle: that against the fascist Axis. . . . [Its] depiction of Black Legion and KKK activities as a grave danger to civil liberties becomes even more meaningful in light of the fact that these forces now join in a conscious, international attack against the allied nations through instigating such acts as the Sojourner Truth Housing riots." Taking the same position on the racist assaults on African Americans in Detroit as that voiced in the CP press, Ellison argues that these Fifth Column–inspired attacks "do not weaken national unity, but strengthen it by giving intensification and direction to honest anger and hate." In the spirit of the toned-down epilogue, Ellison treats the film's harsh representation of native U.S. fascism as not typical but anomalous, the product of isolable enemies; *Native Land* is the sign of "a healthy art, and a healthy art implies a healthy people."[26]

In October 1942 Ellison contributed to a special issue of the *New Masses* devoted to "The Negro and Victory"; the editors, arguing, "This is not the time to stir up the race issue; it's bad for national unity," criticized the "hush-hush attitude" as "a kind of isolationism in respect to the Negro question that is as dangerous in its way as political isolationism was in regard to the fascist menace." In "The Way It Is," an interview with a Harlem resident named Mrs. Jackson, Ellison contributes to this racial anti-isolationism by confronting the widespread ambivalence toward the war among African Americans. Commenting on the recent eviction of a lawyer from his office on 126th Street, Mrs. Jackson recalls her own experiences of being "dispossessed" in the previous decade; things have, she observes sadly, gotten no better. Roosevelt's Fair Employment Practices Committee (FEPC) has not provided work for anyone she knows; in fact a beloved nephew, unable to get a job in wartime industry, joined the merchant marine and died when his ship was sunk by a submarine. "Folks from his union is being very nice to my sister, the whites as well as the colored, [and] sure have shown themselves to be real friends," she notes, but this does not bring him back. Her own son is encountering vicious racism at Forth Bragg in North Carolina. Although she agrees when the "union folks" tell her, "We got to fight the big Hitler over yonder even with all the little Hitlers over here," she still wishes her son would get sent "out of the country": "Cause then maybe my mind would know some ease." Ellison concludes that African Americans are in a paradoxical situation: "Our desire to rid the world of fascism [is] the most burning, and the obstacles placed in our way the most frustrating." The hardships Mrs. Jackson faces can be resolved only by a steadfast backing of "the President's [price and rent] stabilization program." The cost otherwise incurred by the nation's loss of Mrs. Jackson's allegiance, Ellison concluded, is tremendous:

> The Mrs. Jacksons cannot make the sacrifices necessary to participate in a total war if the conditions under which they live, the very ground on which they must fight, continues its offensive against them. . . . Only concrete action will be effective—lest irritation and confusion turn into exasperation, and exasperation change to disgust and finally into anti-war sentiment (and there is such a danger). Mrs. Jackson's reality must be democratized so that she may clarify her thinking and her emotions. And that's the way it really is.[27]

In a draft conclusion, later omitted, Ellison adds a grim analogy: "If one is being dragged by a car that is in danger of being struck by a train, one nevertheless struggles to be free of the car first, regardless of the lesser chance of surviving under the impact of the train." Invoking an image of Jim Crow violence, a lynched man being dragged by a car down a rural road, Ellison's trope equates the car with Jim Crow ("little Hitler") and the train with "the big Hitler." Although the train threatens to wipe out the car, its driver, and the dragged victim alike, from the victim's point of view the car is the more immediate threat. Ellison enjoins *New Masses* readers to appreciate the difficulties involved in persuading African Americans to adhere to the "discipline" needed in the "broader struggle against the fascist Axis." Although his call in the published text for stabilizing rents and prices to produce a "democratized reality" is far less dramatic than the car and train metaphor, the international stakes in Harlem's supporting the war effort are conveyed in the *New Masses* text by a juxtaposed graphic featuring a skeletal Russian mother and child in war-torn Stalingrad; the drawing bears the caption, "But Mother, Don't We Have Allies?" Like Wright, who in fact rewrote Max's speech in the stage version of *Native Son* in 1942 to urge desegregation of the armed forces and full participation in the antifascist war, Ellison agreed, if reluctantly, that the "big Hitler" had to be gotten out of the way before the "little Hitlers" could be confronted. There would be no other way for the Red Army to stand on the banks of the Rhine.[28]

"WHAT IS TO BE DONE?": *Negro Quarterly* and the War

Although after October 1942 Ellison would cease contributing to the CP press under his own byline, he did not sever his ties with the *New Masses*; in November 1942 he was among the new contributing editors honored at a dinner dedicated to the theme "words can be bullets," an event of which the FBI took notice, and served in this capacity for several months more. In early 1942 he had taken the position of managing editor at *Negro Quarterly*, where the famous young Communist Angelo Herndon served as editor in chief. With the support of the Negro Publication Society the two young men produced four issues between spring 1942 and winter–spring 1943. The CP's most prominent political prisoner of the 1930s, the Alabama-born Herndon had joined the Party at the age of seventeen, organized among miners, and participated in the Scottsboro defense. He was nineteen when, in 1932, he led a multiracial march of the unemployed in Atlanta that caused him to be arrested for violating a pre–Civil War statute outlawing slave insurrection. Sentenced to twenty years on a chain gang, Herndon became a cause célèbre of the left—two million signatures were gathered in his support—and with the legal assistance of the young Ben Davis successfully won his freedom in 1934. Describing his reaction to the "spontaneous and moving" demonstrations of support he experienced on his journey from Atlanta to New York, Herndon wrote, "People speak too lightly of the brotherhood of man. That day I experienced it completely. It filled me with a light so dazzling that I felt blinded." After several years of intense activism Herndon would leave the CP without fanfare, or even explanation, sometime in late 1943 or 1944. In both its fervently pro-Communist and its falling-away phases, Herndon's life would supply the basis for several of Ellison's proletarian short stories and the plot of an unwritten novel, as well as various plot threads that Ellison considered weaving into *Invisible Man*.[29]

Scholars commenting on the significance of *Negro Quarterly* in Ellison's career have almost exclusively focused on his editorial in the journal's fourth and final (winter–spring 1943) number, where he called upon those aspiring to "lead" the "Negro masses" to "[learn] the meaning of [their] myths and symbols" and cited the zoot suit and the lindy hop as potential clues to "profound political meaning." Read in conjunction with the passage in *Invisible Man* where the protagonist, after the death of Tod Clifton, encounters the zoot-suited hipsters in the subway and meditates that history may be not a laboratory experiment but instead a gambler, this editorial is routinely viewed as a decisive indicator of Ellison's declaration of political and artistic independence from the left. Ellison here recognizes the barrenness of a scientific approach to Negro life, the argument goes, and grasps the need for a semiotics of culture that can tap into the noneconomic wellsprings of human motivation. A careful perusal of all four issues of *Negro Quarterly*, however, as well as of Ellison's unpublished editorials and correspondence, suggests the continuing relevance of historical materialism to Ellison throughout the entire *Negro Quarterly* period.[30]

In their initial "Statement of Policy" the young editors revealed their intention to pick up the banner of black literary radicalism that had been dropped with the cessation in 1938 of *Challenge* (superseded by *New Challenge*), the periodical edited between 1934 and 1937 by Marian Minus and Dorothy West and, in its final issue in fall 1937, Wright as well. The particular mission of *Negro Quarterly*, more political than literary, would be to address the "rapid change of life introduced by the war." If successful the journal would "not only redound to the benefit of Negroes, but . . . strengthen immensely the democratic ideals of the nation."

> Because our country is now engaged in an all-out war with the Axis forces, the full capacity of its man power must be thrown into the battle in order to insure full victory. This can be done more effectively when the barriers of Jim Crow in the Army, Navy, Air Force, and other national defense bodies are removed. Negroes must share equally in the hardships of war, as well as in the victory that is to come.

Although Abner Berry's greeting to *Negro Quarterly* in the *Daily Worker* stressed the new journal's independence—"There is none of the 'philanthropy' that has shadowed all previous ventures in the publication of Negro literature"—this opening editorial statement affirms the position on the war voiced in the contemporaneous CP press. Notably African Americans are called upon to "share equally in the hardships of war."[31]

Ellison held the secondary position of managing editor, in presumed deference to the better-known Herndon, but solicited most of the journal's contents. Reflecting Ellison's close ties with writers through the *New Masses* and the League of American Writers, *Negro Quarterly* contained poems and short stories by Alfred Kreymborg, Frank Marshall Davis, Waring Cuney, Walter Snow, Langston Hughes, Owen Dodson, Nicolas Guillén, Eve Merriam, and Jorge Amado. The journal's book review section featured Herbert Aptheker on William Blake's historical novel *The Copperheads*; Herndon on Wright's *Twelve Million Black Voices*; Charles Humboldt on Alain Locke's *When Peoples Meet*; Dorothy Brewster on *The Negro Caravan*; Howard Taubman on

Paul Robeson and Earl Robinson's 1942 song fest, "Folk Songs on the Firing Line"; Eugene Holmes on recent books by Edwin Embree, Pearl Buck, and Melville Herskovits; Henrietta Buckmaster on historical fiction; Stanley Edgar Hyman on James Street's *Tap Roots*; and Ellison himself on William Attaway's *Blood on the Forge*.[32]

Longer analytical essays covered contemporary culture and politics: Doxey Wilkerson wrote on Negro education in relation to the war; Harry Slochower on antifascist novelists; Lawrence Reddick on anti-Semitism and racial stereotyping; Louis Emmanuel Martin on the Detroit race riot; Noah Landau on the antiracism of the National Maritime Union; Romulo Lachantanere on the Cuban color line and E. Franklin Frazier on the Brazilian one; Kumar Goshal on the people's war in India; John Pittman on African antifascism; and Edward Bland, who would substantially influence both Ellison's and Wright's views of Negro "preindividuality," on the sociological and historical pressures on Negro novelists. Undervalued to this day as a register of wartime antiracist radicalism and internationalism, *Negro Quarterly* attested to both the critical acuity and political connectedness of its young editors.

The editors' own contributions to the journal emphasize the dialectic of danger and opportunity opened up by the wartime situation. In "Frederick Douglass: Negro Leadership and War" Herndon parallels the new journal with the abolitionist *North Star*, in which Douglass proclaimed his independence from white patronage. Stressing Douglass's break with William Lloyd Garrison and citing, with his own added emphasis, Douglass's statement, "*I am not sure that I was not under the influence of something like a slavish adoration of these good people*," Herndon notes, "It will be found that after almost one hundred years, this pattern of *American thinking* has changed very little, if any. It is based on the presumption of the 'natural' inferiority of the Negro and expresses itself not only among avowedly anti-Negro groups and individuals, but even among . . . well-meaning white groups and individuals" (Herndon's italics). The blame for this situation, he added, is to be shared by "Negro leaders [whose] . . . political ineptness and lack of courage" have "helped to perpetuate this type of thinking among those advanced whites with whom they are associated." That Douglass's battle with racist paternalism even among "well-meaning" white abolitionists resonated with his own experiences with the left is apparent. Herndon finds hope, however, in the coming victory over fascism, which will enable the "non-English-speaking peoples everywhere" to "[march] out of the present hell of slavery into the dawn of a new world." Douglass figures in Herndon's editorial as at once a symbol of Negro autonomy, a reminder of the need to distinguish primary from secondary enemies, an embodiment of the promise of democracy, and a prophet of world socialism.[33]

In his first contribution to the journal Ellison updates his *New Masses* review of William Attaway's *Blood on the Forge* from 1941 to stress the novel's "intensified . . . power" in the wake of Pearl Harbor. Featuring the bosses' cynical use of Negro scabs imported from the South to break the Great Steel Strike of 1919, *Blood on the Forge* points up the current need for African Americans to "discriminate between two types of Western man: the democrat and the fascist." At stake for Negroes in the victory over fascism is the "conquest of nature," the acquisition of "the techniques through which Western Civilization reached its highest development. This they cannot do in the state of constant warfare which fascism would bring, but only in a society wherein they are free to build a philosophy, a political structure and a hope that leads toward peace. They fight against fascism not to protect those in this country who would deprive them of the techniques of modern living, but to safeguard their right to hope." While Ellison links fascism with the destruction of productive forces and what he calls "democracy" with universal access to the means enabling the "conquest of nature," it is evident that "democracy" is a close stand-in for "socialism," and that his conception of the "philosophy . . . political structure . . . [and] hope" of postwar modernity draws heavily upon a Marxist mode of production narrative, which envisions the realm of freedom emerging from the realm of necessity through the abolition of classes and exploitation. "Technique" figures here, we may note, as equivalent to "technology," carrying none of the associations with literary style it would later assume.[34]

Despite Herndon's greater prominence on the masthead, Ellison was the journal's principal in-house political analyst and wrote its remaining three editorials. Emphasizing the international context of the issues facing Negro Americans, in the second number he points out that "the strength in man power and other resources represented by the American Negroes, African, Indians and other oppressed peoples are decisive factors in determining the outcome of this war." The Allied powers' "paternalism," their inability to "base their relations with the darker peoples thoroughly on the Four Freedoms," is producing a "lag between . . . theory and practice" that is being exploited by the Japanese. In a warning directed to not just the American ruling class but also, it seems, the American left, Ellison warns, "All statements that Negroes are 'overwhelmingly' in back of the efforts of the Allies are not only not true, but are misleading." While "the Soviet Union has settled the national question to the satisfaction of its many nationalities," American Negro nationalism, if it is not to become an "unarticulated" force and thus a "danger," will have to be recognized as a legitimate response to African Americans' historical experience as a quasi-colonized people. "If this war is to be a peoples' war based upon the Four Freedoms," he concludes, "then along with the discarded techniques of imperialist domination must go all of the old imperialist definitions and classifications of minority and colonial peoples. All peoples must be allowed to define themselves!"[35]

Ellison's editorial in the third number of *Negro Quarterly* focuses on enfranchisement: "What is the responsibility of the President and the Senate Majority in the anti–poll tax defeat?" Referring to the ongoing C P-led campaign to repeal the poll tax, which served in the Jim Crow South to prevent both African Americans and poor whites from voting, the editorial compares Roosevelt's failure to support the campaign with Churchill's "reaffirm[ed] imperialistic intentions" with regard to India. "If the President cannot master the problem of freedom for all here at home," inquires the young editor, "how can he hope to win freedom for the whole world?" The Senate's failure to pass the bill "has more effectively isolated American Negroes from participation in the Government and its stated aims than ever before. The question they are asking is unmistakable: 'WHAT IS TO BE DONE?'" Ellison ends on a note of warning: "Let the Administration falter in the face of the future if it will, but American Negroes shall continue to seek democratic freedom regardless of where it lies, and the 'common man' of the world will be with them." If Negroes are refused "democratic freedom" in the United States, he implies, they will seek it in alliance with the anti-imperialist movements and nations backed by the Soviet Union. The Leninist bell sounded by the young *Negro Quarterly* editor is at once self-determinationist, anti-imperialist, and pro-socialist; his conceptions of "self-definition" and "democratic freedom" are profoundly at variance with Roosevelt's practical implementation, rhetoric aside, of the Four Freedoms. Although in his introduction to *Invisible Man* in 1982 Ellison would refer to "our beloved F.D.R.," evidently some forty years before his affection had been somewhat muted. As he mulled in his notebook at the time, the developing "concept of a nation" in India and among "the American Negro[s]" gives its possessors the "ability to leap into [a] higher stage of functioning. Soviet mankind." Ellison's notion of freedom was leaping far ahead of the president's.[36]

"A skillful and wise manipulation":
The Zoot Suit Editorial

Ellison's famous statement in his last editorial, the one dealing with myths and symbols, the zoot suit and the lindy-hop, needs to be set alongside these earlier *Negro Quarterly* writings. He designates three "general attitudes held by Negroes toward their wartime experience." The first is "unqualified acceptance of the limited opportunity for Negro participation," the attitude of those who are "comfortable only when taking orders, . . . happy only when being kicked." The second, *"unqualified rejection* of the war," reflects the view of those who "admire men who die rather than compromise their principles." While "during the folk period, before the Negro masses became politically conscious," this view "created folk heroes," it "became impractical . . . on the day John Henry's great heart was burst in his struggle against the machine." These two views are simply "inversions" of one another, ignoring the fact that Negroes *"have their own stake in the defeat of fascism."* Only the third view, advocating "critical participation, based upon a sharp sense of the Negro people's group personality," is viable, being "broader and more human than the first two attitudes, and . . . scientific enough to make use of both by transforming them into strategies of struggle." Referring to the recent angry resignation from the "Black Cabinet" by Judge William Hastie, assistant to Secretary of War Stimson, because of the military's refusal to desegregate, Ellison opines that the "very real class divisions within the Negro group" have been "partially suspended" by "outside pressures" during the current "revolutionary times." The current "centralization of power" among African Americans will enable them to move beyond "playing the role of [an 'expendable'] sacrificial goat" in the "great contest for power between the two large economic groups within the country." African Americans must "[participate] along with labor and other progressive groups as equals with . . . adult responsibility"; such "group unity" will prevent Negroes from being "exploited by others: either for the good ends of democratic groups or for the bad ends of Fascist groups."[37]

In this connection, Ellison proposes, Negro leaders who would take advantage of this opening must "integrate themselves with the Negro masses"; be flexible and alert to "new concepts, new techniques, and new trends among other peoples and nations"; and recognize that postwar advancement will hinge upon Negro workers' becoming acquainted with "the increasing innovations in technology." Above all would-be Negro leaders must "[learn] the meaning of the myths and symbols which abound among the Negro masses."

> [Otherwise] much in Negro life remains a mystery: perhaps the zoot suit conceals profound political meaning: perhaps the symmetrical frenzy of the Lindy-hop conceals clues to great potential power. . . . Our stated war aims, even though . . . essentially correct, . . . will be accepted by the Negro masses only to the extent that they are helped through the fog of their daily experiences. The problem is psychological: it will be solved only by a Negro leadership that is aware of the psychological attitudes and incipient forms of action which the black masses reveal in their emotion-charged myths, symbols and war-time folklore. Only through a skillful and wise manipulation of these centers of repressed social energy will Negro resentment, self-pity and indignation be channelized to cut through temporary issues and become transformed into positive action.

Ellison is sounding several new notes. His accusation that African Americans have figured historically as "sacrificial goat[s]" in the class struggle between the country's "two large economic groups" sharpens his earlier criticism of racism in the labor movement. In his reference to the Negro's "exploit[ation] . . . for the good ends of democratic groups," he extends the domain of white paternalism to encompass the left, presumably included under the rubric of "democratic groups." Also new are his emphasis on "psychology" and his insistence that would-be leaders learn how to interpret "emotion-charged myths, symbols, and war-time folklore" if they would reach the "Negro masses," as well as his notion that, at least for the present, class divisions among African Americans can be sutured in a unified political strategy.[38]

But this last "Editorial Comment" does not constitute a qualitative break with Ellison's earlier writings for *Negro Quarterly*. His description of "democratic groups" as possessing "good ends," to be distinguished from the "bad ends of Fascist groups," hardly indicates that he has written off the Communists, let alone embraced the thesis of "two totalitarianisms." His emphasis on the need for Negro leaders to participate as "equals with adult responsibility" alongside "labor and other progressive groups" does not reject class-based interracial alliances but requires Negro leaders to act with self-confident awareness of their political leverage. His discussion of the need for "psychological" insights that will help leaders guide African Americans out of the "fog of their daily experiences" draws upon the Marxist notion of false consciousness; his urging "wise" leaders to "manipulate" and "channelize" the "myths and symbols" that express mass consciousness bespeaks not a privileging of culture over politics, but a functional view of culture as a means to achieving political ends. "Broad" and "human" do not preclude "scientific," nor does "manipulat[ion]" figure as underhanded. Ellison's designation of the current moment as a "revolutionary time," when the "very real class divisions within the Negro group" have been "partially suspended," indicates that his call for unified Negro leadership is a tactic needed to win the war rather than a strategy for consolidating a Negro bourgeoisie in the capitalist United States. What drives Ellison's argument is his abiding conviction that winning the war will vanquish Jim Crow and open the door to socialist revolution; his differences with the CP line are more rhetorical than substantive.

Ellison's discussion of the "potential power" encoded in mass culture is inseparable from the surrounding context of fascism and war. The zoot suit, whose ballooning trousers and long coats defied wartime austerity measures limiting the use of textiles, was, in the words of Robert A. Hill, "a badge of social defiance . . . signifying the kind of 'cool' rebellion that carried enormous personal as well as symbolic meaning for young African-American and Mexican American males during World War II." Black and brown wearers of zoot suits, many of them draft dodgers, would be attacked by racist mobs in California soon after Ellison's editorial appeared; in 1944 Eugene Talmadge won reelection to the governorship of Georgia in part by campaigning, however fantastically, against "Moscow-Harlem zoot-suiters trying to take over" the state. To plumb the "mystery" of the zoot suit required probing not only the assertion of identity encoded in sartorial style but also the causes and results of the alienation of the costume's wearers from the nation's "stated war aims." While Ellison here manifests the fascination with intercultural mingling that he will later celebrate as the Protean essence of American pluralism—cultural performance beyond the categories of sociological rationality—here he declares that the zoot suit, like the lindy hop, needs to be understood in a "scientific" way if Negro leaders are successfully to move their potential constituencies out of the "fog" of everyday life. The zoot suit needs to be understood in its full significance if Negro leaders are successfully to win its wearers back to the fold of antifascism.[39]

Inviting the sociologist Horace Cayton to contribute to the fourth issue of *Negro Quarterly*, Ellison sets forth his goals. He wishes to analyze "all phases of Negro life, from the economic and political up through the cultural superstructure," thereby exploring "the potentialities of Negroes to function in an organized way on the stage of world politics." His intention is to study "the complex of characteristics which make us an oppressed nation with an eye toward making these findings the basis of new forms of struggle." The current Negro leaders, he complains, are "over-cautious." He hopes his editorial will contain "a pitiless examination of Negro life, its leadership and institutions in terms of the possible strategies and techniques which might be forged in order to create a conscious organism of the whole group. . . . I don't mean to ignore class lines, but to go beneath them with the intention of creating an emotional unity by giving it a consciousness of its potential historical role." He conceives of the issue as "a kind of 'What-are-We-What-are-our-resources-What is-to-be-done?'" Evidently the Communist theorization of Negroes as an "oppressed nation," as well as the methodology for cultural analysis supplied by the Marxist base-superstructure paradigm, assists Ellison as he imagines the "new forms of struggle" enabled by the present historical conjuncture.[40]

"The real problem is class: class: class":
Unpublished *Negro Quarterly* Writings

Ellison's drafts for unpublished editorials, as well as correspondence from his editorial desk, suggest that in his published writings for *Negro Quarterly* he was keeping a good deal of his radical light under a bushel. In an undated piece provisionally titled "Negro Development," he traces the major shifts in the status of the Negro from the Civil War to the present, focusing on the changing nature of Negro leadership and the varying meanings of Negro nationalism. Noting the inadequacies of middle-class leadership—its "contempt for the mass, the folk," its "deriv[ation of] power from [the] white ruling class"—he ponders the complexities of nationalism in terms drawn from the Soviet experience. "Negro nationalism[,] while [it] will build real consciousness among Negroes[,] must come from below," he writes. "From worker intellectuals, articulating [the] feelings and aspirations of [the] masses. Men who come to understand [the] meaning of Negro culture. They will be theoretical Marxists, emotionally Negro nationalists. Negro in form, socialist in content, working class in politics."[41]

Ellison's scattered notes on struggles in the South expand upon the need for class-conscious Negro leadership: "A leader while leading the ruled is still controlled by the laws which rule the group. A revolutionary transcends both the group and the laws. He is under the spell of another picture of reality. He breaks the laws of the status quo emotionally and intellectually under the influence of his will to create the new." Ellison scribbles, "[The] state [is a] coercive apparatus. . . . Spartacus will come." Conjoining a figure

from classical myth with one from history, he adds, "The Promethean instinct will appear again in Negro life," in which case "the South is doomed."
Invoking the Marxist interpretation of the titan Prometheus as the prototype
of proletarian rebellion, Ellison parallels him with Spartacus, the slave rebel
leader of ancient Rome and, not incidentally, Marx's favorite hero in world
history. The heroic figures framing Ellison's portraiture of the revolutionary
leaders needed in the Jim Crow South evidently fire his imagination in a way
that Hastie does not.[42]

In an unpublished editorial examining the grounding of Negro literature
and art in political economy, Ellison further teases out the meaning of nationalism. Identifying Negro culture as the product of "collective" historical
experience, he writes, "Any study of the sources of American Negro cultural
expression must be basically a study of the concept of freedom." Rejecting the notion that the spirituals derive from an African "mythical Sangrila
[Shangri-La]," he dubs this fixation on African roots a "mythical internationalism" that has "hinder[ed] the development of a national consciousness
among American Negroes." He argues, "Internationalism is a land that must
be conquered through the weapons of nationalism [since] . . . man usually
starts from the particular and moves to the general." While back-to-Africa
movements are founded on a false and reactionary internationalism, he sees
emerging a materially based internationalism, one anchored in both deeply
felt national identity and "the need to create a better world" for all oppressed
people. Its exemplar is Paul Robeson, who "as an artist starts at the international and arrived at the national[,] . . . leaping the chasm between the
American Negro experience and that of Africa through the highly intellec-
tualized process of making studies in comparative cultures." In a marginal
notation, Ellison adds, "The working class is the group possessing the type
of consciousness necessary to deal with the new conditions. They have the
toughness necessary to [suck] out the poison which festers [in] the wound."
Although in later years Ellison would become famous—in the eyes of many,
infamous—for his hostility to black nationalist invocations of African roots,
roundly criticizing LeRoi Jones (Amiri Baraka) and others for espousing this
view, it bears noting that this early critique of Afrocentricity is premised
not in American pluralism but in Marxist materialism. *Nation* is a category
of consciousness, a moment of dialectical particularity; the working class,
however, is the "general" agent possessing medicinal powers capable of converting internationalism from myth to reality.[43]

While he was the managing editor of *Negro Quarterly* Ellison wrote a
lengthy letter to an unnamed correspondent who had pressed him about

the possibilities for "equality in outlook and absence of racial prejudice" in an "economically satisfied society." Lamenting the dominance of the "Western and Nordic" notions of beauty that lead Negroes to bleach their skins, straighten their hair, and "marry light," Ellison states that "only a miracle in the form of a strongly nationalist art could change all this." But racial prejudice is a matter of attitudes, "defense mechanisms" adopted by whites and Negroes alike, that are grounded in an "economic basis," namely, the "distinction between haves and have-nots." He devises a provocative metaphor to describe the dissemination of racist ideas and attitudes. This ideological process

> is like the waves of sound produced when a bell is struck within hills[,] productive of echoes. The hammer is applied and sound comes forth in waves which spread out to fall upon the surfaces producing the echo, always spreading, until the sound dies gradually away. The bell becomes silent quite sometimes [*sic*] before the echoes die. But you can't say that the sound came from anything else, even with the bell silent and the echoes still returning.

But the current crisis supplies opportunity:

> White America's attitude is changing toward the Colored one, but only in degree as Colored America becomes aware of its strength when joined to that part of white America with which it has a common cause, and in the degree to which it recognizes its true leaders. We must not be fooled by race; that is a myth, an imbalmed body fallen to dust when exposed to the air. The real problem is class: class: class: whether hidden behind theories of race superiority, or beneath the chronic nationalism of fascism.[44]

Ellison's bell metaphor explores the relationship between temporal and structural causality. The bell is hard, material, and must be struck by an agent—presumably, capital. Once this happens, however, the sound—racism as theory and practice—radiates invisibly over space and time; the ability of surrounding surfaces—people, institutions—to send back the sound creates the false impression that they are its original source. Ellison's ensuing comparison of the "myth" of race with "an embalmed body fallen to dust when exposed to the air" not only riffs on the final scene of James Hilton's novel about Shangri-La, *Lost Horizon*, but also suggests the capacity of materially grounded leftist politics to destroy the chimerical notion of race. "Class: class: class"—when grasped as foundational by both "Colored America" and "that part of white America with which it has common cause"—will vanquish both "race superiority" and the "chronic nationalism of fascism." As he sat at his desk in the offices of *Negro Quarterly*, Ellison was hardly writing his declaration of independence from the left.

"Had the Communists imported a Russian scientist to study the Negro problem": Myrdal's Dilemma

Ellison and Herndon's coeditorship of *Negro Quarterly* came to an end in the summer of 1943. Herndon had been a far from efficient manager of finances; besides, Ellison had been drafted. Despite his and Herndon's promotion of Douglass's views about the need to join the segregated armed forces, the prospect of serving in the Jim Crow army stuck in his craw. Ellison joined the merchant marine as a cook on a Liberty Ship, becoming an active member of the Communist-led National Maritime Union (NMU), and shipped out in late December 1943. Without a typewriter he managed nonetheless to keep writing, sometimes on the backs of ships' menus, as his convoy evaded U-boats on the wartime seas.[45]

That Ellison was by mid-1943 increasingly disaffected with the CP-led left is reflected in a letter to his former lover, Sanora Babb, a white Party member, about his recent experience editing *Negro Quarterly*:

I went into it feeling that it was badly needed, since so little is understood about Negroes even by themselves or by those dedicated, supposedly, to leading us. I tried to translate Negro life in terms of Marxist terminology, hoping . . . by so doing to offer cues and insights to those whose field is that of action. . . . I didn't get very far with those I thought I was working with. The usual distrust of a Negro who dares to attempt to think. I was accused of everything from going over to the talented tenth to being a Trotskyite!

He has also become alienated from his former *New Masses* colleagues. As he writes to Babb later that summer, "I can't write for [*New Masses*] nowadays because they say few things about my people that I can agree with. . . . I'll never waste time with organizations again." That a qualitative change has occurred is obvious; notes to be sounded loudly in *Invisible Man* are beginning to be rung.[46]

Ellison's detachment from the left was neither sudden nor painless. It was after all CP member Add Bates who facilitated Ellison's entry into the merchant marine, recommending him as "one of the boys" to the NMU official in charge of hiring. While the war was on, moreover, Ellison hesitated to criticize the CP in print. In a review of Roi Ottley's *New World A-Coming* for *Tomorrow* in September 1943, Ellison took to task his former FWP boss for reproducing "all the stock, anti-Negro clichés" in his inadequate portrayal of "a people who are evolving from a folk to an industrial consciousness." Ottley gets it all wrong about Negro leadership, Ellison complains, overstating the mass support of Roosevelt's "Black Cabinet," understating the influence of Adam Clayton Powell Jr., and above all failing to appreciate the "problem of identity" confronting Negro leaders caught between "the war, the riots, and their support for the President." Although Ottley gets it right when he addresses "the Negro press, the pro-Japanese movements, . . . conditions in the Army, and police brutality," the book is pervaded by the "false optimism" signaled in its title. "[A] book truly sensitive to the overtones of Negro life today would have ended, not 'with a bang,'" Ellison opines, "but a questioning whisper." In *New World A-Coming* Ottley offers a mixed assessment of the CP that Ellison neither accepts nor rejects: although the CP has "lost ground steadily" among Negroes because of its "quest for national unity," it retains the reputation for having done "more than any other agency in American life toward breaking down the rigid color barriers that once existed between the races." Evidently he turns down this opportunity to lambaste the left, indeed even to insert own "questioning whisper."[47]

In his review of Gunnar Myrdal's *An American Dilemma* (written in 1944 but not published until 1964 in *Shadow and Act*), Ellison charges that Myrdal evades "the question of power and the question of who manipulates that power"; *An American Dilemma* constitutes *"a blueprint for a more effective exploitation of the South's natural, industrial and human resources."* Here Ellison takes some broad swipes at the CP. Pairing "the Left" with "the New Deal," he observes that the former "brought the world view of Marxism into the Negro community, introduced new techniques of organization and struggle, and included the Negro in its program on a basis of equality." The New Deal, "within its far more rigid framework[,] . . . moved in the same democratic direction." Yet both "neglected sharp ideological planning where the Negro was concerned . . . [and] went about solving the Negro problem without defining the nature of the problem beyond its economic and narrowly political aspects. Which is not unusual for politicians—only here both groups consistently professed and demonstrated far more social vision than the average political party." He continues,

> The most striking example of this failure is to be seen in the New Deal Administration's perpetuation of a Jim Crow Army, and the shamefaced

support of it given by the Communists. It would be easy — on the basis of some of the slogans attributed to Negro people by the Communists, from time to time, and the New Deal's frequent retreats on Negro issues — to question the sincerity of these two groups. Or, in the case of the New Deal, attribute its failure to its desire to hold power in a concrete political situation; while the failure of the Communists could be laid to "Red perfidy." But this would be silly. Sincerity is not a quality that one expects of political parties, not even revolutionary ones. To question their sincerity makes room for the old idea of paternalism, and the corny notion that these groups have an obligation to "do something for the Negro."

Ellison castigates the "over-cautious socialism" of the CP and bemoans the absence in the American left of "that cultural sophistication and social insight springing from Marxist theory, which, backed by passion and courage, has allowed the Left in other countries to deal more creatively with reality than the Right." The American CP, he concludes, is unwilling to merge Marx with Freud in confronting "the problem of the irrational," which, in American society, "has taken the form of the Negro problem" and which Myrdal has dubbed the "American dilemma."[48]

Though harsh, these criticisms do not lead to the accusation of treachery and betrayal lodged in *Invisible Man*. Indeed Ellison specifically rejects the charge that the CP's failure to keep its banner aloft during the war is traceable to "Red perfidy"; if anything, he praises the CP, along with the New Deal, which he characterizes, interestingly, as more "rigid," for having "far more social vision than the average political party." He stresses that the CP's inadequacies derive from its members' typical Americanness; it is in fact their unwitting implication in "the moral problem centering upon the Negro [that] . . . disproves the red-baiters' charge that left-wingers are alien." Ellison has some distance to travel before Brother Jack will lose his glass eye and start gabbling in Russian.

In an earlier draft of the Myrdal review, titled "*An American Dilemma*: The Negro Problem and Modern Democracy," Ellison makes a clearer distinction between the failings of the New Deal and those of the left. Alluding to Roosevelt's Black Cabinet, he charges that the New Deal "made blunders in analysising [sic] social trends among Negroes, depending upon a corp[s] of Negro 'advisors' picked for their names . . . rather than an objective knowledge of the subtleties of Negro-white relations." The CP, by contrast, "frequently miss-applied Marxist-Leninist-Stalinist concepts to the Negro situation and discarded them as invalid after they did not fit mechanically into the special grooves of American reality." Ellison continues, "During the vital periods of the New Deal the Left's position on the Negro was revolutionary[;] there were not tactical problems inhibiting [its] program, it demanded complete equality, dramatized the Scottsboro and Herndon cases and fought for Negro jobs." The left's "pragmatic belief in activity," however, led to the "blind belief that the Negro problem consisted solely in those issues where its interests and those of the Negro People coincided." Commenting on the "irrational factors which render black and white solidarity difficult," he credits Myrdal with voicing "a criticism of Marxist failure to consider these factors" and asks, "The Superstructure fallacy?" Remarking on the Carnegie Commission's decision to import the Swedish Myrdal to study the American racial situation, he only half-jokingly observes, "Perhaps had the Communists imported a Russian scientist to study the Negro problem, their work would have been more effective." Noting that Myrdal's mission is to "present the most realistic analysis of the Negro possible and at the same time to discredit the Marxist analysis," he concludes, "The left is called upon to answer this challenge." And he cautions, "Marxism must not be as idealistic as Myrdal would have us believe it is."[49]

Although he does not use the term—it has not yet entered political discourse—Ellison reacts here to the late wartime CP policies that would later be dubbed "Browderism." In the wake of the Tehran Conference in November 1943, Browder declared that socialism and capitalism could co-exist peacefully in the postwar world and that calling for the dictatorship of the proletariat would be *"hostile to the whole of Marxist theory, as well as stupid and—in real effect—reactionary"* (italics in original). Besides resulting in the dissolution of the CP and formation of the Communist Political Association (CPA) in May 1944, this analysis meant that the Black Belt thesis should be abandoned since the Negro people had already exercised their right to self-determination by choosing "to remain part of the American nation." While previously fettered by quasi-feudalist relations of production, the South now had a "limitless . . . future" because "the economic basis for eliminating all [its] social evils [was] being established" through wartime industrialization and mechanization of agriculture. Integral to the "postwar labor-capital cooperation," rather than a blot on the escutcheon of American democracy, the South need no longer be especially targeted for Communist organizing.[50]

Ellison's criticism of CP theory and practice in both drafts of the Myrdal review cannot be read in isolation from his disappointment at these developments. His criticism of the CP's analysis of the "Negro situation" in terms of "Marxist-Leninist-Stalinist concepts" is not that these concepts have been

irrelevant—the Black Belt thesis presumably grounded the Party's "revolutionary position" during the "vital period of the New Deal"—but that they
were mechanically misapplied and then abandoned. Ellison's disparagement
of the left's "pragmatic belief in activity," its "blind belief" that the "Negro
problem" could be addressed only in zones where the interests of African
Americans and the rest of the working class were identical, conveys a critique of the C P's economistic narrowing of the domain of antiracist struggle.
Notably, however, the criticism that he would later invoke—that the authoritarian demands of Soviet foreign policy were responsible for the failings of
the American C P—is absent. If anything, the USSR emerges as a model for
addressing the national question; its leadership role in the world Communist movement is not challenged, nor is the sophistication of Communist
parties elsewhere. It is the reformism and timidity, the "over-cautious[ness]"
of the American branch of the Third International that is at issue; he uses the
same term to criticize the wartime C P as he had used to characterize Negro
leaders in his final *Negro Quarterly* editorial the year before. Ellison's increasing interest in "the problem of the irrational" is inseparable from his critique
of C P economism and productive forces determinism. Freud is summoned
to fill the void left by Marx—"superstructure" becomes a "fallacy"—when
Marxism ceases to offer a critique of dominant ideology or a connection with
revolutionary praxis.

"Not the morality but the methods of American Communism": Wright's Blues

Ellison's review of Richard Wright's autobiography, which appeared in the
Antioch Review in 1945 under the title "Richard Wright's Blues" and was re-
issued in 1964 in *Shadow and Act*, is best known for its formulation of the
blues, as well as its assessment of the origins of Wright's naturalistic method
in the deprivations of his Jim Crow childhood. Earlier drafts of the review,
which was first titled "The Tragedy of Freedom" and then "Wright's Blues:
The Tragedy of Consciousness," diverge dramatically from the published
text. Ellison was invited by *Tomorrow* to review the original text of Wright's
autobiography, which was called *American Hunger* and comprised both the
narrative of Wright's southern youth (published as *Black Boy* in early 1945)
and the account of his northern maturity (published posthumously as *American Hunger* in 1977, though published in a shortened version in the *Atlantic
Monthly* in 1944 as "I Tried to Be a Communist"). In these earlier drafts Ellison focused on Wright's encounter with Communism. Completely excised

from the review that Ellison would publish the next year (since *American Hunger* had been excised from *Black Boy*), "The Tragedy of Freedom" and "Wright's Blues: The Tragedy of Consciousness" reveal at least as much about Ellison as they do about Wright.[51]

Readers familiar with Wright's differing portrayals of his experiences with the CP in "I Tried to Be a Communist" and *Black Boy (American Hunger)* are aware that, in the latter, more extended version, Wright gave a considerably more nuanced, and certainly more generous account of the appeal of Communism. In his commentary on this text Ellison places Wright's especially troubled relationships with other Negro Communists in the context of the American dilemma. Although Wright admired many of his Negro comrades for their "real organizing talent . . . as they led relief demonstrations and built unions," writes Ellison, he disdained their Lenin-imitating behavior and discerned a "lag between their actions and their grasp of the ideology in [the name of which] they acted." Making no "creative use of Marxism" and remaining fixed at the level of "trade-unionism," they "took the form of revolution but not its content . . . ma[king] no revolutions within themselves." Accordingly they brought into their relationships with white Communists "old patterns of response" they had learned in the Jim Crow South: "To be accepted by a group of whites was enough, and regardless of the feelings and wishes of the whites the psychological distance between them and the Negroes remained. . . . The party offered a perfect ambivalent situation whereby [the Negroes] could rebel against white men and conform to the wishes of white men at one and the same time."[52]

In their turn some white Communists, acting out the "moral guilt growing out of the denial of democracy to Negroes," reproduced "counter-stereotypes" of their Negro comrades by "idealizing" them. Because of the resulting "psychological distance," writes Ellison, "It [is] difficult for even the most honest white man to confront the Negro objectively; the critical faculty is undermined and a double standard becomes operative." Thus it appears "as though the well-meaning white individual had consciously encouraged the confusions and shortcomings of Negroes." "[Communists] have fewer *conscious* reservations about Negroes than any other group in the country," continues Ellison. "Fortunately there are some Negroes and whites who, by recognizing the causes [of the double standard], escape this dead-end." But Wright had felt obligated—precisely because he "believed (and still believes) that full democratic rights for Negroes lay in Communism"—to depict both the "horror" and the "glory" he saw dialectically embodied in his experience. He sought to educate the CP about its errors in order to save it; in his text he "functions as a sacrificial animal" in that "he dares the dangers of ostracism to extend the consciousness of the group." Both ironically and tragically, Ellison concludes, Wright ended up being "slapped down by the very group which worked sincerely to create a world into which the possession of such a consciousness as he had won would be neither criminal nor the right of a few, but of all."[53]

Ellison pulls no punches in this portrayal of racial dynamics within the CP; it is evident that in describing Wright's experiences he touches upon his own. It bears noting, however, that he still designates the Party as a group which "worked sincerely" to create a world free of racism. As in the Myrdal review, Ellison describes the CP as "a formerly revolutionary party" and observes with stoical bitterness:

> It was just as inevitable that [Wright's] idealism should die as it was that the party in which he believed would dissolve itself as it has recently done. There is a certain degree of idealism implicit in the most materialistic action, the trick is to expect it. And in the end, the direction of negro destiny must depend upon negroes themselves, regardless of their alliances with other groups. No political party can create character or intellectual quality, it can only help bring about conditions wherein these qualities may emerge. Life in america is such that a negro must either be driven underground into crime, into neurosis, or into the living-death of uncletomism, or else he can develop qualities of self-sacrifice and personal integrity and consciousness which will reject all forms of hampering authority [or] of compromise.

Although anticipating key tropes and themes of *Invisible Man*, this commentary locates the Party's betrayal of Wright's "idealism" largely in its self-dissolution and self-betrayal. Wright's account, concludes Ellison, judges Communists by a Communist standard, "weighing a total individual experience against not the morality, but the methods of American communism."[54]

In his commentary on Wright's draft autobiography Ellison places Wright's personal odyssey in both national and global contexts. Wright's "self-creation" in moving north involved the exercise of a "scientific rebirth technique [requiring] . . . the rapid shedding of every new formulation of the self." Wright repudiated the form of rebirth entailed in "imitating" either capitalist or Communist culture, either by skin bleaching or by adopting Leninist garb, because this role-playing would create internalized "fear and hate" and "a strong tendency toward all forms of ambivalence." Instead Wright opted to shrug off his Jim Crow "preindividuality" and enter the brave new world of modernity, becoming "Westernized" as a "Negro American." The "real and unfulfilled meaning of America's boasted cultural variety," asserts Ellison, is embodied in Wright's achievement of a "cultural richness, an intellectual and emotional flexibility and complexity which, if given a place to function, offers great creative possibilities." But the phenomenon embodied in Wright's transformation goes beyond the geographical borders of the United States and the historical phenomenon of the Great Migration: "This is the method by which backward countries have in our time thrown off the past, by which former Russian peasants lead mechanized armies, by which the level of social and political consciousness of China has outstripped its backward industrial development. Man may use his consciousness to control reality, or he can wander forty years in the desert of his own fears and inertia." The Negro American conscious of his place in historical process, Ellison argues, is positioned to play a vanguard role in the social revolution. On the one hand, the situation in the United States produces frustrating limits: "The dilemma of the American Negro is that he must find himself as a person at the same historical moment in which he must lose himself in the broader struggle of democracy against fascism: he must sacrifice even as he learns what it is he sacrifices." On the other hand, even though the "lag" embodied in the South's quasi-feudal mode of production produces "backward[ness]," it also produces people who can, like the "former peasants" in Russia and China, leap past stages and beyond limits, constituting forces on the leading edge of revolutionary change.[55]

It is in the psychological and political framework supplied by his analysis of Wright's painful encounters with "forms of hampering authority," not just in the Jim Crow South depicted in *Black Boy* but in the politically engaged North as well, that Ellison originally theorizes the blues. The famous passages about "finger[ing]" . . . the jagged grain [of] . . . aching consciousness" and "offer[ing] no scapegoat but the self" that appear in "Richard Wright's Blues" have not yet been written. Instead Ellison defines the "blues mechanism" (originally he calls it the "blues process") as the posture, at once therapeutic and defensive, that Wright "cultivated within himself" first in the Jim Crow South: "his brooding upon his experiences, refusing to repress his deep sense of humiliation, and his incessant concern with transforming it into meaningful images, symbols, and concepts, that saved him from cracking up." When Wright later experienced the tragic contradiction between the "morality" and the "methods" of American Communism in the North, his "need for the fellowship out of which such a morality evolves [was] no less unfulfilled, and it [gave] him the blues." Generalizing upon

Wright's situation, Ellison meditates, "Perhaps for the Negro, the horror of america will for a long time overshadow the glory; and to survive will require much whistling of the blues in the noonday dark." He concludes:

> The traditional blues enhanced the tragedy of unconscious suffering. Wright's blues enhance the tragedy of conscious thought and action. One wonders from what source beyond the area of individual need, out of what humane transcendence of American pragmatic thinking and shallow feeling, out of what inspiring vision, springing from what profound national catastrophe, will come those forms of organized action and understanding that will justify the latent acts of sacrifice and heroism with which Wright's attitude is so painfully pregnant.

The earliest version of this last sentence, while not fully legible, ends with an alternative formulation: ". . . will come those forms of organized action and understanding that will . . . destroy the need of the latent acts of sacrifice and heroism of which this attitude is so painfully pregnant." To "destroy the need" giving rise to the blues is a matter of political praxis, of "organized action and understanding" undertaken in reaction to a "profound national catastrophe." In Ellison's original version of the text the "latent acts of sacrifice and heroism" constituting Wright's blues, as well as the social forces both generating the blues and requiring their abolition, are inseparable from the context of fascism, war, and revolution. Indeed the entire lexicon of terms Ellison uses to define Wright's situation—not just "sacrifice" and "heroism," but also "scapegoat," "ambivalence," "rebirth," and "technique"— reflect upon this context. In 1944 Ellison uses these "god-terms" not to evade or transcend history, but to confront it.[56]

Especially in the drafts of his reviews of *An American Dilemma* and *Black Boy (American Hunger)* Ellison evinced deep disappointment with what he saw as the CP's abandonment of its broad-ranging struggle for Negro rights in the present and for socialism in the future, as well as with the inability of many individual Communists, white and Negro alike, to escape the horns of the "American dilemma." But his standpoint was riddled with ambivalence because the reality with which he was grappling was riddled with contradictions. After all, not even the most fervent advocate of the Double V was calling for slowing war production, much less acceding to the pro-Axis organizing being carried out by various self-described black fascists visible in Harlem and other urban centers. Randolph, once FEPC was introduced, had called off the planned march on Washington. The armed forces continued to be segregated, and black soldiers continued to be subjected to humiliation

and worse; the violence had recently peaked in the summer of 1943. Nonetheless since late 1943 the Tuskegee airmen had taken to the skies; by 1945
some million African Americans were in uniform. While mainly relegated to
unskilled and lower-paying jobs and encountering routine discrimination,
another million African Americans had by this time moved to urban areas
and secured employment in war industries. Hopes for extended postwar
democracy warred with cynicism at the marginal gains being made during
the war.[57]

The prevailing attitude of Negro organizations and newspapers across
much of the political spectrum was perhaps summarized by the prominent Harlem preacher Adam Clayton Powell Sr., who declared in 1945 that
Negroes were resolved to "fight with the United States to beat Hitler and
his idea of a master race into the dust of defeat [and] then . . . fight until
Judgment Day, if necessary, to get the old Simon Legree notion, that everything white represents superiority and everything colored stands for inferiority, out of the heads of a few white Americans." His son, the *People's Voice*
publisher Adam Clayton Powell Jr., already a prominent local politician and
soon to be nationally famous, noted, "Ignoring communists and organizations that include them . . . serves to weaken, not to strengthen." In words
that he no doubt regretted a few years later, when he supported the Korean
War and excoriated Paul Robeson, Powell wrote in 1945, "Red-baiting is born
of the same womb that conceived anti-Semitism, anti-unionism, and Jim
Crow." For all his grousing at the CP for its accessions to American nationalism, Wright allowed advertisements for war bonds to be placed on the dust
jacket of *Black Boy*. In "Richard Wright's Blues," Ellison noted the book's publication "at a time when any sharply critical approach to Negro life has been
dropped as a wartime expendable" and stated that some unspecified "pro-
fessional 'friends of the Negro people' have attempted to strangle the work
in a noose of newsprint." But Ellison refrained from explicit public criticism
of the CP as long as the war continued. It wasn't over until it was over.[58]

"The first truly mature Americans at that":
On the Cusp of "I Am an Invisible Man"

By the time he began concerted work on *Invisible Man* in the summer of 1945,
Ellison's attack on the CP had become frontal, harsh, and unforgiving; what
had started out as a critique from the left was hardening into programmatic
anticommunism. Writing to Stanley Edgar Hyman in mid-September, Ellison lambasted the "so-called left critics" Albert Maltz, Samuel Sillen, and

Isidore Schneider—his former colleagues at the *New Masses*—and dismissed the CP's current "confessing and breast-beating." He fumed:

> In case you haven't heard, they had liquidated the party in the South completely—only no one takes responsibility for that. Can you imagine, abolishing the "vanguard of the working class" in the country's area now undergoing the most rapid industrialization? I was eating and drinking and trying to achieve self-fulfillment with the lynchers of my people. They have done something far worse to the ideas of socialism than the Nazis did to the Jews—worse because so few understand just what has happened. A lot of good-intentioned little people are now falling for Foster just as blindly as they fell [for] Browder, whose crimes they see abstractly as simple evil rather than a smooth job of political betrayal the repercussions of which shall be felt for the next twenty years or more.

Ellison here alludes to events following publication of the letter written by the French Communist leader Jacques Duclos, at the behest of the Comintern, strongly criticizing the CPUSA for having abandoned the fight for socialism during the war. Former Party chair William Z. Foster had taken over the helm from Earl Browder, but there appeared in the CP press for several months a spate of wrenching self-criticism in which prominent Party leaders, Negro as well as white, castigated the organization's "right deviationist error" in believing that the "national unity born of urgent war necessity was an abiding historical phenomenon." As regards the Party's stated intention not to "soft-pedal the fight for Negro rights," there had been, in Doxey Wilkerson's words, a "striking gap between ideological profession and actual performance." But Ellison is having none of it; his cup now runs over with bitterness.[59]

In a letter written in November 1945 to Kenneth Burke, who had just read the published version of "Richard Wright's Blues," Ellison draws lessons from Wright's experience with Communism quite different from those he discovered the previous year in his draft review of *American Hunger*:

> First, the Negro breaks blindly away from his pre-individual condition; next he discovers the organized discipline of communism, but naively believes that he has discovered a utopia in which blacks and whites are magically cleansed of their mutual antagonisms; then reality exerts itself and instead of revealing new forms of man he discover[s] the Negro communists wearing their psychological slave chains and the whites brandishing their psychological bull-whips.

Asking whether a man in Wright's situation should "remain loyal to a political party, accepting it for its stated aims, for its former rather than for its current action, or should . . . remain loyal to his people and to his own experience," Ellison inserts himself into the discussion:

> I believe, for my part, that if one truly believes in communism one ha[s] the obligation to reject the course it has taken in this country since 1937, and that had more of those intellectuals who left it . . . stated their reasons publicly, they might have saved the Left from becoming the farce it has now become. . . . We are afraid to stand alone or to speak alone. And when we sneak away in hurt and outrage we hold our tongues and hope that things will get better with a "change in the political situation," never facing the fact that we, each of us, is the political situation, or that the rejection of an organization is as much a function of belonging and belief as that of accepting its program.[60]

Ellison's postwar letters to Wright draw upon the two men's familiarity with the actors involved. Noting the "failure of guys like Ben [Davis] and the ACP [American Communist Party]" to "build a real organization in Harlem," Ellison gloats, "It seems that the old coalitions are breaking up and the white folks find themselves with a couple of black frankensteins—or black elephants—on their hands. They aren't sure if they have leaders with followers behind them, or simply inflated symbols incapable of functioning in the real world." He adds, "As for the Davises, Fords, Wilkersons, . . . yes, and Robesons, we can laugh those clowns to death." For the post-Duclos letter's "brass confessions" of CP leaders, Ellison has nothing but contempt. "Only men who are not only currupt but whose curruption has frozen over and hardened can confess the things they do and still accept positions of leadership. . . . They're as dangerous as Nazis." Commenting on the falsity of Foster's claim to have rid the Party of revisionist tendencies festering for a decade, Ellison observes that the CP Central Committee has changed hardly at all: "Each new authoritative statement reveals new termite borings of easy, sheep-like belief, vacuity and lack of thought." His tragicomic metaphor for the situation is drawn from western movies:

> The rest of the gang with Foster are in the saddle. Browder ran the nag off a cliff and broke its legs, and left it moaning in the shallow water; Foster has told it the bones have mended, shot it full of dope and God knows whatt'll happen now. A broken swaybacked nag when the times call for a tank coordinated with jet planes of high maneuverability and a speed

faster than sound! Browder is as great an engineer as Hoover; Hoover only drained the country, Browder transformed a locomotive of history into a prairie schooner.[61]

Ellison has clearly changed his tune within the past year. Not some, but all white American Communists are now caught on the horns of the American dilemma; they are in fact "lynchers" and "brandishers of bull-whips." Negro Communists, conversely, are not just inadvertently following "old patterns of thinking" learned in the South, but masochistically kneel down in their "psychological slave chains." The rhetoric of "two totalitarianisms" shapes Ellison's description of the Communists' betrayal of socialism, now seen as equivalent to, even worse than the viciousness of the Nazis. Ellison has, moreover, revised the chronology of Communist failure; apparently the CP has been a "farce" since as early as 1937, the year when Ellison himself first was drawn into its orbit. His rancor is leading him to reconsider and reconfigure how he has spent nearly the past decade of his life.[62]

Although Ellison would meet briefly with Wright and other black radicals in 1946 to explore the possibility of forming a non-Communist-affiliated Marxist journal, he was increasingly relying upon the writing of fiction as a means to "[speak] on the wavelength of the human heart." Hoping "some day . . . to do a surgical job on the repressive effect that c.p. sectarianism had upon [his] sensibilities along with the quickening effects of Marxism," he is delving into his notebooks crammed with materials relating to "psychology, comparative literature and cultural anthropology . . . along with enough notes on the blues to make a book." Finding himself on a "sea of uncertainty," he observes, "The only stable thing I have . . . is the raft of concepts on which I lie as I paddle toward the shore." He forecasts the emergence of a "new humanism," in which it is the destiny of Wright and himself to be not just the "conscience of the Negro people" but the "conscience of the United States":

> The more I think and try to understand the more I tremble before the collosal responsibility we have as Negroes. Nevertheless it won't be the first time in history that the slaves and sons of slaves have risen to positions of intellectual leadership. . . . I'm beginning truly to understand the greatest joke, the most absurd paradox, in American history: that simply by striving consciously to become Negroes we are becoming and are destined to become Americans, and the first truly mature Americans at that.

Rather than driving tanks or locomotives or jet airplanes that will, in both reality and metaphor, "throw off the past" and "leap [toward] . . . "Soviet mankind," African Americans are being transformed from a vanguard historical force into a metonymy of the body politic. The distinction is a crucial one: rather than using "words as bullets" to create a revolutionized reality, he proposes using the existing airwaves to speak for a democratic reality always already coming into being.[63]

"Unless you're prepared to stool on your union":
Notes from the Proletarian Underground

As Ellison pauses on the threshold of writing *Invisible Man*, it is evident that he will not turn back. Yet he remains committed to some of the long-range goals of Communism. The Communists' betrayal is all the more egregious, he anguishes to Wright in 1945, because "they still speak in the name of the only possible future" and are

> responsible to the Negro people at large even if they do spit in the faces of their members. . . . They must either live up to their words or face a relentless fire of mature, informed criticism which will use everything from the many forms of the written word to the platform and the radio. If they want to play ball with the bourgoise [*sic*] they needn't think [they] can get away with it. . . . [A] few good men could change that picture, but it would be folly to try to do it from the inside.

Sharing with Wright his reaction to the recent "explosion of the new atomic bomb," Ellison declares:

> We've got to do something to offset the C.P. sell-out of our people: and I mean by this, both Negroes and labor. With such power in the world there is no answer for Negroes certainly except some sort of classless society. Men are coming into open conflict with the power of the universe again, and although the almost-conquered force is in the "control" of a few, it is so powerful that [it] is an immediate threat even to them. Unity of peoples is more than a political necessity, it has become a matter of life itself.

The Negro leaders who are shilling for U.S. imperialism in this new nuclear age, he adds, provide no alternative to this "sell-out." These are not the words of a man who has abandoned all his leftist commitments. His definition of "our people" is multiracial and class-based; he still sees "some sort of classless society" as the only viable alternative to the threat of nuclear holocaust.[64]

These left-wing sympathies will continue to bob to the surface over the coming years, even as Ellison's raft of concepts takes him downstream (it is tempting to add, deeper into slave territory). In a review in 1946 of John Beecher's autobiographical account of the NMU-led wartime organizing of multiracial Liberty Ship crews, Ellison scolds the author for the sentimental utopianism of his portrayal of "tranquil interracial brotherhood," which avoids the realities of the "rough seas of our race relations." But he accedes to the appeal of Beecher's depiction of the "warmth of human relationships . . . in times of war among soldiers, sailors, and airmen," noting that such relationships are the norm in "pre-industrial societies in which relationships are not based upon an abstract market as in capitalist societies, but upon a more direct and less complex awareness of social necessity." Attributing both racism and alienation to capitalism, Ellison still thinks in historical materialist terms. In a letter to Wright in 1948 largely hostile to the CP, Ellison remarks that the Communists still "stand a good chance to survive and become a force again—if the present trend of events continues long enough." Chester Himes, in *Lonely Crusade*, has misestimated the tenor of the times: "Reality is becoming stern enough to make people reject anti-communist propaganda." Ellison has not yet, it seems, joined the other side.[65]

Perhaps startling to readers familiar with *Invisible Man* is a letter that Ellison published in the *People's Daily World*, a CP-affiliated West Coast newspaper, in November 1954, by which time his raft was well launched into the mainstream of American letters. He had not published anything in the left press for over a decade. Addressing workers who might be approached by the FBI, he warned, "These rattlesnakes are like Anyface. . . . Unless you're prepared to stool on your Union, your friends, or on anyone else they decide you shall finger, they're deadly enough to spit out their fangs at your kids." Not cited in any bibliography of Ellison's work—it is noted only in his FBI file—this anomalous bit of journalism, redolent of the proletarian rhetoric he had presumably abandoned more than a decade before, suggests that, even as he was wining and dining with the New York literati and celebrating the nation's global cold war project, he was disquieted by attacks on class-conscious workers by the repressive state apparatus. He might not be a Communist, but he was still a union man. It had taken a good deal of time for Ellison to wrestle down his Promethean conscience and be reborn as a cold warrior. Even after his rebirth, it seems, he had some residual loyalties. He may even have wondered whether the project of the protean Anyface had been enabled by the words of the invisible man.[66]

Developing an Aesthetic **two**

**Myth, ritual, and revolution
got slammed around.**

—Ralph Ellison, 1977, speaking
of League of American Writers
meetings in the early 1940s

In discussions of literary history and literary craft after he wrote *Invisible Man*, Ellison is renowned—in the eyes of some, notorious—for his distinction between "relatives" (with whom one is stuck, whether gladly or not) and "ancestors," whom a writer is free to choose. Richard Wright was only the most famous of the many African American "relatives" from whom Ellison, in his continuing effort not to be branded a "Negro writer," sought to keep his distance. The "ancestors" with whom he proclaimed closest identity were, among modern writers, Ernest Hemingway, James Joyce, William Faulkner, André Malraux, and T. S. Eliot; among writers of the previous century, Henry James, Mark Twain, Herman Melville, and, at times ambivalently, Ralph Waldo Emerson. Reaching further back, he would invoke Shakespeare, Dante, Virgil, Aeschylus, Homer, and the Bible. As regards the critics and critical schools he had found most valuable, he would mention the theories of the sacrificial hero set forth by Lord Raglan and various Freudian-inflected "myth and ritual" critics drawing upon James Frazer's *The Golden Bough* and the Cambridge School of Classical Anthropology, as well as the treatments of folklore by Constance Rourke and Stanley Edgar Hyman. Above all he would pay homage to Kenneth Burke, whose rhetorical approach to literature as "equipment for living" and whose mapping of narrative along the lines of "purpose-passion-perception" had guided Ellison as he built the novelistic raft that would enable him to navigate his way through the heartland of the American conscience. In conjunction with his chosen lexicon of critical "god-terms," this self-fashioning of his literary ancestry strongly influenced the discourse within which Ellison's oeuvre would be evaluated and celebrated over the years.[1]

Almost completely effaced from this declaration of cultural identity would be an acknowledgment of Ellison's formative years on the literary left. Ellison's sense of belonging within the African American literary tradition would be occluded; his ties with African American Marxist writers other than Wright would drop out of sight, and Wright would be remembered, other than for supplying Ellison with a negative example, for introducing him to the prefaces of James and Joseph Conrad and the letters of Feodor Dostoevsky. The class-conscious theories of literature and culture to which Ellison had been exposed through his participation in the League of American Writers and the *New Masses* editorial board would be effaced, along with the fact that it was in these settings that he first theorized the connections between African American folklore and the myths and rituals examined by comparative anthropologists. As during the 1950s and 1960s the proletarian movement was disappeared from literary history, modernism was conflated with high modernism, and folkloric study divided into anthropology on the one hand and archetypal criticism on the other, Ellison's reframing of his own literary heritage participated in the project of the cultural cold war. It is my purpose in this chapter to read forward through Ellison's early writings about literature and culture, thereby reenvisioning his place in the arc of U.S. literary history and preparing the way for an examination of the creative process resulting in *Invisible Man*.[2]

"The economic basis of Negro personality":
Ellison as Leftist Critic

Although Ellison would later claim that he "never liked, and never believed . . . the facile [idea] . . . encouraged . . . especially [by] the Stalinist Communists" that "the writer owed only a second level allegiance to the art through which he found his identity," his own early critical writings hardly display a first-level allegiance to the realm of artistic formalism. In an unpublished early review titled "New Left Wing American Writers," the tyro critic takes off from Stephen Spender's comment in *The Destructive Element* that the "highbrow" literature of young English Communists "is not in any sense proletarian; it is advance-guard experimental writing imbued with Communist ideology." Applying this statement to radical young American writers who have "taken up the fight of the masses . . . and accepted Marxism as [their] guiding philosophy," Ellison asserts that these misguided leftists "continue to fly over the heads of the audience whose fight they have taken to heart seemingly with as much detachment as some strange bird flying over from Mr. T. S. Eliot's Waste Land." Although he applauds the writers' "interest in experimentation [since] . . . the discoveries and standards of the best bourgeois writers [cannot be] . . . simply label[ed] . . . 'decadent,'" he laments that "the tape worm of literary experimentation seems to deprive the creative body of its nurishment." His biological metaphor continues, "Perhaps the new substance has had the effect of an allegro [allergen?] in their literary systems, reacting against a protein derived from the brilliant but decadent fare of the dying epoch."[3]

Shifting his trope from ingestion to inhalation, the confident young Ellison remarks that the unnamed writers under consideration exist in a "rarified atmosphere . . . in a very small room filled with the cultural bricabrac of a declining era. Such air is for the mountain top and most of us, the masses, live in the deep valleys where such air would be much too thin to go around." The "new left-wing writers" desirous of reaching a popular readership must therefore "descend from their clouds of literary technical abstraction." The model for writers in America, he decides, "is not the method of Proust, nor of Eliot, but of Liberty and True Detective, of Hughes and Sterling Brown." Acknowledging that radical writers may for a while have to write in "two styles," he urges them to undertake "frequent journeys from, and the final abandonment of, the bricabrac fortified room, out into the wide space among the unwashed millions." Ellison was no doubt relieved in later years that these comments had never been published. Although it reveals the self-importance and anti-elitist elitism, not to mention lack of control over wayward metaphors, of a young man struggling to find his radical voice, this review is noteworthy for what it shows about Ellison's felt place in cultural history. For it belies his later claim to have been bowled over in his youth by the example of Eliot; it is Langston Hughes and Sterling Brown — "relatives," we may note — who are given pride of place. Notably too "technique" is reduced to adjectival form and associated with elitist "literary . . . abstraction"; the genres consumed by the "unwashed millions" offer more promising models to writers "desirous of reaching a popular readership."[4]

Toning himself down in his published criticism for the New Masses and other left journals, Ellison contrasted materialist and idealist approaches to culture, demonstrating from the outset a particular interest in folklore. In "Javanese Folklore," a review written in 1939 of Gene Fowler's novel Illusion *in Java*, Ellison criticizes the author's "escapist" romanticism: "It is difficult to believe that almost forty million people living under the colonial rule of the Dutch find their lives as lyrical as does Fowler. . . . Folklore, even those most charming, reveals a contradictory, bitter-sweet quality when something is known of the conditions that give it birth." By contrast, Ellison's report in 1941 on the development of a revolutionary writers' league in the Philippines notes with excitement the "resurgence of Filipino cultural activity" as a result of the "social revolution" accompanying "the growth of industrialization and the activity among workers and farmers." A literature "expressive of the hopes and ideals of the people," he anticipates, will be developed primarily by writers attuned to the proletarianization of the masses through the mounting class struggle; folklore should not be reified through sentimental reflection upon the preindustrial past.[5]

Ellison's early literary reviews stressed the need for novelists to portray the formation of individual personalities in class-based social conditions. Commenting on Len Zinberg's *Walk Hard, Talk Loud*, a novel featuring a black boxer whose career is ruined by racial discrimination, Ellison praises the author for "indicat[ing] how far a writer, whose approach to Negro life is uncolored by condescension, stereotyped ideas, and other faults growing out of race prejudice, is able to go with a Marxist understanding of the economic basis of Negro personality." A similar premise underlies his criticism of Louis Cochran's *Boss Man*, a novel treating the rise of a southern businessman. The author has overrelied on the central character's "unfulfilled desire for a son" to explain his motivations, scolds Ellison. "The South's condition is not due to isolated individuals. . . . No matter how powerful an individual may become, he is dependent upon others with similar interests; it is this group's consciousness of itself as a class—its links lead to Wall Street—that is responsible." *Boss Man* would have been a better novel, Ellison adds, if Cochran had "understood the historical significance" of episodes given insufficient weight, such as "an incident of a white sharecropper protesting his exploitation" and "another of a Negro exerting his will in revolt." Ellison concludes, "The tragedy of the South lies not in the personal frustrations of members of its ruling class, but in the denial of human personality, in the waste of human talent, energy and life, for which it has become a symbol." In his developing aesthetic theory, a text's value as art is inseparable from its capacity to tell the truth, which in turn hinges on its grasp of totality. Rhetoric is intertwined with reference.[6]

"A deeper unity is lost":
Ellison on African American Writers

As a Marxist critic, Ellison put African American writers through a particularly exacting ideological litmus test. Solicited by Wright for inclusion in *New Challenge*, "Creative and Cultural Lag," Ellison's first published review, contained a commentary on Waters Turpin's multigenerational novel of African American life, *These Low Grounds*. Ellison praises Turpin for having set his characters in history but scores him for being insufficiently dialectical:

> It is the Negro writer's responsibility, as one identified with a repressed minority, to utilize yet transcend his immediate environment and grasp the historical process as a whole, and his, and his group's relation to it. This cannot be accomplished with dull sensibilities, or by lagging in the cultural, technical or political sense. . . . It is not necessary for an author to adopt contemporary technical devices to produce novels of distinction. However, Turpin's failure to make use of these devices, and the resulting weakness of *These Low Grounds*, suggest that he might profit by a closer acquaintance with the techniques of his contemporaries.

Although he claims otherwise, clearly the young critic views "technique," signifying experimental means of artistic production, as essential to the production of "novels of distinction"; his advocacy of the artistic avant-garde is inseparable from his call for a dialectics of totality. "Lag," a term signifying uneven development in the base-superstructure relationship, here signifies a backwardness that is simultaneously political and cultural. Two years later Ellison reiterates this judgment when he refers to Turpin as a "clumsy obstetrician," a trope drawn from the Marxist discourse analogizing the movement from one mode of production to another with the process of pregnancy, labor, and delivery, wherein the class struggle functions as midwife. Historical materialism evidently supplied Wright's young protégé with both concepts and metaphors for mapping the relationships among literary texts, authorial consciousness, and "the historical process as a whole."[7]

The Marxist concept of ideology, as well as current Communist theorizing of "the Negro question," guided Ellison's assessment of the Negro Playwrights' performance in 1940 of Theodore Ward's *Big White Fog*. The play's theme, he declares, is "the Negro people's striving to a world in which they can exist as a nation, with the full freedom which the concept implies." He praises the play's "attempt to probe the most vital problems of Negro experience," which include the hardships posed by the Depression and the experience of Garveyism, embodied in Victor, and the emergence of Communism, embodied in Victor's son, Lester. Ellison chides Ward for placing greater emphasis on Victor's "confused Negro nationalism," however, noting, "The Negro people long ago discarded the utopianism of the Garvey movement." The play's plot provides an unrealized opportunity to contrast "the illusory with the realistic, the utopian with the scientific." The story of Lester— which, it bears noting, culminates in a Communist-led multiracial anti- eviction protest—"should have been in the foreground," complains Ellison. "The Negro people's consciousness [of the conditions that produced Victor's tragedy] has increased . . . to the point that they have produced a writer who can objectify those elements once shrouded in a big white fog." Alluding to Ward's borrowing of the phrase "big white fog" to denote false conscious- ness from Wright's "Fire and Cloud"—and anticipating his own use of the phrase in his final *Negro Quarterly* editorial in 1943—Ellison assesses Ward's play in terms that are at once political, formal, and epistemological.[8]

Ellison's comments on Hughes's autobiography, *The Big Sea* (1940), elabo- rated a critique of the legacy of the Harlem Renaissance. The text "offers a valuable picture of the class divisions within the Negro group" and reveals how, in the 1920s, writers had engaged in "a pathetic attempt to . . . wed the passive philosophy of the Negro middle class to the militant racial protest of the Negro masses." Although he views Hughes as "one of the few writers who survived the Negro Renaissance and still has the vitality to create," Elli- son faults him for devoting "too much attention . . . to the esthetic aspects of experience and failing to find a form that would get past the superficial unity of the picaresque." Because Hughes avoids analysis and comment and, in some instances, emotion, "a deeper unity is lost . . . that unity which is formed by the mind's brooding over experience and transforming it into con- scious thought." "Conscious thought," a phrase that will gain in gravitas for Ellison in years to come, here signifies the Marxist framework enabling lit- erary works to possess a "deeper unity." The radical young critic who would sit on the platform among the honored guests at conference in 1940 on the topic "words are bullets" was honing his ax on the reputations of both new and long-established writers.[9]

Ellison's fullest application of Marxist theory in his *New Masses* discus- sions of current African American writing is displayed in "The Great Migra- tion" (1941), his review of William Attaway's *Blood on the Forge*. Although, as we have seen, Ellison would add to the *Negro Quarterly* version of this review (1942) remarks newly linking the novel to the wartime situation, in both its versions the review set forth the young critic's proletarian aesthetic. Ellison applauds the novelist, "one of the most gifted Negro writers," for capturing the assault of industry upon his migrant characters' "folk sensibilities" and showing that "in this world of changing values all the old rules of living are melted away." But he faults Attaway for failing to create a "center of consciousness lodged in a character or characters capable of comprehending the sequence of events." While the Moss brothers' northward migration powerfully portrays "the clash of two modes of economic production," the novel's dialectic is "incomplete," for it represents "only one pole of the contradictory experience from which the novel is composed." Attaway "did not see that while the folk individual was being liquidated in the crucible of steel, he was also undergoing fusion with new elements," and that "the individual which emerged," the "most conscious American Negro type, the black trade unionist," is "better fitted for the problems of the industrial environment." Attaway's "inclusion of such a consciousness would not have been a mere artistic device; it would have been in keeping with historical truth." The novelist of the Great Migration has "grasped the destruction of the folk, but missed its rebirth on a higher level."[10]

Key terms and tropes in Ellison's review of *Blood on the Forge* distilled the principles that guided his practice as a Marxist critic; reconfigured, they would shape the thematics of *Invisible Man*. The equation of "conscious" with "class conscious" signals his conception of the "type" as embodying emergent rather than residual features of the historical dialectic. "Rebirth," which will figure as the dominant trope describing the invisible man's awakening after the explosion in the paint factory (itself probably modeled on the similarly traumatic steel plant explosion in Attaway's novel), here signifies the historical process by which the migrant undergoes negation and emerges, reborn, as the proletarian. The metaphor of melting and re-fusing not only recalls the volatile liquidity of molten steel in Attaway's novel but also signifies the metaphorical liquidity of consciousness produced by the pressures of the Great Migration and anticipates its later reformulation as "fluidity" in the outlines and drafts of *Invisible Man*. The trope may also gesture toward Marx's famous assertion in "The Communist Manifesto" that with capitalism's rupture of older traditions "all that is solid melts into air."[11]

During the period when he was editing *Negro Quarterly*, Ellison published in March 1942 in the *Sunday Worker* under the pseudonym "David Wilson" a review of Sterling A. Brown, Arthur P. Davis, and Ulysses Lee's *Negro Caravan* anthology, titled "Treasury of Negro Literature." Remarking that the anthology contained both "an affirmation of American democracy and a criticism of its limitations," Ellison pronounces that the volume's underlying theme is "freedom," which "gave hope, discipline, and exaltation to the people through their folk art forms." It is necessary, he claims in a noteworthy visual metaphor, to view both history and literature through "the clarifying lens of the Marxist ideology." Alluding to features of the CP analysis of the "Negro question" that would be familiar to *Daily Worker* readers — Reconstruction as "the bourgeoisie's betrayal of its own revolution"; the true identity of Negroes as a "hampered nation" rather than a "race" — Ellison proposes that only recently have writers come to understand the "ambiguity [of] . . . Negro experience" as a "process" rather than "fragmentarily." Writers of the 1920s had stopped at "plead[ing] [their] humanity"; it is writers emerging from the recent wave of class struggle who are positioned to "discipline the emotions and create the consciousness of the whole Negro People — and through them of the entire working class." A weakness of the anthology, however, is that the introductory essays neglect to mention such practical and theoretical contexts as "Negro union activity . . . Allen's *The Negro Question in the United States* and other works of Marxist theory, [and] James W. Ford's candidacy for the Vice Presidency of the United States." In order to carry to a higher level the "discipline" that folk art once gave to slaves, revolutionary writers must now "discipline emotions" and "create consciousness" along distinctly Communist lines. These are hardly the recommendations of a "true outsider of the left," as Ellison would later proclaim himself to have been.[12]

"New proletarian consciousness": The Wright Stuff

The writer who best used "the clarifying lens of the Marxist ideology" to understand and depict Negro experience was, in Ellison's view, Richard Wright, to whom he paid extended homage in 1941 in a *New Masses* review essay titled "Recent Negro Fiction." Ellison chastises Negro writing of the 1920s for having "perceived no connection between its own efforts and the symbols and images of Negro folk forms; it was oblivious of psychology; it was unconscious of politics. . . . Its protest was racial and narrowly nationalistic." By contrast, Wright's "realist" understanding of the "universals embodied in Negro experience" reflects the "new proletarian consciousness" emerging from "the depression years, the movement for relief, the rise of the CIO with the attending increase in union activity among the Negroes, the Herndon and Scottsboro cases, the fight against the poll tax." It was "through exercising his function as secretary of the [Chicago John Reed Club], and through his personal responsibility, forcing himself to come to grips with [the intense issues affecting American life]," wrote Ellison, that Wright gained access to "new techniques," "new themes," indeed "ownership of the means of [literary] production." But the decisive force driving this literary development was the "pressure that was bursting the shell of the Negro people's folk consciousness" and that now "demanded articulation through prose mediums capable of dealing with the complexities of the society in which [the] new consciousness struggled to be born." "Rebirth" and "complexity" are socially determinate phenomena; "universals," in Hegelian fashion, are contained in the concrete experiences of a folk undergoing dialectical transition. Wright's practice reveals the Marxist provenance of terms that Ellison would later rearticulate to serve distinctly non-Marxist ends.[13]

By contrast with recent works by Turpin, Arna Bontemps, and Zora Neale Hurston, which display the "Jim Crow retardation of the natural flow of the Negro folk consciousness into the machines and institutions which constitute the organism of North American society," Wright's work "postulated the existence of a group whose vision rejected the status quo." *Native Son* "represents the take-off in a leap which promises to carry over a whole tradition," enthuses Ellison; the novel blazes a "path which [the Negro writer] might follow to reach maturity." In a world "chaotic with reaction and war" — when, as demonstrated by the recent use of African American scabs during the River Rouge strike, "demoralized and culturally dispossessed Negroes might be used by an American fascism" — fiction like Wright's can help African Americans overcome the "handicap . . . of historically denied opportunities" and "possess the conscious meaning of their lives." "Chaos" is not an undecidable state beyond the realm of Marxist science, but a product of "reaction and war" that must be comprehended and combated from the standpoint of those who, like Wright, possess the "conscious[ness]" and "vision [to] rejec[t] the status quo."[14]

Ellison's appreciation of Wright in both "Recent Negro Fiction" and his other critical commentaries resonates with allusions to Wright's own oeuvre. The trope of Marxism as a "clarifying lens" recalls Wright's statement in "How Bigger Was Born" that his "contact with the labor movement and its ideology" had given him "a pair of spectacles whose power was that of an x-ray enabling [him] to see deeper into the lives of men." Ellison's call on Negro writers to "utilize but transcend" their "immediate environment" recalls Wright's proposition in "Blueprint for Negro Writing" that his peers should acknowledge and absorb black nationalism "in order to transcend it." Ellison's negative — and homophobically tinged — estimate of the New Negroes draws upon Wright's charge that the writers of the 1920s had "entered the Court of American Public Opinion dressed in the knee-pants of servility, curtseying to show that the Negro was not inferior"; his faulting of the editors of *Negro Caravan* for neglecting the context supplied by the Scottsboro and Herndon cases echoes Wright's citation of these same cases as evidence of the growing class consciousness he encourages writers to address. Ellison's criticism of Hughes, Attaway, and Ward for having evaded the "deeper unity" afforded by Marxism recalls Wright's description of *perspective* as the "theory about the meaning, structure and direction of modern society" without which the writer is "a lost victim in a world he cannot understand or control." Above all Wright's insistence upon the typifying and synecdochic status of Negro experience—Bigger Thomas's embodiment of a future either communist or fascist—underpins Ellison's conception of the embeddedness of universals in the dialectic of history.[15]

As we have seen, the correspondence between Wright and Ellison in the early 1940s reveals both men's growing antipathy toward those CP critics, especially African Americans, who failed to grasp the meaning and significance of Bigger Thomas as an embodiment of revolutionary potentiality. Although these negative reactions left a bitter legacy, they did not lead either writer to abandon Marxism as the basis for literary creation or, at least for a time, to jump ship from the CP. Sharing with Wright his reaction to *Twelve Million Black Voices*, Ellison registers not only his profound personal response but also his fortified commitment to the production of revolutionary literature and critical commentary. Acknowledging that Wright's text has made him confront "emotions which tear the insides to be free and memories which must be kept underground, caged by rigid discipline," Ellison expresses his deep sense of "brotherhood" with Wright. "We are the ones who had no comforting amnesia of childhood, and for whom the trauma of passing from the country to the city of distruction brought no anesthesia of unconsciousness but left our nerves peeled and quivering," he writes. "We are not the numbed, but the seething. God! It makes you want to write and write and write, or murder." Wright's text "seizes hold to epochs and a continent and clears them of fog," furnishing "a weapon more subtle than a machine-gun, more effective than a fighter plane! It's like seeing Joe Louis knock their best men silly in his precise, impassively-alert Negro way." Like the "scientific politician," the writer must, in order to "controll reality . . . manipulate it . . . weigh it and balance it, to test it." Indeed, the book supplies "political leaders" with "the essence of what they must work with; all Marx and Engles, Lenin and Stalin wont help them unless they understand this part of the therotical word [made] flesh." Ellison closes on a note of profound gratitude: "I'm better for having read it. Yes, and a better Marxist." Although he would eventually back away from most of this declaration, declaring that Wright, "no spiritual father of mine," had been seduced by "the facile answers of Marxism," this passionate confession, perhaps the most heartfelt writing Ellison would ever produce, suggests the pain that would accompany his own rebirth some years later as a warrior for the other side.[16]

"The whole revolutionary core":
Folk Heroes and Class Struggle

Whether lauded for evading literary ghettoization or criticized for sacrificing blackness on the altar of Eurocentric archetypes, Ellison's use of folkloric motifs has been widely interpreted as his means of transcending (or attempting to transcend) historical and racial specificity. In his writings and interviews after *Invisible Man* Ellison did indeed stress the connections between Negro folklore and transhistorical patterns of myth and ritual, citing Lord Raglan and Otto Rank as his most important theoretical sources and Eliot and Joyce as his most inspirational literary models. Declaring in 1965 that "In folklore . . . we project Negro life in metaphysical perspective," he designated its heroes "our versions of universal figures who repeat the broader patterns of human life on this earth." He later elaborated, "If you put John Henry beside Hercules, they're the same figures given the differences between the cultures out of which they come; they're both men with clubs; they're both heroes capable of fabulous feats of strength, and they're both sacrificial heroes because they die to affirm something about human life."[17]

Ellison's notebooks from the early 1940s reveal that his original interest in folklore had far less to do with cross-cultural universals than with the connection between storytelling and myth on the one hand and rebellion on the other, the particular "something about human life" that the heroes of folklore "affirm." Drawing upon the account of slave rebellions in Thomas Wentworth Higginson's *Travelers and Outlaws, and* especially noting those led by Gabriel Prosser, Gullah Jack, and Denmark Vesey, Ellison meditates that "all the magic, mythology, religion practiced by Negroes was pointed toward freedom." In relation to Vesey—described as "a tireless agitator" whose "whole personality [was] mobilized"—Ellison jotted, "Fable of Hercules and the Wagoner." According to Higginson, Vesey would urge slaves on the docks of Charleston to "'go buy a spelling-book, and read the fable of Hercules and the Wagoner,' which he would then repeat, and apply to their situation." In this legend the hero urges a wagoner stuck in the mud not to rely on the strength of the demigod, but to put his own shoulder to the wheel: Vesey's purpose in invoking Hercules, as well as Higginson's in recounting this tale—and Ellison's in commenting on the slave rebel's strategic invocation of mythology—was, it would seem, to instill in the story's listeners the will to extricate themselves from the mire of oppression. The hero of Greek myth figures here not simply as an analogue to Vesey, but as means to group self-definition; Hercules and Vesey at once personify and create the drive toward freedom.[18]

Contemplating the class-conscious connection between the myth of Hercules and the use to which it was put by Vesey, Ellison concluded, "American Negro culture offers [the] opportunity for study of the intermingling of myth dream and reality, the whole revolutionary core." Because slaves were all subjected to "the same economic conditions," slave culture testifies to the "emergence of a collective consciousness." Despite the development of some class differences among the Negro people since Emancipation, contemporaneous Negro folk culture retains much of this "underground" rebellious quality and points the way toward the "final conflict" embodied in the "mythical age of the revolution." In his lists of Negro leaders, we will recall, Ellison links slave rebels and abolitionists—Gabriel Prosser, Denmark Vesey, Harriet Tubman, Frederick Douglass—with "the Marxists," mentioning specifically James Ford and William Patterson, whom at one point he evidently viewed as inheritors of the mantle of a revolutionary folk consciousness. Before African Americans became redemptive symbols of the "underground logic of the democratic process" they were conductors and engineers on the Underground Railroad and vanguard forces in the revolutionary transformation of society.[19]

In linking the figures of Hercules and John Henry and associating them with past and present leaders of antiracist struggle, Ellison was participating in a discourse familiar to the Depression-era left. The pseudonym "Hercules Armstrong" was assumed by a *New Masses* poet whose chosen theme was radical antiracism. The subject of more songs and tales than any other American folkloric hero, John Henry, the legendary "steel-drivin' man" who beat out the steam drill but burst his heart in the process, was frequently inserted in the red line of African American history. The *New Masses* featured drawings of the well-muscled Negro labor hero by Hugo Gellert. In 1936 the Federal Theater Project put on Frank Webb's play *John Henry*, featuring Paul Robeson in the title role. Langston Hughes's and James P. Johnson's proletarian "blues opera" "De Organizer" (1937), for which Ellison helped write one of the songs, portrayed its leftist protagonist as a latter-day John Henry who has "put his hammer down" to "organiz[e] the poor — And when he gets done organizin' we / Can take this world in hand." "John Henry," either the ballad or the work song version, was routinely sung by Robeson, Josh White, or Leadbelly at leftist cultural gatherings such as the American Writers Congress in 1939, attended by Ellison and Wright. The cultural matrix surrounding the figure of John Henry, bridging the divide between slave and free labor, agrarian and industrial experience, folk and proletarian culture, was the closest approximation to *narodnost* on the American left; that Robeson would routinely juxtapose "John Henry" with Russian folk songs emphasized the internationalism embedded in people's cultures everywhere.[20]

Embodying African American heroism but possessing cross-racial proletarian appeal, John Henry distilled the contradiction between man and machine under capitalism; his fate showcased the threat of advancing technology to labor at the same time that it proudly featured Negroes as participants in the nation's industrial expansion. (That the real John Henry was a diminutive man, consigned to convict-lease labor under the post–Civil War Black Codes, who had died of overwork and silicosis along with at least one hundred other convicts constructing the railroad tunnel system through the Allegheny Mountains had disappeared from view.) The John Henry of Depression-era cultural radicalism was a figure at once tragic and victorious, containing in his Herculean body the dialectic of resistance to oppression and the promise of his class's ultimate triumph. One version of the John Henry "hammer song" asserted, "This old hammer / Killed John Henry, / Can't kill me, Lawd / Can't kill me." Wright had this heroic figure in mind when he called upon radical black writers to draw from the largely oral folklore "which embodies the memories and hopes of [the Negro's] struggle for freedom." He wrote, "The Negroes' most powerful images of hope and despair still remain in the fluid state of daily speech. How many John Henrys have lived and died on the lips of these black people?"[21]

The figure of John Henry as folk proletarian hero melded readily, moreover, with the popular figure of the Negro prizefighter. Ever since the near-indomitable Jack Johnson had flaunted his prowess, wealth, and white women in the face of American racism, black boxers — for decades the only Negroes who could beat upon white men's bodies without prompting retaliatory violence — had symbolized victory over white supremacy. "Hercules Armstrong" doubtless based his pseudonym not only on the physical connotations of his surname but also on the happy coincidence that "Armstrong" signified Henry Armstrong, a prominent Depression-era boxing champion (and Communist Party supporter). The quintessential prizefighter as working-class hero, however, was Joe Louis, whose victory over Max Baer in 1935 was joyfully celebrated in Negro communities, revealing, Wright wrote in the *New Masses*, a "pent up folk consciousness, [a] . . . fluid something that's like iron." Unassuming and clean-living, the "Brown Bomber," who went on to defeat the Nazi icon Max Schmeling in 1938, projected the invincibility and prowess of a Jack Johnson without the interracial sexual bravado. When Louis volunteered to join the army in 1942 and participated in Frank Capra's patriotic documentary film, *The Negro Soldier*—which largely whitewashed the tensions in the Jim Crow armed forces—his canonization as self-sacrificing antifascist Negro hero was complete. That the terms of this canonization were problematic in the eyes of some is registered in a letter to Ellison by Wright from Canada in which he observed, "The film folks here think that THE NEGRO SOLDIER stinks, and they wonder how could Negroes have had anything to do with such a blatant lie about Negro army conditions." Ellison himself, we shall see, tried to bring Louis into *Invisible Man* but could not handle the contradictions involved. In the popular African American imaginary, however, Louis nearly literally embodied simultaneous claims to proletarianness and Americanness: he was John Henry made flesh during the Popular Front and wartime years.[22]

"Myth, ritual and revolution got slammed around":
The Politics of the "Promethean Urge"

Besides signaling his interest in locating contemporary African American radicalism in the red line of history, Ellison's preoccupation with the connections among such figures as Hercules, John Henry, and Joe Louis reflects his participation in the discussions about literature, anthropology, and mythology that were occurring in leftist circles. In one of his rare later allusions to his days as a literary radical, Ellison recalled in 1977 that, at League of American Writers functions where "the craft of fiction was passionately discussed," often "myth, ritual, and revolution got slammed around." While this "slamming" was evidently a collective activity, the figure who more than any other helped Ellison relate Negro folklore to cross-cultural patterns of myth and ritual was the literary critic and folklorist Stanley Edgar Hyman, who introduced Ellison to the doctrines of the Cambridge School of Classical Anthropology. Familiar to most of Ellison's readers as the addressee of his polemical essay, "Change the Joke and Slip the Yoke" (1958), Hyman was a comparative folklorist with a broad-ranging knowledge of literary theory, ancient and modern. Although not a Party member when Ellison met him,

Hyman was a man of the left: he had been a member of the Young Communist League as an undergraduate at Dartmouth; Ellison was first pointed out
to him in 1941 by the Communist poet Isidore Schneider at the American
Writers Congress; the two would come into contact through Hyman's writing of a review for *Negro Quarterly*. Hyman's *The Armed Vision: A Study in the
Methods of Modern Literary Criticism* (1948) — which contained commentaries
on all the major critics and critical schools of the day, including Maud Bodkin
and archetypal criticism; Constance Rourke and folk criticism; Christopher
Caudwell, George Thomson, and Marxist criticism; and Kenneth Burke and
rhetorical criticism — would significantly influence Ellison's thinking about
literary theory in general, and the universal dimensions of folklore in particular, as he composed his novel. Along with his wife, the fiction writer
Shirley Jackson, Hyman would play a significant role in Ellison's revisions
of the manuscript of *Invisible Man*; the two men maintained a close, if somewhat edgy, friendship for many years.[23]

Since both Hyman and the Cambridge School have been viewed as principal influences on Ellison's turn away from proletarian realism and toward
a depoliticized mythic universalism, their principal doctrines warrant a brief
recapitulation and perhaps re-visioning. The sharp-tongued Hyman was in-
tolerant of what he called the "current cult of the folksy" among the Popular Frontist left, criticizing the sentimentality of the music compiler Alan
Lomax, the composer Earl Robinson, and the folklorist B. A. Botkin, who
headed the folklore division of the Federal Writers Project during Ellison's
years as an interviewer. As a scholar of folklore Hyman was still more critical
of myth and symbol theorists who denied the material grounding of myths
in rituals central to the production and reproduction of life among primitive
peoples. *"Myth is neither a record of historical fact nor an explanation of nature,"* he
wrote in 1948 in an essay that Ellison acknowledged as indispensable to his
own thinking. *"It is the spoken correlative of a ritual, the story which the rite enacts or once enacted. It arises out of the ritual, and not vice versa"* (Hyman's italics).
Myths depart from their origins, registering "increased misunderstanding of
the ancient rite, and a compensatory transformation for intelligibility in new
terms." But their psychological and ideological function of "collective rationalization" abides. Ellison would differ with Hyman regarding the importance of determining the origin of a given myth, professing a greater interest
in structure and function. Shirley Jackson's recently published short story
about modern-day scapegoating, "The Lottery," Ellison complained, presented its stoning ritual in too "archaic" a form, thus preventing the reader's
"full identification with the 'dedicated and set aside' scapegoat," for Ellison

the key feature permitting the sacrificial narrative to assume the "propor-tion" of "tragic action." But Ellison was hooked. "If Shirley does anything else along this line let me know," he wrote to Hyman. "We're beginning to work the same vein" (*sparagmos* [Greek for "scapegoat"], he jotted).[24]

More a synthesizer and explicator than an original theorist, Hyman based his formulation of the relationship between myth and ritual on the find-ings and arguments of the Cambridge School of Classical Anthropology. For the most part literary classicists who had turned to anthropology for an understanding of the origins and functions of myth, literature, and the plastic arts, members of the Cambridge School had developed and system-atized the connections between myth and ritual set forth in James Frazer's enormously influential *The Golden Bough*. The Cambridge School theorists discerned the roots of mythology neither in attempts by primitive people to explain natural phenomena nor in actual events retold in fantastic form, but in rituals symbolically associated with collective activities necessary to the life of the group. Contemplating the near universality of the figure of the murdered, tortured, and dismembered god in cross-cultural mythology—whether Osiris, Attis, Adonis, Dionysus, Prometheus, Hercules, or Christ—the classical anthropologists described the sacrificial function of this "year-daimon" in rituals of initiation, purification, and rebirth that symbolically enacted the group's attempts to gain the favor of the gods in the hunt or the harvest. These post-Frazerian scholars theorized the sacrificial scape-goat not as a victim to be ostracized and maligned, but as an honored hero, sometimes chosen to be king; as hanged god, the hero is chopped to pieces and totemically consumed at a beast-dancing feast that celebrates at once his necessary death and his esteemed social role. "Le roi est mort, vive le roi! Ave Maria!" ("The king is dead, long live the king! Hail Mary!") reads the finale of *The Golden Bough*.[25]

Jane Harrison issued the manifesto of the Cambridge School in *Themis* (1912) and its popularized version in *Ancient Art and Ritual* (1913, revised edi-tion 1918). Arguing that art, as an outgrowth of myth, should be understood as expressive rather than mimetic, she proposed that, in both Greek trage-dies and their theorization in Aristotle's *Poetics*, the object of representation was not an extratextual entity existing in the natural world, but the feelings aroused by the enactment of a ritual now forgotten: all art is a "thing done," a form of symbolic action based, in however distorted a form, in myths that are in turn based in primitive tribal rituals. In class societies, she pointed out, such myths and artworks could be reconfigured to serve ends quite differ-ent from their original communalist functions. Cambridge School members and followers—including Gilbert Murray, Rhys Carpenter, Jessie Weston, and Francis Fergusson—would explore the implications of this myth-ritual argument for a range of genres, from Greek tragedy to primitive bear cults, medieval mummery, and Elizabethan and modern drama. The anthropologist Bronislaw Malinowski developed a view of myth as "a vital ingredient of practical relation to the environment" that would accord in significant respects with the functionalist view of mythology set forth by Harrison.[26]

Clearly this theory of the relation of myth to ritual was not intrinsically radical and could be inflected in a variety of ways. Lord Raglan and Otto Rank discerned timeless formal and psychoanalytical patterns in heroic quest narratives; Maude Bodkin found in the "rebirth archetype" a "supra-personal experience . . . of the tidal ebb toward death followed by life renewal." Weston's theorization of the relationship between the fisher king and the grail legend is deployed by Eliot in *The Waste Land* for ideological purposes that are hardly subversive of the status quo. By the mid-1950s myth-and-symbol criticism had almost completely devolved into archetype hunting. The original Cambridge School theorists, however, eschewed idealism and interpreted rituals in relation to sociopolitical configurations of preclass and early class societies. Murray analyzed Hercules as "the hero of a subject peasant population in a low state of culture." Harrison, a feminist and Fabian socialist, viewed Dionysus as the favored god of the working classes and stressed the central role of the matriarchal pre-Olympian Themis as the "collective conscience" presiding over the totemic feast in primitive communalist Greek society.[27]

Several of the leftist literary theorists whom Ellison was reading during his apprenticeship years, usually at Hyman's recommendation, extended the historical materialist implications of the Cambridge School's approach to myth and literature. William Empson described proletarian literature as "covert pastoral" and discerned significant links between the proletarian hero and the figure of the hanged god. Christopher Caudwell, in his *Illusion and Reality: A Study of the Sources of Poetry* (1937), argued that poetry expressed "the emotional, social and collective complex which is [the] tribe's relation to the harvest"; his contention that poetry's "truth" consists not in its "abstract statement" but in its "dynamic role in society" drew upon the classical anthropologists' functional view of culture in relation to production. Caudwell's discussion of the decline of myth into folk "superstition" and "legend" as an "adaptation to the role of an exploited class," one whose lore became "tainted with the idiocy of exploitation," aligned with Harrison's views on the differing ideological functions of myth in preclass and class societies.[28]

George Thomson, the dean of Marxist classicism, acknowledged Harrison and other Cambridge School theorists—alongside Marx, Engels, and Caudwell—in his study *Aeschylus and Athens: A Study in the Social Origins of Drama* (1940). Arguing that the ritual practice of dismembering and consuming the totem animal was linked with the "equality of the common meal," Thomson analyzed the intergenerational mentoring occurring in the "men's houses" of primitive Greek society as the groundwork for celebratory rituals of initiation. As societies developed class hierarchies, he argued, the religious cult of Orphism, focusing on the figure of Dionysus, reflected the class outlook of slaves. Especially prominent in Thomson's discussion was the figure of Prometheus. This rebellious titan, Thomson wrote, was the "the patron saint of the proletariat" because he brought to man the gift of fire, that is, the gift of intelligence, thereby making "man free, because it had enabled him to comprehend, and so to control, the laws of nature. Freedom consists in the recognition of necessity." Punished for his transgression by Zeus, king of the Olympians, Prometheus was impaled upon a rock, his liver continually consumed by an eagle; it was Hercules, the laboring demigod, Thomson pointed out, who finally freed him. As myth became detached from ritual, however, and Dionysian energies were channeled into the production of drama, rebellion was converted into catharsis. Aristotle correctly discerned that tragedy was "conservative of the established order," Thomson argued; antagonisms between social classes were displaced into the realm of aesthetic response. In the hands of Caudwell and Thomson, the Cambridge School's theorization of myth and symbol not only anchored art and literature in material production but also limned their roles in social reproduction and ideological legitimation.[29]

While most of Ellison's critics, taking him at his word after 1952, have traced his interest in myth and ritual to Raglan, Rank, and Eliot, the Cambridge School scholars and their Marxist descendents figured prominently in Ellison's thinking during the period when he was conceiving and composing *Invisible Man*. References to Caudwell and Thomson are sprinkled throughout his outlines and notes from the 1940s; long passages from Harrison and Murray are copied out in his notes and notebooks. Contemplating that "heroes must be what Cambridge school calls the Eniauto-daimon or Year Spirit," he quotes at length from Murray's description of Hercules: "He is worshipped by the Phythagoreans [*sic*] as the power of nature or growth; he carries a horn of plenty and a club which was once a green brough [bough]. He is burned each year, but reborn. He is both a dead man and a living god." As a consequence of Hercules's immense strength and fearlessness, writes Murray, "his master is frightened of him." Ellison inserts the parenthetical comment, "John Henry is perhaps our version of Hercules" and further remarks, "The secret of John Henry lies not only in his universality, but in the fact that while a Negro Hercules he dramatizes nevertheless the conflict between the man and the machine—which is and remains a problem of all Americans." For Ellison, what connected the various figures whom he termed "broad men"—Hercules, Dionysus, and Prometheus on the one hand, and Denmark Vesey, John Henry, and Joe Louis on the other—was not, as he would assert in 1954, their participation in "the great human joke directed against the universe . . . which is the secret of all folklore and myth: that though we be dismembered daily we shall always rise up again." It was instead these figures' common status as heroes reflecting the needs of the "broad" masses of humanity and willing, when necessary, to sacrifice themselves in service to these needs.[30]

Wright, like Ellison fascinated by the figure of the Negro rebel as an avatar of Prometheus, recommended that his young friend read *Psychology and the Promethean Will* by the psychologist William Sheldon. Sheldon argued that both societies and individuals are torn between Epimethean and Promethean tendencies. (In Greek mythology Epimetheus was Prometheus's brother, and in almost all respects his antithesis.) According to Sheldon, the Epimethean will reflects a "conservative idealism," a "backward straining element" embodying the "wish for safety and for the security of righteousness." The Promethean will, by contrast, contains "the forward straining dream of a better world. . . . When dominant, [it] gives rise to radical idealism." Although not a leftist partisan of the Promethean urge, which he saw resulting in "futile protest movements" and "dreams of heroic, spectacular sacrifice," Sheldon proposed that both societies and individuals act out the conflict between these two tendencies. The implications of this theory for an exploration of consciousness as a zone of class struggle are not far to seek. Bigger Thomas was evidently in Wright's eyes a misguided Promethean rebel; Ellison would draw upon Sheldon in his portraits of more disciplined Negro radicals. For these two Marxist African American writers, Western mythology supplied not a way out from blackness, but general patterns by which to connect the "indignant consciousness" produced by capitalist racism with the thread of rebellion running throughout the history of class society.[31]

The French writer André Malraux, who in the 1930s authored several novels focused on international antifascist activity, further shaped the young Ellison's awareness of how novels could convey forms of Promethean heroism in the historical present. In his comments on Malraux's oeuvre, written after *Invisible Man* was published, Ellison emphasized the non-Communist features of Malraux's protagonists and the largely depoliticized aesthetic theory set forth in *The Psychology of Art* (1949), published several years after Malraux had abandoned his leftist sympathies. Occluded in these retrospective accounts of Malraux's initial impact is Ellison's early attraction not only to Malraux's unabashedly revolutionary heroes, a number of whom are not just antifascist but Communist, but also to the French writer's fervent embrace in the 1930s of Soviet aesthetic theory. Preserved in Ellison's files is an interview with Malraux in 1934 for *International Literature*, the journal of the Comintern-sponsored International Union of Revolutionary Writers, in which Malraux declared himself "absorbed by the new, forthcoming personality" embodied in "the Communist man, the man of the classless society." The artist who would attempt to "find a form" adequate to the task of representing this emergent social reality—as well as the "inner world of naked feelings" that is portrayed in "psychological literature"—must don the "spectacles [of] ideology." (Underlining Malraux's statements about psychology, Ellison jotted his own name in the margin.) Ellison also preserved two essays by Malraux from the *Partisan Review* of 1935, in which the French writer explored the different relations between the artist and society in the capitalist West and the USSR. "Humanism well may be man's fundamental attitude toward a civilization which he accepts," wrote Malraux, "just as individualism is his fundamental attitude toward a civilization which he refuses. . . . Restor[ing] a meaning to the idea of manly brotherhood, [this humanism] . . . enables the creation of the positive hero, the only true one always, the one who risks his life for other men." Malraux writes, "The absence of money as an intervening factor restores to the heroic deed all its primitive significance, such a significance as it might possess in war, if the cannon-merchant did not exist, and if no one drew any profit from war—a Promethean significance." Garnering ideas from sources as diverse as Harrison and Thomson, Wright and Malraux, the young Ellison sought out models of Promethean rebellion ranging from Denmark Vesey and John Henry to the "positive man" of Soviet socialism. He was pursuing the red line of heroic history.[32]

"Like fetid bodies of the drowned":
Psychologizing the Political

Even as his search for cross-cultural cognates to the figure of the Negro folk proletarian rebel led him to comparative folklore and cultural anthropology, Ellison's concern with the rise of fascism, and especially the appeal of black fascists to sectors of Harlem's alienated migrant population, led him to psychoanalysis. In this interest he was not alone among leftists: the felt urgency of coming to terms with fascism, with which American racism was in many ways aligned, prompted a number of Marxists to overcome their skepticism about ego psychology and turn to Freud for a fuller understanding of the workings of ideology. Caudwell and Thomson both invoked Freud in their discussions of the ideological functions of catharsis. Edward Bland's formulation of "preindividuality," which significantly influenced both Wright's and Ellison's views of Negro consciousness in the Jim Crow South, was indebted to Erich Fromm's exploration of preindividuality in relation to the "totalitarian flight from freedom," itself a distorted expression of the "need for social solidarity," involved in the rise of Nazism. Wright's project in *Lawd Today* and *Native Son* was patently Freudian in its examination of the potential attraction of fascism to black men symbolically castrated by American racism. Before explorations of the "authoritarian personality," invoking the discourse of "two totalitarianisms," focused on the homologous personality structures presumably discoverable in Communists and fascists alike, theorists grounded in historical materialism displayed a strong interest in psychologizing the political. The antifascist motivation for finding a rapprochement between Freud and Marx would be another casualty of the cold war.[33]

While Erich Fromm and Wilhelm Reich had a significant impact on American Marxists interested in conjoining politics and psychology, two lesser-known American Marxist Freudians were also widely read in the leftist circles where Ellison moved in the late 1930s and early 1940s. One was Reuben Osborn, whose *Freud and Marx: A Dialectical Study* was recommended to Ellison by Hughes and assessed favorably by Hyman in *The Armed Vision*. Osborn's study made the case that Freud and Marx were not merely compatible but, in combination, necessary for "a full understanding of man." Citing the Freud of *Totem and Taboo* and the Engels of *On the Origin of the Family, Private Property and the State*—as well as an array of theorists from Frazer to Lenin to Dimitrov—Osborn argued that Freudian ego psychology furnishes a necessary supplement to the Marxist theory of the state. In particular an understanding of the workings of the superego on the individual level is vital to the Communist movement's grasping "the irrational conservatism which compels the perpetuation of an outworn social system"—namely, fascism. Marxism is needed to explain the preconditions of fascism, he argued, but psychoanalysis is needed to explain its coming into being. Without heeding this complex causality, warned Osborn in a telling formulation, "a psychologically blind leadership may hold back revolution for years." That Osborn's call for articulating historical materialism with psychoanalysis had the blessing of the Third International is indicated by the fact that *Freud and Marx* contained a preface by the prominent British Marxist John Strachey, who acknowledged that Marx had neglected the "formal side" of the formation of consciousness, which is "precisely the subject of psychoanalysis." Both Osborn and Strachey were Marxists first and foremost; their audience was assumed to be leftists, and the problematic they featured—the conundrum of the appeal of fascism—was framed by Popular Frontist concerns. But Osborn's notion that Marxism can and must make use of psychoanalysis evidently was not seen as a threat to revolutionary praxis; both provided scientific means for mapping and explaining human behavior.[34]

A Marxist Freudian colleague in the League of American Writers whose influence on Ellison is palpable was the literary critic Harry Slochower. Author of *Three Faces of Modern Man* (1937), *Thomas Mann's Joseph Story* (1938), and *No Voice Is Wholly Lost* (1945), Slochower, like other critics of the Popular Front era, claimed for socialist humanism the heritage of the best in bourgeois liberalism. Since art by its nature gravitated toward universalism, he argued, and since only Marxism could realize a universalism that would be concrete and material rather than abstract and utopian, Marxism supplied the only context within which art could thrive. Indeed, and this would be crucially important for the young Ellison, it was only in the context of socialism, or at least the fight for socialism, that true tragedy was possible, since only here could individuals freely choose to challenge the limitations on their humanity. Although he granted that there was both "clash and congruence between Marx and Freud," Slochower viewed their relationship as contradictory in the dialectical sense. He was perhaps somewhat fanciful when he suggested that "Freudian regression" has its analogy in the Marxist proposition that the future classless society has its "historic prototype in the primitive commune." As with the antifascist Osborn, however, Slochower's penetration "into the Fascist Styx" produced some provocative analogies between the projects of Marx and Freud. The Freudian notion of unconscious motivation, he proposed, was akin to the Marxist notion of false consciousness; Freud's view of the Id as "a chaos, a cauldron of seething excitement" had its counterpart in Engels's view of the "unconscious blind agents" in nature and history. "The Marxian formulation that freedom is the cognizance of necessity," wrote Slochower, "has its Freudian counterpart in the notion that consciousness of the causal factors leads man to free himself from their neurotic effects." Devising a Marxist therapy that might expose and decathect the ideological demons haunting the political unconscious was, in Slochower's view, the urgent task confronting both writers and critics of literature.[35]

Even as Ellison distanced himself from his leftist associations in 1944 and 1945, he took it upon himself to devise such a therapy, or at least further highlight its necessity, in relation to the role played by racism in the American political unconscious. His review of Myrdal's *An American Dilemma*, we have seen, called for investigation of "the problem of the irrational . . . [that] has taken the form of the Negro problem," that "blind spot in our knowledge of society where Marx cries out for Freud and Freud for Marx." In "Richard Wright's Blues" Ellison invoked the full range of Freudian concepts—trauma, repression, displacement, masochism, hysteria—to describe the psychic dynamics of Wright's tortured childhood in the "pre-individual" environment of the Jim Crow South. In "Beating That Boy" (1945), a review of Bucklin Moon's *Primer for White Folks*, a compilation of writings about race mainly by white liberals, Ellison observes that "what was opportunistically labeled the 'Negro problem' is actually a guilt problem charged with pain." In this first attempt to apply psychoanalysis to the problem of American racism—a concern that would motivate Ellison for the rest of his life—he wrote, "[Although] ceaseless effort [is] expended to dull [the problem's] throbbings with the anesthesia of legend, myth, hypnotic ritual and narcotic modes of thinking, [the United States is] . . . a nation of ethical schizophrenics. . . . Imprisoned in the deepest drives in human society, it is practically impossible for the white American to think of sex, of economics, his children or womenfolk, or of sweeping socio-political changes, without summoning into consciousness fear-flecked images of black men." As a result, the "racial situation . . . is like an irrational sea in which Americans flounder like convoyed ships in a gale." When the literary artist, reflecting the guilt-ridden preoccupations of the culture at large, "attempts to tap the charged springs issuing from his inner world, up float his misshapen and bloated images of the Negro, like the fetid bodies of the drowned." By evading the looming presence of the Negro, literature trivializes itself, producing "precise and complex verbal constructions for converting goatsong into carefully modulated squeaks." Not just the typical American psyche, but also its high modernist representations, it appears, are founded upon racism.[36]

Although this diagnosis of white American racial consciousness invokes the Freudian paradigm, Ellison grounds the "racial situation" in historical materialism. It was in the wake of "the return of the Southern ruling class to power in the counter-revolution of 1876," he writes, that the "Negro issue" was "pushed into the underground of the American conscience and ignored." Racist ideology is not a cultural residue, moreover, but undergoes regular reinforcement: "Not only have our popular culture, our newspapers, radio and cinema [been deployed,] . . . but even our social sciences and serious literature have been conscripted—all in the effort to drown out the persistent voice of outraged conscience." The texts gathered in *A Primer for White Folks* display "something practically missed from American writing since *Huckleberry Finn*: a search for images of black and white fraternity." These texts possibly forecast a "superior society and . . . more vital literature." But the political unconscious of the United States must be probed, and its demons released, if fascism is to be defeated—not just across the ocean, but in the "irrational sea" that threatens the convoy of the antifascist cause. The war is still on. And Ellison is still Freuding Marx and Marxing Freud; he has some distance to travel before he posits the Negro as the sacrificial figure that will redeem the nation from its sins.[37]

"Some group profits by it": Kenneth Burke and the Left

The elephant in the room of this discussion of Marx, Freud, and the literary unconscious is Kenneth Burke, whose influence on Ellison's entire project, critical and novelistic, has been widely acknowledged, not least by Ellison himself. In 1945 Ellison thanked Burke for the "amalgam of sociology, psychology, Marxism and literary criticism" without which he "would not be at home in this rather cock-eyed world." Subsequently he would credit Burke not only as the source of the "purpose-passion-perception" plot structure of *Invisible Man* but, more centrally, as the basis for his understanding of "the nature of literature and the way ideas and language operate in literary form." He would characteristically describe Burke's influence in liberal pluralist terms, however, proposing that the "integrative" work undertaken in fiction by "symbolic action" is comparable to the "centrifugal force that inspirits the democratic process." Largely because they read both writers' early work through the lenses supplied by their later commentaries, most critics discussing the Burke-Ellison relationship have examined it, and celebrated it, in liberal terms. A reexamination of the distinctly leftist rhetorical theory that Burke developed in the 1930s and early 1940s, as well as of the leftist commitments that helped to guide him to this theory, is indispensable to an understanding of the aesthetic principles guiding the creation (and subsequently the revision) of *Invisible Man*.[38]

Ellison encountered Burke, whom Michael Denning considers "the most important communist cultural theorist in the United States" during the period of the Popular Front, through the institutions of the literary left. Although in his letter to Burke in November 1945 he remarked that it was necessary to "reject the course [Communism] has taken in this country since 1937," this was the year when, at the American Writers Congress, Burke first impressed the younger man with his astute rhetorical analysis of "Nazi magic" in "The Rhetoric of Hitler's 'Battle.'" Burke had been active in the New York chapter of the John Reed Club in the mid-1930s and a member of the League of American Writers since its inception; in 1939 he was editor of the League of American Writers organ *Direction*, where Ellison published his first short story. Burke published extensively in the *New Masses* in the 1930s and served as its book review editor for several years. While commentators on Burke's relationship to the CP-led left have emphasized his "maverick" and "independent" status, this characterization significantly underplays the extent of his involvement with Communist causes. Burke supported the Nonaggression Pact, criticizing his friend Malcolm Cowley, who quit the CP at the time, for the "red-baiting-ish quality" of Cowley's projected position statement. "Though never having been hunky-dory with the Party," he remarked of himself, "I now find no occasion to welch." To Ellison he criticized Wright's decision to publish "I Tried to Be a Communist" in the *Atlantic Monthly*, noting that, in relation to "the quarrels with the Communists," while "there is something unsatisfactory about remaining silent, there is something much more unsatisfactory in selling one's grievances to an audience which loves to hear of them for wholly reactionary reasons." In response to the Trotskyists' criticism that the CP continually changed its positions in relation to fascism and war, he justified these changes on dialectical grounds — as reality changes, so do the terms in which it is analyzed — and to the end of his life enjoyed the antipathy of the editors of the *Partisan Review*.[39]

Burke was an exacting critic of proletarian literature but offered encouragement to its practitioners. In 1934 he positively reviewed "Rubicon or The Strikebreaker," a play depicting "the story of a marine worker's conversion to sympathy with the Soviet way of life." In a *New Masses* review in February 1936 of Muriel Rukeyser's *Theory of Flight*, Burke praised the poet for linking dialectics with the "strange initiation rite" of conquering the air. "In having such a writer on their side," he wrote, "Communists have a most worthy ally." In a review later that year of James T. Farrell's *A Note on Literary Criticism*, a text largely hostile to the proletarian literary movement, Burke faulted Farrell for "attacking Left critics who have been attempting to discover how effectively the literary weapons may be 'taken over' for purposes of *here* and *now*." Burke evidently had no quarrel with the notion that literature has utility in the class war.[40]

In his Depression-era and wartime writings Burke unabashedly proclaimed his pro-Communist proclivities. In a contribution to the *New Masses* in 1934 titled "My Approach to Communism," he stated, "Communism alone provides the kind of motives adequate for turning the combative potentialities of man into cooperative channels. . . . The Communistic orientation is the only one which successfully produces the combative-cooperative fusion under conditions of peace, hence the only one upon which a permanent social structure can be founded." In *Permanence and Change* (1935) he asserted, "A sound system of communication, such as lies at the roots of civilization, cannot be built upon a structure of economic warfare. It must be economically, as well as spiritually, Communistic." In "Twelve Propositions by Kenneth Burke on the Relationship between Economics and Psychology" (1938), appearing in the new Marxist theoretical journal *Science & Society*, Burke responded to Margaret Schlauh's somewhat skeptical review of his recent *Attitudes toward History* (1937). He had never "den[ied] the reality of . . . proletarian . . . exploitation," wrote Burke, but simply stressed how it "takes shape when filtered through a complex human consciousness." In *A Grammar of Motives* (1945) he set forth "A Dramatist Grammar for Marxism," in which he emphasized Marxism's "poignant concern with the ethical" and defended "the whole purpose of materialist criticism" as "the bring[ing]about [of] such material conditions as are thought capable of releasing men from their false bondage to materials."[41]

Antifascism and antiracism figured centrally in Burke's analysis of the workings of ideology. The essence of fascist propaganda, he argued, was its creation of a false inclusiveness that was in turn grounded in the imperatives of class rule. The targeting of the Jew as the "international devil" produced a "noneconomic interpretation of a phenomenon economically engendered." Linking the "current distress in Germany" with Jim Crow, he argued that in both cases the "scapegoat mechanism" functioned as a "rationalization" that reinforced "trained incapacity." In a critique of the deeply conservative Southern Agrarians as "a heretical sect reaffirming orthodox commercial values," he pointed out that their elevation of "property as an *absolute*," contrasted with "the collectivists' treat[ment of] property as a *relationship*," was premised in their anti-Negro assumption that "some are endowed by natural quality to rule, and others are endowed to be hired." The "cultural lag" embodied in the "fossil-like" behaviors of Jim Crow was not residual but

continually reinforced: "Some group . . . profits by it." Burke's class-based
antiracism was a central feature of his appeal to the young Ellison.[42]

Although Burke has been read as a proponent of pluralistic American democracy, in his early writings he directed attention to the slippages and contradictions in the rhetoric of nationalism, as articulated by both rulers and their leftist opponents. During the 1930s he stressed the dangers of "misused nationalism." Hitler deployed "Nazi magic" in his appeal to a specious sense of national unity; U.S. capitalist advertising proposed a comparably "specious concentric identity" between "business and nation." But leftists should not respond to this specious universalism by engaging in a nationalist homogenization of their own. Burke criticized Granville Hicks's Popular Frontist U.S. literary history, *The Great Tradition*, for celebrating "nay-saying" to injustice as a "peculiarly 'American'" quality and "trying to claim nearly every outstanding American of the past for the cause of revolution." He analyzed the function of the U.S. government's wartime propaganda in "confronting the need to change from a commercial-liberal-monetary nexus of motives to a collective-sacrificial-military nexus of motives as the principle shaping the logic of the nation's efforts." To this end it was necessary that the term *democracy* be invoked as a collective emotion, an "ideal," one which "the disenfranchised, such as the natives of India or the Negroes of the South, can logically be asked to defend as a purpose even when they could not be asked to defend it as an actuality." At the same time he criticized Roosevelt's refusal to invoke even "the mildly collectivist slogans of the New Deal"; by substituting for the slogan "All Out Aid to the Democracies" the slogan "Win the War," the president was cynically yoking the popular willingness currently to engage in collective sacrifice with a postwar "return to an economic order which was already proving unworkable." Even as Burke granted the need for a class- and race-transcending nationalist rhetoric of sacrifice as an expedient to aid the wartime effort, he remained acutely aware of the ways this rhetoric strengthens class rule. Hardly the assertions of a liberal pragmatist, Burke's wartime writings recall Ellison's editorials for *Negro Quarterly* and reveal that in the early 1940s the two men were very much on the same wavelength.[43]

During the Depression and wartime years, and somewhat beyond, Burke envisioned revolutionary social transformation as a real, and desired, possibility. In his speech at the Writers Congress in 1935 Burke argued that the term *the people* constituted a "psychological bridge," linking "two conflicting aspects of a transitional, revolutionary era, which is Janus-faced, looking both forwards and back." In *The Philosophy of Literary Form* (1941) he observed, "Periods of social crisis occur when an authoritative class, whose purpose and ideals had been generally considered as *representative* of the total society's purposes and ideals, become considered as *antagonistic*. Their class character, once felt to be a *culminating* part of the whole, is now felt to be a *divisive* part of the whole." In 1947, on the defensive as he contemplated the epic pretensions of the emergent Pax Americana, he queried whether "the Nazi methods had been eliminated" and proposed that the "ideal citizen" would be "at once ruler and ruled" and that the "neo-Virgilian epic" needed in the postwar world "must transcend nationalism." As late as 1950 he defined ideology as the "myth of the state" and praised Marx's work on "mystification," observing that it is a "sign of flimsy thinking to let anti-communist hysteria bulldoze one into a neglect of Marx."[44]

Burke himself felt the effects of the cold war: in 1952 he was denied a position at the University of Washington because of his former political affiliations. He removed from the second editions of both *Permanence and Change* and *Attitudes toward History* numerous passages indicating his Marxist leanings; subsequently his rhetorical theory became increasingly formalistic and abstract and his politics increasingly pragmatic and pluralist. His writings of the 1930s and 1940s, however, had aimed at elucidating the interrelations of literature, psychology, and ideology largely in order to strengthen the movement for revolutionary social transformation. As he wrote to Cowley in 1950, he had assessed the literary radicals as being "strong on relations between literature and society, but weak on internal analysis"; he envisioned his role as helping to "bridge this gap. To this end the theory of 'clusters,' 'equations.'" The "internal analysis" that Ellison drew from Burke as he undertook *Invisible Man* — in both its original drafts and its subsequent revisions — was guided by this understanding of the inevitably political deployment of all language.[45]

"Functioning of a structure": Rhetoric as Ideology

The rhetorical theory that Burke developed in the 1930s and 1940s is dispersed, some might say scattered, throughout his writings. The key features that would be of particular usefulness to Ellison, who would unabashedly term himself a "rhetorician," can be summarized in six propositions. While Burke's tendency to invent neologisms to define the terms in his critical lexicon can at times make for rough sledding, an understanding of these key concepts is indispensable to a grasp of his importance to Ellison's creative process.[46]

First, Burke held that all literary discourse, and much discourse that would not be considered literary, is a "strategy for encompassing a situation." He developed different phrases to describe his view of texts as interventions in specific historical contradictions and debates: the "dancing of an attitude," "equipment for living," the "functioning of a structure," and "symbolic action." Consisting largely of paired synchronic and diachronic terms, these formulations suggest the mutual determination of categories and processes. While literature renders knowledge—Burke did not reject the cognitive dimension of discourse—above all it functions as persuasion: "Effective literature could be nothing else but rhetoric." Rhetoric in turn is inseparable from ideology, which Burke defines as "the nodus of beliefs and judgments which the artist can exploit for his effects." In order for art to be objective, it needs to draw upon a widely shared ideology; "in proportion as the ideology which the dramatist relies upon is weakened," art becomes "subjective," possessing a narrower appeal.[47]

In Burke's overlapping definitions, "ideology" is variously defined. Sometimes it signifies resistance to oppressive modes of thought; at other times, simply shared assumptions bearing political implications. More often it signifies legitimation, requiring "a highly developed money economy, with its extreme division of labor and a maximum of abstract relationships for which the ideologist seeks to compensate by all the deliberate subterfuges for persuading people to 'identify themselves' with the faction, doctrines, or policies he represents." Any handler of words is therefore a "medicine man," dealing in discourses that can either poison or heal. Fascism is a poison; it retards change and forecloses inquiry. Marxism is a "social therapeutic" because it instills the "reclassification-consciousness" necessary for grappling conceptually with the dynamics of crisis and transition. But there are no neutral uses of language; its "manipulation" (not, for Burke, a pejorative term) entails either acceptance or rejection of dominant systems of belief.[48]

Equations, Representative Anecdotes, Associational Clusters: Synecdoche as Coercion

The principal means by which a writer rhetorically effects the "functioning of a structure" include "associational clusters," "symbolic mergers," and "equations." Although a given symbol makes singular appearances in any given text, it acquires meaning only insofar as it connects with "a particular grouping or pattern or emphasizing of experiences." "Equations," wrote Burke, "cause us to collapse into a single chord a series of events that, by the nature of the literary medium, must be strung out in arpeggio." Equations thus convey meaning by implying the general through the particular, the diachronic through the synchronic. Burke supplies an example relevant to the patterning of *Invisible Man*: the "representative anecdote" of the Bellerophontic letter[49]—which sets up ostensibly different situations in which a character unwittingly "dig[s his] own grave"—points to a "recurrent [pattern] of experience" carrying thematic chordal resonance. Each time the motif appears, cognition of its immediate meaning is reinforced by re-cognition of its position in a larger pattern. Characters function as subsets of character systems; images function as parts of signifying chains.[50]

All representational processes, for Burke, can be grouped under four "master tropes": metaphor, metonymy, synecdoche, and irony. Of these the most important is synecdoche: "To say that one can substitute part for whole, whole for part, container for the thing contained, thing contained for the container, cause for effect, or effect for cause, is simply to say that both members of these pairs belong in the same associational cluster." Synecdoche implies what Fredric Jameson, building upon Burke, has called the "paradox of rhetorical realism": rhetoric and reference are conjoined in a process that simultaneously asserts the writer's partisan relationship to reality and the objective status of that reality. Frank Lentricchia points out that, in Burke's formulation, synecdoche lays claim to both "epistemological and ontological universality" insofar as it proposes that "some part of the whole *really does* stand in for the whole—participates in the whole." The procedure of asserting that a given particular typifies a given whole is, he concludes, implicitly coercive; synecdoche functions to impose one view, one interpretation, at the expense of others. For Burke rhetoric is not pluralist in its effects, a feature that Ellison well understood when he referred to the symbolism in *Invisible Man* as "a hook to snare errant fish." The key question is not whether rhetoric entraps, but what ends, and whose ends, are served by this entrapment.[51]

"Ritual drama as the Ur-form": Dramatism

While associational clusters and equations characterize a wide range of discourses—poetic, narrative, expository, argumentative—the distinctive feature of texts with a significant diachronic component is, for Burke, dramatism, wherein the "representative anecdote" serves as the key to the unfolding of symbolic action. Burke describes the conceptual components of dramatism as a pentad—consisting of act, scene, agent, agency, purpose—each of which tends toward a particular philosophical emphasis. Materialism, for instance, would correspond with scene, stressing environment, while idealism would correspond with agency, or willful subjectivity. The "very center of dialectical motivation" in the forward movement of narrative or drama, by contrast, is the triad: "Out of the agent's action there grows a corresponding passion, and from the sufferance of this passion there arises a knowledge of his act, a knowledge that also to a degree transcends his act." The categories of classical tragedy—*agon*, reversal, recognition—are repeated at each stage in the text's temporal progression. The perception attained at the end of one phase prepares for the purpose and passion of the next. The reader (or audience) is carried along in this succession of reversals and realizations, attaining catharsis through identification with the protagonist.[52]

Burke affirms that ritual drama constitutes "the Ur-form, the 'hub,' with all other aspects of human action treated as spokes radiating from this hub." But the rhetorical power of dramatism consists in the fact that "*the imaginary obstacles of symbolic drama must, to have the relevance necessary for the producing of effects upon audiences, reflect the real obstacles of living drama.*" Key rituals such as initiation and rebirth, amounting basically to "socialization," are neither survivals from a primitive past nor ahistorical archetypes detached from social causality, but fundamental principles structuring all human interactions that are in turn necessarily grounded in particular social formations. Burke's doctrine of dramatism is unapologetically materialist; although values form the "'objective material' with which the artist works in constructing symbols that appeal," the "objective factors giving rise to a code of moral and esthetic values are of course, *economic*. They are the 'substructure' that supports the ideological 'superstructure.'" Burke's stipulation that "all the world's a stage" does not preclude the historical circumstances producing the roles acted out, or indeed the labor process creating the physical stage itself. From his early proletarian fiction to the completion of *Invisible Man*, Ellison, who always called himself an unabashed "Aristotelian," would substantially alter the extent and manner in which the *agons* experienced by the protagonists in his "symbolic dramas" would correspond with "the real obstacles of living drama." He would be a highly conscious practitioner of the rhetoric of fiction.[53]

"Weighting and counter-weighting": Dialectic

Central to both synecdoche and dramatism, and hence to all representation, synchronic and diachronic, is the principle of dialectic, which for Burke comprises a wide range of meanings, ranging from Platonic conversation to Hegelian contradiction. "In the most general sense," he writes, dialectics signifies "the employment of the possibilities of linguistic transformation." While terms like *apple* and *house* require "no counter-words like 'anti-house' or 'un-apple' to define them, dialectical terms, like freedom, perfection, or the terms for social movements, . . . derive their significance from their relation to opposite terms." The intrinsically political nature of language derives from its dialectical character. What Burke calls "perspective by incongruity" is this "weighting and counter-weighting" intrinsic to language, a characteristic denied by the "liberal ideal of *neutral* naming in the characterization of processes." The acts of acceptance and rejection that constitute political practice thus both precede and flow from the ways the meanings of these acts have been linguistically framed. Notably the "social movement" in relation to which he distinguishes "anti-house" and "non-apple" from "freedom" and "perfection" is "Hitlerite anti-Semitism."[54]

Rather than making him a proto-poststructuralist, Burke's dialectics of language was premised upon the view of "history [as] a 'dramatic' process, involving dialectical oppositions." All social phenomena, he wrote, contain their opposites: in drama, "the *agon* . . . is analytically subdivided into competing principles, of protagonist and antagonist. Their competition sums up to one over-all cooperative act." This cooperation is, however, continually undergoing change along the lines of thesis-antithesis-synthesis; the diachronic triad, "purpose-passion-perception," is not a formalistic principle, but a literary means of enacting the motion of contradiction. Ellison's notes for *Invisible Man* are replete with references to cycles of "purpose-passion-perception" enacted on multiple levels, from the chapter to the section to the novel as a whole; the structure of the novel is in fact one large dialectical spiral, containing loops within loops. Although the invisible man would end up disparaging the view of history as a spiral and voicing a profoundly antidialectical view of contradiction, he would owe his very existence to his creator's Burkean grasp of the dialectics of narrative development.[55]

"Psychoanalysis must face another birth trauma":
Marx and Freud

It is in his "Freudo-Marxism" that Burke's relationship to historical materialism is more problematic. Since rhetoric invokes emotions and attitudes often existing at an unconscious level, psychology remains for Burke indispensable to an understanding of the workings of ideology. Focusing less on the "psychology of information" than on the "psychology of form," Burke explored the linguistic dimension of the unconscious, proposing that dream mechanisms such as condensation and displacement enact the psychic functioning of equations and clusters. At times he proposes what looks like a dehistoricized Freudianism. While it constitutes for the individual the core of revolutionary praxis, the choice between acceptance and rejection can also be understood, he argues in 1937, as enacting the opposition between symbolic castration and parricide. The "identifications" produced by various rituals of membership are not just ideological positionings, he argued in 1950, but forms of "compensation for division."[56]

Mainly, however, Burke's writings of the 1930s and 1940s stress that Marxism is needed to correct the "preforensic" (that is, private) emphasis of Freudian psychoanalysis, which arbitrarily narrows the domain of causality, "essentializing" the realm of personal experience rather than "proportionalizing" this experience in relationship to society at large. In "Twelve Propositions" he insists that "men must throw off old and deceptive modes of identification and take on new ones"; the Marxist critique of alienation is indispensable to this project. In a critical review of Otto Rank's *Birth and Death of the Hero* titled "Without Benefit of Politics" Burke acknowledges the relevance of Rank's emphasis on Freudian birth trauma to the "current conditions of crisis" generating so much talk about rebirth. He observes, however, that "Freud's and Rank's emphasis seems equally 'infantile' in the sense that they consider human relationships in terms of non-political or pre-political coordinates." He concludes, "Psychoanalysis must face another birth trauma, so modifying its identity as integrally to encompass economic and forensic thought." In the drafts of *Invisible Man* the motif of rebirth aligns the protagonist's personal traumas with larger historical "conditions of crisis" that are effaced in the published text. Many of Ellison's revisions would be directed toward "essentializing" the invisible man's rebirths and "de-proportionalizing" their relation to his environment.[57]

"Ritualistic" and "Pseudoscientific":
The Dual Nature of the Scapegoat

The figure of the scapegoat is, for Burke, at the center of the "Ur-form, the 'hub,'" of both social reality and its literary representation. Although based in ancient collective rituals surrounding the figure of the sacrificial king, the scapegoat is not an oddity imported from anthropology, but a current presence as "the 'representative' or 'vessel' of certain unwanted evils, the sacrificial animal upon whose back the burden of these evils is ritualistically loaded." In the "dialectic of the scapegoat" there occurs a process characterized by "(1) an original state of merger, in that the iniquities are shared by both the sacrificers and their chosen vessel; (2) a principle of division, in that the elements shared in common are being ritualistically alienated; (3) a new principle of merger, this time in the unification of those whose purified identity is defined in dialectical opposition to the sacrificial offer."[58]

Burke draws a crucial distinction between two types of scapegoats, ritualistic and pseudoscientific (or "factional"), that were routinely conflated by the Cambridge School. "A ritualistic scapegoat is felt both to *have* and *not to have* the character formally delegated to it. . . . In universal tragedy, the stylistically dignified scapegoat represents everyman. In his offence, he takes upon himself the guilt of all—and *his* punishment is *mankind's* chastening. . . . We are not onlookers, but participants." By contrast, the "pseudoscientific scapegoat, endowed by 'projection' without an explicit avowal of the process, is felt purely and simply to have the assigned character." In preclass societies "all were implicated in the guilt that went with the strength-giving killing and eating of the totem animal. Perhaps we may note the emergence of the 'factional' scapegoat when, instead, he is ritualistically loaded with the burdens of collective sin and driven off." In contemporary Marxist discourse associating rebirth with revolution, the reborn proletarian hero can signify as the ritual scapegoat of the historical dialectic. In the rhetoric of Hitler, by contrast, the scapegoat functions as a "projection device," resulting in "purification by dissociation" and a false sense of rebirth in the racialized collective. Burke's use of the terms "pseudoscientific" and "factional" to designate the scapegoat-as-maligned-victim links the key scapegoat in contemporaneous American society, the African American, with the racist pseudoscience aimed at producing "trained incapacity" in the white population, as well as with the politically divisive effects of the scapegoating process. The present-day scapegoat can thus signify either voluntary self-sacrifice in service to collective needs or coerced blood sacrifice in service to authoritarian rule; it can perform either a revolutionary or a fascist social function.[59]

Burke's analysis of the dual nature of the scapegoat, while filling key critical voids left by the Cambridge School, had limitations of its own. One was, perhaps paradoxically, rhetorical. A deeply antiracist man of broad sympathies, Burke was aware of his inability to identify with Ellison's situation as a Negro. He told Ellison, "The indignities you suffer, you suffer not as an individual, but as a member of a race. . . . Whenever I am with a Negro, I think of myself as white. . . . If I forget that I am a white man, and burn merely from the sense of inadequacies as an individual, it is only because I am not surrounded by a set of customs that continually reminds me of my color." His task, he concluded, was to "do what [he could] to weaken the magic of any such classification." While Burke's distinction between "pseudoscientific" or "factional" scapegoats on the one hand and "ritualistic" scapegoats on the other is crucially important—and will be invoked throughout this study— his terms are so arcane that they diminish the power of the racist magic that they seek to counter. Orlando Patterson's term "American Dionysus," while not based in Burke's materialist social analysis, more effectively captures the *agon* and, at times, the agony accompanying the black scapegoat's status as at once human exile and dying god. Where appropriate throughout this study, this term is substituted for Burke's less felicitous language.[60]

The other shortcoming of Burke's analysis is, again perhaps paradoxically, theoretical: despite his cagey understanding of the role of texts in enforcing rites of consensus, Burke did not distinguish between what René Girard would later designate the scapegoat *in* a text, the character shown to be enduring the scapegoating process at the hands of other characters, and the scapegoat *of* a text, the figure (or figures) onto whom the text itself rhetorically loads blame for the represented scapegoat's suffering. In *Invisible Man* Ellison would place Burke's dual-natured scapegoat at the center of his commentary on American racial rituals, showing the potential for both heroism and victimization in the sacrificial situation faced by the American Dionysus in his different modes. At the same time he would enact purification rituals of his own by invoking cold war rites of consensus to designate Communists as the aliens to be expelled from the novel's implied community. In its expert representation of scapegoats both *in* and *of* the text, Ellison's novel exhibits the political power of Burkean rhetorical theory in the hands of a writer highly conscious of its premises and skilled in its application.[61]

"Calling the tune of the ritual dance":
On the Cusp of *Invisible Man*

As he began work on *Invisible Man,* Ellison expressed gratitude for the "amalgam of sociology, psychology, Marxism and literary criticism" he had found in Burke's work. But he reminded his friend of the distinct pressures he faced as a Negro writer striving to find and reflect universals through the prism of race. Referring to the recent "smug embod[iment of] an unconscious, culture, prejudice etc" expressed by the likes of the Agrarian critic Donald Davidson, Ellison declares, "I must, if I am to survive and struggle against them, be *conscious* of every idea, insight and concept that I am able to grasp, every second as though they were spread upon a parapet like so many rifles waiting to be fired." Although he would "like to write simply as an American, or even better, a citizen of the world," he found himself "forced to arrive at . . . universalism through the racial grain of sand." He would prefer to use the term "nation" rather than "race" to signify "Negro," he went on, "but the Fascists have rendered it [nation] confusing." He concluded, "To throw away the concern with the racial (suppress national) emphasis would for me be like cutting away the stairs from my situation in the world to that universalism of which you speak . . . for in the dialectical sense the two are one." While Burke's critical apparatus gave Ellison some important tools with which to confront the task of representing Negro humanity to a broad, transracial audience, the task, formidable in its dimensions, remained to be confronted. Burke was aware of the dimensions of the task facing Ellison and wished him well on his journey.[62]

I close this discussion of the aesthetic theory that Ellison had largely worked out by the time he began work on *Invisible Man* with a glance at the published text and drafts of "Twentieth-Century Fiction and the Black Mask of Humanity," an essay in which he expanded the historical-cum-psychological argument adumbrated in "Beating That Boy." For the great writers of the nineteenth century, who had access to "a body of unassailable public beliefs upon which [they] could base [their] art," Ellison wrote, the Negro was "a symbol of Man." By identifying with Jim, Twain's Huck had been "like Prometheus," defying "the judgment of his superego" and "dramatizing the clash between the direct, human relationships of the frontier and the abstract, inhuman, market-dominated relationships fostered by the rising middle class—which in Twain's day was already compromising dangerously with the most inhuman aspects of the defeated slave system." In almost all twentieth-century literature, however—the more recent works by Faulkner constitute honorable exceptions—the Negro has been "rigidly tabooed" and pushed into the underground of the American psyche, thence to be projected outward once again as a stereotype "in a magic rite by which the white American seeks to resolve the dilemma arising between his democratic beliefs and certain antidemocratic practices." Not simply "racial clichés introduced into society by a ruling class to control political and economic realities," these "projected aspects of an internal symbolic process [spring] . . . not from misinformation alone, but from an inner need to believe."[63]

Although Ellison would later forgive Hemingway for ignoring Negroes—and in fact proclaim in 1965 that the "grace under pressure" manifested by Hemingway's heroes "tells us a hell of a lot about the way Negroes were feeling and acting" in the 1920s—in 1946 he viewed Hemingway as Exhibit A of American literary racism. Hemingway's evasion of American social reality, and especially of the figure of the Negro—epitomized in his obsession with the fatalism of being "gored by a bull, hooked with a fish"—reveals his "attitude of rejection" and his identification "not with human heroes, but with those who are indeed defeated." This defeatism, argues Ellison, reveals the moral, political, and psychological quandary of a society in which the "great social myth [of the] . . . democratic dream" has lost universal currency: "By our day the democratic dream ha[s] become too shaky a structure to support the furious pressures of the artist's doubt." When a "great social myth declines, man without myth is Othello with Desdemona gone: chaos descends, faith vanishes and superstitions prowl in the mind." While the "hard-boiled writer" purports simply to "[present] sheer fact," Ellison is aware that

> one "fact" itself—which in literature must be presented simultaneously as image and as event—[becomes] a rhetorical unit. And the symbolic ritual which has set off this "fact" . . . is the rite of superstition. The superstitious individual responds to the capricious event, the fact that seems to explode in his face through blind fatality. For it is the creative function of myth to protect the individual from the irrational, and since it is here in the realm of the irrational that, impervious to science, the stereotype grows, we see that the Negro stereotype is really an image of the unorganized, irrational forces of American life.

Writing that sustains superstition rather than myth, he concludes, "serves to justify and absolve our sins of social irresponsibility."[64]

In his 1953 preface to "Twentieth-Century Fiction and the Black Mask of Humanity," Ellison apologized for the "bias and shortsightedness" of the "young member of a minority" who had authored the essay. His notes and drafts indicate, however, that he originally intended to pose a still sharper critique of the role of modern literature in promoting and sustaining racist inequality. Observing that the "literary imprisonment of Negroes [is] a 'conditioner' for the use of the atom bomb," he launched the essay with a startling Gothic metaphor:

> Somewhere in Slavic folklore we encounter the perfectly normal man who after being bitten by a vampire has the horrible experience of looking into a mirror and discovering that it will no longer cast a reflection of his image. You will remember, of course, that one of the identifying characteristics of the vampire is that he can never be seen reflected in a mirror and that it is the fate of his victim to take on the vampire's qualities. Now if we think of the victim as the American Negro, 20th century American writers as the vampires (which incidentally are really rather unhappy ghosts who aspire to return to life), and 20th century writing as the mirror, this Gothic concept becomes highly useful for getting at some of the aspects of the American Negro's segregation in words.

While the published essay begins with the observation, "Perhaps the most insidious and least understood form of segregation is that of the word," here Ellison compares writers purveying anti-Negro stereotypes with predators living off the blood of the living and their texts with mirrors producing not images but invisibility. The universals of folklore are being invoked with a vengeance. Ellison's original title, "Imprisoned in Words," suggests further that writers are the jailers of the Negro, the disciplinary authorities who would keep Jim as well as Huck pent up in the cabins of the present-day racial regime.[65]

Both the published text and the notes and drafts of "Twentieth-Century Fiction and the Black Mask of Humanity" reveal the extent to which Ellison had absorbed both Burke and the Cambridge School theorists. He explicitly maps his argument along the lines of the Burkean pentad, jotting, "I—Act—Distortion; II—Scene—20 vs 19 cent; III—Agent—Writer; IV—Agency—Novels with Negro Scapegoats; v—Purpose—To back status quo, to absolve personal guilt." His discussion of the scapegoat as an "irrational" figure "impervious to science" recalls Burke's distinction between the ritualistic and the pseudoscientific scapegoats; the term *projection* indicates a psychoanalytical conception of the "scapegoat process." Ellison's insistence that facts are rhetorical units in larger patterns draws upon Burke's theorization of equations and associational clusters as the constitutive features of textual representation and persuasion. His steady focus on ritual invokes the notion that all writing, as symbolic action, not only describes but enacts rituals: "Rhetoric is the key to ritual," he writes, "for just as the stereotype calls racial prejudice into action, so does the rhetorical flourish [*sic*] call the tune of the ritual dance." His rebuke of Hemingway's "attitude of rejection" and abandonment of "broad social responsibility," moreover, invokes the Burkean doctrine of frames of acceptance and rejection, as well as the notion that the writer is, as either doctor or poisoner, a medicine man.[66]

"Twentieth-Century Fiction and the Black Mask of Humanity" displays the distance Ellison has traveled since he wrote dismissively of the "strange bird flying over from Mr. T. S. Eliot's Waste Land" and called upon writers to situate themselves in the "wide space of the unwashed millions." Where once he praised a novelist for depicting the "economic basis of Negro personality," he now caricatures the Marxist view of ideology as constituted by "racial clichés introduced by a ruling class in order to control political and economic realities." Freud is pulling away from Marx: the "inner need to believe" in white supremacy can be disarticulated from the imperatives of capitalist ideological rule. But Ellison has not so much abandoned as reconfigured the proportionality of elements in his earlier radicalism. The universals he discerns in folklore point to the coercive mechanisms and psychic effects of oppression. He envisions Huck Finn, in his rejection of racist interpellation, as an avatar of Prometheus; he locates the capacity for Promethean rebellion on the part of "human heroes" in an abidingly historical materialist interpretation of pre– and post–Civil War history. Even the need to "absolve personal guilt" involved in the scapegoating mechanism, described as "purpose" in his pentad, is paired with the need to "back [the] status quo," that is, ideologically sustain the hegemonic racial and class order. Ellison's analysis bears distinctly upon the postwar scene, where, as he worried to Wright in 1945 and 1946, there lurked the danger of a resurgent American fascism. The "great social myth" that has declined is, if not socialism, at the very least the expanded notion of democracy that guided the left during the war and raised hopes for the postwar era. The chaos that has descended, and the superstitions prowling in its wake, have everything to do with the spate of postwar lynchings. Although Ellison is avoiding Marxist terminology, it is evident that, as a conscious opponent of the Donald Davidsons of the world, he still draws upon his leftist training for a good deal of the conceptual artillery "spread upon a parapet like so many rifles waiting to be fired." For the writer compelled to view social reality through the "racial grain of sand," words are still bullets.[67]

Writing from the Left

three

> Experimentation is Prometheus;
> the inspired application of
> experimental method; the will
> to discover new knowledge.
> —Ralph Ellison,
> notes to "Slick" manuscript

In his interviews and essays after 1952 Ellison would routinely speak with contempt of the project of proletarian literature. Noting that he "rejected Marxism . . . because it cast the Negro as a victim and looked at him through ideology," he also held that left politics inspired poor writing: "What was written by proletarian writers was so empty that I could tell they weren't interested in art at all." He pitied Richard Wright for having "believed in the much abused idea that novels are 'weapons,'" while of himself he said, "[For a time I] wrote what might be called propaganda having to do with the Negro struggle . . . I never wrote the official type of fiction. . . . My fiction was always trying to be something else. . . . I never accepted the ideology which the *New Masses* attempted to impose on writers." When queried about his own forays into the writing of fiction before *Invisible Man*, Ellison would at times refer to a novel about a Negro aviator in a German prison camp during the Second World War; he would also occasionally mention a cluster of stories drawing upon his childhood experiences in Oklahoma, as well as another group, including "In a Strange Country" (1944) and "Flying Home" (1944), that featured the ironies facing African Americans in the armed forces during the antifascist war. But while he referred to some unnamed early experiments that he termed—alluding to his musical training—"five finger exercises," he never spoke of the short stories he had published in the *New Masses* ("The Birthmark," 1940) and the League of American Writers organ *Direction* ("Slick Gonna Learn," 1939) during the years when he was try-ing his wings as a Marxist critic. Nor did he subsequently mention that he had written more than a dozen other tales, most of them in publishable or near-publishable form, that could best be described as proletarian; gathered in a folder marked "Early Stories," these would be discovered in his apart-ment only after his death. When a number of these tales appeared in 1996 in *Flying Home and Other Stories* alongside previously published works, it was clear that Ellison had in fact been quite a talented practitioner in the genre that he would subsequently derogate.[1]

In this chapter I examine a range of texts drawn from the corpus of Elli-son's early fiction (considerations of space necessitate selection of a repre-sentative sample). These include tales, both previously published and newly discovered, drawn from *Flying Home and Other Stories*; the early published stories omitted from the volume; a number of narratives still available only in manuscript at the Library of Congress; and notes and outlines for what appear to have been at least two unwritten novels. While all this material is of relevance to the project of understanding more fully the author of *In-visible Man*, the previously unpublished texts, as well as the drafts of "Flying Home," the most important of the early published tales, are of particular interest in connection with Ellison's politics, for they display his fascination with the figure of the African American leftist as Promethean rebel. Despite its usefulness in gesturing toward the political and artistic radicalism of the young Ellison, *Flying Home and Other Stories* cannot fully introduce readers to the aspiring proletarian writer, who was engaged in a project in some ways more revolutionary than anything ever attempted by Richard Wright.[2]

The body of early writing to be examined here in certain ways sustains Ellison's assertion, made both at the time and in retrospect, that at some point in the early 1940s he consciously changed the direction of his writing away from the school of social protest and literary naturalism. He noted to Sanora Babb in the summer of 1943 his determination "to map a new course for [his] writing, based upon those things that are abiding in Negro experi-ence in the U.S.": "It will be harder than before, there'll be no token fame to go with it nor pictures in [*New Masses*], but I'll learn to write so that it will be read because it is true and perhaps now and then with a streak of beauty." He recalled in a letter in 1948 to Wright that in 1942 he had found it necessary, "at the expense of much wrenching of emotions and intellectual convictions, to change the direction of [his] writing." The stories published in or after 1943 do indicate that Ellison was undertaking new explorations of the mythic dimension of folklore and new experiments with stream of consciousness and surrealism; these texts are in various ways transitional to *Invisible Man*.[3]

"Transitional" should not be taken in a teleological sense, however; as with other aspects of Ellison's thinking and writing during the 1940s, there is a danger involved in reading backward from a standpoint defined by the 1952 novel and cherry-picking those features of his early work that can be read as anticipating later developments. If we read forward through Ellison's early fictional oeuvre, we see that after 1943 he was not so much altering course as modulating the direction of his craft, which continued to be moved along by historical currents that he made no major effort to resist. Even Ellison's earliest stories reveal his preoccupation with myth, ritual, and Freudian psychology, as well as with the relevance of folklore to the fight for freedom, past and present. And while some of these apprentice works could hardly be termed experimental, as he developed his technique he sought the means of representing the "emotions and intellectual convictions" of fictional characters themselves seeking to change the course of history. Some of these characters partake of the political doubts Ellison himself was entertaining during the war years; the notes for the uncompleted novels in particular reveal his interest in portraying a Communist hero torn between doubt and commitment. By no means is Ellison's Promethean hero lacking in a sense of irony; indeed much of his wrestling is not so much with external antagonists as with inner demons. Read in tandem with the contradictory views that Ellison continued to articulate into the late 1940s, however, his early fictional writing displays not the substitution of a simplistic naturalism by a nuanced modernism, an immature Marxism by a seasoned humanism, but his continuing, if finally failing, struggle to find a ground where his warring tendencies might coexist in dialectical tension.

A point on critical procedure. While the discussion of *Invisible Man* in Part II of *Wrestling with the Left* assumes that the reader is familiar with the novel, this chapter clearly cannot be premised upon the reader's acquaintance with the fiction under examination; only the tales gathered in *Flying Home and Other Stories* are readily available, and these probably will not have been perused by many readers of this study. A brief summary of each text thus precedes commentary and analysis; it is hoped that the necessity for this approach will compensate for its occasional awkwardness.

"A color other than white on the old ball":

Proletarian Short Stories

"The Birthmark" tells of a brother and sister, Matt and Clara, coming to terms with the lynching of their brother, Willie. A mere page and a half in its original *New Masses* publication in July 1940, the story is straightforward and wrenching. On a rural southern roadside Matt and Clara have been brought by a patrolman and the local coroner to identify the body of their brother, who was, they are told, accidentally hit by a car. The face has been badly disfigured, so they must seek to verify the body's identity by looking for a birthmark below the navel. While Matt tries to shield Clara from the horror, she insists upon viewing the body. Willie's loins are blood-soaked; he has been castrated. Clara passionately declares, "They asked us last month to sign a piece of paper saying we wanted things like this to stop and you was afraid. Now look at my brother, he's laying there looking like something ain't even human. And these white folks talking 'bout a car hit him. He was lynched. Lynched! I'm gonna tell everybody, HE WAS LYNCHED!" The story ends with the figures who embody state power insisting that Matt and Clara agree that Willie was hit by a car, to which Matt bitterly accedes.[4]

In Nathaniel Hawthorne's tale bearing the same title, the "birthmark" signifies the precious flaw, disregarded by Aylmer, the seeker for scientific perfection, that makes all people human; in Ellison's tale of Jim Crow the "birthmark" of the Negro is his designation as what Burke called the "pseudoscientific" or "factional" scapegoat. Willie's birthmark is what allows him to be turned into something that "ain't even human." Yet the hand of the oppressor is if anything weakened by this act of castration, for Ellison implies that the antilynching campaign to which Clara alludes—*New Masses* readers would recognize it as a project of the CP-affiliated National Negro Congress—has gained a new recruit in her. Although murdered and dismembered, the American Dionysus—who was lynched, Ellison implies, because he would not abide by the ethics of living Jim Crow—is reborn in his sister. As in Wright's "Bright and Morning Star," it is the continuation of the left-led movement against racism that enables the resurrection of the lynched man: "The king is dead. Long live the king."

In an early draft, it bears noting, the motif of rebirthing is connected with Matt rather than Clara. Instead of ending with the words "'I'll remember, suh,' Matt said bitterly, 'he was hit by a car,'" the text continues: "Matt began pushing Clara gently along, his arm around her waist and his hand over her mouth to keep her from saying what he wanted to say and what from now on he would feel. He felt the soft warm flesh of her body and knew he would have to be a different man, like the boy back there on the ground, come out of her into a different world." The original version of the ending treats Willie's sacrifice and Clara's resistance as an initiation ritual enabling Matt to "become a different man." The sister, here silenced, figures primarily not as an actor in her own right, but as a medium through which male martyrdom can be redeemed and male radicalism reborn. As Ellison prepared the tale for publication, he evidently decided to feature female heroism; possibly the examples of strong Negro women's leadership he had witnessed at the NNC convention of May 1940 influenced his revisions.[5]

"A Party Down at the Square," one of the stories discovered in the folder marked "Early Stories" and published for the first time in *Flying Home and Other Stories*, further displays the young writer's attempt to link proletarian realism and class-conscious critique with symbolism based in myth and ritual. The first-person narrator, a young white boy from Cincinnati visiting relatives in Alabama, is taken by his uncle one evening to witness the burning alive on the town square of an anonymous African American man, whom he continually refers to as "that Bacote nigger." Men and women throng to get a closer look as the sheriff and his deputies stand guard, apparently to safeguard, not stop, what is going on. When the lynching victim calls out in agony, "Will someone please cut my throat like a Christian?" a lyncher calls back, "Sorry but there ain't no Christians around tonight. Ain't no Jew-Boys either. We're just one hundred percent Americans." The "party" is interrupted by the heavy winds and rains of a cyclone that has blacked out the nearby airport and forced the pilot of a plane to swoop low over the lit-up town square, which he mistakes for the runway. He zooms upward without crashing, but the plane's wing breaks an electric power line which, whipping like a snake, electrocutes a white woman, who turns "almost as black as the nigger." The armed sheriff forces the crowd back to the bonfire, and the lynching is completed. The boy observes that the burning man's back "looks like a barbecued hog"; he vomits but is reassured by his uncle, who jokes that his nephew, though a "gutless wonder from Cincinnati," will "get used to it in time." The story ends with a conversation in the town's general store between two white sharecroppers who look, the boy thinks, "hungry as hell," like "most of the croppers." One observes that another "nigger" has been lynched (lynchings are always done in pairs "to keep the other niggers in place"). The second remarks that "it didn't do no good to kill niggers 'cause things don't get no better"; he is told by the first that "he'd better shut his damn mouth." He has been silenced. "But from the look on his face," the boy surmises, "he won't stay shut long." The story ends with the boy think-ing, "It was my first party and my last. God, but that nigger was tough. That Bacote nigger was some nigger!"[6]

This wrenching tale of Jim Crow sacrificial practices addresses the scape-goating process on the levels of both ritual and ideology. The lynchee is here not a redeemer, but a victim, a pseudoscientific scapegoat, whose fate illus-trates the "trained incapacity" of the mob. As in "The Birthmark," however, Ellison implies that the violent practices of Jim Crow have limited power to terrorize and control. The sheriff's herding the townspeople toward the lynching demonstrates the coercive role of the state in rallying them around their whiteness. The references to the ritual as a "barbecue" suggest that the victim's killing and dismemberment are an ideological substitute for food that might otherwise fill empty bellies: a false totemic consumption. The closing dialogue between the hungry sharecroppers suggests that the ritual's days even as surrogate symbolic action may be numbered; material necessity cries out for a class-conscious repudiation of the myth of Negro inferiority that sustains the ritual sacrifice. And the defiant refusal of the lynchee to cry out in pain marks him as a hero to the young boy, who, in Ellison's nod to *The Adventures of Huckleberry Finn*, recognizes in the victim a humanity lack-ing in his torturers. What was to have been an initiation into the consensual rites of whiteness has become instead an initiation into universal humanity. While it remains unclear whether the boy will assume the Promethean role Ellison later assigned to Huck, the frame of acceptance imposed by his uncle is being supplanted, it appears, by one of rejection; Burke's rhetorical cate-gories have been concretely dramatized.

Besides commenting on the role of racializing rituals in the Jim Crow South, "A Party Down at the Square" alludes to the trajectory of global poli-tics. The cyclone suggests the cataclysmic coming of fascism, which the Jew-baiting "little Hitlers of the South," preoccupied with scapegoating the Negro, do not see as a threat to themselves. The electrocution of the white woman, who is even dressed in white, reveals the high price paid by those who, implicated in "100% Americanism," align themselves along the same side of the color line as their rulers. With her exposed breast, she is violated not by the Negro, but by the very men self-designated as her chivalric protec-tors. The snakelike whipping of the power line—which leads from the urban industrial center of Birmingham—signifies the danger that modern forces of production become destructive, a source of evil, when fettered by capitalist social relations. The airplane, potentially a symbol of modern technological advancement, seeks the light of civilization but finds only the fire of barba-

rism. The statue of the Confederate general presides over the horrific consequences of cultural and material lag: the Civil War, it would seem, was won
by the other side.[7]

"The Black Ball," another previously unpublished story first appearing in
the 1994 anthology, features a more mature and politically aware—and initially cynical—protagonist. The tale is narrated in the first person by John,
a young father who, while ambitious to return to college, is working as a
janitor in an unnamed town in the Southwest. A single parent, he ponders
how to introduce the realities of Jim Crow to his four-year-old son. When
the child, who plays regularly with Jackie, the white son of a neighboring
gardener, asks whether brown is better than white, his father replies, "Some
people think so. But American is better than both." John is continually anxious that his son's vigorous playing with a white ball will disrupt the resident
building manager and imperil John's job. Wary of whites, John is at first put
off when a unionist, whose "lean" face has "a redness [that] comes from a
long diet of certain foods," approaches him with an invitation to join a building service workers' union. All unions, John declares, exclude black workers
from membership. The organizer, who, it emerges, initially organized among
"croppers" but now concentrates on urban proletarians, proclaims that his
union is different. As proof of his sincerity he displays his badly burned
hands, injured, he relates, in a fruitless attempt to prevent a black fellow
sharecropper from being lynched in Macon County, Alabama.[8]

As John reads André Malraux's *Man's Fate* during his lunch break and
meditates upon the unionist's message, he sees a nursemaid shepherd her
white charges away from Jackie, who disconsolately "drag[s] his toy, some
kind of bird that flapped its wings like an eagle." Asked by his son what he is
looking at, John replies, "I guess Daddy was just looking out on the world."
When an older white boy seizes the white ball from John's son and accidentally throws it through the manager's window, the boss angrily warns John
that he will find himself "behind the black ball" if his child, presumed guilty,
shows his face again. Queried by the child about why the boss thinks the
white ball is black, John ruefully thinks, "My, yes, the old ball game," and
tells his son that he himself will play with the black ball "in time." The story
ends with John putting iodine on his hand, which he has cut cleaning up the
broken glass: "Looking down at the iodine stain, I thought of the fellow's
fried hands, and felt in my pocket to make sure I still had the card he had
given me. Maybe there was a color other than white on the old ball."[9]

In "The Black Ball" sacrifice signifies both brutal ritual and conscious
commitment: the white unionist's "fried hands," injured in his attempted

interference in the lynching of a Negro comrade, signify his self-sacrifice in the fight against racism. (It is noteworthy that Macon County is specified as the site of racial violence; the Alabama county where Tuskegee Institute is located, it will figure prominently in Ellison's fiction about the Jim Crow South.) That the organizer's past action may lead to John's future political activism is suggested in Ellison's original ending to the story, which reads, "The ball game had begun already." The Popular Frontist inflection of the theme of rebirth is signaled not only through the allusion to the great American game but also through John's stated desire to embrace an American identity beyond white or brown. Presumably the rediscovery of authentic Americanism will restore life to the "crippled" eagle dragged through the dust by Jackie, a member of the white working class evidently spurned by his middle-class peers. Yet the iodine with which John will heal his cut hand implies that the "old ball game" of racial division will end only when the American working class is healed of its wounds by the red antibiotic of communism. John is holding the entire globe in his bloodied hands, which link him with the white unionist; it will be "man's fate" to gain possession of a world beyond nations. Drawing upon the revolutionary standpoint of the early Malraux, Ellison shows his protagonist on the cusp of becoming the "new man" of a transformed world. Verbally confined to the sphere of Americanism but iconographically reaching toward proletarian internationalism, "The Black Ball" displays the melding of democracy with hopes for socialism that engaged the hopes and imaginations of many radicals during the Popular Front and wartime years.[10]

"Prometheus in the Chicken Yard":
Buster, Riley, and Crushed Rebellion

In his four stories featuring Buster and Riley, Ellison drew upon memories from his childhood in Oklahoma City, deploying folkloric references to highlight issues largely beyond the boys' necessarily limited conceptual range. "That I Had the Wings," the third in the series, portrays in tragicomic terms the two boys' attempt to get some baby chickens to fly by attaching makeshift parachutes to them. The story opens with Riley identifying with a fledgling robin struggling to fly: "Yuh had me fooled. . . . Yuh wuzn't really scaird. Yuh jus didn't want no ole folks messin with yuh." When the boys chant a defiant song in which they imagine themselves "President of these United States [and] . . . Great—God-a-mighty . . . swing[ing] on them White House gates!," Riley's aunt Kate reprimands them for their disrespect and blasphemy, instructing them to sing instead about flying up to Jesus. In an early draft the boys' play is extended, and they are shown pretending to be Kingsberry, a gunfighter famed in Negro folklore for having stood off the Texas Rangers.[11]

Tired of make-believe, the boys recall the "white guys [who] jump outa them airplanes in them parachutes" and decide to engage in flight experiments with the birds in the yard. They first grab Ole Bill, the spur-footed rooster whom Riley has described as "the Louie Armstrong of the chickens playin' 'Hold that Tiger'. . . . [He's] good-lookin' an' he can fight like Joe Louis!" When Buster challenges, "But he caint fly!," Riley tosses the rooster off the roof; he hits the dust hard but survives. The boys then attach pieces of cloth to some chicks and toss them; the baby birds are killed. When Aunt Kate chastises the boys, Riley bitterly exclaims, "I wish yuh had died back in slavery times." The story ends with Ole Ben viciously attacking Riley with his spurs; bleeding, the boy cries, "We almost had 'em flying."[12]

That Ellison viewed his story as more than a childhood reminiscence is signaled by the range of titles he considered: "Wings of the Spirit"; "All Birds Like to Fly"; "A Morning's Flight"; "Ole Bill the Mighty Chanticleer"; "Parachutes for Two"; "The Outlaw"; and, last but not least, "Prometheus in the Chicken Yard." The first three titles would have paralleled the chicks with the boys and stressed their sense of earthbound confinement, clearly linked to the "grounding" effects of Aunt Kate's discipline in the ethics of living Jim Crow. "The Outlaw" would have emphasized the boys' identification with Kingsberry and highlighted the challenge to the state, embodied in their taunting chant about the president and the White House gates. Other titles link the tale more specifically to the context of the Second World War. "Parachutes for Two" recalls the boys' longing reference to the white paratroopers and directs attention to the segregated armed forces; in particular it invokes the ambiguous situation of the Tuskegee Air School, which Ellison angrily dismissed as "window-dressing" in the final *Negro Quarterly* editorial, where he praised William Hastie for resigning from the War Department. "That I Had the Wings," implying the prefatory words "I Wish," signifies the airmen's desire to "have the wings," that is, not just control of bombers and fighter jets but also badges indicating their accepted proficiency as military pilots. Ellison's eventual choice of this title emphasizes the historically specific connection between the boys' yearning for freedom and the situation of the Tuskegee airmen; had he written not "the wings" but "wings," the tale's Icarian motif would have prevailed.[13]

But what of the titles "Ole Bill the Mighty Chanticleer" and "Prometheus in the Chicken-Yard"? Riley's laudatory comparison of Ole Bill with the tiger-taming Louis Armstrong and the Brown Bomber Joe Louis suggests that the rooster signifies a defiant, and decidedly masculine, alternative to Aunt Kate's repressive regime. Yet Ole Bill is unable to fly and ends up viciously attacking Riley with the spurs Aunt Kate has provided. Ellison's marginal notations to the story illuminate the rooster's symbolic role in connection with Tuskegee, the site of wartime "window-dressing": "NAACP prospering . . . Tuskegee revived by air school, Carver, with attempt to work out new methods . . . Middle class bargaining, through rejection, self-pity, now pleading, now threatening, but with no real weapon because no real control of power." Unable to use his wings for flight but armed to suppress those below him, the rooster is associated with the famous Tuskegee scientist and administrator George Washington Carver, whom Ellison described contemptuously to Kenneth Burke as "a symbol of the achievement possible for negroes who stayed in their place, bowed to the white folks, prayed to God and left politics alone." In their childish attempt to master the basics of flight, Buster and Riley have, like the would-be Tuskegee airmen, challenged the gods of white supremacy and their surrogates in both Aunt Kate and Ole Bill. In Armstrong and Louis they have chosen culture heroes who embody a success circumscribed by the rules of the entertainment and boxing worlds. But Ole Bill, who works for the other side, rules the roost, and if necessary threatens circumcision (or is it castration?) of those who would rebel. Ellison's elimination of references to Kingsberry and Prometheus in the story's dialogue and title underlines the limits within which not just the Tuskegee airmen, but young black men in general, are allowed to move. Beneath its vernacular re-creation of childhood experience, "That I Had the Wings" is a bitter allegory of the defeat of the titans by the Olympian gods, the crushing of wartime hopes by the continuing rule of Jim Crow.[14]

"Until I use my plane for killing":
"Flying Home" as Revolutionary Parable

The preoccupation with the Tuskegee airmen adumbrated in "That I Had the Wings" occupies center stage in "Flying Home," which appeared in *Cross Section* in 1944. Narrated in the third person, the story opens with Todd, a young pilot in training, having crash-landed in a field in Macon County after his plane has been disabled in a bloody collision with a buzzard (a "jim-crow"). Todd comes back to consciousness in the company of Jefferson, an old Negro sharecropper, who evokes in the young man not solidarity but shame at the backwardness of "peasant" Negroes. Recalling a conversation with his northern-born girlfriend about the psychological costs of undergoing military training in the South, Todd contemplates the humiliation he will experience when the word of his crash gets out. A series of italicized stream-of-consciousness flashbacks reveals that Todd's passion for flying goes back to his childhood; we learn that a traumatic incident in which KKK-authored leaflets warning African Americans not to vote were dropped from a plane is what inspired him to achieve mastery of modern aviation technology.[15]

While they wait for a boy to bring help, Jefferson informs Todd of the brutality of Dabney Graves, the local plantation owner—he has recently murdered five sharecroppers—and then entertains, or possibly cautions, Todd with a folk "lie" about dying and going to heaven, where Jim Crow still reigns. In defiance of rules ordering Negroes to wear special restraining harnesses, Jefferson purportedly angered St. Peter by shedding his harness and speeding around on only one wing; he was expelled from heaven and, Jefferson explains amid gales of laughter, sent back to Alabama. At first interpreting Jefferson's story as a mockery of his own aspirations—"We can hope to be eagles, can't we?" Todd shouts—the younger man comes to see the similarity between Jefferson's dream and his own. When help arrives in the form of Graves bearing a straitjacket—he declares, "You can't let the nigguh git up that high without his going crazy"—it is now Todd who bursts into uncontrollable laughter. As he is carried away, he feels "as though he had been lifted out of his isolation, back into the world of men. A new current of communication flowed between the man and boy and himself." Seeing another buzzard, he expects "the horror" of his fall to return. But instead, "like a song within his head he heard the boy's soft humming and saw the dark bird glide into the sun and glow like a bird of flaming gold." The closing mention of music recalls the provenance of the tale's title in Lionel Hampton's "Flying Home," a jazz composition popular in wartime Harlem.[16]

Critical commentary on "Flying Home," noting the tale's folkloric and mythic resonances, has generally interpreted its ending as an affirmation of the cultural and psychological homecoming, the "flying home," of its previously alienated protagonist. Read backward from *Invisible Man*, the story has been seen to anticipate the invisible man's rediscovery of his southern roots when he bites into the hot yam and thinks, "I yam what I am." Jefferson's trickster tale and ironic folk humor signify a zone of vernacular freedom exempt from the control of authoritarian gatekeepers and straitjacketers, both heavenly and earthly. Todd parallels Icarus in his belief that he can escape his common identity with the old man; Jefferson brings him to earth. Bearing as he does the name of the country's third president, the old man emerges as a carrier of the legacy of the Founding Fathers, a precursor of the grandfather of the 1952 novel. The story's closing image, which transmutes the buzzard of oppression into a phoenix of hope, suggests Todd's ritual rebirth into the folk he has formerly abandoned; although his name signifies death (in German, *Tod*), he will regain life. "Flying Home" is routinely read as a culturalist text in which African American vernacular and folklore emerge as quintessential embodiments of the promise always present, if not always recognized, in American democracy.[17]

With its allusions to myth and folklore, jazz-like shifting of time frames, surreal humor, and invocation of the vernacular as a repository of transcendent wisdom, "Flying Home" would seem to bear out Ellison's claim to have changed course in his fiction by the time he composed this tale. The notes, outlines, and multiple drafts of the story reveal, however, that the published version was the product of extensive rethinking and reframing. Other titles contemplated by Ellison suggest a range of emphases: "A Harness for Wings"; "A Yoke for Wings"; "A Joke for Wings"; "A Yoke No Wings"; "The Black Eagle"; "The End of Flight"; "The Humanization of the Aeroplane"; "The Meaning of Sacrifice." Some of these titles relate clearly to themes in the published version: "harness" and "yoke" indicate the constraints of Jim Crow; the various plays on "wings," as in "That I Had the Wings," signify Todd's yearning for freedom; "joke" suggests the Negro's status as the butt of humor but also the power of folk laughter to slip the yoke; "black eagle" alludes to a common nickname for the Tuskegee aviators as well as the tale's Icarus motif. But the other titles remain somewhat mysterious until viewed in the contexts supplied by different drafts of the tale.[18]

Ellison originally conceived of Todd (in early drafts he is named "Mead") as a more politically conscious character and heightened the historical tensions informing the young man's environment. As he pilots his plane before the accident, Todd/Mead recalls, "There was a lynching the first month, but we were far enough away as not to be bothered." He thinks about "John Brown and slavery" and reminds himself, "You're being trained for war so remember and keep yourself alive." Glorying in the "delicate adjustment" between man and plane, Todd/Mead ponders, "No black man's got the right to feel this free. . . . What really did it mean, why was he here so free in this broad blue expense of endlessness? It was like the dreams in which he constantly [was] going to a destination he did not know, on a mission he could not discover." In the "clear blue singing sky," he intuits both "great danger" and "great promise." While Todd's yearning to fly historically connects the current antifascist war with the war against slavery, his hubris consists in his illusion that mastery of aviation technology (the "end of flight") can separate him from the lynch violence of the Jim Crow world below, his conviction that he is "exceptional," exempt from the fate of "ordinary men." Just as Icarus's idealism led him to forget the material qualities of wax, the young pilot's fascination with the "broad blue expanse of endlessness" tempts him to think that freedom consists in his own "delicate adjustment" with the plane and to forget that he is "being trained for war."[19]

The young aviator—in some versions speaking in the first person—is supplied with a fuller personal background in early versions of the tale. When his girlfriend complains about his acceptance of southern racist practices, she asks, "Don't you, whom I love, by accepting their chauvinism, humiliate me more?" It was principally Communists who used the term "chauvinism" to refer to white supremacy; the couple appears to have moved in leftist circles. The aviator's childhood memories, moreover, combine his longing to pilot planes and his fear of the messages they drop with his proud recall of his parents' resistance to Jim Crow. His mother, like Ellison's own, defied racists refusing her and her children entry to the local zoo; his father and uncle shouldered guns when the Klan planted a burning cross in front of their house. While it is clear that, as in the published version of the tale, the young "black eagle" needs to overcome his arrogant attitude toward the sharecroppers on the ground below if he is to achieve his mission, in the drafts he is supplied with a personal and familial history of militant antiracism. He is not simply an alienated elitist awaiting rebirth through rediscovery of the blues-inflected laughter of the folk.[20]

Technological modernity, the force that defeated the folk hero John Henry, undergoes different treatments in successive versions of the tale. In the published version the airplane figures as a site of humiliation and illusion; it is the closing image of the mythical phoenix that supplies compensation for the young man's defeat by the buzzard of Jim Crow. In an earlier draft, Todd/Mead recalls:

> Once I took a trip to the country and saw a rich farmer having his crops dusted from a plane. The pilot flew low over the fields, sending a white spray that caused me to remember the falling cards as it made the plants snap back and forth under a cover of whiteness. I was dumbfounded,

shocked that a plane should be used in such an unworthy manner. To me it was sacrilege. But the farmer I was visiting did not think so.

"Lawd," he said in a tone of reverent yearning, "dont I wish I had money to hire one of them things to spray *my* crops with!"

Where in the published version airplanes are linked with crushed ambitions and white supremacist intimidation, here modern technology can be a force for good; its "sacrilege" consists not in its association with a "cover of whiteness," but in its being reserved for the rich. It is capitalism that prevents "the humanization of the aeroplane," which, as in "A Party Down at the Square," becomes an instrument of destruction only when yoked to the regressive imperatives of Jim Crow.[21]

Piloted by an aviator who dares to shed all yokes and harnesses, the plane affords access to an understanding of the social totality, both geographical and structural, shaping the terrain below. Todd/Mead thinks:

> The plane gives us again our heritage—no forty acres and a mule but many acres and many mules. Not a sense of detachment, of irresponsible freedom, but one of profound attachment to the earth. And always black faces looking upward.
>
> The plane is a builder of contrasts, where from the air one sees the pattern of our southern living. . . . The croppers' shacks, the mansions cresting the hills, the new factories blowing smoke no planter ever blew, fox hunting lands with miles of roaming fences. Once I saw the red coats riding to the hounds through a gunsight, played war games high above the Georgia pines, and saw the tracks dividing black streets from white as I dived like a stuka on the town, while all the black faces were looking upward. And both plane and I are no longer simply pilot and plane. We are vessels for their hopes.

Ellison here offers a perspective on both social structure and historical process that carries strong Marxist overtones. The pilot's view from above allows him "possession" of a truth about social relationships that is obscured at close range on the ground. The desire for "forty acres and a mule," the program of Reconstruction historically limited to the goal of private "ownership of land," gives way to the "many acres and many mules" of collective ownership. As a "builder of contrasts," the airplane affords understanding of the dialectical unity-and-conflict of the divided social world: countryside and city, poor and rich, black and white. The pilot reminds himself not to revel in the "irresponsible freedom" afforded by his "detachment" on high, but instead to reaffirm his "attachment to the earth" below; he and the other "black eagles" are "vessels for the hopes" of the masses. That the pilot has aimed at the red-coated fox hunters through his gun's sight reveals that, as a bearer of the legacy of John Brown, he has been training himself to take action against not just the fascists overseas, but their analogues at home. Dabney Graves's violence will beget its own gravediggers.[22]

As he revised "Flying Home" with the assistance (or perhaps interference) of Stanley Edgar Hyman and Shirley Jackson, Ellison seems not to have tinkered with Jefferson's "lie," which remains essentially the same in all the drafts. But he considered having it precede the entire account of Todd/Mead's crash, serving "by contrast [to] show the limits of flying as freedom." "Swing low, sweet chariot," jotted Ellison on this outline, perhaps also implying the limitations of spirituals as a means to freedom in the era of the airplane. Short-circuiting Jefferson's mentoring role, this version strongly suggests that initially Ellison was far from viewing the old sharecropper as his persona; indeed, Ellison scribbled, the old man's "folk tale . . . sugarcoats bitterness." Once he decided to situate Jefferson's folk fable at the heart of the story, however, Ellison considered various endings. In one version Todd/Mead is shown reflecting, "The others walked ahead as Jefferson and his boy carried me gently along in silence and I felt bound to them as I had never felt bound to anything. Bound by an anguish that throbbed within me as sharply as the pain in my foot. Jefferson's shoulders were sagged at the points his wings should [be] pictured as growing, and I realized that I must fly for him, that I must give him back his wings." In the published text Todd has abandoned his stance of superiority to the folk, but what will result from his "silent communion" with the old man and the boy is not clear: the closing image of the phoenix construes rebirth as transcendence, not negation. Here, by contrast, Ellison posits an interactive relation between the masses, the "black faces looking up," and the pilot, the "vessel for [their] hopes." The "end [that is, the goal] of flight" is a world in which Jefferson, no longer harnessed to the plow, regains his wings. For such a world to emerge, pilots must not only heed the wisdom of the folk but also "fly home" to them with the knowledge gained from aerial vision; the buzzard of Jim Crow will not be eliminated by simply flying into the sun.[23]

In still another draft ending, Todd/Mead, apparently not seriously injured, gets back into his plane and flies off. There is no "communion" with Jefferson and the boy, no lyrical moment when the buzzard is transmuted into a phoenix. Instead, as he looks down, the pilot's thoughts are not epiphanic but grim:

The shadow against the earth seemed more real than the plane. But the folk wish-dream had moved between me and the plane. The plane became an alien thing, as alien as when it was falling. I headed for the airport. Gunsights were before me, suggestively. My hands fingered the trips of the guns that were filled with blank ammunition. And irony rides with me as passenger, irony pilots the plane, *my* plane until memory spoke through that old man who might have been my grandfather. The plane had fooled me with the complex perfection of its being. . . . And now I know that wonderful adjustment can not be again, ever—until—and this be our pity and this our irony and this our danger and our promise—I shall never, never possess the delicate adjustment that is the plane again until I use my plane for killing.

Here the "black eagle" returns to his alienation in the sky; the "meaning of sacrifice" is that he must, like a Malrauvian hero, prepare himself to enact antifascist, and possibly revolutionary, violence. Rather than experiencing oneness with the "black faces looking upward," Todd/Mead finds that Jefferson's "folk wish-dream" has rendered his connection with technological modernity "an alien thing." "Irony" both "pilots the plane" and "rides . . . as passenger," as the "blank ammunition" in his guns reminds him of his powerlessness: he has, after all, been grounded by Jim Crow. It is only when he "use[s his] plane for killing"—not just overseas, it seems, but against the red coats at home as well—that he will recover his "delicate adjustment" with technological modernity. An act of concrete negation, the deployment of guns, is what will reconcile the "folk-wish dream" of the old man and the technological expertise of the young man; technique is meaningless, an Icarian illusion, when divorced from Promethean political practice. As he composed the various drafts of "Flying Home," Ellison may have been experimenting with myth, folklore, and narrative form, but he was hardly abandoning his revolutionary political vision. Indeed Prometheus had left the chicken yard and taken to the sky.[24]

"And then put out their eye": "In a Strange Country" and the Problematics of Patriotism

"In a Strange Country" addresses frontally the bitter contradictions facing African Americans involved in wartime service to the state. Based on Ellison's own experiences in the merchant marine, the tale takes place in an unnamed Welsh port city, probably Swansea, where the protagonist, a black merchant marine sailor named Parker, has just been assaulted by white American soldiers. Sporting a bruised eye, Parker enters a pub, where he is treated with warmth and kindness by some Welshmen, for whom music is evidently the food of internationalist love. A group bridging class differences, containing both "the leading mine owner" and a miners' union official, the Welsh singers evince familiarity with Negro spirituals and fondly call Parker a "black Yank." Parker thinks to himself that these Welsh are "a different breed; even from the English"; though white, they are not *white*. As he listens to them sing there arises in his mind's eye the image of "a Russian peasant kneeling to kiss the earth and rising wet-eyed to enter into battle with cries of fierce exultation." And as he wrestles inwardly there come to his mind various lines from *Othello*, ending with the ironic reflection, "Do the state some service, Parker. . . . Put out that light, Othello—or do you enjoy being hit with one?"[25]

The story ends with a nationalist-internationalist songfest. The Welshmen sing their national anthem with gusto and then strike up "God Save the King," which, Parker notes, is "not nearly so stirring." They next sing the "Internationale," which makes Parker recall *when he was a small boy marching in the streets behind the bands that came to his southern town.* Finally the choir takes up "The Star-Spangled Banner." First feeling "as though he had been pushed into the horrible foreboding country of dreams and they were enticing him into some unwilled and degrading act," Parker sings "our flag was still there" in what feels like "the voice of another, over whom he had no control." Feeling "a burst of relief," he realizes that "the melody seemed charged with some vast new meaning. . . . For the first time in your whole life, he thought, the words are not ironic . . . [and] hoped his black eye would hold back the tears."[26]

A tale of political rebirth, "In a Strange Country" explores the paradoxes of "win the war" patriotism away from the terrain of Jim Crow, as well as the difficult relationship between nationalism and internationalism in the antifascist crusade. As the story's title suggests, the defamiliarization afforded by being overseas enables its protagonist to understand that the identity of "black Yank" can be a contradiction rather than an outright oxymoron. While Parker has experienced a "degree of understanding" with white fellow sailors in the merchant marine because of "the common danger and a fighting union"—clearly he is a member of the left-led National Maritime Union—he has refrained from "approaching white men so closely" before: "That's a unity of economics, he said to himself. And this a unity of music, a 'gut-language,' the 'food of love.'" There resonates in the background, however, the voice of Paul Robeson, an honorary member of the NMU and its favorite singer, whose multilingual concerts epitomized the Popular Frontist view of proletarian internationalism as the braiding of multiple indigenous national cultures. The scattered lines from *Othello* that run through Parker's mind come from the tragic hero's closing soliloquy, where he contemplates that he has "done the state some service." A standard item in many of Robeson's wartime performances, this soliloquy clearly pertained to the situation of Negroes as Jim Crow participants in an antifascist war. The Welshmen's identification with Parker and seeming inability to think of themselves as white derives from their history of colonization under British rule and current embrace of leftist politics. (Wales was one of few places in the United Kingdom where Communists were elected not as Labourites but as open reds.) In turn the Welshmen call to mind for Parker the image of a Russian peasant passionately kissing the ground before going to war, an image that not only brings to mind Robeson's internationalist *narodnost* (he often sang Russian folk songs) but also wartime propaganda movies like *The Battle of Russia* that featured the Russian people's "love of their soil." All the nationalisms of the Allied forces are affirmed: if half-heartedly, the Welshmen sing the anthem of the British Empire, while Parker finds "vast new meaning" in an anthem he has been tempted to associate with Jim Crow. It is the singing of the "Internationale" that connects the Welsh and U.S. national anthems and transports Parker back to the streets of the southern town of his youth. The red-led crusade against fascism is what enables this metonymic linkage of otherwise incommensurable patriotic identities.[27]

That Ellison had to struggle to achieve this linkage, however, is suggested by his revisions of "In a Strange Country." In an earlier draft the Welshmen who in the published text join in the singing of "God Save the King" without enthusiasm are initially simply silent, presumably unable to overcome their hatred of the colonizer. In his childhood hometown memory Parker recalls not following the band, but being Jim-Crowed:

> And that night he sat outside that sub–Post Office building with his battered cornet, reading the stolen score by the dim light from the window as he played softly along with the band rehearsing inside, and [he remembered] the way the white face thrust itself through the window and cried, "Hey fellows! It's a little shine!" and him running away in embrassment and self-loathing and calling back "I can play as well as you!" But that was the last time he had played for several years.

In this version of the tale Parker's anger at his racist white kinsmen remains unalloyed to the end: "*Put out that light, Othello, he thought, placing his hand over*

his eye, and then put out their eye." The Othello with whom he identifies is one
who, having done the state some service, still follows the rule of Mosaic
revenge. Like the drafts of "Flying Home," these alternative passages from
"In a Strange Country" reveal Ellison's win-the-war patriotism to be laced
with ambivalence. Just as his editorials in *Negro Quarterly* muzzled some of
the revolutionary views articulated more freely in the unpublished writings
composed at his editorial desk, the published versions of his wartime stories
repress the decidedly unpatriotic speculation that violence is needed to abolish not just international fascism, but its Jim Crow equivalent.

"Experimentation is Prometheus":
The Unpublished "Slick" Novel

"Slick Gonna Learn," a short story drawn from Ellison's novel-in-progress
that appeared in 1939 in *Direction*, gestures toward the issues that he was
attempting to explore in the longer text. Set in an unspecified northern
industrial city, the story opens with the unemployed protagonist having
just gambled away his last few dollars in an effort to get money with which
to send Callie, his ailing pregnant wife, to the hospital. After fighting with
Bostic, the gambler who fleeced him, Slick is arrested by policemen, who
take him to the edge of town and throw him in a roadside ditch. They are on
the verge of seriously injuring, and perhaps killing, him when they are called
away to quell the mounting violence of striking workers at a local factory.
Slick is picked up by a friendly white truck driver wearing a union logo on his
cap, who expresses sympathy for both the strikers and his battered passenger. The story ends with Slick wondering whether he can trust the driver; the
reader infers that Slick, like the protagonists in "The Birthmark" and "The
Black Ball," is "gonna learn."[28]

Both the desperation of Slick's situation and the necessity for his taking
radical political action are developed in the unfinished novel. The narrative opens with an extended description of Slick's fight with Bostic, during
which, to the tune of the blues, Slick recalls past humiliations by racists,
longs to get hold of one of the machine guns he had assembled in a factory
during the Great War, and fantasizes that Joe Louis is at his side. As he is
being brutalized by the police, more memories stream in: of the postwar
lynching of a friend, of his own unwitting participation in postwar strikebreaking, of his subsequent work shining shoes and waiting on tables. In
one draft he remembers the fires and lynchings in Greenwood, the Negro
section of Tulsa, Oklahoma, which was assaulted by racists in 1921; Slick can

clearly become either more class-conscious or more antiwhite. After a brief flashback conveying the tenderness of Slick's and Callie's marriage—a rare romantic scene in Ellison's oeuvre—the text focuses on her terror at going to the Catholic hospital where Slick has managed to get her admitted by begging a favor from the paternalistic doctor whom he has in the past served as a hunting guide. Callie's fears prove well-founded: the only thing that will save her life is an abortion, and this the hospital, with its brooding iconic figures of the Virgin and saints, will not perform. She dies.[29]

Ellison was undecided about how to end Slick's story. Callie's death would "dramatize the need for socialized medicine," Ellison jotted. "Hospital must affect the entire community." After Callie's "mental derange[ment]" and death, Slick might be "driven to violence" to support his children and be killed. Or perhaps, mulled the young writer, the workers' strike would "[give] Slick his life; he must realize it! The strike theme must become a life principle." There might be an episode in which Slick and some Negro friends, fleeing gunfire, would attempt to help a white man hurt in a car accident; his blood on their hands would result in their being held responsible for his death. A less gruesome ending, somewhat anomalous in the light of the story's anticlericalism, would have shown Slick "find[ing] his way to religion and through religion to communism." He would either die or be reborn.[30]

That union activism and left politics might supply the basis for a hopeful outcome to Slick's situation would be due to the efforts of one Booker Small, a young African American Communist strike organizer who takes the political baton from the Good Samaritan truck driver appearing in the short story version. Emphasizing that Slick's life was saved by the greater urgency of the cops' suppressing the strike, Booker serves as a classic proletarian mentor. Raised by a mother who held up Angelo Herndon as a model and herself went to jail seven times for protesting segregated housing, Booker exemplifies the radicalized middle-class Negro who has come to view his formal education as a "farce" and has cast his lot with the "common people." He fulminates against the black bourgeoisie. "[Those who] taught you in school or . . . wear [goatees] and write longwinded books and hold government jobs," he tells Slick, are "the ones who betray, they're the ones who make Negro life [incestuous]. . . . Thats when you screw your own mother. . . . They have nothing new to offer us to solve our problems. . . . [These bastards are] smooth boys. The white folks who run the country are crazy about them. . . . Theyre crabs . . . off the toilet seat of American history." For Booker class betrayal is sickness and obscenity.[31]

By contrast, Booker holds up Marx and Douglass as joint exemplars of the leadership needed by the working class:

> Douglass was of the same type as Marx. He liked to fight, he was quick tempered and he had a great mind. And just like Marx he was for the oppressed, not just the black but the white as well; and not only in the United States but all over the world. He just didn't have the education that Marx had and being black kept him from getting the people around him like Marx. . . .
>
> They looked very much alike. They both looked like lions . . . [with] big heads, thick manes of hair, with large beards and bushy eyebrows. And in the pictures I've seen of Marx he was almost as dark as a Negro, not that I'm trying to make him one, though I wish he had been, but it's the truth. Both of them had fierce eyes and both looked like they would fight a circle saw.

Booker evidently is—at least Ellison wishes him to be—an organic intellectual, using pungent vernacular metaphors as he explains the relevance of abolitionism and communism to the dilemmas confronted by his confused and angry listener.[32]

We learn that Booker has taken part in class struggles in Birmingham, where the police fired into the homes of workers trying to form unions. He has lived in New York and has fond memories of the Apollo Theater, Central Park, and breakfasts with "comrades," as well as more bitter recollections of the "meaninglessness" of the narrow lives of the Harlem migrants hemmed in by economic hardship and police brutality. After he and Slick have gone hunting in the snow—the vivid passage reproduces some of the minimalist grace of the autobiographical sketch "February" that Ellison would publish many years later—Booker expresses his frustration at being unable to go to Spain to fight fascism. The first among several of Ellison's protagonists who hunger to fight in Spain, Booker thinks, "Here is the true farce . . . starting off to shoot fascists in Spain and end up shooting little rabbits in Ohio. Little furry behinded agents of reaction. Left-right deviationist bastards. Enemies of the people." Booker clings to the science that Marxism can supply: "Funny, there was a time that would have been magic. Magic is now become science. . . . All Europe is haunted by a specter." While Ellison left the ending of Slick's story open, his notes indicate that Booker's odyssey would entail further political activism. The young organizer would go "South to fight poll tax battle," Ellison jotted, joining those who "believe that the South is our country and national home and want to make it free." Booker is, it would seem, an amalgam of Angelo Herndon and Ellison's own idealized self.[33]

Although these fragments of the "Slick" novel suggest Ellison's adherence to a fairly straightforward conception of proletarian realism, the text indicates that the young writer has various arrows in his literary quiver. Freud is present explicitly, Joyce and Shakespeare implicitly, in Booker's riffing meditation on his sense of inner division: "Why should anything be confounded by anything Freud believed died sugar coated cats and doggies must like undertakers come to dust, the id libido and alter ego." The hunting scene creates a Hemingwayesque interlude with flashes of lyrical intensity. Booker's stream of consciousness as he contemplates the "farce" of hunting rabbits rather than shooting fascists shows Ellison blending the rational and irrational in interior monologue. Ellison demonstrates an early interest in incorporating blues lyrics into fictional narrative when he includes in the pool room scene a Victrola playing the song about the "devil's son-in-law" and the woman with "feet like a frog" that will be sung over a decade later by Harlem's Peter Wheatstraw. Ellison's "experimental attitude" is already in evidence.[34]

In this first attempt at a novel Ellison is also already working the Promethean theme: myth and Marxism go hand in hand. He notes that the reciprocity between Slick and Booker—worker and intellectual, practice and theory—should embody "the unity of opposites. Prometheus and Epimethius. . . . Experimentation is Prometheus; the inspired application of experimental method; the will to discover new knowledge." Long passages copied and cobbled together from Sheldon's *Psychology and the Promethean Will* show the young Ellison seeking a materialist psychology that can be applied to his fictional creations—and perhaps himself:

> The real function of psychology has always been to formulate a systematic conception of mental life, and the central difficulty in such a task lies in building a system which will apply equally well to the inner and to the outer world of consciousness. A psychology which fails to describe individual human motivation and the outer patterning of the social order as coordinate and intimate reflections of each other, can be of little use to the student of conflict. The latter needs a systematic classification of mental life in which individual and social psychology are seen as inevitable reflections of each other.

A psychology doing justice to the dialectic of the individual and the social, demonstrates Sheldon, gives one the "discipline" to develop "elasticity and toleration of conflict farther out at the periphery of consciousness":

Without this discipline, every temptation of the day can throw the mind off center, creating chaos and frustration. To resolve deep lying conflict is death to the soul. *To intellectualize it and carry it at higher levels is life abundant.*

The Promethean conflict is the strife which takes place in the human mind between the yearning for understanding, and the weaker more immediate pull of those living affections and desires which are conditioned upon the good will and the support of fellow beings. (Ellison's italics)

For the young Ellison, the universals of myth provide access to a dialectical psychology that maps the conflicts within individuals along the axes of contradiction in society at large.[35]

While Ellison worked on the "Slick" manuscript his own Promethean impulses plunged considerably ahead of his ability to embody them in fiction. Clearly, however, his notions of discipline and chaos and "life abundant" are deeply politicized. Ellison scribbled on the manuscript, "Democracy [is] built upon splits between whites and blacks. . . . Slavery is death. Under capitalism man is dominated by death. One strives to escape from capitalism so as to escape from death. To conquer fear of death one goes to meet it face to face. Communism is only effective when it raises consciousness of man to higher level." Reflecting back on the struggle to end slavery, he jotted, "Douglass made mistake of trying to work on inside when outside was where he belonged." As Ellison sought to create in his own fiction the "conscious hero" whose absence he, as a "student of conflict," was lamenting in the work of other radical black writers, democracy was linked with capitalism and consciousness with communism. Ellison was evidently pressing against the limits of Popular Frontist reformism.[36]

"To make every death have a meaning":
Red Black Organizers

In several short stories apparently written in the early 1940s and left in varying stages of completion, Ellison pursued the revolutionary themes adumbrated in "Slick" while developing the folkloric and mythic allusiveness that was becoming his trademark style. Variants on Booker would preoccupy the young writer as he attempted to recreate in his fiction the figure of the African American trade unionist he had glimpsed at the gathering of the NNC in 1940 but found lacking in such novels as *Blood on the Forge*. Inspired by Malraux's examples of revolutionary heroes who are at once introspective and committed, conflicted and disciplined, Ellison aspired to create Communist Negro heroes who would be both "conscious" and "complex."[37]

"The Dream," a partially completed coming-of-age story set in a southern town in late 1941 or early 1942, is narrated primarily from the point of view of Lonzo Jefferson, an adolescent boy who has been befriended by an NNC organizer named Jim Napue. Esteeming the bold Jim, "who was'nt stuck-up like the other guys who went off to school," over his own meek father, Lonzo assists the Congress by distributing leaflets that call upon the town's African American population to "vote and demand jobs at the new defense plant." Tensions in the town are high; the mayor, representing the interests of the local plantation-owning elites, uses his power to keep African American labor bound to the land. Jim struggles against the pro-Japanese sentiment of the African American population, who fail to see that, should the Japanese Empire triumph, "they'd do the same thing to us that the crackers have done." Jim works closely with a white organizer, Bradshaw, who is attempting to win the white workers to support the hiring of Negroes. Evidently both Jim and Bradshaw are Communists.[38]

The tale opens with a dialogue in which Bradshaw questions Jim about the wisdom of involving young Lonzo in their dangerous activity; there follows a conversation in which Lonzo and his friends display a somewhat clouded understanding of the NNC's goals. The tale's climactic action is precipitated by the boys' discovery of a landed homing pigeon. Motivated by a combination of "revenge" and "nationalism," as Ellison comments in the margin, as well as by a felt need to prove their manhood, the boys attach to the bird's foot a message threatening to blow up the plant; they sign it with Bradshaw's name. When the bird delivers the message — in an early instance of birds functioning as omens of doom in Ellison's fiction — the town goes into a panic. Anti-aircraft guns are trained on the sky; the white workers refuse to enter the factory. Lonzo, under suspicion for distributing the leaflets, is brought in for questioning; he remains silent while Bradshaw is interrogated and beaten. Only when Jim is brought in and tortured does Lonzo confess his inadvertently destructive prank; the town government subjects the boys to a "public whipping" which, Ellison comments in the margin, is equivalent to "an act of lynching. Back of it is psychological fear of Negro revolt, i.e., as saboteurs, spies, etc." The boys' initiation into manhood, a rehearsal of *Invisible Man*'s battle royal minus the comedy, is a scapegoating ritual designed to castrate them as future political actors.[39]

The father-son relationship between Lonzo and his proletarian mentor Jim conjoins Marx and Freud. When Lonzo asks Jim the meaning of a wet dream in which he found himself running naked through the plant, Jim's description of wish fulfillment links personal with collective desires:

> Dreams are made out of the things you want most of all, Lonzo. And sometimes when you want to do things that youre afraid to do when youre awake you sometimes dream about it and do it when youre asleep. Sometimes you're afraid to go after it because its so much against the law, and sometimes because its against what they call peace. Then theres the kind of dreaming you do in church and where everybody is dreaming out loud and singing and shouting and the preacher gets to describing something out of the Bible or about heaven and some of the people get to see and feel the dream so strong that they shout and jump around and faint, and foam at the mouth. That's the kind of dream that makes everybody get together, get organized, and they want heaven so much that if right then when theyre all worked up, if at just that moment they could go out and get their hands on heaven they'd take it for themselves, even if the angels had machine guns and tried to shoot them away from the pearly gates.

If the symbolic castration of the boys reveals the political unconscious of the town's rulers, Lonzo's dream reveals a longing for freedom that is the personal and sexual equivalent of the collective yearning expressed in the Negro spirituals about which Ellison was at this time writing in his notebooks. Jim's task as mentor is to decode his acolyte's dream; as organizer, it is to take those impulses that are repressed and displaced and channel them into political action.[40]

Just as in one draft of "Flying Home" Todd/Mead must harden himself in order to carry out his revolutionary mission, Jim has desensitized himself to violence in order to fight fire with fire. In response to Bradshaw's concerns about Lonzo's safety, Jim replies, "Hell they kill us every day. And with all this new industry coming down here there'll be even more killing. The important thing now is for us to make every death have a meaning." When Bradshaw objects that he sounds like "a terrorist or a suicide," Jim remarks, "Lynching's the terror I'm concerned with."

> No matter how many jobs we get for my people unless they learn to sacrifice for what they get we wont get anywhere. And the young guys are the ones who'll have to be taught first. . . . That's what I mean . . . a tragic symbol. You see, Brad. A naked image of Christ nailed to a cross is just as repulsive as a naked Negro swinging from a tree, but Christians call

it beautiful, while they turn away from a lynched Negro. Now when it comes so that everytime black folks see a black body hanging from a tree limb they will see it as the symbol of the all out fight against the kind of fascism we have down here then we'll be getting somewhere.

Jim explicitly counterposes the two functions of the scapegoat. The Negro can, as "a black body hanging from a tree limb," serve as a pseudoscientific scapegoat legitimating white supremacy. Or the Negro can be a tragic symbol, a hanged god whose resurrection will consist not in a skyward ascension but in the "all out fight against . . . fascism" undertaken by those remaining below.[41]

Another variant on the figure of the red black hero is presented in an untitled story beginning "The cars finally came to a stop" (which I will refer to as "The Final Destination"). Ellison here portrays the graveside responses of different family members, especially a young radical named Bishop and his bitterly skeptical uncle Charles, to the recent suicide of another uncle, Paul. As the mourners warm themselves with whisky in the cold wind while the grave is being dug, Bishop ponders the meaning of Paul's "final destination." Musing about the death of "Comrade Lenin in Russia"—"More than twenty years and *he's* still here"—Bishop remarks to Charles, "All of us wish that there had been some sacrifice we could have made to save him. We are united in regret by death. . . . But I can't help thinking that if we had been united in an effort to make jobs and do away with the conditions which led him to this act, he would be with us today." When Charles reacts cynically, Bishop continues, "It's like them asking us Negroes to join in National unity for war when there's dying to be done and refusing us that unity in times of peace." As the conversation turns to religion Bishop asserts that Paul's suicide affirms not the presence but the absence of God:

> Maybe [Paul] had a right to take his life. . . . In the last ten or fifteen years his God left him to himself. He had no job and had spent his savings. And God did nothing about it. Maybe he had a right to embarass his God. . . . There are many dead gods. And each time a thing like this happens it isnt true what the preachers tell us, that the soul is condemned to eternal punishment. It is the god who dies.

In the South there are "thousands who are ready to die, be shot, lynched, in order to live. . . . The death of the fighting spirit is the only death from which there can be revival."[42]

The conversation turns to Hemingway's fiction. When Bishop claims that he can envision a revolutionary future with "the crackers retreating from Atlanta like the Italians retreated from . . . Caporetto," Charles, mistaking *A Farewell to Arms* for *The Sun Also Rises* ("[the one about] the guy getting his balls shot away"), grimly observes, "Thats what'll happen to you Negroes who try to start something down South." Bishop, correcting his uncle about the Hemingway title, asserts, "There's a Dr. Bogaroz in the Soviet Union who can give that back to you. . . . It's the truth. . . . It is to be found in the medical journals here in this country. And it is not a miracle but a scientific fact, just as an airplane is a scientific fact." The tale ends on a mellower note as the young radical reverts to thoughts of Paul: "I loved him. My favorite uncle. Why must you die?" The grave now dug, the other mourners return: "This time each carried a small bunch of carnations in his gloved fist . . . their pink and white petals sharp and clear. The wind seemed to grow stronger and he watched petals burst from the flowers and sail away."[43]

It is difficult not to be somewhat irritated by Bishop, this self-important young man who, at the graveside of a beloved uncle, corrects an unbeloved uncle's literary lapses and lectures him about "scientific fact." But the text sends out no signals that Bishop is being ironized; he sounds like Booker Small and indeed like Ellison himself in some of his *New Masses* critical commentaries. As in "The Dream," Ellison conjoins the notions of initiation and rebirth with radical political practice. Paul's suicide was a meaningless gesture, reflecting his defeat; only those who die in a "fighting spirit" can experience revival through the secular activism guided by the science to which the aptly named Bishop is committed. Socialism is the antidote, both symbolically and, it seems, literally, to the castration that is the fate of lynchees in the U.S. South. The closing image—in its lyricism recalling the closing image of "Flying Home"—suggests transcendence through negation, implying that petals from the flowers of mourning will be scattered throughout the South and generate new life. What Sheldon was calling "life abundant" may yet come from Paul's death; the regime of Jim Crow may yet be buried by the gravediggers it creates.

"The Final Destination" evades easy dating. Bishop's ironic comments about the demand for national unity in time of war may refer back to the Great War, suggesting that the story was authored during the "Yanks Are Not Coming" period, September 1939 to June 1941. Since Lenin died in January 1924, however, the young man's reference to the Bolshevik leader's having been in his tomb "more than twenty years" indicates that the story could have been written as late as 1944 or even 1945. Of course it is possible that Ellison simply made a mistake about the year of Lenin's death, in which case the story could have been written in or around 1940. If the story was written sometime after January 1944, this would mean that Ellison was, through Bishop, commenting sardonically on the national unity called for not just by the U.S. government but also by the CP during the Communist Political Association (CPA) period. Yet if *this* is the case, the story's evident leftism — not just Bishop's enthusiasm for Soviet socialism, but also his identification with the Leninist tradition in the United States — presumably conveys Ellison's own continuing commitment to revolutionary politics during the last year of the war. The former option is the more likely one: the story bears the stylistic marks of apprenticeship, and Ellison could certainly have been wrong — or have opted for Bishop to be wrong — about the year of Lenin's death. Either way, however, "The Final Destination" is a testament, more than any of the equally polished stories chosen for inclusion in *Flying Home*, to Ellison's early commitment to a specifically Communist political radicalism; it could readily have been included in the anthology from 1994.

A more nuanced portrait of a red black organizer is contained in a long fragment from a projected short story or novella about rural southern organizing; untitled, it is designated in the Ellison archive as "Paul Character." The action centers on a crisis in a campaign against the poll tax and lynching that is being implemented through the NNC and other unspecified mass organizations that apparently receive financial support from wealthy liberals. The main organizer, an older man named Oscar, has just been killed; the task of leadership has been passed to Paul, a young Communist filled with revolutionary fire but uncertain about his standing in the eyes of those whom he would lead. (There is no connection between this character and the deceased uncle named Paul in "The Final Destination.") Airplanes are dropping intimidating leaflets; the sharecroppers are gathering arms. Confronting Paul is the necessity, in the face of the planters' terror, to "keep up the morale of the people" while restraining them from retaliatory violence. Some unspecified mistaken action on the part of a militant sharecropper named Tab requires that Paul consider sacrificing his own life in order to save his comrades. The efforts of the NNC have resulted in only "piecemeal" changes; what is needed, he believes, is "some dramatic action of such significance that the resistance of Negroes throughout the country could be steeled." Ellison's sketched notes for the ending indicate that Paul will "go out shooting." The question of revolutionary choice and sacrifice assumes classically tragic dimensions; it is no accident that Ellison describes the farmer conveying the news of Tab's error as a "messenger of Fate."[44]

Paul is cut of the same political cloth as Booker Small, Jim Napue, and

Bishop; though college-educated, he has acquired, in Ellison's echo of Melville's Ishmael, his real "college in the mill and factories and his teacher in the trade union." Although his years in the North offered respite from Jim Crow, they left him feeling excluded from his own life; he gave up a civil service job to fight in Spain (an experience that is mentioned only in passing). Paul has remained "skeptical, encased in the cold, impassive anger of his kind, believing nothing, and honoring nothing, waiting only for some blind power to blot the whites from the face of the earth." Feeling an "almost physical need to be back again with his people," Paul returns South as an NNC organizer to help construct "a new underground railroad." The leaflets proclaiming the movement's slogans "pierced him with an intensity that made his bones ache. . . . [In] these words lay the passionate message which his whole life had taught him and which in turn he must give back to those from whom he came." Yet even now he feels like an "exile . . . separate . . . from folk Negroes." Although he admires Oscar's ability to "brave the anger of the lynch mobs," he resents the older organizer's "clinging to an old pattern of obsequiousness [toward the] . . . whites who backed the organizations." Paul himself can barely bring himself to speak with one such wealthy supporter who is pulling away because of the rising level of violence. "He's evading the issue," thinks Paul in a flashback. "Probably liberal. Look at his lips. Lisps. Mother complex." Anticipating *Invisible Man*'s young Emerson in the implied equation of homosexuality with guilt-ridden liberalism, this character functions as a lightning rod for Paul's antiwhite anger.[45]

Paul's literary derivation in Wright's protagonists is evident. A passage from "Fire and Cloud" is copied onto one draft; the situation requiring Paul's sacrifice closely resembles that facing Aunt Sue in "Bright and Morning Star." In his blind hatred of whites and suppressed violence, Paul suggests a politicized Bigger Thomas or Jake Jackson of *Lawd Today*. But in both his alienation and his revolutionism Paul is more self-aware than any of Wright's protagonists and more closely resembles a Malraux hero: Kyo or Ch'en in *Man's Fate*, Kassner in *Days of Wrath*, Manuel in *Man's Hope*. Like Malraux's revolutionaries, Paul has found in Communism "a force for changing the world[,] a force which was necessary and absolute": "For him the participation in the struggle liberated his own sense of dignity, he became a Man. Through it he was able to see the meaning of Negro life, its past present and future. As an individual he saw in it a force which linked him to the rest of the universe. The sprawling chaos of America had assumed a shape, a form when he had begun to look upon it through the dicipiln [*sic*] of the Party." "Chaos" signifies the oppressive reality awaiting transformation; "discipline," a term especially resonant in Malraux's Spanish Civil War novel, signifies the means by which individuals choose to channel their energy into the collective agent of that transformation: the Party. While positioned in a mere plot fragment—"Paul Character" hardly stands alone as a story—Paul is Ellison's fullest fictional embodiment of his prediction, jotted in his notes as *Negro Quarterly* editor, that "Spartacus will come."[46]

"Not enough energy to use Marxism in a creative manner": "The Initiation"

Although Ellison was evidently drawn to the figure of the red black union or NNC organizer, the radical professor also attracted him as a possible fictional protagonist; as early as April 1939 he remarked to his old friend Joe Lazenberry that he was "mapping a novel of the Negro college." Among the materials related to this "mapping" is a nearly completed short story, "The Initiation," which features Bard, a southern-born professor of literature who has moved north, joined the Communist Party, and returned to the college near his hometown to organize among students. His teaching the "literature of protest and rebellion" has inspired some students to put his pedagogy into adventurist practice; they have assassinated a local "cracker" politician, closely resembling Louisiana's Huey Long, and have been speedily hanged. Bard's demoralization is compounded by the Party's recent decision to close down its southern branches. Although he regarded it as a "sacrifice of Negro interests," he "agreed to the . . . imposed but not unwelcome . . . dissolution." "The Initiation" shows Ellison working out in fiction some of his growing political ambivalence during the wartime years.[47]

Bard's distress is compounded by his difficult relationship with his brother Giles, whose life reflects—Ellison in his notes directly quotes from Wright's description of his sharecropper father in *Black Boy*—"the narrowness [of Negro life], its cruelty, its poverty of westernized culture, its lack of a sense of honor, love . . . and loyalty." Bard's decision to join the Party is motivated not just by "the excitement of being part of a globe-encircling movement possessing an articulate philosophy" but also by his need to "thrust [political activity] between himself and his life, more as a defense than as a weapon of change." His desire to come to terms with Giles is intertwined with his own need to open "the underground doors of his consciousness" and acknowledge his oneness with his brother, whose latest letter home he has not yet read. Bard's alienation is at once internal, interpersonal, and political, fulfilling Sheldon's dictum that "individual human motivation and the outer patterning of the social order [are] coordinate and intimate reflections of each other."[48]

The story focuses on a single night of crisis: Giles has somehow aroused the ire of local Klansmen, who, mistaking Bard for his brother, have forced the professor into a car and plan to lynch him; in his terror, for a few moments he even hallucinates that he has become Giles. Managing to convince the mob of their mistake, Bard, who thinks Giles is still safely in the North, tells them that his brother is at their mother's house nearby. Bearing the mark of the rope on his neck, he makes his way to a roadhouse where Jerry, a sympathetic Negro truck driver, takes him back to the campus, braving more vigilantes on the way. Cautioning him that the mob, if it can "pull niggers outa jails and courthouses and outa hospitals even," can come to get him on campus as well, Jerry says he would have done the same for anyone, white or black. Through the selfless courage of Jerry, whose scarred ear and lacerated neck are "badges of honor," testaments to a shared "world of unspoken meaning," Bard feels reintegrated with the folk and, by extension, with his brother. Having now "understood something of sacrifice," he feels "re-born." The story concludes tragically, however: Giles is lynched at their mother's house, his unread letter having contained the news of his plan to return home early. Instead of being crushed by guilt, however, "in the end [Bard] incorporates his brother's characteristics into his own personality transformed and now made articulate." The doubling of the brothers, at first ironically signaling their mutual alienation, now indicates their dialectical unity; as happens between the siblings in "The Birthmark," Giles is reborn in Bard, whose "initiation" has entailed an appreciation of heroic sacrifice in the fight against Jim Crow.[49]

Already preoccupied with the tripartite dramatistic categories that would guide the construction of *Invisible Man*, Ellison jotted notes to himself about the arc of "purpose-passion-perception" inscribed in Bard's experience; writing that "EXERTION OF WILL is the motive force of tragic plots," he compared Bard with heroes ranging from Macbeth and Wright's Aunt Sue to Dostoevsky's convicts in *The House of the Dead*. Evidently not just Burke but also Aristotle, Wright, and the Western classics were clamoring for Ellison's attention as he composed "The Initiation." Freud also made his presence felt. As Bard lies helpless on the floor of the Klansmen's car and later in Jerry's truck, he "regresses psychologically . . . to [the] stage of [an] infant." He dreams that some black Jews who are about to circumcise him turn into a "cracker" who is about to castrate him. He then sees the "determined, and formal, distant [face of] . . . Sanford the organizer . . . a white man's face which had been the face of a comrade." Presumably the Party leader who informs him that the Party's southern operations have been shut down, Sanford tells Bard that the "historical situation" requires the "liquidation of his mother." The trauma of the kidnapping, with its very real threat of castration and lynching, has evidently brought to the surface repressed infantile fears, a loss of ego identity, and a yearning to return to the womb. That a "cracker" lyncher is associated with a white Party organizer hardly suggests that Marx, at least as embodied in the CP, is going to rescue Bard from the toils of his unconscious. Yet it is the class-conscious proletariat in the form of Jerry (who would have rescued a white victim of Jim Crow fascism as readily as a black) who rescues Bard from the return of the repressed. Through Jerry's willingness to sacrifice, Bard takes on his brother's working-class identity without losing his own; doubling functions not to haunt, but to heal the fragmented self.[50]

The political ambivalence informing "The Initiation" sets this story apart from the other tales featuring red organizers in the South; the cold-eyed Sanford, who in Bard's nightmare even wields a castration knife, anticipates *Invisible Man*'s Brother Jack. But Sanford remains external to the story's principal focus on the contradictions internal to Bard. Ellison jotted, "Contact with the c.p. provided [Bard] with a philosophical (conscious) orientation" but then "restricted [his] growth" because "American color conditioning became operative." It is because he reacted passively to the Party's southern dissolution that Bard himself "must be prepared for sacrifice": he is complicit in his own scapegoating. In language closely resembling his, and Wright's, description of the Lenin-imitating Negro soapbox speakers who "failed to make a revolution in themselves," Ellison describes Bard as able "to reject a naïve Marxism" but having "not enough energy to use Marxism in a creative manner, applying it to the conditions of his own life. . . . Communism creates fear in him not freedom because he had not faced [the] meaning of his individuality." Ellison also faults Bard for too readily viewing the situation facing African Americans as "just another version of that one universal problem facing all men" and for "ceas[ing] to plum [the] meaning of Negro's perdicament after becoming [a] communist, since he felt this made Negro problem superfluous. He could never bring himself to consider that his teachings applied here and now to the conditions of the South." The primary source of his own alienation, Bard is guilty of premature universalization.[51]

Apparently composed around the same time as Ellison was drafting his reviews of *An American Dilemma* and *Black Boy (American Hunger)*, "The Initiation" exposes the growing fault lines in his relationship with the CP. As in these essays, however, Ellison stresses the liberatory potential of Communism, along with the accountability of white and Negro comrades alike for the failure to sustain and build the left movement in the South, a failure all the more ironic because class-conscious workers like Jerry already practice much of what the Party preaches. Bard's initiation into the realities of Jim Crow violence and Giles's rebirth in his brother suggest that Ellison continues to explore the politics of doubling raised in "The Birthmark," where one sibling's ritual sacrifice enables the other to emerge as a committed and conscious opponent of Jim Crow. The death and (re)birth of the hero remain linked with the refusal of assent to the dominant social order.

"Forms of Negro heroism":
Notes for Unwritten Novels

In an interview in 1955 Ellison remarked that it had taken him five years to write *Invisible Man*, "with one year out for a short novel which was unsatisfactory, ill-conceived and never submitted for publication." In his introduction to the 1982 edition of *Invisible Man*, he stated that the text had "erupted out of what had been conceived as a war novel," one that "focused upon the experiences of a captured American pilot who found himself in a Nazi prisoner-of-war camp in which he was the officer of highest rank and thus by a convention of war the designated spokesman for his fellow prisoners." It has been generally assumed that the so-called airman novel and the never-published short novel are one and the same. But while in 1944 Ellison sketched out a coherent plan for the airman novel for the Rosenwald Fund, from which he won a grant the following year, his papers contain no draft of this novel, or indeed of any novel other than *Invisible Man*. Instead they contain fragmentary notes and drafts for what appear to be several different possible novel-length narratives that overlap in some respects but remain distinct in others. Fleshed out in various ways, the protagonists of these novels would have substantially developed Ellison's conception of the Malrauvian "conscious hero" that is partially portrayed in Todd/Mead, Booker Small, Jim Napue, Bishop, Paul, and Bard.[52]

One of these novels would have focused on a protagonist named "Gann Wilson"—Wilson also being, we will recall, Ellison's surname for his pseudonymous *Daily Worker* article of 1943—who traces his radical commitments in part to the legacy of his father. Like Ellison's own father, Gann's "old man" had fought in the Philippines and then settled his family in Oklahoma, aiming to avoid the harshest rigors of Jim Crow. Refusing to kowtow to the boss but "weakened by his old soldier's wounds," Gann's father was "crushed by a machine on his job." The fighting spirit of the father lives on in his son, who has become involved with the left and yearns to fight in Spain. In a brief dramatized flashback Gann recalls the government officials who refused his visa request: "They had told him that 'Uncle Sam is interested in protecting the lives of his people, even against themselves.' . . . He thought of Scottsboro. Protection my ass! The only time they give a dam [*sic*] whether you die or not, is when dying might lead to a higher consciousness among those interested in your death. 'Nigger, don't go over there dying and getting the niggers at home stirred up.'" These bitter thoughts about the representatives of Uncle Sam are compounded by memories of two white fellow radicals—one, notably named Todd, has "cold grey eyes"—who also discouraged him from going to Spain. Their "impassivity" was "maddening," and Gann wonders whether it was simply their attitude toward money that separated them from their white counterparts in government surveillance. Clearly the Gann Wilson novel would not have contained an unproblematic portrait of black-white relationships in the C P, or indeed of the Party's attitude toward potential volunteers for the antifascist struggle in Spain.[53]

At one point Ellison imagined that Gann, like Bard, might be a professor, this time not of literature but of sociology, an older man who is "aware of [the] ideological role he plays" in promulgating the doctrines of the "Chicago School." While he was "35 years ago handsome," he is now a wreck, "given to psychotic headaches" caused by his "consistent compromises of personality i.e. agreeing with whites." He has holes in his socks and, notably, carries a "new shiny briefcase . . . [a] symbol of authority, a gift from [the] 'Foundation.'" In a fragment titled "Burr Bullet-Head," Gann-the-professor reacts to the authoritarianism of an unnamed college administrator:

> It was well known among the faculty that ___ used his position as distributor of scholarships to seduce male students. He was the trustees' man . . . [a] tall black man with a bald, bullet head. . . . Gann had been told how as a boy ___ had walked to the school penniless and illiterate and how he had worked his way steadily up to a position of control over the president. . . .
>
> [The resigned faces of the teachers] were the tired, passive faces like those Negroes whom [Gann] had seen on the subways of New York. Yet they were supposed to be the emancipated ones. . . . ___ exerted his power against their will as he did against the students, sparing them only his sexual advances. . . . It was ___'s idea that the school made no contracts

with the teachers. They were hired for one year only and at the end of each those who were to be kept the next year were sent a formal announcement. Commencement week their one topic of conversation was "Did you get your 'ask-back'?" They pronounced it "ass-back." "You get your ass back if you give them your ball," Gann thought.

Ellison jotted in the margin, "sharecropper same way." Apparently drawing upon J. Saunders Redding's harshly satirical description of a Negro college president in *No Day of Triumph* (1942), as well as upon his own experiences with sexual harassment by a male dean at Tuskegee, Ellison here rehearsed the appearance of Bledsoe.[54]

In most notes and fragments, however, Gann is a younger man, college-educated like Ellison, committed to revolutionary practice like Herndon. Ellison ponders:

> How can a Negro American master his fate? That is the main theme. It will be an attempt to probe the secret of what it is that leads various American Negro types to revolutionary action. In the fore ground will be Gann Wilson, a young Negro with a college background and his attempts to master his fate as a Negro and to attain a sense of his dignity as a man. The action of the story arises out of Gann's attempts to carry out revolutionary activity in the South, which is his way of escaping submitting to the fate of the middle class Negro; and at the same time of overcoming his fear of death. In his efforts he will learn to act as a member of a larger political group and to discover a faith in the Negro people and their ability to take part in a larger revolutionary struggle. In leaving the North with its capitalist deathhold upon his personality, he goes into the South, where he must face the physical death [left] to those who pit themselves against the feudal system. It is in facing death that Gann proves his own personality. In seeking an individual solution he arrives at the correct group solution.

Ellison's skeletal notes for the plot take Gann to New York, where he encounters the "narcotic effect" of "Harlem, Housing, Sex, [and] Music." While "obsess[ed]" with going to Spain, he would return south, where a "Preacher, Sharecroppers [and a] Chain Gang" would be elements in a plot resulting in "Death [and] Consciousness," whether for Gann himself or his comrades is not clear. It was clear, however, that Gann was to engage in "revolutionary action . . . against capitalist society."[55]

Apparently leaving aside Gann Wilson, Ellison also considered writing a novel that would have merged multiple autobiographical elements, from the death of Ellison's mother in Dayton through his wartime experiences in Wales, with an ambitious mythic scheme invoking Dante's *Inferno*. Ellison's mapping suggests interconnections between geography and history, psychology and myth:

Lesson V. the Family	Father
Oklahoma	Area of Childhood
Marginal Statement of Problem	College
NY	Radical Period; apocalypse
Spain	Discovery of guide, Virgil
London	
	Is through inferno only
South Wales	dead foolishly in Spain
Ohio	then London for relics of Virgil in vain
Problem of Girl	London during War

s.w. [South Wales] discovery of kindred people, culture.
Revolution of personal values, self
Return—Ohio—death of mother
Dispossession and maturation in the snows.
Scenes of hunting. Quest for father, really.
Cultural hero.

From "Negro" optimism through defeat of success to optimism based
   upon mature attempt to analyse his situation.

Gesturing toward a considerably less radical novel than the Gann Wilson text—someone, presumably not the protagonist, is "dead foolishly in Spain," and the plot hinges on the "revolution of personal values" rather than the class struggle—this narrative would have treated the war as a symbolic inferno. The protagonist would descend and, after a "radical period," emerge stronger and wiser; the identity of his Virgilian guide is unclear.[56]

The war would have figured centrally in still another novel whose scattered notes suggest Ellison's intention to feature a Communist protagonist whose failing marriage embodies a host of larger political contradictions. The protagonist is a political organizer who, in one variant, has been "stationed in the South" as a soldier; his wife is "for him blind, mute and inar-

ticulate, symbolic of [a] large section of [the] Negro people." In another variant, set in the North, the wife functions as an antidote to the protagonist's
cynicism, having "converted him from his [hatred of] the people for their
backward crudeness and for their preindividualism and for attacks upon his
ambition." Although he is a "failure as an organizer," his "protected position
in [the] party keeps him from realizing it" until, weary of his neglect and
emotional abuse, she confronts him with the news that she is having an affair with another man. At first he is "not aware of his suffering," feeling that
"only his pride is hurt." But she "tells him he has met his fate," and "a riot
occurs." In this wartime Harlem version of Henry James's "The Beast in the
Jungle," the fate of the alienated male protagonist who refuses a woman's
love is inseparable from his fate as an elitist who has rejected the people he
is supposed to serve. The leap of the beast is embodied in the class revenge
of the riot.[57]

Notes for a narrative titled "Where the Shadow Lay upon Her Face,"
possibly the title of the text just described, indicate that the plot revolving
around the married organizer would have anticipated some key concerns informing both the drafts and the published text of *Invisible Man*:

> The need to come into possession of one's identity, both personal and
> political, in [a] world in which it is denied by the conscious enemy and
> unrecognized by one's allies.
>
> Political factors: the focusing of ones personality within a revolution-
> ary political structure wherein one operates on a plane which does not
> always jibe with the general political level of ones group. 2. the dangers
> of this i.e. where one is psychologically so insecure that one can bear no
> questioning of one's actions, no criticism of the policy and the essentially
> uncreative effect upon the personality. 3. The general weakness of politi-
> cal strategy of childishness. The general organization must falter because
> the national factors of Negro life are not sufficiently understood.
>
> The Riot.
>
> The War.
>
> The search for human dignity upon the sea at a time when all the world
> fights for these things in armies.
>
> The needless sacrifice of a revolutionary situation.

Ellison pondered, "What are the forms of Negro heroism? [It] must speak
both for Negroes and for the broadest number of whites, i.e., must be national and international, specific and universal. One must not worry about
'narrow Negro nationalism,' for if one speaks thoroughly for Negroes then

the larger understanding of humanity will have been served." What prevents a man from attaining heroism is his "inability to perform necessary tasks because [he is] pulled in too many directions by money, by selfishness, by foster child psychology." The weaknesses of the individual and the group jointly contribute to the "sacrifice of a revolutionary situation," a "needless" sacrifice and a tragic one. This association of the "forms of Negro heroism" with both the opportunities and the constraints opened up by war and revolution would be much on Ellison's mind as he began work on *Invisible Man*.[58]

"An ironic comment upon the ideal and realistic images of democracy": The Airman Novel

In the "Statement of Plan of Work" for the "airman novel" that Ellison submitted in 1945 to the Rosenwald Fund, he supplied a plot summary and thematic commentary that elaborate upon the description briefly given in the 1982 introduction to *Invisible Man*. Set in a Nazi prison camp, this "novel of ideas" was to "determine what type of democratic relationships are necessary for a highly conscious Negro to function with white men and at the same time exercise the fullest potentialities of his humanity." The hero, nameless here, elsewhere designated "Sheppard," was to "be representative of that growing group of young black Americans who in their various forms of isolation are slowly mastering the meaning of their experience in the United States, and who are mastering Western concepts, techniques, etc. . . . who are too wise to accept the status quo, but have not yet conceived the new." Having "bailed out of a disabled plane," this young aviator is placed in charge of his fellow prisoners, Negro and white, by the "satanic" Nazi camp commander, who, as a "psychologist given to ceaseless intrigue," wishes to "[express] . . . his contempt for white 'democrats' and . . . prove to the Negro hero his own racial inferiority and unfitness for rule or participation in government." The airman is thus "given the power of life and death over his group of fellow nationals, several of whom are southerners; his problem is to overcome the deep feelings of humiliation which have led to his intellectual development and create within the camp a functioning democracy" in a setting where "relationships are not blurred by sleazy American prejudices and worshop [*sic*] of 'progress.'" The young airman succeeds in his venture by "evolving a broader concept of freedom. . . . Regressing like T. E. Lawrence among the Arabs, he will find the most satisfying relationship with white Americans in the very teeth of the Nazi." Yet "after plotting the escape of several important airmen he refuses to follow at the last minute and is killed. . . . The novel, in effect, will be an ironic comment upon the ideal and realistic images of democracy."[59]

While Ellison's papers contain only fragmentary passages of narration and dialogue from the novel, he apparently was fascinated by the experience of U.S. soldiers, especially Jews and Negroes, in Nazi prison camps and gathered a small archive of newspaper and magazine clippings. He saved a profile written in June 1944 of a former POW named Herbert Ehrich, who, having been wounded and captured in Sicily, ended up spending two and a half months in a German camp near Munich. Ehrich especially recalled his warm relations with Russian and Serbian members of forced labor battalions and noted that he had not been subjected to any particular discrimination on the basis of his Jewish background. (Anticipating the radio motif central to the 1952 novel, Ehrich noted his informants' wildly discrepant accounts of current events; determining that he was as qualified as they to promulgate his view of what was happening beyond the camp, he concluded, "There was nothing left but for Herb Ehrich himself to go on the air!") Ellison also gathered information on one Capt. Henry Weintraub, who had spent nineteen months in a prison camp in the Polish corridor south of Danzig before being released in a prisoner exchange. Weintraub made public statements thanking the Red Cross and the War Fund for supplying the POWs with not just adequate food but also books and even musical instruments; like Ehrich, Weintraub noted that Jewish soldiers were subjected to "very little discrimination." Apparently drawn to Weintraub's story, Ellison went so far as to contact him personally and borrow some of his correspondence with friends of still interned POWs.[60]

Most of the articles that Ellison saved, however, documented the experiences of Negro airmen shot down in the European theater. One clipping reported on Wilbur F. Long, a member of the 332nd Fighter Group who had been shipped in a boxcar to a German camp after crash-landing in the Hungarian countryside. Thanking the Red Cross for supplying badly needed food rations to the American captives, Long noted that "many of his fellow internees were Southerners who were surprisingly decent and on many occasions shared their rations with him." Ellison saved a *Pittsburgh Courier* account of seven Negro airmen who were liberated from a German POW camp in May 1945. One recalled that, when "some white soldiers attempt[ed] to set up a 'jim crow' section in the camp . . . this was quickly erased by the German officers." (These airmen "were all quick to admit that there was no segregation demanded by the Germans except on the part of Jewish soldiers who were removed completely from the camp and were never seen there again." Apparently Ehrich's and Weintraub's experiences were not universally characteristic of Jewish POWs.) Ellison was also interested in the case of First Lt. Herbert V. Clark, a veteran pilot of the 332nd Mustang Group, who, when shot down over northern Italy, was picked up by a band of partisans; retaining his rank among the antifascist guerrillas, he spent the rest of the war harassing enemy supply lines. This was the same "quiet and unassuming" airman, the *Courier* noted, who "had revolutionized flying habits when he landed his P-40 Warhawk on one wheel while returning from a dive bombing mission over Anzio Beachhead" the year before. Showing that the real-life analogues to Todd/Mead had finally taken to the skies and been permitted to fire their guns, these news stories display Ellison's continuing interest in the historical experiences and political outlooks of the Negro airmen, especially once removed from the home front of Jim Crow.[61]

As both his plot outline and his accompanying notes reveal, Ellison was bent above all on exploring the contradictory situations—moral, political, and psychological—confronted by such young men. For the novel's scenario was rife with irony. It was in the hellish camp presided over by the "satanic" German commander that the Negro airman was able to undertake his experiment in constructing democracy. Ellison jotted, "real comradeship . . . the joy returned to work." It was only when this multiracial group of American POWs were isolated from their native land—and able to play music and "give theatricals, i.e. microcosm of culture, Negro and white"—that they could at least begin to discover one another's humanity. Aware that the logic of his narrative might imply the superiority of Nazism to American capitalist democracy, Ellison cautioned, "This must not be mistaken for a recommend[ation] of fascism." But Sheppard's death would be necessary in order to reinforce this point: since his refusal to escape along with the other internees constitutes a kind of suicide, bespeaking his deep skepticism whether the democracy within the camp can be reproduced back in the United States, "he must, of course, be murdered by the Nazis so that they may be dramatically negated."[62]

Leftist politics as the source of both commitment and existential dilemma were not to have figured as prominently in the airman novel as in the other novel outlines Ellison sketched in the early to mid-1940s, from "Gann Wilson" to "The Shadow Lay upon Her Face." Ellison noted at one point that his hero, seeking "some means by which he could challenge the whole structure of his world," had previously "joined organizations and movements, all in vain." He jotted to himself, "Include homefront disillusionment[;] criticism of party necessary." If Sheppard was ever part of the Communist movement, this identity presumably no longer figures centrally in his consciousness. But radical politics nonetheless inform his situation as leader of the internees. Not only does Sheppard have to mediate differences between conflicting groups—"labor-capitalist, worker-intellectual, liberals-communists"—but Ellison himself mapped these contradictions in an ascending order, moving from "Nazi x Democrat" to "Negro x white" to "Negro Socialism x Democracy," a scale suggesting his abiding view of socialism as both the dialectical negation of democracy and the means of Negro liberation, even if democracy had first to figure as the dialectical negation of fascism. When the Nazi camp commander attempts to frighten the Negro internees with threats of torture in order to turn them against Sheppard, moreover, they "sing the International in their cells." Ellison still had some distance to go before he would disarticulate the fight against racism from the goal of socialism, turning "democracy" into an all-encompassing "god-term."[63]

Ellison never took the airman novel beyond its rudimentary stage. Perhaps, once the war was over, he found it difficult to sustain narrative interest in his character's conflicts, both internal and external. Perhaps the war itself had brought Ellison to a stalemate: he wished to believe in the promise of postwar capitalist democracy, but the echoes of the "Internationale" still rang through his brain. *Invisible Man* would get him past this deadlock, but not without considerable blood, sweat, and tears.

PART II

Living Jim Crow four

Denounce [the radicals], spurn
them as you spurn a water moc-
casin. Grind its head into the
dirt as I mean to grind any sign
of radicalism that rears its head
here upon this campus!

—Ralph Ellison, Bledsoe to the
invisible man, "Campus" episode
of *Invisible Man*

Unity = Incest

Contradiction = Aristocrat vs. sharecropper

Out of decadence   out of degradation

Monopolist of finance monopolist of emotions.

—Ralph Ellison, notes to "Trueblood" episode of *Invisible Man*

In retrospective accounts of the writing of *Invisible Man*, Ellison stated that
the words "I am an invisible man" came to him as he sat in a barn doorway
in Waitsfield, Vermont, in July 1945, contemplating the Green Mountains.
The implication of the anecdote is that the novel emerged from the conjunction of the New England past with the "new world a-coming" after the war.
Repressed in what Arnold Rampersad has called this "myth of origin," however, was Ellison's own insertion in recent history: the hosts of Ellison and
his partner Fanny McConnell Buford were the Communist Party fellow travelers Amelie and John Bates, the brother of Add Bates, the CP activist who
had called upon his NMU comrades to help Ellison evade the draft by ship-
ping out in the merchant marine. Ellison had been relocated, but not reborn.[1]

Although at the end of the novel's prologue the invisible man asserts,

"The end is in the beginning and lies far ahead" (6), Ellison admitted in August 1945 that he had little idea of where his hero was going to take him; as he wrote to Hyman, "This section of the novel is going very well—though God only knows what the hell it's all about. Of one thing I'm sure, any close symbolic analysis of it will reveal how completely crazy I am. Anyway, its fun." In a draft version of a letter to Peggy Hitchcock of Reynal and Hitchcock (undated, but evidently written several months later), Ellison briefly sketches his protagonist's character, alludes to sections of the novel's southern portion he has apparently already sent to her, and elaborates on his intentions for the rest. The invisible man will return

> briefly to the South where [the] pressures of [the] Negro community become too painful and he goes to live in Atlanta or Birmingham, where at the lowest point of his personal disintegration, he steps in front of [a] mixed relief parade and is exclaimed a Hero by [a] left-wing group. He is arrested, charged with treason, thrown in jail. After his release he returns north and becomes [a] political figure; a leader who discovers soon that he leads no one, but is in reality a figure-head.

Although this protagonist lacks the commitment and verve of a Paul or a Jim Napue, there was at this point no firewall in Ellison's mind between the red organizer protagonists of his earlier fiction, especially those resembling Angelo Herndon, and the hero of his novel-in-progress. In a later version of the letter to Hitchcock he describes a plot more familiar to readers of the 1952 text: rather than moving from south to north, then back to the South as an organizer before returning to the North, the invisible man "hop[es] to redeem himself and return to the South as a leader" but instead remains in New York, where he "becomes one of the leaders of a left wing political organization, . . . which position of prestige he loses just at the point that he thinks he has at least achieved an identification against the negative pressures of the world." Ellison adds, "This, I'm afraid[,] is as far as I have concieved the structure, for the end, the climax, evades me."[2]

At this point Ellison has his plot only vaguely in mind, but he is clear on his larger intentions, political and rhetorical. Contradicting his later insistence that the novel is not to be bound to direct historical representation, he informs Hitchcock that his work-in-progress is "a sort of political allegory of the Negro in American life," in which a number of distinct "levels" will "make [the novel's] meanings universal rather than just racial." These levels of allegory will include that of the psychological in which I describe the physical and psychological changes which occur in Negroes when they move from the South to the North; on the level of racial psychology, the level of a folk Negro with interracial contacts; another level will concern itself with the man's search for self-definition in a world of swirling values. On another level it will be the story of a man of good will who attempts to function idealistically in a political organization which cannot afford the luxury of idealism.

Because he wishes to "write of Negro life in terms of broad meaning so that those meanings will be grasped by [a] white American reading audience," Ellison writes, "I . . . load my material in such a way that when a scene or an action is presented it sounds 'not as a single melodic line but a series of chords.'" The result will be, he states, a "truly progressive novel of Negro life."[3]

Writing to Hitchcock when he is now well into the novel, Ellison voices a conception of the "political," the "racial," and the "universal" that has clearly moved away from the doctrines that guided his *New Masses* criticism. But neither are his various levels of allegory arranged in the Chinese-box formation described in his lecture at West Point in 1969: namely, that in representing "the complex unity and diversity not only of Americans but of all human life," the writer's task is to move "from the specifically imagined individuals to the group, to the nation and, it is hoped, to the universal" in order to "creat[e] and broade[n] our consciousness of American character . . . creat[e] and re-creat[e] the American experience." Describing to Hitchcock the project taking shape in his mind, he asserts that the appeal to the white reader will consist in finding in the life of a Negro character a meaning that is "broad" (his favored term for describing the class-conscious and transracial signification of such folk proletarian heroes as John Henry and Joe Louis). Ellison is still much preoccupied with how to establish the "accord of sensibilities" he valued in Malraux's revolutionary fiction and to explore the synecdochic possibilities in the "racial grain of sand" he described to Kenneth Burke. His goal is not to map the lineaments of "*the* American experience," much less to transcend historical particularity through ahistorical archetypes, but to produce "a truly progressive novel of Negro life."[4]

In the early days of composing *Invisible Man*, Ellison thinks of the universal not as the final end of mimesis, but as the linchpin of an antiracist rhetorical strategy: it is the means by which a black writer can reach out to and make connection with a nonblack readership. In the letter to Hitchcock his unattributed quotation from Burke's description of "chordal collapse"—"not a single melodic line but a series of chords"—reveals that he will be relying on Burkean strategies of textual patterning, equations, and associational clusters to convey the novel's intricately layered sociopolitical message. The dialectics of symbolic action will convey the dialectics of historical process. Ellison's unabashed claim to be writing "political allegory" asserts his abiding view of literature as a means of conveying knowledge of social reality; it unapologetically invokes a reflectionist epistemology. The theory of representation he devised after writing *Invisible Man*—positing artistic experimentalism and democratic pluralism as twin antidotes to the chaos of reality—is hardly in evidence.[5]

In what appears to have been the late spring of 1947, Ellison sent to his new publishers at Random House a two-part text titled "Working Notes for *Invisible Man*," in which he elaborates upon the character profile and plot outline sketched in his letter to Hitchcock. In the first part he supplies a description of the protagonist that situated the invisible man's unmoored psychological state in historical context. Deploying a naturalistic metaphor similar to that used in his review of *Blood on the Forge*, Ellison writes, "Negro life is psychologically apart. Its tempo of development from the feudal-folk forms of the South to the industrial urban forms of the North is so rapid that it throws up personalities as fluid and changeable as molten metal rendered iridescent from the effect of cooling air." Alluding to the southern chapters that his editors have already seen, he notes that although "our character" is a "Negro individualist" who "breaks away from the preindividual community of southern Negro life," he is also "a man born into a tragic irrational situation who attempts to respond to it as though it were completely logical."[6]

In the second part of "Working Notes" Ellison focuses on the New York section of the novel, for which a climax has now apparently been imagined. In this plot outline he makes no mention of the paint factory explosion, Mary Rambo, Tod Clifton, Ras the Exhorter, or the invisible man's discovery of his betrayal by Jack. While the protagonist becomes involved with the left—he has a love affair with a young white woman in the Brotherhood but subsequently realizes that he has been a mere figurehead—his disillusionment with radical politics does not culminate in realization of his invisibility. Instead, going underground during the riot, he emerges to take up various roles, including that of a cult preacher; he writes his memoirs in the hope that they will "serve to define himself" but "doubts that they will be read." For the creator of the invisible man, the end, at least the end with which readers of the 1952 text are familiar, was clearly *not* in the beginning.[7]

In this chapter I focus on the process by which the section of the novel set in the Jim Crow South came into being. Although Ellison's communications with his editors in 1946 and 1947 convey the impression that the novel's opening section came to him fairly quickly and underwent little revision, his drafts and outlines reveal that his original conception of the protagonist's youth contained a far bleaker and more deeply traumatizing encounter with the realities of Jim Crow than appears in the published text. Moreover, the campus section renders a considerably harsher portrayal of the role of the Negro college in perpetuating white supremacy and the miseducation of the Negro. Reading forward through Ellison's jottings and erasures, we will see that, even after he first heard the ghostly voice of his protagonist, he had to fight down the impulse to depict more explicitly, indeed more naturalistically, the historical forces constituting the social "substance" of the invisible man's "flesh and bone" existence.

"Another incident of brutality to mother and father": The Youth of the Invisible Man

Although the entirety of the prologue to *Invisible Man*, containing the narrator's provocative opening words, came to Ellison only late in his compositional process, the smoker scene—which in subsequent commentaries he variously termed the text's "governing ritual," "representative anecdote," and "metaphor for the whole situation"—was apparently clear in his imagination from the outset. When "The Battle Royal" appeared in 1948 as a short story in both *Horizon* and *'48: Magazine of the Year*, the American flag on the belly of the stripper was removed, as was the erection of one of the boys. But almost all the other details are identical, from the dancer's caricature of the white goddess to the Cyclopean jack-in-the-box popping out of the invisible man's eye, as the battle royal ritually enacts the psychological castration signaling the young men's initiation into manhood according to the ethics of living Jim Crow. "White rules reward Negroes for humiliating themselves," jotted Ellison. "Negro individualists receive petty rewards." An African American Candide, the invisible man is launched into his career as the protagonist of a half-picaresque, half-bildungsroman memoir in which the mature retrospective narrator will only occasionally intrude.[8]

In one draft the class hierarchy of the town is etched more sharply, as are the dynamics of the protagonist's humiliation. The men who praise the invisible man's glossing of Booker T. Washington's famous "Atlanta Compromise" speech of 1895 are described not as the "most lily-white men of the town," but as the "most reactionary." The original lineup of dignitaries, em-

phasizing brute class power rather than the finer distinctions of caste, designates "rich men" rather than "doctors" and omits "teachers" and "merchants";
the white school superintendent, we learn, "has sexual relations with wife of
leading Negro of community—who accepts it." The text of the young man's
speech, initially titled "Black Humility versus Political Action: or, the Advan-
tages of Staying in Our Place," stresses—arguably overstresses—the youth's
Washingtonian sycophancy. "Mr. President and Gentlemen of the Board of
Directors and Citizens," the young man declares through bloody lips, "two
thirds of the population of the South is of the Negro race. You know it and
we know it. But two thirds black is not as good as one third white. You have
taught us that and we have been willing pupils and we love you." When he
receives the first of the Bellerophontic letters that will keep him running, his
internalization of white supremacy is still more pronounced than in the 1952
text.[9]

In the published novel there occur a few Proustian moments when
memories of childhood flash across the invisible man's mind, but the smoker
scene, coupled with the flashback to his grandfather's death, furnishes the
only dramatized portrayal of the protagonist's youth. Ellison's notes and jottings reveal that he at first considered fleshing out those early years. The invisible man would recall that, because he was "small and weak in comparison
with most of the iron armed boys [he] grew up with," he developed an "interest in speech-making. . . . . [He] discovered that [he] could confuse others
and could completely overcome them with words." Some of the boys called
him "Rev." In another version he "lived in a storefront glass house on edge
of white neighborhood"; since his mother "worked for a broker" as a domestic and "brought [him] cast off suits and shirts bearing Brooks Brother's and
Sulka's labels," he "was the envy of the boys who hung around the corner";
indeed he "wanted to be a Wall Street broker" himself.[10]

Ellison also considered supplying his protagonist with a less elitist childhood, one more resonant of Wright's youth in *Black Boy*, Lonzo's experiences in "The Dream," or, for that matter, Ellison's own early years—which,
as Arnold Rampersad has shown, were hardly lived in the lap of luxury. The
invisible man recalls a high school football game in which, as he ran for a
touchdown, he was accosted on the sidelines by a white man with a pistol,
who threatened, "Nigger, if you cross that goal line don't think its going
to be so healthy for you." He associates his "mother father sister brother"
with memories of "pistol / levee camp / cotton pick" near Charleston, South
Carolina, a site locating the protagonist's youth in the heart of the Deep

South. The young man has "seen violence done his mother" which he has "pushed out of consciousness"; he has witnessed "another incident of brutality to mother and father." His cousin Preston has been jailed for some unspecified act of defiance. In one version the scene is set in "Greenwood," the name of the Negro neighborhood near Tuskegee, but also, we will recall, the name of the neighborhood that was the blood field of the Tulsa riot of 1921, which Slick sees in a fiery nightmare vision in Ellison's unpublished novel of 1939–40.[11]

Contemplating the irony that racial stereotypes portray Negroes as "associated with the tom tom, with spontaneity, with the deep instinctive centers of emotion," Ellison noted that the Negro's "position in the U.S. has made him a model of repression in the South, and in the North he is a neurotic who does not recognize his neuroticism." He contrasted his protagonist with Camus's Meursault in *The Stranger*. While both appear "frigid," he noted, Meursault is at least in "very mild revolt"; the invisible man, however, has been "confronted . . . with violence from his birth" and has "learned to supress the better part of humanity." Ellison introduces a trope that will be key to his protagonist's characterization:

> He sees but he doesn't see, he hears yet doesn't hear; he feels, but immediately short-circuits his feelings and thus he maintains a precarious stability. He is mechanized, wired for sound, air conditioned, shock-absorbed, proofed against emotional storms and fires, guaranteed to stick to the groove. There is only one flaw in all this—even in the mechanized human being there is no way of insuring against internal combustions within his brain. And that is where the drama starts.

The young man's flat affect, described in a series of mechanical metaphors, is traceable to the violence of his Jim Crow environment; emotional and sexual repression is a function of "conditioning."[12]

In the published text Ellison's decision not to flesh out his hero's "confrontation with violence since his birth" indicates his increasing dissociation from naturalism; the symbolic castration of the young men at the battle royal stands in for a whole history of racial and sexual humiliation that it is left to the reader to infer. While this stripping away of the protagonist's past has the advantage of dramatic compression, to a degree it abstracts the smoker scene from the political economy of the Jim Crow South. This abstraction in turn allowed Ellison to state, in later influential commentaries, that the scene portrays an initiation process "to which all greenhorns are subjected," a "keeping of taboo to appease the gods and ward off bad luck," a "ritual beyond the racial identities of the actors involved." Reading backward from these statements, various critics have construed the battle royal not so much as the protagonist's induction into the disciplinary regime of Jim Crow as his first halting step toward participation in the potential reciprocity, however abused in this instance, of American democracy. Had Ellison chosen to develop more fully the narrative materials describing the protagonist's Jim Crow childhood, the text's "governing ritual" would have been governed by a logic less assimilable to ideological legitimation.[13]

"Spurn the radicals wherever you meet them!":
Campus Politics

Although Ellison would repeatedly deny that the college represented in *Invisible Man* was Tuskegee Institute, which he attended from 1933 to 1936, his notes to the novel make it evident that he very distinctly had his near-alma mater in mind:

> FIRE AT TUSKEGEE
> CHAPEL—PURITANISM—
> KIDS CAUGHT IN BUSHES DURING FIRE EXPELLED.
> ATTEMPT TO ORGANIZE
> SENSE OF MORALITY
> GIRLS SENT HOME PREGNANT.
> CYNACISM OF TEACHERS
> SNOBISM OF TEACHERS & STUDENTS.
> PARK
> WASHINGTON'S GRAVE
> JOKE ABOUT STATUE
> STUDENT CYNACISM
> JIM CROW GUEST HALL.

Some of these items would pertain to any number of Negro colleges: the sexual Puritanism, enforced religiosity, demoralization of the faculty, and segregation of white guests from the campus black community. Others, however, explicitly signify Tuskegee. A series of mysterious fires had struck the campus in 1933, the year of Ellison's arrival. The theories of the sociologist Robert Park, Booker T. Washington's former secretary, were routinely taught at Tuskegee, causing the young Ellison no end of anguished rage. The "joke about the statue" at "Washington's grave"—Was the Founder raising or lowering the veil over the face of the former slave? — was a jest widely shared among Tuskegee's cannier undergraduates.[14]

In the 1952 text of *Invisible Man* Ellison would direct his satire toward the figure of Hebert ("A-Bear") Bledsoe, who is a composite of Robert Russa Moton, Washington's successor at Tuskegee from 1915 to 1935; Frederick D. Patterson, president during Ellison's last year; the nameless college president in Jay Saunders Redding's *No Day of Triumph* (1942); and Ellison's own earlier profile in "Burr Bullet-Head": "College President might be a study in humiliation and spite, [of] a masochism which becomes sadistic in relation to students, Negroes." In the 1952 text Bledsoe is despicable for his ambition and kowtowing to wealthy whites; the "small replica of a feudal castle" (102) in his office aquarium signifies his role in maintaining the neofeudal sharecropping economy. Yet he is never seen to do any direct harm (other than to the invisible man, of course) and plays a quasi-trickster role, paralleling the protagonist's grandfather and supplying the young man with some valuable lessons about how to survive in a white man's world. Looking back upon his creation in 1972, Ellison noted, "Bledsoe is cynical, but . . . never lied to this guy. And Bledsoe's acceptance was based on rebellion too. . . . Bledsoe lived within and manipulated the credibility gap."[15]

Bledsoe, at first named "Crump," plays a significantly more retrograde role in the early drafts, where it is difficult to credit him with being in rebellion of any kind. In one version a professor who resembles Bard of "The Initiation" relates to the invisible man the fate of a student who sought protection from the college president after having been falsely accused of rape in the nearby town. Abandoned by the president, the student seized from the campus ROTC building a gun with which to defend himself, only to find that its pin had been removed; he was shot down by a pursuing mob. The name of this rebellious student is Napue; Ellison's antifascist organizer hero, who in "The Dream" fights to open up wartime factory jobs to Negro workers, was apparently to make a cameo appearance (presumably dating back to his Depression-era college years, before the events of the story) in *Invisible Man*. In another version, this one closely resembling "The Initiation," it is the professor who is seized by the mob, who are angered at his radical teaching. In still other versions the fleeing man is a sharecropper involved in union organizing. The invisible man, watching the mob and Dr. Crump from some bushes, "could see that they had been drinking and hear them demanding that a wounded sharecropper be turned over to them. And before my eyes I heard the president agree with them and saw him . . ." Ominously the text breaks off here. Such fragments account for Ellison's otherwise enigmatic jotting of "attempt to organize" among his list of possible plot elements in the college section. The southern college was originally envisioned as the site of considerable violence.[16]

Ellison toyed with the notion that the invisible man might himself be touched by this violence; the president's betrayal would threaten not just his career but his life. Upon his arrival as a freshman, the young man would be badly beaten up by railroad police—as was Ellison himself upon arriving at Tuskegee—and flee to a nearby funeral home, where he watches the undertaker embalm a sharecropper who has died "with his hands on the plow" from a stroke brought on by chronic malnutrition. The undertaker, whose breath smells of whiskey, warns the young man, "Don't let yourself have to work for the other fellow, like me." In another variant the young man is apprehended by a mob invading the campus after the debacle at the Golden Day (where Norton has died of a heart attack). In still another version, the invisible man "sees student cadets marching with rifles. Gets into fight with whites because he believes that College is haven. President offers to turn him over to mob (sheriff). Wants to fight. Asks student for rifles learns there is no ammunition and only five rifles have firing pins. Escapes North." In these drafts Ellison had hardly dispensed with the themes and concerns of his radical fiction. Jim Napue's cameo appearance speaks for itself; the sexual-cum-political symbolism of the guns without pins recalls the disabled guns—and the enforced impotence of the Negro in the fight against fascism—in Todd/Mead's plane in early versions of "Flying Home." That the protagonist of *Invisible Man* might have played the role of student rebel, challenging both the campus administration and the Jim Crow state apparatus, suggests the Promethean lineaments of his original conception.[17]

In featuring the college president's handing over a transgressive rebel to either the vigilante mob or the sheriff, Ellison was not simply imagining a characteristically cowardly act; he was invoking an actual early Depression-era incident in which Tuskegee's President Moton handed over an undefended black man to a rampaging mob. Readers of *Invisible Man* will recall that, in his speech at the Harlem eviction, the protagonist stirs up the crowd by mentioning a "wise leader, you read about him, down in Alabama . . . [who] . . . when that fugitive escaped from the mob and ran to his school for protection, . . . was strong enough to do the legal thing, the law-abiding thing, to turn him over to the forces of law and order." A knowing voice responds, "Yeah, . . . so they could lynch his ass" (276). Although twenty-first-century readers are unlikely to catch Ellison's historical reference, the invisible man's Depression-era audience would have been familiar with a notorious incident in which a wounded sharecropper was denied sanctuary at Tuskegee. In December 1932 Clifford James, a member of the Communist-led Sharecroppers Union (scu), had been seriously injured during a shootout with sheriff's deputies in Reeltown, in nearby Tallapoosa County. James walked seventeen miles to seek aid at Tuskegee; he was treated for his wounds but then handed over to the Macon County sheriff. He died that night in the Montgomery County jail of gunshot wounds, as did another scu member, Milo Bentley. In Birmingham a few days later,

> the [International Labor Defense] . . . protest[ed] the arrests and . . . censure[d] Robert Moton and staff members at Tuskegee Institute for their complicity in the deaths of James and Bentley. . . . A mass funeral was held for the two martyred union organizers. Pallbearers carrying two caskets draped with banners emblazoned with deep red hammers and sickles led a procession of three thousand people, most of whom were black.

Reported in the *Daily Worker*, the *Southern Worker*, the *New Masses*, and the national black press, Tuskegee's role in the sharecropper deaths became widely known, and Moton received hate mail from around the country.[18]

Ellison originally portrayed Crump/Bledsoe as not only an abettor of sharecropper repression but also a red-baiter and opponent of antilynching activism. The Scottsboro defense campaign supplies the probable context for Crump/Bledsoe's declaration in an early draft:

> We live in a time of hardship and in these times a new evil has raised its head among us. Outsiders have come into the land to lure the young and foolish away from the sane and intelligent path lain down by our founder. Radicals, whispering false ideas into young brains that the white man will never accept and which no one with intelligence that God gave a mule would ever expect him to! They are attempting for their own selfish purposes to use you, to turn you against the white men whom we know, against our proven friends. . . . I warn you to spurn the radicals wherever you meet them. Denounce them, spurn them as you spurn a water moccasin. Grind its head into the dirt as I mean to grind any sign of radicalism that rears its head here upon this campus!

The "outsiders" and "radicals" who would protest lynch violence are, presumably, the likes of Napue and Paul, as well as the petitioners who approached Matt and Clara in "The Birthright" and the man with the "fried hands" who approaches John in "The Black Ball." In the context of this speech, Bledsoe's blunt declaration in the 1952 text—"I'll have every Negro in the country hanging on tree limbs by morning if it means staying where I am" (143) — takes on added resonance; his textual predecessor has already contributed to at least one lynching and is prepared to contribute to more. Had the original characterization of the college president survived into the final drafts of *Invisible Man*, it is unlikely that Bledsoe would have garnered such a reputation among critics as a system-beating trickster, or that Ellison himself would have been able to look back upon his creation with such ironic admiration.[19]

A point on chronology. At the beginning of chapter 1 of the 1952 text, the invisible man states that eighty-five years have passed since his grandparents "were told that they were free, united with others of our country in everything pertaining to the common good, and in everything social, separate like the fingers of the hand" (15). This allusion to the Emancipation Proclamation of 1863, accompanied by a swipe at the famous hand metaphor in Booker T. Washington's "Atlanta Compromise" address of 1895, situates the narrator's approach to the reader in 1948. Since he tells us that his story goes back some twenty years, his graduation from high school occurs in or around 1928. The task of chauffeuring Mr. Norton would be given to an upper classman, either a junior or a senior; presumably, then, the campus action takes place in the early years of the Depression, when the Scottsboro case and the violent suppression of Alabama sharecroppers were much in the news. As we shall see, Ellison will soon throw a monkey wrench into his historical chronology.[20]

"Can a Negro be a man?": Campus Sexuality

Although the left-wing professor who is seized by a mob invading the campus never made it into even a rough chapter draft of *Invisible Man*, Ellison evidently had Bard of "The Initiation" in mind. Ellison's notes show him contemplating including a portrait of a "Negro teacher" who would be a "true teacher"; he would be seen as "a threat to the whole Southern system," since his teaching is "the equivalent of a crime, in that all acts which enlighten the Negro student are against the state." This radical professor was reconfigured and fleshed out as Woodridge, a flamboyant homosexual who, more cynical than Communist, initiates the invisible man into some of the harsher realities of campus life. A composite of several professors and administrators whom Ellison encountered at Tuskegee, Woodridge was presented in a fully dramatized, and highly dramatic, scene that would eventually be eliminated from the novel. The two passing mentions of Woodridge remaining in the published text, which depict him as a passionate lover of literature and proponent of the neo-Joycean project of "creat[ing] the race by creating ourselves" (354), barely gesture toward his far more ironic mentoring role in the early drafts.[21]

In the excised "Woodridge" episode, the protagonist, lonely and desperate for support in the aftermath of Norton's collapse and Bledsoe's castigation, visits the silk-gowned professor in his campus residence. Noting something "almost feminine" about the room, the youth sees a "nude Greek torso" and "an ugly primitive African statue" on a chest. Reassuring him, "I don't hurt little boys," the professor taunts the invisible man as "an idealist and a slave . . . the model student of the college . . . a machine-made man, created in a region in which machines are few!" Woodridge then tells the tale of Napue's murder, mentioning Napue by name, and concludes, "Moral: This is no place to get lead in your pencil, bullets in your gun, wad in your pocket, sense in your head. Our job is to take it out." Woodridge queries the limits of his own role as a teacher of literature. "Can a Negro be a man?" he asks. "Can a Howard man be a teacher in hell?" He rants against "the obscene optimism of these 'great' writers" and exclaims, "I spit on all these books, these writers, these dreams, these insults! What do they know of life? . . . . It's all a fucking lie. . . . I wipe my ass with this literature, this condom to abort reality!" The drunken professor advises the youth to become a "raper of babies" and tears up volume upon volume of Western classics, from Shakespeare to Balzac to Conrad. He relates a recurrent dream in which he scoops out his students' eyes, remarking bitterly, "They don't even feel the pain." After driving the invisible man from his room, he apologizes the next day, gives him a list of books to read, and sadly remarks, "Something so vast has happened to our people that the more I realize of its dimensions the more helpless I become."[22]

Woodridge's query, "Can a Negro be a man?"—followed by the declaration, "If you belong to the lady of the races, isn't it all right to become a 'lady'?"—supplies Ellison with artillery to go after the sociologist Robert Park. Ellison's well-known antipathy to sociology began at Tuskegee, where he was exposed, by a Negro professor, no less, to Park's notorious characterization of the Negro as the "lady of the races"—an experience compounded by the efforts of a male dean to seduce Ellison during his freshman year. Ellison's characterization of Woodridge is conceived from an indisputably heteronormative standpoint; the English professor's inability to rebel anywhere other than on the "level of ideas," Ellison jotted, reflected the homosexual's typical practice of "intercourse without generation." As in "Burr Bullet-Head," he saw reflected in Woodridge's situation the "role of homosexuality in Negro college emphasizing lack of manhood, systematizing it." Indeed, Ellison speculated, Crump/Bledsoe might also be a homosexual, albeit closeted from both the world and himself. "Fear and uncertainty among Negroes in South, lack of identity," Ellison ruminated. "No one is sure of anyone else and thus is uncertain of him self, thus passive and feminine leader, who *is* homo, capitalizes upon condition (fear as means of control, psychological uncertainty to satisfy his own hostility toward whites, his fear of whites and his self-hate; i.e., hate of Negroes and their fear and helplessness)."[23]

Despite, or because of, his neurotic behavior, Woodridge is or would have been the first of Ellison's Jamesian "super subtle fry": characters who, like the vet, force the invisible man to face uncomfortable truths. Indeed Woodridge's designation of the protagonist as a "machine-made man" nearly replicates the vet's later claim that the youth is a "mechanical man" (94). Woodridge's status as sexual outsider positions him to expand upon the cultural dimensions of the powerlessness, sexual and political, embodied in the bulletless guns in the campus ROTC arsenal; the male students may "drill four abreast . . . uniforms pressed, shoes shined," but with "minds laced up, eyes blind like those of robots," their militarism part of their subordination to the "visitors and officials on the low, whitewashed reviewing stand" (36). Although Woodridge's nightmare invokes both *King Lear* and *Oedipus Rex*, the great classics of the Western tradition are linked with the campus's blinding role, also embodied in the statue of the Founder. Ellison tinkered with Woodridge's destruction of his library, at one point deciding that "not Shakespeare—only naturalism, Zola and American," would be torn to pieces. Nonetheless he eventually decided to excise from his novel the drunken homosexual professor who views white-authored literature as complicit in the mental castration of young African Americans and to put in his place a culturalist seer who urges the invisible man to follow in the footsteps of Joyce's Stephen Dedalus. Along with heteronormativity, Ellison's beloved classics had to be preserved.[24]

In drafts of the campus chapters Ellison also explored the connection between the disciplinary suppression of heterosexuality and its indoctrination of cynical young adults in the ethics of living Jim Crow. In the published text a glancing reference is made to the fact that the grass surrounding the Founder's statue is the students' favorite site for sexual trysts. In an earlier version the invisible man attends a dormitory bull session where red-blooded male prankishness takes on a more predatory cast. His roommate, Jack Maston, is an experienced operator, boasting that he is about to "snatch

. . . the draws . . . of a 'little chick'" he has been pursuing for months. This conquest, to be secretly witnessed from the bushes by members of his fraternity, will be his "last frat test." The female students are apparently equally eager for sexual activity. "Hell, didn't I have one slip me into Old Buckethead's house when she was on duty over there and into his own righteous bed!" declares Maston. "All [these old bastards who run the school] . . . think about is keeping the boys and girls separated and pleasing the white folks." Casting down one's bucket where one is apparently can take many forms.[25]

The hypocrisy fostered by the college's sexually sanitized atmosphere encourages the young men's "preindividual attitudes," Ellison wrote. Maston intends to go to Chicago, where "niggers . . . who never looked inside a college are cleaning up, making all the money, getting into politics and everything." He announces, "You guys can believe in this stuff they teach you down here, but me, I'm through with it soon as I leave the campus." Maston's friend, who plans to get an ugly woman to support him through medical school, replies, "My folks sent me here so I could work part of my way and because they believe in the crap the founder put down. They want me back to save our people." Although the youths think they are rejecting the ideology of the Founder and striking out on their own, Ellison pondered, they are actually reproducing his values, minus the "idealism" accompanying the college's origination, as described in Barbee's sermon. That the young men's cynicism might even take violent form is suggested in Ellison's note that the invisible man might see "Negro boys raping women near where he hides; sees someone dear to him raped before his eyes."[26]

The women students apparently so eager to be deflowered by the likes of Maston are also sketched in the drafts of Invisible Man. According to their male peers, they are subjected to the custodianship of the aptly named Miss Whitesides, the dean of women, "fat and indolent, with all the mannerisms of a southern white lady. She went about dressed in white and [was] so tightly corseted that she always appeared short of breath. Her complexion was very light to which she added so much white powder that she looked like a ghost most of the time." Whitesides habitually selects dark-skinned female students to wait on her, compelling them to help her remove her corsets, from which, the dozens-playing young men joke, roaches crawl out. Miss Whitesides "is more interested in seeing that we dont get close to the boys than she is in seeing that we learn anything," one young woman is reported saying. "[She] make[s] us take off our bloomers . . . to see if we been with any boys."[27]

In the 1952 text the only woman associated with the campus is Miss Susie

Gresham, a "grey-haired matron in the final row" to whom the invisible man pays ambivalent tribute in an italicized retrospective riff that sounds a somewhat odd blast during the chapel scene. Noting Miss Gresham's role as the sex police—she is the *"guardian of the hot young women on the puritan benches . . . [who is] looking at that co-ed smiling at that he-ed"*—he imagines her receiving his heretical words *"with [her] dear old nod of affirmation."* She was, he decides, a *"relic of slavery whom the campus loved but did not understand . . . yet bearer of something warm and vital and all-enduring"* (113–14). Such a fond appraisal could not so readily have been made of the maternal Miss Gresham if the text had retained Miss Whitesides, whose control of the women students' sexuality underlines the college's role in coupling puritan discipline and white supremacy with perverted voyeurism. Conjoined with the portrayal of Woodridge, this revelation of the students' cynical attitude—toward success, toward sex—expands the text's commentary on the campus's role in the ideological reproduction of elitist, misogynist, and racist consciousness; preindividuality is linked not just with defensive group solidarity in the face of Jim Crow violence, but also with the herd-like and sordid ambitions of the Negro middle class.

Ellison's notes indicate that, in contrast to the published text, where he implies that the invisible man has done some trysting of his own, he considered characterizing the invisible man as a sexual neophyte. In "Working Notes" he wrote that he had "omitted from the first section . . . an affair which ends in failure when he approaches a folkish girl with a version of romantic love which he has gleaned from his reading. She is amused at his antics and rejects him." Another note posits that the invisible man is a virgin. As he crafted his portrait of the memoirist as a young man, Ellison avoided undue sexual humiliation; accompanying the banishment of Woodridge was the attribution to the protagonist of appropriate male heterosexual credentials.[28]

"No grass grew beneath the tree":
Trueblood and the Waste Land

Most of the dialogue and narration in the episode where Norton encounters Trueblood underwent little revision; once Ellison allowed Trueblood to speak, the sharecropper's voice took over. Ellison's notes explicitly link the Trueblood chapter with the "governing ritual" of the battle royal: "Theme: Degradation leads to help of whites. Trueblood Boy & prizefight. Politics."

"Politics," however, apparently entailed a greater emphasis on Trueblood's sharecropper status. In the 1952 text Trueblood claims, "When I feels po'ly in my gut I takes a little soda and it goes away" (51); Ellison originally observed that the sharecropper "suffers from hypertension or even a stroke" and that "his speech, voice quality is effected by his relations with his environment." Such details link Trueblood with the deceased sharecropper whom the invisible man viewed in the funeral home upon arriving at the campus. Next to an outline of the Trueblood episode, Ellison jotted, "sharecroppers union." There is no evidence that he intended to portray Trueblood as a member of the SCU, but the sharecropper was evidently aligned in Ellison's mind with Clifford James, the organizer handed over to the sheriff by Moton in 1932, as well as with the social conditions prompting the emergence of the SCU. We are reminded that the SCU attracted white as well as black members, moreover, by the initial description of the "lean, hungry face" of the sleeping white oxcart driver whom the protagonist sees on the road to Trueblood's cabin. Only later did Ellison pencil in the words "he was the kind of man I feared"; at first, the sleeping man as readily evokes the white sharecropper who, at the end of "A Party Down at the Square," has no interest in the false barbeque offered in the lynching and looks "hungry as hell."[29]

The context supplied by these allusions to Jim Crow oppression and resistance illuminates a passage in Trueblood's monologue that otherwise makes little sense. As he describes his situation in bed with his daughter, when he has to "move without movin'," Trueblood alludes to "that feller . . . down in Birmingham. That one what locked hisself in his house and shot at them police until they set fire to the house and burned him up" (60). His remark has clear sexual meaning: the fact that he is about to shoot his own bullets in his daughter, no matter what the consequences, links his incestuous desires with his earlier fantasy of invading the bedroom of Mr. Broadnax, the plantation owner, and seizing the diaphanously garbed Mrs. Broadnax. But Trueblood's reference to the man in Birmingham, besides recalling the death of Silas in Wright's "Long Black Song," gestures toward the violent class struggles being waged in the city that was the center of red-led Alabama activism. Especially when coupled in early drafts with the guns lacking firing pins seized by Jim Napue in the ROTC arsenal, Trueblood's allusion to the Birmingham incident suggests his awareness of current proletarian resistance and reinforces the links between social rebellion and sexual transgression implied in his dream invasion of the master's house.[30]

Trueblood is not the only character aware of Alabama violence. In an early draft the invisible man's confused motives in taking Norton to Trueblood's cabin are traced to a cause that is eliminated from the 1952 text. The young chauffeur is driving while Norton pontificates about racial destiny:

> [We drove past] a spot where I'd been told a wife had climbed a tree and cut her husband down, alone, the body falling heavily and leaving the imprint of a man in the soft clay that had remained until the first rains came and filled it in with leaves and loose soil washed from the hillside. No grass grew beneath the tree and its branches were scorched and bare of leaves. I pressed my toe on the throttle.

Distracted—or perhaps subliminally motivated—by these memories, the young man takes a wrong turn and ends up in Trueblood's front yard; the troubling political unconscious that compelled him to utter "social equality" in the smoker scene erupts again. The centrality of the hanging tree to the day's crisis is emphasized in a draft of the passage describing the young man's moonlit walk later that evening. In the 1952 text he recalls the "mad surreal whirl" surrounding "Trueblood, Mr. Norton, Dr. Bledsoe and the Golden Day"; in the earlier version he agonizes over "Trueblood, the road-side tree, and the Golden Day."[31]

The critical role played by the lynching tree in early drafts of *Invisible Man* requires us to rehear the echoes of T. S. Eliot's waste land in the retrospective narrator's description of the campus on the day of the trustees' arrival: "the school a flower-studded wasteland, the rocks sunken, the dry winds hidden, the lost crickets chirping to yellow butterflies. . . . And oh, oh, oh those multimillionaires!" In early notes Ellison wrote:

> Waste land Money = shit
> Sacrifice = hanged man = lynching.

Conjoined with the image of the barren earth under the scorched lynching tree, these linked words and phrases inject historical specificity into the metaphor equating the college with the waste land. Grass fails to grow beneath the tree not because the land lacks fertility, but because the body of a lynched man has obliterated the growth of new life; the hanged man is not an archetypal fisher king but an American Dionysus whose sacrificial death is intended as a warning to those who would interfere with the foul-smelling capital accumulation of the multimillionaire trustees. The Ellison who had written in 1939 that the "boss man" produces the real "waste" of the South here proposes a political allegory effaced from the 1952 text.[32]

It may seem anomalous that Ellison would choose to invoke Frazer's archetypal myth of the dying god to comment on the "hanged man" of Jim Crow violence. We will recall, however, that "myth, ritual, and revolution were slammed around" during Ellison's League of American Writers days; as both Cambridge School theorists and Marxist critics pointed out, rituals of purification, initiation, and rebirth needed to be understood in historical materialist terms. That Ellison was consciously attempting to fuse myth and ritual with political critique is illustrated in what appears to be a very early draft of the college section, where the narrator states, "I discovered my invisibility in a strange way." Explaining that he "landed in college during the early days of the Depression," he goes on to describe the campus's lush beauty and relate that one evening he waded into a spring, "cleansing" his feet in "an unconscious reproduction of a primitive ritual I had read about somewhere." Noting that he feels himself "surrounded by mirrors" that convey to viewers only their own reflections, the narrator then recounts seeing a "car load of red-faced white men [demand] something of the school's coal-black president . . . round as a beer barrel in his white nightshirt, a regular shadow in human form." Although the text is cut off here, presumably this is another version of the episode in which Crump/Bledsoe hands over the victim sought by the mob. The invisible man's rite of purification prepares him for his initiation into invisibility, which here entails being at once not-seen and subjected to racist terror. The prose in this draft passage is awkward and the symbolism obvious. But Ellison's intention is an ironic yoking of cross-cultural rites of passage described by anthropologists with a young Negro's coming of age during the Depression. His allusive goal is not, it seems, to transcend or evade history, but to investigate the universal dimensions of the scapegoated hanged man in the "racial grain of sand" lying on the terrain of Jim Crow.[33]

"Not biology, but class, is destiny":
The Sharecropper and the Millionaire

Commenting in 1971 on the Trueblood episode, Ellison noted that, while he had been "working consciously out of [the] idea of tragedy as it becomes entangled with notions of race in the South," he had not "been able to convince many people that Trueblood is a tragic man." Perhaps his revisions of the episode were partly to blame. For one thing, he originally stressed Trueblood's purposive, and hence hubristic, transgression of the incest taboo. In one draft the sharecropper admits to an investigator from the college that— speaking of his wife and his daughter—he "wanted both of them for himself." The daughter is at first complicit as well. "Eden. She hugs him and he takes her in sleep: dream symbolism," mulled Ellison. "Both give into subconscious wishes during sleep. Censor is down." Although he jotted, "Float in Oedipus joke," the Freudian dimensions of the Oedipus story were of less interest than its tragic dimensions. Ellison reminded himself: "*Things to be done in this chapter*: balance the tragic ingredients in the sharecropper; build up suffering of wife and daughter; construct scene of violence when his incest is discovered." Trueblood's tragedy is that "he must expect punishment but it doesn't come because his punishment is not to be punished but helped by whites."[34]

Perhaps paradoxically this greater emphasis on Trueblood's tragic stature would also have dignified Norton, whom Ellison described as Trueblood's "double . . . fascinated by actual incest of ignorant and morally brutalized Negro peasant." More pathetic than tragic in the 1952 text, Norton was originally conceived as partaking in the aura of Trueblood's blues-inflected heroism.

> [He] encounters tradegy [*sic*] in that he persists in the direction in which he loves, he drives his error to its tragic, agonizing conclusion. Persistence is the key word. Edipus persist[s] and insists upon discovering the guilty person. King Lear persists in his mistaken way, Macbeth piles murder upon murder. All create conflict, sustain it, heighten it, until it shatters them apart.
>
> Thus my task is to see to it that Mr. Norton carries through his mistake. The beast is ever waiting to spring and bear him to earth while he, unknowing, continues through his self-created jungle.

In this Jim Crow version of Henry James's "The Beast in the Jungle," Norton, like John Marcher, inhabits the psychological wilderness of an uninterrogated life. Norton's "error" is that he "asks ivm [the invisible man] to reveal to him his fate." The millionaire should be "allowed to assume a more human character," jotted Ellison, who even contemplated abandoning the novel's first-person narration in order to "dramatize" the internal struggles of the trustee.[35]

As Ellison's notes and drafts reveal, this more sympathetic conception of Norton's humanity would not have precluded a harsher assessment of the millionaire's determining role in the capitalist system producing Trueblood's degradation. If anything the original version would have more fully enacted Wright's dictum, in "Blueprint for Negro Writing," that the Negro artist needs to establish the causal connection between the fates of the share-cropper and the Wall Street financier. In the published text the tin red apple on Trueblood's porch suggests a transhistorical notion of original sin that places the two men in parallel rather than dialectical relationship. In an early version, by contrast, "Apple" is the brand name on the tin of chewing tobacco from which Trueblood extracts a plug. As part of his reward for confirming white supremacist fantasies of black degradation, Trueblood can now avail himself of products of sharecropping labor that were previously beyond his budget.[36]

In the published text we are told that Norton is "forty years a bearer of the white man's burden and for sixty a bearer of the Great Tradition." If "sixty years" refers to the abandonment of Reconstruction in 1877 and "forty years" to the official institution of Jim Crow in the *Plessy v. Ferguson* decision of 1896, Ellison features Norton's status as a "bearer" of the history of racism. (The reader may also note that this recalibration of chronology somewhat disrupts the early-1930s dating implied by the drafts' veiled references to Scottsboro and Reeltown.) Ellison's notes stress Norton's connection with nineteenth-century history: "Norton's ideas are those of abolitionist who won war through Negro, and then sold him out with hypocritical moral reasoning." In their "endless curruption [*sic*] . . . Norton and his kind control consciousness of Negroes. Condition them to passivity, provincialism, servility. . . . Norton must embody Puritan Calvinist streak. Moral concern disguising economic motive. Secularization of capital. Interest in Negroes characterized by sentimentality hiding selfish motive." He adds, "Norton is puritan abolitionist spirit transformed into its mechanical object. . . . Jamesian Problems: New England sensibility floundering in its own vomit. Trustee failed to live." Norton's "fail[ure] to live" is a function not just of his repressed incestuous desire but also of the unacknowledged relationship of New England capital to the betrayal of Reconstruction. His Jamesian "floundering in vomit" is tied to the legacy of past and present exploitation, both material and psychological. Trueblood is Norton's political unconscious.[37]

In doubling the sharecropper and the multimillionaire Ellison explores the political economy of incest: "Incest is the ultimate expression of monopoly. Trustee must reveal monopolistic spirit in his conversation and action." Norton's longed-for daughter, clad in wispy white, figures in the novel's "political allegory" as an ideological mechanism by which the multi-millionaire's parasitic relation to black labor, which furnishes the past and present basis of his wealth, can be at once fetishized and hidden:

Norton's daughter might be a projection of bourgoise technology and the disguised ethic which appeared historically as a humanistic abolition disguising it[self as] disgust with value. Thus she is sentimental, full of curls and frills, having no interest in suitors. She thus appears in our period streamlined, sterile, looking more like a castrated boy than a female, but also interested now in ethical responsibility.

While in the 1952 text Norton's daughter becomes ill in Italy and collapses at an embassy party in Munich, originally her death is "due to [a] machine accident." Norton's association with machinery connects the source of his wealth with Trueblood's reference to himself as a "cotton-pickin' machine," as well as with the background droning of the campus power plant—"All operated by *black hands*," Barbee boasts—throughout the scene (65, 133). Although Norton is fascinated by the fact that the sharecropper cabins date back to slavery, their present-day decrepit state is traceable to the present-day poverty of their inhabitants, which is in turn traceable to the predominant control of the southern economy by northern finance capital. (The cabins had not been whitewashed since before Washington's death in 1915, according to a study of Macon County by the sociologist Charles S. Johnson.) In relation to both the campus and its environs, Norton's interest—in both senses of the word—is hardly innocent.[38]

Ellison's notes indicate his Marxist-Hegelian conception of the identity of Norton and Trueblood:

Unity = Incest
Contradiction = Aristocrat vs. sharecropper
             Out of decadence   out of degradation
             Monopolist of finance   monopolist of emotions.

Norton's "decadence" is the dialectical counterpart of Trueblood's "degradation." White supremacist doctrine would attempt to essentialize a binary opposition between finance and emotions, positing that the sharecropper's incestuous act is "true to his blood," while the trustee's philanthropy is an emanation of his "Northernness." But the meaning of the encounter between Norton and Trueblood, Ellison jotted, is that "not biology, but class, is destiny. . . . Norton's is the fate of absolutes of 'purity.' Interestingly enough incest the way to familial purity, is condemned by most societies. Class thus becomes the strategy of obtaining that which is denied by biology. Needless to say it too is destiny once it is achieved." In the published text Trueblood's incest is rewarded because, like the battle royal, it confirms white supremacist stereotypes while permitting powerful white men vicarious enjoyment of their own repressed sexual impulses; the text's "governing ritual" creates myths enabling ideological legitimation. At the same time, Norton and True-blood are paralleled as fathers commonly embroiled in incestuous desire: Marx and Freud are set side by side. In the "political allegory" of the early drafts of *Invisible Man*, Marx and Freud interpenetrate: Norton and his class have historically created and presently perpetuate the social conditions that impel Trueblood to transgress the incest taboo as a way of defying the rule of the Great House.[39]

Ellison originally reinforced this emphasis on the economics of the Trueblood-Norton relationship in a brief coda to the Trueblood episode. While in the published text Norton gives Trueblood a hundred-dollar bill with which to buy toys for his children, in early drafts he has the invisible man drive him into town to a toy store, where he buys "dolls and wagons, tractors and airplanes, fire engines and trains, little sets of dishes and doll furniture, and cowboy chaps and coiled lariats"; the invisible man mean-while "picked up a toy cash register and turned the handle, hearing a tiny bell as its cash drawer sprang open." Back at the cluster of sharecropper cabins, a cluster of blank-eyed and fearful children refuse the toys and ask Norton whether he is "the bossman . . . the sheriff, or 'the law.'" The invisible man places most of the toys by the highway: "The little white dolls with pink cheeks looked stonily into the sun as we drove away."[40]

Displaying Norton's "sincere philanthropy reduced to its most pathetic extreme," this conclusion to the Trueblood episode reinforces the economic nature of the relationship between the doubled men. For the philanthro-pist's decision to buy gifts for the children rather than pay the man directly in cash for the service rendered suggests the northerner's oneness with southern plantation owners, whose coercive relationships to their tenants routinely took the form of payments in scrip rather than money. This point is reinforced by the fact that the only cash register in the scene is a toy. Like the dolls that "[look] stonily into the sun," the rosy-cheeked Norton is in-capable of seeing that he is indeed the bossman and the law. His position of power has made him blind.[41]

"Home economics": The Golden Day

From the outset Ellison realized that "[w]hat [the invisible man] does to re-veal fate of trustee must motivate his explusion and trip north." His notes and outlines for the Golden Day episode show that he considered various alternatives. Norton might "drop dead of heart failure," and the invisible man and Halsey would "hide [Norton's death] from vets because they fear lynch mob." The vet might even kill Norton. As he gravitated toward less apocalyptic scenarios, Ellison decided that, whatever the result, the scene would show Norton's illness resulting from his being unable to "bear [the] knowledge" with which he is confronted. His feeling "'safe' only with Negroes" because they "seem stable, loyal, completely dominated, nailed in place [is] . . . a mistake which he discovers too late in the Golden Day." The second and final jump of the Jamesian beast would occur in the Alabama roadhouse.[42]

A motley crew of middle-class Negroes driven insane by the ethics of living Jim Crow, the vets at the Golden Day are even more obstreperous in Ellison's early drafts. There is "a painter-sculpt[or] who was never too careful of the material he used and who made the most striking surreal images out of fresh excrement"; a "legless man a symbol"; a "preacher . . . who thinks he's seeing Jesus Chirst" and declares, "Here comes the Messiah, you all!"; a chaplain who "claimed he invented a bomb"; and a sociologist, evidently another variant on Woodridge, who "reveals a definite homosexual personality and 'acts out' his acceptance of Park's theory that Negro people are the 'lady of the races.' . . . In relation to trustee . . . this can take form of maschoism 'beat me daddy' he said, extending poker." "These bastards aren't nuts, aren't shell-shocked, because of the war," the psychologist explains. "They only got set off by the war." The chapter contains the "same symbolism as battle royal," Ellison jots, "only more surreal." The "governing ritual" of castration here extends to Negro artists, intellectuals, and professionals, recalling Wright's portrait of the maddened imprisoned intellectual in Native Son.[43]

Ellison originally expanded the list of world-historical figures with which the ailing white trustee is tauntingly associated by the throng of vets and prostitutes. Besides resembling Thomas Jefferson and John D. Rockefeller—who, charges the vet named Burnside, stole the formula for turning blood into money—the millionaire bears a likeness to "President Wilson, Vardaman or Bilbo, Jesus Christ, Abraham Lincoln, . . . Andrew Carnegie, Henry Ford, George Washington." With what Edna calls his "billy goat balls," the wealthy philanthropist wants to "fuck the whole world." Supercargo's role as the superego enforcer of Jim Crow rule is rendered still more explicit. One vet comments, "He's like a slave driver inside one's head and an especially evil one because he pretends to be black, like us, but if you rub him a bit the blackness comes off and you see his true whiteness." Supercargo's racial identity might even have been kept ambiguous. "Attendant is a huge character (white or black)," Ellison wrote, "a personalization of the [mental] censor. Censor appears on balcony in his shorts, without his white uniform and hell breaks loose." It is his uniform, rather than his skin color, that defines his disciplinary role.[44]

The early versions of the Golden Day episode further stress the implication of the campus in the exploitation, both economic and sexual, of the local community. Jokingly referred to in the published text as "the best little home-maker in the business" (96), Edna, a former home economics major at the college, initially

> lost no opportunity to tell us of her various clandestine experiences with various members of the faculty. She was an attractive girl, still young, and might have pursued her profession far more successfully in a large city, but she preferred to remain at the Golden Day in order to be near the school and to embarrass it. They had tried to have her removed, but she was the mistress of a promenient white man and that setteled that.

Another prostitute, who calls Norton "Hokey pants," tells him, "You white folks think you pulling the strings up there, but those [mammy] scratchers up there are pulling you. You better git hipped, Pops. Get you some rubber boots and keep your eyes peeled. Drop downt here when they don't expect you and then look around. Maybe you'd see why I had to practice home economics with the dean in order to stay in school." Playing upon the *homo economicus* of classical economic theory, the student-turned-prostitute exposes the real contract between students and administrators, as well as the illusory contract between administrators and trustees. As the financial supporter of a college invested in the production of prostitutes, Norton is forced to see that he has indeed sown "endless curruption." While the chaotic uprising of the vets at the Golden Day has been read as a celebration of heteroglossia, anticipating the carnival atmosphere of the Harlem riot in the novel's closing pages, Ellison's early drafts emphasize the degradation of the roadhouse's inhabitants and guests; surrealism is mobilized for purposes of satiric critique.[45]

"Reach out to the future and transform it":
The Vet and His Mentor

The nameless doctor who is dubbed "the vet"—and, having called Norton a "lyncher of souls" (93), is exiled along with the invisible man—is a more fully politicized figure in the novel's early drafts. "Obsessed with political terrorism," mulled Ellison, the vet "concentrates upon transferring [this] obsession . . . to someone capable of carrying it out." Ellison's character sketch explains why "these hands so lovingly trained to master a scalpel yearn to caress a trigger" (93). The vet is a former "Negro soldier, a doctor, who remained in France after last war, but retained his citizenship; he returned to States after the Depression swept Europe. He is hungry for conversation, is articulate, conscious, his science reduced to ineffectuality by political support of American industrialism. Speaks in humanistic vein but Norton fails to understand him." In the 1952 text the vet explains, "Ten men in masks drove me out from the city at midnight and beat me with whips for saving a human life" (93); in the draft we learn that he was beaten "for having operated upon Negro and white whom Southerners wish to die." As a result of this trauma he "breaks down and enters hospital"; it is evident that both his patients and he were targets of the mob's wrath. In the context supplied by other references to SCU organizing, it is probable that the "Negro and white whom Southerners wished to die" were radical activists opposed to the "political support of American industrialism." The vet's obsession with terrorism, which links him to Booker Small and Jim Napue, is a response to the vigilante (or perhaps state-sponsored) terrorism he has directly experienced.[46]

The vet's sympathy with the radical opponents of Jim Crow is connected with the left-wing political theories imparted to him by the French doctor under whom he trained after the war. Reminding himself to "couch [the] old Frenchman's argument in metaphysical terms," Ellison has the vet recall the doctor's words. Remarking to his pupil that the American "obsession with whiteness and purity would give a certain Viennese named Freud an interesting problem," the doctor described his own background:

> I was a peasant and then later I came to work in a factory. Most of what are called my "intentions" are merely adaptations of processes I learned about [on] my father's farm in Normandy, and later in a small factory here in Paris. I merely took advantage of my beginnings. You see, the earth and man's fingers are the beginnings of all science. You will make a contribution only if you face squarely your beginnings and then with your feet firmly planted in the human necessities of that beginning you reach out to the future and transform it. A technique is no more than a means of taking[,] channelizing the harsh shock of naked reality, of protecting this tender bundle of nerves and blood vessels called man.

The doctor's peasant proletarian origins, coupled with his evident reading of Marx and Engels, supplied him with a "technique"—both a materialist epistemology and a radical politics—enabling him to "reach out to the future and transform it." In his proposition that grounding in "human necessities" supplies the basis for revolutionary practice, the doctor articulates the connection between necessity and freedom that Ellison often cited in his writings of the early 1940s.[47]

Viewing "technique" as a means to the end of improving life, the French doctor expresses his amazement at its characteristic perversion in the United States: "I am not too certain whether your obsession with technique is actually what it seems; whether it isn't realy a desire to be mastered *by* technique and thus by things, machines, rather than to master Nature and to organize, or mechanize it as it appears." Addressing his student specifically as a Negro, the doctor asks, "Where all this passion of Americans to become tools? Why is it that *you* of all Americans cannot possess yourselves to the point of refusing to be further brutalized? You whose beginning lies in a state of humiliation, why must you work so fervidly to render that humiliation more complex?" Next to the vet's report of the doctor's words, Ellison mused:

> Men by becoming the supreme value thus become non-value or valueless. Negroes by being regarded as human, were thus sucked into a movement of thinking which was to regard all men as tools. . . . Negroes used as instrument of primative accumulation, then as a bridge from slave economy to industrial economy. . . . Negroes are not animals, but men. Men are machines, ergo Negroes are machines. "God's law" to "natural law" to "market law." From slavery to "freedom" of the market to drudgery to amusement industry.

Evidently the French doctor is playing the role of a ventriloquist in relation to his creator.[48]

Besides gesturing in the direction of Marxism, the French doctor articulates key theses of Lewis Mumford. Commentary on Ellison's use of Mumford has been generally confined to analysis of Ellison's designation of the roadhouse as the Golden Day, thereby alluding to Mumford's famous discussion of the American Renaissance as a "golden day" preceding the incursion of industrial civilization. (That Mumford gave scant attention to both slavery and abolition irked Ellison, who invested the allusion with considerable irony.) The French doctor's disquisition reveals Ellison's significant agreement with Mumford's more extended critique of mechanized modernity. Not only did Mumford write in 1926 that the Civil War was "a struggle between two forms of servitude, the slave and the machine"; in 1939 he applied his analysis of mechanization to fascism, which he viewed as "accept[ing] the automations that capitalist industry has created . . . and mak[ing] them universal." In the published text Ellison reassigns a small portion of the French doctor's mini-lecture to the vet, who speaks regretfully of having forgotten "things about life [that] . . . most peasants and folk peoples almost always know through experience, though seldom through conscious thought" (91). But when the vet proclaims the invisible man to be "the perfect mechanical man," much of the substance of Ellison's commentary on specifically capitalist, as opposed to more broadly industrial, dehumanization is lost.[49]

"Cut out the bombast!" Ellison noted in the margin by the doctor's words. The novelist was evidently under pressure from his editors to reduce the episode involving the "vet-doctor, Norton, narrator." "Less overt irony and philosophy and more straight recital of events will allow the reader to see what is after all implicit in the story," urged Harry Ford of Knopf. Ellison's rationale for going along with this "show-not-tell" advice may have been stylistic; the doctor's ideas are, after all, conveyed through a speech within a speech. But then the familiar text of *Invisible Man* is full of much longer (and hardly unbombastic) disquisitions, not least those by Trueblood and Barbee that frame the Golden Day chapter. The effect of Ellison's excising the French doctor's words to the vet, as well as the vet's explanation of why he was forced to quit his profession, is not to eliminate redundancy but to depoliticize the scene.[50]

In eliminating the French doctor and toning down the vet, Ellison also altered the causality of Norton's collapse. For the drafts of the encounter between the vet and the millionaire reveal that what Norton learns at the Golden Day is what precipitates his heart attack, and, in the earliest versions, his death. The revelation of his commonalty with Trueblood constitutes the first leap of the beast in the "self-created jungle" of his tangled psyche. But the realization that he has "sown corruption" is what smites him at the Golden Day; not just the mechanized young chauffeur, but also the prostitutes and the crazed inmates are the product of the campus and the Jim Crow social order that it legitimates and sustains. It is because he and his class have turned these people into "tools" that they constitute his "destiny." The vet's words, as well as the transmitted wisdom of the French doctor, occasion the second leap of the Jamesian beast that brings on the perception following the purpose of Norton's trip south and the passion of his interrogation of the sharecropper. What Norton has learned from both the sharecropper and the veteran helps to account for Ellison's choosing as one of the novel's epigraphs the quotation from Melville's "Benito Cereno": "What is it that has cast such a shadow over you?" The answer is, of course, "the Negro." Like Melville's Spanish slave ship captain, Norton has been faced with irrefutable proof that his very existence is based upon racist dehumanization and violence. In the 1952 text Trueblood's residence in the underground of Norton's psyche is comprehensible in Freudian terms; in the drafts it can be accounted for only by a substantial Marxing of Freud.[51]

"Something extremely old and meaningful":
The Alternate Founder's Day

Like Jim Trueblood's dream narrative, Homer Barbee's Founder's Day speech seems to have sprung full-grown from Ellison's imagination, undergoing virtually no significant revision in either Barbee's testimony to the "black arts of escape" (122) or the narrator's assessment of the sermon as a "black [rite] of Horatio Alger" (111). In early drafts, however, the ironic disparity between the Founder's ideals and their sordid realization is enhanced by the juxtaposition of the chapel scene with another rite attended by the invisible man. After Barbee's sermon the disconsolate youth follows the sound of "banjos plucking through the light staccato clapping of hands" and arrives at the football practice field, where a group of "farm people from miles around" are having a Founder's Day celebration of their own. The children chant, "Buckeye the rabbit, shake it, shake it," while the adults perform "circle group dances [he] had never seen before": "It was like a dream, or a scene from my grandfather's description of the old days. . . . It was as though I had intruded upon something extremely old and meaningful which I had no right to see." A farmer tells him, "Long before they had the college or anything else, we useta have camp meetings on this spot and we celebrated the first Juneteenth after freedom right down there where they dancing now." Irene, his wife—who contrasts dramatically with Miss Susie Gresham—gives the young man some food and remarks on his appetite: "Probably got plenty field hand in him. Take more than a few years or generations of living in town and rubbing his head on them books to take that outta him."[52]

The invisible man is then treated to the trickster tale of one Polk Millsap, who during the Civil War reportedly absconded to Canada with a "potbellied stove full of gold dollars and silverware" entrusted to him for safekeeping by his former master. Remarking that for years "white folks around here [were] spitting mad if you called Polk's name," the raconteur concludes:

"You say 'Polk Millsap' and you was liable to git your head knocked off. Oh he was a thickheaded sonofa gun! But . . . he mighta done some good after all" (winking): "Well, maybe that's how they decided to see that young fellers like this here got a little education. Why doggone, they couldn't have 'em going round messing up the orders like Polk did, could they now? . . . . [Polk] was just naturally dumb. These boys today is too smart to git things mixed up like that."

When the invisible man declares that he has to leave, the farmer inquires, "Afraid they'll git you for breaking discipline, eh?"[53]

The invisible man's coming upon the farmers' Founder's Day celebration was drawn from Ellison's own experience; the story of Polk Millsap was based on the "bad Negro" reputation of Ellison's maternal grandfather of that name. Had Ellison retained this episode in the published text, he would have supplied a fuller frame for the dual valence of Barbee's chapel speech. The published text of *Invisible Man* wavers between appreciation of Barbee's eloquent idealism and ironic recognition of his blindness, which is imagistically linked with the lowering of the veil on the Founder's statue. The farmers' relishing in the exploits of Polk Millsap reflects their admiration for his outwitting of the master; beyond mere tricksterism, Millsap's theft of the silver delegitimates private property based on the theft of labor. The farmers' skepticism toward the "discipline" of the campus suggests their embrace of a vastly different conception of education than is promulgated through the "black rites of Horatio Alger." In both their mode of transportation and their circular dances, the farmers gathered on the campus athletic field embody a direct connection between the collectivity imposed by slavery and the "human collectivity of the future" that Ellison meditated upon in his notebooks during the early 1940s. Hastened into exile by the "discipline" of Bledsoe, the invisible man is incapable of understanding the position of these rural folk in the red line of history, the "something old and extremely meaningful" that they embody. Had Ellison left the farmers in the novel, the reader would have been invited to ponder this connection; the text's dramatic irony would have included awareness that our Candide-like hero fails to appreciate not only the capitalism-driven perfidy of his foes but also the communist (or at least communistic) proclivities of his friends.[54]

"A hook to snare errant fish": The Politics of Rhetoric

I pause before our hero's northward migration and consider the significance of the revisions that Ellison made in his text as he prepared it for publication. Reading forward from the notes and drafts, we have learned that Ellison excised multiple fictional elements—characters, scenes, and motifs accruing symbolic resonance—which, had they been retained and their patterning extended, would have supplied the novel with a substantially different political inflection. Evidently Ellison intended from the outset that the battle royal would serve as the text's "governing ritual." But the domain over which this ritual would govern was by no means predetermined.

The many references to exploitation, violence, and class struggle that Ellison excised in the course of producing the 1952 text indicate that a number of themes and character types etched in his proletarian writing remained in the front of his mind as he began work on *Invisible Man*; the carryover of Jim Napue from "The Dream" to the novel's early drafts shows that the links were at times direct. Ellison's continuing emphasis on environmental causation in his notes and early drafts did not mean that he approached his novel in the naturalistic mode: Woodridge's rant is as surreal as anything in the published text. Nor did Ellison's abidingly Marxist perspective entail a diminution of the novel's mythic dimension; if anything, the early notes and sketched passages are more explicitly preoccupied with rituals of purification and myths of hanged gods. Nor did Ellison's initial concern with the political economy of the South preclude attention to the psychological mechanisms of repression and sublimation: both Trueblood's distorted rebellion and Norton's distorted domination act out the lived dimension of monopoly. While confined for the most part to notes that were never dramatized and short passages that were never extended—the Woodridge chapter is the only omission of significant length—Ellison's original conception of the dynamics of life in the Jim Crow South was clearly an ambitious amalgam of Frazer, Freud, and Marx. But Marx's guiding hand is visible in many places.

Ellison's continuing commitment to a leftist political perspective in the early drafts of *Invisible Man* had implications not only for the novel's characters and incidents but also for its guiding tropes. Surrounded by multiple references to sharecropper organizing and state repression, the "representative anecdote" of the battle royal, repeated in Norton's exploitation of Trueblood and the situation of the crazed vets at the Golden Day, is originally anchored in political economy. There is a gruesome link between the symbolic castration of the boys at the battle royal and the "imprint of the man in the soft clay" beneath the scorched tree that the invisible man passes on his way to Trueblood's cabin. The Burkean associational cluster connecting the many references to machines in the notes and drafts also takes on a materialist dimension largely absent in the published text. The vet's assertion that the protagonist is a "perfect mechanical man" is linked, in the 1952 text, with other references to machines: the power plant built "by black hands," Trueblood's description of himself as a "cotton-pickin' machine." This trope is significantly extended in the drafts and notes: Woodridge's charge that the product of Negro miseducation is a "machine-made man"; the French doctor's disquisition on the strange desire of Americans "to be mastered . . . by machines" that is linked with the mythology of the "freedom of the market"; the "machine accident" causing the death of Norton's daughter, herself an embodiment of fetishized surplus value; even the missing firing pins on the guns in the campus ROTC office. Rhetorically conjoined in what Burke called an "equation," these narrative details constitute a trope that reinforces the commentary on the connections between capitalism and Jim Crow, economics and ideology, that is articulated more explicitly on the level of character and action. This trope would be substantially etiolated in the published text.

A student not just of Burke but of Wright, Dostoevsky, Conrad, and James, by the time he began work on *Invisible Man* Ellison was a highly conscious practitioner of the art of fiction. Acutely aware of the challenge he faced in persuading his non–African American readers to see shared, "broad" human significance in the experiences he was refracting through the "racial grain of sand," he made use of every fictional device at his disposal. Representation entailed collaboration, and collaboration entailed manipulation; as he put it many years later, images and symbols were "hook[s] to snare errant fish" among his readers, and the more subliminally they worked, the better. He was also aware that the meanings attached to individual narrative elements are fluid and situational. "When you put a detail in its proper place in an action, it gathers up associations and meanings and starts speaking to the reader's sense of significance," he remarked. "Place[d] in the right context, and at the optimum state of an action, [the detail] vibrates and becomes symbolically eloquent. . . . It's symbolic action." The reader's "sense of significance," while reliant on prior experience, does not wholly preexist engagement with the text; it is produced in the process of reading, just as the meaning of each detail is inflected in relation to every other. When Ellison declared in 1955 that, as he started to write his novel, "the symbols and their connections were known to me," he was, we have seen, only partially telling the truth. The associational clusters to which the separate symbols belonged were as susceptible to manipulation as were the people and situations he was creating and eliminating as he worked with characterization and plot. As we read forward through the invisible man's entry into the world of multiple machines, we must pay close attention to the changing politics his creator was encoding and embodying by means of symbolic action.[55]

Becoming Proletarian five

LeRoy bore the stamp of
destiny; he was "dedi-
cated and set aside."
— Ralph Ellison, notes
for "LeRoy's Journal"
episode of *Invisible Man*

Le roi est mort. Vive le
roi! (The king is dead.
Long live the king!)
— James Frazer,
The Golden Bough

Although Ellison had decided upon the key events occurring in the southern portion of his novel by the time he sent "Working Notes" to his Random
House editors in 1947, the plot of the northern portion evidently remained
sketchy in his mind. The invisible man would eventually be apprised of Bledsoe's treachery, but it would be the "secretary of the seventh trustee," and
not young Emerson, who served as messenger. The invisible man would
experience in the traumatic hospital sequence a "form of rebirth" recalling the sensation of the "charged carpet after the Battle Royal," but it is a
"severe attack of nervous indigestion," not the paint factory explosion, that
precipitates his hospitalization. He would then live not with Mary Rambo,
but with a recently migrated family whose members are "involved in matters as tragic as those he discovered in Trueblood." Less monkish than in the
1952 text, he would have "his second affair with a girl." This provisional plot
outline is supplemented in "Working Notes" by a character sketch analyzing the invisible man's situation as a migrant. The "tempo of development
[of Negro life] from the feudal-folk forms of the South to the industrial
urban forms of the North is so rapid," writes Ellison, "that from it personalities of extreme complexity emerge, personalities which in a short span
of years move from the level of the folk to that of the sophisticate." These

are "as fluid and changeable as molten metal rendered iridescent from the effect of cooling air." Later denoting the "pluralistic turbulence of the democratic process," the term "fluid" originally signified the historical dialectic whereby one mode of production transforms into another. A world of difference would accompany Ellison's migration from one meaning to the other.[1]

Much of the material contained in the notes, outlines, and drafts of the section of *Invisible Man* portraying the protagonist's experiences as a recently arrived migrant in the urban North departs dramatically from the plan laid out in "Working Notes"; after undergoing extensive revision, a good deal ended up being jettisoned. Ellison continued to map the invisible man's growth and development as a daimon hero out of the pages of the Cambridge School. One outline aligns the arc of "purpose-passion-perception" within this section with "puberty-death-rebirth" and the four seasons. At the same time, Ellison stressed to himself the typicality of the invisible man's life as a migrant wrenched from the preindividuality of life in the Jim Crow South and "plunge[d] into the reality of [the] city," ranging from the "churches, bars, tea pads, dance halls, [and] middle class homes" of Harlem to "[political] organization . . . and the depression C.P." As the invisible man "step[s] from feudalism over to capitalism," noted Ellison, he "faces [the] possibility of personality disorganization [and] . . . brutalization," as well as a "new moral orientation." Ellison wondered, "How has [the] Negro dealt with [the] problem of individuality as he stands in [a] marginal position between preindividuality and individuality, between the theories of the American Creed and the realities of Jim Crow practices? . . . His contact with labor a process of discovery of new social identity." History supplied the matrix of rebirth: "The experience of Depression and the War represents the slow painful cutting of the umbilical chord releasing him into the fearful world of individuality." Evidently Wright's *Twelve Million Black Voices* and Drake and Cayton's *Black Metropolis* were as much on Ellison's mind as Raglan's *The Hero*.[2]

A useful register to the conception of Harlem guiding this section of *Invisible Man* is Ellison's essay "Harlem Is Nowhere" (1948), which details the challenges facing the new LaFargue Clinic, a center providing "psychotherapy for the underprivileged" directed by the radical psychiatrist Frederick Wertham. Observing that Harlem, "overcrowded and exploited politically and economically, . . . is the scene and symbol of the Negro's perpetual alienation in the land of his birth," Ellison stresses that the "surreal fantasies acted out upon the streets [arise from a] . . . vast process of change that has swept [American Negroes] from slavery to the condition of industrial

man." Harlem is both "the scene of the folk-Negro's death agony . . . and the
setting of his transcendence. Here it is possible for talented youths to leap
through the development of decades in a brief twenty years, while beside
them white-haired adults crawl in the feudal darkness of their childhood."
While sharing in "those conflicts created in modern man by a revolutionary
world," the Negro, "barred from participating in the main institutional life of
society," is unable to "participate fully in the therapy which the white American achieves through patriotic ceremonies and by identifying with American
wealth and power." Hence the "constant threat of chaos . . . the irrational,
incalculable forces that hover about the edges of human life like cosmic destruction lurking within an atomic stockpile." As he probes the social psychology of Harlem, Ellison acknowledges its residents' existential experience of chaos while grounding the surreal in a Marxist mode of production
narrative. The possibility for "transcendence" is both individual and social,
moreover, linked to the "revolutionary" nature of the postwar world. While
Ellison would many years later compare his own entry into Harlem with the
exploratory activity of a "pioneer," this earlier account places the experience
of migration in world-historical perspective.[3]

Before we join the invisible man as he enters this revolutionary world edged
by the threat of chaos, a brief comment on "purpose-passion-perception," the
Aristotelian structure theorized by Burke as the basis for narrative dialectics.
Ellison's notes to *Invisible Man* are replete with references to this tripartite
plan, which he consciously deployed to structure not only individual chapters
and the novel's overall arc, but also the pattern shaping each of the novel's
three major sections. Originally designated "Book I: College," "Book II: The
City of Invisibility," and "Book III: Political Life," these sections were the re-
spective correlates of the major stages of purpose, passion, and perception in
the invisible man's odyssey from naïveté to wisdom. Although Ellison's commentaries after 1952 tended to describe this structure in purely formal terms,
his original conception of these cycles within cycles linked the "purpose-
passion-perception" of the protagonist's experience with historical cycles of
thesis-antithesis-synthesis. The designation of one nodal point or another as
the site of transition from one phase to another was hardly a purely formal
matter: the various insights that the protagonist attains, as well as the developments that produce these moments of realization, describe a trajectory
that is simultaneously personal, political, and historical.[4]

Ellison's steadfast commitment to patterning his text along the lines of
"purpose-passion-perception" bears note because he not only revised, re-
ordered, and rejected much of the material originally intended for inclusion

in the New York section of *Invisible Man* but also ended up shifting the nodal point where the second section ends and the third begins in the novel's overall arc. In early drafts "Book II: The City of Invisibility" comprises a number of episodes that terminate with the invisible man's meeting with young Emerson; "Book III: Political Life" begins with the protagonist's appearance on Mary Rambo's threshold. Rather than constituting a site of folkish nurturance essentially sealed off from the struggle going on in Harlem's streets, Mary's apartment—and its inhabitants—provide access simultaneously to politics and perception. The correspondence of "The City of Invisibility" with the stage of passion is equally significant, since it is the invisible man's experiences as a migrant among other migrants that prepare him for "The Book of Politics"; far more than in the 1952 text, proletarianization is key to the protagonist's development. While Ellison had abandoned the project of writing a proletarian novel by the time he sent his hero into northern exile, the themes and tropes of his earlier fiction continued to shape his creative process.

"Presided over by a group of very old men":
New York Arrival and Men's House

In the published version of *Invisible Man* the protagonist's departure from the South is rapid, underlining the abruptness of the transition from country to city. The vet, also banished for telling too much truth, winks at him as they both board the bus. Prophesying that the protagonist will soon be dancing with white women, the vet advises, "Be your own father, young man. And remember, the world is possibility if only you'll discover it" (156). Soon, however, the vet is forgotten; the young man has arrived in the city, ridden in the subway close to a white woman, witnessed a black policemen in Harlem directing cars driven by whites, had his first view of Ras the Exhorter, and found himself a room at Men's House.

In an earlier draft the specter of the state looms over the invisible man's departure from the South. On the bus the vet comments on a roadside chain gang; possibility is apparently constrained by necessity. After the older man leaves the narrator recalls, "I had never seen such a man before—or since. And I'm not altogether sure that I didn't dream him. Since I've been invisible I've written the government in an effort to find him, for I believe there was much more to him than I could then understand." As the bus approaches New York the invisible man has a strangely cinematic dream in which he imagines himself an undercover FBI agent. He fools his Peter Lorre–like antagonist by rolling his eyes and acting like Stepin Fetchit; just as his partner, fatally shot, asks him to report to J. Edgar Hoover, the protagonist awakens from his slapstick nightmare. While in his fantasy the invisible man is incorporated into rather than targeted by the state's surveillance apparatus, the surfacing of the FBI from his political unconscious suggests an awareness of governmental authority that would be utterly implausible in the protagonist of the 1952 text. However faintly, this young man retains features of Jim Napue and Gann Wilson, whose encounters with the disciplinary regime of the state were anything but cartoonish.[5]

In the 1952 text Ellison focuses his ironic commentary on the inhabitants of Men's House in the scene midway through the novel where, after learning from young Emerson of Bledsoe's betrayal, the protagonist contemplates his fellow residents with newfound contempt: "[They are] still caught up in the illusions that had just been boomeranged out of my head." They are, he thinks "a group of janitors and messengers who spent most of their wages on clothing such as was fashionable among Wall Street brokers . . . who never read the financial pages though they purchased the Wall Street Journal religiously and carried it beneath the left elbow" (256–57). Hallucinating that a prominent Baptist preacher is the nefarious college president, the invisible man dumps on the minister's head the foul contents of a spittoon, an act that gets him expelled from the building for the next ninety-nine years; a porter jokes, "You really baptized ole Rev!" (258). Although in the light of his recent encounter with young Emerson the young man's enraged rechristening of "ole Rev" is psychologically plausible, his sudden insight into the pretensions of the inhabitants of Men's House, who have barely been described up to this point, rings somewhat false. Something is missing.[6]

What is missing is supplied in earlier drafts, where the critique of Men's House as a site of generational betrayal is integrated into a more fully elaborated anatomy of the failings of the aspiring Negro middle class. Explicitly identifying the building as the Harlem YMCA—where Ellison himself first stayed upon his arrival in New York in the summer of 1936—the narrator describes it as "the tallest building in the community; the place where almost all the college men stopped upon coming to New York. . . . A convenient place to live with barbershop, restaurant, tailor and shoe repair shops; a chapel, lodge rooms, swimming pool and gymn; many indeed, most of community efforts not confined to churches took place here. . . . [It was] presided over by a group of very old men." The narrator recalls in another draft that the Y "was the stopping place of most important men when visiting N.Y. and the permanent home of a great many unmarried ones"; the common shower, he notes, was the most popular place for sexual trysting. At Men's House the protagonist meets up with Pemberton, a former student from the college, who is mesmerized by the crude boasting of the older residents, one of whom claims to get stock market tips from his white lover, the wife of a Wall Street financier. The passage describing the speech and accoutrements of the inhabitants of Men's House—which Ellison was to rewrite and reposition many times—first appears at the very beginning of the New York section of the novel; there is no reference yet to the "boomeranging" of illusions. When the invisible man later "baptize[s] ole Rev," his anger at the black bourgeoisie, or more precisely, its wannabe imitators, has been festering for a long time.[7]

Ellison's emphasis on the failure of the Y's older inhabitants to furnish the younger ones with meaningful models of leadership accounts for his decision to designate it "Men's House." As the Marxist classicist George Thomson pointed out in *Aeschylus and Athens*—a study locating myth, ritual, and ancient Greek tragedy in historical materialist context that Ellison perused with interest during his days at the League of American Writers—Men's House was

> usually the largest building in a tribal settlement. It belongs in common to all the villagers; it serves as a council chamber or town hall, as a guest-house for strangers, and as the sleeping resort of the men. . . . When marriage and the exclusive possession of a woman do not follow immediately upon initiation into the tribe, the institution of the Men's House becomes an effective restraint upon the sexual proclivities of the unmarried youth. It then serves as a club-house for the bachelors.

It was at the Men's House that, in the Greece of clan and tribal society, youths undergoing initiation into manhood were guided through rituals of purification, renaming, and rebirth by their elders. In Harlem's Men's House, by contrast, initiation consists in the inculcation of habits of slavish imitation of white elites—even, on occasion, confirmation of membership in the "lady of the races." The members of the aspiring Negro middle class gathered at the Harlem Y join the growing cluster of characters thematizing the misleadership of the young by the old. Ellison's allusion to the rituals of tribal Greek society thus serves not to collapse history into myth, but to highlight the difference between the gendered social relations in preclass and class society.[8]

As he wrote and rewrote the New York section of his novel Ellison contemplated having the invisible man undergo a range of initiations at Men's

House. In one version the young man shares Pemberton's illusions: "I dreamed of becoming rich . . . through guile and cunning. . . . I dreamed at first of inventions that would secure me a fortune. Then I dreamed of developing a foolproof system for beating the numbers and the horses. . . . But those were too flimsy to occupy me for long . . . They contained no women and no richness of depth." In another version he continues to frequent Men's House even after he has moved out—"into squalor in which Negroes dwell, a slum"—and "[hears] boys discussing [Spain] on various levels of political maturity." The Spanish Civil War, a preoccupation of the leftist heroes of Ellison's early fiction, indeed of Ellison himself, might also absorb the invisible man. In still another variant, while staying at the Y the young man "reads revolutionary literature by accident. Wants to become like Chinese Terrorists, dreams of throwing bombs in Senate at Bilbo, Rankin, instead assaults whites on subways. Throws brick into car of Negro leader." Suggesting that the young man may have absorbed the vet's "terrorist" inclinations— and recalling the young students of Bard who, in "The Initiation," assassinate the southern politician—these actions, whether fantasized or real, further display the invisible man's politicization. They also suggest his kinship with his creator, who, soon after his arrival at the Harlem Y, was introduced by Langston Hughes to Malraux's *Man's Fate*, in which a central character is in fact a Chinese terrorist. Men's House would have exposed the young protagonist not only to middle-class misleadership but also to antifascism and international revolution. He would not need to meet the Brotherhood in order to start thinking about leftist politics.[9]

The invisible man also does not need to meet the Brotherhood to realize that a "death on the city pavements" awaits migrants unable to adjust to the whirl of urban life. Unable to sleep one night at Men's House because of the digestive problems accompanying his transition from south to north, he imagines that if his parents made the trip to New York they would be "simply knocked off their feet by the bigness of the city. . . . It would be like a trip to the moon." He compares his parents' generation with his own: "Their kind were dying off and we were taking their places." His grandfather, though "grumbling" and "dissatisfied," would have been better able to "take it in stride." Reflecting that he never really knew the old man, he falls asleep, reverting in a dream to a painful memory in which his grandfather finds a nest of baby sparrows that have been washed to the ground in a storm. The old man declares that the birds "carry message[s] to white folks about Negroes" and crushes them with a brick. The dream-memory turns into a nightmare as the invisible man feels himself slammed by the brick; he awakens and vomits. While demonstrating the old man's violent hatred of whites, the nightmare also displays his superstitious preindividuality; he is one of the "white haired adults crawl[ing] in the feudal darkness of their childhood" whom Ellison describes in "Harlem Is Nowhere." The invisible man has moved, indeed leaped into the world of modernity; he can't go home again, nor, at least at this point, can memories of the folk sustain him in the brave new world. Nor can the old man, if he is to emerge in the epilogue as a carrier of the truth of democracy, be portrayed as a killer of helpless baby birds. The nightmare at Men's House would have to go.[10]

"Sap from the hanging pine": The Paint Factory

Although in the 1952 text the episode at Liberty Paints follows the invisible man's encounter with young Emerson, who recommends him for the job, Ellison originally portrayed the young man's stint in the paint factory as one of several short-term jobs that he takes while still waiting to hear from his prospective Wall Street employers. He is taken to the factory by an acquaintance from Men's House—in some versions by Pemberton, in others by Cato, another graduate of the college who proudly testifies to Bledsoe's close relationship with the factory's owner and is not disquieted by the knowledge that he is helping to break the union. Jotting in the margin, "Black makes white whiter; black makes white dry (Collaboration and conspiracy)," Ellison evidently had in mind from the outset the trenchant symbolism of Optic White, which achieves its perfect whiteness by incorporating a touch of blackness. In all versions of the text Optic White has been used to whitewash the campus and, years before, the Golden Day and the sharecropper cabins nearby, but Ellison considered different names for the company: "Lumiere Paints" and "Tottle's (the patriotic paint)." He also specified the site and date of the planned repainting in Washington: the Department of Labor on Decoration Day. Decoration Day, the original name of Memorial Day, paid tribute to the northern victory in the Civil War; the Department of Labor building supplied the site of Depression-era Labor Secretary Frances Perkins's attempts to reconcile capital with labor, especially the anticommunist leadership of the AFL. Kimbro, the invisible man's irascible boss at Liberty Paints, initially curses not only the bungling workers in his lab but also the "bastards" and "fatasses in Washington" who demand the rush job. Ellison originally specified connections among the various modes of whitewash that are less explicitly conveyed in the 1952 text.[11]

Despite Ellison's evident pleasure in riffing on the whiteness of Optic

White, the paint factory episode does not originally precipitate the invisible man's hospital stay and subsequent sojourn with Mary Rambo. Although he learns that an unnamed elderly Negro, complete with handkerchief-bound head, works in a key position at the plant, this forerunner of Lucius Brockway does not actually appear. Nor does the invisible man come across the union meeting in the locker room or descend into the factory's basement. Instead, fired at the end of the day for having botched his batch of paints, he returns to Men's House. The episode simply figures as the first in a series of failed attempts by the invisible man to find work while he awaits word from his saviors on Wall Street.[12]

Later versions of the paint factory episode, which include Brockway and the union meeting and end in the explosion, differ from the published novel in some key details. While in the 1952 text it appears that some young Negro workers have joined the union, a development bemoaned by Brockway, Ellison earlier noted, "Don't forget to stress the scabbing element in his being hired"; in fact a ruckus occurs outside the personnel office where the invisible man is being signed up. Ellison also sharpened the debate among the unionists in the locker room. The workers' contempt for antiunion "finks" and anger at their bosses are more pronounced; the union leader who chairs the meeting refers to the "class struggle" rather than the "labor movement." When the workers vote on whether or not to permit the new Negro worker to join the union if he passes muster, however, they vote not "Aye," as in the published text, but "Nay." Ellison stresses not only the use of black workers as scabs but also the self-destructive racism of AFL craft unionism; we are reminded that the only unions with which Ellison ever affiliated himself were the Communist-led American Writers Union and the National Maritime Union.[13]

Brockway, the exemplar of invisible black labor inhabiting the basement of American industry, in the 1952 text wears "dirty overalls" and a "striped engineer's cap" but barely reaches five feet. In drafts he is variously "hardly four feet tall" or "over six feet tall." His complexion, unspecified in the final version, is "unbelievably black." The proud formulator of the slogan "If it's Optic White, it's the right white," he is in one draft explicitly associated with the entire "childhood jingle" that runs through the protagonist's mind: *"If you black / Stand back / If you brown / Hang a round / But if you white / You right."* The proud originator of the "good strong base" of brown crystals that give Optic White its glorious whiteness, Brockway in another draft heaves enormous brown clumps of pine residue into a machine that is "big enough to kill a man." The legend of the railway worker John Henry is obliquely invoked, but Lucius Brockway is no John Henry; in his satisfied awareness that African Americans are *"the machines inside the machine"* and his alignment with white supremacy, he embodies not proletarian heroism but its negation. Ellison's notes stress that Brockway embodies the "older generation" that "threatens" and "attacks" the invisible man but ultimately "is weak"; he is one more elder who fails to supply a model for the young, one of the "black straw-bosses" whom Wright described in *Twelve Million Black Voices* as being strategically positioned to control black workers and "tell [them] what to do."[14]

In the context of Brockway's still more explicit collusion with white supremacy in the novel's early drafts, the "familiar" smell the invisible man discerns in the basement fumes assumes ominous implications. While in the published text this smell is simply that of the pine used to make turpentine, in an early draft the invisible man thinks, "It smelled like sap from the Hanging Pine." When the machines explode, the invisible man feels himself

> falling so swiftly or so swiftly falling into a suspension with such a weight upon one's middle, or floating in anything so dense, be buoyant in anything so buoyantless, for it was hard, it was steel or stone or lost, strayed in the piney woods at midnight after rain and the earth sweating blackness, steaming thick, the pain in the heel where the rusty nail had puncturing while soaked, must be, whole body all but eyes, in turpentine smell, that flowed one, floated one, steel and stone and aching bone past buildings gleaming optic whitely on a campus hill, moon-white, like glue the blackness gloating goolyly past a constellation of glum faces "as though the sky had shut its eyes."

The details buried in this nightmarish vision—a body soaked in turpentine, a heel punctured by a nail, the moonlit campus, the crowd of melancholy onlookers—connect the northern paint factory with southern racial violence; they particularly invoke the hanging tree that set the young man on the road to Trueblood's cabin and later haunted him during his moonlit walk. The college that sends young men to scab in northern industry and abets the suppression of sharecropper organizing is covered with the same whitewash as the Department of Labor on the one hand and a sharecropper's cabin on the other. The pine trees that supply the turpentine at the base of the paint not only mask the blackness within whiteness but also furnish the means to lynching; the invisible man's olfactory nerves register a political unconscious that his conscious mind cannot admit.[15]

In this context the insertion into the protagonist's hallucination of a phrase from Homer Barbee's sermon, "as though the sky had shut its eyes," takes on an ominous resonance. For Barbee utters these words as he re-calls the train trip with the dying Leader; looking out the window, he "saw the looming great North Star and lost it, as though the sky had shut its eye" (127). Barbee's later blindness enacts his loss of the vision of freedom; the campus buildings that gleam "optic whitely" in the background of the southern lynching tree are implicated in the invisible man's current crisis in the world of the machine. Where in the 1952 text the surreal factory explo-sion portrays a reified and chaotic encounter between man and machine, in the earlier drafts the exploitive social relations underpinning the relation of north to south and capital to labor, as well as their deathly consequences, are kept to the fore. Surrealism affords access to a social totality that can be repressed for only so long.

"Some anti-human, labor-saving device": "Wheelchair"

In the 1952 text of *Invisible Man* the protagonist learns about Bledsoe's Bel-lerophontic letter soon after he arrives in New York; he endures the hardship of unemployment only after he has spent several weeks under Mary's roof. Originally, however, he is shown to be increasingly lost, hungry, and desper-ate while, still living at Men's House, he takes a series of short-term jobs. He is aware of not being alone in his Depression-era poverty: "There were many evictions taking place and much protest over them," recalls the nar-rator. "Black and white crowds battled the police, replacing furniture after it was set out upon the street. There was also much marching and soap-box speechmaking which I listened to but barely heard." Feeling himself "a better speaker than most," he "paid them little heed" and "preferred taking long walks back and forth across the many bridges" where he orates to the empty air. Policemen suspect him of being suicidal since "many were jump-ing from bridges in those days"; he stops visiting the bridges but engages in colloquy with an ironic inner voice that continually asks who he is and what he is doing. He is in a state of "lostness."[16]

Ellison's jottings stress the typicality of his protagonist's situation. Re-minding himself, "Keep it psychological! And philosophical," Ellison wrote, "He must undergo a conversion of disillusionment and during that period he wanders within the formless, institutionless jungle, his personality be-coming as changeable as the environment is plastic, and shapeless." He re-minded himself that if his character "gets past [this state of disorganization] then all will be smooth sailing." The invisible man's disorientation seems to have reflected that of his creator. "It shouldn't be difficult," scribbled Ellison. "But it is. I find I look at a blank sheet of papper [sic] day after day. . . . The job is to keep trying."[17]

As he kept trying Ellison sent his protagonist out on other jobs. In an episode titled "Wheelchair," variously positioned early or late in the job search, the invisible man takes a one-day job as a dishwasher for a banquet held at an East Side mansion owned by a wealthy woman philanthropist who is confined to a wheelchair. The source of the family's wealth is not revealed, but Ellison suggests that it derives from the manufacture of "some anti-human, labor-saving device." The job placement desk at Men's House informs him that the woman, descended from "revolutionary stock on both sides," had fallen from her horse years before, ended her engagement, and, mourning the death of her idealized father, turned to philanthropy, especially in relation to Negroes. (In versions where "Wheelchair" follows the visit to Emerson, the invisible man is originally suspicious of the "neatly folded assignment slip," since "no sealed or folded reading matter escaped my careful scrutiny.") Upon arriving at the mansion the young man receives mixed signals. There is no servants' entrance, and the icy-toned butler tells him, "We are all human beings." But after working double the job for which he was hired—he mops the ballroom floor besides busting dish suds—he is scantily fed and discovers only $1.50 in his pay envelope; he explodes in angry mirth.[18]

Trying to find the exit he wanders past an equestrian portrait of the "founder of the line," a "fat man in a powdered wig," and onto the flower-covered terrace, where he meets his employer. She mistakes his ironic laughter for Negro cheerfulness; tossing the money onto her lap, on an impulse he grabs the wheelchair and propels her out of the garden and down the hill toward the river; the traffic cop greets the woman but ignores the protagonist: "Invisible, I thought. Invisible." A narcissistic and guilt-ridden liberal, she parallels her status as a cripple with his as a Negro and claims that his brusqueness is giving her a "lesson in humility." Denouncing her as a "hypocritical hypochondriac" and "invalid invalid," the invisible man dares her to confess her fraudulence by getting up and walking. Calling "Father, Father!" she in fact rises from her chair and stumbles toward him, crying out her thanks. Ellison contemplated several possible endings to the episode. The invisible man might return the woman to the mansion without incident. He might escape back to Harlem by subway but get expelled from Men's House for his outrageous behavior on the job. He might simply return to Mary's (where, in some variants, he already lives). Most dramatically he might duck the blows of a policeman and jump into the East River, to be rescued by a tugboat captain named, of all things, Jack. Ellison's imagination was running as wildly as the invisible man himself.[19]

Ellison worked and reworked the tragicomic "Wheelchair" episode with the model of Greek drama in mind. His notes map out a trajectory from *agon* to *peripeteia* in which the invisible man is explicitly assigned the role of the *sparagmos*, and his emotional exploitation by the "wealthy cripple" is paralleled with the "governing ritual" of the battle royal. "Wheelchair" extends the critique of philanthropy as a form of ruling-class neurotic displacement earlier articulated in the relationship between Trueblood and Norton; the woman's therapeutic use of the invisible man as an instrument for release from her obsession recapitulates Norton's use of Trueblood as a surrogate for his own inadmissible longings. With her hysterical paralysis signaling her repressed desire for (or perhaps fear of) her idealized father, and her sublimation of her sex drive desire as philanthropy, Ellison's "wealthy cripple" comes straight out of the pages of Freud.[20]

But "Wheelchair" displays the ideological connections among sexual repression, guilty liberalism, white supremacy, and the imperatives of class rule. The woman's repressed sexual desire for her father—she is Norton's adult daughter, surviving and reciprocating his lust—reiterates the link between incest and monopoly capital. Her blue-blooded connection with the founding fathers and policy of admitting servants through the front door do nothing to mitigate the paltry wages she pays; her pretensions to democracy render her patrician liberalism all the more repellent. Her insistence that her physical disability gives her privileged understanding of her employee's racial situation equates being Negro with being crippled and renders invisible the particularity of his experience. The fact that her family's fortune has been created through the production of "some anti-human, labor-saving device" not only recalls Norton's daughter's death by a "machine accident" but also links her wealth with the job-destroying mechanisms that brought on the death of John Henry. In her ignorance of the material sources of her comfort and leisure, the "wealthy cripple" embodies the Jamesian "sensibility floundering in its own vomit"; the text's political allegory addresses not only the material practice of exploitation but also its ideological legitimation.[21]

"I was dematerialized": "Uncle Charles"

In "Uncle Charles," a much-rewritten and often relocated episode evidently composed early in the creation of *Invisible Man*, Ellison again featured a humiliating interaction between a Negro worker and a liberal white boss who bends the rules of racial interaction while maintaining a position of class power. In most versions the narration consists of a flashback to the invisible man's teenage years (Tatlock is mentioned), when on the Fourth of July he accompanied his uncle Charles on a country club waiting job; the host is young Mr. Kinkaid, the northern-educated son of an established club member. Quoting Booker T. Washington, Uncle Charles instructs his nephew that his goal is to make money; the boy feels that he is "being initiated into mysteries which [he] had never suspected." "Priestlike" in his ritual gestures, Uncle Charles has mastered the performance of blackness; like Babo in "Benito Cereno," he is an "actor . . . who helps the illusion along," taking care to dress in black and white clothing stressing at once the inseparability and the separation of white masters and Negro servants. The nephew is appalled at the transformation Charles undergoes at work: "At home he spoke a beautiful English, but now he spoke in a thick dialect; his feet, of which he was very vain, were fine and slender, but now he shuffled as though his arches were broken. Instead of the deep mellowness of his voice, I now heard him whining several registers higher in the most obsequious intonation."[22]

In full view of the young Mr. Kinkaid, Uncle Charles—the youth hallucinates that he wears the "dark red lipstick . . . of a black-face comedian"—drinks heartily from his host's cocktail glass. To see the old Negro waiter steal alcohol, Uncle Charles informs the boy, will flatter the employer, not anger him. But the strategy boomerangs: Kinkaid, fearing that his northern guests will think him an "an unreconstructed slave driver," publicly chastises the grinning old man, whose "teeth [reflect] the red white and blue lights." Devastated, Charles mutters, "Who would have thought that going north would spoil a good southern boy like that." The invisible man's iconoclastic new alter ego whispers to him that the liberal host was not a humanist but a sadist; by ritually castrating the old man in front of the boy, to him just "another pair of black hands," Kinkaid rendered them both invisible. The narrator concludes, "I was dematerialized, float[ing] off into the smoke that hung like a haze above the red-white-and-blue decorations."[23]

Ellison considered various ways to work Uncle Charles's story into the novel. One possibility was that the elderly waiter was not the protagonist's uncle, but an inhabitant of Men's House named Charles Dupré whom the narrator assists on another one-day job. Another version of this material, titled "Uncle Charles and the Humanistic Host," eliminates the narrator's internal colloquy, cancels any explicit links with the novel, and is essentially a free-standing short story. Other versions feature the invisible man's internal division during his period of "lostness" and are prefaced by the heading "Book II, No. 3: Perception," indicating that the invisible man's painful memory of his uncle's humiliation was to supply the final stage of the tripartite arc of "The City of Invisibility" and prepare the way for "Book III, Political Life." Ellison scribbled in the margin to this episode, "the author of my birth and my death"; originally it would be neither the conversation with Emerson nor the hospital episode, but instead the act of recalling Uncle Charles's symbolic castration, that motivates the invisible man's rebirth as questioner.[24]

"I have [not] seen black hands": Eliminating "Wheelchair" and "Uncle Charles"

Why did Ellison decide to eliminate from the novel's final version the chapters dealing with the rich woman in a wheelchair and Uncle Charles? There is admittedly a degree of repetition and overlap in the omitted episodes, which play out the battle royal's "representative anecdote" of the Negro male as scapegoat. "Wheelchair," with its exposé of ruling-class sexual corruption and philanthropic hypocrisy, elaborates on the portrait of Norton as a "sow[er of] corruption." "Uncle Charles," with its display of verbal ritual castration, re-creates the claustrophobia and barely disguised sexual sadism of the smoker scene. The analogous forms of control exercised by the "humanistic host," the "wealthy cripple," Norton, and the town fathers stress the continuity between southern racists openly endorsing the ethics of Jim Crow and northern-educated liberals who follow an updated set of rules. Perhaps Ellison concluded that "Wheelchair" and "Uncle Charles" were redundant.

What "Wheelchair" and "Uncle Charles" add to the novel's congruent portraits of the humiliation of Negroes by powerful whites, however, is a fuller depiction of the centrality of the exploitation of labor to the dynamics of American racism. The dishwasher and the waiter perform tasks that are at once ideological—they confirm their employers' sense of the naturalness of social hierarchy—and material: if unable to purchase these servants' labor, the employers would have to wash the dishes, mop the floors, and obtain the food and drink themselves. The $1.50 paid to the invisible man for more than eight hours' labor reveals the closeness of wage slavery to chattel slavery; Uncle Charles's ostentatiously subservient black hands recall the anonymous black hands that built the power plant droning in the background as Norton listens to Trueblood. The labor of the sharecropper, the paint factory worker, the dishwasher, and the waiter together constitute the means by which capital is accumulated and consumed, whether by the "Lords of the Land" or the "Bosses of the Buildings," as Wright wrote in *Twelve Million Black Voices*. That these workers are not-seen by those who benefit from their expenditures of energy, a situation made explicit by the protagonist's realization that he is invisible and has dematerialized, expands the meaning of invisibility. The specifically racist invisibility of the black worker contributes to the more general fetishization of the products of all labor in a capitalist society. In its early drafts *Invisible Man* is a novelistic counterpart to Wright's proletarian poem "I Have Seen Black Hands," in which the visibility of all the activities undertaken by the hands of African Americans, whether reproducing labor power, laboring, or struggling to appropriate the products of their labor, is made manifest. Rather than detracting from the existential dimension of invisibility, this material grounding of the phenomenon of being not-seen enhances the urgency of the protagonist's need to rebel and prepares the way for "Book III, the Book of Politics."[25]

Perhaps Ellison eliminated "Wheelchair" because its portrayal of ruling-class sexual guilt was redundant with the characterization of Norton. But there was another reason why Uncle Charles would have to be excised from the novel's final draft. Especially when juxtaposed with Woodridge and other male characters more fully etched in the drafts, from Bledsoe and Brockway to the Wall Street wannabes at Men's House, Uncle Charles reconfigures the cluster of older African American men upon whose shoulders the mantle of leadership might rest. Yet his humiliation graphically illustrates the limits of trickster subversion through role-playing; the grandfather's recommended strategy of "overcom[ing] them with yesses" has not made Charles into a "spy in the enemy's country" or initiated the young man into the mysteries of adulthood. It has instead boomeranged, for uncle and nephew alike. When the humiliation of the Washington-quoting Uncle Charles is added to the college president's complicity in the death of the nameless sharecropper, Brockway's pathetic antithesis to John Henry, and the failed manhood (according to Ellison's sexual calculus) of Woodridge and the inhabitants of Men's House, the novel's character system suggests anything but an affirmation of Washingtonian yessing as a means to survival. If the narrator's grandfather is to emerge in the epilogue as the carrier of affirmative wisdom, not only does his crushing of the sparrows have to be excised, but his parallelism with Charles, the quintessential Uncle Tom, needs to be removed from view.

Accompanying the intensified critique of black misleadership in the opening New York chapters is an imagistic cluster thematizing the text's satirical commentary on American patriotism. In the 1952 text the ironic reach of this trope is limited: the American flag is tattooed on a white dancer's belly; Norton resembles Thomas Jefferson; Liberty Paints whitewashes the nation's capital. The drafts add images that significantly extend the Burkean equation: the bunting at the Fourth of July celebration where Uncle Charles is stripped of his manhood; the portrait of the wheelchair-bound philanthropist's bewigged ruling-class ancestor; Optic White's association with the betrayal of Decoration Day, labor-capital class collaboration, and the pine-harvesting economy that produces lynch violence. In its original conception, the rhetoric of symbolic action in *Invisible Man*, conveyed through a tightly woven set of tropes and a carefully aligned character system, conveys a profoundly antipatriotic discourse. As Ellison moved toward the final draft of *Invisible Man*, these materials would be either entirely occluded or substantially etiolated in their rhetorical range.[26]

"A tabloid representing the U.S. flag": Peter Wheatstraw

While Ellison considered situating the invisible man's encounter with young Emerson at various points in *Invisible Man*, in all versions of the text he meets up with Peter Wheatstraw, the "blueprint man," on the same day he meets his destiny on Wall Street. The name chosen by Ellison's street peddler refers, notes Steven Tracy, to "the popular St. Louis blues musician William Bunch, who under the name 'Peetie Wheatstraw' produced some 164 recordings between 1930 and his death in 1941. Calling himself the 'Devil's Son-in-Law' and the 'High Sheriff from Hell,' Wheatstraw was a powerful outlaw figure, a trickster, one who both embraces and transcends his association with the devil because the devil is an authority figure to be resisted." In one draft the peddler's whistling makes the young man wonder, "Whom had I known who had gone whistling like that, walking loose-jointed down the alleys . . . with a gunny sack across his shoulder, filled with brass? It was my cousin Preston who had been caught and jailed and my father had cursed and my mother had cried. Preston had never stopped whistling, though it was the whistle chords that gave him away." Wheatstraw the folk outlaw evokes the memory of a cousin admired for both his cool demeanor and his disrespect for private property; the silver-appropriating Poke Millsap and Leo Gurley's bank-robbing "Sweet-the-Monkey" also come to mind. Wheatstraw's wordplay about the woman with "feet like a monkey / legs like a frog" echoes the blues song "Boogie Woogie," recorded in 1936 by Jimmy Rushing, that Slick hears in the poolroom as he gambles for the money to pay for his wife's medical care. Evidently Ellison associated the vernacular riffing of his brash street peddler with at once the harsher and the more creative features of migrant life.[27]

Besides exhibiting a verbal wizardry that puts the invisible man's muted speech to shame, Wheatstraw in all versions of the episode signifies on the notions of "blueprint" and "plan." He remarks, "Folks is always making plans and changing them"; when the young man replies, "You have to stick to the plan," Wheatstraw ripostes, "You kinda young, daddy-o" (175). Wheatstraw's ambiguous speech has fed a small critical mill. Do his enigmatic words allude to specific texts, such as Wright's literary manifesto of 1938 about the aims of black proletarian literature, or Myrdal's sociological tract? Do they refer to a blues identity that defies blueprinting? Might his words glance, self-reflexively, at Ellison's cavalier attitude toward his own blueprint in "Working Notes"? Or might they gesture more portentously toward the superiority of vernacular folk culture to any and all attempts at foundational reasoning, whether the countinghouse logic of Norton or the revolutionary scientism of the Brotherhood? Ellison's comment in 1974 that Wheatstraw is a "kind of messenger, such as you get in Greek tragedy[,] who . . . reminds the hero in an ambiguous way of the time of day or the tonality that experience is turning into" suggests Ellison's post-1952 archetypal standpoint but yields few interpretive clues.[28]

Wheatstraw's riddling manner leaves meaning open, but a draft of the episode suggests an early guide. The invisible man notices on the top of the peddler's pile of "abandoned plans" the "cover of the magazine section of [a] tabloid representing the U.S. flag." The icon signifying the ideals presumably laid out when the nation was founded—now the emblem of a sensationalist newspaper—points to what has been relinquished and embeds itself in the text's accreting antipatriotic associative cluster. In pointing up the young man's naïveté about "stick[ing] to the plan," the iconoclastic Wheatstraw suggests the advisability of jettisoning confidence in American democracy. As a "messenger" of this view, Wheatstraw resembles not so much a figure from Greek tragedy as Ellison's FWP interviewee Eli Luster, who informed his young interlocutor, initially a naïf like the invisible man, that God "step[ped] in" to sink the *Titanic* because it carried "all big rich folks." But "God's time is coming," predicted Luster, when "won't be no men down in Washington making fifty thousand dollars a week and folks cain't hardly make eighteen dollars a month. Everybody'll be equal, in God's time. Won't be no old man Rockefeller, no suh!" As Jerry Watts has pointed out, after *Invisible Man* Ellison's celebration of folklore as indicative of "black American creative endurance and American possibility" was often accompanied by

only a "perfunctory mention of the dire plight of many blacks." The tabloid
American flag on the junkman's wagon suggests Ellison's earlier awareness
of the limits to discursive resistance from behind the veil: Wheatstraw may
signify upon the ever-changing nature of blueprints, but American democracy is one blueprint that has been tossed into the trash.[29]

"Revelation and revolution": Emerson and Wall Street

Once Ellison decided that it would be the son of the Wall Street mogul Emerson who delivers to the invisible man the news of Bledsoe's treachery, the
scene assumed its key components: the Statue of Liberty barely visible in the
fog; the portraits of the "Kings of the Earth" (181); the world map with pins
attached by ribbons to samples of extracted products; the cage full of shriek-
ing exotic birds; the copy of *Totem and Taboo* on young Emerson's desk; the
invitation to visit the Club Calamus; the revelation of Bledsoe's letter; and
the invisible man's realization that, like "poor Robin," he has been "picked
. . . clean" (191). Ellison's additions and subtractions were relatively minor.
The young millionaire's reference to himself as "Huckleberry" and to the invisible man as Jim—Ellison's joking allusion to Leslie Fiedler's famous reading of Twain's novel as a tale of homosexual friendship (1948)—was added
only after Ellison had come across Fiedler's essay. The invisible man initially
thinks to himself that Emerson "talks like Woodridge" and wonders, somewhat implausibly, whether the young millionaire might be Jewish. More significantly Ellison contemplated having his protagonist knock over the bird
cage, freeing its imprisoned multicolored inhabitants; later that night he
would dream that he bears a letter to Norton requesting that he "clip to
death" the bearer's nails. Castration and homosexuality were clearly much
on Ellison's mind as his protagonist approaches his first major moment of
recognition.[30]

Ellison's invitation to the reader to analyze Emerson's behavior in explicitly psychoanalytic terms is indicated not only by the presence of Freud's
text on the young man's desk but also by Ellison's own notations. Regarding "young Emerson's motivation," he jotted, "Father antagonism with implied Oedipus complex. Undergoing analysis. Compelled to make positive
act against father. Takes this form because he identifies himself with boy's
Negro status." In *Totem and Taboo* Freud, referring extensively to Frazer's *The
Golden Bough*, argued that sons, deprived of the opportunity to possess the
mother but prohibited from killing their father, are banished. They learn to
displace their hostility and guilt onto a totem representing the "ancestor and

primal father"; under normal circumstances their participation in the collective sacrifice and symbolic consumption of the totem commits them to the incest taboo and allows them to forget the "homo-sexual feelings and activities which probably manifested themselves among them during the time of their banishment." However ambivalently, they are thereby reconciled with the father. Evidently young Emerson, who is undergoing Freudian psychoanalysis, realizes that his homosexual orientation enacts his rejection of identity with his father; his desire to help the invisible man signals his attempt at an alternative identification, as well as a belief that, as a "neurotic," he can bond with the "savage" sitting across his desk.[31]

That Ellison feels some sympathy for young Emerson is evident from the Huck-Jim parallel, as well as from his jotted comment, "Just as IVM [invisible man] enacts universal problems in terms of their relevance to Negro experience, I must have [a] white character obsessed with [the] same problems on a slightly different level; thus he will be a psychologically crippled white man . . . who in grappling with his personal flaw—which can be homosexuality, a stutter, physical ugliness, etc—come[s] to identify himself with Negroes." But just as Norton and Trueblood cannot be simply paralleled in their yearning to consume the transhistorical apple of incestuous carnal knowledge, Emerson and his Negro guest cannot, as the ruling-class scion imagines, celebrate their unity at the Club Calamus. Ellison concludes that Emerson "fails and is ironic because he really never succeeds in losing himself and actually becoming interested in Negroes, except as a symbol of his own unhappiness." Like the wealthy woman in the wheelchair, young Emerson is confined to the limits of his race and class. His ahistorical reading of *Totem and Taboo* is self-serving, for it prevents him from realizing the extent to which his office high above Wall Street is sustained, in the era of imperialism, by the exploitation of "primitives," noted on the world map and symbolized by the captured tropical birds. Ellison's mulling the possibility that the invisible man would knock over the bird cage indicates that the protagonist's political unconscious might register the totality that his conscious mind cannot yet grasp.[32]

As with Trueblood, Ellison discovered in the Aristotelian rather than the Freudian dimension of the Oedipus story a means of generalizing his protagonist's situation. Describing the tripartite structure of the Wall Street episode, Ellison designated "purpose" as the invisible man's attempt to meet the various trustees, "passion" as his insistence on learning the truth from young Emerson, and "perception" as the ensuing destruction of his "old formulation of personality." In this "climactic scene," Ellison asked himself,

"Where are the elements of terror and pity? For Oedipus it lay in his discovery that he himself is real culprit. Thus he becomes a destroyer of himself, in form of blinding. In this case father principle is couched in form of trustees. His tragedy is to discover that he has been betrayed by these father principles." Noting that the invisible man was not at this point capable of "discover[ing] his mistake himself," Ellison named young Emerson the "messenger," observing that "it is not the messenger that is of primary importance, but the message[, which] produces the turn in events that makes for revelation and revolution . . . changing [the invisible man] from believer into questioner." After the dialectic enacted in the encounter the protagonist would undergo a "leap in consciousness" constituting psychological rebirth; repeating the formulation from the now-excised chapter on Uncle Charles, Ellison jotted, "'This day shall give you birth and death!' Emerson tells [the invisible man] in effect."[33]

In all its variants the invisible man's encounter with young Emerson figures as a critical moment of transition: recognizing that he has been "betrayed" by the "father principles" embodied in the trustees, the protagonist is changed "from believer to questioner." In the 1952 text the episode occurs early in the New York section, preparing the way for the paint factory explosion, the hospital scene, the meeting with Mary Rambo, and the "baptiz[ing of] ole Rev." In most earlier versions, by contrast, the invisible man's discovery of Bledsoe's perfidy occurs only after he has endured several painful experiences as a migrant seeking work in Depression-era Harlem. His realization that he has, like "poor Robin," been "picked clean" is accompanied by the impulse to free the incarcerated tropical birds. As a messenger Emerson seconds the lesson of Wheatstraw, who has just delivered the news that the blueprint of American democracy is a mere icon on the trash heap of history. The young millionaire's "revelation" of the collusion between the trustees and Bledsoe leads to a "revolution" within the invisible man for which the way has been in large part prepared by his recent proletarianization.[34]

"We seemed as unrelated as a seat on the stock exchange and a stool in a sharecropper's cabin": Hospital and Rebirth

No section of *Invisible Man* underwent more rewriting than the chapters depicting the protagonist's hospital experience and subsequent encounter with Mary Rambo: material occupying little more than twenty pages in the published text ran to several hundred handwritten and typewritten manuscript pages. Ellison initially planned that the hospital episode would occur soon after the invisible man's arrival in New York: the explosion sending him to the hospital would take place not at the factory, but in his gastrointestinal tract. Rather than snobbishly ordering orange juice and toast and repudiating pork chop breakfasts, while living in Men's House the invisible man "chewed the pig, so to speak seven days a week. . . . Pig meat and corn bread and greasy greens, red beans, turnips and rice became too much for my digestive system[,] . . . too powerful for the type of life I now led. . . . It was as though I had kept pressing explosives into a weak shell casing—either some kind of a release was necessary, or an explosion was inevitable." When one night "rumblings like a minute Mexican revolution had broken out inside [him]," he is taken to the hospital from Men's House.[35]

In the drafts the hospital episode is still more surreal than in the published text. Sedated, the invisible man has strange dreams. First, Norton and Bledsoe are sitting on his belly. Then he takes the place of "the Negro in the white marble statuary group [at the Lincoln Memorial] which depicted Abraham Lincoln freeing a kneeling slave—only now the chains had been removed from [his] feet and placed around [his] head and tightened." The invisible man shouts, "Do I have to make you a speech? All right, Lincoln freed the slaves and I'm getting out! Say amen! You didn't cure me, you took all my energy. That's it, you probably have a whole hospital full of us, using our energy to run your stupid machinery." The questioning of his identity is bizarre; the technician in charge is accompanied by a "little brown man" who asks the invisible man whether he is "Booker T., Frederick D., W. E. B., Walter W., Phillip R., Mantan M., Joseph L., Richard, Roland, Lester G., Thomas B. [originally Richard B.], Charles S., Eugene K., Langston H., Bert W., Weldon J., John Henry, Moses T." Only when the invisible man fails to respond is he asked about the folkloric rabbits, Brer and Buckeye.[36]

The invisible man is then asked about another animal in Negro folklore, the text's omnipresent "Jack-the-Bear," and imagines "a big man wearing striped trousers and a swallow tailed coat; a man who seemed small despite his great stature and ludicrous despite his grave expression." With a "full-bosomed" and "light-skinned" matron on his arm, this dignified Negro, identified in an extended Joycean riff as "Booker Taliaferro [Washington] ALA BEARA," would have been "anything but amused had he heard himself called 'Jack-the-Bear.'" The distraught patient then envisions a group of railroad workers stripped to the waist, rhythmically chanting, "Jack the Rabbit / Jack the Bear / Caint you lift it / Just a hair?" as they lift the lid from his coffin-like box. He recalls childhood playmates with rural nicknames like "sisretta, lolly, cabby, louella," and notably "huck"—"little jokers, teasing tar babies . . . bounding their bottoms there below." He sees himself among them: "It was no mistake, there beneath the bubble-radiated hair, plastered to his skull like the hair of a new-born babe[,] was my own face." This reborn infant self taunts the forceps-wielding obstetrician who has just brought him into the world: "Gee, doc, I didn't know that was you. With all that white on I'd swore you was the Ku Klux Klan." This is quite a rebirth.[37]

In the passage where the invisible man experiences shock therapy (or whatever it is), feeling "disconnected" (237) from the anger that he knows he feels, Ellison added the marginal comment, "John Henry a tragic hero." As he gradually recovers, the invisible man recalls fragments from American history, elementary Latin, and the Bible. There come into his mind the words of victorious generals—General Pershing's pronouncement on arriving in France in the First World War, "Lafayette, we are here"; Julius Caesar's words of victory in Gaul, "Veni, vidi, vici"; and St. Paul's meditation on rebirth: "For we know in part, and we prophesy in part. But when that which is perfect is come, then that which is in part shall be done away. . . . When I was a child, I spoke as a child, I understood as a child, I thought as a child: But when I became a man, I put away childish things. . . . For now we see as through a glass, darkly; but then face to face." Recalling hazily that as a child he had heard the biblical passage spoken to him by "someone whom [he] had known and respected," the invisible man feels that the words contain a "magic clue." Gradually recovering consciousness, he sees a "man in a white jacket" who, "manipulating the dials and flickering lights before him," appears unaware of his presence, and he wonders whether the man "had any connection at all with the pressures I felt, for we seemed as unrelated as a seat on the Stock Exchange and a stool in a sharecropper's cabin."[38]

Ellison had in mind a wide range of literary and historical allusions to accompany the "political allegory" of his protagonist's emergence as a modern man. Kafka was on his mind: "The 'machine' must as much as possible reproduce the effect of society as a whole upon semi-folk personality when it comes to city," he noted. "It is the battle-royal write [*sic*] large, a 'womb' and something like the machine in the *penal colony*" [Ellison's italics]. So was the German movie director Fritz Lang: the doctors treating the invisible man recall the "abstract[ly] . . . motiv[ated] people in 'Metropolis.'" The invisible man's juxtaposition of phrases from General Pershing and Julius Caesar links the protagonist's present situation with the cane-wielding, Pershing-obsessed veteran outside the Golden Day and suggests the imperial motivations of U.S. participation in the Great War. The quotation from St. Paul associates rebirth with both the rejoining of a previously fragmented self and the vision of a reintegrated totality, "that which is perfect."[39]

Despite their fragmentation—the young Ellison is experimenting aggressively (and perhaps excessively) with stream of consciousness—these jottings and allusions suggest the historical and political dialectic shaping the invisible man's entry into urban modernity. His dietary crisis reflects the contradictions of his identity as a migrant; the fact that the explosion results from internal rather than external forces suggests the traumatic impact of the transition from preindividuality to proletarianism. While his recall of his playmates' folkish names suggests that his former personality is a "childish thing" that, in St. Paul's words, he will have to "put away," the memory precipitates a Bugs Bunnyesque challenge ("Gee, doc") to the white-sheeted medical authority towering over him. The doctor's mention of Jack-the-Bear brings to mind not only the figure of Booker T. (Taliaferro) Washington, dressed like a capitalist in a *New Masses* cartoon, but also the image of John Henry, who inspires the sweating railroad workmen to liberate him from the box of preindividuality. By contrast, the memory of the veil-manipulating campus statue of the Founder spurs the protagonist to discern a parallel with Lincoln, who removes the former slave's shackles from his feet only to bind his mind. While in Ellison's later writings Lincoln would emerge as a beloved martyr, indeed as a surrogate African American lynchee, in this draft of the hospital scene the Great Emancipator is aligned with forces of oppression and exploitation. Nor is he the "Old Abe Lincoln . . . thin and long, [whose] heart was high and . . . faith was strong, [who] hated oppression [and] hated wrong [and] went down to his grave to free the slave" celebrated in "Ballad for Americans." As he endures his ordeal the invisible man is decidedly antipatriotic; the flag is on his mental trash heap.[40]

Critical readings of the hospital scene often conflate the machine with scientific rationalism as such, pointing up analogies between the electric shock rug in the South, the North's more modern method of torture and dehumanization, and the Brotherhood's aspiration to subject all reality to Science. This reified reading of the machine, while largely appropriate to the published text, has little applicability to the drafts, which, albeit in surrealist style, continue to manifest the influence of historical materialism, especially as articulated by Wright. Not only has the machine explosion propelling the invisible man into the hospital physically enacted Wright's portrayal of migrants "project[ed] into the vortex of modern life" in *Twelve Million Black Voices*; the invisible man's inability to grasp what is happening to him displays to the reader the need for the totalizing consciousness that Wright alluded to in "Blueprint for Negro Writing." For when the protagonist thinks that he and the white-coated technician "seemed as unrelated as a seat on the Stock Exchange and a stool in a sharecropper's cabin," his words very nearly echo Wright's call upon writers to reveal the relationship between the financier swiveling in a chair on Wall Street and the sharecropper standing in the field: without such a perspective, social relations remain fetishized and opaque. The relation between Norton and Trueblood also remains in view. When Ellison first imagined the invisible man's hospital stay, Wright's "Blueprint"—and along with it, the science of the laws of motion in capitalist society—were not yet among the plans abandoned on Peter Wheatstraw's wagon.

"Now you're arguing politics":
Toward a Formalist Epistemology

But neither was Ellison at this point advocating Wright's revolutionary alternative. While the most dramatic changes in the hospital scene center on the invisible man's frazzled interior state, a small revision in the conversation between the doctors warrants more than passing notice. In the 1952 text the doctor in charge of the therapy claims that his "little gadget will solve everything"; when the other, who prefers surgical castration, questions whether the machine's "cure" will apply equally to the man on the table and a Harvard graduate, the first replies, "Now you're arguing politics" (236). The invisible man is mystified—as is, most likely, the reader. Earlier drafts clear up the confusion. We learn that "psychiatrists and socialists" have been assigned to the team working on the patient. The first doctor, who boasts that his "little machine" will "deliver the Cure" (here capitalized) is, presumably, the socialist; when the other doctor questions whether one cure will work equally in "primitive instances" and "advanced conditions," the first banters, "Now you're arguing politics. . . . The old socialism in one country argument."[41]

Although his comment will be mysterious to many present-day readers, what the "socialist" doctor alludes to is a debate that would have been familiar to many of Ellison's readers in the middle of the past century. Trotskyists, citing the theory of permanent revolution, asserted that socialism could not be built and maintained in one country. In particular it would not succeed in the USSR unless the revolution spread to advanced industrialized countries; the USSR's large peasant population and low level of development of productive forces, they predicted, would result in bureaucratic deformations and reverse the revolution. Stalinists maintained that socialism could be successfully established and maintained. The lag created by uneven development could be compensated by rapid industrialization and collectivization of agriculture; the only hope for world socialism consisted in the defense of the bastions where it was already existing. During the Depression and the Second World War this was hardly an academic debate, for the "socialism in one country" argument supplied much of the basis for the primacy placed upon defending the USSR that motivated the various changes in the Communists' line and practice from 1935 onward. The first doctor, who believes his "Cure" is equally applicable to all members of society, is evidently identified with the pro-Soviet position; the other, believing that the different capacities of different classes of human beings preclude the success of the experiment, is skeptical.[42]

In both the drafts and the published text the doctors dehumanize their patient: the first, a caricature of materialist determinism, breezily suggests that the "psychology" of the patient is of no importance, that he will "experience no conflict of motives"; the second, an out-and-out racist, equally breezily advises not just surgery but castration (236). The versions of the hospital scene in which the socialist is present lampoon the notion that Marxist science will solve the problems of the world, revealing the distance Ellison has traveled since the somewhat callow Bishop in "The Final Destination" believed that Soviet science could even reattach a severed penis. Given Ellison's growing anticommunism as he revised his novel, we might expect that he would have retained, and if anything expanded, this satiric depiction of the socialist doctor in the 1952 text. But instead he chose to depoliticize the doctors' discussion, removing the reference to "socialism in one country" and jotting to himself that the passage "must dramatize, on one level, the psychosomatic changes incurred by urban environment; on another it must treat of the irony involved in the old fallacy of science as a cure of human ills—science meaning technology, anti-humanism."

Why did Ellison eliminate the critique of the socialist doctor, substituting for it the formalistic equation of science with antihuman technology and leaving as residue only the mysterious reference to "arguing politics"? Perhaps, on the level of verisimilitude—to which he maintained some allegiance even in his surrealistic whirl—Ellison questioned the plausibility of placing a pro-Soviet doctor in charge of operations in a capitalist hospital. Perhaps abiding sympathies with the USSR, which for several years he largely dissociated from the theory and practice of the CPUSA, made him reluctant to include a critique that might brand him a Trotskyite. Or perhaps the depoliticization was itself an aspect of Ellison's growing anticommunism. As the dehumanizing doctors are linked through the signifying chain of the governing ritual with the text's accumulating lineup of antagonists, the binary oppositions accompanying this signifying chain undergo a subtle shift: now science versus humanism is added to the list. The scene with the doctors functions as a crucial linchpin connecting the protagonist's domination by small-town racist businessmen, millionaire philanthropists, and sell-out Negro educators on the one hand with his coming domination by Communists on the other: for while one doctor appears motivated by down-home old-style racism, the other, the egalitarian believer in the Machine as the "Cure" for all, appears motivated not by humanism but by abstract logic. In the 1952 text it is through this doctor, no longer identified as a socialist, that the satiric target apparently migrates from political economy to epistemology: not exploitation and its rationalization, but the notion that human behavior can be studied, and shaped, according to laws of necessity, emerges as the object of critique.[43]

As we shall see, Ellison would prove reluctant to locate his critique of the left on the terrain of the left: fascism and war, and the response they generated in the Brotherhood's real-life analogue, the CP, would be effaced from the novel, even as it invokes the world of the 1930s and 1940s. Ellison would locate his critique of the left in the realm of behavioral description. The doctors wish to control their patient; the Brotherhood wishes to control social reality: Power is an end in itself, and Science, associated with hunger for power, takes shape as the antithesis to humanism. In their clinical discussion of the invisible man's cure in the published text, the doctors *are* in fact "arguing politics." The apparent depoliticization of the hospital scene is a repoliticization, preparing the way for the invisible man's confrontation with a leftist authoritarianism that is its own end. A formalist epistemology posited on the dualism of "two cultures" stands in for a substantive critique of actual policies and programs adopted under the aegis of Marxism.

"Folk element in a state of brutalization":
Enter Mary Rambo

In the drafts of *Invisible Man* the invisible man's awakening to Communist perfidy is deferred, in large part through the substantially expanded role played by Mary Rambo and the inhabitants of her rooming house. In the 1952 text the invisible man first encounters "Old Mary" when, emerging from the subway after his factory hospital ordeal, he faints and she comes to his aid; after "baptiz[ing] ole Rev" in a last visit to Men's House, he goes to live with her. In earlier versions, however, the invisible man is not released from the hospital immediately after his ordeal but instead is placed in the glass-covered box. He is not in the factory hospital but in Harlem Hospital; it is Mary, a custodial worker wearing a "harsh blue uniform," who as midwife to his rebirth sets him free. Described as having "oily neatly straightened hair" and "work-swollen fingers"—in other variants, impish, hog-like, and belching, with eyes "round and bright as a treed raccoon's" and spitting "brownish saliva"—she holds up a sign asking whether he has landed in the hospital because of "TOO MUCH WOMENS, TOO MUCH MUSTARD." She remarks, "They must think you awful strong for them to have put you under all this pile of junk. Awful strong. They must think you John Henry or somebody."[44]

The invisible man garners Mary's sympathy by inventing the story that he ended up in the hospital because he was injured while repulsing the advances of a white homosexual in a back alley. "What kind of man am I?" the white man presumably asked. "Don't you know I can have you lynched? . . . Stand still, it won't take long." A former southerner—"You should have known my Mammy. She was good to me"—the fictitious man attempted to bribe the invisible man with twenty dollars, a microscope, and (in a detail recalling the interracial sexual bribery in Wright's "Long Black Song") a "chronograph with four hands." Aware that he is inventing the story, the invisible man nonetheless "feels gripped by a feeling that I was relating an actual happening"; he subsequently dreams of "an [Arctic] seashore inhabited by penguins that smoked cigarettes and talked in deep southern voices" and wakes up wondering why he had "told that particular lie to old Mary." Had the encounter with the man in the alley "actually happened"? "[The man's] delicate features that had been brutalized, scarred [and his] . . . distorted, wild-eyed face [reminded me of] someone I had known before he had lost his mind." He ponders, "Who was it there behind the glaring glass of my memory?"[45]

Like Todd/Mead upon encountering Jefferson in "Flying Home," the invisible man is initially alienated by Mary's folkishness. "Though I wanted release, I realized I did not want it through this ignorant, unscientific old woman," recalls the narrator. "Would she electrocute me?" When Mary engineers the invisible man's escape by strengthening him with a folk remedy sent north by her 104-year-old mother, he gratefully wonders whether she might be a long-lost relative. Heaving off the box lid, he "topple[s] into the machine the body of a dead boy his age" that was left on an operating table in the hospital basement. The invisible man flees and finds himself in the basement of an adjoining nightclub, where the jukebox plays a song that "sounds like Jack-the-Bear." Chased by security guards, he runs past a "series of furnaces" to the "slowing hum of the dynamos" and hides in a pile of coal. His pursuers consider giving up the chase, remarking that he must be a "missing labor leader" (in one draft, "that Brotherhood labor leader").[46]

"Naked as a jaybird" the invisible man emerges in the rainy nighttime street; he accounts for his unclothed state by claiming to some passersby that he was interrupted while having sex with a friend's wife. An admirer hails him as a "stud" and supplies him with a pair of pants. Fighting his way through the storm to Mary's apartment, he helps a cane-tapping blind man cross the street; he is jolted by the man's observation, "I guess they keep a young fellow like you moving." The man reminds him of his grandfather; the meeting jogs memories of a cataclysmic rural flood he witnessed as a child, especially the haunting image of a black stallion that thrashed through the rising waters and made it to higher ground. Drenched, the invisible man arrives at Mary's building, where a purple wreath marking a recent death covers the door. It has been quite a night.[47]

Although Ellison reworked the invisible man's hospital escape many times, he eventually omitted it from the novel, publishing a version of it in 1963 under the title "Out of the Hospital and under the Bar." In his preface to the published story he remarks on the importance of the invisible man's being freed by Mary, "a woman of the folk." Yet while Mary strengthens the young man by means of a folk cure and invokes the presence of John Henry, the narrator's description of her verges on the grotesque. That Ellison initially shared his hero's ambivalence is suggested by his comment that the "old cleaning woman is principle of the irrational, the unrecognized and unorganized areas of experience which nevertheless makes itself felt—usually in a detrimental manner. She is also folk element in state of brutalization—she looks a bit like mother Gresham." Both the white homosexual predator and the Negro hospital worker are described as "brutalized"; the midwife of the hero's rebirth is an overworked proletarian.[48]

The invisible man's escape through the interconnected urban basements highlights the working-class context of his emergence. Evidently drawing upon Wright's description of Fred Daniels descending through a manhole and discovering the substratum of capitalist society in "The Man Who Lived Underground" (as well as, perhaps, the basement in *Native Son*), Ellison introduces narrative details—the furnace, the coal pile—that reiterate the key role of Negro labor in powering the dynamo of northern industrial production. The fact that the guards who pursue him mistake him for a labor leader, indeed a Brotherhood organizer, reveals that class struggle is part of the underground of Harlem life. The text also points up the continuities between South and North. The image of the cigarette-smoking penguins with southern accents conjured up by thoughts of the homosexual predator recalls the opening smoker scene; the playing of Duke Ellington's "Jack-the-Bear" on the jukebox indicates that southern folklore is being retained and transfigured in the jazz enjoyed by urban sophisticates. The corpse encountered in the hospital basement recalls the dead sharecropper the protagonist viewed in the funeral home upon arriving at the campus. As he emphasizes the theme of rebirth—the invisible man substitutes the dead man for himself and leaves the hospital naked—Ellison insists upon the dialectical emergence of the new from the old.[49]

Ellison's focus on the historical dimension of the invisible man's northward odyssey did not preclude attention to its mythic and psychoanalytic dimensions. The omnipresence of water—the rain, the triggered memory of the flood from which the stallion valiantly escapes—signifies, Ellison jotted, that "initiation approaches." Unaware that he echoes Bledsoe's request to keep the protagonist running, the blind man is invested with a prophetic quality, recalling Tiresias in Eliot's "The Waste Land." His stick, which Ellison describes as "apotropaic . . . magical . . . [not] a regular cane . . . but the dried branch of a tree," invokes the Golden Bough. At once a means of warding off bad luck and a symbol of male fertility, the cane links with the sexual anxieties that have permeated the invisible man's recent trauma: his fears of castration and homosexuality, his identification with the stallion, his gratification at being called Tyrone.[50]

Ellison took care, however, to avoid loading too much mythic and Freudian baggage on the blind man's frail shoulders. "[The] blind man is blind because although he thinks he sees present and future, he sees actually only the past," he jotted. He "might remind [the invisible man] of one of the veterans who marches [with] a cain which he calls a rifle. This man's sanity exists in his insanity: He insists that life is a war." The blind man is linked with the Pershing-haunted vet at the Golden Day through their common obsession with the past. The prophetic powers of the cane-tapping urban resident are limited; sometimes a cane is just a cane. The protagonist's coming purification and initiation will take place not in an abstracted archetypal realm, but in a history-haunted world where "life is a war."[51]

"Our people are really beginning to act radical":
Mary Rambo's Rooming House

As both a folk character and a woman, Mary Rambo has figured prominently in critical commentaries on *Invisible Man*. Her vernacular speech is routinely counterposed to the coercive discourses of the hospital doctors and the Brotherhood; contrasted with the text's array of false fathers, from Norton to Bledsoe, Emerson to Brother Jack, Mary is seen as the embodiment of a valorized female principle, a "symbol of unsullied, redemptive, universalized love." Although the invisible man proclaims himself alienated by her constant talk about his becoming a "race leader" (316), his desire during the riot to return to Mary's apartment registers his realization that he must return to his roots. In the 1952 text, however, Mary appears in few dramatized scenes and does relatively little to earn her inflated critical reputation, which often derives from some fairly stereotypical expectations of her symbolic nurturing role as an elderly black woman. In the novel's drafts, which take us far beyond the terrain of "Out of the Hospital and under the Bar," Mary's role is considerably more compelling, in both its mythic and its historical dimensions.[52]

Ellison considered the possibility that after leaving Men's House the invisible man would live with a recently migrated family contending with "the blasting pressures of the city"; he might even, like Ellison himself, take a job as the superintendent of a large Harlem building. Once he created Mary, however, Ellison gave her a fuller profile. She is of mixed-race background, remarking, "[Papa] and old man Faulkner was kin. All you had to do was look at em and the only difference was one of em fell in the flour barrel and one in the tar." As a teenager she worked as a domestic: "I used to live their lives during the day, but doggone it I lived my own at night!" At the age of seventeen she left the South, married, had four children—one of whom, notably, she named John Henry—and spent twenty years in Baltimore. She moved to New York because "in a town like [Baltimore] you can't change but so much. They too much like where you come from." She recalls her "greenness" on arrival: at Radio City Music Hall she was so astounded by a naked male statue that she lost her balance, broke her spectacles, and rolled down the stairs. She also recalls an incident when she and her daughter Lucy thought they had found on a street a huge bag of coins, only to discover that it held snow chains for automobile tires. Excised from the 1952 text, some of this material would be included in a story titled "Did You Ever Dream Lucky?" that appeared in 1954. Evidently a composite of various migrants whom Ellison interviewed as an FWP worker and *New Masses* journalist, Mary supplied him with a rich array of materials.[53]

Although Mary may say, like the FWP interviewee Lloyd Green, "I'm in New York, but New York ain't in me" (255), she apparently abandoned both the rural South and Baltimore for the greater challenge of the northern metropolis. Her lineage from a plantation owner named Faulkner—Ellison is wisecracking here—has produced no abiding loyalties to the South, which she associates with hard labor. Her decision to name one of her sons John Henry, coupled with her reference to the "steel-drivin'" folk hero when she helps the invisible man escape from his hospital coffin, indicates her valuation of the proletarian heroes of Negro folklore. Ellison noted that, in her "tale of coming to [the] city," Mary, like the invisible man, moves "from purpose, to passion to perception"; her spectacles symbolically break because, having completed her northward journey, she "doesn't need them any longer." She may sing the "Backwater Blues," but she is now a woman of the city.[54]

While in the 1952 text the invisible man notes that Mary has other roomers, they never appear; for all practical purposes the young man and his landlady live alone. In earlier drafts the other inhabitants of Mary's rooming house are given names, faces, and voices. The roomers include Mr. Portwood, a retired railway worker; Mrs. Garfield, a former Oklahoman and a widow; and Cleo, a "plump young brownskinned woman" who works as a domestic; her "strangely lovely face" greets the invisible man when he rings Mary's doorbell. Other roomers might have been Bouchet, a jazz trumpeter whose riffs recall "gutbucket music and Trueblood behavior," as well as several nameless characters: "a numbers runner, a seaman, a West Indian lawyer, a Negro girl who returned to US after Europe," even a "white girl, married to Negro, who unconsciously hates Negroes." Ellison noted, "Perhaps Old Mary's apartment might contain a graded series of types, leading from extremely Harlemized to folk"; the "sound of [the] Elevated" would supply an "urban background to all of the folk business in Mary's apartment."[55]

This "graded series of types" links Harlem's proletariat to its preindividual past. A painting on the wall titled *Harvest Home* evokes for Mrs. Garfield childhood memories of Oklahoma harvests with ripened crops gathered amid "blood-red leaves"; she remembers "a bunch of little white and colored children, all playing together in the crowd," and "a great tall old chief of an Indian . . . standing on a corner wrapped in a blanket." During harvest season the community's preacher was sustained by "a share of what [everybody] got for themselves." As Mary's roomers put on blues records and dance the "old dances"—the "Eagle Rock," the "Turkey Trot," the "Black Bottom," Buddy Bolden's "Stinky Butt, Funky Butt"—the narrator recalls, "I was overcome with a feeling of opportunities lost and a deep nostalgia for those past times when I had ignored such music, rejecting it out of a belief that there was something better, more meaningful, more enobling. What, I did not know. I had rejected it and the comradship out of which it was created and of which it was evocative." Mary comments on white hipsters who have been scouring Harlem for old blues recordings. "I guess it must be gitting kind of hard to be white these days," she observes. "Looks like to me that when them boys starts to doing things like that, acting like our boys, something must done hurt em real bad. . . . Looks like to me they suppose to imitate folks like John D. Rockefeller instead of Cootie Brown and Mose Jones." Unlike the musician Jim Barber, the FWP interviewee who acknowledges the class position he shares with his white fan though he spurns his friendship, Mary empathizes with these white enthusiasts of the blues; Negro culture serves to bring together the disenfranchised of all races.[56]

Mary's apartment rings with talk about the present. The roomers discuss a recent incident when Harlemites threatened a policeman who took aim at three men who had just broken a store window and stolen a ham. Mr. Portwood observes, "Negroes are getting tired of taking it. Somebody don't come soon and show 'em what to do, hell's going to pop." Mary's renters compare North and South and talk about "how increasingly ['the race'] were concerned with politics and hard times": "Long discussions were held in which it was debated whether there was real freedom in the north and what was the worst drawback to living in either region. There was also a great deal of talk about the evictions that were now taking place daily about Harlem. Groups were organizing and replacing furniture in evicted apartments." Mrs. Garfield recalls that her husband had "worked with his hands and believed in unions and strikes. . . . He was way ahead of his time." Most notably, the Brotherhood appears to be a regular a topic of dinnertime conversation. Remarking on the "colored and white . . . Brotherhood people" who can be seen "holding meetings together," Mrs. Garfield concludes, "Our people are really beginning to act radical." The apolitical Cleo, observing that the Brotherhood "don't seem to be getting very far," concedes that "they give some pretty nice dances." Mr. Portwood, who expatiates on the qualities of the ideal Negro leader, mentions the Brotherhood and suggests that the invisible man "maybe . . . oughta join up with them. Or maybe be a union leader so our folks can get some of the good jobs." Mary urges the invisible man to become "a preacher, a new Garvey, a new Douglass, a unionist," anything that will show him to be a "strong intelligent man who ain't afraid to make a fool out of the white folks." What the invisible man in the 1952 text refers to as Mary's "constant talk about leadership and responsibility" (258) derives from these discussions. Originally designating the protagonist's arrival at Mary's as the beginning of the novel's stage of perception, Ellison noted that the conversations among the roomers would furnish the "preparation for the political section." Rather than a womb-like space exempt from Harlem's class struggles, Mary's rooming house is the site where the invisible man is readied for his initiation into leftist politics.[57]

"Some of us are trying to make that brotherhood grow": LeRoy and Treadwell

By far the most important of Mary's roomers is an absent presence, a young man named LeRoy whose room the invisible man inhabits and whose clothes he wears. Ellison provided a character sketch of the man who would function as the invisible man's absent double:

> [He is] distinctly different from those who like him were born in South. He has learned to read, and has linked up his humanity with that of Humanity generally. He is interested in problems of leadership. He is Leader, psychologically, who has seen the dichotomy of his position as consisting of a need to act on folk level, or of building up organization whereby he can cooperate on more sophisticated urban level. In folk he can see only limited possibilities, which are nevertheless vital. On the other hand he feels need to possess the meaning of the entire American culture, if not emotionally, intellectually—although he does not believe that such a division is necessary.

Born and early orphaned in the rural South, LeRoy "escaped a mob and changed his name" when he was fifteen. He moved to Birmingham and then to New York; he took college courses but quit, becoming active in a maritime workers union. Two days out during his last voyage he was murdered by company thugs and thrown overboard during a storm; his body was gruesomely sliced in two by the ship's propeller and then swept back onto the deck by a massive wave. The news of LeRoy's death is brought by Treadwell, a "tall, windblown white man" who has just returned from accompanying the body back to the South. LeRoy's closest shipboard friend, Treadwell says that he has "never seen a crew so upset over a man's death."[58]

LeRoy went to sea, Treadwell relates, because "he felt that if he stayed ashore he would die. He couldn't stand the way he had to live and the more he learned the more [he] became convinced it would kill him. He felt the need of a broader, a more human kind of life but he saw no possibility of achieving it." LeRoy despised the "calculated [obsequiousness]" of the "leaders of those organizations" opposed to the union, Treadwell continues. But even though "the union was as close as he could come," it was "too narrow," for "one of the things [LeRoy] despised was the assumption that all men need is a job, economic security." LeRoy's friendship changed Treadwell's life, forcing him to rethink what it meant to be a white southerner, a worker, and a man. LeRoy was, Treadwell explains to his Harlem listeners, "my friend . . . my brother," at once a "symbol of freedom" and a "kind of warning *against* revolt":

> We're trained to hate you, to suppress and repress you. Its our major dicipline our equivalent of a state church, or a recognized military cult, or . . . entering the service of a king. . . . Everything else that we're trained to suppress becomes mixed up with it—hate for father, mother, brother, sexual urges, unclean thoughts. . . . So that its hard to change anything deeply within us without images of you rushing into our minds—Why when I first became friends with LeRoy I began to dream that I was fighting with my father, trying to kill him!

Treadwell may not have read Marx or Freud, much less Wilhelm Reich, but LeRoy evidently enabled his shipmate to grasp that the white supremacy and sexual repression embedded in his political unconscious constitute the "discipline" of ideology.[59]

Treadwell's memory of a conversation about some young white American tourists whom he and LeRoy watched disembarking in Le Havre distills what the white seaman learned from his Negro comrade. Observing that the young Americans, "convinced that they are about to visit an inferior people," are "unconscious vessels of our whole way of life," LeRoy pitied them for their inability to "experience raw emotions": "I'm not condemning the kids, so much as trying to evaluate what put me on the deck and them in the first class cabins." By contrast with the rich, LeRoy declared to his friend, "There are only two really and deeply human groups in the whole country[:] . . . yours and mine. We fight each other and hate each other and fear [one] another. And yet our hope lies in the fact that we do. We're the only two groups that aren't ashamed to admit that we're the most miserable bastards in the world. And that all the money and power in the world is no cure for it." In one variant LeRoy is said to have suggested that this class-based comradeship may be continuous with comradeship of a more Whitmanian kind: "Sometimes we even love one another, though we seldom admit it since we have dirty words for those who admit their interest openly." Treadwell concludes with the hope that his and LeRoy's friendship portends future possibilities. Although LeRoy was murdered by those who are "against the union and against any friendship between the colored and white crew members," the white sailor states, "Things do change, Miss Mary. They change quite fast nowadays. Times are very hard now but just the same a kind of brotherhood is growing up between our people and some of us are trying to make that brotherhood grow."[60]

While Mary and her roomers continue to speak with Treadwell, the invisible man subjects himself to a "real ritual of cleansing" and puts on LeRoy's "white on purple dressing robe." He views in the mirror his head, shaved from the operation, and sees "a new man . . . bald as a new born baby": "[I discerned] a new intensity in the eyes, as though another contradictory spirit had taken possession of my face. 'Who the hell are you,' I whispered." He joins the others for dinner, where purple flowers adorn the table. As they consume a turkey that Mary calls "King Tom," she serves wine with "an elegant ritual motion." The meal finished, Treadwell gives Mary a package containing a portrait of LeRoy painted by a fellow sailor clearly conversant with Picasso and Braque; replacing *Harvest Home* on the wall, the portrait brings cubism to Harlem. Mary exclaims, "This don't look no more like LeRoy than it does Jack-the-Bear or Cootie Brown. . . . Here he got one eye over here and the other way over yonder." Mr. Portwood comments that it looks as though LeRoy "was beat up by a bunch of meat cleavers"; he sees in the corner a "man that's done been hanged." Treadwell declares that LeRoy had borne the "stamp of destiny"; he had been "dedicated and set aside." Mary, recalling her past conversations with LeRoy about leadership, says to the invisible man, "LeRoy goes, you come. I got an idea, like I say, that you something special too." Treadwell then half-jokingly tells the invisible man, "You can't avoid it . . . for now you are the dedicated and set aside." For the person so designated, "his life is not his own. . . . [He] arous[es] expectations of some exhilerating act of grandeur from people who hate him though they hardly know him, and love and the enthusiasm of those who can find in him no external reason for their great expectations." Treadwell is clearly another messenger, though bearing a different kind of news to the invisible man than was carried by the scion of Wall Street.[61]

"'Dedicated and set aside'":
LeRoy as Ritualistic Scapegoat

Down to his chosen name (in old French LeRoy means "the king"), Ellison's heroic mariner is recognizable, albeit in twentieth-century African American guise, as an avatar of the dying king or god described by Frazer, Raglan, and the Cambridge School. Like Raglan's hero, he knows nothing of his parents, travels to another land, does great deeds, is honored as a king, then falls out of favor with the gods and meets with a mysterious death. Like the dying gods of ancient myth, whose bodies were "torn in pieces, scattered over the fields, lost, sought for, discovered and recognized," LeRoy is the classic *sparagmos*. The purple wreath and flowers, signifying his royal status, associate him with Adonis of Greek myth; his death by water links him with both Osiris, the Nile god, and Dionysus. Occurring in the fall, LeRoy's death, like that of the year-daimon, is aligned with cyclical patterns of death and rebirth; the cubist portrait featuring the hanged man in the corner has replaced *Harvest Home*, with its gathered abundance amid the "blood-red leaves." At the feast memorializing his death and celebrating his life, LeRoy is ritually consumed as the animal totem "King Tom." Along with cubism, the hanged god has come to Harlem.[62]

In the light of LeRoy's status as honored scapegoat, Mary's role expands. In her "ritual" serving of the wine and carving of the turkey, she presides over the "communal feast of the primitive clan" as a present-day Themis, the prepatriarchal goddess whom Jane Harrison described as the "force that brings and binds men together . . . the collective conscience, the social sanction . . . the social imperative." Some of the "old dances" performed in her living room are named after animals and suggest the "beast-dances" of totemic ritual: the turkey trot, the eagle rock. Mary's name suggests her identity with the mother of Christ, the son who at the last supper was ritually consumed as bread and wine. As Frazer had written of the dying god in *The Golden Bough*, "Le roi est mort, vive le roi! Ave Maria!" But *Invisible Man* is not a disguised Christian allegory; or, to put it another way, to the extent that it invokes Christian myths it does so anthropologically. In her symbolic register Mary is a cross-cultural figure based in ancient rituals of purification, initiation, and sacrifice; her folkishness connects the preindividuality of Negro folk culture with the communalism of the earlier preclass societies whose remnants are celebrated in *Harvest Home*. Indeed other names for Themis are Demeter and Gaia—"Mother Earth"—whose son (according to Aeschylus) is Prometheus. Mary's symbolically maternal position in relation to LeRoy thus links him, on the one hand, with her biological son, John Henry, named after the foremost martyr in both Negro folklore and proletarian legend, and, on the other hand, with the Titan who enabled humans to rebel against the limits constraining their acquisition of knowledge. The political implications of Mary's role as Themis-Demeter-Gaia are not far to seek, adding a distinctly revolutionary dimension to the otherwise stereotypical notion of her function as a "Mother Earth" figure.[63]

That Ellison had the doctrines of the Cambridge School explicitly in mind as he created LeRoy is evidenced in his comment to himself that "LeRoy is several things: hero and scapegoat; drowned sailor; promise of racial success and leadership; the good man cut off in youth, in springtime of life." Ellison also assigned roles to the other inhabitants of Mary's apartment. In accordance with the descriptions of ritual and tragedy outlined by Francis Fergusson in *The Idea of a Theater* and Gilbert Murray in his contribution to *Themis*, Ellison summarized the "types of ritual" as "initiation, fertility; totemic feast; purification; expiation; sacrifice; and killing of the God-king-scapegoat." The "stages of ritual," corresponding with "purpose-passion-perception," consisted of *agon, pathos*, arrival of the messenger; *thernos* or lamentation; and *anagnoris* or *peripeteia*. The dismemberment and consumption of the *pharmakos* or *sparagmos*, whose totemic meat gives energy to the ritual's participants, especially drew Ellison's attention. He wrote, "In meal with Treadwell, they divide up turkey, tear a fowl between them, each selecting meat they like. . . . Later they are attracted to, or call attention to identical parts of portrait of LeRoy. . . . Cleo must see his legs, Miss Mary consider him wholly, Sam [Portwood] his hands." When he wrote to Hyman in 1948 that he was "beginning to work the same vein" as had Shirley Jackson in "The Lottery," Ellison was understating the situation; he was utterly absorbed with his mariner scapegoat.[64]

Ellison's figuring of LeRoy as ritualistic scapegoat is echoed in a cluster of literary allusions linking water, death, sacrifice, and the brotherhood of man; he turned to a number of his "ancestors" for advice about how to make his drowned African American mariner hero resonate with "universal" meaning. He builds off his own earlier work. The extended nautical metaphor in "Beating That Boy," of the "pounding irrational sea" bringing up the "fetid bodies of the drowned," is reinflected as symbolic action in Treadwell's description of LeRoy's death at sea, as well as the key situation of the Negro in the political unconscious of the white working class. In his function as the savior of Treadwell, LeRoy invokes James Wait, the title character of Joseph

Conrad's *The Nigger of the "Narcissus,"* upon whom the white members of the ship's crew load their guilt and through whose death they seek redemption. In his willingness to immerse himself in the "destructive element"—a phrase appearing repeatedly in Ellison's notes to *Invisible Man*—LeRoy acts out the injunction of Trader Stein in another Conrad novel, *Lord Jim*. LeRoy's dismemberment and death by water resonate with Eliot's drowned sailor and fisher king in *The Waste Land*. Above all, the multiracial friendship of Treadwell and LeRoy calls to mind the water-borne relationships between Queequeg and Ishmael on the *Pequod* and Huck and Jim on the raft; these allusions rescue from the realm of "dirty words" the homosocial bonding alluded to in Treadwell's remark, "Sometimes we even love one another." In the case of LeRoy and Treadwell, however, the racial roles are reversed: the former is unambiguously the tutor, the latter the pupil.[65]

As avatar of the dying god, LeRoy functions as a tragic figure; nonetheless some humor accompanies his doubling with the invisible man, especially in relation to Cleo, Mary's winsome young roomer. In the 1952 text the invisible man is a strangely asexual creature. The narrator implies that he had some sexual experience at college, but in the North he develops no romantic attachments; his only sexual experiences are with middle-aged white nymphomaniacs married to Brotherhood functionaries or wealthy fellow travelers. Especially noteworthy is his apparent lack of attraction to (or for) any black women in Harlem. In the novel's drafts and notes not only is he supplied with a former girlfriend in the South, but he becomes involved with Cleo, who, it turns out, was formerly involved with LeRoy. Although LeRoy was the king in many respects, he was apparently no sexual superman, having been unable to penetrate her tight hymen. The invisible man is a new prospect for the job: "You can burst it, I know you can," she sweetly suggests as they lie together on his (formerly LeRoy's) bed. "If LeRoy hadn't spent so much time fooling with those books he might have too. He didn't try but once a week." The new lodger does his best to rescue the damsel from her distress but encounters the same barrier as had LeRoy; he solves the dilemma by deflowering Cleo with LeRoy's pen.[66]

Cleo's role was envisioned as mythic as well as comical. Ellison jotted, "Cleo and the pen: substitute phallus, related to LeRoy as Osiris figure?" Like the Nile god, LeRoy would be dismembered, but his phallus-turned-fetish would be used to generate renewed life, in this case through his writing. Ellison considered emphasizing Cleo's Greek rather than Egyptian associations, calling her either Io (who in Greek mythology was informed by the rock-bound Prometheus that she would be the ancestress of the greatest hero of all, Hercules), or Delphenia (whose name suggests Delphinia, the festival when young women would entreat Apollo to be gentle with the sea). Biblical associations would be suggested in Cleo's attempts to induce both young men to deflower her: the phrase "dedicated and set aside" echoes the Hebrew designation of the Sabbath, where it is stipulated that young men seeking to purify themselves for priestly functions should avoid sexual contact with women. These mythological associations, ranging from Egyptian to Greek to biblical, show Ellison perhaps overreaching in his attempt to endow Cleo with mythic meaning. It bears noting, however, that he intended her to play a role in the invisible man's political initiation and meditated that "perhaps Cleo (or Delphenia) should be a more complicated character. Folk transformed by city, she might foreshadow his political *agon*." The young man's inability to penetrate her hymen, along with his resort to "mechanical manipulation, substituting an instrument for his body," might display his "fear of responsibility" and constitute "a failure to establish creative communication with folk." Ellison evidently encountered difficulties reconciling the various roles to be played by the young female roomer.[67]

Although in the 1952 text the invisible man's complaint that Mary badgers him with her talk about leadership is not borne out by any dramatized evidence, the passages eliminated from earlier drafts explain his uneasiness: the pressure not just to lead, but to lead as LeRoy has done, is intense. The invisible man grasps neither the importance of LeRoy to Mary's roomers nor the difference between the scapegoat as victim and the scapegoat as hero; when he first hears the phrase "dedicated and set aside" all that comes to mind is "the powerful whites who gave him the scholarship." Nor do Mary and her roomers themselves understand the effect of their "ritually load[ing] upon him their hopes and fears. . . . They want him to represent them, although they never state it consciously, for perhaps they do not realize it themselves. . . . He is dedicated and set aside. . . . He understands his role deep down, but feels they have no right to control him. . . . Old Mary and group think they celebrate a resurrection, when he is still undergoing dismemberment." It will take more than their unconscious ritual actions to make the invisible man appreciate his new role.[68]

"Symbol of freedom": LeRoy as Proletarian Hero

The leadership role modeled for the invisible man by LeRoy may be outlined in terms of anthropological universals, but it is located in a distinct historical context. Noting to himself that the memorial dinner for LeRoy will "establish the folk nature of these city Negroes among whom IVM is briefly to live," Ellison wrote that it will also "carry forward the mythical elements on a new level [and] introduce the political theme." Central to this political theme is the fact that LeRoy's murder, his sacrificial death, has resulted from his leadership in building a multiracial mariners' union; though unnamed, this is clearly Ellison's fictional version of the National Maritime Union. Left-wing sailors had played a key role in organizing support for the Scottsboro Boys and Angelo Herndon; Ellison had been impressed by the militancy and class consciousness of the maritime workers at the National Negro Congress in 1940. Founded in 1937 and electing as its secretary the Jamaican-born Communist Ferdinand Smith, the first black to occupy high union office in the United States, the NMU called for the "brotherhood-of-the-sea" in its constitution. The union prevented ships from sailing if they did not hire Negroes and expelled its own members if they manifested white chauvinism. In 1943, the year Ellison joined the merchant marine to evade the draft, the NMU insisted that a nondiscrimination clause be a standard feature of its contracts. As a result of NMU pressure the first Negro ever to serve as captain of an American ship, the Caribbean-born Hugh Mulzac, assumed the helm of the Liberty Ship *Booker T. Washington*. Mulzac and his multiracial crew "made twenty-two round trips, transported 18,000 troops, shot down two enemy aircraft, and did not sustain a single accident, loss of cargo, or human casualty," leading Mulzac to become "a civil rights activist, Popular Front idol, and Black war hero." The friendship between LeRoy and Treadwell was not an anomaly, at least not on ships where the NMU represented the sailors.[69]

Rank-and-file members of the NMU figured prominently in the international causes of the day; CP Chairman Earl Browder declared, "[Seamen are] the truly international members of our Party and the vanguard of the vanguard." Some nine hundred volunteered and three hundred died fighting the fascists in Spain; during the Second World War sailors in the merchant marine died at higher rates than did members of any branch of the armed forces. The NMU paid the price for its radicalism: during the postwar red scare thousands of rank-and-file members were screened by the Coast Guard under a new "port security" program, and the radicals among the union's leaders were targeted by the House Un-American Activities Committee. The NMU president, Joseph Curran, who had grown increasingly anti-Communist over the years, proceeded to purge most of the union's fifteen thousand foreign-born members; Ferdinand Smith, declared an immigrant troublemaker, was deported in 1949. By 1951, when Ellison was nearing the end of *Invisible Man*, having himself purged the last traces of LeRoy from his text, hundreds of Negro and Puerto Rican sailors had been brutally beaten, thousands had been fired, and most passenger and cargo ships had returned to being all-white preserves. As both a dying god and an actor in history, LeRoy was "dedicated and set aside"—indeed, he dedicated and set himself aside—in the effort to make a living reality the image of "black and white fraternity" that Ellison found so compelling in Melville and Twain, but which in practice required sacrifice of the most heroic kind.[70]

Ellison was fully cognizant of the NMU's left-wing associations: he had secured his position on the *Sun Yat-Sen* through the agency of the Communist organizer Add Bates and had begun *Invisible Man* while staying on the farm owned by Bates's fellow-traveling brother and sister-in-law. That Ellison for some time continued to honor the NMU, even as he was venting his anger at the CP in correspondence with his friends, was displayed in "The Booker T.," his review in February 1946 of John Beecher's *All Brave Sailors*, an autobiographical account of the author's experiences as a rank-and-file sailor on the Liberty Ship that was captained by Mulzac and celebrated in the left press as a symbol of the democracy for which the war was being fought. Perhaps it bears noting that the militant unionist serving as first engineer on the *Booker T.* was named—in what may have been an instance of life imitating art—Leroy King. While the NMU performed the usual functions of a union in defending the interests of its members, it clearly embodied the promise of a better world in a larger, broader sense. In submitting himself to the "destructive element," Mary Rambo's former roomer and quasi-son— the quasi-brother of John Henry and double of the invisible man—was a modern-day Prometheus.[71]

"A way of life more universal, more human, and more free": LeRoy's Journal

LeRoy leaves behind not only an indelible imprint on the memories of those who knew him but also a journal in which he meditated on philosophy and politics. His library reflects his eclectic interests:

> There were volumes of history, english, one titled "Black Heroes now and Then." Works of Darwin, Marx and Freud, Frazier, Malinowski and Ragland, one called "Folklore in the Old Testament," a study of Luther Burbank, a work on navigation, the Aneid, a Shakespeare, a book on mathematics, something called "How to Abandon Ship[,]" one called "Sickness

unto Death," a Dictionary, a Thesaurus, Bulfinch's Mythology and many others. "He had broad interests," I thought as my eyes rested upon a work titled Myth and Leadership, a study of the leader and his mission.

Serving as a kind of "play within the play," LeRoy's collection of books contains clues not just to LeRoy's preoccupations—and "ancestors"—but also to the novel in which it self-reflexively appears.[72]

It is LeRoy's own text, however, presumably written with the same pen the invisible man uses to penetrate the redoubtable Cleo, that shakes the protagonist's structure of beliefs and effects the transition, begun in Emerson's Wall Street office, "from believer to questioner." While feeling competitive with LeRoy—"I would read every book on the shelves, I would know more than LeRoy ever knew"—the invisible man also feels a "dependence" on him, for "although he was drowned, he was the only influence I had ever encountered who justified the feelings that I had [kept] repressed within myself." This LeRoy, he thinks excitedly, "wrote like a criminal or an invisible man." He becomes, Ellison jotted, a "benchmark" by which the protagonist's progress might be measured. Some journal entries allude to LeRoy's personal experiences. Working as butler to "Gabby," the mistress of a powerful ambassador, for example, he had seen the ambassador naked and had sneaked a look at the "diplomatic double-talk" recorded in the ambassador's diary. LeRoy concludes:

> It is a fallacy to say that people participate in their government. The people are governed: only those like Gabby participate—perhaps; the rest of us seldom get a glimpse. Three cheers for Gabby, diplomatic representative of the people. . . . Must we always take the backdoor to knowledge? . . . Without the possibility of action, all knowledge comes to one labeled "file and forget." I can neither file or forget. Nor will certain ideas forget me, they keep filing away at my lethargy, my complacency.

In one variant on this trio of butler, mistress, and ambassador Ellison contemplated the possibility that the invisible man, not LeRoy, would be the butler; that the naked ambassador and his mistress would involve him in a sadomasochistic sexual ritual; and that the "diplomatic double-talk" would be the planned collusion of the Western capitalist nations with Hitler at Munich. LeRoy's inability to "file and forget" is situated in the prewar collusion between fascism and democracy. Notably Ellison wrote "secret sharer theme" in this section of his notes; like the paired characters in Conrad's maritime story bearing that name, the invisible man and LeRoy would participate in an unspoken understanding of the failings of the society they inhabit.[73]

Several of LeRoy's entries address the politics of revolt and revolution, past and present. Recalling Booker Small's critique of Frederick Douglass in Ellison's early "Slick" manuscript, LeRoy decides that Douglass was a "typical 19th century idealist" who "made [the] mistake of throwing his best energies into speeches. Had he spent his time in organizing a revolt he would have been a far more important man today; he would have fathered a tradition of militant action around which men could rally today." For all their "present day validity," LeRoy writes, Douglass's speeches bear witness to the "ineffectuality of their . . . eloquence." By contrast, John Brown was "more reasonable in his so-called madness" because he advocated "guerrilla warfare. . . . No matter if a million had died, but died with guns in their hands, a tradition of responsible civic action would have been established that would have become a living force in our national life." He concludes, "In case of emergency a machine gun is good insurance. Don't recommend quoting Thoreau, or Ghandi [sic], for though their words be weapons, in some instances bullets are the only effective words." LeRoy's formulation recalls Ellison's featured guest status at the "words can be bullets" *New Masses* dinner and conference in 1942.[74]

LeRoy ponders the connection between the particular and the universal in the status of African Americans. "[It is] part of the character imposed upon us as a people to be a 'race'—that vague term without cultural or geographical, or psychological boundaries," he writes. "[But] it is my nature, my internal compulsion, to be a man, a member of a culture, a civilization, a citizen of the world." Not only does LeRoy's "belief in this idea" make him "morally stronger than the most vicious mob"; it also leads him to contemplate the possibility that Negroes are "the true inheritors of the West, the rightful heirs of its humanist tradition," and why that is so: "[The West] has flourished through our own dehumanization, debasement, through our being ruled out of bounds; since we have been brutalized and forced to live inhuman lives so that they could become what they consider 'more human.'" He ponders, "Not because we are humble shall we inherit [the] earth but because we are kept, forced into a position in which we are uncorrupted, forced outside, alienated from outlook, policy, etc., forced into an identity of experience with [the] whole non-European world." He asks, "Isn't the whole pattern of our history away from authoritarianism either of the left or right? . . . Doesn't the pattern of our experience insist that we seek a way of life more universal, more human and more free than any to be found in the world today? If only it were not inevitable that in order to achieve the consciousness of the West one must also absorb its corruption!" He decides, "[The paradox of being a Negro stems from] the constant remembrance that even the best that the Western world has attained—art, science, culture— even religion—has been attained through our degradation[.] There is black blood alike in bullion cubes and in bullion gold, and in the bulls of popes and bulletins of state, and the loftiest arguments by the loftiest minds."[75]

For all this despair about the present, LeRoy imagines reaching out to fifteen million listeners, presumably through the medium of radio, and postulates a vastly transformed future, domestic and global. "After we have rejected this way of life completely," he writes, "someday there might be a black secretary of State, even a black President. How insane this seems, but it is merely logical. And especially will it be after we are no longer effectively aggressive. Douglass was sent to Haiti—who will be sent to industrialized India? Africa? Palestine?" He asserts that he would like to be president himself, "not for the power and the alleged glory but for the perspective." He wonders, "What does he feel when he sees my black, questioning face of negation staring out of the crowd? Not smiling, just staring, the nature of my questioning revealed without a mask." In order for his life to be truly "redeemed," however, it "demands something far larger, broader":

> A change in the rules by which men live. For now for me to be more human is to be less like those who degrade me. . . . I wish to be, in my thinking, neither black nor white, and in my acting, neither exploited nor exploiter. And yet I'm willing to accept the human responsibility of soiling my hands with the blood of those who spill my blood whether wearing a hood and using a gun or sending out the orders in a telegram.

In the margin next to this last sentence Ellison scribbled, "Bosses."[76]

LeRoy carries within himself the trauma of the South: "Sometimes . . . I am overcome with the passion to return into the 'heart of darkness' across the Mason Dixon Line, but then I always think that the true darkness lies within my own mind. . . . I feel the need to reaffirm all of it, the whole unhappy territory and all the things loved and unlovable, for all of it is part of me. . . . Of course all this is absurd, but then all life is absurd." As he faces the challenge of becoming "a human being," moreover, rather than just "Negro or American, of a race or of a nation," LeRoy at times feels "like a man forced to assemble himself out of disparate and misfit parts. A man, that is, who must 'put himself together with monkey wrenches.' Still the pain which others inflict upon his unformed structure and that which he inflicts upon it himself, is most human. Are there no *humane* wrenches in this world? Can a man be assembled with a monkey wrench—even on an assembly line?" The task of being human cannot be separated from the era in which one lives; the Hegelian "unhappy consciousness" LeRoy experiences as one who is "dedicated and set aside" takes a form specific to the industrial age.[77]

While LeRoy is not a ventriloquist's dummy—he is attributed traits of character separating him from both his double and his creator—he nonetheless figures crucially as a barometer of Ellison's politics as he drafted *Invisible Man*. Some of LeRoy's comments can be read as indicators to the liberal pluralist, even anticommunist turn in Ellison's thinking from 1943 onward. The young diarist's claim that "black blood" suffuses the achievements of the West anticipates Ellison's insistence after *Invisible Man* on the necessary hybridity of all cultures. His proposition that Negroes may be the "true inheritors of the West, the rightful heirs of its humanist tradition," recalls Ellison's statement in 1945 that he and Wright might emerge as not just the "conscience of the Negro people" but also the "conscience of the United States." His reference to the "authoritarianism either of the left or right" gestures toward the "two totalitarianisms" thesis. LeRoy may be a card-carrying member of the NMU, but not of the CP.

Yet LeRoy's views are far distant from the cold war liberalism that his creator will eventually embrace. LeRoy mentions the "authoritarianism" of the left, but his journal contains nothing supporting this claim; all his examples of authoritarianism point instead to the ruling class and its henchmen. His caustic comment that "the people are governed [and] only those like Gabby participate" indicates a cynical assessment of democracy that has nothing in common with Ellison's later view of democracy as a "rock [amid] chaos"; if anything, LeRoy's comment recalls Ellison's note on the "Slick" manuscript associating democracy with capitalism and capitalism with death. The young diarist's stated willingness to take up arms against both Klansmen and the bosses who send them their orders by telegram exhibits a Leninist view of the state and class rule. His preference for the insurrectionary strategy practiced by John Brown over the rhetorical suasion advocated by Douglass conveys a revolutionary connection between theory and practice. Negroes are the "true inheritors of the West," he believes, not because they metonymically signify the body politic, but because they have been excluded from it, do not partake of its corruption, and have it in their interest to create a world "more universal, more human, and more free." He attributes the black presence in "bulls of popes and bulletins of state" not to cultural osmosis, but to the embeddedness of black labor—that of American Negroes and the world's colonized masses alike—in bullion. He keeps alive the accusation of Burnsides, one of the crazed vets at the Golden Day, that John D. Rockefeller stole the formula for turning blood into money.

Indeed LeRoy's views are to the left of some of the CP doctrines and positions that stuck in Ellison's craw during the wartime years. LeRoy's preference for Brown's actions over Douglass's words not only counterposes revolution with reform but also recalls the CP's deployment of Douglass's Civil War–era speeches to encourage African Americans, swallowing their resentment, to join the Jim Crow armed forces in order to defeat the greater enemy. His chafing against the "narrow" limits of unionism, the notion that "all men need is a job, economic security," as well as his willingness to give up his life in the struggle for a class-based universalism, contains an implicit critique of the Browderite call for peaceful coexistence between labor and capital both during and after the war. Even his speculation that there might one day be a black secretary of state—which, when attributed to the invisible man in the 1952 text, merely affirms his naïve faith in the Brotherhood—is premised upon a radical anticolonialism. It is only "*after* [Negroes] have rejected this way of life completely"—that is, overcome capitalism—that there could be peaceful international relations in which envoys of color from the United States might be sent to the dark-skinned nations of the world. Although LeRoy, like the vet's French mentor, deploys the vocabulary of humanism, this is a rhetorical choice; he voices values and aspirations that are largely congruent with those expressed in Ellison's *Negro Quarterly* writings of 1942–43. LeRoy's presence in the drafts of *Invisible Man* reveals the extent to which Ellison continued to embrace a Marxist paradigm well into the late 1940s and could not readily banish it from his novel's ethical frame.

By creating in LeRoy a modern African American avatar of Raglan's hero and Frazer's hanged god, Ellison was not trying to evade history and flee to the realm of myth and ritual; his invocation of the discourses of anthropology and mythology was inseparable from his "political allegory," which was in turn inseparable from the historical context of fascism, Communism, and war. Aware that universals can be mediated and represented only by particulars possessing shared cultural currency, Ellison held up his class-conscious Negro proletarian as a concrete means of access to the realm of the deeply and broadly human. Enacting Harry Slochower's dictum that it is only in the fight for the "better world" of socialism that man finds freedom, LeRoy is Ellison's Malrauvian "conscious hero," inheriting the mantle of Napue and Paul, Bard and Sheppard. While garbed in the purple robes of an archetypal king, LeRoy embodies the conscious working-class hero for whom Ellison first issued a call in his 1941 review of *Blood on the Forge*. LeRoy's anguished sense of being "assembled with a monkey wrench . . . on an assembly line" reveals the modernity of his situation; the ship's propeller that grinds him to pieces is not a fetishized Machine, but a material historical force. Mary Rambo's absent roomer is a present-day John Henry, a Promethean scapegoat whose death signals at once the tragedy and the necessity of working-class sacrifice in the process of transforming the world, of making it "more human."[78]

Before we leave LeRoy, one final observation. Ellison clearly entrusted the invisible man's double with a number of locutions and observations that echoed Ellison's own writings from his earlier radical days. In his aspiration to find a way of life "more universal, more human and more free," the journal-writing mariner spoke for one aspect of his creator: the radical internationalist, the questioner of the meaning and limits of democracy. That the phrase "dedicated and set aside" had additional personal resonance for Ellison is indicated in a poem titled "Deep Second" that he sent to Albert Murray in 1953 after visiting the Oklahoma City neighborhood around Second Street where he had spent his childhood. Reflecting on his triumphant return as a prize-winning favorite son, yet stirred by nostalgic pain, Ellison wrote of the "child father to the childish man," presumably his own fatherless self: "[He] dedicated me / And set me aside to puzzle always the past and wander blind within the present / Groping where others glide, stumbling where others stroll in pleasure." Returning home, which he calls "my second coming into deep second," he recalls the people of his past: "In me and only me . . . [they] live forever[,] I who can give no life but of the word would give them all." The poem is not Ellison's finest effort; he joked, "This ain't much but it's probably the first time anyone was mad enough to try to get Deep Two into a poem." But its echo of the phrase Treadwell lovingly used to describe LeRoy suggests Ellison's deep identification with the invisible man's secret sharer—even if, in 1953, this prophetic figure has been transmuted from a radical activist who wished to spur his fifteen million listeners toward present and future action into an artist hero who speaks for the mute multitudes of his past.[79]

"An invaluable tightening of the narrative":
LeRoy's Second Death

Even as LeRoy testifies to Ellison's abiding Marxism, his confinement to the memory of his friends and the pages of his journal reveals the impasse beyond which his creator could not proceed. By the time he wrote about his radical mariner, Ellison had burned his bridges to the left. During the Popular Front and the wartime years the Third International had indeed been severely hobbled by its conflation of democracy with antifascism on the one hand and the "better world" of socialism on the other; it would continue to pay the price for this theoretical and strategic mistake in years to come. But in the wake of the Duclos letter, the old nag picked itself up—not just because Foster shot it full of dope—and started to address many of the concerns raised in LeRoy's journal. For all the CP's weaknesses, there was at the time no better means for seeking out "a way of life more universal, more human, and more free." Because LeRoy had been confined to memory and memoir, however, and was never given a role to play in the novel's narrative present, he could eventually be excised from *Invisible Man*, "filed and forgotten," leaving behind only the haunting phrases "more human" and "dedicated and set aside" with which his creator could not, it seems, bear to part.

Ellison evidently eliminated LeRoy from his text only quite late in his compositional process; in the original typescript LeRoy's journal is among the contents of the invisible man's briefcase when he descends into the manhole. The purging of LeRoy was strongly urged by Harry Ford of Knopf, who read a midstage draft and urged multiple cuts and revisions:

> Careful reading leads me to feel quite strongly that Leroy's diary should be dropped entirely. Prolix, didactic and inimical to the narrative—[it is] a crutch for the narrator which never entirely works (at least for this reader), and which remains simply a device. It seems to me that either LeRoy has to be introduced as a character (if it is really necessary to project his highly sophisticated viewpoint) or eliminated entirely. I would prefer the latter.

Aware of the centrality of LeRoy to the entire rooming house episode, Ford observed, "If LeRoy goes, then it seems to me that Mary has no reasons for being, and all passages relevant should be deleted. I would see this as an invaluable tightening of the narrative, which is much too loose and shifty from here on."[80]

Ellison eventually chopped apart his novel, tossing Mrs. Garfield, Portwood, Cleo, and Mary into folders from which Mary alone, in dismembered form, would emerge. LeRoy, whom he would designate a "stillborn hero," would be buried at sea; there would be no Treadwell to bring his body home. As he engaged in his own act of ritual sacrifice, however, Ellison eliminated the possibility that his novel would contain a hero "dedicated and set aside" for any purpose other than victimization. The dual nature of the American

Dionysus would be collapsed into one; the "governing ritual" of the battle royal would be limited to repeated acts of castration; the search for leadership would entail not tragedy but irony. Once readers know of LeRoy's sacrificial murder, however, his ghost haunts not just Mary's boardinghouse but the novel's entire domain. *Le roi est mort. Vive le roi!*[81]

Finding Brotherhood

> A few of us stepped forth and accepted within the confines of our personalities the death of our old folk lives, an acceptance of a death that enabled us to cross class and racial lines, a death that made us free.
>
> —Richard Wright, *Twelve Million Black Voices*

> To act scientifically in regards to such a situation would be to take action to *prevent it before it happened* . . . to swerve the developing forces away from the destructive event and transform it into [a] socially useful one.
>
> —Ralph Ellison, advice of Hambro in the "Brotherhood" episode of *Invisible Man*

In the published text of *Invisible Man* the protagonist's encounter with the Brotherhood is shadowed from the start by the reader's apprehension that something sinister is in the works: the "governing ritual" of the battle royal is about to be repeated, if in a new and different register. Brother Jack hires the protagonist not for his intelligence and initiative but for his voice; the young man's oratorical abilities are being turned against him once again. The protagonist is supplied with his new name on another one of those ominous slips of paper; when another message arrives, cautioning him to go slow in a white man's world, the handwriting is, as it were, on the wall. As ignorant armies of punch-throwing black men clash by night in the streets of Harlem, and as the invisible man finds himself blinded by bright lights in the boxing arena while Brotherhood officials look on, we know that sacrificial rituals are once again—indeed still—in process. In short, much of our cognition in this section of the novel is based in re-cognition. The text's careful rhetorical patterning enables us to view new characters and situations as supplements to familiar clusters and equations; repeated tropes, character types, and incidents channel, in fact govern, our response to the invisible man's entry into political life.

Our ease in making connections among parallel and analogous symbols and incidents is reinforced by our knowledge, or what we believe to be our knowledge, of history. We are aware, even if the invisible man is not, that he has landed in a nest of Communists. LeRoy may not have limned for us the "authoritarianism of the left," but we know a red when we see and hear one. We wink and nod when Ellison identifies his leftists as the "Brotherhood," just as we previously winked and nodded at his dissociation of the Founder from Booker T. Washington and of the campus (even with its signature statue) from Tuskegee. It does not matter that in postpublication commentaries Ellison continually denied that the Brotherhood is the C P. Like the reviewers who greeted *Invisible Man* back in 1952, virtually all of whom made this association, we discern the historical identity of the radicals the invisible man encounters in Depression-era Harlem. We know that they protest evictions and profess themselves friends of the Negro people, but also that their motives are tainted and their friendship false. When red-headed Brother Jack follows the invisible man over the rooftops and offers him a job, this is, we acknowledge, typically opportunistic and cynical Communist behavior. Rhetoric is compounded by reference, re-cognition via textual patterning with re-cognition via invocation of a fund of common knowledge. If we identify with the cold war–era reader who is assumed and greeted in the 1952 novel, textual rites of consensus are operating with a vengeance.[1]

In this chapter I examine the process by which Ellison creates an apparently seamless homology between the northern urban left and the series of antagonists the invisible man has encountered, starting with the town fathers at the battle royal. As we may anticipate, given the harshness of his criticisms of the Communists in his correspondence in 1945, Ellison from the outset intended to subject his protagonist's experiences with the Brotherhood to critical scrutiny. In one early outline the protagonist, after learning that he has been "given the run-around" by the trustees, returns to the South, either Atlanta or Birmingham, where, in a partial parallel with Angelo Herndon, he

> steps in front of [a] mixed relief parade and is exclaimed a Hero by [a] left-wing group.

He is arrested, charged with treason, thrown in jail. After his release he returns north and becomes [a] political figure; a "leader" who discovers soon that he leads no one, but is in reality a figure-head.

In a draft of his letter to his publisher, Peggy Hitchcock, in 1946, Ellison remarks that his novel's "political allegory" will entail describing "a man of good will who attempts to function idealistically in a political organization which cannot afford the luxury of idealism." Although "allegedly democratic," he continues, the organization "observ[es] the ritual of jimcrow custom," thereby "mak[ing] for situations of such absurdity that they [be]come the antithisis of anything progressive." The hero loses his position of leadership in the organization "at the point when he truly begins to understand something about himself and the world." Ellison added, "This, I'm afraid[,] is as far as I have concieved the structure, for the end, the climax, evades me."[2]

While consistently stressing the ironic disparity between the Brotherhood's theory and its practice, Ellison's notes and outlines indicate his original intent to spread the blame for the invisible man's never attaining the standing of a genuine leader. When he is "picked up by the radicals" who find him "useful because he is young, handsome, [and] can speak[,] it does not occur to them," notes Ellison, "that he is an opportunist, disorganized and unreliable." "The democracy which he discovers in his political milieu is not that of its written program, but of its human exponents"; nonetheless he "fall[s] into the uncle tom pattern again, . . . creat[ing] ambivalence in order to feel comfortable." Expanding on this contradiction in "Working Notes," Ellison writes that the invisible man, upon learning that "he is a leader in name but not in fact, gives in to his passive drives . . . fail[ing] to see that he is dealing with well-meaning but blundering human beings, most of whom have misunderstood him because of the unconscious assumption that they knew what was best." Accordingly he "phones his office several times a day to ask for himself . . . finding reassurance in hearing the girl use his title." When he becomes romantically involved with Louise, a white Brotherhood member, he "cannot accept himself nor believe that anyone like Louise could find him attractive," a psychological complex that Ellison refers to in his notes and letters to Hyman as the novel's "Othello theme." As in the early drafts of Ellison's reviews of *Black Boy* and *An American Dilemma*, as well as in "The Initiation" and other proletarian short stories, both African American and white Communists are shown to be toting considerable baggage as they journey toward a better world.[3]

Besides depicting the invisible man and his comrades as beset by comparable contradictions, the outlines and drafts of the novel's New York section contain a number of episodes—eliminated from the published text—that substantially remold the portrayal of the Brotherhood's relationship with Harlem's migrant population. At least half of the section of the novel that Ellison variously titled "Perception," "Book III," and "Political Life"—itself occupying the second half of the 1952 text—originally contained quite a sympathetic depiction of leftist political organizing among urban African Americans. Accompanying this added material is a reconfiguration of certain key tropes. As we shall see, the positive characterization of Louise ruptures the text's portrayal of white Brotherhood members as racists and of white women as tools of power-hungry white men. The novel's symbolism of blindness and invisibility is complicated by a cluster of images that associate Marxism with a lens affording special insight into reality. Injecting greater complexity, to use Ellison's favorite evaluative term, into the published text's more reductive treatment of the left, these omitted episodes and readjusted tropes afford insight into the reasons why the novel's climax may have continued to "evade" Ellison. For some time he was apparently unable, or unwilling, to skewer the left: LeRoy's inability, or unwillingness, to illustrate concretely the "authoritarianism of the left" may have affected his creator as well.[4]

"What is to be done?": Yam Man and Eviction

In the text of *Invisible Man* from 1952, the working-class character of Harlem's migrants is emphasized on the day the invisible man encounters the Brotherhood. In his Men's House days the protagonist had breakfasted on toast and orange juice; now, with the blasting of his bourgeois expectations, he is prepared to acknowledge his abiding love of southern foods and buys two hot buttered yams from a street peddler. His declaration of identity—"They're my birthmark . . . I yam what I am" (266)—has been widely hailed as signaling his willingness to return to his roots. This gesture not only prepares him, and us, for his upcoming defense of the Provos, the elderly evicted couple, but also indicates his growing oneness with the migrant folk from whose vernacular traditions he has to this point separated himself. For many critics his punning consumption of the yams also portends an opposition between the signifying fluidity of folk or migrant speech and the rigidity of the Brotherhood's scientific discourse. A good deal of political and cultural resonance has been detected in those yams.[5]

While the invisible man's delight in the steaming yams signals his yearning for home in all versions of the text, Ellison at first framed the yam seller's situation in more starkly economic terms. In answer to the invisible man's inquiry about the source of the yams, the man tells him, "Before I came North I used to raise em. Had me a forty acre farm. . . . Then I got into some trouble and had to leave. So I came up here and went to work in a factory. Then I was out of work and hit upon this idea." He says, "With all the home boys round these parts [business] aint so bad. Don't look like I'll ever get away from yams though." Although he received part of the promise of Reconstruction (forty acres) the yam seller's inability to abide by the ethics of Jim Crow—"I got into some trouble"—has driven him northward to join the industrial proletariat. The Depression, however, has interrupted that trajectory: selling yams is not a folkish vocation but his way of surviving in the informal economy on the fringes of crisis-beset capitalism. In the 1952 text a close-to-the-soil character linked with other migrants—Peter Wheatstraw, Mary Rambo—who exude folkish authenticity, the yam man earlier figures as a laid-off proletarian. As Paul notes in Ellison's early fictional sketch of the radical organizer hero, having forty acres is no solution to the problem of systemic racism, which requires a more fundamental challenge to class rule.[6]

In the 1952 text the invisible man's decision to speak out at the eviction is spontaneous; in fact in his ignorance he has to be informed of what an eviction is. In earlier treatments of the young man's period of urban wandering Ellison stresses his needy narcissism. "The only thing left was the desire to make speeches," recalls the narrator. "In spite of Bledsoe, Norton and the others I felt myself to be a leader and a speaker of some eloquence." Having discussed the Harlem housing crisis at Mary's, and having himself come across many an eviction protest since his arrival in New York, he wonders, "Where had all the soap-box speakers gone, now that winter had come? Did they go south with the birds or keep silent until the spring? What if they made their same angry speeches down south, and had been doing so for years without my knowledge? Or did they now make their proclamations in well-heated meeting rooms, now that no one lingered on the windy corners?" When he speaks at the eviction protest, Ellison jotted, the invisible man's words are "mainly a projection of his own anger and bitterness. . . . He speaks out of lostness and vanity."[7]

The eviction episode itself underwent little revision; in all the drafts Ellison's portrayal of the Brotherhood-led multiracial solidarity dramatizes the testimony of the composite "we" in Wright's *Twelve Million Black Voices*: "[We] black folks smashed the marshals' locks, picked up the paltry sticks of furniture, and replaced evicted families" with the support of "white workers" who "differed from those we had known on the plantations; they were not 'po' white trash." Ellison initially stressed the immediacy of the southern memories evoked in the invisible man by the Provos' plight. The young man's sharp visual image of his mother, *"hanging wash on a cold windy day, so cold that the warm clothes froze even before the vapor thinned . . . her hands white and raw in the shirt-swirling wind"* (273), is followed by a memory of his father, whose "last years" were nothing but "straw whirling away in the wind." When the young man sees the Provos' possessions "as behind a veil *that threatened to lift, stirred by the cold wind in the street"* (273), windblown images of both parents thus press upon his consciousness. We are reminded that the invisible man has not just generalized roots in the South but family members still trapped by Jim Crow.[8]

This "veil" is more than the veil of private memory; as the narrator relates, "The new voice in my head was about to attack the Founder." He soon finds himself speaking mockingly of the "great leader whose wise action was reported in the newspaper the other day" (275). The historical referent of this "wise leader" is almost surely Tuskegee's President R. R. Moton, whose action in surrendering the wounded Sharecroppers Union organizer Clifford James to the Macon County sheriff closely resembles the invisible man's ironic praise of the "leader [who] . . . when that fugitive escaped from the mob and ran to his school for protection . . . was strong enough to do the legal thing, the law-abiding thing" (276). When the invisible man asks the angry Harlem crowd, "What is to be done?" his echo of Lenin invokes the revolutionary phrase that was a favorite of Ellison's in his *New Masses* and *Negro Quarterly* days. The veil that "threaten[s] to lift" in the published text is not just the veil of a generalized Du Boisian double consciousness, but the veil covering the invisible man's painful personal remembrances, as well as the veil ambiguously positioned by Washington on the Tuskegee campus statue. The South is very much alive in the North; not just the scattered memorabilia of the Provos, but also the recent collusion of Washington's legacy with the suppression of sharecropper organizing, probe and poke at the historical consciousness of the invisible man from behind his memory's windblown veil.[9]

Although Ellison never worked this material about penetrating behind the veil into a dramatized narrative, his jottings reveal that doing so would have repositioned the text in history, moving it forward by several years. In one variant the scene included "old folks, soldier, white aggressor, mother father sister brother"; in another variant, "black woman, a sweetheart, a mother, possible a grandmother, 'big mamma,' stressing emotional elements of Harlem riot. White man, Negro mother, Negro soldier . . . Perhaps old man could have been or there could be a disabled son present." These notes indicate that Ellison considered situating the Provos' eviction not during the early years of the Depression, as is implied by the historical references to Clifford James and R. R. Moton, but during the wave of wartime evictions about which Ellison had written in 1942 in his *New Masses* profile of Mrs. Jackson, "The Way It Is." The presence of the soldier in particular would have pointed to the tensions over segregation in the armed forces that contributed to the Harlem uprising in 1943; the references to the "white aggressor" and the "black woman" suggest a more specific connection with the catalyst of the riot, namely, an encounter in which a black soldier was shot by a white policeman after interceding in an altercation between the policeman and an African American woman. Ellison was clearly pondering whether—and if so, how—to relate the war abroad to the war at home.[10]

"History has passed them by":
Encountering the Brotherhood

According to all of Ellison's notes, outlines, and drafts, the eviction episode is what brings the invisible man directly into contact with the Brotherhood. But Ellison considered various possibilities for how this might happen. Instead of escaping over the rooftops, the protagonist might "[find] a gun, [be] arrested, held in jail"; it would be this display of militancy—and not his speech-making ability—that results in his being "picked up by group." Ellison supplied an additional impetus for his hero's pursuit of a connection with the Brotherhood. In the published text he briefly encounters a young white woman in the Provos' emptied apartment. Congratulating him on the effectiveness of his speech, she advises him to escape over the rooftops but is never glimpsed again. In early drafts, however, the invisible man thinks:

> She was very pretty and I felt my throat tighten with swift fear and shame as I realized that I was alone with her. *If the police caught me here it would be really bad for me,* ran through my mind. *But isn't she pretty! What is she doing up here / Who's she with, why would he bring her up there and get mixed up in something like this? She's not afraid and I'm trembling. But look at that face! And that tone of voice. It's like we've known one another a long time. . . . It's just*

like I've heard, here they don't know to be afraid. Just like I heard. These northern ones are crazy.

The prophecy of the vet is on the verge of being fulfilled.[11]

In all the dramatized versions of the text Brother Jack is described as a politician, bent upon recruiting the young man for his rhetorical skills. Resenting the invisible man's racial identification with the Provos—evidenced in his assertion that "We were burned in the same oven"—Jack states, "You were watching a death, . . . meta-phor-ically speaking. . . . History has passed them by. . . . They're like dead limbs that must be pruned away so that the tree may bear young fruit or the storms of history will blow them down anyway. Better that the storm should hit them." In the published text, Jack's assessment that the Provos are "living, but dead[,] dead-in-living . . . a unity of opposites" displays an objectifying scientism in which "individuals . . . don't count" (290–92). But in the context supplied by the invisible man's dream at Men's House—in which he imagines that his parents would be utterly lost in the city, and even his grandfather would prove unable to shed his superstitions—Jack's analysis of the Provos' preindividuality is shown to be largely accurate, even if his conclusion that they "don't count" reveals his robotic rationalism. The invisible man's very recent memory of his father's "last years" as "straw whirling away in the wind," moreover, draws upon the same imagistic matrix as Jack's description of the "storms of history"; Ellison's elisions detach Jack's statement from a trope that might otherwise give it greater credibility.

Even as Ellison reconfigures the context framing Jack's view of historical necessity, however, he gestures toward its continuing relevance. For through Jack, who claims to have been reading "a detective story or something" titled *A Death on the City Pavements*, Ellison teasingly alludes to the section treating northern migration in Wright's *Twelve Million Black Voices* bearing that designation. Wright writes, "A few of us stepped forth and accepted within the confines of our personalities the death of our old folk lives, an acceptance of a death that enabled us to cross class and racial lines, a death that made us free." Ellison, we will recall, admired *Twelve Million Black Voices* more than any other work by Wright; by making him confront the "trauma of passing from the country to the city of distruction [that] brought no anesthesia of unconsciousness but left our nerves peeled and quivering," he wrote to Wright in 1941, the text made him a "better Marxist." Like the "scientific politician," Ellison learned from reading Wright's text, the writer must "manipulate . . . weigh and balance [and] test [reality] . . . in order to control it." The analysis offered by the "scientific politician" in the 1952 text further echoes Ellison's own assertion in his essay "Harlem Is Nowhere" (1948) that Harlem is both "the scene of the folk-Negro's death agony . . . and the setting of his transcendence. Here it is possible for talented youths to leap through the development of decades in a brief twenty years, while beside them white-haired adults crawl in the feudal darkness of their childhood." Read in the context supplied by these texts, Jack's commentary on the Provos' place (or lack of place) in history sounds a good deal like something Ellison himself thought and wrote; the only difference is that in Jack's voice the invocation of science and dialectics comes across as an inhumane proclamation of necessity rather than a rational grasp of the process, at once painful and redolent of possibility, whereby the old gives birth to the new.[12]

Noting the rhetorical pattern that makes teaching *Invisible Man* an English professor's dream, Pancho Savery has observed of the eviction episode, "By this point of the novel, if not earlier, students are usually having fun. They easily recognize the various manipulations of the Brotherhood and can connect them to those of the men at the battle royal and to Bledsoe, Brockway, Kimbro, Emerson, and Norton. This part of *Invisible Man* can be taught very quickly." For Savery and many other critics, the process of interpretation goes on automatic pilot once the text moves into the Brotherhood section. Had *Invisible Man* retained the episodes and characters that Ellison left on the cutting floor, the process of recognition and connection would have been fraught with difficulty, requiring slowing down rather than speeding up.[13]

"Struck down by History": Last Rites

In several drafts of *Invisible Man* the motif of death on the city pavements undergoes further elaboration when, soon after parting with Jack, the invisible man comes across an old white man who has just been hit by a truck and lies dying on the sidewalk. The young man thinks, "Everyone was being dispossessed. . . . Pruned away, as the man in the cafeteria had said. 'Struck down by History.' . . . *Elderly abstract white man struck down by History at the wheel of two ton truck.*" The truck driver, a white man whose jacket sports "a row of green and black union buttons," calls the invisible man "Mac" and asks him to pretend to be a priest and perform the last rites. First refusing, the protagonist gives in: "I had grown so used to fantasy, had become so fragmentized that with the dead language on my tongue I fell into the priest's role with a certain ease." He substitutes a deck of playing cards for a Bible and dredges up all the Italian and mangled Latin he can remember, from "Allegretto . . . Moderato . . . Legato con fuoco" to "Allia Gallia est . . . divisia enter tertia partem" to "Ultima Thule in Excelsis, E Pluribus Unum, mater, mater, Maria." A fragment of Proverbs comes to him "out of the past: . . . 'Man's despair is God's opportunity.'"[14]

As he leaves the dead man, the protagonist finds himself imitating the stride of a man he had known as a child:

> A tall, fastidious Jew (even taller and more fastidious than Uncle Charles) for whom I'd worked as an adolescent. He was a man who walked with a stately stride, a very kind man, and more aristocratic than all the aristocratic Southerners in the town put together. . . . I had admired him because when the others called him Christ Killer I knew that they hated him and to me he was a figure who seemed more like Christ than they and yet free of Christ because he was a Jew. . . . By identifying myself with him I had found one way of defying the others.

Frightened by both the people who assumed he was a priest and his own readiness in assuming the role, he wonders:

> What had happened to people that they couldn't see me. Didn't they know that I was nothing like the figure they assumed? First the eviction and now this. One group as confused as the other! Had I become invisible? And then a truly terrifying thought: Perhaps I was everything, anything or nothing, depending upon who was looking upon me at the moment! Hadn't I acted the role of priest as quickly as I had played—what was the term?—a rabble-rouser?[15]

As in the draft version of the hospital scene, the invisible man's political-cum-mythic unconscious is hard at work. The conquest-celebrating words of Julius Caesar, who was previously associated with General Pershing, here coexist not only with directions in Italian for musical performance but also with "E Pluribus Unum," the Founding Fathers' proclamation of unity in diversity. "Ultima Thule in excelsis" couples the mysterious geographical limits of the known world with divine sanction to explore them. The sudden memory of the "aristocratic" Jew shows the protagonist coupling anti-Semitism with anti-Negro racism, an association that would have been heightened had Ellison retained the wartime context of the eviction protest, and that would have added a grim historical footnote for readers in 1952 to the invisible man's claim to have been "burned in the same oven" as the Provos. His identification with the Jew, whom he considers "more like

Christ" than his persecutors, reinforces his emerging sense of himself as a "dedicated and set aside" subject-object of sacrifice; his call upon "mother Mary" is at once a cry for Mary Rambo and a call upon the mother of the dying god. Mid-twentieth-century readers might have caught Ellison's further allusion to the popular Harlem evangelist Father Divine, for the biblical phrase "Man's despair is God's opportunity" closely approximates the title of this cult figure's famous sermon in 1947 about the moral blessings of poverty. Through the invisible man's cobbled-together string of biblical and Latinate words and phrases, Ellison suggestively associates Christianity with empire, anti-Semitism, Negro invisibility, and the sacrifice of the dying god. The ideological critique he had embedded in such early naturalistic works of fiction as "A Party Down at the Square" is still being voiced, albeit in a heavily allusive high-modernist idiom.[16]

Ellison's notes indicate that he considered situating the priest scene at many different points in the text, from the invisible man's early days at Men's House to his time at Mary's to his full involvement in Brotherhood activity. Ellison's eventual decision to locate the episode right after the eviction reveals the text's hardening emphasis on the politician's opportunism:

> If [the] priest scene comes after he [is] approached by politician, it will be given an added irony; i.e., he has really lost integrity and will play any role. . . . "Man's dispair is God's opportunity," comes into his mind, ironically, while he is giving last rites to old man (who reminds him of Old Man Norton in the Golden Day). Ironically, for in his own dispair he goes to see [the] politician, thus it is [the] politician's opportunity.

Despite Ellison's evident attachment to the priest scene—it appears in multiple plot outlines—he eventually left it out. Perhaps he felt that the episode's modernist allusiveness, like that associated with Cleo/Delphenia or various elements in the hospital dream sequence, was overly dense. In the search for "universals," it was one thing to invoke John Henry; it was quite another to appeal to more obscure Western cultural and intellectual traditions familiar only to elite audiences. Perhaps he was influenced by the Knopf editor Harry Ford's comment that the episode should be "sacrifice[d] . . . in the interest of the forward movement of the narrative. Loss of identity and personal confusion of the narrator seems strongly established without it." While *Invisible Man* suffers no irremediable damage—indeed the text probably benefits—from Ellison's decision to excise the priest episode, the comment quoted above reveals the deliberateness with which he approached the task of structuring his text. He was well aware that, immediately following the protagonist's encounter with Jack, the priest episode would resonate with an ironic political implication it would lack in other settings. Ellison was a highly conscious practitioner of symbolic action.[17]

"All Americans joining hands against their oppressors and dispossessors": The Brotherhood Parade

Ellison's decision to excise another episode that would have followed the eviction scene is considerably more crucial. The invisible man is shown encountering a multiracial march of protestors streaming down Lenox Avenue toward Mount Morris Park; the successful eviction protest is inspiring mass activity. Curious, but also wondering whether "that nameless girl, with a warm voice, a pleasant face," is somewhere in the parade, he follows:

> There were hundreds of them, marching six or eight abreast in a kind of wild discipline beneath a blaze of phosphorescent flares. . . . I now saw the whites, not old and at the head, as they would have been at the campus, but young, of all ages and mixed indiscriminately throughout the procession. . . . At the head of the procession a group of men stood on the bed of a truck, surveying the gathering crowd. "They must be the leaders," I thought. . . .
>
> Their chanted words were now becoming distinct:
> *"No more dispossession of the dispossessed!"*

Noting that the men in the truck are a mix of black and white, with one looking "like an Indian or a Chinese," he sees a sign bearing the image of a locomotive and the words, "The History Train is Moving, Get on Board, Harlem, Get on Board," as well as other placards proclaiming, "YOU HAVE A DATE WITH DEMOCRACY" and "A RENDEZVOUS WITH HISTORY!"[18]

Although some onlookers disparage the whites in the march as "just some *more* white folks making some more fools out of some *more* Negroes," a group of boys do a riff on the marchers' slogans in the parade's wake:

> *I dispossessed your mama 'bout half past nine,*
> *She said, "Come back, daddy, any ole time."*
> *I dispossessed your sister at a quarter to two,*
> *Said, "If you stay 'til six, daddy, you will do."*
> *I dispossessed your grandma at a quarter to one,*
> *She said, "Daddy, daddy, daddy, thy will be done."*

Jesus Christ, I thought, looking at the strutting, nose thumbing boys. I
haven't heard anything like that since I left home. They were playing the
dozens in the same rhythm as the chant.[19]

The invisible man is not deterred by a woman in a hot dog stall who urges
him instead to join Father Divine; he would then be "possessed by father, . . .
and there ain't no room for worldly dispossession." The march and subsequent rally at Mount Morris Park have him enthralled, and he recalls, "Something which I could not define took hold of me. Perhaps this is something
like what I had made them feel today." Hearing the crowd sing "one of our
songs . . . but with a different set of words," he at first feels "somewhat indignant," as if "tricked into singing something as new which [he] had known all
along." Watching the group on the speakers' platform, consisting of "twenty
men . . . one white woman and one black woman," he sees Brother Jack, looking down "as though he saw each member of the crowd separately and in infinite detail." A bushy-bearded white man addresses the crowd

> in economic terms, . . . painting a picture of bad conditions which ex-
> tended not only over the North but over the entire world. He described
> scenes of eviction and dispossession and men laid off from jobs, and the
> work of unions and the activities of strike-breakers and the attempts to
> set white workers against black workers. "There is only one America," he
> said. "And it's not a white America nor a black America, it's the America
> of equality, where everyone should be guaranteed the right to live in
> peace and prosperity, an America to be won by all Americans joining
> hands against their oppressors and dispossessors."

When the crowd sings "John Brown's Body," the invisible man remembers that his grandfather "had often sung [the song] in a quavering voice
when by himself." After the national anthem is sung, he ascends the windblown speakers' platform; the man who greets him is at first "cold-eyed" but
warmly calls him "Brother Key" when he recognizes the young man as the
speaker at the eviction. "If you want me, I'd like to work with you," the protagonist offers. "All you have to do is speak, brother," he is told. "You just
keep the door unlocked and we'll do the rest."[20]

The man's cold eyes recall the stare of the party leader in "The Initiation";
his statement that the invisible man needs only to speak signals troubles
to come. Nonetheless white members of the Brotherhood are shown here
not as aliens mysteriously popping up at Harlem evictions, but as activists
at ease marching down Lenox Avenue alongside their black comrades. The

Brotherhood's slogan about dispossession is not foreign to Harlem ears, but assimilable to the verbal play of the dozens. The Brotherhood's call for "an America to be won by all Americans joining hands against their oppressors and dispossessors" carries nonironic force; Ellison would later scoff at Communist claims to embody "twentieth-century Americanism," but the white-bearded speaker, who appears both persuasive and sincere, utters words similar to those Ellison himself had penned during the late 1930s and early 1940s. Most important is the fact that the invisible man joins up with the Brotherhood not several weeks later, because he is broke, but immediately, because he is attracted by what he has seen and heard. Despite its faint hints at the "authoritarianism of the left," the parade episode contains a highly sympathetic representation of the Popular Front–era CP. Had it been retained in the published text it might have recalled for some of the novel's first readers not only the vigorous left-led Depression-era activism but also the recent Harlem nighttime vigils of thousands in support of Willie McGee and the Martinsville Seven, cold war–era victims of racist attack. The passage had to be expunged.[21]

"We're not interested in his looks but in his ability":
Induction into the Brotherhood

In the 1952 text the invisible man is inducted into the Brotherhood at the Chthonian several weeks after the eviction episode; in the drafts this scene occurs on the same evening as the eviction, parade, and rally. LeRoy is on the protagonist's mind, for the cubist paintings on the walls of the wealthy fellow traveler's apartment remind him of the portrait now on Mary's wall. The other guests are approachable. One, who, the young man thinks, may be passing over the color line, is a "pleasant man with dreamy gray eyes"; perhaps he offsets the "cold-eyed" man at the rally. The "plain" woman who asks about "the state of women's rights" (311) in the 1952 text is earlier described as a "feminist fighter" who inquires into the "conditions of domestic workers." It seems unnecessary to stipulate that she is not attractive.[22]

In the 1952 text Jack's designation of the invisible man as "the new Booker T. Washington" (305) indicates that the smoker scene is about to be replayed; the invisible man, we anticipate, will again imitate Washington's "Atlanta Compromise" address of 1895, albeit in an altered idiom, to please those with power. But Jack's proposition that this new Booker T. Washington will "work for the poor" is initially accompanied by the explicit statement, "The old Washington worked for the rich. You will be . . . even greater than he. Because you today will speak not just for one race, but for all the dispossessed. . . . You shall be one of a collectivity of heroes of the people!" Jack's choice of Washington is anomalous; not Washington but Douglass, as Ellison well knew, was the African American at the center of the left's pantheon of historical heroes. While Jack's opportunism is blatant, it is evident that what he admires in Washington is his capacity to lead, not his politics. His admission that Washington "worked for the rich" recalls Ellison's own earlier estimate that Washington, as a tool of the "counter-revolution" in the post-Reconstruction South, had "betrayed not only the Negro but also the working class and the northern farmers as well." At least no punches are being pulled.[23]

Jack is evidently obsessed with a view of History that is both apocalyptic and mechanical: a "supreme world crisis" must be faced, and only the Brotherhood can offer the necessary "scientific explanation" (307). This statement is supplemented in a draft, however, by his observation that in times of crisis "the people . . . [demand] the resurrection of the dead," and that "the dead will answer":

> Thus the question is whether we who represent the living, we who are the consciences of the people are to stand by and allow the dead to come forth with their old false answers, the answers made invalid by historical developments or whether we shall teach the dead the new answers, the new truth, so that they can give the people the new truth in their old names? We say no! For if we fail to win the ears of the dead, the enemies of the people will take advantage, they will write the speeches of the dead.

Although Jack arrogantly considers himself to be in possession of "the new truth," he evinces a certain degree of epistemological sophistication. He sees that history is both past events and the way they are narrated; the class struggle is fought out in the streets and in the realm of discourse. In the battle of representation, figures from the past, especially the past of a nation, are always being reconfigured for present uses: hence his placing alongside Booker T. Washington such figures as Jefferson, Jackson, Pulaski, Garibaldi, Sun Yat-sen, Danny O'Connell, and Abraham Lincoln (307). Typical of the Popular Front–era CP's advocacy of popular nationalism, Jack's statement is not one with which Ellison, as he revised his manuscript, would likely have quarreled; perhaps it needed to be struck from his increasingly negative portrayal of Jack precisely because he agreed with it.[24]

Jack's interchange with Emma further indicates Ellison's initial intention to invest the Brotherhood leader with greater credibility. In the original typescript, when Emma expresses her wish that the young man were "a little blacker," Jack angrily responds, "Don't be a damn fool. . . . We're not interested in his looks but in his ability." The word "ability" is crossed out, and "voice" is penciled in. In the first version Jack apparently has made a positive estimate of the young man's potential that is not restricted to his verbal facility. Emma's comment raises serious doubts about the Brotherhood's integrity; the invisible man catches its imperialist overtones and thinks, taking a stiff drink, "What was I, a man or a natural resource?" (303). What Emma says moreover is not Ellison's own invention: in 1944 it was reported in the right-wing *New York World-Telegram* that the light-skinned Angelo Herndon had heard the CP leader Anna Damon utter words to this effect when, several years before, he had been greeted by a CP-led delegation in New York's Pennsylvania Station after being freed from prison. If Damon had in fact made the statement about Herndon's complexion, Ellison would probably have heard the story from Herndon himself during their time as coeditors of *Negro Quarterly*. Apparently, however, this offensive comment, even if authentic, did not turn Herndon away from the CP; in *Let Me Live* his claim to have been "dazzled" by the multiracial display of the "brotherhood of man" referred to his experiences on the very day he arrived in New York. It was only when Arthur Schlesinger, drawing upon the *World-Telegram* reportage, featured Damon's comment in a *Life* magazine article about the CP in 1946 and subsequently in his *The Vital Center* in 1949, that Damon's remark assumed synecdochic status as a register of the racial outlook presumably widespread among white Communists. Ellison's original intention to feature Jack's valuation of the invisible man's ability rather than his looks (or for that matter his voice) would have suggested, at the very least, that, within Brotherhood circles, there was a range of racial attitudes, some more emancipated than others. This was an estimate that Ellison himself had in fact aired in the draft of "Richard Wright's Blues," where he stated that although some white Communists, acting out of guilt, "idealize" their Negro comrades, thereby producing a "double standard," there are "fortunately . . . some Negroes and whites who, by recognizing the causes [of the double standard], escape this dead-end."[25]

It could be argued that Ellison's substitution of "voice" for "ability" in the published text is not all that significant; Jack is, after all, characterized as a politician and shown to be manipulative from the outset. But characterization is dialectical and situational; depending on where a writer places emphasis at a given moment, either negative or positive qualities can predominate. In the context supplied by the 1952 version of the library scene, where it is patent that Jack intends the invisible man to function as a ventriloquist's dummy, the Brotherhood leader's subsequent condemnation of the short drunken white man who asks the protagonist to sing spirituals constitutes further evidence not of Jack's antiracism, but of his inhumanity. Although the drunk's statement that invisible man, *qua* Negro, must be naturally musical recalls Emma's whispered comment about his complexion, the new recruit is shown reacting to the two assertions quite differently. Emma's racism places her beyond the pale, while the drunk's invites the compassionate thought, "Shouldn't the short man have the right to make a mistake without his motives being considered consciously or unconsciously malicious?" (314). Presumably the drunk is an object of sympathy because he has also been the object of Jack's attack. By this logic, however, Jack is both damned if he does react and damned if he does not. Had he, or some other Brotherhood representative, not intervened, the drunk's stereotypical remark would have gone uncontested; yet Jack's shouting at the drunk leads the invisible man to conclude that the Brotherhood's programmatic condemnation of white chauvinism is a sign of an unforgiving rigidity, not of an authentic dedication to equality.[26]

This scene contains one other small revision with large ramifications. When Jack hands the invisible man his new Brotherhood name, it is at first "typed on a slip of paper"; "typed" is crossed out and "written" is penciled in. In the 1952 text, the protagonist's crowning realization of Jack's betrayal will occur when, having fled underground during the riot, he matches the handwriting on the warning note he received as Harlem organizer with the handwriting on the slip containing his Brotherhood name: it is a moment of consummate re-cognition, the falling into place of the final piece in the jigsaw puzzle of treachery. In Ellison's original conception of his plot, however, there was evidently no plan that *perception* would hinge on this visual clue, for there is no direct evidence that Jack is the supplier of the new name. Indeed while it is evident that the invisible man has not chosen his own party name, for readers familiar with leftist organizing this assignment of an alternate political identity would not necessarily set off alarm bells; in order to evade surveillance it was routine for Communists to assume different names, and often to play no role in choosing them. Indeed in one of Ellison's favorite novels, Malraux's *Days of Wrath*, the Communist protagonist Kassner is saved from execution by an imprisoned comrade who self-sacrificially assumes Kassner's name; falsifying and exchanging names can save lives. As Ellison later remarked about his rhetorical strategy as a practitioner of symbolic action, "Place[d] in the right context, and at the optimum state of an action, [a detail] vibrates and becomes symbolically eloquent."

It is the inclusion of the name-bearing paper within the associational cluster of Bellerophontic letters, rather than the paper's possession of intrinsic significance as a marker of red perfidy, that invests it with "symboli[c] eloquence."[27]

"Oh you fair warrior": The Othello Theme

In the earliest versions of the Chthonian chapter there appears to have been no induction in the library, no toast to History. Instead the invisible man has already joined the Brotherhood after the torchlight parade; at the party he is absorbed by his reencounter with the pale young blonde woman he met at the eviction earlier that day. Her name is Louise; he flirts with abandon. She is idealistic; speaking of "the movement" she says, "It's our only hope! And our people are the best people in the country. Really selfless and devoted and truly democratic. You're sure to like it." The narrator recalls, "'Yes, I'm sure,' I said, looking boldly into her eyes, 'Because you're a part of it, I'm sure I will.'" As he looks at her "gently throbbing and upward sweeping throat," he is infatuated:

> And I knew at that moment that it was not her color, but the voice and if there was anything in the organization to which I could give myself completely, it was she. If I could work with her, be always near her, then I could have all that the Trustees had promised and failed to give, and more. And if she was not the meaning of the struggle for the others, for me she would be the supremest prize of all. "O you fair warrior," my mind raced on, "You dear, sweet, lovely thing, for you I'd rock the nation with a word. You'll be my Liberty and Democracy, Hope and Truth and Beauty, the justification for manhood, the motive for courage and cunning; for you I'll make myself into this new name they've given me and I'll believe that Brother Jack and the others mean what they say about creating a world in which even men like me can be free."

Well tutored by Woodridge, the invisible man replays in his mind Othello's greeting to Desdemona: "O my fair warrior." He remembers the vet's laughter but thinks, "So I would *play* the fool, and if it was that my being black made me desire the white meat of the chicken, then I'd accept my desire along with the chitterlings and sweet potato pie."[28]

The Othello theme is extended as the invisible man and Louise converse. She speaks of her wealthy father, a variant on Shakespeare's Brabantio, and declares that her political participation is "a means of balancing up some

of the harm he does." Her white handkerchief recalls for the young man a
story about an aunt of his, a laundress who, offended by her employer's demand to know the secret of her spotless washing, claimed that she added
coal oil; when her employer tested the technique (one apparently less effica-
cious than the admixture of black to white at Liberty Paints) and chastised
the laundress, the black woman beat the white woman "to a fair thee well."
Nothing daunted by the challenge implicit in the story—will she identify
with the rebellious black laundress or the overbearing white employer?—
Louise responds, "We must act in order to do something about the hateful
things." Louise is no mere liberal or fellow traveler, the invisible man learns;
according to Jack, "[She] works closely with the strategy committee and
many of our directives will come to you through her." When the protagonist
and Louise leave the party together, she, driving a Lincoln convertible purchased by her father, drops him off at the subway; a man asks whether he is
"the one they used to call Petey Wheatstraw back down in Dallas" and con-
gratulates him on having snared a "little pink-toe." Nodding off on the train,
the invisible man dreams briefly of Tatlock, as well as of signs reading "*No
niggers or dogs allowed*" and "QUIT DISPOSSESSING THE DISPOSSESSED."
His mind is spinning; he has met up with his own version of Mary Dalton,
red rather than pink.[29]

Back in LeRoy's former room the protagonist ruminates on his day:

> I'd have to learn that "scientific" language to speak to the people; and I'd
> have to find words to make her understand how I felt about her. All this
> time I'd wasted fooling around waiting for the trustees to recognize me!
> But I'd make up the lost time, now that I knew better; and it was good
> that I'd been given a new name, I'd be able to lash out at them and they
> wouldn't know who I was, or from where I'd come.

His motives are, to say the least, mixed. He is driven by the desire for revenge; while he claims that her color is not what draws him, it is evident
that his attraction to Louise the woman cannot be separated from his es-
timation of Louise as the "prize," the "white meat of the chicken." Besides
setting up an implied comparison between the invisible man and Paul Robeson—whose Broadway performance as Shakespeare's Moor of Venice had
met with great popular acclaim, but whom Ellison was to view over the years
with a combination of awe, contempt, and not a little envy—the *Othello* allusions position him as one who will, we fear, love not wisely but too well. But
if the protagonist in some sense *is* Othello, then Louise *is* Desdemona, a
figure beyond irony who embodies genuine innocence. Where the figure of

a white woman used as bait to draw in black recruits was a familiar trope in such anti-CP texts as J. Saunders Redding's *On Being Negro in America* (1951) and Chester Himes's *Lonely Crusade* (1947), Ellison's Louise would appear to be cut from a different political cloth.[30]

"Working Notes" indicates that Ellison initially assigned to Louise an important role in *Invisible Man*. A "young woman of great charm," Louise "is the one person in the [Brotherhood] whom [the invisible man] can believe accepts him as a human being. He regards her as a symbol of democracy, of freedom and fertility." As we shall see, her figure would continue to appear in various sketches and outlines for subsequent plot developments. Aside from the description of their encounter at the Chthonian, however, the only other sustained passage focused on Louise is a long Joycean ramble, apparently part of the invisible man's meditation the night they have met, in which he free-associates from the white woman featured in beer advertisements to Miss Anne to Primus Provo to Macon County to the blue eagle rock to John Brown to being higher than a Georgia pine, with many other connections in between. Ellison wrote to Hyman in the fall of 1949, "[I have decided] to leave out the 'Othello' theme, which I'm now convinced would complicate thing[s] too much. I'll just save it for the next novel."[31]

In deleting Louise, Ellison no doubt simplified his task. But he also effaced from the text a female character who, linked with Mary Rambo, expands the locus of rebirth beyond the purely male domain; just as Mary serves as surrogate mother to LeRoy, Louise serves as erotic partner and spiritual companion for the invisible man as he strives to meet the demands of his double. She also supplies a compelling instance of at least one Brotherhood member for whom the invisible man is not invisible; that she functions as a symbol of democracy to him, as LeRoy did to Treadwell, alerts us to her vital role in the novel's political theme. Above all she is a white woman who breaks the mold of objectification and stereotype supplied by the other appearances of white women in the novel: the naked dancer and, later, Sybil and the woman in the red robe. To the extent that she is confined to stereotype, this occurs primarily in and through the tortured consciousness of the invisible man.

Commentators on the Chthonian chapter of *Invisible Man* have frequently noted the reference to Greek mythology in the name Ellison chose for his protagonist's site of initiation: because the term refers to the underworld presided over by Hades, it has been taken to suggest the hellish nature of the Brotherhood's domain. The fact that the invisible man later encounters Sybil (Sibyl) at Emma's apartment in the Chthonian underscores the mythologi-

cal allusion and further connects the narrative with Eliot's *The Waste Land,*
where the poet hero descends into the half-classical, half-Christian inferno
of the modern "unreal city." If we bear in mind Ellison's interest in the Cambridge School, however, the Chthonian takes on less demonic connotations.
According to Jane Harrison, the chthonic deities were pre-Olympian figures,
daimons associated with the earth rather than authoritarian gods associated
with the heavens, who embodied the direct relationship between humanity
and nature in preclass societies. The figure of Dionysus distilled this relationship; his yearly initiation at the time of spring planting, entailing sacrifice by dismemberment, signaled the process by which deities are made, and
then used up, in order to meet communal human needs. Harrison points out,
moreover, that the "civilization of the worshippers, quite other than patriarchal," was reflected in the relative positions of male and female deities. In
the underworld, from which new life emerges every spring, Harrison writes,
"two goddesses reign supreme: Demeter and Kore, the Mother and the Maid;
Hades . . . never disputes their sway."[32]

The all-male lineup of Brotherhood leaders in the library indicates that
patriarchy rules supreme; Emma is barely even Hera to Jack's Zeus, serving
as at most his secretary and mistress. But Louise's prominent role in the
earliest versions of the Chthonian episode suggests her connection with the
chthonian deities, especially with Kore (more commonly known as Perse-
phone), whose emergence from the underworld every spring accompanies
the renewal of life and the promise of agricultural bounty, especially corn.
Louise's "fall of light hair" reinforces her resemblance to Kore/Persephone
of the corn-silk hair and links her with Mary Rambo, a Demeter/Themis/
Gaia figure, in a symbolic daughter-mother relation. Their nurturing relationships with the doubled figures of LeRoy and the invisible man testify to
the central role of women, as both mothers and lovers, in the birth, growth,
death, and rebirth of male heroes. It is perhaps no accident that the invisible
man thinks of LeRoy's picture when he sees Emma's cubist paintings; his
secret sharer, the proletarian hanged god, is witnessing the invisible man's
initiation in this new variant of Men's House. Ellison's interest in the matriarchal configuration of the chthonian deities may motivate the otherwise
anomalous comment that, in an early version of the library scene, is assigned
to one of the Brotherhood leaders: he declares not "We believe in brotherhood," but "We believe in motherhood." The site of initiation into the band
of false fathers in the published text, the Chthonian figures as the site of a
more ambiguous entry into the tribe in the novel's early drafts. It is where
the invisible man meets a white goddess whose mythical whiteness is asso-

ciated not with castration and control—as are, in their different ways, both the dancer of the battle royal and Sybil—but with rituals stemming from the collective needs of a nonhierarchical social order.[33]

"Tell us what we need to know":
Meeting Brother Hambro

The invisible man's fondness for his fellow roomers makes him regret "having to leave this old house with its close, intimate community, even though it was often too close for me." Regarding Cleo, he thinks, "God knows I don't owe *her* anything. . . . Except . . . that which a man owes any woman, every woman, if he thinks he does and she thinks he does, which I don't, which she would, but I wont. . . . And yet I'll be leaving something unfinished with her." He dreams that he is on stilts and that, taking him for LeRoy, she calls him down. Leaving Mary's the next morning, he carries not only the iron-cast Sambo bank but also LeRoy's journal. "Where else could you get a job beating your gums?" he ponders, banishing his doubts. "You're—what's the phrase—dedicated and set aside, for whatever and you'd better hurry and learn for what. Brother Jack's made a date for you with history." He leaves behind his old hat, "its green felt . . . sunfaded and dust coated though [he] had worn it only a year": "Now it hung shapeless and brown, like a leaf struck by the winter's snow. I would buy a new one for my new name." An avatar of the year-daimon, he has been reborn and is entering a cycle of activity where the words "dedicated and set aside" will rearticulate his role as scapegoat—whether as fall guy or dying god remains to be seen.[34]

Ellison considered inserting at this point a short comic scene in which the invisible man attempts to change the hundred-dollar bill given to him by Brother Jack. Some midtown jewelers attempt to swindle him, but he is wise to their game. The episode plays off the battle royal scene—this time he can tell fake money from real—but adds little to the novel beyond making the obvious point that he is now in the big money and has become somewhat cagier. In the published text the invisible man immediately enters the tutelage of Brother Hambro, a "tall, friendly man, a lawyer and the Brotherhood's chief theoretician" (357). The older man does not appear in a dramatized scene, however, until he coldly explains the necessity for sacrificing Harlem. By contrast, Hambro's precursor is named Stein; the "third joint of his right index finger" is "permanently crooked"; he bears "three blue stars tattooed on the back of his left hand." This "almost Lincolnesque" teacher stresses the unity of theory and practice, noting that "action without theory [is] a riot; theory without action, that's kibitzing." The invisible man finds himself "working harder than [he] ever had at college," during the day "reading and discussing theory" and in the evenings "attending rallies and meetings in the various districts." Stein/Hambro urges his student, "Listen to the people talk, get their grievances, their protests." He acknowledges, "[The Brotherhood has] tried on several occasions to move the people to action and each time we've failed . . . [because we had the] wrong approach—not to the historical forces, but to your people."[35]

Stein/Hambro's explanation is worth quoting at length:

A people may exist during a historical period and still not be of that period, just as the Plains Indians are still with us but not a part of the present day historical movements. To be part of a historical period a people must be organized and able to make themselves felt as a force. To do this a group must find its voice. . . . It must be able to effectively accept or reject the basic issues of its time, and thus it must learn to act.

In answer to the invisible man's query, "But don't we act?" Stein/Hambro replies,

Yes, but not historically. . . . I refer to *decisive* action. Perhaps it would be more correct to say that your people *react* rather than act—insofar as they express themselves after events which profoundly effect their destiny have occurred. *After* a lynching or a riot they protest, and sometimes quite vigorously. But to act scientifically in regards to such a situation would be to take action to *prevent it before* it *happened.* At the first hint they would arm themselves or take whatever action that would be effective— asking for police protection, where that is possible—although we know it seldom is; calling upon friendly white people—whatever is necessary to swerve the developing forces away from the destructive event and transform it into [a] socially useful one.

Noting that the group behavior of the Negro people "has nothing to do with race"—the "labor unions were like that until recently"—Stein/Hambro concludes with a warning and a plea:

We don't know too much about your people. We thought we did but we don't, even though some of us still think we do. What we have is a theory. It's a good theory, but it's up to you to put it into action. So instead of trying to tell you how or what to do I'll tell you to work it out your own way. Only don't say that I told you, because some of our brothers wouldn't understand. . . . And one final thing, Brother: don't tell us what we want to hear, tell us what we need to know.[36]

Ellison's decision to exclude this conversation from the 1952 text substantially alters the invisible man's introduction to the left. Where Brother Jack seems to have all the answers and simply wants the invisible man to rubber-stamp his conclusions, here the principal Brotherhood theorist evinces a good deal of humility, stressing the need for theory to be informed by practice. His analysis of the requirement that African Americans "make themselves felt as a force" recalls a principal concern of Ellison's *Negro Quarterly* editorials. Stein/Hambro's assertion that the purpose of such historical engagement is to act proactively in order to "prevent [a lynching or riot] from happening" contrasts dramatically with the 1952 text's portrayal of radicals wishing to profit from racial violence. Stein/Hambro advocates that Negroes "act historically" so that they may make their own "destiny" rather than have it made for them; he turns Norton's formulation on its head. As a sympathetic mentor Stein/Hambro resists incorporation into the cluster of false fathers who reenact the battle royal's governing ritual. Like Trader Stein in *Lord Jim*, Stein/Hambro is instructing the young man how to survive in the "destructive element" into which he is being initiated, indeed how to transform the "destructive event" into its opposite.

But Stein/Hambro is not just a wise mentor. Notably he is most likely Jewish, as his name suggests, and he bears on his hand what appears to be a concentration camp tattoo as well as evidence of torture. Stein is aligned with other references to Jews and anti-Semitism—the "tall, fastidious Jew" of the protagonist's childhood, the protagonist's claim to have been "burned in the same oven" as the Provos—that suggest parallels between the "Nazi persecution of Jews" and "the persecution of Negroes in the United States" that Ellison had examined in one of his first pieces of political journalism. In the 1952 version of *Invisible Man* Hambro's largely unsympathetic characterization suggests an ironic inflection to his name; his claim to being a brother to the sons of Ham is specious, indeed hammy. If we recall his earlier incarnation as the largely sympathetic Stein, however, Hambro's name suggests the kinship between the sons of Ham (who was after all a son of Noah and brother to Shem, biblical ancestor of all Semitic peoples) and modern Jews, as well as the speciousness of the racist discourse proclaiming their difference. Ellison's original portrayal of Stein/Hambro thus suggests his continuity with such positively rendered left-wing Jewish characters as Wright's Boris Max in *Native Son* and Himes's Abe Rosenberg in *Lonely Crusade*. Compounding the omission of references to Spain and Munich, the conversion of Stein into Hambro removes *Invisible Man* from the international context of fascism and war, the "supreme world crisis" to which Brother Jack referred.

"The great groping of the blind for sight":
The Arena Speech

With the elimination of the antieviction parade, the arena rally is the novel's only dramatized representation of the appeal of the Popular Front-era CP to New York's working class. The invisible man is mesmerized by the heady atmosphere in the hall: the singing of "John Brown's Body," the enthusiasm of the "uncommon people" determined to be "dispossessed" no more. Yet the protagonist is both caged and blinded in the circle of artificial light; his recalling that "years ago" a famous boxer was "beaten blind in a crooked fight . . . right here in this arena" implies—for the reader, if not the Candide-like hero—that the novel's governing ritual is about to be replayed. Over several drafts Ellison converted an uplifting experience into one tinged with threat. At first Brother Jack contributes to the oratory, "speaking in terms of economic[s], history, international trends[,] . . . of the necessity facing the people, of what they must do." For the young man on the stage Jack "seemed to roll the world into a circle of meaning, then took a segment of the circle and pulled it until it was like a pointer that [led] to each individual in the arena." This conjunction of individual and collective identities gives the invisible man "the sense of being intimately connected with events and people abroad."

> I no longer lived upon a fragment, but in a total world, the revolution of which, with its surge of events, through the correct and combined action of others, I could help control. For the first time I seemed to have a hand in my own destiny. Old Norton had spoken of me as *his* destiny, now Brother Jack was giving me a sense that I was my own—no, that we, here in the arena were *our* destiny. We had only to combine and act. . . . I listened completely absorbed, my respect for him growing.[37]

Although Jack's speech does not stir the audience emotionally—"No shouts of 'Amen' interrupted him, nor spontaneous singing"—the invisible man initially thinks, "He's giving them too much to absorb at once . . . the analysis is too profound." Ellison revised this passage to read, "I listened carefully to his analysis. He went into minute detail, speaking coldly in terms of economics." Finally, however, Ellison removed Jack's entire speech, along with the protagonist's reaction to its content, and portrayed the Brotherhood leader as a "father listening to the performance of his children," penciling in "bemused" before "father," "adoring" before "children." He added the concluding words, "'Listen to them,' Brother Jack said. 'Just waiting to be told what to do.'" The Brotherhood's Marxism has been transformed from a means of grasping totality to an instrument of totalitarian control.[38]

Ellison initially placed considerably more emphasis on the rally's display of class-based multiracial unity. "Lord, Our God, we are assembled here tonight with the lines thrown down," intones the preacher who opens the rally. "I mean the color lines, Lord. Tonight, Lord, there will be no color line for we know that in your sight no colors exist. We are assembled, Lord, in the spirit of brotherhood." Sounding much like the invocation uttered by the preacher-turned–Workers Alliance organizer that Ellison recorded in "No Discrimination," the opening prayer shows the Popular Frontist appeal of the "spirit of brotherhood." As soon as he enters the arena, the invisible man sees "row after row of faces, black and white." ("Black and white" was crossed out of a subsequent draft.) In the published text, the theme of class-based solidarity can be inferred from his parable of the two one-eyed men who stop "walking down opposite sides of the street" and combine their vision to fight back against the "smooth, oily scoundrel running down the middle of the street . . . [who] claims he needs the space—he calls it his *freedom*" (344). But the phrase "black and white" explicitly describes the audience only once in the published text, when, near the end of his speech, the protagonist tells his listeners that he feels "your black and white eyes upon me" (345). Expanding the speech in the drafts, Ellison contemplated that, as he stands in the spotlight, the invisible man might conjure up a "picture of [a] flood with people of both races fighting the force of nature, lined up with spades repairing a broken levee." The invisible man would link this image from a transformed South with his own remembered picture of "Negroes and whites with flares winding up . . . Mount Morris Park . . . in the cold."[39]

These utopian visual images of black and white, dark and light, Ellison jotted, would be accompanied by literary images of "black and white fraternity," recalling "Huck and Jim," the "Negroes in Moby Dick," and Faulkner's "kids in Intruder in the Dust." The speech would also draw upon the invisible man's memories of his "grandfather's friendship for his young master; how they hunted, played, fought and ate and were punished together; and how later the grownups intervened and destroyed their friendship, destroyed their innocence and dropped the curtain of hate between them." The young orator places this somewhat idealized account of antebellum trans-

black and white fraternity has been an unlawful thing." That the movement
exemplified at the arena rally is to complete the unfinished tasks of the Civil
War, and make real the fictional utopia imagined by Ellison's cherished "ancestors," is clear.[40]

In the published text the invisible man's leaning forward and confessing
that he feels "more human" is prompted by an eruption of his subconscious,
a feeling of being "naked" in the bright lights (345). In an earlier version he
confronts the electricity of the situation in terms that explicitly recall the
battle royal:

> I had to seize the ends of the broken power line and allow it to flow
> through myself—otherwise failure and profound embarrassment. And
> even as I felt the words returning I sensed that I was about to say some-
> thing that shouldn't have been revealed. I leaned forward, straining to
> see through [the] barrier of light, feeling the hot swift terror that comes
> when technique fails, when the machine collapses and you see the blood
> shoot from your exposed flesh. It was one of those moments when, with
> the [mechanism] thrown out of gear there is left nothing to fill the gap
> but the tender naked self.

Declaring, "Our common dream [has become] . . . a fighting reality," he concludes, "You've given me back my anger and the old human vision. I've been
reborn. I've been reborn in you and you in me and we witness an American
miracle. I feel the great deep ache of the land for fraternity, the great groping of the blind for sight."[41]

In the 1952 text the protagonist is wholly unprepared for the arena speech,
which he delivers the day after his induction at the Chthonian; although
he has glanced at some Brotherhood pamphlets, he knows nothing about
left politics. Yet he undergoes severe chastisement all the same; evidently
his lapse into the vernacular has pushed the sectarian buttons of several
Brotherhood leaders. In earlier drafts, by contrast, he has studied with Stein/
Hambro for four months and has sat silently on rally platforms analyzing the
strengths and weaknesses of other Brotherhood speakers. When he speaks
in the arena it is not a sink-or-swim situation, nor is there a postmortem.
"The others were waiting in the dressing room," recalls the narrator, "and
as we got into the car and started away I could hear the audience still cheer-
ing behind us." In a subsequent version containing the post-rally meeting,
Brother Jack offers a mild criticism: "You did well. . . . But you must study
our literature because you must never fail to get over our ideological mes-

sage." The other leaders are "more enthusiastic." The "brother with the pipe" drops his initial criticism, the "short bald man" affirms Jack's overall positive assessment, and "the others made sounds of agreement." Although in these early versions of the episode the Brotherhood leaders would presumably have firmer grounds for criticizing the "unscientific" nature of the invisible man's speech—he has, after all, been studying both theory and practice for several months—they are relatively positive; perhaps they actually appreciate his ability rather than just his voice.[42]

Later that evening the invisible man reflects upon the reaction of the audience: "I had spoken for them and they had recognized my words. I belong to them. . . . Perhaps this was what was meant by being 'dedicated and set aside.'" Wondering, "What had I meant by saying that I had become 'more human'?," he dismisses the possibility that he had picked up the phrase from another rally speaker, his grandfather, or Woodridge. Racking his brain, he decides, "It was a mystery once more, as at the eviction I had uttered words that had possessed me" (353-54). While the source of the phrase "dedicated and set aside" is equally a mystery to the reader of the 1952 text, a reader acquainted with the drafts recognizes their provenance in Treadwell's description of LeRoy. The phrase "more human" comes from LeRoy himself, as he meditates in his journal about the need for "a way of life more universal, more human and more free than any to be found in the world today." To be "more human" involves laying claim to a kind of freedom very different from that enjoyed by the capitalist whose freedom consists in keeping the workers visually impaired by racism and confined to different sides of the street.[43]

Still mulling the uncanny way in which LeRoy's words have worked their way into the back of his mind, the invisible man reads further in the journal and comes across the entry in which LeRoy imagines being able to reach fifteen million listeners. The protagonist ruminates:

> If I could get only a million to listen to me I could get something done. What if one could get the 15 million to listen, he could help get something done. What if I could become known to each and every one of them, could become a meaningful name in their mouths? That was something worth working for, and a way to make the world spin faster. If I could reach each of these and bring them into the movement.

Next to the text describing the invisible man thinking, "Ally the one tenth of the population with those conditioned to brotherhood and there'd be no worry about race," Ellison scribbled in the margin, "Dies Irae."[44]

It is noteworthy that LeRoy's conceit about radio broadcasting, the trope that famously ends the novel, occurs in the aftermath of the arena rally. The protagonist dreams of reaching an audience of millions — of "raising hell with radios!," as Langston Hughes exclaims in "Good Morning, Revolution!" — on the day when he feels he has "become 'more human'" and, as a Brotherhood representative, "spoken for" his audience of "uncommon people." Ellison's jotting "Dies Irae" next to the invisible man's vision of a Brotherhood-led movement of millions alludes to the antifascist theme effaced from the published text. For the Latin phrase "Dies Irae," in religious discourse associated with the Day of Judgment, translates as "day [or days] of wrath," the English title of Malraux's novel (translated in 1936) about German antifascists. While this historical reference point, coupled with the Popular Frontist theme of dispossession, would seem to locate the arena rally in the 1930s, as in the early sketches of the eviction scene Ellison blends the Depression and wartime years. For the invisible man's statement that for seventy-nine years "black and white fraternity has been an unlawful thing" — most likely a reference to the Emancipation Proclamation of 1863 — situates his speech in 1942, in which case the "supreme world crisis" that laps at the novel's edge is not the rise of fascism in the 1930s but the antifascist war of the early 1940s, with all the complications posed to the left by the Nazi invasion of the USSR. The invisible man's desire to reach fifteen million listeners by radio is thus a more ambitious version of Ellison's and Herndon's project in *Negro Quarterly* of persuading African Americans that they have "their own stake in the fight against fascism."[45]

In the published version of *Invisible Man* the arena rally figures as an ambiguous event; heady and exciting, it is shadowed by memories of the battle royal. In his subsequent meditation the protagonist catches at straws of memory, unable to recall where he came up with the phrase "more human" or to fathom how or by whom he has been "dedicated and set aside." His excitement at being accepted and celebrated is offset by the cold reception of his speech by several Brotherhood leaders who promise to figure as future competitors and antagonists. His success is fraught with anxiety.

In the drafts, by contrast, the invisible man accepts the role proposed to him by Treadwell and acknowledges his oneness with LeRoy. He recognizes the danger of electrocution but volunteers to be the conduit of electricity connecting the platform with the rest of the arena; where at the battle royal his conduction of electricity was a means of surviving a ritual directed against him as a "pseudoscientific" scapegoat, here it is dialectically transformed into a strategy for purposively aligning the individual with the collective. The electricity generated at the power plant operated by black hands need not be utilized only for purposes of exploiting labor or, as in the hospital episode, assuring ideological domination; it can be turned against its owners and supply light for those who dwell in darkness. On the day of the invisible man's emergence into the spotlight as a Brotherhood organizer, LeRoy has been reborn in him. The repressed alter ego that had burst out with the words "social equality" at the smoker, led him down the road to Trueblood's shack, tormented him during his days of "lostness," and prompted him to "attack the Founder" at the eviction, has emerged from the depths of his political unconscious. Through LeRoy's analysis of the sources of black leadership, the invisible man grasps the connections among fighting "dispossession," becoming "more human," and being "dedicated and set aside." The ominous similarities between the arena rally and the battle royal indicate that the novel's "governing ritual" may well still prevail. But irony and destiny contest with hope and possibility; the "great groping of the blind for sight," coupled explicitly with the "deep ache for the land of fraternity," is not an individual but a mass historical need, one for which the Brotherhood is shown to possess a solution of considerable appeal. Not all boxers end up blinded; the invisible man is willing to fight for sight. He is not, at least at this moment, the scapegoat as victim, but the scapegoat as sacrificial hero, consciously willing to subject himself to modern forces of production if these can provide the energy for movement toward a better world.

"I could make them forget black and white":
Organizing for the Brotherhood

Ellison considered various possibilities for the invisible man's activities as a Brotherhood organizer. There might be a "mass meeting at Columbus Circle where he discovers American political violence. Goons come to break up meeting, he fights . . . [is] arrested under old law against masking in public because he appears on platform wearing dark glasses. Case fought to supreme court. Won." This victory would be followed by a "campaign to have Negroes hired as bus drivers, other city jobs." Or, "badly beaten at a demonstration, [he] lies between life and death. Survives a hero." Or again, feeling the need to redeem himself after his "failure to use scientific language," he might engage in some "heroic action[,] one in which he performs self sacrifice[,] . . . refus[ing] to give information under torture." He "might return South for a time; he might go to prison to make it possible for more important leader to continue his work." In one way or another, Ellison decided, the plot "demands a dramatic, climactic action," one enabling the invisible man to "act heroically" and at the same time "suspect that he is invisible exactly at the moment of his triumph."[46]

That the invisible man's "days of certainty" will end in doubt and then disaster is forecast in the published text at the end of chapter 17, where the retrospective narrator recalls that "for one lone stretch of time" he lived in a magical haze, subjecting himself unquestioningly to a regimen of "pattern and discipline" (380–82). The phase of "purpose" within the arc of "Political Life" has been established quickly; almost immediately problems arise, and the "passion" begins. The first dramatized passage depicting the protagonist's Brotherhood work, his and Tod Clifton's encounter with Ras the Exhorter, ends with Clifton's foreboding comment about the need to "plunge outside of history" (377). The note warning the invisible man that "this is a *white man's world*" then appears on his desk (383), and, as Douglass gazes down from his portrait on the wall of the Harlem office, the long journey toward disillusionment begins. The reader, positioned alongside the ironic narrator in his basement, remains ahead of the naïve protagonist all along, wondering when he will wake up and smell the coffee.

The drafts of *Invisible Man* indicate that Ellison initially planned a fuller description of the "purpose" guiding his protagonist's work as a Brotherhood organizer. Not only does he organize the People's Hot Foot Squad, a "drill team of six-footers . . . striking up sparks with their hob-nailed boots" (379); in the narrator's retrospective summary of the "days of certainty," the activity surrounding the stepped-up campaign against evictions is elaborated:

> It was nothing for our group to pull five thousand men and women into the streets on short notice; or to lead them to mass with groups from other sections for a ringing march straight down Broadway or Fifth, or even Park, to City Hall. We must have worn an inch or two off the surface of the streets. Just give me the hungry and dispossessed and I could make them forget black and white and rush a squad of police, or throw an iron picket line around City Hall or the Mayor's Mansion.

The Brotherhood's activities are shown to produce positive results. After one demonstration of ten thousand "there was a lessening of police brutality, and an ordinance passed against evictions. And most of all more relief was provided." The invisible man manifests heroism in battle—"I continued speaking. Bricks could fly, hostile cops could shatter heads and I'd hold my ground"—and evidently takes seriously his assignment to place his finger on Harlem's pulse:

I began to be quite popular with the membership. Especially with that of Harlem. They were my secret. For it was by talking with them, standing in their bars, visiting [their] homes, listening to their problems, discussing their likes and dislikes that I was able to make fruitful suggestions to the top committees when policy was being made. Besides I reacted to events much as they did themselves. Thus whenever we launched a slogan it was forged so as to express their hopes as well as those of other groups and their support for most issues was won.

Ignoring, however, the most important part of Stein/Hambro's advice—that he should tell the truth—the invisible man acts manipulatively in relation to these "top committees": "I learned to talk only after I had listened to them and when I talked I knew what they wanted and what they wanted to hear; thus in the big committee meetings of the leadership I knew what to say and to get our demands fitted into the general program. Oh I loved the role I played—or thought I played, and I played the role I loved." Even more than in the published text, the invisible man of the drafts is a contradictory figure, in part opportunistically playing a role and in part committed to making the role a reality.[47]

The ironic perspective of the narrator in the 1952 novel guides the reader's attention toward both the illusion-filled protagonist and the menacing circles in which he moves. Ellison's sentence-level additions and substitutions reveal, however, that the retrospective narrator had to undergo considerable refashioning in order to perform this rhetorical function. In a passage describing the narrator's recollection of Brotherhood members from "the other sections," Ellison made the following changes:

> They were like no other people I had ever known. I liked their ability to organize[,] their selfless acceptance of human equality, and their willingness to get their heads beaten to bring it a fraction of a step closer. They were [*substituted: seemed*] willing to go all the way. Even their wages [*substituted: a great part of their wages*] went into the movement. And most of all I liked [*added: what I thought was*] their willingness to call things by their true names. Oh, I was truly carried away. For a while I was putting most of my salary back into the work [*substituted: Money was not so necessary when we found so much in our group*].

The narrator's observations of selfless behavior, originally presented as objective statements of fact, are altered to stress their subjectivity; he now sees the reality behind appearance. Eventually, however, Ellison omitted the entire passage. Even in its qualified form this description of Communist self-lessness supplied perhaps too compelling a rationale for the invisible man's decision to accept his new identity and role. Instead the reader is left with the distinct impression that the Brotherhood has money to throw around; the invisible man's astronomically high salary of sixty dollars per week suggests that he is being bribed by a corruption widespread in the organization.[48]

Even the invisible man's assuming a new name upon joining the Brotherhood takes on a different valence in the novel's earlier drafts. As he watches the "watery play of light" on the portrait of Douglass, he thinks:

> How magical it was that [Douglass] had talked his way from slavery to a government ministry, and so swiftly. Perhaps, I thought, something of the kind is happening to me. Douglass came north to escape and find work in the shipyards; a big fellow in a sailor's suit who, like me, had taken another name. What had his true name been? Whatever it was, it was as Douglass that he became himself, defined himself. And not as a boat-wright, as he'd expected, but as an orator. Perhaps the sense of magic lay in the unexpected transformations. "You start Saul, and end up Paul," my grandfather had often said. (381)

This passage in the 1952 text exhibits the seductiveness of the notion that one can assume an identity, even so heroic an identity as that of Frederick Douglass, when it is supplied by others; the invisible man is repeating his old errors and riding for a fall. In an earlier version, however, between the phrases "is happening to me" and "Douglass came north" are injected the words, "Only I knew more about how things were done than Douglass knew. I was no 19th century idealist, as LeRoy had written of Douglass, and in the Brotherhood we were dedicated to the fight for our beliefs. . . . Yes, there was magic about it."[49]

With the addition of these words, the ensuing reference to Douglass as "a big fellow in a sailor suit" not only recalls that in the previous century Douglass escaped from slavery with the help of abolitionist sailors but also connects him with the twentieth-century radical mariner who reflects upon the limitations of oratory in the absence of action and ponders how best to carry forward the combined legacy of Douglass and Brown. That Douglass had changed his name several times in the course of his escape—and allowed Nathan Johnson, his abolitionist host in New Bedford, to select the name "Douglass" for his final incarnation—further validates name changing as a feature of initiation into a new social role. The evident approval of

Douglass's transformation by the invisible man's grandfather, whose favorite song was "John Brown's Body," further valorizes the practice of changing identities in altering historical circumstances. The allusion to St. Paul (formerly Saul), whose words about rebirth, sight, and totality resonated in the protagonist's mind during the hospital scene, suggests that he is entering a phase when "that which is in part shall be done away"; he will stop "see[ing] as through a glass, darkly," and will encounter the world "face to face."[50]

At least so he hopes. Even in the drafts the invisible man's feeling that his transformation is "magical" bodes ill; in the published text he is closing his eyes to signs of trouble that are all too clear to the reader. To view his sense of transfiguration in an entirely ironic light, however, is something that even the retrospective narrator of the 1952 text cannot fully manage to do. Chapter 17 ends with the protagonist's confident statement, "Life was all pattern and discipline; and the beauty of discipline is when it works. And it was working very well." In an earlier draft Ellison penciled in the words, "If only it could have stopped right there." This observation lacks the ironic intonation of the narrator's other retrospective assessments of the "days of certainty." One wonders whether his creator at one point shared this regret, and with difficulty expunged it from the final draft.[51]

"A lens is forming out of our scars and bruises":
The Magazine Interview

Struggling to truncate "purpose" and get into "passion" as he revised the novel's political section, Ellison omitted several episodes dramatizing the Brotherhood's activism in Harlem. Occurring in the period following the invisible man's reception of the poisoned pen letter warning him, "This is a *white man's world*" (383), these passages elaborate upon the young man's goals and achievements as an organizer. His interview with the magazine reporter—which, summarized rather than dramatized in the 1952 text, leads Wrestrum to accuse his rival of being a "dictator" and an "opportunist" (401)—is initially rendered as a conversation with Miss Laurel, an attractive young woman from *Brown Success* magazine. Asked where he was born, he jokes, "The Arena . . . right on the platform with the spotlight on me"; pressed, he states, "On one of those little Sea Islands off the coast of South Carolina." Remarking on the "traces of African culture to be found there," she proposes, "Maybe you're the descendant of an African king." He replies that he was an orphan, raised by "an old woman called Aunt Mary" and taught to read by "some of the boys at the shine parlor." Denying that he ever "studied under Dr. Bledsoe"—the reporter seems to have gotten wind of his past—he asserts, "Well, for a time I went to sea. . . . I was an ordinary seaman."[52]

He then lays out the philosophy of the Brotherhood:

Freedom is not only the consciousness of necessity, Miss Laurel. It is also the recognition of possibility. First must come the recognition of the possibility of freedom. . . . Without the recognition of *possibility* freedom might lie close at hand unrecognized. A new ideal of freedom must at first be abstract, an idea; but with possibility it is different. Possibility must always be concrete, a technique, a body of concepts, a vision and since these can't exist within the pure air, possibility means people, organized people. . . .

Growth is implicit in man, for he is born not in sin, but in discontent. He wants to move toward the light from the darkness. . . . Just let the mind get a peep at the possibility of freedom and it emerges cautiously from its world of darkness and looks around for a lens through which it can focus its sight. That lens is possibility. Sometime the lens lies right at hand and we fail to see it, or else we're too timid.

His metaphors become wilder. "They say pearls come from grains of sand falling into the shell and irritating the delicate flesh of the oyster. Maybe that's the way with consciousness. Your mind has to be bruised until it develops the pearl the eye is capable of seeing, accepting the vision that will melt the iron, crack the iron rock of reality." The Negro people, he tells Miss Laurel, "have given birth to the pearl, and a lens is forming out of our scars and bruises, and soon we'll all see that Brotherhood is the vision that will transform the world." The scene ends with his failed attempt to secure a dinner date; Miss Laurel, it turns out, is married.[53]

The magazine interview features the invisible man's giddy egotism: he pontificates, flirts, throws his weight around. But the interview reveals the extent to which he has accepted his doubling with LeRoy. He thinks, "My background came over with that vague, unreal twist that LeRoy's had, and in fact, it read more like LeRoy's real life than my own except for some things which I had said about brotherhood and consciousness." In concocting for himself a history of being raised by a woman named Mary and then going to sea, he obviously has on his mind not just LeRoy but also LeRoy's books about the hero; the invisible man's fictional pedigree is straight out of Raglan and Rank. His claim to have come from the Sea Islands, with their strong folkloric ties to Africa, signals his identification with a cosmopolitan blackness (one that the older Ellison would insistently disavow). His assertion that he learned to read and write at a shoe shine parlor recalls Douglass's narrative of how he acquired literacy. His comments on freedom, necessity, and possibility are an amalgam of LeRoy, the vet, Marx, and Engels, as well as Ellison's own writings for the *New Masses* and *Negro Quarterly*.[54]

Of special interest is the invisible man's somewhat convoluted metaphor about the pearl and the lens, which contains a Marxist reformulation of LeRoy's analysis of the basis for African Americans' role in creating a "better world." LeRoy had written that it is the Negro's experience with "brutalization," the extraction of bullion from blood, that yields particular insight into the current social order, as well as the need for a "more human" mode of existence. In an analogy drawn from the dialectics of nature, the invisible man here describes the emergence of the pearl out of the irritation produced by a grain of sand; the pearl beyond price is the negation of negation. In the same way, he proposes, the lens of class consciousness can be fashioned from the "scars and bruises" of Negro life. This metaphor suggestively recalls Ellison's *Daily Worker* recommendation in 1942 that both history and literature be viewed through "the clarifying lens of the Marxist ideology," which itself recalled Wright's description in "How Bigger Was Born" of how it felt when he envisioned Bigger Thomas's life from the standpoint of class consciousness: "[It was] as though I had put on a pair of spectacles whose power was that of an x-ray enabling me to see deeper into the lives of men."[55]

While the young man's enthusiasm is somewhat manic, it is difficult to view with irony his epistemological-cum-political formulation; it sounds too much like what Ellison used to proclaim. We are reminded of Ellison's statement to Burke that he felt compelled to approach the "universal" through the "racial grain of sand"; that grain of sand is no discrete or inert entity, but an agent capable of producing revolutionary insight. Perhaps Ellison's own political unconscious is at work as he narrates the invisible man's speech on behalf of LeRoy.

"We decided we was goin to join": Hattie and Julius Franklin

The Brotherhood's poster campaign, which features the multiracial "Rainbow of America's Future," plays a minor role in the 1952 novel. Disappearing as soon as they are put up, the posters are the locus of mystery until it is discovered that, as Brother Tarp says, Harlemites are "taking them rainbow pictures and tacking 'em to their walls 'long with 'God Bless Our Home' and the Lord's Prayer" (386). The episode serves mainly to fuel Wrestrum's envy and hostility. Originally, however, the posters' disappearance generates suspense—the Brotherhood fears sabotage, even F B I interference—until the invisible man, engaged in door-to-door canvassing, spots one of the posters in the apartment of a couple named Hattie and Julius Franklin. Hattie, who reminds him of Mary Rambo, recognizes him as "that speaking brother"; he is, she says, familiar to "everybody who knows how much good the brotherhood is been doing." Complaining about Negro relief investigators "spying on their own folks," as well as about white store clerks who call her "Honey," Hattie prods her six-foot-four husband into confessing that he took the poster. She declares, "At least four of my friends got them on their walls. Hester Cook and Lizzie Sanders even had theirs framed." She and her husband are not members of the Brotherhood, Hattie states, "But we believe in it and we supports everything youall do. I guess we never got around to joining."[56]

The poster campaign, by virtue of its immense popularity, generates controversy in the mainstream press. While one newspaper attacks the Brotherhood as "subversive," another attempts to co-opt the issue. Professing distrust of the "motives [and] questionable methods [of] . . . this increasingly conspicuous group," the second paper asks, "Is this not a glimpse, garish though it may be, of our great and fecund American dream?" Dismissing the Brotherhood as "latecomers," the editorial concludes, "We say let our slogan be, the American Dream achieved in the good American way!" The narrator recalls, "It gave us quite a laugh, we had them fighting among themselves and the fact that the placards were my project worked very well for me." While the episode further illustrates Jack's opportunism and vanity—in one version he takes credit for the poster campaign once he learns of its success—the "Rainbow" poster's popularity also displays Popular Front propaganda at its most effective, as well as the genuine appeal for Harlemites of the left's multiracial approach to the fight against racism.[57]

The Franklins do not make just a cameo appearance. When the invisible man returns to Harlem after his assignment downtown, he finds them active in the Brotherhood's "Don't Buy Where You Can't Work" campaign, which is demanding jobs for Negro workers in Harlem stores. Hattie remarks that it was because of this activism that "we decided we was goin to join." When during the riot the invisible man is attacked by Ras, Julius is shown defending him physically from Ras's "private strongarm squad." Ellison's exclusion of the Franklins from *Invisible Man* effaces concrete and dramatized evidence of the Brotherhood's success in reaching Harlem's working class. Hattie's resemblance to Mary is telling, for it expands the text's typifying range. While Mary largely remains, at least in the published text, a preindividual migrant, insisting that New York has not penetrated to her core, Hattie develops into a class-conscious activist. Julius, with his marked resemblance to the mythic John Henry, presents a black man in overalls other than Lucius Brockway. The image of this quintessential proletarian physically defending a fellow Communist from a band of Garveyites would have to be expunged from the 1952 text; when one of his editors suggested that the Franklins be eliminated from the manuscript, Ellison agreed.[58]

"We building the movement together":
The Fired Tenement

Hattie and Julius Franklin were not to be the only supporters of the left among Harlem's working class. In another episode eliminated from the 1952 text the Brotherhood calls upon the city government to "provide more housing for the people" and pressures landlords to clean up their tenements; the focus of the campaign is a huge slum apartment building called the Jungle. Ellison notes that the building is "full of rats, vermine [sic]. Prostitution. Storefront church. Plagued by numbers runners, wineheads, . . . and politicians. . . . People too brutalized to fight against it." Hoping to supply Harlem with what one organizer calls "a living demonstration to others that [the Brotherhood is] for the man lowest down," the tenement campaign will guarantee that they "will always have allies, and will always be in touch with reality." The tenement episode could have been based upon any number of CP organizing efforts in Harlem between the time Ellison arrived in 1936 until he left for the merchant marine in 1943.[59]

Thinking that he has seen Louise enter the building, the invisible man loses sight of her but overhears two tenants talking:

> "Look here man," I heard, "You know these here fays don't act like ofays, they act like people!"
> "What kinda people?"
> And I bent closer, excited, as he said,
> "Real people. The other night a couple of em invited me to go home with em, and I started not to go; then I changed my mind. I said to myself, If they can ask me, then least I can do is go."

Responding to his friend's skepticism, the first speaker continues:

"Now the last thing in the world I wanted out of the Brotherhood was to go sitting up in some white man's house. All I wanted was the sonsa-bitches whats poor as me to take off some of that pressure sos I could get myself something. Cause I always figures I could get mine if they left me alone. But this is something much bigger than I thought. I'm in it for good now. They invite me to they house, I invite them to mine; they serve me sauerkraut and winnies, I serve em red rice and beans, and we building the movement together."

The inhabitants of the Jungle enact the hospitality extended toward class-conscious whites that the composite *we* of Wright's *Twelve Million Black Voices* recognizes as key to the migrants' emergence into modernity: "We invited them into our homes and broke our scanty bread with them, and this was our supreme gesture of trust."[60]

Ellison imagined different outcomes to the episode, all involving fire. In one draft, when the fire breaks out the invisible man helps people escape and becomes "a hero by default." In what appear to be later versions, Brotherhood organizers "see [the] fire and allow it to burn. Then . . . it must be decided whether they do so through callousness or out of their belief that large numbers will benefit from its destruction." In a variant of this debate, "one group thought of burning building [but] are stopped by danger to people, tenants' possible loss of life." Ellison eventually decided that the fire would be deliberately set by members of the Brotherhood: "Fire grows out of conflict between two factions: out of color situation; out of efforts of some members of faction to create incident that will bring Harlemites to pitch of indignation." The invisible man's heroic saving of lives would be manipulated: "They must *use* him just as they use the event of the fire. . . . They burn houses and risk lives of tenants in order to do good. He saves lives at risk of his own. . . . He reveals the essential anti-humanity of their humanism." An episode originally intended to demonstrate the Brotherhood's sincere concern over poverty is transmuted into proof of its perfidy.[61]

"The bear that was a man": Brotherhood and Sacrifice

At some point during the composition of *Invisible Man* Ellison abandoned a fragmentary, and more than slightly bizarre, episode that was variously titled "Barbecue," "The Bear That Was a Man," and "Bear in Window." To be located after the invisible man has gone downtown and then returned to Harlem, the unevenly sketched chapter shows him learning from Brother

Tarp that Harlemites are tiring of the new Harlem leaders' abstract verbiage and hungering for the kinds of parades and actions previously organized by the protagonist. The invisible man hatches a plan for a huge Brotherhood-sponsored barbecue, to be held in the park under the George Washington Bridge, to which all of Harlem will be invited; the chief attraction will be a barbecued bear. When the bear arrives from Alaska "in a box like a coffin," it is discovered that the bear is frozen and has already been skinned. The "naked" bear is placed in the refrigerated display window of a restaurant, with a sign reading, "YOU HAVE A DATE WITH JACK THE BROTHER-HOOD BARBECUE BEAR—FREE." People in the crowd remark that the bear resembles a man; the invisible man assures them, "That's Jack the Bear standing there." The text breaks off after an old woman peers through her spectacles and proclaims, "He might not be a *bear*man . . . but he sure is a *man* bear." The actual cooking and consumption of the bear are not portrayed, although in another sketch of the problems facing the invisible man on his return to Harlem Ellison jotted, "Barbecue makes people sick."[62]

It is not clear how this strange episode was supposed to align with other elements in Ellison's contradictory patterning of the Brotherhood's relationship with Harlem, let alone with the many references to the folkloric Jack-the-Bear scattered throughout the text. On the one hand, the eerie resemblance of the bear to a man, compounded by its having been skinned and readied for public cooking and consumption, suggests a human sacrifice, even a lynching; we recall Ellison's chilling comparison of a lynched man with a barbecued hog in "A Party Down at the Square." That this ritual would be carried out in the name of the Brotherhood is indicated by the jotted words beneath the title "The Bear That Was a Man": "The Brotherhood has invited you to eat one of your own. That's what it wants you to do." This grim association of the Brotherhood with murder, even cannibalism, anticipates the invisible man's closing nightmare of castration by the lynch mob led by Brother Jack. That both events take place in the shadow of the bridge named after the first of the Founding Fathers suggests the Brotherhood's betrayal of the democratic legacy. Especially when read backward from the standpoint of Ellison's anticommunist American nationalism post-1952, the "Bear in Window" episode can be taken to indicate that, from the outset, he intended to condemn the Brotherhood as "lynchers of my people," as he had railed in the letter from September 1945 to Hyman accusing the Communists of having "done something far worse to the ideas of socialism than the Nazi did to the Jews."[63]

On the other hand, the bear's ritual association with death and rebirth—as the Cambridge School theorist Rhys Carpenter put it, "Death in the midst of life, and some hope of life even after the crushing calamity of death"—makes it difficult to read the "*man* bear" as simply a victimized scapegoat. Ellison indicated various alternative possibilities when he wrote, "What if in story of the barbecued bear he is treated as Manna? This requires context of some kind—political? It is, after all, a context, an agon. Bear a sacrifice? What if bear actually is a—man? What consequences other than the legal?" One possibility is that sometimes a bear, even if it looks like a man, may be just a bear. Ellison's notation that a context which is political is required implies another possibility: that he came up with the bear-sacrifice theme when thinking in another context, perhaps biblical, as is intimated by the reference to manna, the divinely supplied food that sustained the Israelites during their flight from Egypt. But insofar as Negro folklore analogized African Americans under slavery with Israelites under Pharaoh's rule—and CP-inflected updatings analogized slaves with present-day workers and Pharaoh with capital—the notion that the barbecued bear would supply necessary nourishment on the journey to a better world dramatically reconfigures the episode's political context, transforming it from an allegory of lynching into one of emancipation. The interpretive possibilities are dizzying.[64]

LeRoy may help here in synthesizing what are otherwise two utterly incompatible readings. For the radical mariner was totemically consumed as "Tom the turkey" by those who had dedicated him and set him aside. The notion that the Brotherhood would invite Harlemites to "eat one of [their] own" might signify not the murder and cannibalism of a victimized scapegoat but the sacrifice of an honored god. As symbolic action the barbecue would thus embody not a lynching but a counterlynching: the ritual consumption of the cooked and dismembered bear would, like the symbolic ingestion of the sacrificed king, serve to affirm and strengthen the community's communalism and communion. From this standpoint the protagonist's plan to locate the barbecue in the shadow of the George Washington Bridge reveals the representational contradictions accompanying Popular Front nationalism, but not necessarily in an ironizing way. Does the archetypal Founding Father look down kindly on this bonding ritual of his people? Or does he aim to keep in the shadow of his iron might the descendants of his slaves? "Bear in Window," while a source of comic relief, contains a host of ambiguities barely resolvable even in the context of the richer and more complex treatment of myth, ritual, and politics shaping the novel's early drafts. One thing is clear: once LeRoy was killed off there remained no means by which the "Bear in Window" material could be effectively related to the rest of the novel. It was fated to join the many other narrative elements, realistic and allegorical alike, that would be excised by Ellison's editorial knife.

Ellison's decision to omit many Harlem-based episodes—the parade, the magazine interview, the poster campaign, the encounter with the Franklins, the tenement organizing, the bear barbecue—has an impact on *Invisible Man* that is both quantitative and qualitative. In the 1952 text, with the exception of Brother Tarp, the only migrants encountered by the invisible man before the riot—Mary without her roomers, Peter Wheatstraw without his discarded flag, the yam man without his factory worker history—are folk figures who seem largely out of touch with the proletarianizing forces of modernity. Along with the youths playing the dozens with Brotherhood slogans in the antieviction parade, however, the Franklins, the inhabitants of Mary's apartment, and the unnamed dwellers of the Jungle leave a concrete visual and aural impression of the relevance of the Brotherhood's theory and practice to many of Harlem's inhabitants. It was one thing for the narrator to summarize in ironic retrospect his memories of the "days of certainty" preceding his downfall. It was quite another thing—as Ellison, a careful reader of Henry James's prefaces, well knew—to dramatize and flesh out the Brotherhood's interactions with Harlemites who assume a reality of their own.

Ellison's omission of these working-class episodes and characterizations is compounded by the conversion of Stein into Hambro, the increasingly robotic characterization of Jack, the elimination of Louise, and the excision of LeRoy as the protagonist's abiding secret sharer—revisionary acts that profoundly transform the text's carriers of a leftist political vision. On another rhetorical level (more subtle and subliminal, but for that reason far harder to detect), Ellison's cancellation of the reference to Marxism as a clarifying lens removes from the novel's guiding trope of blindness and vision the dialectical possibility that vision can be magnified and focused by science. His comparable reworking of the motif of electric power in the arena rally episode negates the possibility that industrial technology can function as a means of both individual development and collective working-class resistance. In his revisions of the first half of the Brotherhood section, the way is being prepared for the lowering of the political boom in the second half.

Up to this point, however, Ellison's shuttling back and forth between the mid-1930s and the early 1940s has not posed any significant problems to his "political allegory." The Brotherhood activities he has featured are fairly typical of the Popular Front left. As long as "purpose" and "passion" dominate the invisible man's motivations, the larger historical forces shaping his radical activism—the Depression and the war—can remain largely unspecified. When he is moved into the phase of "perception," however, history comes to the fore; occlusion becomes repression. Let us keep in mind which gods rule the seas as we move into the gathering storm.

seven

Recognizing Necessity

Note: make Thrilkild a
totalitarian type, eager to
regiment all aspects of life.

—Ralph Ellison, notes for
"Brotherhood" episode
of *Invisible Man*

Red-baiting is born of the
same womb that conceived
anti-Semitism, anti-
unionism, and Jim Crow.

—Adam Clayton Powell Jr.,
Marching Blacks (1945)

In the familiar text of *Invisible Man* the protagonist's honeymoon as a Brotherhood organizer is cut short. Just as he concludes that "it was working very
well," he receives the anonymous handwritten note advising him, "*Do not go
too fast*." His informant—"a friend who has been watching you closely"—tells
him, "This is a *white man's world*" . . . The colored people do not want you to
go too fast, and will cut you down if you do" (383). From this point onward
the action descends through the *agon* of his duping and manipulation to the
peripeteia of his learning the depth of the Brotherhood's opportunism and
treachery. The plot abandons its picaresque features—episodic plot, humor-
ous tone—as each situation contributes to the movement toward revelation:
the growing envy of Wrestrum; the demeaning assignment to lecture on the
"woman question" downtown; the disappearance and death of Tod Clifton;
the meditation on the hipsters in the subway; the scene when Brother Jack's
eye falls out; the discovery, through Rinehart, of a fluidity and chaos beyond
the ken of Brotherhood scientism; the riot and the final encounter with Ras;
the invisible man's arrival—epistemological, political, and psychological—
in the netherworld of existential possibility.

The homologous characters and guiding tropes in the 1952 text are pat-
terned to reinforce the themes of revelation and betrayal conveyed in the

intensified movement toward closure; the rhetorical powers of dramatism and synecdoche are harnessed as "perception" emerges with felt inevitability from "purpose" and "passion." Jack, Wrestrum, Hambro, and Ras, as antagonists, join the ranks of Norton, Bledsoe, Brockway, and Emerson; Sybil, Tarp, and Rinehart align with such bearers of insight as Trueblood, the vet, Wheatstraw, and young Emerson. Clifton's murder plays out the potential for death always embedded in the symbolic ritual of the battle royal. The imagistic equations focusing on castration, blindness, invisibility, and Bellerophontic letters achieve their climactic synthesis in Clifton's dancing dolls, Brother Jack's false eye, and the identical signatures on the anonymous warning note and the slip of paper containing the invisible man's Brotherhood name. These carefully orchestrated elements of plot, character, and symbol reinforce the protagonist's delayed but hard-fought perception that history is not a spiral but a boomerang and that freedom is the recognition not of necessity but of possibility. The stage has been set for the invisible man's lynching nightmare and descent to the American underground, where, in the epilogue, he will rediscover the sagacity of the Founding Fathers and offer himself as a spokesperson for universal humanity. For a text embracing antideterminism as a politics and an epistemology, the ideological trajectory described for the reader of *Invisible Man* is highly deterministic; perhaps paradoxically, the recognition of possibility on the level of theme is, on the level of rhetoric, the product of a disciplined recognition of necessity. The novel's embrace of chaos is highly structured.

Like the earlier portions of the novel, however, the closing section of *Invisible Man* is the product of multiple revisions. What the reader experiences as a seamless conjoining of idea and form was labored over at length. Characters and events occupying central places in the published text—the death of Tod Clifton, for instance, and the hostile encounters with Ras—were added either midway or late in Ellison's compositional process. Meanwhile Louise, LeRoy, and the Brotherhood's Harlem base gradually disappeared. While Ellison planned all along that the protagonist would discover his invisibility and figurehead status in the Brotherhood, the novel was originally to end on a significantly different note. The invisible man's political career would be "short and fast and furious," Ellison noted. Fleeing into a basement during the riot, he subsequently emerges "covered with dirt and blackness, completely unrecognizable as the once suave politico." With "his political personality . . . dismembered, . . .[he] decides to become a preacher, the leader of a cult," and sets up a "small store-front church" where he "exploits the congregation" by means of such "technological gadgets" as "recording machines [and] . . . p.a. systems." Now "embrac[ing] his invisibility, . . . [he] wanders up and down the many social levels of the city." He is "compelled by his loneliness to probe the forms of personality and experience developed by urban Negroes and to relate them to more universal patterns." He writes his memoirs in the hope that "once . . . read, [they] will allow him to enter the world of things known and define himself." The novel ends on an ironic note: "Characteristically, he doubts that [the memoirs] will be read." Ellison's early outlines do not focus on the protagonist's political crisis as the principal cause of his alienation. Rather it is the historical experience of migration, producing the "forms of personality and experience developed by urban Negroes," that provides both the locus of the invisible man's personal narrative and the key to the "more universal patterns" it aspires to contain. In its original version *Invisible Man* was envisioned as a specifically African American supplement to and commentary on the Marxist modes of production narrative.[1]

As *Invisible Man* undergoes its own migration from historical materialism to high modernism, from Prometheus to Proteus, two related features of the closing chapters are of central importance. One is the text's intensification of the rhetoric of anticommunism, indeed its movement from anti-Communism to anticommunism. At issue here is not simply the increasingly negative portrayal of individual Communists, especially Brother Jack; embedded in their reductive stereotyping is a shift in the patterning of causality in the text, such that the Brotherhood is now held responsible for the sacrifice of not just Clifton and the invisible man but all of Harlem. To recall the formulation of René Girard: the ritual scapegoats *in* the text emerge as the prime scapegoats *of* the text. Not simply the culminating figure in the novel's lineup of antagonists, but a synecdoche that absorbs most of their combined negativity and bears most of their combined weight, the Brotherhood functions, through the rhetoric of guilt by association, as the epitome of a brutally scientistic antihumanism. Not only does this move deflect a substantive critique of white supremacist exploitation into a formalist critique of rationalist epistemology; it also lifts the burden of responsibility for the perpetuation of this exploitation by the Bledsoes, Nortons, and Emersons of the world, thus fulfilling the principal purpose of anticommunism in the cold war and beyond.

This deflection of responsibility and blame is closely related to the second key feature of the novel's closing section, namely, its increasingly problematic relation to the history of the 1930s and 1940s. Up to this point the text's occasional transposition into the 1940s of typical Depression-era activities and situations in order to meet the overall chronological requirements of the narrative has not proven particularly disruptive. In the novel's final section, however, the demonization of the Brotherhood is contingent upon a distortion—not just an imaginative reshaping, but a distortion—of the historical record. The scapegoating of the Brotherhood relies upon the postulation of certain negative traits as being typical of the left, and this postulation of typicality in turn rests upon an unspoken allusion to actual wartime events. But because the relevant historical framework is invoked without being named, the text is placed under no requirement to confront the basis upon which its claim to typicality largely rests.

In the closing section of *Invisible Man* rhetoric occludes reference, re-cognition edges out cognition, and anticommunism displaces the novel's critique of the social and historical origins of invisibility.

"Lousy bourgeois": The Invisible Man as Antihero

In the 1952 text the invisible man is portrayed as vain, narcissistic, and above all infuriatingly naïve. Whatever his weaknesses, however, they pale in comparison with the paranoia of Wrestrum and the authoritarianism of Brother Jack, as well as the megalomania of Ras the Destroyer. Ellison's early drafts of and notes on the novel's Brotherhood section indicate that he considered making his protagonist a significantly more flawed and unlikable human being; his doubling with LeRoy both opens up the possibilities for heroism and sets a standard by which he will be measured when he falls short. Not only does the invisible man "give in to his passive drives" and feel "at peace" only when "he is treated as an inferior," but he craves recognition, going to church only "[to have] the deacons seat [him] on the rostrum, where [he] could be introduced to the congregation." He "begins to travel in sophisticated Harlem circles," fooling himself that he is trying to gain their political support; during the period when he is a "political bigshot, supposedly dedicated to the overthrow of such people," he is "actually . . . drawn to [their] values and . . . forms of disintegration." Even as he recognizes that he has no real power or influence in the Brotherhood, he "ruthlessly expels a group of Negroes critical of some of the organization's policies," especially its lack of democracy. His "cynacism toward [the] masses" makes him complicit in the "exploitation of folk Negroes," which in turn compounds his sense of fragmentation: "I was a man of parts, I had more parts than Old McDonald had chicks. Here fragment/part, there fragment/part, everywhere, part part."

The protagonist may be experiencing dismemberment, but it is difficult to feel much compassion for the unprincipled character sketched here.[2]

While Ellison did not draft many dramatized episodes wherein the invisible man manifests this degree of cynicism and vanity, he sketched several possibilities. In one, having been fired by the Brotherhood, the protagonist is "surprised at the generous amount of the check" constituting his severance pay. "The joyride was over," he states. "I was back where I started. Only where before I was blind now I could see. . . . This time I knew that I was invisible." He decides to "live while the money lasts" and "force [him]self into visibility in terms of society." He does a physical and mental makeover: "[I] conked my hair and read the avant-garde writers and sang the blues and despised myself." The self-humiliation is painful:

> I dressed fastidiously, spending tedious hours on my toilet. I tried all of the preparations for straightening the hair. I piled them on until my hair turned dry and red and fell out by the handsful. I smeared strong bleaching ointments upon my face until it was for a time a mass of running sores which forced me to stay within the house for months, but at best I could achieve only a muddy, green-tinged complexion. Yet I kept trying; for what profiteth a man if he gain the shores of democracy and slip back upon the rock of the Anglo-Saxon aesthetic? What type nose wears well with the Constitution? What grade of hair blends with the Bill of Rights?[3]

Ellison considered placing this passage at various points in the text. In an early version the money is compensation for the accident at the paint factory; he has not yet met the Brotherhood. He thinks, "I hated myself, for while I rejected Emerson and Norton's world I came to suspect that I was reaching out for it in the very gesture of my rejection." This version is followed by a brief scene in which he makes a comic attempt at visibility. He has been following the latest Brooks Brothers fashions, reading bestsellers ("LeRoy's journal was not enough"), and going to the theater. One evening he enters Sardi's, the posh midtown restaurant frequented by celebrities, and demands a drink; he is refused, gets into a fight, and is ejected. Two workers, "scholarly gentlemen in sandhogs' helmets," notice him in his tuxedo on the sidewalk: "The lousy bourgeois," one of them [says]. "Yeah, the sure sign of a decadent class," replies his companion.[4]

In later versions of the much-transposed passage about the skin and hair treatments (Ellison clearly loved it and wanted to use it somewhere), the narrator inspects his blisters and thinks that aesthetics "is a subtle matter. . . . Regardless of what the Brotherhood argues, economics might be a function of aesthetics rather than the other way around." About the "illogicality" of his contradictory aspirations, he asks, "What logic lay between Jack and Emerson? They were equal, they were white, and I was invisible." After leaving the Brotherhood he dresses in an outrageous zoot suit again to visit Sardi's, where several people nod and smile in his direction. The reason for his friendly reception is revealed when the doorman greets him as "Bojangles," a "recognition" that sends him into gales of ironic laughter and convinces him more than ever of his invisibility. The Brotherhood's negation of his humanity, Ellison implies, is what has driven him into the clownish imitation of an entertainer who was himself expert at blackface role-playing.[5]

The satirical standpoint in these variants on the Sardi's episode alters significantly between the two drafts. In the first version Ellison targets the racism of the bourgeoisie and their hangers-on, as well as the invisible man's self-destructive worship of whiteness. The fact that the workers on the street view him with contempt supplies a class-conscious evaluative framework; the invisible man is not paying enough attention to LeRoy's journal. By contrast, the later draft pairs Jack and Emerson as the key antagonists. What matters is that they are both powerful and white; that they are presumably on different sides in the class struggle is "illogical" but irrelevant. The materialist approach to aesthetics (implicitly sustained in the first version by the negative judgment of the tuxedo-wearing conked-hair protagonist by the "gentlemen in sandhogs' helmets") is lampooned in the second, where the narrator suggests that the dominance of the "Anglo-Saxon aesthetic" is the cause rather than the result of economic forces. (It was precisely this idealist view of the origins of racism that Ellison had vigorously contested in his *Negro Quarterly* writings.) Although Ellison considered various uses of the episode treating the invisible man's cosmetic and sartorial attempts at combating invisibility, he eventually tossed it out. To function as a spokesperson for universal humanity at the novel's finale, the invisible man had to be invested with a certain degree of credibility—and dignity. Whether in its pre- or post-Brotherhood variants, the passage portrays the invisible man as pathetic to the point of repulsion; memories of his burned hair and green-tinged complexion disqualify him as a speaker for the reader, on the lower frequencies or anywhere else along the band.[6]

Besides exhibiting a fragile sense of racial identity, the invisible man is shown to make some serious mistakes in judgment and strategy during his time as a Harlem organizer for the Brotherhood. As he hobnobs with the black bourgeoisie on the side, he "becomes acquainted with one Dr. Chom-

boir, a southern Negro college administrator noted for his conciliatory policies" and "deni[al of the] reality of Negro life." When the invisible man requests support for the antieviction campaign, Chomboir replies, "You'd
better stick with the folks who have the money. Poor colored folks are bad
enough, but poor colored folks and poor white folks, that's a farce." His inquiry becomes personal: "What did they do to get you? They put you next to
some of that Jew pussy?" Teaching the invisible man "the technique of exploiting the fear operative in the Negro community," this Bledsoe avatar, jots
Ellison, "for a short time becomes a model for the invisible man." Their relationship ends, however, when the invisible man "discovers that the southerner comes to the city and spends his nights in white whorehouses where
the girls tie him, dress him in a red bandanna and flagellate him verbally and
physically." Too much is too much even for our ambitious protagonist.[7]

The invisible man further errs when, later in the novel, he attempts to
gain back some of the favor he has lost in the eyes of the Brotherhood leadership by "mov[ing] in opportunistically" to take up the case of a Negro writer,
a murderer incarcerated in Sing Sing who has written a novel based on his
life and now agitates for release: "We backed his book, we publicized his
boyhood, sent reporters and photographers to his home town for descriptions of his background. And we did much talk about the suppression of
Negro culture and launched a program to encourage the Negro writer to
voice the best interests of the NEGRO PEOPLE." Although the campaign
helps the organization win back some of their "lost prestige," the writer, it
turns out, "has nothing but contempt" for the Brotherhood, and "his speech
is crude and folkish and profane." The campaign implodes when the writer,
having been released, commits a murder "similar to that for which he was
first convicted"; a psychiatrist has to be called in to "save him from [the]
chair." Recalling an incident in Wright's career—in 1941 he advocated on behalf of Clinton Brewer, an incarcerated musical composer who killed again
upon being freed from prison—the episode reveals the shallowness of the
invisible man's judgment and helps to "put an end to [his] usefulness, as
Brother Jack and others see it." While the Brotherhood's motives in approving the backfired campaign are clearly in question, it is also evident that they
have some justification in questioning the invisible man's leadership abilities. Such proof of his incompetence had to be eliminated if he were to be
viewed as one more sinned against than sinning.[8]

"Bed struggle . . . and bread struggle":
White Women of the Brotherhood

Although the 1952 text displays the protagonist's invisibility to the white members of the Brotherhood—the men exploit him for his prowess in the streets, the women for his prowess, real or imagined, between the sheets—Ellison first had to expunge from the text various traces of a more mixed and complicated state of affairs. Early notes and drafts are guided by the assessment of race relations on the left set forth in "Working Notes," namely, that the white members of the Brotherhood are "well-meaning but blundering human beings . . . still prejudiced, opportunistic and paternalistic, despite their good intentions." The organization, notes Ellison, is "not itself perfect, but guided by men whose motives like [the invisible man's] own are mixed." The poster campaign is originally not a debacle resulting in his punitive reassignment downtown, but a "minor triumph . . . mak[ing] it easier for [him] to leave Harlem"—a move that, in this version, the protagonist welcomes. He is given "no set district" but moves "from section to section"; his lectures to citywide audiences address not just the "woman question" but "all the forms of prejudice to be cleansed from the Brotherhood." As he speaks he feels that "The white brothers and sisters seemed to undergo a strange unburdening whenever I appeared before them. . . . I was truly loved and respected." There are no ironic textual markers indicating that his perception here is to be seen as mistaken; he may be unduly respected, but he is not exactly invisible.[9]

As in successive drafts the assignment downtown turns from reward to punishment and the lecturing assignment is reduced from "all forms of prejudice" to the "woman question," the protagonist's relations with white women highlight his degradation. In the published text, as the ass struggle gets comically confused with the class struggle, even sexual conquest results in castration. The invisible man is seduced by the woman in the red robe but, when discovered in her bed by her husband, ignored; the fact that the husband is "some important member of the Brotherhood—someone so familiar that my failure to identify him was driving me almost to distraction" (418) only reinforces the protagonist's sense of invisibility. In earlier versions of this episode the "jungle fever" theme also prevails, but the protagonist retains more control of the situation and emerges with his male ego substantially less bruised. He at first successfully resists the call of the flesh—initially designated the confusion of the "bread-struggle . . . with the bed-struggle"—and is "careful to keep the biological and the ideological carefully

"Brother Tabu," and discovers, "When [the] decorum [of the ladies Bella-donna] collapsed . . . sentimentality oozed into the room with the soft flesh released from their girdles. . . . They expected me to be as they imagined Joe Louis or Robeson would be. . . . Either they wanted you to sing Old Man River and just keep rolling along or to do tricks with your muscles." When the woman in the red robe takes him into her bed, her untroubled husband is not a Brotherhood leader but a businessman; the couple are wealthy fellow travelers who have an open marriage. After the experience the invisible man believes himself to be "the most sophisticated man in the world" and accepts her invitation to come back the next week. "Such incidents . . . were few [but] I considered them a sign of growth," he recalls with pride. "For although I considered them dangerous it was not out of the old combination of Puritanism and racial fear, but out of self respect and political caution."[10]

The invisible man's vanity and casual misogyny are unmistakable. Yet it is evident that his sexual experiences with white women help him escape the hold of Jim Crow; while his lover is absorbed in primitivist fantasy, he too is getting what he wants. Only after the first draft did Ellison designate the husband "strangely familiar" and jot in the margin "naked dancer." The assignment to lecture on prejudice in all its modes, which testifies to the Brotherhood's valuation of the protagonist as a leader and allows him to "throw off the old southern ways," eventually devolves into a replication of the battle royal.[11]

The early versions of the invisible man's relationships with Emma and Sybil, while displaying mutual cynicism and manipulation, also show him largely in control of what happens to him. Seeking information about the Brotherhood leadership that will enable him to take revenge, he approaches the hapless Sybil because the cagey Emma, his first choice, is not forthcoming. While in the published text Emma and the invisible man flirt but never cross the line, one draft passage shows them kissing hungrily in the same library where he was inducted into the Brotherhood. Another outline indicates that Emma, here married to Jack and not his mistress, comes to visit the invisible man frequently; he is "deliberately careless . . . call[ing] her when [he] knew [Jack] was home . . . and writ[ing] her indiscreet letters." Apparently Emma has not withheld everything.[12]

Married to an unspecified Brotherhood leader in the published text, Sybil is initially either the wife of the white Brotherhood leader MacAfee or Jack's secretary. In all versions of the sex scene the nymphomaniac Sybil is obsessed with mythic notions of black male potency; Brotherhood leaders, it would appear, leave a good deal to be desired in bed. The original sex scene, which contains the Santa Claus surprise, is raunchier still. Sybil asks him to "do fancy tricks" with not his "muscles" but his "muscle"; she keeps mumbling "shit, piss, fuck, shitpiss fuck"; he calls her a "funky bitch"; when she demands that he rape her, she strikes him "where it hurts." While in the 1952 text they appear to make amicable love after the play-acting ("She moved into my arms" [526]), in earlier drafts he accedes to her brutal request: "I gave it to her. Yes, it cost me a lot but it calmed her and I decided to end the farce." When Sybil, clad in chthonian garb, later that evening haunts the invisible man as he traverses the netherworld of the riot, they both have been previously involved in decidedly nonmythic rituals.[13]

"To end his conflict he drives her away": Leaving Louise

The absent presence in this cluster of white female characters is, of course, Louise. As Ellison indicated in "Working Notes," Louise was to figure crucially for the protagonist as a "symbol of democracy, freedom, and fertility." But for the invisible man her whiteness

> is quite a problem. He is proud of it and he hates it. He receives pleasure from the resentment of those who object when they walk down the street. He is also afraid of the danger which he feels this involves and insists that she spend long hours beneath the sunlamp, baking her complexion painfully close to that of a mulatto. Like Othello, whose situation he now parodies, he cannot accept himself nor believe that anyone like Louise could find him attractive. Finally, to end his conflict he drives her away.

In this reading of *Othello*, which emphasizes racial self-doubt, larger social forces condition the protagonist's situation, but the principal barrier to the lovers' relationship is internal to him.[14]

Ellison never dramatized any scenes between the invisible man and Louise after their encounter at the Chthonian. But his notes indicate that she was to figure prominently in the protagonist's motivations for involvement in the Brotherhood. He searches for her at the parade and at the arena rally. At first worshipping her from afar, he enjoys his downtown assignment because it supplies frequent opportunities to see her. "I missed no opportunity, although I could bring myself no closer to telling her how I felt," he relates. "It was as though by moving large numbers of people, by blasting them with brotherhood I was bringing her closer to me." Ellison notes, "He does his job well so that he can be with Louise without difficulty." They dance closely at subsequent parties at the Chthonian, and she awakens "all manner of tender feelings" in him; he buys her roses on the way to a rally, but the stems are broken when a fight breaks out. Over time he and Louise become intimate. In one sketched outline they live together; in another they get married. This is not a one-night stand with a middle-aged sexual adventuress, but a serious interracial romantic relationship.[15]

Although the *Othello* motif suggests a tragic trajectory, Ellison considered various directions that the relationship between Louise and the invisible man might take. He might gain maturity and self-confidence in the relationship: "Getting in [a] situation wherein he overhears [a] group of leaders talking to Louise and realizes their intentions, [he] is struck by their adolescence, and decides he will treat her like a woman and not a goddess." She might demonstrate her personal courage by insisting on going into the Jungle unaccompanied and, in one variant, saving people's lives. She might demonstrate her political commitment by accusing him of being "defeatist and anti-Negro," thereby serving as his revolutionary conscience. In one extraordinary turn of the plot, their relationship helps him eventually to "[accept] the humanity of whites" and see that "they're weak, heroic, etc, like himself." Although he has previously left her, at the end of the novel he "decides he'll try to reach Louise on the phone." To say the least, this version of Louise's role would have produced a very different book.[16]

But most of Ellison's notes link the invisible man's neurotic inability to overcome the "Othello complex" with his political insecurities in dealing with white men. The novel is "not a study of jealousy, but of insecurity, self-distrust, self-rejection," Ellison wrote. "If he believed in himself he might then believe that she loves him." Not only does the invisible man subject Louise to the torture of the sunlamp; he might accuse her of "having Negro blood and of hiding it" or of having an affair with Jack, charges that the invisible man does not believe but cannot help making. Toward the end he has a nightmare in which he visits Louise in a luxurious bedroom with a clock prominently placed over the door. Her hair "swirled out in ringlets," she sleeps in "an enormous ivory bed in the shape of a barge" surrounded by candles. She awakens and beckons him to join her. But as he is about to enter her he sees that "her legs [are] completely covered by coarse brown hair" and that "one long, mishapened foot dangl[es] from the bed." He awakens in horror from his vision of Louise as demon. From her original appearance as an avatar of Kore/Persephone, she has descended into the Hades of his anxious imagination.[17]

Evidently not just the invisible man, but his creator as well, had trouble seeing Louise as something other than "the white meat of the chicken"; she is well-nigh buried alive under a mound of literary references. When they meet she sparks a Joycean monologue; now she alludes to Shakespeare's Desdemona, Cleopatra, and the monstrous daughters of King Lear. Also thrown in are a dose of Poe's Ligeia and Eliot's woman with the Medusa-like hair in "The Waste Land"; in his nightmare the invisible man now groups Louise with the other "ladies Belladonna." For all her unreality, however, Louise is shown to be passionately committed to the Brotherhood; her innocence consists in an integrity that is both personal and political. Ellison drives her away to end not only his protagonist's internal conflict, but also, perhaps, his own.

"Make him a totalitarian type":
Delegitimating Black Communists

The process of divesting the Brotherhood of moral and political authority entailed not only reshaping the descriptions and functions of various white characters but also reconfiguring the roles of the organization's black members. The loyalty of the older members needed to be qualified. Brother Maceo, who in his hostile encounter with the invisible man disguised as Rinehart is described as "a game old brother" (488), is previously designated "a kind old man who believed strongly in Brotherhood." Brother Tarp, with his memories of the chain gang from which he broke free, is the character most fully embodying the appeal of the Brotherhood to the black working class; the scarred and broken shackle that he gives to the invisible man, signaling his desire to pass along the legacy of struggle to his young comrade, establishes Tarp's difference from Bledsoe, whose smooth chain links indicate that, by contrast, his break with slavery is mere performance. When Brother Tarp silently disappears in the period leading up to the riot, apparently taking back his gift of the Douglass portrait, the Brotherhood, Ellison implies, has lost its claim to legitimacy in the struggle for Negro rights.[18]

Tarp is more fully fleshed out in earlier drafts. The sketched episode about the barbecued bear begins with Tarp and the protagonist going out for ribs in a Harlem restaurant. It is Tarp's fond memories of southern picnics sponsored by "preachers and politicians . . . and what a time's we'd have" that inspires the invisible man to attempt the same thing; they leave the restaurant together singing "Solidarity Forever." Tarp is also indirectly linked with LeRoy since he wears "a sailor's watch cap on the back of his bald head"; by extension both the Brotherhood custodian and the radical mariner would have been linked with Douglass, the "big guy in the sailor suit." In early drafts Tarp, along with other "disciplined ones," adheres to the Brotherhood's program to the end, working in the Harlem office even as the majority of older members fall away; there is no mention of the portrait of Douglass disappearing from the wall. Early drafts thus negate the dichotomy between experience and science, immediacy and theory, underlying the reading of Brother Tarp as an embodiment of "concrete experience" that subversively negates the Brotherhood's "abstract, ideological view of man's position and possibilities in the world."[19]

Brother Wrestrum, with the obvious pun on his name, is conceived as a nefarious character from the outset; his physical resemblance to Supercargo suggests their comparable roles in disciplining African Americans to conform to the rules made by powerful whites. His earlier names bear note: first he was Elmo, then Thrilmort, then in several drafts Thrilkild, the latter two names pointing quite obviously to the sadistic pleasure he takes in playing his role. The growing influence of cold war discourse as Ellison worked on the portrait is indicated in his marginal note next to a passage describing Thrilkild/Wrestrum's bullying behavior: "Note: make Thrilkild a totalitarian type, eager to regiment all aspects of life, along with MacAfee." Presumably the novel's audience will recognize this "type," which conjoins fanaticisms of the left and the right and collapses politics into character structure, formalistically conceived. The specific beliefs that might motivate Thrilkild/Wrestrum fall out of view; all that matters is his apparent need to "regiment" the lives of others.[20]

Always a repellent character, Thrilkild/Wrestrum in early drafts at least manifests more agency in his villainy. The invisible man notes upon meeting him that Thrilkild/Wrestrum "in a way . . . seemed to take quite a bit of authority upon himself, reminding even the top leaders of the necessity of acting like brothers. . . . And he seemed to have a nose for rooting out unbrotherly attitudes. The thing that surprised me about him was that he sometimes went so far as to criticize Brother Jack and Brother Hillard and the others." Thrilkild/Wrestrum is here a self-appointed policeman of brotherliness, it seems, rather than one of the "servile black functionaries" Ellison later claimed to have seen working in the Harlem office of the CP. Several other drafts and notes stress factionalism within the Brotherhood and designate Thrilkild/Wrestrum as the head of a Harlem clique seeking to amass power. While unremittingly negative, this earlier portrayal suggests that all power in the Brotherhood is not in the hands of whites; indeed it reminds us that, in *Black Boy (American Hunger)*, Wright's principal opponent in the Chicago CP was not a white leader but one "Buddy Nealson," a powerful African American representative of the CPUSA to the Comintern.[21]

Most important, Thrilkild/Wrestrum emerges as an antagonist in his own right in relation to the poison pen letter that the invisible man receives at the beginning of chapter 18 of the published text. While the reader is quickly disabused of the notion that Thrilkild/Wrestrum could have written it—the protagonist is "more disappointed than relieved" (393) that his interlocutor does not recognize it—originally the invisible man for a long time entertains the suspicion that Thrilkild/Wrestrum authored the letter. In an early draft it is possible that it *was* indeed he who wrote the letter, since the letter's author is never revealed. At first Ellison appears not to have intended the note to have come from Jack at all. In an outline of incidents following the placard episode, Ellison jotted, "Jealousy over his success . . . Some one warns him of danger. Old member warns him. Refuses to give his name." If this "old member" is Thrilkild/Wrestrum, the invisible man's enemy emerges as an Iago-like figure rather than a mere puppet who, in a consummate irony, plays out the battle royal in the ranks of an organization dedicated to the eradication of Jim Crow.[22]

"Something had driven him away":
Tod Clifton's Death on the City Pavements

As Ellison heightened his novel's anticommunist theme, LeRoy and Louise were his most important exclusions; his most important inclusions were Tod Clifton and Ras. In the 1952 text the street fight between the Brotherhood and Ras's supporters dramatizes their hostile relationship. Clifton lunges at Ras when the black nationalist challenges, "What they do to you, black mahn? Give you them stinking women? . . . A pat on the back and a piece of cunt without no passion?" (372–73). (Ellison at first inserted in Ras's speech the words "Sour cream in the blasted vagina" but removed them, he wrote to Albert Murray, at the behest of his publisher.) Yet Ras's repeated description of Clifton as a "black king" (372–73), as well as his accusation that they are "three black men fighting in the street because of the white enslaver" (372), indicate his awareness of the "governing ritual," to which the invisible man remains oblivious. Clifton's acknowledgment that it may sometimes be necessary to "plunge outside history" (377) foreshadows the sacrifice for which he has been dedicated and set aside. Since Ras and Clifton occupy mutually dependent novelistic functions, it comes as something of a surprise to learn that Ellison created them separately and aligned them only gradually.[23]

In the published text Clifton disappears for no apparent reason; when the invisible man discovers him in Bryant Park, spieling out of the corner of his mouth about brotherhood and dispossession and manipulating the Sambo dolls with hidden strings, his self-negating behavior testifies to an unspecified but profound betrayal by the Brotherhood, one that has destroyed the very basis of his being. Ras's "black king" dies victimized by both the black-shirted, stiff-armed agent of the New York police force and the organization presumably dedicated to fighting fascist violence; indeed Clifton's death suggests that the two institutions party to it are totalitarian mirror images of one another. Clifton's tragic "death on the city pavements" is not meaningless, however, for it precipitates the invisible man's recognition of the depths of Brotherhood perfidy and eventual rebirth as a broadcaster on the lower frequencies. Clifton plays the role of the sacrificial scapegoat in the rhetoric of *Invisible Man*.[24]

In the light of his key role in the 1952 text, as well as in interpretive commentary on the novel, it bears noting that Clifton is not mentioned in "Working Notes" and is absent in the early outlines and drafts. When he first appears he is summarily sketched:

> Brother Clifton had had some rough times about which he'd never talk but there was something powerful propelling him forward. He was our best speaker in the youth division, and showed a great concern with ideology, leading several study groups both in the district and in neighborhood clubs. And when things became rough on the streets he was one of the most courageous, except that he was sometimes too violent.

Initially there is no confrontation with Ras; instead, during an antieviction rally where the Brotherhood members are "attacked by a gang of hoodlums," the protagonist watches Clifton "go wild in the fighting": "[I] had to leap in and stop him from battering one of our own brothers, after which he . . . suffered with remorse and regret." The only other thing we initially learn about Clifton is the somewhat anomalous information that "he had a pleasant voice and had hoped to get a job in a musical."[25]

As Clifton's role in the novel gets more fully dramatized, he sounds somewhat like Jack, telling the invisible man, "Just keep speaking and pick up on ideology"; in the coming encounter with Ras, he urges, "Your voice . . . [will] just keep rousing things up." The confrontation with Ras originally ends with Clifton punching Ras, who falls to the pavement, a "thick black man with a bullet head and . . . tears on his face"; Clifton here says nothing about plunging outside of history. When Clifton disappears, the invisible man is confused: "I thought of all the girls who might have set him off, but he'd never been seriously involved with any of them. Nor had he had any political disagreements with any of the leaders; I would have been told of that if he had. It made no sense; he had every reason to go on to become important in the Brotherhood. Something had driven him away."[26]

The account of Clifton's death went through several drafts. Originally it is not Clifton who is the "spieler," but an unnamed "youth leader . . . one of the most enthusiastic"; the invisible man is "about to ask about Clifton, a youth member of the Harlem district," phrasing suggesting that Clifton has not been introduced to the reader. In this version the anonymous young man's chant makes no ironic reference to left politics:

> *He's more than a toy, he's Sambo the dancing doll.*
> *He lives in the sun shine of your smile, thats his secret[.]*
> *Ladies and Gentlemen, only 25 cents, because he likes to eat!*
> *Shake it Sambo, Shake it and take it . . . Thank you.*

Ellison wrote, "I was sure. He was one of the most promising members, one who'd shown a passion for ideological discussion." He crossed out "I was sure" and substituted "It was Clifton," and added to the chant the words, "the dancing doll, the 20th century miracle . . . he'll kill your depression, and your dispossession. . . . And only twenty-five cents, the brotherly two bits of a dollar because he wants me to eat." The tragic ending—and anticommunist implication—of the episode were evidently not foreordained. In the earliest version there occurs no police murder. Thinking that "Perhaps I could get in touch with him and bring him back, find him a job," the invisible man leaves to get a cold drink and "call the District." Ellison next opted to have the young man killed, writing, "[The] spieler runs around corner runs into cop tries to fight is shot." In the published text this young Harlemite turns into Clifton's lookout; it is Clifton who satirizes the Brotherhood and is murdered. The metamorphosis of the passage is quite extraordinary.[27]

Although the reader of *Invisible Man* never discovers the "something" that drove Clifton away from the Brotherhood, Ellison initially supplied his character with two intertwined motivations. These emerge in a scene where Clifton confronts the invisible man the evening he has moved back to the Harlem office from downtown. One motivation involves Louise, or a nameless variant on her: it is not the invisible man, but Clifton, who marries a

"Othello complex." Clifton bitterly says,

> First they build you up as something special, then they come along and
> try to make us believe that when we get one we've got all there is to get.
> Well, I had one . . . and I wanted her because she was the woman but
> they wouldn't let it go at that. Everywhere we went they had to make
> something of it. We had to be symbolic of this and symbolic of that. We
> couldn't go to a party or a downtown rally without being reminded that
> she was white and I was black. Pretty soon I got to feeling like a piece of
> bait. I got so sick of it that I bought a sun-lamp and made her lie under it
> for hours. . . . And she dyed her hair. . . . I still love her, but I sent her away.

Penciled-in editorial changes show Clifton voicing suspicion that Louise may
have married him "under orders [from] the committee"; the invisible man
thinks, "He hates himself. . . . He doesn't believe that she—any white girl—
could love him simply because she is white." In successive drafts Clifton
charges that the Brotherhood has used Louise as "nigger bait." "I didn't know
whether we were together for love or for discipline," he despairs. "We were
like that couple in a sign advertising one of those jungle movies; she was the
blonde and I was the gorilla." Ellison penciled in the words, "There was a
pained expression on his face, and I thought, he sounds like the Exhorter."[28]

The catalyst of the crisis in Clifton's marriage, it emerges, is the Brotherhood's decision to stop its antieviction and welfare campaigns, thereby
greatly damaging the organization's standing in Harlem. "What else could I
do? What else, with her still disciplined and things going to hell up here?"
exclaims Clifton. "I couldn't stand being so close to what I knew was betraying me. I might have hurt her." Responding to the invisible man's confusion, Clifton continues, "Do I have to draw you a picture? They've sold
us out and I took part. . . . I took part and you're taking up where I left off.
I didn't disappear, I quit. I hope everyone in Harlem quits!" The Harlem
leadership, he charges, has been left to take the blame for the organization's
shift in strategy: "They're playing some game and we are the goats. . . . They
make their moves behind a screen of 'dicipline' and we're supposed to forget
everything and go along."[29]

Why did Ellison omit this late-night conversation between the two men?
After all, it not only accounts for Clifton's impassioned response to Ras's
comments about interracial sexual relationships but also supplies a concrete motivation for Clifton's "plunge outside history." Perhaps Ellison's past
romantic relationship with the white Communist Sanora Babb made him

balk at reproducing the anticommunist doctrine that white women function as bait to draw black men into the radical movement. Or perhaps, as Ellison observed to Hyman in late 1949 about the "complicat[ions]" introduced by the Othello theme, Othello and Desdemona, as symbolic vehicles, may simply have been getting out of hand. In any event, by removing the Othello theme Ellison further etiolated the novel's potentially sympathetic connection with left politics. In his essay "Twentieth-Century Fiction and the Black Mask of Humanity" (1946), we will recall, he had written, "The democratic dream has become too shaky a structure to support the furious pressures of the artist's doubt. And as always when the belief which nurtures a great social myth declines, large sections of society become prey to superstition. For man without myth is Othello with Desdemona gone: chaos descends, faith vanishes and superstitions prowl the mind." Clifton's loss of faith in the Brotherhood is analogous to Othello's loss of faith in Desdemona; his caricatured reversion to the preindividual realm of minstrelsy is analogous to Othello's descent into the madness of unbounded jealousy. Yet Desdemona is by definition an emblem of purity and loyalty; to imagine her corrupt is to invalidate the premise of Shakespeare's tragedy. As the rhetoric of anticommunism increasingly shapes Ellison's revisions of *Invisible Man*, however, Louise, as a symbol of the "great social myth [of the] . . . democratic dream," cannot be allowed to retain her wifely purity along with her red identity. Both Louise and LeRoy, who function as symbols of democracy for the protagonist and Treadwell, respectively, have to be removed from the novel if the "democratic dream" is to be severed from the egalitarian aspirations of political radicals. That the Popular Front icon Paul Robeson had broken the color barrier on Broadway with his performance of Shakespeare's hero may also have entered into Ellison's decision to excise the Othello theme from the novel; memories of Robeson's achievement in 1943 might not have jelled well with his stigmatization in the year of *Invisible Man*'s publication.

Ellison's decision to eliminate from his novel the specific reason for Clifton's plunge outside of history shrouds the young Harlem organizer's death in mystery. But perhaps this vagueness is precisely what Ellison eventually wished. Clifton's self-derogating chant suggests that his loss of identity stems not just from distress at a change in political strategy but from his shattering recognition that his humanity has been stolen from him; before he is murdered by the policeman he is in some sense already dead. The reader of the published text, by this point expert in picking up reiterations of the "governing ritual," knows how to supply the missing causal links in the "political allegory." Clifton's murder reenacts the battle royal, now migrated to the ranks of the left; the manipulators of the situation are not the local bourgeoisie or the Wall Street "kings of the earth" but the pullers of strings at the CP headquarters downtown on Union Square. No more need be known; Clifton, for all his objections to being seen as "symbolic of this or that," is, ironically, the text's consummate symbol, operating at the highest possible level of generality to signal the Brotherhood's ruthless subordination of the individual—especially the black man—to its mechanistic scientism. As the American Dionysus, the sacrificed black king, Clifton becomes the novel's substitute for LeRoy; as tragic scapegoat *in* the text he enables the scapegoat *of* the text, the Brotherhood, to take increasingly distinct shape.[30]

"Yellow and brown allies": From Ras the Killer to Ras the Exhorter/Destroyer

Although he makes few dramatized appearances in the published text of *Invisible Man*, Ras the Exhorter, later dubbed Ras the Destroyer, plays a critical role in establishing one of the extremes of fanaticism in relation to which the invisible man's closing embrace of ambiguity takes rhetorical shape as a golden mean. Ras is first glimpsed by the invisible man on the day of his arrival in Harlem, "a short, squat man shout[ing] angrily from a ladder to which were attached a collection of small American flags" (159). When the invisible man, now a Brotherhood organizer, and Clifton confront Ras several months later, Ras's castigation of the invisible man for his ginger-colored skin highlights the absurdity of what Ellison would later call "blood-thinking." Yet in his wild comments about race and sex Ras manages to plant the seeds of doubt, in both Clifton and the reader, about the Brotherhood's integrity. Ras is next shown gaining support in Harlem when, in the wake of Clifton's funeral, he taunts the invisible man about the Brotherhood's failure to oppose police brutality. When Ras and his supporters are seen for the last time during the riot, he is on horseback, dressed as an African warrior and brandishing a spear, while they move militaristically "in a tight-knit order, carrying sticks and clubs, shotguns and rifles" (556). It is also implied that Ras is, if unwittingly, being used by the Brotherhood: addressing a group of hostile Harlemites, the invisible man pleads, "'Use a nigger to catch a nigger.' Well they used me to catch you and now they're using Ras to do away with me and to prepare your sacrifice" (558). Finally showing up in the invisible man's lynching nightmare, the black nationalist has evidently become American enough to join the phalanx of castrators.[31]

Although Ras figures crucially in the novel's closing lineup of antagonists, his full portrait was inserted into the text only in 1950, when most of the novel was substantially complete. In the earliest drafts, where Clifton has not yet joined the novel's cast of characters, the invisible man first encounters Ras's anonymous predecessor on emerging from the subway after the funeral and seeing "a short bald-headed man" making a speech; the narrator says, "I didn't know the man." A revised version reads, "I was passing a nationalist street meeting with a group of brothers when the speaker, a short baldheaded man, leaned down." "Ras the Killer" is penciled into this draft; then "the Exhorter" is added, and the man is additionally described as a "radical race [agitator] who proposed that Negroes migrate to Africa." This meeting is the invisible man's first and only encounter with Ras; when he descends into the manhole he is running not from Ras and his henchmen, but from the wild gunfire and confusion. In a subsequent version where Clifton and the invisible man confront Ras in the nighttime streets, Ellison prepares for this encounter by having the invisible man first glimpse Ras on the day he arrives in Harlem. Here, it bears noting, the orator does not shout from "a ladder to which were attached a collection of small American flags" (159), as in the published text, but simply is seen clasping a "small strange flag" in one hand.[32]

Ellison's decision to describe his black nationalist agitator more fully, but to change his name from Ras the Killer to Ras the Exhorter/Destroyer, at once gestures toward and withholds direct reference to an actual historical figure. "Ras the Killer" was the sobriquet of Randolph Wilson, a virulently anti-Semitic and anti-Communist African American fascist who was prominent in Harlem street agitation during the Second World War. An FBI agent assigned to follow Wilson reported in August 1941 that, at a rally on Lenox Avenue at 127th Street, he "openly confessed his hate of the President and of the Jews and made favorable remarks about Hitler." In his muckraking bestseller, *Under Cover* (1943), the journalist John Roy Carlson reported hearing Ras the Killer state in a street rally, "I was happy to see Hitler declare war on the white man. I'm mighty happy to see him winning." Lashing out at miscegenation, Wilson concluded, "When I sleep I want to sleep with a woman of my own blood. I don't want the white woman to sleep with." Another speaker at the Ras-sponsored rally warned, "Don't you believe all these things about brotherhood. There ain't no brotherhood for the colored man, except in his own kind."[33]

Notable for his incendiary rhetoric, Ras the Killer was only one of several right-wing latter-day followers of Marcus Garvey who were active in Harlem during the Depression and wartime years. These included the street agitators Arthur Reid and Ira Kemp; Sufi Abdul Hamid, variously dubbed the "Harlem Hitler" and the "black Hitler," who injected anti-Semitism into the "Don't Buy Where you Can't Work" campaign and was brought to court on charges of "fomenting racial strife between Negroes and Jews"; and Leonard Robert Jordan, the "Harlem Mikado," who advocated wartime support for Japan and warned that, after the defeat of the United States, Roosevelt would be "picking cotton" and his two top cabinet ministers "would be riding [Jordan] around in rickshaws." As the FBI reported, in a Harlem speech in the summer of 1941 Jordan stressed that "Jews were the enemy of all Negroes"; he was convicted of sedition and sentenced to prison in 1943.[34]

Ellison was well acquainted with such figures; in his article "Anti-Semitism among Negroes" (1939) he had targeted both Reid and Hamid. That year he also joked in a letter to Hughes, "I, Muhammed Ras de Terror, come to the mountain." He was familiar with the fictional portraits of Harlem fascists by Carl Offord in *The White Face* (1943) and Wright in his unpublished novel *Black Hope*, written right after *Native Son*. As coeditor of *Negro Quarterly* he had overseen the publication of Lawrence Reddick's essay on Negro anti-Semitism. Ellison's Ras is a composite figure, alluding in his name to Wilson/Ras the Killer and in his flamboyant dress suggesting Hamid, who characteristically walked through Harlem dressed in a "turban, green velvet blouse, Sam Browne belt, riding habit, patent leather boots, [with] a black crimson-lined cape carelessly around his shoulders." While Ellison clearly lampoons his black nationalist's biological notion of race and sartorial choices, he almost completely effaces his pro-Axis politics, which are reduced to a vague reference to blacks' need for "yellow and brown allies" (373). The anti-Semitic and pro-Japanese fascism constituting the most dangerous feature of the historical Ras the Killer is almost entirely eliminated from his fictional portraiture.[35]

Why would Ellison gesture in the direction of one of Harlem's most renowned Negro fascists by naming his character Ras, but then refrain from displaying some of the most infamous features of his character's historical prototype? After all, Ras fits into the logic of the "two totalitarianisms" thesis. As Thomas Schaub has noted, the closing description of Ras's disciplined followers, which "situates Ras within the set of all those characters and scenes in the novel that embody order and repression," from the robotic college students marching in formation to the People's Hot Foot Squad, ends up "tuck[ing] Ras within the discourse of totalitarianism." Ras's final appearance during the riot inspires the invisible man to contemplate the blindness to individuality shared by all his antagonists and prepares the way for the epilogue's meditation on the enduring legacy of the Founding Fathers.[36]

But Ras can perform this synthesizing ideological function in the 1952 text largely because his attack on the Brotherhood has been justified in the reader's eyes: Clifton does end up betrayed by his white allies (even if we never learn exactly why or how), and, as the woman in the red robe has shown, the movement's white men do make their wives available to African American men. If Ras were shown to be virulently anti-Semitic and pro-Axis, however—in fact an active partisan of Hitler and Hirohito—he could hardly figure as the means to the invisible man's realization during the riot of the "beautiful American identity" that he, Ras, and the other antagonists presumably have in common. (It bears noting that Ellison revised the original typescript from "the beautiful absurdity of their identity" to "the beautiful absurdity of their American identity and mine.") If Ras the Killer's full range of beliefs were attributed to Ras the Exhorter/Destroyer, the reader might even be reminded of the historical role played by Communists in the fight against fascism. Had the torchlight parade and Mount Morris rally been retained in the 1952 text, the reader might recall the considerable appeal, to both Ellison and the invisible man, of Popular Frontist "twentieth-century Americanism." Had Stein/Hambro and Louise been retained as characters, moreover, the novel would contain concrete instances of Communist Jews and white women that would undermine Ras's rhetoric: he would be not just rigid and fanatical, but wrong. Ras's grouping with Jack in the published text is accomplished through the formalist positing of totalitarianism as the authoritarian personality writ large but lacking specific political contents. The fact that Ras was added to the novel only toward its completion, and shown to be less a carrier of dangerous black nationalism than a pawn of the Brotherhood, suggests that as a character he is the offspring of cold war ideology. In the published novel Ras is tarred with the brush of anticommunism and at the same time incorporated into the text's anticommunist rhetoric. Once the logic of guilt by association dictates rhetorical policy, a truly diverse array of people, it seems, can be drawn into the dragnet.[37]

"Like the dodo bird": The Men of Transition

In commentary on *Invisible Man* much has been made of the passage where, after witnessing Clifton's murder, the protagonist encounters the zoot-suited hipsters in the subway. He realizes that these "men of transition" who speak a "jived-up transitional language" carrying "remote, cryptic messages" have never heard of the Brotherhood, but may be nonetheless "the saviors, the true leaders, the bearers of something precious." He then conjectures that history may be after all "a gambler, instead of a force in a laboratory experiment" (440–41). Linked with the invisible man's comment in the epilogue that history is neither a spiral nor an arrow but a boomerang—and at times also connected with Ellison's final *Negro Quarterly* editorial, where he wrote of the mystery potentially embodied in the zoot suit—this passage has been widely interpreted as the crucial turning point in the protagonist's *agon*, the beginning of *peripeteia*. While the passage's principal target has been recognized as Marxism's spiral theory of history—the implied referent of the "laboratory experiment" comment—its locus of critique has been expanded to encompass progressivism and sociological rationalism, with their implied arrow theories of history.[38]

Originally Ellison situated the subway encounter with the hipsters not after the death of Clifton but in the prologue. Not only are there no references in this draft to "my fallen brother . . . running and dodging the forces of history" (441); there are no references to the Brotherhood at all. The young men's "remote, cryptic messages" are here "remote, meaningless messages"; the entire passage describing history as a gambler is penciled in only later. When in the 1952 text the narrator wonders what future historians would think of the "transitory ones[,] . . . such as [he] had been before [he] found Brotherhood," the invisible man distances himself from the zoot suit–wearing migrants: the men on the platform who "know nothing of Brotherhood" are referred to exclusively as "they" (439). In earlier drafts, however, his identity with them is retained as he challenges the reader, "What about us who you see sometimes waiting still and silent in the subway?" Stating that he too is a "throwback" to an earlier time, he compares himself not with a "small distant meteorite that died several hundred years ago" (442) but with a vanished species: "Perhaps I should have disappeared around the first part of the 19th century, like the dodo bird."[39]

Ellison was aware that the passage would carry different valences in different locations. "Decide whether hipsters dress, etc, should come before or after political experience," he mulled. "Irony and truth if it comes after." In the earlier versions—the ones containing no allusion to the Brotherhood, no connection with the death of Clifton, and no mention of history as a gambler—the subway encounter does not invite the antimaterialist reading to which it is frequently subjected. When he initially identifies himself with these "men outside of historical time" as a fellow migrant and charges the reader with having "failed to see them" and "failed to understand [their] . . . transitional language," the narrator implies that their, and his, invisibility consists in the inability of northern sophisticates to acknowledge the humanity of the "men of transition" emerging from the preindividuality of the Jim Crow South. By designating the migrants' language as "meaningless" rather than "cryptic," however, the narrator indicates that the "something precious" contained in their speech may not hold the key to an encoded vernacular wisdom, even if it does embody a folk legacy in danger of being lost on the mean streets of industrial society. In its original version the passage addresses the issue of identity, but more in the discourse of social science than in that of metaphysics.[40]

The invisible man's initial comparison of himself with a dodo bird reinforces the passage's connection with the discourse of scientific rationalism. A large flightless bird that was rendered extinct within a century of its initial contact with the humans who relentlessly hunted it down in the seventeenth century on the Indian Ocean island of Mauritius, the dodo figures in discussions of natural selection as Exhibit A of the vulnerability of certain species to rapid historical change. Early anthropologists not infrequently analogized the dodo bird to primitive societies threatened with extinction in the modern world. James Frazer referenced such a comparison when he wrote in 1927, "The most urgent need of anthropology at present is to procure accurate accounts of the existing customs and ideas of savages before they have disappeared." The "philosophic historian" who obtains such accounts "will be able to formulate, with a fair degree of probability, those general laws which have shaped the intellectual, social, and moral evolution of mankind," he wrote. Should the anthropologist fail in this venture, "the savage . . . will then be as extinct as the dodo." The comparativist thrust of Frazer's evolutionary anthropology was the source of its value to the scholars of the Cambridge School, who sought to anatomize the "general laws" guiding the parallel developments of ritual and myth in different civilizations. Raglan's hero, based on examples abstracted from multiple cultures, embodies the epitome of this effort; the concept of preindividuality theorized by Fromm and applied to African Americans by Bland was based on similar evolutionist premises, as was Wright's formulation of the meaning of migration in *Twelve Million Black Voices*. And as was, for that matter, Ellison's own formulation of the process by which "the folk individual was being liquidated in the crucible of steel" that he set forth in his review of *Blood on the Forge*, notably titled "Transition." Ellison may or may not have come across Frazer's article as he browsed among the writings of the Cambridge

School, but he invokes the same evolutionist discourse in his original description of the hipsters in the subway. When in the published text the invisible man dismisses the scientific view of history, he rejects an analytical standpoint his own creator had occupied only a few years before.[41]

"Confusion over communism":
Rinehart and Lawrence Dennis

The precipitant of the invisible man's realization that freedom is the recognition of possibility, the Protean figure of Rinehart has been variously interpreted as the embodiment of relativist decadence and the epitome of trickster subversion. Ellison considered various locations of the episode in which the invisible man takes on the identity of this quintessential confidence man; these were all located toward the novel's end. The invisible man's encounter with "Rinehartism" would be central to the "perception" stage of his psychological and philosophical odyssey. "Through Rhine," noted Ellison, the protagonist discovers "the formlessness of the Negro community. Class lines are meaningless, status becomes a matter of the will and the imagination. Rhinehart has made himself what he wanted to be, and he has willed to be several different conflicting types simultaneously." Rinehart prompts the protagonist to reconsider the meaning of the phrase "plunging into reality": "It is reality that does the plunging and unless you have a thicker skin than I, it eventually penetraits you. . . . Something gives, something changes. . . . The difficulty lies in our insistence upon their being a correspondence between cause and effect, [for] causes might become short circuited and produce uncalled for effects—or no visible effect at all." He concludes, "I put on a pair of dark glasses and became educated, aware of myself, while clearly there is no connection between self-awareness and green glass." A veritable workshop has been established in Ellison criticism dedicated to commentary on this shape-changing con artist, who, it is sometimes argued, challenges not just the Brotherhood's rationalism but the stability of all foundational knowledges. But while Rinehart emerges as a deconstructionist *avant la lettre*, he also serves, however paradoxically, to reinforce the liberal conception of America as a land of opportunity. Frequently cited in the critical commentary on Rinehart is Ellison's statement in 1955 that, although the Harlem con man is "a personification of chaos," he also, as a "figure in a country with no solid past or stable class lines[,] . . . is intended to represent America and change." Epistemological indeterminacy and American social mobility, both embodied in the notion of fluidity, take shape as flip sides of the same coin.[42]

As he composed *Invisible Man*, Ellison was initially uncertain about the meaning and role of this character, jotting in the margin of the original typescript, "What kind of man is Rhinehart (sp) anyway?" In an early draft the Brotherhood member Julius Franklin has a pretty clear idea. Condemning Rinehart as "a dog . . . a slickster, a confidencer," Julius tells the invisible man, "Rinehart's been around here for a hell of a time, taking advantage of the people and everything. He's in every racket you can shake a stick at, including the preaching racket. He's got him an after hours night spot; he's mixed up in the numbers; I heard he's got him a stable of two white women; he's a gambler AND he's got him a couple of them storefront churches." Julius also has personal memories of Rinehart in the South, where he was "one of these here little boy preachers [whose] daddy used to carry him around all over. . . . [He] could sing like a bird." He compares Rinehart with one "Disciple William Love," a cult preacher who "converted one thousand men women and children in about a month" while being "one of the biggest dope peddlers in the country." Julius's memories prompt the invisible man to recall a story he had heard about "another [boy preacher] who had grown up and passed for white and become a wealthy broker, a country gentleman, and a reactionary writer on politics—with no one except a few Negroes the wiser; yes, and they [were] amused and silent at the deception." In the 1952 text the antipathy of class-conscious Harlemites toward Rinehart is confined to Brother Maceo's hostile reaction when he mistakes the invisible man, wearing a hat and dark glasses, for the preacher-pimp-hustler. In earlier versions Julius's account of Rinehart's parasitism, especially when coupled with the narrator's own memories, makes it less possible to celebrate Rinehart as a transgressive epistemological hero and prophet of existential possibility.[43]

Readers familiar with *Juneteenth* immediately recognize that, when he created Rinehart, Ellison was already thinking ahead to his next novel; especially in light of the backstory about the "boy preacher" supplied by Julius Franklin, the connection between the Reverend Bliss Proteus Rinehart of *Invisible Man* and the Bliss/Sunraider of the posthumous text is patent. Ellison's notes reveal that he in fact considered making the protagonist of his next novel the "natural son" of Rinehart; in a plot involving "a masquerade and a chase" the son (presumably Severen in *Juneteenth*) would seek the truth about his father, who had moved from his church to Wall Street and then "into government." Ellison added, "Rhinehart must function politically, on confusion over communism. A false fellow [who] manipulates chaos." In this formulation Rinehart's relationship to chaos is one of political instrumentalism, not existential embodiment. Chaos moreover, here associated with "confusion over communism," suggests not so much a society in which "class lines are meaningless" as one in which the apparent permeability of class lines can be deployed in the authoritarian social project of fascism. That Wall Street would be implicated in this Rinehartesque figure's "manipulat[ion of] chaos" further suggests that, even as he moved toward the equation of fluidity with status-transcending individual acts of will, Ellison continued to be drawn to the Marxist view of fascism as a chaotic manifestation of monopoly capitalism in crisis that he had articulated in his *New Masses* writings.[44]

In supplying the Rinehart of *Invisible Man* with such shady connections, Ellison was not only foreshadowing his next fictional project but also alluding to a real historical prototype. For while the enigmatic preacher-turned-power broker sketched in his notes for *Invisible Man* and fleshed out in *Juneteenth* is a composite of various notorious Harlem religious hustlers, he also quite specifically calls to mind Lawrence Dennis, a light-skinned African American who, passing over the color line, emerged as the most prominent Depression-era political theorist of American fascism, bar none. Paraded by his mother around the United States and Europe as a child prodigy preacher, Dennis as an adult cut his family ties and built a career as a diplomat, a dabbler in high finance, and a prophet of "the coming American fascism," the title of a book published in 1936 that was preceded by *Is Capitalism Doomed?* (1932) and followed by *The Dynamics of War and Revolution* (1940). Consorting with the likes of Benito Mussolini and Rudolf Hess, Dennis advocated a Hitleresque conjunction of the state with big business minus the more virulently racist features of the current fascist regimes in Europe. Although, as Gerald Horne has pointed out, much of the "confluence of fascism and passing that drove Lawrence Dennis's life" derived from his antipathy to the deep-seated racism in American society, central to his success in the 1930s was not just his unflagging hostility to the labor movement and the left but also his flirtation with white supremacists and anti-Semites. As the United States became embroiled in the Second World War, however, Dennis's fortunes faltered; identified by the FBI as a danger to national security, he ended up as one of the defendants in the mass sedition trial of 1944–45. Astute observers like Horace Cayton and George Schuyler had known for years of Dennis's racial background, but by 1946 he had been all but outed as a Negro, although even then the mainstream press remained curiously reluctant to accept that he was black.[45]

Ellison's reading notes indicate that he was acquainted with *The Coming American Fascism*; the parallels between Dennis and *Juneteenth*'s Bliss/Sunraider are too close to be coincidental. Ellison's decision not to include in his fictional portrayal of Rinehart any allusion to the pro-Nazi beliefs and activities of his prototype-by-association suggests that, as *Invisible Man* approached its finale, he wished to detach his confidence man's exploitive mode of operation from its specific political contents. Rinehart could figure as a "personification of chaos" as long as chaos signified a state of being and perception isolable from historically specific social and political practices. Just as Ras needed to be stripped of his anti-Semitism if he were to be posited as Jack's totalitarian twin, Rinehart needed to be divested of the power to harm the body politic if his Protean shape-changing were to present a challenge to the Brotherhood's scientism. If Ras and Rinehart were to inspire in the invisible man a recognition of the Americanness of his situation, these figures had to be dissociated from the anti-Americanism that Popular Frontist leftists, advocates of the view that Communism was "twentieth-century Americanism," so vehemently opposed.[46]

"Did it signify love or politics?": Clifton's Funeral

In prefatory remarks accompanying "A Lament for Tod Clifton," the section of *Invisible Man* that he originally selected for inclusion in an anthology of writings on race edited by Whit Burnett in 1971, Ellison explained why he chose the funeral scene:

> It seems to represent the moment in the plot wherein the narrator becomes aware of the basic irony of his political role and begins to move painfully from a state of illusionment to a sense of reality.... He stumbles to a depth of human experience which renders both the superficiality of the Brotherhood's program and the duplicity of its leaders inescapable. Indeed, he plunges into that realm beneath the level of the merely rational where men, aroused by the sight and smell of blood and knowing themselves to be in the presence of (and the possible victims of) violent and unjust death, are moved to an awareness of the necessity for human fraternity which overrides all considerations of race, class, creed or color.... By attempting to dignify and politicalize Tod Clifton's slaying he discovers that the Brotherhood which has sought to teach men how to live possesses no ceremonial forms for dealing with death.

The *peripeteia* described here hinges on the invisible man's simultaneous discovery of human authenticity and Communist duplicity; indeed the one realization is contingent upon the other.[47]

Critical commentaries on the funeral scene frequently emphasize the invisible man's newfound humanism. His seeing "not a crowd but the set faces of individual men and women" (459) exhibits the rediscovered capacity for warmth and spontaneity that he has hitherto suppressed in the name of rationalism and discipline. The statements from his inner meditation most frequently cited are his query, "Could politics ever be an expression of love?" (452) and his confession that he experiences a "transcendent emotion . . . deepened by that something for which the theory of Brotherhood had given [him] no name" (453). Given the prominence of these passages in interpretations of the funeral scene, it bears noting that neither is included in the original text. The invisible man, wondering at the size of the crowd, first thinks, "Why were they here? Because they knew Clifton, or because his death gave them the opportunity to express their mass protest against the police department?" Ellison crossed out this last sentence and penciled in, "Did it signify love or politics?" He later added the skeptical query about whether politics could ever express love. Deeply moved by the singers, the invisible man at first thinks, "They touched upon something deeper than protest, or religion . . . and yet it had aroused and joined us all." Ellison penciled in the observation, "[This emotion is] something for which the theory of Brotherhood had given me no name." While the invisible man's oration itself underwent little change from draft to draft, its original framing did not hinge on the separation of the emotional from the political, the experiential from the theoretical.[48]

Ellison crucially altered the Brotherhood's relationship to the funeral. In the published text the invisible man pulls together the funeral march without the permission, much less the blessing, of the citywide leadership of the Brotherhood; in fact it is for organizing the event on his own responsibility that he gets called onto the carpet. Here he marches at the head of the procession not with Brotherhood members, but with various "old community leaders" (450). Somewhat oddly, however, it seems that the event "was arranged to attract the largest number" and that "an appeal went out for all former members to join the funeral march"; the use of the passive voice obscures the agency of these arrangements and appeals. "[When so many] brothers and sisters whom I hadn't seen since my return . . . turned up, [as well as] . . . members from downtown and outlying districts," the invisible man says, "[I] watched them with surprise as they gathered and wondered at the depths of their sorrow" (450). The reader too might be wondering why these "brothers and sisters" are there at all. If, as it turns out, Jack and the other leaders are so vehemently opposed to honoring the renegade

Clifton with a mass funeral, why would so many rank-and-file members violate Party discipline in order to attend?

The passage's drafts help to resolve this ambiguity. In its earliest version, when the march memorializes not Clifton but the nameless spieler killed by the police, the funeral is unambiguously the product of Brotherhood activity, organized to dramatize the death of its young member at the hands of New York's finest; that the young man was selling the Sambo dolls apparently does not trump his having been the victim of a northern lynching. The invisible man at first marches with "the other district leaders" of the Brotherhood; presumably a decision has been made at the leadership level to support the event. The choice of Mount Morris Park as the site of the funeral ceremony recalls the winter evening antieviction parade and rally that inspired the invisible man to join the Brotherhood. His perception of individual faces—a register to his departure from Brotherhood habits—may even recall his earlier description of Jack looking out on the nighttime crowd "as though he saw each member of the crowd separately and in infinite detail." The early drafts of the funeral scene remind us that it would have been only under the aegis of the Communist movement that a multiracial crowd of thousands would have gathered in Harlem to protest the police murder of a young black man. Ellison's later observation that leftists had no rituals for mourning runs counter to his own original representation of the funeral for the anonymous spieler, which far more accurately describes the typical reaction of leftists to racist police murder during the 1930s and 1940s. Harlem funerals for the victims of state violence were often recorded in the pages of the *Daily Worker*; Wright had penned a number of articles featuring the multiracial character of the crowds in attendance at these events. Ellison knew better.[49]

"We have given them the possibility of a choice": The Eye Scene

In the published text of *Invisible Man* the protagonist's moment of truth comes when, having organized the funeral for Clifton, he is harshly criticized by the Brotherhood leadership for acting out of his "personal responsibility" (463) rather than adhering to "discipline" (465). When Brother Jack's glass eye falls out and he starts "spluttering and lapsing into a foreign language . . . the language of the future" (473, 476)—which is presumably Russian—what has been clear to the reader all along finally becomes clear to the invisible man: having traveled from "purpose" through "passion" to "perception," he has "boomeranged around" (476) to a realization of his invisibility. Antagonists align and symbols cluster. Jack's assertion that the invisible man was hired to speak and not to think goes back to the young man's speech at the smoker: "personal responsibility" is apparently as noxious to Communists as "social equality" is to Jim Crow racists. Jack's not-seeing the protagonist through his glass eye completes the associational cluster associating blinding and blindness with misleadership and illusion. Here blindness, as in Arthur Koestler's *Darkness at Noon* and other cold war texts, emerges as a metaphor for Communism. The Cyclopean appearance of the Brotherhood leader thus designates him as the principal antagonist of our "no name" but increasingly wily protagonist. Jack's insistence on "sacrifice" in the name of "discipline" means that, as he undergoes his Kafkaesque trial, the invisible man has been "dedicated and set aside" not as an honored figure embodying collective values and needs of humanity as a whole but as a fall guy upon whom are being heaped the collective shortcomings and failures of a political organization. Ellison jotted, "They tear him apart verbally for funeral . . . passion, [sparagmos], dismemberment"; the "governing ritual" is reenacted by white men of the northern urban left. If a workshop has been convened around the figure of Rinehart, the eye scene has given rise to a veritable industry.[50]

The climactic role of this revelatory chapter, which in his notes Ellison usually dubbed the "eye scene," was not planned far in advance; there is no mention of it in either "Working Notes" or the novel's early plot outlines. As the scene took shape in his imagination Ellison considered situating it at various points in the narrative, even as early as the aftermath of the arena speech. Asking himself, "Does eye scene have feeling of end?" he worried, "What if he breaks during eye incident goes underground? What of riot then?" Ellison eventually decided that he would "start at end and plot backwards." As it became clearer to him that Jack would be designated the Cyclopean antagonist to the protagonist's Ulysses, he revised the invisible man's recall of their past associations. When the narrator returns to Harlem after his assignment downtown, he initially thinks, "When I met Brother Jack he was as bland as ever, but now that I admitted to myself that I no longer liked him I told myself that I was being subjective." This was revised to read, "When Brother Jack visited the section he was as bland as ever, but now as I admitted the uneasiness to myself, I discovered that my first dislike of him had returned."[51]

The eye scene itself was reworked several times. Originally, as he enters the room the protagonist sees MacAfee talking with a "tiny Japanese brother who gestured passionately with his delicate hands." Jack then "bounces in" and offers an explanation about why Harlem has to be "sacrificed." "[A] major change in policy," he says, "[will require] deals and alliances with other political groups. As for the purely local aspects of such issues as relief and dispossession most of the struggle of this nature will be carried on by our brothers working in the unions. Our job now is to raise the conscious-ness of the people to a higher level. We must teach them to think not locally, but nationally." Jack describes the situation facing Harlem's inhabitants as a war: "It isn't that they are to be held back, but that they are to be brought ahead more slowly. It's like a battle, one unit can't be allowed to get too far ahead of the rest, otherwise it's destroyed. A tempo must be maintained or we upset the total strategy. We must retreat in order to advance." He con-joins the battle metaphor with one of vision:

> We gave them a mirror, theory, and then showed them . . . a sword, prac-
> tice, with which to hack their way out of their condition. . . . We stepped
> into a chaotic situation, and created a firm center, brothers. Due to our
> efforts the people now have a new rallying point. We have given them the
> possibility of a choice. We have placed their history, their destiny, into
> their own hands. . . . And in keeping with [this new period] we are called
> upon to apply a new flexibility to our approach to the general political
> situation.

Jack makes no mention here of sacrifice, but instead stresses that Harlemites will create their own "destiny"; he talks about "choice" and "possibility," not History. His implicit allusion to Perseus's fight with the Gorgon—the mir-ror of theory enables the sword of practice to vanquish the gorgon (whether of democratic capitalism or fascism is not clear)—names African Americans as heroic agents. Like the invisible man in his interview with *Brown Success* magazine, Jack believes that the Marxist grasp of historical necessity is the key to historical possibility. That Jack's words radiate arrogance is undeni-able; it is after all the Brotherhood that provides the mirror of theory in which the possibilities for action will be refracted. The notion that the lens of Marxism might supply a means of overcoming poor vision and changing reality—the possibility previously suggested at the magazine interview—is here subjected to ironic critique. But Jack's unbounded confidence that the Brotherhood's mirror and sword will enable Harlemites to achieve their own destiny is more paternalistic than demonic; these do not sound like the words of a man who is planning to "murder" Harlem.[52]

In what appears to be the earliest dramatization of the eye scene, the in-visible man enters the room:

> [The leaders were sitting] around the table in their shirt sleeves listening to a brother who was so angry about something that in the middle of his burst of words he lapsed into a foreign language, stopped[,] choked, began shaking and shook his head so violently that I saw something fly out of his face and land upon the table and roll a ways as he reached out, still speaking American now, picked up the object and dropped it into a glass of water that stood on the table before him. "Here he is now," he shouted, pointing in my direction, "Here's the corruptor of discipline!" But I was so surprised to see the collapse of his eyesocket that I didn't realize that he was referring to me.

The one-eyed Brotherhood member—notably *not* Jack—does not enter into a diatribe about sacrifice. Nor does the invisible man think to himself that the foreign language into which the man has lapsed is the "language of the future," even though he does stipulate, rather oddly, that the man switches back to speaking "American." Instead Brother Jack, "rapping for order," tells the man to sit down and the meeting continues.[53]

Ellison's changes in the eye scene, which guarantee that the invisible man finally emerges from his big white fog and grasps the depths of Communist perfidy, are especially significant in the light of events unfolding in the late 1940s. In the margin of a subsequent draft of the eye scene where it is Jack, and not an unnamed Brotherhood member, who loses the eye and starts gabbling in "the language of the future," Ellison jotted, "Jack has red hair." In turning Jack into a Russian-speaking redhead, Ellison obliquely suggested his resemblance to a prominent figure in the discourse of the early cold war. In 1948 Elizabeth Bentley, a former Communist turned FBI informant, testified before HUAC that her onetime Party lover, whom she first knew as an American named Teddy, turned out to be Jacob Golos, a Russian-born naturalized American citizen who was, she claimed, the key figure in a secret network of Communists working for the federal government and passing information to the Soviets. Described by Bentley as short and shabbily dressed, with "bright red" hair, Golos emerged as a key figure among the more than eighty people, including Alger Hiss and Julius Rosenberg, whose names she gave to the FBI. With his perfect English and deceptively American demeanor, Golos, the enemy within, was indistinguishable from an authentic American. The narrator's speculation that Jack obtained his glass eye at the same place where "he learned the language he lapsed into" (476) strongly suggests that, even if he is not Russian-born, Jack has been to school in Moscow and, in moments of stress, thinks in Russian. Jack may accuse Clifton of having been a "traitorous merchant of vile instruments" (466), but the reader knows the identity of the real traitor in the room.[54]

The counterpart of Jack's transformation into an alien is Stein/Hambro's Americanization. Visiting Hambro in the aftermath of his mock trial and hearing Hambro's child chant Humpty-Dumpty's classic tale of decline and dismemberment, the invisible man listens in disbelief as the Brotherhood theorist calls for Harlem's "sacrifice." He at first thinks, "I like him [Hambro], he's really a kind and sincere man." This is changed to "I might have liked him, I thought, he seems to be kind." Finally the invisible man is shown "shak[ing] with rage" as he "think[s] of Jack and Hambro": "I looked around a corner of my mind and saw Jack and Emerson merge." Ellison added the words "into one single white figure"; in the final text Norton would be added to the group. No longer a radical Jew who has been interned in a concentration camp for his opposition to Nazism, Hambro (no longer Stein) inspires the invisible man to envision the cluster of white supremacist "men without faces." The totalitarian reconfiguration of the Brotherhood is complete.[55]

"Leaders are sacrificed, aren't they?":
Revenge in Mount Morris Park

During his period of "yessing" the Brotherhood after he returns to Harlem, the invisible man originally experiences nightmares and hallucinations. "One morning I noticed a mysterious white spot forming on my cheek as I shaved," he recalls. "A spot the size of a small coin, and of an unhealthy whiteness." He has a dream in which "his face is painted and they're pitching baseballs at his head." He receives threatening phone calls; Jack responds by promising him protection but telling him, "Leave the police alone. We don't go to our enemies for protection." As the protagonist becomes "aware of his figurehead role[, a] Negro tries to shoot him . . . does in fact, but wound isn't serious." He attempts to join a group of young African Americans "dedicate[d] to doing something violent." When he "offers his platform experience" they turn him down, "laugh[ing] at his naivete and threaten[ing] him with knives."[56]

A fully dramatized scene omitted from the closing portion of the published text is one—in some versions a nightmare, but in others a real occurrence—showing the invisible man approached in Mount Morris Park by "four young fellows" with conked hair, "peg-topped trousers," and shoes with "hard square flat toe caps." Proclaiming themselves "the avengers" who plan "an orderly liquidation," they call him a "brown nose artist": "[You sold] us out and pretend[ed] to lead us. . . . But when the white folks said stop you said 'Yassuh' and stopped." The invisible man thinks, "Something strange was happening in Harlem. They . . . looked like any sharpies and yet they were trying to carry out an assassination. Where did they get such ideas?" Hanging around his neck a "white placard on which the single word 'TRAI-TOR' was neatly lettered," the "avengers" take him up the park tower and wrap a bandanna around his head, telling him, "[It's] your uniform . . . the emblem of your trade." In response to the invisible man's desperate plea, "You don't know what you're doing," they say that they have "reached po-litical maturity [and] . . . accept the responsibility of doing the dirty work." They declare, "So now you're going to be a real leader. Leaders are sacrificed, aren't they? . . . He's joining our club, we're initiating him." In both the dream and the real-life versions of the passage, which Ellison dubbed "Revenge in Mt. Morris Park," the invisible man is saved by a groundskeeper; "[But] the bandanna was still on my head and the placard with the word 'Traitor' hung around my neck."[57]

In one variant of the nightmare the occasion for the invisible man's pro-posed assassination is that he has bet against Joe Louis; it is Cleo who places the bandanna around his eyes. She accuses him of "selling out the champ." "You hate the champ and you hate us," she says. "We trust you and you vote against our Joe. You hit below the belt. . . . Don't feel bad. . . . We have reached political maturity. You gave my basket to Ella and my bottle to Betty and my key to Louise." The invisible man's guilt at abandoning his black lover for a white one, compounded by Cleo's invocation of famous female jazz and blues artists, reinforces his guilt at abandoning the modern folk hero who embodied for Harlemites victory over white supremacy at home and, during the wartime years, fascism abroad.[58]

Situated in most drafts between the eye scene and the riot, the at-tempted assassination, whether real or dreamed, aligns the invisible man as handkerchief-head with the cluster of Negro traitors who aid and abet the perpetuation of white supremacy: Bledsoe, the Men's House wannabes, Brockway, Dr. Chomboir. The incident's transparent political message, that the invisible man has been a willing dupe in the Brotherhood's "sell-out" of Harlem, underlines the betrayal theme; its mythic and ritual references— Mount Morris as Calvary, the assassins as Christ killers, the invisible man as a "dedicated and set aside" scapegoat—reinforce the sacrificial trope. Why then, other than to streamline his plot, did Ellison eliminate the episode? Perhaps because its portrayal of politically conscious "sharpies" runs counter to the 1952 text's depiction of hipsters as migratory "birds of passage" wholly unaware of the world of Brotherhood. Perhaps because the elimination of the earlier Mount Morris Brotherhood rally removed the irony of the invisible man's near-crucifixion at the site where he had sworn his fealty to the Brotherhood and, in a ceremony originally organized by the Brotherhood, mourned Clifton. Or perhaps because the CP—both during the 1930s when Louis defeated Baer and Schmeling and during the 1940s when he exemplified win-the-war patriotism—was a consistently strong supporter of the iconic "our Joe," who was just about the last prominent African American the left would historically have accused of "selling out." While Ellison and Wright shared a distaste for Louis's performance in Frank Capra's *The Negro Soldier*, as well as for the CP's celebration of the documentary in its promotion of wartime unity, such reservations about Louis's public image put them at odds with the vast majority of African Americans. If the invisible man's loss of faith in the Brotherhood is, during the riot, to be compensated by his rekindled respect for working-class Harlemites, he cannot derogate the favorite son who was also a favorite of the Brotherhood's real-life analogue. Actual historical allegiances were too dramatically at variance with the increasingly Manichaean alignments rhetorically shaping in the text; once again, Mount Morris had to go.[59]

"A naïve, peasant-like act of revenge": The Riot

In the published text of *Invisible Man* the riot furnishes the culminating confirmation of the Brotherhood's treachery; the protagonist sickens as he realizes that he has unwittingly aided and abetted in Harlem's "sacrifice." The riot reenacts on a mass scale the ritual of the battle royal; the spectacle of blindfolded boys fighting one another for the entertainment of Jim Crow racists is magnified into the phantasmagoric violence of an entire community dismembered and destroyed in order to advance the Brotherhood's purported will to power. Personal revelation is coupled with political understanding as the invisible man witnesses Harlem go up in flames: "It was not suicide, but murder. The committee had planned it. And I had helped, had been a tool. A tool just at the very moment I had thought myself free" (553). In the darkened, glass-filled streets he expects further deception, looking for Jack and thinking, "If he wished really to hide his strategy he'd appear in the district, with a sound truck, perhaps, playing the friendly adviser with Wrestrum and Tobitt beside him" (565). No motive for Harlem's "murder" is supplied; none is needed as catastrophe proceeds inevitably from climax and the character system elaborated up to this point goes on automatic pilot.

This portion of the published text is a well-wrought Aristotelian urn, onto which are inscribed multiple allusions to biblical, Homeric, and Dantean mythology that heighten its archetypal resonance and sense of felt inevitability.[60]

Originally, however, Ellison had no intention of portraying the riot as the result of a deliberate Brotherhood plot to sacrifice African Americans to its "new program." He jotted, "Riot could be unforeseen event, misjudged by whites, understood by him." After the invisible man loses credibility with the organization because of his botched advocacy of the writer and freed prisoner turned murderer, he hands in a falsified report indicating that all is well north of 110th Street; he is not listened to when he then conducts a survey of Harlem for the Brotherhood and exclaims, "They're going to explode. People will be killed! They're going to run amuk. Can't you understand?" He sees "the alarm seep into their eyes" but is countered by Tobitt, who declares his report "unscientific," a slander on "the great Negro people of Harlem." The invisible man sadly concludes, "I had been given my chance and I had failed. I had failed to make them see." Fooled by the invisible man's own falsified reports, which they have been only too willing to believe, the Brotherhood leadership are shown here to be politically blind. But their eyes manifest "alarm"; what prevents them from acting on this alarm is not a malevolent disregard for the lives and welfare of Harlem's inhabitants, but, if anything, a romantic overestimation of their powers of endurance, as well as a tragic underestimation of the depth of their outrage and despair.[61]

Ellison only gradually decided to blame the riot on the Brotherhood's subordination of Harlem's needs to its larger international strategy. Originally the narrator recalls, "We had been so successful in our fight that immediate objectives were being won faster than we could educate our following to fight for new and broader issues. We were ready and our program was worked out—but we couldn't move faster than the membership." This earlier rationale warrants quoting at length:

> We had grown too comfortable in the strategies of battles that were for the most part won. And it was at this point that the opposition went into action [and] picked Harlem for the showdown and we were given a shock. They made us discover that what for a long time had been our strongest district was now our weakest. It came upon us slowly. First membership began falling off, but we were unaware because for some reason the Harlem committee falsified their reports, making it appear that things were going smoothly, or were at least stable. But History forced the truth.

I learned that a deal had been made with a congressman back during the time of my first speech and now when with elections drawing near . . . we would have to throw our support behind him, the people were not responding.[62]

The narrative voice heard here recaptures some of the invisible man's pre-"perception" callowness: he cannot figure out why the Harlem reports might have been "falsified," and he speaks of "History" with a capital *H*—Jack's way of designating his favorite locomotive force—without irony. Nonetheless it is clear that the Brotherhood is losing support principally because it has been fighting too many of its battles on the terrain of the enemy, what Ellison termed "playing ball with the bourgeoisie" in a letter to Wright in 1945. The Brotherhood relies on opportunist ties with politicians rather than mass protest from below: "With the new program there were no more marches, no charging of police lines, no rallies, no delegations storming the welfare department." Only after several drafts of this material did Ellison determine that international considerations would be shown trumping local priorities. "Change comes when there is a pact made between leaders of brotherhood and administration (city)," Ellison ruminated, "and it is decided that for reasons of foreign policy the ills of mose [the Negro] can no longer be stressed." While he clearly alludes here to the "soft-pedaling of the struggle for Negro rights" during the "win the war" period, this critique is congruent with the objections to CP wartime policy, largely from the left, that Ellison had formulated in the last two years of the war and that the CP itself acknowledged in the wake of the Duclos letter. It is a far cry from an accusation of murder.[63]

Ellison gets away with the accusation of murder, however, by stripping the wartime Harlem uprising of its historical and political context. He accomplishes this in part by commingling details from the riots of 1935 and 1943; his practice of casually conflating events and situations from the Depression and wartime years now serves a distinct political end. From the troops carrying machine guns to the white manikins hanged from lampposts, the text replicates much of what Ellison himself witnessed on the streets of Harlem and reported in the *New York Post* on 2 and 3 August 1943. But he omitted from the 1952 text the catalyst of the riot in 1943, namely, the rumors of a white policeman's murder of Pvt. Robert Bandy, a soldier who stepped in to defend from abusive treatment a woman named Marjorie Polite. The incident brought to a boil resentments at the wartime economic duress disproportionately experienced by African Americans, as well as at the indignities and worse suffered by black members of the segregated armed forces. Ellison substituted for the Bandy-Polite incident a cause more closely resembling the event that triggered the Harlem riot of 1935: the rumored police killing of a child who had engaged in minor theft in a store on 125th Street. Several of Ellison's notes for the riot chapters of *Invisible Man* indicate his original intention to show one or more soldiers participating in the fray, as well as "cops using billies to knock anyone not in uniform"; though fragmentary, these descriptions reinforce the earlier portraits of soldiers involved in anti-eviction demonstrations that were also omitted from the published text. Ellison's decision to excise all references to the Second World War enabled him to avoid confronting the crisis about the meaning of democracy that the antifascist war posed to large numbers of African Americans. This omission also made it possible to evade the complicated matrix of local, national, and international considerations that had challenged the political judgment of a wide range of actors and organizations (not just Moscow-affiliated Communists) during the war—not least Ellison himself during his time at the editorial desk of *Negro Quarterly*. In the early years of the cold war it was easier simply to accuse the Communists of wishing to "murder" Harlem.[64]

In the commentaries Ellison wrote after the publication of *Invisible Man* he routinely denied that the novel engaged directly with specific persons and events of the twentieth century; many critics, understandably loath to obligate him—or any other novelist—to an unwelcome pledge of verisimilitude, have allowed him his fictional license. Yet much of the critical commentary granting Ellison his donnée also takes as unproblematic and self-evident not just his generalized depiction of the left's robotic inhumanity but also the validity of the invisible man's charge that the Harlem riot was indeed an act of "murder . . . planned by the committee." The specific charge, rarely queried, is thus taken as further evidence to validate the typicality of the caricature. Circularity reigns supreme.

A methodological proviso is in order here. Throughout most of the portrayals of Brotherhood characters in *Invisible Man* Ellison's revisionary process entails distortion and caricature for the purpose of retypification; that is, it functions both to invoke and to reinforce negative generalizations about how leftists characteristically act and think. In the library recruitment scene, for instance, where Ellison replaces Jack's initial respect for the invisible man's "ability" with an ambition to exploit his "voice," the change compounds the emerging portrait of Jack as a manipulator. But Ellison did not alter the publicly known historical record (although the salary offered to the invisible man significantly exceeds what was routine for red organizers); instead he deploys the conventional fictional arsenal of the novelist—ironizing characterization conveyed through details of dialogue, action, and physical portraiture—to render persuasive the version of historical reality that he wishes to convey. One can take umbrage at his portrayal, but one cannot accuse him directly of *lying*. In his published treatment of the Harlem riot of 1943, however, the accusation of planned murder is so wildly at variance with the historical record as to count as not merely fictional improvisation, but plain old falsehood. For Ellison well knew that the last thing that the left affiliated with the Third International wanted to see in 1943 was any activity among African Americans that was, or could be interpreted to be, antipatriotic or pro-Axis. When Klansmen attacked Negro defense plant workers attempting to move into the Sojourner Truth Housing Project in Detroit the previous year, the *New Masses* had denounced the situation as "more than a national scandal": "This is treason. This is the fifth column in the flesh." In relation to Harlem the CP adopted the slogan "No Detroit Here!" When the riot broke out the CP leader and NMU official Ferdinand Smith went on the radio—presumably on the higher frequencies of mainstream stations—and rode through the streets on a sound truck with Mayor La Guardia, pleading with Harlemites to return to their homes. In the riot's aftermath Smith, in an interview in Powell's *People's Voice*, condemned Jim Crow in the armed forces and discrimination in the Red Cross blood banks; Ben Davis led a delegation of community leaders to address with particular severity the consumer issues affecting Harlem's inhabitants; and the CP press contrasted the Detroit and Harlem uprisings, insisting on the latter's causality in police brutality and "rent, prices, jobs." If anything, the CP can be accused of "playing ball with the bourgeoisie" both before and during the riot: the image of Smith and La Guardia riding around Harlem and going onto the airwaves together more than slightly smacks of class collaboration. But it is simply not true that the Brotherhood's historical prototype wished for, much less intended wartime Harlem to erupt. When Ellison describes the protagonist awaiting the appearance of the Brotherhood leadership in a sound truck, he presents what actually happened—the CP's fervent attempt to cool things down—as simply one more deception. History becomes mirage, while anticommunist fantasy becomes reality.[65]

Except for the publishers of explicitly right-wing newspapers like the *New York World-Telegram*, which carried on its witch hunt against the CP throughout the war, commentators at the time, regardless of their attitude toward Communists, were agreed that the riot had nothing to do with the left. Referring to the likes of Hamid, Jordan, and Wilson in an analogy with Civil War–era Copperheads, La Guardia blamed the riot on "snake agitators" seeking to "start racial trouble." The main debate among analysts writing for the *Crisis, People's Voice,* and the *New York Amsterdam News* was over whether or not the participants had been "hoodlums" or otherwise stable members of the working class. In his *New York Post* reporting Ellison himself proposed that the riot had been "a naïve, peasant-like act of revenge"—a formulation that echoed Wright's characterization of the Harlem riot of 1935 as an expression of "naïve, peasant anger" in *Twelve Million Black Voices* and suggested Ellison's own view of Harlem's migrants as largely preindividual and unsophisticated in outlook. (Notably in the *Daily Worker* Mike Gold sharply upbraided Ellison for portraying the riot as "a spontaneous, unorganized revolt of dumb masses against economic conditions.") As late as 1948, in "Harlem Is Nowhere," Ellison referred to the riots of both 1935 and 1943 as "spontaneous outbreaks."[66]

The disingenuous thesis that the Detroit and Harlem wartime riots had been engineered by Communists gained widespread currency only with the heating up of the cold war, when it would be baldly asserted, without evidence, in such propagandistic texts as the *Saturday Evening Post* serial "I Was a Communist for the FBI" (1949). As Ellison's revisions indicate, he did not originally intend to accuse the Brotherhood of murder; the 1952 text reflects not his own perceptions at the time, let alone those of practically every other commentator on the riot of 1943, but his deliberate alteration of what he knew to be the historical record. This was at a time when the Rosenbergs were convicted on charges of conspiracy to commit espionage and "there were no means for distinguishing between accusatory statements and accuracy of charges."[67] By the time Ellison produced the final draft of the riot, no proof was needed to back up the assertion that communism was equivalent to treason.

In his treatment of the Harlem riot of 1943 Ellison re-creates its surface details, minus the participation of soldiers, but effaces its causality, which cannot be separated from the crisis opened up by the international antifascist war. He drops hints that the Brotherhood is dominated by international concerns and is run by men who think in Russian. He also portrays the organization as fundamentally racist, using African Americans, in their yearning for freedom, as pawns in its master plan to control the direction of History. Synthesizing these two key tenets of cold war ideology, he projects them back upon a historical screen sufficiently concrete and realistic to evoke memories of the wartime uprising but sufficiently abstract and surreal to evade direct identification of the event portrayed in the novel with its historical prototype. In so doing he manages to rewrite the historical episode and to invoke it as evidence of the very portrait of the left that enables his rewriting in the first place. His strategy is consummately self-confirming, illustrating Kenneth Burke's thesis about the coercive role of synecdoche in transforming cognition into re-cognition.[68]

An undated note that Ellison wrote to himself indicates that at one point he even considered retaining in the riot episode the Marxism-as-lens trope that he had introduced in the invisible man's magazine interview: "Riot / Leader goes on drunk / Symbols: Cash register / Camera. Sensitive mechanism capable of recording reality = Marxism. Irony through analogy between useless instrument of thought which he will not 'will' to use and child's ignorance of power of lens." The reference to "child's ignorance of power of lens" probably refers to an incident in Ellison's childhood, when he was fascinated but confused by a photographic lens that he discovered on the street. "Leader goes on drunk" may allude to the saturnalian aura of the riot that is pictured in the novel, although the woman sitting on the milk truck swigging beer hardly figures as a leader. The cash register recalls both the toy cash register in the omitted episodes depicting Norton at the toy store and the protagonist's interaction with the moneychangers, symbolic elements which, had they been retained in the novel, would have underlined its commentary on the hegemony of Wall Street. Most important, however, is the notion that Marxism might have supplied the protagonist with an "instrument of thought . . . capable of recording reality" that he "will not 'will' to use." Even as Ellison revised his text to portray the Brotherhood leader as quintessentially blind, some part of him, it appears, retained confidence in historical materialism as a means of comprehending reality—and chastised his protagonist for being incapable of using it. We are reminded of his comment that Bard in "The Initiation" lacked the "energy to use Marxism in a creative manner." Suggesting that Ellison had to struggle to subject himself to the discipline of another way of seeing (or not-seeing) the world, his decision to eliminate the notion of Marxism as a clarifying lens from the novel's motif of vision and blindness reduces the dialectical complexity of the central trope in *Invisible Man*.[69]

"He burns the paper with his Brotherhood name":
The Politics of Re-cognition

The crowning moment of perception in *Invisible Man* occurs when, having descended into the manhole during the riot, the protagonist decides to burn the documents in his briefcase in order to light his way out of the darkness.

As the fire consumes each item, starting with his high school diploma and Clifton's doll, he reencounters the iron weights—Mary's bank, Tarp's chain link—signifying the baggage of slavery and Jim Crow borne by his illusion-ridden consciousness. The scene culminates with his recognition that the handwriting on the note bearing his Brotherhood name is identical to that on the message warning him that the Brotherhood is a white man's organization. The last secret of the Bellerophontic letters has been revealed. Jack has doubly betrayed the invisible man, first by supplying him with still one more contrived identity and then by denying that identity any agency; worse than the rest of the antagonists precisely because he claimed to be different, the Brotherhood leader has "kept this nigger boy running" longer than any other.

It is thus no wonder that in his subsequent nightmare the invisible man envisions Jack as the knife-wielding leader of the lynching party that tosses his privates over the George Washington Bridge. The castration ritual symbolically adumbrated in the battle royal has been literally enacted; the invisible man has been not just picked clean, but dismembered. Like Joe Christmas in *Light in August*—a text that Ellison had in mind when composing the castration nightmare—the protagonist has been butchered by a figure who epitomizes the traits of ruthlessness, brutality, and authoritarianism informing the cluster of antagonists aligned in the novel's character system. In the horror of this nightmare its victim is largely absolved of responsibility for his destiny. However much his own ambitions and illusions contributed to the preceding sequence of events, the reader feels, surely the protagonist does not deserve the fate of an American Dionysus, castrated in view of the bridge named after the nation's first president. The protagonist's designation as the lynch mob's "dedicated and set aside" scapegoat *in* the text thus enables the reader to construe the mob, and especially its leader, as the rhetorical scapegoat *of* the text. By a turn of the ideological wheel, the revolutionary organization that Ellison had portrayed in his early proletarian fiction as the foremost opponent of lynch violence has here metamorphosed into its foremost exponent. Ellison's comment in a letter to Hyman in 1945, "[The Communists are] lynchers of my people," here achieves fictional fulfillment. It has been a long struggle to wrestle down Prometheus, but Ellison has finally prevailed.[70]

Precisely because the published novel's denouement is overdetermined by this aggregation of symbols and motifs, however, it bears remembering that Ellison did not initially envision the unveiling of Jack's treachery as the culmination of the text's arc of "purpose-passion-perception"; his intentions changed as history (History?) changed. That Ellison retained some awareness of the ad hoc nature of his compositional process many years later is indicated in an interview he gave in 1974. In response to a query about how the poison pen letter fits in with the identity-bestowing pieces of paper beginning each of the novel's major sections, he replied, "Well, let's try not to make this too neat; when you are giving an interview you don't always remember how many tags and errors you leave as you structure your plot." Not only did he consider bringing the invisible man aboveground for a closing performance as a Rinehartesque preacher, or, still more dramatically, having him phone Louise; even after he opted to terminate the novel's action in the manhole he did not feature the invisible man's discovery of the handwriting. In one variant nothing is left in the briefcase after the bank is abandoned. In another the invisible man cannot bring himself to burn LeRoy's journal and instead "burns the paper with his Brotherhood name," wondering whether the note "could be" from Jack; the protagonist "recognizes [the] writing on [the] letter of warning," adds Ellison, but still does not identify the author. In the original typescript the information that the handwriting "looked familiar" is penciled in. When we recall that Ellison originally intended to have the invisible man's name handed to him typed rather than handwritten on a slip of paper in the Chthonian scene, it appears that, for quite some time during the creation of *Invisible Man,* he was not planning to end the novel's action with the protagonist's shattering realization of his betrayal by the Brotherhood leader.[71]

By 1952, however, Ellison had access to an audience, both actual and implied, that had not existed when he began work on *Invisible Man* in 1945. Even the business of recognizing the handwriting on a slip of paper resonates with the discourse of the cold war, for the proposition that Alger Hiss's handwriting was discernable on key espionage documents was central to the government's prosecution in the Chambers-Hiss trial. The invisible man's recognition of Jack's handwriting entails a simultaneous act of a posteriori re-cognition on the part of the reader. The last Bellerophontic letter delivers not news but confirmation of what has been always already known. Reference bows down to rhetoric. The wheel has come full circle. The end is in the beginning.[72]

We now return to Ellison's boomerang of history.

eight

Beginning and Ending **eight**

This end is our beginning.

—Paul Robeson, narrator,
Native Land (1942)

Things were getting back to normal—
reaction was mobilizing again for the
right war—against labor, the Negroes,
the people at home; and against the
socialist, colonial and anti-fascist
movements abroad. The Communists
and other progressives, having been
among the foremost fighters against
Hitler, were now to be the new victims of the monopolists' wrath. New
scapegoats had to be manufactured.

—Benjamin Davis, *Communist Councilman
from Harlem: Autobiographical Notes Written
in a Federal Penitentiary*

"The end is in the beginning and lies far ahead," remarks the narrator in the prologue of *Invisible Man* (6). He is preparing to re-create for the reader the sequence of events landing him in his basement—which is, if not a particularly clean place, a well-lighted one—and giving him the blues. When the reader encounters a near repetition of this assertion right before the epilogue—"The end was in the beginning" (571)—the invisible man's meditations on a range of subjects, from personal rebirth to national redemption, presumably emerge from the journey from "purpose" through "passion" to "perception" that has transformed the naïve protagonist of the picaresque into the cagey if still ambivalent narrator of the bildungsroman. Whatever specific "socially responsible role" (581) he settles upon, his first step has been the writing, indeed the publication of his memoir, which bears witness to his movement "from ranter to writer."[1]

Although the invisible man has been addressing readers from his basement lair for over half a century, we need to remind ourselves of the historical context from which the narrator immediately speaks in the prologue and epilogue of Ellison's novel. His den resonates with the archetypal echoes of a chthonic underground; the impending emergence of his Jack-the-Bear persona invokes both the myth of the seasonal rebirth of the bear and the redemptive associations of "an Easter chick breaking from its shell" (6). But the narrator's marijuana-scented den is haunted by history—not only the suppressed history of slavery and abolition, "shut off and forgotten during the nineteenth century" (6), but also the currents roiling the aboveground world, where a "socially responsible role" (581) awaits him when he chooses to return. The long narrative bookended by the prologue and epilogue, we have seen, has largely evaded historical determinacy. The "slightly different sense of time" (8) experienced by narrator and reader alike in the surrealistically lit basement continues to discourage pinpointing the historical moment, although the narrator's reference to "the chamber with the deadly gas that ends in the oven so hygienically clean" (575) suggests that, even if the protagonist has not been shown going through the war, he has endured that historical *agon*.

The implied reader of the published text, however, lives in a world that is not just postwar but cold war. By 1952 he or she has witnessed the detonation of the USSR's first hydrogen bomb, the first wave of the Smith Act trials, the passage of the Taft-Hartley Act and mounting expulsion of Communists from the CIO, and the beginning of the Korean War. If inclined to keep up with the latest wisdom emanating from New York–based intellectuals, this reader has learned from the young James Baldwin that "those categories which were meant to define and control the world for us have boomeranged us into chaos"; from Arthur Schlesinger that the classic totalitarian personality—of the right or the left—is a "tight-lipped, cold-eyed, unfeeling, uncommunicative man" who denies "anxiety" and clings to "certitude"; from Hannah Arendt that the "tyranny of logicality" leads man to "surrender his inner freedom"; from Lionel Trilling that the finest writers are those who avoid the "dark and bloody crossroads where literature and politics meet" and instead embody the "yes and no" of their cultures. If concerned about the current and future direction of Negro leadership, this reader is aware of Ferdinand Smith's deportation and Du Bois's expulsion from the NAACP, as well as of the diplomacy on behalf of the State Department conducted officially by Ralph Bunche and unofficially by Adam Clayton Powell Jr. (who has evidently reconsidered his 1945 assertion that "red-baiting is born of the same womb that conceived anti-Semitism, anti-unionism, and Jim Crow"). This reader may feel sympathy with the thousands of demonstrators who gathered in Harlem the previous spring to protest the legal lynching of William McGee but knows that those red protestors are themselves facing the loss of jobs or worse under the provisions of the Smith Act; speaking out against racism, especially in the company of Communists, has become a dangerous activity. It is for this troubled and fearful reader that the invisible man offers to speak in the resonant final sentence of *Invisible Man*.[2]

The novel's prologue positions the reader to accompany the retrospective narrator as he recounts his zigzagging odyssey through time and space. The invisible man's personal experiences apparently constitute both history and History; his opening remark that "the world moves . . . by contradiction . . . not like an arrow, but a boomerang," along with his warning to "beware of those who speak of the spiral of history" and to "keep a steel helmet handy" because they are "preparing a boomerang," suggests that his life has turned him into something of a philosopher. The prologue's reader is invited to consider the narrator's skeptical attitude toward not just bourgeois progressive notions of history (the arrow) but also toward Hegelian Marxist conceptions (the spiral); the latter, he warns, is especially dangerous, requiring armament of the vulnerable brain. Until readers learn how he came to be so blue, however, they will have to keep in abeyance any questions about his somewhat confused and confusing historiographical metaphors. How exactly does his version of "contradiction" differ from that of the "spiralists," who also purport to be dialecticians? Is the boomerang a weapon, ideological or otherwise, being prepared for use in an attack by the spiralists? Or does it signify everyman's necessary encounter with the circular workings of History? Does the boomerang signify teleology (it will have to come back to where it began) or contingency (you never know when it will be thrown, perhaps by that gambler, History)? To the extent that the invisible man's own text resembles a boomerang—it has after all returned to its starting place—is this reversion one more painful "[boomerang] across [his] head," or is it a welcome return, enabling his final rebirth and emergence? And, given that the narrator has returned on another level to his point of departure, does his memoir itself resemble a spiral, more than he may wish to admit?[3]

The reader accompanies the invisible man through the epilogue as he attempts to discern the larger figure in the carpet of the experiences of which he is now the memoirist. Although, like Eliot's fisher king, he hesitates to distill formulable lessons from what has come before—almost all of his speculations and assertions take the form of questions—his very posture of indecision is part of what he has learned and wishes now to share. The reader, who has been somewhat impatient throughout the narrative with the protagonist's Candide-like naïveté, is now eager to hear what, if anything, he has learned. It still may not be clear what the invisible man means when he says that history is a boomerang, or what his "socially responsible role" will now entail. But he has been run from pillar to post by a set of antagonists, different in social station but possessing homologous character structures, who surely describe a variety of undesirable roles. If he decides that he must say yes and no at the same time, he must have good reasons for his temporizing. The reader who encounters the novel after its thirtieth anniversary has the added experience of hearing Ellison's own voice in the introduction written in 1982, his own Jamesian counterpart to Wright's "How Bigger Was Born," where he echoes many of the phrasings and overtones of the narrator of the epilogue. When he speaks, the voice heard at the end of *Invisible Man* has both street credibility and ex post facto authorial sanction.[4]

That the *you* inscribed in Ellison's text has not fully corresponded with the *we* of the novel's actual readers is attested to by the controversy that has swirled around the novel's framing passages, especially the epilogue, since its publication. Readers amenable to the narrator's final stance—whether interpreted as "affirming the principle" of American democratic pluralism, asserting nonconformist individuality, and positing invisibility as a universal condition, or as contesting possessive individualism and celebrating indeterminacy and heteroglossia—generally have not found the epilogue disquieting. The invisible man can speak for them. Readers not so readily interpellated by the text, however—those who take exception, from a range of standpoints, to its politics, its psychology, or its philosophy—have been troubled by the narrator's presumption that he takes to the radio waves on their behalf. In their very divergence, what these reactions commonly testify to is the forceful (one might say, coercive) rhetorical role of the novel's framing passages in positioning the reader as a partner (one might say, a secret sharer) in the narrator's retrospective commentary on history and History.[5]

Ellison's often repeated assertion that he first heard the haunting voice of his narrator when he sat in a Vermont barn door in the summer of 1945 has led many readers to assume that, in some fundamental sense, the novel's beginning and ending were already in mind when he began to write. As readers of this study are by now aware, the rest of Ellison's novel emerged only after prolonged travail. The process by which the prologue and epilogue came into being was no different.[6]

329

BEGINNING AND ENDING

"Millions live under such conditions":
The Shadow of Wright

Readers familiar with "How Bigger Was Born" hear in the reference to Poe in *Invisible Man*'s second sentence—"No, I am not a spook like those who haunted Edgar Allan Poe" (3)—an echo of Wright's closing assertion that the oppression of the Negro, a "shadow athwart our national life," means that "if Poe were alive, he would not have to invent horror; horror would invent him." In earlier drafts of Ellison's opening, Wright's presence is more palpable still. One early version, immediately following the handwritten header "Introduction," reads:

> Just as people shout to make themselves understood by those who do not know their language, so in trying to make myself seen I have sharpened my own eyesight. It is as though my eyeballs have been sandpapered like the tips of a safe cracksman's fingers and I see that which is only just becoming to be. It has become like a disease and I have tried to get rid of it, but it is more than a disease, it is a way of life.

Sharing with the beginning of the published text the key motif of seeing and being seen, this version invokes not just Wright's preface to *Native Son* but also "The Man Who Lived Underground." Like Fred Daniels, the invisible man has entered his basement lair through a manhole while fleeing from antagonists and has undergone an existential rebirth; his reference to safecracking recalls Daniels's jewelry and cash burglary, for which an innocent man dies in his stead. Theft of money—not ectoplasm and circus sideshows, but money—contextualizes the initiatory metaphor of *Invisible Man*. We hear in both versions of the novel's opening the narcissistically self-ironizing voice of Dostoevsky's underground man, especially his contention that "a great deal of consciousness . . . is a disease"; but in the earlier draft this disease is linked with the invisible man's sense of himself as criminal outsider. Like Du Bois in the famous passage about double consciousness that begins *The Souls of Black Folks*, the narrator stresses the "sharpened . . . eyesight" afforded him by the state of being unseen. Where in the published text the invisible man asserts that it is "sometimes advantageous to be unseen" (3), here he treats his enhanced vision as an extension of his disease. There is no benefit to being behind the veil—only the advantage of irony.[7]

In other drafts of the novel's opening section Ellison highlights the centrality of race to his narrator's conception of invisibility. The passage recounting the invisible man's experiments with skin bleaching and hair straightening, later resituated among his Brotherhood-era experiences, at first appeared in the prologue. His series of questions—"What profiteth a man if he gain the shores of democracy and slip back upon the rock of the Anglo-Saxon aesthetic? What type of nose wears well with the Constitution? What grade of hair blends with the Bill of Rights?"—departs dramatically from the largely nonracialized formulation of invisibility contained in the opening pages of the 1952 text. He then describes the clothes he used to wear:

> I had recently purchased the latest extreme in zoot-suits. It was an apple green material with white chalk stripes, the pants five inches at the cuffs and ballooning to thirty inches at the knees. The coat was padded at the shoulders, which were broad enough to give courage to even a Casper Milktoast, and the skirts of the coat dropped elegantly to my knees. I wore a large, snow white felt hat set off by a blue white polka dotted band. My shirt was magenta and my tie brown with green stripes. I dressed with meticulous care, trousers creased to a razor edge sharpness, shoes shined to gleam like flame. And to top it off I wore a blue, white dotted show handkerchief in my breast pocket, scented with Black Narcissus perfume.

Caricaturing the sartorial rituals enacted at the opening of Richard Wright's *Lawd Today* by Jake Jackson, whose urban alienation replaces but cannot efface his bitter memories of the Jim Crow South, this satiric description then leads into the "birds of passage" meditation which, in the 1952 text, accompanies the invisible man's encounter with the hipsters in the subway after the death of Clifton. The invisible man's use of "we" to describe his identity with the hipsters—somewhat anomalous in the published text—in this draft fits in with his memory of his own ballooning pants and padded jacket. Proclaiming his oneness with these creatures of historical lag who "speak a transitional language [and] think transitional thoughts," the invisible man ponders, "But then again perhaps I'm not exclusive." In the 1952 text his encounter with the zoot-suiters engenders doubt about the Brotherhood's scientism and speculation that history is a gambler. In its original placement at the novel's beginning, the "birds of passage" meditation emphasizes the connections between invisibility and migration, as well as the historical typicality of the invisible man himself.[8]

Other possible beginnings of the novel, not separated out as elements of a prologue, show the narrator dwelling on his state of internal division. One reads:

So far away, so long ago. It's difficult to recognize myself. That "I" can hardly have been me, and yet it was, *he* was. But that is all part of invisibility. I have lived so many lives, and so rapidly, so much has been jammed into so tight a space of time that it's as though I've become a walking hotel for ghosts—and all these mean and evil fellows none of whom can stand the sight of the other. It is an awful situation, for they fight with one another like a family of evil brothers forced to live with one another crammed together in a small house.

In the 1952 text the brothers living in the same house are engaged in an Oedipal celebration after their mother's murder of their slave-master father. Here the familial overcrowding in the house of the historical self produces tensions more reminiscent of Bigger Thomas's explosions in his family's kitchenette apartment than of the collective surrogate patricide acted out in *Totem and Taboo*.[9]

Another possible opening would have involved transposing a passage originally intended to be located during the protagonist's stay at Men's House after he has exhausted his options with the Wall Street–based trustees: "What brought on the crisis? One moment you believe, you're willing to throw yourself beneath the juggernaut, to lie upon the blazing coals, and the next you're done with it, through. You're come on to something else and [are] completely cynical toward the old beliefs—or at least you like to believe you are." In its original location this passage relates only to the invisible man's disillusionment with the "old beliefs" of upward mobility that he absorbed from the campus's enactment of the "black rites of Horatio Alger"; this disillusionment prepares him for his political awakening. Resituated in the prologue, however, the text would imply that the "old beliefs" comprise not just bourgeois aspirations but also leftist politics, the totality of experiences landing him in his hole. As with other passages that Ellison considered shifting around the novel, the valence clearly changes depending on their location: a critique of the false consciousness generated by capitalism is here rendered coterminous with a critique of the illusions attendant on political radicalism. Even with this homogenization, however, the dichotomy between belief and cynicism was too mild for Ellison's developing ideological purposes; the passage would have to be excised.[10]

In what appears to be the very earliest version of the novel's opening, the invisible man describes the dizzying succession of identities he has inhabited or which have inhabited him:

> It is difficult to keep the chronology straight. . . . I've been too many people, died too often, known too many rebirths. And even that is not exact, because so many of those selves I have been were never quite born and again some were never quite dead when the other emerged to take its place. And I am not speaking of a case of "multi-personality." I am speaking of something which happened in the real world. I went to college and became disillusioned and before I had time to learn the lesson of disillusionment I was snatched up and made a radical political leader [this is crossed out and "into other experiences, discovered new ways of life" is substituted]. And the amusing, pathetic, horrible, and pitiable thing is that all the time, during all those ten years that seemed like a century, and in which I died a thousand deaths, I didn't know who the hell I was!

The text then switches to the third person, offering a fragmentary account of the young man's arrival on the campus. In this version there is no smoker scene, no presentation of the briefcase; instead the narrator speaks in generalities of his "many rebirths." While the prose of this opening is flat and we greatly miss the drama and irony of the battle royal, this rudimentary opening passage reveals Ellison's insistent location of his protagonist's fragmented identity in the rapidity of historical change. Political radicalism here appears not to figure — either positively or negatively — in the invisible man's drama of identity.[11]

Accompanying this early sketch of the invisible man's distraught frame of mind is a passage stressing the extreme psychological repression of his Jim Crow childhood:

> I took my conditioning seriously. I could not afford to do otherwise. Suppose all the little boys, such as I was, in the South, should have started thinking and feeling in reaction to the reality in which they found themselves? Suppose there actually did exist a mechanical equation between environmental cause and human affect [sic]. Could you imagine the explosions that would occur? Both within their minds and within the body politic?

Boys like himself, he continues, could not afford to "become conscious of the world around them," for this would entail:

becoming conscious that that world is one of impossibility. The amazing thing is that millions live under such conditions as though they were unaware that anything was unusual about them. Just as I did, myself. Peel the onion of experience of its layers of time and what do you get? Incidents toward which for safety's sake you could not afford to react. (He sees his mother done violence when he is adolescent. . . . He sees uncle humiliate himself before whites for money as waiter.)

The influence of Wright is again palpable: the analysis of "conditioning" as repression invokes *Black Boy*; the invisible man's positioning as one of "millions liv[ing] under such conditions" recalls the central numerical trope of both *Twelve Million Black Voices* and "I Have Seen Black Hands." Gesturing toward the omitted chapter about Uncle Charles as well as other unexplored childhood incidents set in the Jim Crow South, this introduction would have launched *Invisible Man* on a very different trajectory, making it considerably more difficult for the narrator later to conclude that his life underground is one of "infinite possibility."[12]

"Not even the war must get in the way of our need for light": Later Beginnings

Once Ellison had decided that a prologue was in order and had positioned his loquacious narrator in his basement den, the novel's familiar opening started to take shape. Remaining references to Louise, which lasted into the original typescript, were cleared away. The beautiful woman on the slave block in the narrator's pot-induced dream, originally his sister, became his mother. His being surrounded by "newspapers from the 1860s, temperance and abolitionist tracts" devolved into a generalized proposition that he inhabits a site cut off in the past century. The music filling his cellar, at first the Funky Butt of Buddy Bolden, transmuted into the "bad air" of Louis Armstrong.[13]

Ellison continued, however, to emphasize his underground narrator's status as a bird of passage. Incorporating into the novel a passage based on his unpublished journalistic commentary on Harlem's "crime wave" of 1943, Ellison shows the invisible man meditating on the constipating effects of coffee and the appeal of marijuana. "[Weed] has such an attraction for certain city Negroes," the narrator observes, "[because] it creates a kind of hysterical tranquility, relaxing the sense of time, placing them fully outside a reality which only incompletely accepts them. . . . The hitch comes when you realize that for most of us in our time there is no tranquility, no relief. . . . Beneath the tranquility I found even more noise, clashing and conflict. All the past and present was struggling one with the other along with echoes of the future—and that's the thing you've got to watch." The "slightly different sense of time" that in the 1952 text has been taken to imply an existential rejection of linearity and Western rationalism is here traced to the recent migrant's sense of being rendered an outsider in the brave new world of the urban North. As one of these "certain city Negroes," he experiences a disorientation produced by his decidedly linear movement from south to north.[14]

In one draft the streets above are still in wartime. As he sets in place his 1,369 lightbulbs, the invisible man wryly notes, "Not even the war must get in the way of our need for light and ever more and brighter light." Each bulb, he jokes, "stood out clearly from all the rest, said its piece, and waited patiently like women in a ration queue, for the other voices to speak." This early incarnation of the invisible man conveys a feisty radicalism; later presenting himself "in the great American tradition of tinkers that makes [him] kin to Ford, Edison, and Franklin" (7), here he opposes not just monopolized utilities, but monopoly capitalism:

> I only regret that I cannot use some of the power to operate machines. Say to design clothes. Imagine the creations I might send up out of this hole! Or say that I made kitchen ware, so cheap as to revolutionize the market. Think of what would happen should some hole-dweller like me get his hands upon some of the suppressed inventions lying dry and sterile among the blue prints locked in the vaults of some of the huge manufactures. With my power he could flood the market with better and cheaper and more efficient and more beautiful machines. Of course this is all talk and foolishness. He'd only be caught and sent either to the bug-house or to prison.

He adds, "They'd finance an entire army with the latest, yet uninvented weapons to keep that from happening." While the narrator is situated in the midst of the war, Ellison has him gesturing toward Hiroshima; the gassed and burned bodies of the recent global holocaust haunt the novel's retrospective frame, even as it gestures toward postwar consumerism.[15]

A lover of technological gadgets but an opponent of machine civilization in the 1952 text, the narrator in this version of the prologue seeks to develop machines that are "better and cheaper and more efficient and more beautiful." The problem with blueprints is not that they supply logical schemes for organizing society, but that they are "suppressed" by the "huge manufactures" bent on protecting their profits. The "they" who would wage war against the invisible man's attempt to appropriate the means of production and produce everyday commodities "so cheap as to revolutionize the market" are the "huge manufactures" who evidently wield state power. From this vantage point Ford, Edison, and Franklin are not mere "tinkers," but originators of the inventions and technology enabling the production of the instruments of war. In this version of the prologue the narrator refers to his time on the left not as "Brother Jack and all that sad, lost period of the movement" (13) but simply as "Brother Jack and all that period." It has been argued that the invisible man's "act of sabotage" through his "cagey rewiring" points to the need to "disrupt established forms of power from within" rather than to "master the social, political, and technological apparatuses of white America." In this early draft, however, he dreams of something more than tricksterish subversion. His period of radical activity is clearly in the past, but this class-conscious incarnation of the invisible man appears not yet to be "completely cynical about the old beliefs."[16]

That Ellison originally viewed the novel's wartime context as central to his narrator's perspective is indicated by the inclusion among the novel's drafts of an episode titled "Blues." Claiming that he has been living in a "hole in the ground" in Harlem for a year ("three years" is crossed out) "since [he] accepted [his] invisibility," the nameless narrator recounts meeting a friend named Russell, evidently a CP member, who "had been sent down to Mississippi" to organize in the army. ("In the old days when I had known him," he notes, "he had a reputation for courage based upon his activities as an organizer in the lynch land.") This tragic tale-within-a-tale (Russell narrates most of it in the first person) describes the events leading to his murdering his wife, Velma, while he is back in Harlem AWOL from his military base in the South; the invisible man wonders to himself at the irony that Russell, presumably an "integrated personality," would be "coming to me, an invisible man, for understanding." Russell explains why he loved Velma: "She symbolized a large section of our people." But he became alienated from her, in part because, though formally a Party member, she "neglected Marx completely," and in part because during the Harlem uprising she joined in the looting of stores. He then had an affair with a white woman. After Velma left him Russell came under the influence of a mysterious "big black man" who called himself "Blues" (here the story veers into the realm of the Gothic). At the prompting of Blues, Russell killed Velma when he learned she had turned to prostitution.[17]

Evidently told to the invisible man after he has starting living in his basement but before the war is over, Russell's sad story provocatively links the blues with Party politics, the Jim Crow army, the ass-class struggle, and the Harlem uprising. Recalling Ellison's fragmentary notes on a novel about a married Communist organizer living in wartime Harlem, "Blues" indicates that Ellison had by no means relinquished the concerns of his early revolutionary fiction when he started to conceive the notes from underground that would become *Invisible Man*.

"Bring in grandpa": The Principle Affirmed

Ellison closed an early draft of the familiar prologue with a one-page summary of events and meditations that would eventually be expanded and re-situated at the novel's finale: the invisible man has been clubbed into the cellar; he wonders whether he is in the "rear or in the *avant garde*"; the stench in the air must be let out; he will shake off his old skin; he will emerge from hibernation and play a socially responsible role. Ellison added by hand, "And who knows that but that I speak for you?" He scribbled at the top of the page, "Out. Put [in] Epilogue." Originally, however, there was no epilogue at all.[18]

Ellison's notes and outlines highlight the process by which he radically transformed the ending of his novel. In one commentary on the meaning of "perception" he noted that the invisible man will "refuse to be exploited" and "must organize Negroes among themselves"; this will give him the "determination to return." Elaborating upon this possibility, Ellison speculated that, after descending into the manhole and "burn[ing] the paper with his Brotherhood name"—unsure, in this version, whether or not the other note in similar handwriting could have been from Jack—the narrator concludes:

> 1. Visibility accepted. Life seen from invisibility. The fluid character of reality.
>
> 2. Perception that there must be a part of oneself that must not be surrendered. They must refuse to be either sacrificer or victim. That power is only thing that others respect, otherwise you're expendable. His determination to end his hibernation and return.
>
> Traitor to individual groups of organization when you accept invisibility.
>
> Understand grandfather at last. He's been a traitor through agreeing and now he accepts the humanity of whites. They're weak, heroic etc like himself. It is a betrayal of self to regard themselves as anything else. Decides he'll try to reach Louise on the phone.[19]

While the 1952 text strongly suggests that none of the "infinite possibilities" facing the invisible man includes a "determination to return" to the political realm, these notes imply Ellison's early intention to have his protagonist reenter that realm, albeit on his own terms: some of the "individual groups" within the "organization" warrant his loyalty and require that he break out of the passive mode. We are reminded of Ellison's statement in *Negro Quarterly* in 1943 that African Americans need to develop the "group unity" enabling them to "participat[e] along with labor and other progressive groups as equals with . . . adult responsibility"; such unity will prevent their being "exploited by others: either for the good ends of democratic groups or for the bad ends of Fascist groups." Implied in this early ending to *Invisible Man* is a contradictory attitude toward multiracial solidarity. On the one hand, the invisible man has come to see politics as a matter of group power: African Americans, it is implied, need to constitute, as needed, a self-determining political bloc. On the other hand, the invisible man "accepts the humanity of whites" and will "try to reach Louise on the phone," a gesture at least as political as it is romantic, since there are no indications that Louise has herself abandoned the organization. Notably the term "traitor" appears in the context of treachery *to*, not *by*, the left.

By the time he completed the original typescript Ellison had decided to transfer to the end of the novel—in a section still not designated as the epilogue but set off by asterisks—the material relating to music (Old Bad Air here takes the place of Funky Butt), the smell of spring, and the protagonist's decision to emerge from hibernation. This closing material is at first much briefer than the 1952 epilogue, in one version consisting of only a single page. Beginning with the invisible man's descent underground and his discovery that it was Jack who both supplied his Brotherhood identity and then took it away, the final section shows the infuriated invisible man "bang[ing] around in the dark" and "making steaks of [the briefcase's] strap." But there is as of yet no castration nightmare, no encounter with Norton in the subway, and no memory of the grandfather's dying words. The original typescript ends with the words, "And who knows but that I speak for you?" with "on the lower frequencies" penciled in and then crossed out.[20]

Next to this truncated ending Ellison jotted, "Too condensed; bring in grandpa." At this point he began to create the passage about "affirming the principle" that has drawn so much attention, positive and negative, among his commentators. Given its importance as a distillation of the invisible man's—and, many have speculated, Ellison's—political philosophy, the passage's evolution bears careful tracing. At first it read:

And then I saw the joke of all my running and puzzled his deathbed advice. Could he have meant—he *must* have meant to affirm the principle and not the men, meaning to affirm the principle which was greater than the men, greater than the numbers and the vicious power and all the methods used in its name, the principle which they themselves had dreamed out of the chaos and darkness and violated and compromised but to which we fell heirs, not for the power or vindication but because for us, given the particular circumstances of our origin, it was the only way, the only way. And not because we were weak or afraid or opportunistic, but because too much that motivated others had been exhausted, burned out, negated in our living. And more, because we, hardly through any fault of our own, linked those to all the others, despite Jack and their own refusal to see, to all the loud clamoring semi-visible world too long used as mere pawns in a futile game. "Agree 'em to death and destruction," he had advised, but they were their own death and their own destruction except as the principle lived. But what do I want, really want, I asked myself. Certainly not Rinehart or invisibility nor simply not to run. But the next step I didn't know and that kept me in the hole.[21]

Although much is familiar here, several key assertions are absent. There is as yet no claim that "we," at this point clearly African Americans, are to "take responsibility for all of it, for the men as well as the principle, because we were the heirs who must use the principle because no other fitted our needs." Nor does the invisible man ask, "Weren't we part of them as well as apart from them and subject to die when they died?" Nor is the passage followed by a call for the weaving of America from many strands, for rejecting conformity, or for affirming diversity. Nor does the somewhat confusing formulation about the relation between African Americans and colonized peoples (the "loud clamoring semi-visible world"), who have all been "used as mere pawns in a futile game," target Jack as the chess player who manipulates these pawns; Jack is chastised for the lesser crime of "refus[ing] to see" the links between and among the world's people of color (574–77). Several important steps are thus missing in the process by which the invisible man, through reinterpreting his grandfather's words, affirms that African Americans are the chosen carriers of the American democratic legacy and Communists their sworn antagonists. Although this draft version ends with the words "And who knows but that I speak for you?" the signifying chain still misses some crucial links in its outreach to the reader. Not yet does the grandfather enable his grandson to perform the published novel's ultimate task of reading backward, that is, re-cognizing that the sphinx-like old man always already had the answer the invisible man has been seeking.[22]

"Diversity stuff": From Integrated Self to Body Politic

In the 1952 epilogue the narrator's statement "I know that men are different and that all life is divided and that only in division is there true health" is followed by the observation that he has stayed in his hole because "up above there's an increasing passion to make men conform to a pattern." He points out, "Jack and the boys [are waiting, knives in hand, to] 'ball the jack,' and I do not refer to the old dance step, although what they're doing is making the old eagle rock dangerously." He then asks, "Whence all this passion toward conformity anyway?" and proclaims, "Diversity is the word. Let man keep his many parts and you'll have no tyrant states." Asserting his own lack of interest in "becom[ing] white," he concludes, "America is woven of many strands; I would recognize them and let it so remain" (576–77). In this sequence of ideas, while there is reference to the "many parts" within the individual, the terms "difference" and "division" are associated primarily with social groups. "Diversity" is the key to American pluralism and freedom; "Jack and the boys," by contrast, are associated with conformity, "tyrant states," and the castration of the American eagle.[23]

Initially the narrator's recognition that "all life is divided and that only in division is there life" is followed not by the image of Jack and the rocking eagle but instead by this observation: "I am amused at those who credit the Napoleons and Lenins and Roosevelts with 'integrated personality.' These were—like Christ, who broke his heart trying to be both man and God— three of the most divided men ever to walk the earth. . . . [They were] men of ambivalence, torn in a million directions yet trying to go in only one." This is the original context in which the narrator remarks, "But diversity is the correct word, let man be made of many parts, and you'll have no Hitler states. Why, if you follow this integration business they'll end up forcing me, an invisible man, to become white." He jokes, "None of that for me. Like America I am made up of many strands, most of which conflict with one another." Criticizing those who would "tabulate, file, stipulate, and catalog," he confesses:

> Even those who declare themselves dedicated to the recognition of man's right to be different and who claim that they would not have this as the basis for the smooth functioning of society, fall into this error. I know. I

took part with them in activities and found the same old errors slipping in. . . . And yet my own diversity expressed itself in spite of my efforts to respond as I felt I was expected to respond.

What Ellison referred to in his notes as the "diversity stuff" initially focused on conflicts internal to individuals, not to the pluralist construction (e pluribus unum) of the United States.[24]

This earlier meditation on diversity carries implications quite different from those conveyed in the 1952 text. The invisible man's allusion to famous political leaders as instances of "ambivalence" displays his abiding preoccupation with the nature of leadership, and particularly the fragmentation and dismembering of the self that threaten all those who have been "dedicated and set aside." His grouping of Lenin with Napoleon and Roosevelt—he later adds Churchill to the list—suggests his interest in leaders of various political stripes who emerge in times of revolution, crisis, and war. Ellison's eventual elimination of this reference to actual figures, along with his substitution of "tyrant states" for "Hitler states," dehistoricizes his protagonist's meditation and implicitly invokes the thesis of "two totalitarianisms," which characteristically deployed the term "tyranny" to describe the twin monstrosities of fascism and communism. By erasing the invisible man's admission to having made the "same old errors" as others who thought they could reorganize society on the basis of scientific analysis, Ellison further erodes the grounds upon which the reader might distinguish rather than equate communism and fascism; errors, after all, are not crimes. The invisible man is speaking like a cold war liberal.[25]

The narrator's original emphasis on division as an internal state suggests that he sees the principal threat to diversity not in the dehumanizing scientism of "Jack and the boys," but in the felt compulsion of individuals to override their own internally contradictory states in the dubious quest for "integrated personality," the psychological state so alien to the narrator in "Blues." The invisible man's counterposition of "ambivalence" with "integrated personality"—which, valorizing the latter at the expense of the former, is suggestively akin to Schlesinger's privileging of "anxiety" over "certitude"—hardly offers a probing analysis of the psychology of leadership. But neither does it deny to a Communist the same complexity of self that it attributes to rulers of bourgeois regimes; nor does it collapse the notion of wholeness into that cold war–era whipping post, "conformity." As he substituted "conformity" for "integration," however, Ellison penciled in the margin, "conformity, standardization, blind discipline"; the narrator's initial statement—"Like America I am made of many strands, most of which conflict with one another"—becomes the proto-multiculturalist declaration "America is woven of many strands." Internal contradiction is reconfigured as liberal pluralism. Diversity, the demographic ideal now enshrined by "affirming the principle," converts the American dilemma, that is, its past and present practice of racism, into the basis for American exceptionalism, indeed national redemption. In this conflation of personal and social diversity the Negro stands forth as a metonymy of the nation as a whole, what Ellison would later call the contribution of the "harsh discipline" of African American experience to the "American heritage." The figure of the Negro, who for Ellison at one point signified a vanguard force, capable of "leaping over" the preindividuality caused by lag and heralding the classless society of the future, now contains multitudes by embodying the diversity of America.[26]

In the published text the narrative's previous alignment of antagonists is continually alluded to in the epilogue, which refers to "Jack and his ilk" (572), "Jack and his kind" (574), and "Jack and the boys" (576). Since in the preceding nightmare scenario Jack is portrayed as the head of a mob containing the principal figures who have kept the narrator running—"old Emerson and Bledsoe and Norton and Ras and the school superintendent and a number of others whom I failed to recognize" (569)—it would appear that the subsequent mentions of "Jack and ___" in the epilogue are intended to underline the fundamental kinship of the members of the lynch mob, diverse as they may appear. In that nightmare sequence, however, only Jack and Tobitt threaten the invisible man, who addresses the mob as "you scientists," a term that hardly applies to any of his other enemies. (Bledsoe in fact is mentioned only insofar as the protagonist himself utters "a Bledsoe laugh," which if anything suggests a newfound identification with the college president [570].) The epilogue's constant reference to "Jack and ___" further positions Jack as at once ringleader and epitome; the other members of the mob effectively fade from view. The only time the narrator distinguishes between Jack and any of the others is when, evidently referring to postwar anticolonial movements, he notes that the "loud, clamoring semivisible world" is seen as a "fertile field of exploitation by Jack and his kind" and "with condescension by Norton and his kind" (574–75). This opposition lets the Nortons and Emersons of the world off the hook; the narrator has apparently forgotten his meditation on the "kings of the earth" displaying their exotic trophies in their offices high above Wall Street. Instead Communists, who in fact were giving substantial support to anticolonial struggles around the world, are shown here as supplanting the imperialists in using people of color as "mere pawns in a futile game." International cold war politics decisively shape the text's revisions, and the capital accumulated off the backs of sharecroppers like Trueblood and as the far-flung producers of the commodities featured in Emerson's suite fades from view. The altered text has enlisted itself in what Ellison would call three years later "the struggle of the West to gain the allegiance of the remaining non-white people who have thus far remained outside the Communist sphere."[27]

Even the implied parallel between Jack the exploiter and Norton the condescender is largely effaced by the invisible man's subsequent encounter with Norton in the subway. For the aged trustee here appears more obtuse and foolish than dangerous; it is hard to recall that he is a personal friend of the John D. Rockefeller who stole the formula for turning blood into money and, as Edna originally remarked in the Golden Day, wants to "fuck the whole world." The "chordal collapse" about which Ellison wrote to Peggy Hitchcock in 1946 here resounds with a crash. The extended Burkean equation that has linked Jack with the likes of Bledsoe and Norton around homologous traits of character—manipulation, arrogance, denial of individuality—now coalesces around a single figure, Jack, who carries on his back the entire weight of their collective transgressions. Once the hegemonic rhetoric of the cold war has produced an audience largely conditioned into a state of "trained incapacity," the Brotherhood leader can be "dedicated and set aside" for sacrifice. The principal agent of scapegoating *in* the text emerges as the principal scapegoat *of* the text: at the moment when Jack assumes leadership of the lynching party he becomes, paradoxically, the novel's principal lynchee.[28]

"I can neither file nor forget":
Dismembering LeRoy's Journal

As he composed the epilogue Ellison not only transferred large chunks from his draft prologue to the novel's finale but also ransacked LeRoy's journal, juxtaposing passages in new combinations to produce meanings that his seagoing organic intellectual and union organizer could hardly have intended. After his funny but sordid account of the Munich-planning diplomat and his mistress Gabby, we will recall, LeRoy concludes, "It is a fallacy to say that people participate in their government. The people are *governed*." He then ruminates, "So why do I write, torturing myself to put it down? Because in spite of myself I've learned some things. Without the possibility of action, all knowledge comes to one labeled 'file and forget,' and I can neither file nor forget. Nor will certain ideas forget me; they keep filing away at my lethargy, my complacency." In another entry he confesses to an overwhelming sense of despair—"All life is absurd. . . . The true darkness lies in my own mind"—and expresses the need to return to the "'heart of darkness' across the Mason-Dixon line" and "reaffirm all of it, the whole unhappy territory and all the things loved and unlovable." This meditation is followed by his stated wish to be president—not for the power, but for the "perspective"—so that he might be confronted with his own "black face of negation" staring at him out of a crowd. LeRoy's anger and despair are shaped both by his radical skepticism about democracy and by his awareness of himself as a "black face of negation"; these are the reasons he cannot "file and forget."

In the 1952 epilogue the narrator reproduces LeRoy's statement about the absurdity of life and "the true darkness [that] lies within [his] own mind" but adds, "Till now, however, this is as far as I've ever gotten, for all life seen from the hole of invisibility is absurd" (579). He then repeats LeRoy's words about being unable to "file and forget" and goes on to ask, "Why should I be the one to dream this nightmare? Why should I be dedicated and set aside— yes, if not to at least *tell* a few people about it?" (579). As if acknowledging the sacrificial hero LeRoy to be the source of the language that he—or rather his creator—has pillaged, the invisible man informs his readers that the task for which he has himself been "dedicated and set aside" is to share with them his "nightmare" and "give pattern to the chaos which lives within the pattern of [their] certainties" (580–81). Clearly the "possibilities of action" imagined by LeRoy and his double ended up leading them in very different directions.

We hear another echo of LeRoy in the invisible man's closing declaration of ambivalence. During the memorial dinner in which LeRoy is symbolically consumed at Mary's, Treadwell reported his friend's words to him at Le Havre:

> We fight one another and hate one another and sometimes we even love one another. . . . And yet our hope and our humanity lies in the fact that we know that we hope and that we hate and that we fear and that we love. Anyway we're the only two groups in the country that aren't ashamed to admit that we're the most miserable bastards in the world, and that all the money and power in the world is no cure.

For LeRoy contradiction requires not just conflict but sublation: hope and fear, hate and love can undergo dialectical transformation only when white and black workers like Treadwell and himself realize what has made them "the most miserable bastards in the world" and act upon this knowledge. But there is "no cure" for their misery under capitalism; the implied negation of present misery is future revolutionary transformation of the social order.

In the published epilogue, by contrast, the invisible man muses on the existential implications of "affirming the principle": "I denounce and defend, or feel prepared to defend. I condemn and affirm, say no and say yes, say yes and say no. . . . And I defend because in spite of all I find that I love. In order to get some of it down I *have* to love. . . . So I approach [life] through division. So I denounce and I defend and I hate and I love" (579–80). Here contradiction is framed as paradox and oxymoron; like a New Critic, the invisible man cherishes the ambivalence that enables him to oscillate between the poles of antinomy and avoid the dull certainties of political commitment. Indeed the narrator's statement prefigures Ellison's later critical prescription that novels are "ritualistic and ceremonial to their core[,] . . . preserv[ing] as they destroy, affirm[ing] as they reject." Where LeRoy's conception of contradiction is dynamic, requiring negation and transformation, the invisible man's is homeostatic, entailing a ping-pong motion within overall stasis. Their reasons for refusing to "file and forget" are profoundly different, premised on antagonistic assumptions that cannot be made to cooperate. The invisible man's formulation of contradiction as oscillation draws upon the discourse of antipolarity, the denial of classes and the diffusion of class struggle, that was integral to the cold war ideological assault on labor. Whereas LeRoy was pushed to his death in the "destructive element" by enemies of interracial unionism, the invisible man, who now apparently defends and loves what he claims also to denounce and hate, urges what Simone de Beauvoir called the "ethics of ambiguity."[29]

Ellison further borrows from LeRoy's journal to rework the meaning of the crucial phrase "more human," which bursts out from the invisible man during the arena speech. Discovering the provenance of the phrase in LeRoy's statement that African Americans "have been brutalized and forced to live inhuman lives so that [the West] could become what they consider 'more human,'" the protagonist reads on. "Doesn't the pattern of our experience insist," LeRoy asks, "that we seek a way of life more universal, more human and more free than any to be found in the world today?" For LeRoy the project of becoming "more human" entails the abolition of the social conditions that make the enhanced humanity of the few contingent upon the degradation of the many; his unhappy consciousness is an indignant one.

In the published epilogue, by contrast, the invisible man, reflecting upon his newfound ability to denounce and defend and hate and love all at once, thinks:

Once I thought my grandfather incapable of thoughts about humanity, but I was wrong. Why should an old slave use such a phrase as "This and this or this has made me more human" as I did in my arena speech? Hell, he never had any doubts about his humanity—that was left to his "free" off-spring. He accepted his humanity just as he accepted the principle. It was his, and the principle lives on in all its human and absurd diversity. (580)

What enables the narrator's rebirth—he will, he decides, "shake off the old skin and come up for breath" (580)—is the discovery that "humanity" and "the principle" are coterminous: his trickster grandfather, superficially an Uncle Tom, all along embodied the essence of the democracy that he was de-nied. There is no need to think in terms of "more human" (and its dialectical correlate, "less human"); LeRoy's project of social transformation is irrele-vant if the "death in the smell of spring" is the same in "thee" and in "me" (580). LeRoy's indignant consciousness has been reformulated as ambiva-lence and complexity. And his status as a historically concrete avatar of the dying god, his bid to universality as a modern embodiment of Prometheus, Thomson's "patron saint of the proletariat," is diffused in an archetypal in-vocation of seasonal rituals of emergence removed from social and political practice. The text's severing of its tissue of mythic and ritual allusion from a historical materialist base accords with its closing embrace of the liberal pluralism that posits the American nation as the chosen site of "diversity," "humanity," and "the principle." The closing formulation of rebirth as sea-sonal archetype symptomatically enacts the pressures of the cold war mo-ment; its apparent ahistoricity is profoundly historical.[30]

One last motif cherry-picked from LeRoy's journal relates to the famous last sentence of *Invisible Man*. Perusing the journal during his "days of cer-tainty" as a Brotherhood organizer, the protagonist comes across LeRoy's entry about having access to an audience of millions and thinks, "If I could get only a million to listen to me I could get something done. What if one could get the 15 million to listen, he could help get something done. . . . That was something worth working for, and a way to make the world spin faster. If I could reach each of these and bring them into the movement." By 1952 the icon of the red fist grasping the radio microphone has alerted the U.S. population of the dangers of leftist subversion; when at the end of *Invisible Man* Ellison's narrator asks whether, on the "lower frequencies," he may be "speaking for" his readers, he is certainly not trying to "bring them into the movement." In fact quite the opposite is the case; he warns them of the movement's treachery.

The invitation that the invisible man holds out to the epilogue's readers, while apparently ecumenical, is not an entirely open one. Here he extends an olive branch to readers of European descent who might have been put off by the text's harsh portrayal of virtually every white character appearing in its pages. (Somewhat ironically, had Ellison decided to retain Treadwell and Louise such an olive branch would not be necessary; but then, the basis for these characters' inclusion—their embrace of a class-conscious multi-racialism—had to be ruled out as the basis for "images of fraternity" in the published text.) Invisibility, the narrator now announces, is not the exclusive province of those who have endured the humiliation—and worse—of the racial rituals governing American life; it is a universal human condition. When Wright addresses his multiracial audience as "you" at the end of *Twelve Million Black Voices*, he does so on the basis of class solidarity; Ellison, by contrast, expands his audience on the basis of patriotic identity. For the narrator has equated "humanity" with "the principle" and has portrayed "Jack and the boys" as castrators of not just the African American protagonist but also the American eagle. A nonblack (especially a white) reader, uncertain about the degree of his or her identification with the novel's protagonist but certain about dangers posed by Communists and Communism, can thus request entry into the text's charmed circle of initiates and reply affirmatively to the narrator's closing invitation. Anticommunism enables Ellison to secure the "accord of sensibilities" with his readers about which he expressed concern when writing to Kenneth Burke and Peggy Hitchcock at the very outset of his project. In order to secure and invoke the universals necessary for successful artistic communication, Ellison has sutured the disparate elements in his audience by expelling from the tribe those members who can be "othered" as un-American.[31]

"And now you know who I am!":
Echoes from the Antifascist Underground

For readers familiar with Ellison's frequent homages to T. S. Eliot, the narrator's closing verbal play with the boomerang structure of his tale invokes the sonorous metaphysics of "Little Gidding": "What we call the beginning is often the end / And to make an end is to make a beginning." For readers encountering the novel in 1952, however, the invisible man's repeated assertions about beginnings and endings may have invoked not so much the voice of Ellison's "ancestor" Eliot as the echo of his "relative" Paul Robeson, who concluded his voice-over narration of violent labor struggles in the documentary *Native Land* (1942) with the promise, "This end is our beginning." Referring to the state-sponsored and vigilante opposition to the Depression-era movement for interracial unionization, Robeson's narration vowed to extend the battle against domestic fascism into the international arena: one cycle of class warfare was ending, but a new one had begun. Robeson's fans, if regular radio listeners, would also have been attuned to his frequent presence on the wartime airwaves. Declaring, "Today's struggle of the Negro is part of the worldwide struggle against fascism," he reminded his listeners that African Americans deeply grasped the meaning of the war out of an "awareness born of their yearning for freedom from an oppression that predated fascism." Robeson's voice had embodied the Popular Front for Ellison, as for many others. Ellison had quoted Robeson's finale to *Native Land* in his *New Masses* review of the film; Robeson's voice had resounded in the background of "In a Strange Country"; Ellison had praised Robeson's blending of nationalism and internationalism in his unpublished *Negro Quarterly* editorial about American Negro culture; several of Ellison's writings in the early 1940s had been drafted on the back of advertisements for the "Folksongs on the Firing Line" songfest, that had been cosponsored by Earl Robinson, who composed "Ballad for Americans," and had featured songs that Robeson routinely sang. Above all, Robeson, whose Broadway appearance in Shakespeare's tragedy had boldly transgressed the theatrical color line, had figured as a shadowy presence throughout the Othello theme central to the tales of both the invisible man and Tod Clifton in early drafts of *Invisible Man*. Although by the time he began work on the novel Ellison was dismissing Robeson to Wright as a "clown," the invisible man continues to contend with the reverberations of Robeson's voice in his basement lair; Armstrong's "Black and Blue" is, imaginably, not the only music that he hears. When proposing himself as a spokesperson for the reader, the invisible man has not in fact given up ranting for writing; still speechifying, he offers to substitute his boomeranged and cyclical version of beginnings and endings for the spiral version enunciated by Robeson a decade before.[32]

There is a more than passing irony in the fact that, when he offers to speak on behalf of the reader, Ellison's narrator represents himself as an authentic bearer of the legacy of the Founding Fathers. For the Popular Frontist left had also laid claim to being the true voice of America. In the finale to *Native Land* Robeson had proclaimed that, although "there were many casualties, many wrongs" in the previous decade's class war, the result was that "American labor and the American nation are stronger for having passed through this fire": labor and the nation emerged from the fray as, if not identical, coterminous entities. In "Ballad for Americans" Robeson's voice not only contained the nation's anonymous working-class multitudes, the "everybody who's nobody" and "nobody who's everybody," but also praised its common dedication to the "mighty fine plan" laid down by "Mister Tom Jefferson, a mighty fine man." When his call-and-response ended with the words "And now you know who I am. / Who are you? / America! America!," the politics of Popular Frontist metonymic nationalism received their fullest and perhaps most eloquent expression. The rhetorical ripples between the discourses of Robeson and the invisible man thus speak volumes about the class-collaborationist risks entailed in Popular Front and wartime patriotism. Arguably the most injurious boomeranging that takes place at the end of *Invisible Man* is not the head-bopping experienced by the protagonist—who, hard-headed anyway, emerges from his basement pretty much unscathed to take up his "socially responsible role"—but the ironic return of the CP's slogan of "twentieth-century Americanism," now used to hunt down the very radicals who once purported to use it as a weapon in the struggle against fascism.[33]

But language, even for singers and writers, is not everything; what Robeson meant by "America" and what the invisible man means are very different propositions. When in the "Ballad for Americans" Robeson spoke of democracy, he included the deeply radical proposition, closely echoing Marx, that "a man in white skin can never be free while his black brother is in slavery." When in his wartime speeches he referred to the historic role of African Americans, he viewed them not just as contributors to the nation's pluralistic culture but, from their collective memory of slavery and continuing battle with Jim Crow, as leading participants in the world-historical process that would free all dispossessed people from their chains. Robeson's postwar support of the inhabitants of the "semi-visible world" would lead to his hounding by the FBI and the ruin of his career. When the invisible man, by contrast, affirms the legacy of the Founding Fathers, he celebrates the "fluidity" of American society and beckons the world's people of color away from anticolonial rebellion and socialism—indeed, into the arms of the U.S. State Department. Ellison's joining the CIA-backed Congress for Cultural Freedom soon after the publication of *Invisible Man* made it clear where he situated himself in the hardening political alignments of the cold war.[34]

The invisible man speaks hesitantly in 1952, emphasizing his marginal position along the lower frequencies of the radio band. As it happens, however, he will soon be recognized as the spokesperson for an ever-widening circle of listeners nodding their heads in agreement. When his creator receives the National Book Award a year later, William O. Douglas, the keynote speaker, emphasizes the importance of understanding the cultural texts of Asian peoples "not as Americans write or translate them, but as the Asians write them," if the United States is successfully to aid the Asian "counter-revolution against Communism"; diversity and vernacular culture have socially responsible roles to play in the realm of global politics. Although in the past Ellison scored the CP for giving secondary priority to the demands of African Americans during the war, he has no difficulty now in sharing the ceremonial dais with Archibald MacLeish, who, as head of the Office of War Information, sought to bolster Negro morale without doing anything to contest segregation of the armed forces or discrimination in wartime industries. (Both MacLeish and Bernard DeVoto, the third NBA recipient, Ellison writes to Albert Murray a few days later, were good company, "both easygoing and friendly men, nothing stuffed shirt about them.") Within a decade *Invisible Man* will be recognized as one of the most important novels to emerge since the war; within twenty years the novel will be adjudged one of the best novels of the twentieth century. More than a half-century after his first broadcast the invisible man occupies the very center of the radio band, his voice a required presence in many classrooms around the United States.[35]

But as we listen to the wry, haunting voice of the invisible man and contemplate his offer to speak for us, we should recall that he once viewed Brotherhood as the route to becoming "more human" and that his creator once "dedicated and set aside" a proletarian radical to be his protagonist's secret sharer. Inasmuch as the crisis-ridden system presided over by the Nortons and Emersons inflicts ever-increasing misery upon the Marys, Truebloods, and Treadwells (not to mention the beleaguered inhabitants of the still "semi-visible world"), the invisible man's original plan for expanding his own and others' humanity, suitably updated to encompass the historical conditions and political landscape of the twenty-first century, continues to require our serious consideration. That we have witnessed over the past decade the readiness of not one but two black secretaries of state to affirm the imperatives of Wall Street in relation to the "semi-visible world," and have since then elected a black president who looks through and past the "black face of negation" staring back at him both at home and abroad, indicates the need for fundamental systemic change—not simply "change that we can believe in." This study of the political odyssey portrayed in the making of *Invisible Man* will have accomplished one of its principal goals if it reminds us that, as LeRoy urged, we cannot afford to file and forget.

Introduction

1. The National Book Award was instituted in 1950; in 1973 the critic Maxwell Geismar noted, "For the last twenty years of cold war culture, I consider [both the Pulitzer and the National Book Award] a fraud." Quoted in Joseph F. Trimmer, *The National Book Awards for Fiction: An Index to the First Twenty-Five Years* (Boston: G. K. Hall, 1978), xv. (The closing section of chapter 8 deals with the National Book Award and with William O. Douglas's keynote address at the ceremony in 1953.)

2. Harvey Breit, *New York Times Book Review*, 4 May 1952, 26–27; Eloise Perry Hazard, "The Author," *Saturday Review of Literature*, 12 April 1952, 22; Lloyd Brown, "The Deep Pit," *Masses and Mainstream* 5 (June 1952), 62–64; John Oliver Killens, review of *Invisible Man*, *Freedom* 2 (June 1952), 7; Abner W. Berry, "Ralph Ellison's Novel 'Invisible Man' Shows Snobbery, Contempt for Negro People," *Daily Worker*, 1 June 1952, section 2, p. 7.

3. Ellison, "The World and the Jug," *The Collected Essays of Ralph Ellison* (hereafter CE) rev. ed., ed. John F. Callahan (New York: Modern Library, 2003), 167; Ellison, introduction to *Shadow and Act*, CE, 58; Ellison, "Remembering Richard Wright," CE, 667; Ellison, introduction to *Invisible Man* (New York: Random House, 1982), xvii; Michel Fabre, "In Ralph Ellison's Precious Words," unpublished manuscript.

4. Ellison, "A Very Stern Discipline," CE, 745, 748.

5. For discussion of Ellison's reception by African American critics, see Charles "Pete" Banner-Haley, "Ralph Ellison and the Invisibility of the Black Intellectual: Historical Reflections on *Invisible Man*," *Ralph Ellison and the Raft of Hope: A Political Companion to* Invisible Man, ed. Lucas Morel (Lexington: University Press of Kentucky, 2004), 158–70; and Jerry Gafio Watts, *Heroism and the Black Intellectual: Ralph Ellison, Politics, and Afro-American Intellectual Life* (Chapel Hill: University of North Carolina Press, 1994). In *Daggers and Javelins: Essays, 1974–1979* (New York: Quill, 1984), 146, Amiri Baraka sharply criticized Ellison for "trying to steer Afro-American literature away from protest, away from the revolutionary concerns of the 1930s and early 1940s," but did not mention Ellison's own writings of that period. Ellison himself in 1977 noted the former leftist associations of various black nationalist critics later associated with *Black World*. Maryemma Graham and Amrijit Singh, eds., *Conversations with Ralph Ellison* (Jackson: University Press of Mississippi, 1995), 347–48.

6. Ellison, *Flying Home and Other Stories*, ed. John F. Callahan (New York: Modern Library, 1996); "Ralph Ellison Rediscovered: His Unpublished Letters on Race and Identity in America," *The New Republic*, 1 March 1999, 36–37; Lawrence Jackson, *Ralph Ellison: Emergence of Genius* (New York: John Wiley, 2002), hereafter RE:E; Arnold Rampersad, *Ralph Ellison: A Biography* (New York: Knopf, 2007), hereafter RE:B. Robert O'Meally's 1980 study notes the early writings but treats them, except for those he terms "vernacular," dismissively. *The Craft of Ralph Ellison* (Cambridge, Mass.: Harvard University Press, 1980).

7. Instances of twenty-first-century criticism acknowledging the importance of Ellison's relationship to the left include Jesse Wolfe, "'Ambivalent Man': Ellison's Rejection of Communism," *African American Review* 34, no. 4 (2000), 621–37; Frederick T. Griffiths, "Ralph Ellison, Richard Wright, and the Case of Angelo Herndon," *African American Review* 35, no. 4 (2000), 615–37; William J. Maxwell, "'Creative and Cultural Lag': The Radical Education of Ralph Ellison," *A Historical Guide to Ralph Ellison*, ed. Steven Tracy (Oxford: Oxford University Press, 2004), 59–84; and Christopher Z. Hobson, "*Invisible Man* and African American Radicalism in World War II," *African American Review* 39, no. 3 (2005), 355–76. For an overview of the main trends in recent Ellison criticism, see Barbara Foley, "The Ellison Industry," *Symbolism: An International Annual of Critical Aesthetics*, vol. 8, ed. Rüdiger Ahrens and Klaus Stierstorfer (New York: AMS Press, 2007): 323–41.

8. Ellison, "The Little Man at Chehaw Station," CE, 506; Ralph Ellison, "Brave Words for a Startling Occasion," CE, 151–54. For instances of "reading backward" Ellison's "god-terms" in analyses of *Invisible Man*, see John F. Callahan, "Chaos, Complexity, and Possibility: The Historical Frequencies of Ralph Waldo Ellison," *Speaking for You: The Vision of Ralph Ellison*, ed. Kimberly W. Benston (Washington, D.C.: Howard University Press, 1987), 125–43; and Horace A. Porter, *Jazz Country: Ralph Ellison in America* (Iowa City: University of Iowa Press, 2001).

9. See, for example, Ellison, "The Little Man at Chehaw Station," CE, 504–7; Ellison, "On Initiation Rites and Power," CE, 532–33; "The World and the Jug," CE, 171–73; and Ellison, "Perspective of Literature," CE, 781–83. Rampersad complains that, by the mid-1970s, Ellison "essentially had no other topic . . . [than] 'the very complex nature of American reality'" (RE:B, 517). For a discussion of the American exceptionalism undergirding Ellison's and James Baldwin's view of the Negro as a redemptive figure, see Michael Nowlin, "Ralph Ellison, James Baldwin, and the Liberal Imagination," *Arizona Quarterly* 60, no. 2 (2004), 117–40.

10. Ellison to Murray, 6 June 1951, in *Trading Twelves: The Selected Letters of Ralph Ellison and Albert Murray*, ed. Albert Murray and John F. Callahan (New York: Random House, 2000), 19.

11. Gerald C. Horne, *Black Liberation/Red Scare: Ben Davis and the Communist Party* (Newark: University of Delaware Press, 1994), 137–66; Martha Biondi, *To Stand and Fight: The Struggle for Civil Rights in Postwar New York City* (Cambridge, Mass.: Harvard University Press, 2003); Robbie Lieberman, "Communism, Peace Activism, and Civil Liberties: From the Waldorf Conference to the Peekskill Riot," *Journal of American Culture* 18, no. 3 (1995), 59–65. While the terms are easier to separate in theory

than in practice, I use the term *anti-Communism* to designate hostility specifically toward the CPUSA and the term *anticommunism* to designate a more generalized antipathy to leftist movements and ideas. See Joel Kovel, *Red-Hunting in the Promised Land: Anticommunism and the Making of America* (New York: Basic Books, 1994), 3-5. The ideological dimension of the distinction between "historical" and "implied" readers, first elaborated by Wolfgang Iser in *The Implied Reader: Patterns of Communication in Prose Fiction from Bunyan to Beckett* (Baltimore: Johns Hopkins University Press, 1974), has been explored by Peter J. Rabinowitz in *Before Reading: Narrative Conventions and the Politics of Interpretation* (Ithaca: Cornell University Press, 1987).

12. Gerald Horne, *Black and Red: W. E. B. Du Bois and the Afro-American Response to the Cold War, 1949-1963* (Albany: State University of New York Press, 1986), 151; Louis Budenz, *Men without Faces: The Communist Conspiracy in the U.S.A.* (New York: Harper and Brothers, 1950); Richard Crossman, *The God That Failed* (New York: Harper's, 1950); Arthur Schlesinger, *The Vital Center: The Politics of Freedom* (Boston: Houghton Mifflin, 1949); Eric Hoffer, *The True Believer: Thoughts on the Nature of Mass Movements* (New York: Harper and Row, 1951); Hannah Arendt, *The Origins of Totalitarianism* (1951; rev. ed., New York: Harcourt Brace Jovanovich, 1973); American Business Consultants, *Counterattack: The Newsletter of Facts to Combat Communism* (New York: RAND, 1950). *I Was a Communist for the FBI* was initially a series of articles in the *Saturday Evening Post* based on the testimony of the FBI mole Matt Cvetic, who appeared before sixty-three government committees and fingered approximately three hundred Communists. The movie became a radio series in 1952. See Stephen J. Whitfield, *The Culture of the Cold War* (Baltimore: Johns Hopkins University Press, 1991), 21-22, 133-35; and Daniel J. Leab, *I Was a Communist for the FBI: The Unhappy Life and Times of Matt Cvetic* (State College: Pennsylvania State University Press, 2000). For more on the formalist dynamics of anticommunism, that is, its reduction of politics to a matter of authoritarian character structure, see Philip Selznick, *The Organizational Weapon: A Study in Bolshevik Strategy and Tactics* (New York: McGraw-Hill, 1952); for a critique, see Peter L. Steinberg, *The Great "Red Menace": United States Prosecution of American Communists, 1947-1952* (Westport, Conn.: Greenwood Press, 1984). On the evolution of the term *totalitarian*, see Benjamin L. Alpers, *Dictators, Democracy and American Public Culture: Envisioning the Totalitarian Enemy, 1920s-1950s* (Chapel Hill: University of North Carolina Press, 2003).

13. David Riesman, et. al., *The Lonely Crowd: A Study of the Changing American Character* (New Haven: Yale University Press, 1950), 252, 238.

14. John F. Callahan, "Ellison's *Invisible Man*," in Callahan, ed., *Ralph Ellison's Invisible Man: A Casebook* (New York: Oxford University Press, 2004), 313.

15. Graham and Singh, *Conversations with Ralph Ellison*, 347.

16. The drafts of *Invisible Man* occupy some 4,000 pages of text; the novel outlines and early fiction are scattered among some 2,000 pages of rough manuscripts and random notes.

17. Jackson, *RE:E*, 426-31.

18. The precise quotation from Marx is: "Men make their own history, but they do not make it just as they please; they do not make it under circumstances chosen by

themselves, but under circumstances directly encountered, given and transmitted from the past." *The Eighteenth Brumaire of Louis Bonaparte* (New York: International Publishers, 1963), 15. For citations relevant to the discussion here and in the following paragraphs, see chapter 1, below.

19. James S. Allen, *The Negro Question in the United States* (New York: International Publishers, 1936), 33–34, 62, 178, *et passim*; William Z. Foster, *Toward Soviet America* (New York: International Publishers, 1932).

20. Manning Marable, "The Cold War in Black America, 1945–1954," in *Race, Reform and Rebellion: The Second Reconstruction in Black America, 1945–1990*, rev. 2nd ed. (Jackson: University Press of Mississippi, 1991), 13–39. When the aged Du Bois was handcuffed and arrested in March 1951, he received widespread support from the black press; the *Pittsburgh Courier* editorialized that his arrest was "meant to serve as a gag on any Negro leadership that is disposed to 'shoot the works' for freedom" (quoted in Horne, *Black and Red*, 165). After joining the Communist Party, Du Bois spent his final years away from the United States, in Ghana.

21. Frank Marshall Davis, *Livin' the Blues: Memoirs of a Black Journalist and Poet*, ed. John Edgar Tidwell (Madison: University of Wisconsin Press, 1992); Oliver Harrington, *Why I Left America and Other Essays* (Jackson: University Press of Mississippi, 1993). For more on Killens, see Alan M. Wald, *Trinity of Passion: The Literary Left and the Antifascist Crusade* (Chapel Hill: University of North Carolina Press, 2007), 50–62. Hansberry, later famous for *A Raisin in the Sun* (1959), was assistant editor of Robeson's strongly anti-Korean War *Freedom*; Brown was an editor of *Masses and Mainstream*. *Iron City*, Brown's 1951 novel about racist political and legal repression during the "mini-red Scare" of 1939–1941, remained buried for many years.

22. For an instance of the continuing influence of inherited anticommunist and formalist paradigms—as well as of Ellison's own post-1952 commentary—upon the secondary-school-level teaching of *Invisible Man*, see P. L. Thomas, *Reading, Learning, Teaching Ralph Ellison* (New York: Peter Lang, 2008).

23. Ellison, "Beating that Boy," *CE*, 150. For a sharp critique of the published novel's "cartoon-like" portrayal of African-American life as "no more than a black battle royal," divested of the potentiality for historical agency, see Houston Baker's "Failed Memory: Black Majority Modernism and Mr. Ellison's *Invisible Man*," in *Critical Memory: Public Spheres, African American Writing, and Black Fathers and Sons in America* (Athens: University of Georgia Press, 2001), 21–40, quote p. 26.

Chapter One: Forming a Politics

1. Whether or not Ellison ever joined the Communist Party is unclear. Both Jackson and Rampersad hedge their bets. Among Ellison's papers is a ledger-style record, titled "Branch Control Record," where, in what looks like Ellison's handwriting, "Initials of Members" are followed by "Date Registered" and dates for November 1941 are entered. Included among the score or so of initials are T. W. and A. B., possibly signifying Ted Ward and Abner Berry, both African American CP members. Included here are small chits reading "dues" and "international solidarity," as well as

a pamphlet, "The Road to Liberation for the Negro People," signed "Your comrade, Mike Gold." The folder also contains a document signifying Ellison's membership in the International Workers Order and a death benefit, dated 1 April 1939, made out to his wife at the time, Rose Poindexter. Box 215, F. 2 and 4, Ralph Ellison Papers, Library of Congress (henceforth RE P). The International Workers Organization was a broad-based organization consisting mostly of non-Party members. Ellison's involvement in the business of a branch, however—the unit of organization higher than a club—suggests a much closer relationship with the Party.

2. Ellison to Ida Ellison, 30 August 1937, in "Ralph Ellison Rediscovered: His Unpublished Letters on Race and Identity in America," *New Republic*, 1 March 1999, 36; Ellison to Wright, 8 November 1937, Wright Papers, Beinecke Library, Box 97, F. 1314; Rampersad, RE:B, 81–113. Thompson was prominent in black cultural and political movements, from the Harlem Renaissance to the civil rights movement and protests against McCarthyism in the 1950s. When Josie Craig Berry, the wife of Ellison's high school English teacher, noted in her column in the *Black Dispatch* that Oklahoma City's native son had published a review in *New Challenge*, Ellison wrote back proudly of his association with both *New Challenge* and the *Champion*, the latter of which he described as "a youth magazine with popular appeal and a bias against war and fascism, and all the latter term implies." See Josie Craig Berry, "Over My Shoulder," *Black Dispatch*, 20 November 1937, 6; Ellison to Berry, 22 November 1937, Josie Craig Berry Papers, University of Oklahoma.

3. Federal Writers Project, "The Negro in New York," Reels 2 and 3, Schomburg Center for Research in Black Culture (SRBC), New York City. The work of Ellison and other researchers would eventually be published by Roi Ottley and William J. Weatherby as *The Negro in New York* (New York: New York Public Library, 1967).

4. Ann Banks, ed., *First-Person America* (New York: Random House, 1981), 250–52, 243–45. See also the treatment of urban folklore at the Congress of American Writers in 1939 in Donald Ogden Stewart, ed., *Fighting Words* (New York: Harcourt, Brace, 1940), 7–31. For more on the state and city guides written by FWP writers, see Christine Hold, *The WPA Guides: Mapping America* (Jackson: University Press of Mississippi, 1999), especially 92–122, "New York City"; and Jerrold Hirsch, *Portrait of America: A Cultural History of the Federal Writers' Project* (Chapel Hill: University of North Carolina Press, 2003). Wright authored the section on Harlem in the guide to the city, *New York Panorama* (1938; rpt. St. Clair Shores, Mich.: Scholarly Press, 1976), 132–51.

5. Banks, *First-Person America*, 254–57.

6. Ibid., 257–60. For more on the sinking of the *Titanic* in African American folklore, see Lawrence Levine, *Black Culture and Black Consciousness: Afro-American Folk Thought from Slavery to Freedom* (New York: Oxford University Press, 1977), 427–29.

7. "Their Arms Are Strong," Box 166, F. 2, RE P. A number of Ellison's untitled sketches have been supplied with titles by Library of Congress archivists; a few FWP and *New Masses* journalistic writings are misfiled as fiction.

8. Ellison, "No Discrimination," Box 163 (filed under "I'm in New York but New York Ain't in Me"), RE P; Hosea Hudson, *Black Worker in the Deep South: A Personal Record* (New York: International Publishers, 1972). See also Robin D. G. Kelley, *Hammer*

and Hoe: Alabama Communists During the Depression (Chapel Hill: University of North Carolina Press, 1990). "No Discrimination" may have drawn upon Ellison's experiences as a publicist for the Greater New York Committee on Unemployment in 1939 (Rampersad, *RE:B*, 128–29).

9. Ellison, "The Little Man at Chehaw Station," *CE*, 253.

10. Ellison, "Practical Mystic," review *of Sojourner Truth: God's Faithful Pilgrim, New Masses*, 16 August 1938, 25–26. Seventy-six years old in 1938, Ella Reeve "Mother" Bloor was a seasoned labor organizer and founding member of the CPUSA. The anthropologist, educator, and folklorist Arthur Huff Fauset, the half-brother of the Harlem Renaissance novelist and one-time *Crisis* literary editor Jessie Redmon Fauset, was a teacher's union leader and active in Philadelphia politics in the Popular Front era.

11. Ellison, Notes 1942–50, F. 11, Box 152; F. 2, Box 151, REP. Another, more current list started with the NAACP leader Walter White and ended with Ferdinand Smith, an activist Communist official in the National Maritime Union (Notes 1942–50, F. 8, Box 152, REP). James W. Ford, the CP's vice-presidential candidate in 1932, authored *The Negro and the Democratic Front* (New York: International Publishers, 1938). William Patterson was the International Labor Defense lawyer in charge of the *Scottsboro* defense.

12. Ellison, "Anti-Semitism among Negroes," *Jewish People's Voice*, 3 April 1939, 3, 8. This was the publication of the Jewish People's Committee for United Action against Fascism and Anti-Semitism, founded in 1936. Reid called himself "the black Hitler." See John Roy Carlson, *Under Cover: My Four Years in the Nazi Underworld of America* (New York: E. P. Dutton, 1943), 154–63; Claude McKay, *Harlem: Negro Metropolis* (1940; rpt. New York: Harcourt Brace Jovanovich, 1968), 181–262; and Robert A. Hill, compiler and editor, *The FBI's RACON: Racial Conditions in the United States During World War II* (Boston: Northeastern University Press, 1995), 1–72.

13. Ellison, "Judge Lynch in New York," *New Masses*, 15 August 1939, 15–16.

14. Ellison, "Judge Lynch in New York" (draft) quoted in Jackson, *RE:E*, 220. Lawrence Jackson opines that the *New Masses* editors, Joseph North and Samuel Sillen, "revised the piece to conform to the journal's political agenda." Ellison recalled in 1971 that the article "caused much protest to be directed at the police precinct" and brought the police to his own door. Maryemma Graham and Amrijit Singh, eds., *Conversations with Ralph Ellison* (Jackson: University Press of Mississippi, 1995), 200.

15. Georgi Dimitrov, *The United Front against War and Fascism* (New York: International Publishers, 1936), 8; Earl Browder, *The People's Front* (New York: International Publishers, 1937); James S. Allen, *The Negro Question in the United States* (New York: International Publishers, 1936), and *Reconstruction: The Battle for Democracy 1865–1876* (New York: International Publishers 1937). At the Seventh World Congress the Comintern explicitly posed the Popular Front as a choice between the class-against-class politics of the preceding Third Period (1928 to mid-1935), set forth in R. Palme Dutt's *Fascism and Social Revolution* (New York: International Publishers, 1936). Dimitrov stated, "Now the toiling masses in a number of capitalist countries are faced with the necessity of making a definite choice, of making it today, not between proletar-

ian dictatorship and bourgeois democracy, but between bourgeois democracy and
fascism" (111).

16. Ellison, "The Negro and the War," Box 20, F. 11, REP. Although much has been made of the post-Pact defection from the League of American Writers by various prominent writers and critics, the membership declined only from 820 to 700. Franklin Folsom, *Days of Anger, Days of Hope: A Memoir of the League of American Writers, 1937–1942* (Niwot: University Press of Colorado, 1994), 180.

17. Wright to Ellison, undated [spring 1940], Box 76, REP; Ellison to Wright, 14 April 1940 and 15 May 1940, F. 1314, Box 97, RWP; Wright, "Not My People's War," *New Masses*, 17 June 1941, 8–9. Ben Davis's commentary on *Native Son* appeared in the *Sunday Worker*, 14 April 1940, 4–7, and 23 June 1940, 4–5. Samuel Sillen analyzed the national press reaction to the novel and provided his own commentary in "The Response to *Native Son*," *New Masses*, 23 April 1940, 25–27; 30 April 1940, 26–27; and 21 May 1940, 25–27.

18. Ellison, "Camp Lost Colony," *New Masses*, 6 February 1940, 18–19. Recently declassified documents from the Russian Foreign Intelligence Services reveal that a year before the Nazi invasion of the USSR, the United States and Britain had approved the Soviet occupation of the Baltic states; a staple element in the anti-Communist narrative of the Second World War has been called into question. See Tom Parfitt, "Moscow Dossier Embarrasses U.S. and Britain ahead of Riga Summit," *The Guardian*, 24 November 2006, online.

19. Ellison, "The 'Good Life,'" *New Masses*, 20 February 1940, 27; Ellison, "Anti-War Novel," *New Masses*, 18 June 1940, 29–30.

20. Ellison, "Hunters and Pioneers," *New Masses*, 19 March 1940, 26.

21. Ellison, "Argosy across the USA," *New Masses*, 26 November 1940, 24. For a reading of "Let America Be America Again" as a critique of "Jeffersonian platitudes," see Jonathan Scott, *Socialist Joy in the Writing of Langston Hughes* (Columbia: University of Missouri Press, 2006), 88–94.

22. Ellison, "A Congress Jim Crow Didn't Attend," *New Masses*, 14 May 1940, rpt. in CE, 5–18, quotes on 13–14. Randolph worked with the CP in the National Negro Congress until shortly before the meeting Ellison attended; thereafter he functioned in the labor movement as an anti-Communist and was roundly attacked by the CP. For an account sympathetic to Randolph's perspective, see Andrew E. Kersten, *A. Philip Randolph: A Life in the Vanguard* (Lanham, Md.: Rowman and Littlefield, 2007).

23. Ellison, "A Congress," 8, 10, 16–18; Ellison to Wright, 11 May 1940, F. 1314, Box 97, RWP. Ellison's letter replays a number of Wright's words in his account of African Americans' ecstatic reactions to Joe Louis's victory over Max Baer. "Joe Louis Uncovers Dynamite," *New Masses*, 8 October 1935, reprinted in Joseph North, ed., *New Masses: An Anthology of the Rebel Thirties* (New York: International Publishers, 1969), 160–64. The address delivered by Owen Whitfield featured a political allegory in the form of a folk fable in which two donkeys, black and white, "gnawed the rope from each other's necks and together . . . went and kicked the man's hips who had tied them together in the first place" (F. 9, Box 6, Richard B. Moore Papers,

SRBC). Ellison's enthusiastic notes record the broad range of issues addressed at the National Negro Congress: "democratic Spain"; the Domestic Workers Union; the Workers Alliance Rental Allowance Program; the vanguard role of Negroes in maritime unionism ("National Negro Congress," Box 91, REP).

24. The notion that African Americans might figure as a metonymy of democratic possibility was not born with the Popular Front; an earlier variant was central to the discourse of the Harlem Renaissance. See Barbara Foley, *Spectres of 1919: Class and Nation in the Making of the New Negro* (Urbana: University of Illinois Press, 2003). Ellison evinced little of this ambivalent patriotism in an unpublished article written for the Federal Writers Project in 1940 titled "The Negro and the War," in which he argued forcefully that only the Negro middle class, never the masses, had benefited from Negro participation in the nation's wars. Referring to the current conflict as a reflection of the fact that "the contradictions of capitalism are much sharper today," he bluntly concluded, "The Negro people are against this war" ("The Negro and the War," Box 20, F. 10, REP).

25. James Ford, "The Negro People and the New World Situation," *Communist* 20 (August 1941), 696–204; Frederick Douglass, "Negroes and the National War Effort," speech of 6 July 1863, rpt. in *Communist* 21 (April 1942), 262–69; Ben Davis Jr., "The Communists, the Negro People, and the War," *Communist* 21 (August 1942), 633–39; "Have Communists Quit Fighting for Negro Rights?" *Negro Digest* 3, no. 2 (December 1944), 56–70. For the argument that the wartime CP channeled but did not abandon the struggle against racism, see Maurice Isserman, *Which Side Were You On? The Communist Party During the Second World War* (Middletown, Conn.: Wesleyan University Press, 1982), 55–82, 141–43; and Philip W. Foner, *Organized Labor and the Black Worker*, 2nd ed. (New York: International Publishers, 1982), 278–85. For a highly critical account, see Earl Ofari Hutchinson, *Blacks and Reds: Race and Class in Conflict 1919–1990* (East Lansing: Michigan State University Press, 1995). Racial violence during the war and the track record of the FEPC are discussed in Gary Gerstle, *American Crucible: Race and Nation in the Twentieth Century* (Princeton: Princeton University Press, 2001), chapter 5, "Good War, Race War"; and Daniel Kryder, *Divided Arsenal: Race and the American State During World War II* (Cambridge, England: Cambridge University Press, 2001). For more on the Negro press during the war, and especially the Double-V campaign, see Lee Finkle, *Forum for Protest: The Black Press During World War II* (Rutherford, N.J.: Fairleigh Dickinson University Press, 1975). See also Barbara Dianne Savage, *Broadcasting Freedom: Radio, War, and the Politics of Race, 1938–1948* (Chapel Hill: University of North Carolina Press, 1999).

26. Ellison, "Native Land," *New Masses*, 2 June 1942, 29. On the wartime Detroit riots, see Max Weiss, "Fifth-Column Diversion in Detroit," *Communist* 22 (August 1943), 698–710; and John L. Spivak, "Unmasking the KKK," *New Masses* 21 (April 1942), 4–9. For a detailed description of the making of *Native Land* over several years (it was in fact begun in 1939), see William Alexander, *Film on the Left: American Documentary Film from 1931 to 1942* (Princeton: Princeton University Press, 1981), 206–42. Produced before Pearl Harbor, the film, which featured many episodes of violent racism and anti-unionism, flopped in 1942; CP leaders Earl Browder and William Z.

27. "Let This People Fight," editorial, *New Masses*, 20 October 1942, 2; Ellison, "The Way It Is," *New Masses*, 20 October 1942, rpt. in CE, 310–19, quotes on 312, 315, 316, and 319.

28. Ellison, "You Can't Get Around It" (original title of "The Way It Is"), F. 1, Box 166, REP; John Randolph, "'Native Son' Down Below," *New Masses*, 10 March 1942, 21. For the argument that in "The Way It Is" Ellison "intrudes on the boundaries of [Mrs. Jackson's] personal identity" with a "political program [that] seems somewhat externally imposed," see William R. Nash, "*Invisible Man* as 'a Form of Social Power': The Evolution of Ralph Ellison's Politics," *Ralph Ellison and the Raft of Hope: A Political Companion to* Invisible Man, ed. Lucas Morel (Lexington: University of Kentucky Press, 2004), 11.

29. "Ralph Ellison," Report by Office of Naval Intelligence, FBI File, Request Number 1046404–00; Angelo Herndon, *Let Me Live* (New York: Random House, 1937), 304; "Words Can Be Bullets," *New Masses*, 28 November 1942. Marlon B. Ross's otherwise useful introduction to the reissue of Herndon's autobiography in 2007 contains no information about Herndon's life after he quit the CP. Angelo Herndon, *Let Me Live* (Ann Arbor: University of Michigan Press, 2007), vii–xli. In his autobiography the poet and journalist Frank Marshall Davis berated Wright for publishing his anti-Communist essay, "I Tried to Be a Communist" (1944), noting that Wright was "paid for his attacks at very nice rates" while Angelo Herndon had "turned down an opportunity to 'tell all' to the Hearst press for substantial financial gain." Davis, *Livin' the Blues: Memoirs of a Black Journalist and Poet*, ed. John Edgar Tidwell (Madison: University of Wisconsin Press, 1992), 243–44. While Herndon apparently got involved in some shady and embarrassing business dealings in Chicago in the 1950s, he remained in contact with various African American CP leaders (e.g., William Patterson, Claude Lightfoot) and, according to the *Chicago Defender*, in 1963 participated in a Negro History Week celebration at the Hopewell Baptist Church (*Chicago Defender*, 9 February 1963). In *Black America and the World Revolution* (New York: New Outlook, 1970), 39, Lightfoot alluded to the Herndon and Scottsboro cases as "significant turning points in the struggle for black liberation in the United States." For more on Herndon as a model of Ellison's invisible man, see chapter 7; and Frederick T. Griffiths, "Ralph Ellison, Richard Wright, and the Case of Angelo Herndon," *African American Review* 35, no. 4 (2001), 615–37. Lawrence Jackson asserts that for several months after ceasing to publish in the *New Masses* Ellison continued to contribute "unsigned editorials" (RE:E, 279). I am indebted to Dick Johnson Reavis for a copy of Ellison's FBI file (personal communication, 7 June 1999). For an astute assessment of Ellison's connection with the CP, see Reavis's M.A. thesis, "Defamatory Man: Ralph Ellison and the Communist Party (University of Texas at Arlington, May 1998).

30. Larry Neal's seminal essay "Ellison's Zoot Suit" (1970) broke ranks with the black nationalist critiques of Ellison hitherto prevailing among African American critics (with few exceptions, such as Ishmael Reed and the circle around Yardbird).

Neal's essay has supplied the locus classicus of culturalist readings of the fourth and final *Negro Quarterly* editorial, reprinted in Kimberly Benston, ed., *Speaking for You: The Vision of Ralph Ellison* (Washington, D.C.: Howard University Press, 1987), 105–24. This editorial from 1943 is the only one that has been republished. Eric J. Sundquist, ed., *Cultural Contexts for Invisible Man* (Boston: Bedford Books, 1995), 233–40.

31. "Statement of Policy," editorial, *Negro Quarterly* 1, no. 2 (spring 1942), 3; Abner W. Berry, "The *Negro Quarterly*: A Vigorous Journal," *Daily Worker*, 15 September 1942, 7.

32. In an interview with John Hersey in 1982 Ellison noted that Herndon had invited Ellison onto *Negro Quarterly* because he "wanted someone who was familiar with literature to work with him" ("A Completion of Personality," *CE*, 815).

33. Angelo Herndon, "Frederick Douglass: Negro Leadership and War," *Negro Quarterly* 1, no. 4 (winter–spring 1943), 311, 323. Ellison's journal from this period contains sections copied out of Benjamin Quarles's "The Breach between Douglass and Garrison," *Journal of Negro History* 23 (April 1938), 144–54 (Notes 1942–50, F. 11, Box 152, REP). As Ellison's close colleague, Herndon was probably familiar with this essay.

34. Ellison, "Transition," *Negro Quarterly* 1, no. 1 (spring 1942), 87, 91, 92. For a discussion of Ellison's original *New Masses* review of *Blood on the Forge*, see chapter 2.

35. Ellison, "Editorial Comment," *Negro Quarterly* 1, no. 2 (summer 1942), i–iv.

36. Ellison, "Editorial Comment," *Negro Quarterly* 1, no. 3 (fall 1942), 195–96, 240; Notes 1942–50, F. 6, Box 152, REP; Ellison, introduction to *Invisible Man*, 1982, xxi.

37. Ellison, "Editorial Comment," *Negro Quarterly* 1, no. 4 (winter–spring 1943), 295–300. For more on William Hastie and the Black Cabinet, see Richard Dalfiume, "Military Segregation and the 1940 Presidential Election," *Freedom's Odyssey: African American History Essays from Phylon*, ed. Alexa Benson Henderson and Janice Sumler-Edward (Atlanta, Ga.: Clark Atlanta University Press, 1999), 353–69; and Kryder, *Divided Arsenal*, 35–38.

38. Ellison, "Editorial Comment," *Negro Quarterly* 1, no. 4 (winter–spring 1943): 301–2.

39. Hill, *RACON*, 41; Talmadge quoted in Thomas Borstellman, *The Cold War and the Color Line: American Race Relations in the Global Arena* (Cambridge, Mass.: Harvard University Press, 2001), 44. For more on the politics of the zoot suit and the zoot suit riots, see Robin D. G. Kelley, *Race Rebels* (New York: Free Press, 1994), 161–81; Lawrence Jackson, "Ralph Ellison, Sharpies, Rinehart, and Politics," *Massachusetts Review* 40, no. 1 (1999), 71–95; and Stuart Cosgrove, "The Zoot-Suit and Style Warfare," *History Workshop Journal* 18 (1984), 77–91.

40. Ellison to Horace Cayton, n.d., F. 6, Box 60, REP.

41. Ellison, *Negro Quarterly*, F. 1, Box 96, REP.

42. Ibid.

43. *Negro Quarterly*, F. 2, Box 96, REP. Jones set forth his analysis of the slave roots of African American culture in *Blues People: Negro Music in White America* (New York: William Morrow, 1963). Ellison's review in 1964 would sharply criticize Jones's book for its "distracting . . . straining for a note of militancy" ("Blues People," *CE*, 279).

44. Ellison, *Negro Quarterly*, F. 2, Box 96, REP.

45. Rampersad, *RE:B*, 170–86. For more on the N M U and antiracism at sea, see chapter 5.
46. Ellison to Babb, quoted in Rampersad, *RE:B*, 158, 165. The term "talented tenth" referred to the elitist doctrine that only one of ten African Americans was qualified to lead the rest; it was first given widespread circulation in W. E. B. Du Bois's essay of that name published in *The Negro Problem* (James Pott and Company, 1903).
47. Add Bates to "Brother Campbell," 19 February 1943, F. 5, Box 60, R E P; Rampersad, *RE:B*, 167; Ellison, "New World A-Coming," *Tomorrow* 3 (September 1943), 68; Roi Ottley, *"New World A-Coming": Inside Black America* (Boston: Houghton Mifflin, 1943), 242, 243. Ottley's book would become the basis of a New York-based radio program in 1944–45 largely focused on civil rights concerns; it was broadcast over W M C A (Savage, *Broadcasting Freedom*, 246–60).
48. Ellison, *"An American Dilemma*: A Review," *CE*, 337–38, 333–35.
49. Ellison, *"An American Dilemma*: A Review," F. 10, Box 105, R E P. In a preface apparently intended for the review's publication in *Shadow and Act* in 1964, Ellison asserted that the piece had been written from the vantage point of a "vague anti-Marxist Marxism" and claimed that he had been "disenchanted with politics following 1939 and 1940 when Richard Wright left the C.P." This statement is of dubious value, since Wright, as Ellison well knew, did not leave the C P until 1943. Michel Fabre, *The Unfinished Quest of Richard Wright*, trans. Isabel Barzun, 2nd ed. (Urbana: University of Illinois Press, 1993), 229–32. Ellison's commentary on *An American Dilemma*, while more sympathetic to Myrdal's psychological emphasis, was in several key points aligned with Herbert Aptheker's Marxist polemic of two years later, *The Negro People in America: A Critique of Gunnar Myrdal's "An American Dilemma"* (New York: International Publishers, 1946).
50. Eugene Dennis, "Postwar Labor-Capital Cooperation," *Political Affairs* 24, no. 5 (1945), 415–22; "The Path to Peace, Progress and Prosperity: Proceedings of the Constitutional Convention of the Communist Political Association," New York, May 20–22, 1944, 83, 115 (New York: Communist Political Association, 1944). See also Isserman, *Which Side Were You On?*, 187–213; Harry Haywood, *Black Bolshevik: The Autobiography of an Afro-American Communist* (Chicago: Liberator Press, 1978), 529–69; James W. Ford, "Tehran and the Negro People," *Communist* 23, no. 3 (1944), 260–66. Reflecting this reformist shift, the *Communist* was renamed *Political Affairs* in January 1945.
51. Ellison, "Richard Wright's Blues—Drafts and Partial Drafts," F. 3, Box 105, R E P; Fabre, *The Unfinished Quest of Richard Wright*, 253–54. The manuscript can be dated by its reference to the Harlem uprising of August 1943 as having happened within the last year. The entire text of Wright's autobiography was published as *Black Boy (American Hunger)* by the Library of America in 1993; the two sections were titled "Southern Night" and "The Horror and the Glory." For a comparison of the different versions, see Christopher Z. Hobson, "Richard Wright's Communisms: Textual Variance, Intentionality, and Socialization in *American Hunger*, 'I Tried to Be a Communist,' and *The God That Failed*," *Text* 6 (1994), 307–44. While there are some small differences between the two versions published under the title "I Tried to Be

a Communist" in the *Atlantic Monthly* in 1944 and in *The God That Failed* in 1950, the dramatic difference is between both of these on the one hand and the *American Hunger* version on the other. Wright settled on the title *Black Boy*, as well as the relatively upbeat ending of the 1945 text, at the suggestion of his publisher.

52. Ellison, "Richard Wright's Blues—Drafts and Partial Drafts," F. 3, Box 105, REP. Large hunks of the last fifteen pages of the longer text were pared away from the version published in "I Tried to Be a Communist"; the omitted materials stress the pull of the CP's interracialism, intellectualism, atheism, and spirit of self-sacrifice. The Communist cartoonist and illustrator Ollie Harrington reported that, on the tenth anniversary of the publication of *The God That Failed*, Wright was invited to submit an updated version of "I Tried to Be a Communist." Living in Paris Wright expressed regret at having made the original contribution and declared that "he would write an essay on racism and the cloak and dagger terrorism that was poisoning the climate around the expatriate Paris community.... They can publish that in their goddam 10th anniversary issue." Oliver W. Harrington, *Why I Left America and Other Essays* (Jackson: University Press of Mississippi, 1993), 23. Despite his growing alienation from the CP, in 1944 Ellison continued to refer to Trotskyists as "wreckers," a view he had previously expressed to his friend Joe Lazenberry in April 1939 (Rampersad, RE:B, 123). While in 1971 Ellison referred to "Stalinist Communists" and after the publication of *Invisible Man* was on friendly terms with a number of New York Intellectuals who were former Trotskyists, his stated antipathy to Communists and Communism did not routinely invoke the discourse of anti-Stalinism (Graham and Singh, *Conversations with Ralph Ellison*, 200).

53. Ellison, "Richard Wright's Blues—Drafts and Partial Drafts," F. 3, Box 105, REP.

54. Ibid.

55. Ibid.

56. Ellison, "Richard Wright's Blues," CE, 129, 143; Ellison, "Richard Wright's Blues—Drafts and Partial Drafts, F. 3, Box 105, REP. Wright approved Ellison's use of psychoanalysis and "the individualistic and pre-individualistic concepts" in the review, but wrote to Ellison, "I do see the blues concept, but only slightly" (Wright to Ellison, 25 July 1945, F. 1, Box 76, REP). For more on the disparity between Wright's and Ellison's blues (in the published essay of 1945), see Adam Gussow, "'Fingering the Jagged Grain': Ellison's Wright and the Southern Blues Violence," *boundary 2* 30, no. 2 (2003), 137-55.

57. Reportage in the 1944 *Daily Worker* indicates that many rank-and-file Communists continued the fight against Jim Crow in the military and the factories. See Judith Stepan-Norris and Maurice Zeitlin, *Left Out: Reds and America's Industrial Unions* (Cambridge, England: Cambridge University Press, 2003), 253-58; Neelson Peery, *Black Fire: The Making of an American Revolutionary* (New York: Free Press, 1994); Interview with Howard "Stretch" Johnson, 6 June 1988, by Richard Wormser, part 2, Oral History of the American Left, Tamiment Library, New York University. Johnson stated, "I was actively trying to organize the [Black] enlisted men in the 92nd [Division] to struggle against Jim Crow and segregation.... White officers were

being fragged in the 92nd because they had generated so much hostility in the enlisted men. . . . When we got overseas, where we were dealing with live ammo, a lot
of white officers got popped by our side. . . . There was a lot of respect for the Rus-
sians. . . . So that being a Communist did not operate against me among the men. I
had their respect."

58. Adam Clayton Powell Sr., *Riots and Ruins* (New York: Richard R. Smith, 1945), 102;
Adam Clayton Powell Jr., *Marching Blacks* (1945; rev. ed., New York: Dial Press, 1973),
141; Ellison, "Richard Wright's Blues," CE, 128.

59. Ellison to Hyman, 16 September 1945, F. 1, Box 51, REP; Jacques Duclos, "On the
Dissolution of the Communist Party of the United States," *Political Affairs* 24, no. 7
(1945), 656–72; Doxey Wilkerson, "Speech by Doxey Wilkerson," *Political Affairs* 24,
no. 7 (1945), 619–21. The Duclos letter was extensively commented on in the *New
Masses, Daily Worker,* and *Political Affairs* starting in mid-1945. For an astute analysis
of the issues involved, see Haywood, *Black Bolshevik,* 529–604.

60. Ellison to Burke, 23 November 1945, F. 1, Box 38, REP.

61. Ellison to Wright, 22 July, 18 August, and 5 August 1945, F. 1314, Box 97, RWP.

62. In 1957 Ellison would push back the date marking the bankruptcy of the left by still
another decade, remarking that the level of discussion at an abidingly left-leaning
PEN conference that had just readmitted Hungary was "abysmally low . . . thanks
to much repetition of politico-cultural theories discredited some thirty years ago"
(Rampersad, RE:B, 365).

63. Ellison to Wright, 18 August 1945, F. 1314, Box 97, RWP. For more on the Ellison-
Wright correspondence of the mid- to late 1940s, see Michel Fabre, "From *Native
Son* to *Invisible Man*: Some Notes on Ralph Ellison's Evolution in the 1950s," in
Benston, *Speaking for You,* 199–216. The black intellectuals interested in publishing
the magazine included Horace Cayton, St. Clair Drake, Lawrence Reddick, Elmer
Carter, C. L. R. James, Wright, and Ellison; the former Trotskyists Bernard Wolfe
and James T. Farrell expressed interest in supporting it. Titled *American Pages,* the
journal would have focused on the implications of the theory of "lag." Constance
Webb, *Richard Wright: A Biography* (New York: G. P. Putnam's Sons, 1968), 214–20.
While it has been speculated that Ellison developed the view of African Americans
as at once rearguard and vanguard through contact with James's application of the
Trotskyist view of "permanent revolution" to the Negro question, Ellison encountered James only in the mid-1940s, some seven years after he first articulated the
view (see chapter 2). See William J. Maxwell, "'Creative and Cultural Lag,'" *A Historical Guide to Ralph Ellison,* ed. Steven Tracy (New York: Oxford University Press,
2004), 59–83.

64. Ellison to Burke, 23 November 1945, F. 1, Box 38, REP; Ellison to Wright, 18 August
1945, F. 1314, Box 97, RWP.

65. Ellison to Wright, 1 February 1948, F. 1314, Box 97; RWP; Ellison, "The Booker T.,"
New Republic 114 (1946), 262.

66. Ellison, "Beware of the Snake Who Dresses Like a Man," *People's Daily World,*
17 November 1954, 5; Ellison, FBI File.

Chapter Two: Developing an Aesthetic

1. Ellison, "The World and the Jug," CE, 155–88, quote p. 185; Ellison, "Hidden Name and Complex Fate," CE, 189–209; Ellison, "The Art of Fiction: An Interview," CE, 210–24. Other Euro-American writers whom Ellison claimed as nineteenth- and twentieth-century ancestors are Gertrude Stein, Henry David Thoreau, Søren Kierkegaard, Joseph Conrad, Feodor Dostoevsky, Leo Tolstoy, Nikolai Gogol, Franz Kafka, Isaac Babel, Maxim Gorki, Mikhail Sholokhov, Marcel Proust, Thomas Mann, Jean-Paul Sartre, André Gide, and Albert Camus. Much has been written about Ellison's multiple literary influences; the most comprehensive studies are John S. Wright, *Shadowing Ralph Ellison* (Jackson: University Press of Mississippi, 2006); and Alan Nadel, *Invisible Criticism: Ralph Ellison and the American Canon* (Iowa City: University of Iowa Press, 1988).

2. Regarding the centrality of the African American literary tradition to *Invisible Man*, see Robert B. Stepto, "Literacy and Hibernation: Ralph Ellison's *Invisible Man*," *Speaking for You: The Vision of Ralph Ellison*, ed. Kimberly W. Benston (Washington, D.C.: Howard University Press, 1987), 360–85.

3. David L. Carson, "Ralph Ellison: Twenty Years After," *Conversations with Ralph Ellison*, ed. Maryemma Graham and Amritjit Singh (Jackson: University Press of Mississippi, 1995), 200; Ellison, "New Left-Wing American Writers," F. 2, Box 103, REP.

4. Ellison, "New Left-Wing American Writers," F. 2, Box 103, REP.

5. Ellison, "Javanese Folklore," *New Masses*, 26 December 1939, 25–26, quote p. 26; Ellison, "Philippine Report," *Direction* 4 (summer 1941), 13.

6. Ellison, "Negro Prize Fighter," *New Masses*, 17 December 1940, 26–27, quote p. 27; Ellison, "Ruling-Class Southerner," *New Masses*, 5 December 1939, 27. Len Zinberg was a Communist novelist who changed his name to Ed Lacy during the cold war. See Robert Niemi, "Ed Lacy 1911–1968," *American Writers: A Collection of Literary Biographies*, ed. Jay Parini (Detroit: Gale, 2006), 193–96; and Alan M. Wald, *Trinity of Passion: The Literary Left and the Antifascist Crusade* (Chapel Hill: University of North Carolina Press, 2007), 1–15. For more on the intertextual relation between Zinberg's novel and *Invisible Man*, see Joseph Ramsey, "Red Pulp: Radicalism and Repression in Mid-Twentieth-Century U.S. 'Genre Fiction,'" PH.D. dissertation, Tufts University, 2007.

7. Ellison, "Creative and Cultural Lag," *New Challenge: A Literary Quarterly* 2, no. 2 (1937), 90–91. The early twentieth-century sociologist William Ogburn, while not a Marxist, developed a theory of *lag* in relation to social and cultural processes that was influential in left and progressive circles. See "The Hypothesis of Cultural Lag," *The Making of Society*, ed. V. F. Calverton (New York: Modern Library, 1937), 719–30.

8. Ellison, "Big White Fog," *New Masses*, 12 November 1940, 22–23. For more on the production of Ward's play, see Rena Fraden, *Blueprints for a Black Federal Theatre, 1935–1939* (Cambridge, England: Cambridge University Press, 1994), 115–35. Ellison later wrote to Wright that the *New Masses* editors had asked him to remove from his review consideration of the play's tragic dimension (5 August 1945, F. 1314, Box 97, RWP). Abner Berry, a Communist leader in Harlem, recalled that during a late-night discussion among Wright, Ward, Ellison, and himself each writer described

a favored trope to signify the situation of African Americans. Wright designated a cage; Ward, a fog; Ellison, a road that was "fraught with dangers at every turn [and] had no end." Oral History of the American Left, interview with Abner Berry, 5 September 1977, tape 1. Ward evidently recalled this discussion in 1947 in his attack on Wright, whose choice of the cage he criticized as defeatist. "Five Negro Novelists' Revolt and Retreat," *Masses and Mainstream* 1 (winter 1947), 100–109.

9. Ellison, "Stormy Weather," *New Masses*, 24 September 1940, 20–21; Ellison, FBI File, FIOA Request 1046404–000. "Stormy weather" was a phrase from the CP songbook (1940), revised—in acknowledgment of hard times following the Nonaggression Pact of 1939—from "Now is the time to get together / This is anti-fascist weather" to "Now is the time to get together / This is stormy weather." Maurice Isserman, *Which Side Were You On? The American Communist Party During the Second World War* (Middletown, Conn.: Wesleyan University Press, 1982), 55.

10. Ellison, "The Great Migration," *New Masses*, 2 December 1941, 23–24.

11. Karl Marx, "Manifesto of the Communist Party," 1848, *The Portable Karl Marx*, ed. and trans. Eugene Kamenka (New York: Penguin, 1983), 207.

12. David Wilson, "Treasury of Negro Literature," *Sunday Worker*, 8 March 1942, 6. Ellison identified this review by "David Wilson" as his own in a letter to Kenneth Burke (4 December 1946, F. 1, Box 38, REP). Allen's *The Negro Question in the United States* (New York: International Press, 1936) was the principal CP official statement until it was replaced by Harry Haywood's *Negro Liberation* (New York: International Press, 1948).

13. Ellison, "Recent Negro Fiction," *New Masses*, 5 August 1941, 22–26. A shorter version of the essay was published as "Richard Wright and Recent Negro Fiction" in *Direction* 4 (summer 1941), 12–13. Fragmentary comments on Wright's short stories among Ellison's notes indicate that he may have planned to write a review of *Uncle Tom's Children* that would have stressed the meaning of "tragic action" as "the price one may have to pay for the satisfaction of living according to one's ever-expanding convictions, of challenging what is for one's own good because it is for the common good" (Notes 1942–50, F. 2, Box 151, REP).

14. Ellison, "Recent Negro Fiction," 22–26.

15. Richard Wright, "How Bigger Was Born," *Native Son* (1940; revised and reprinted, New York: Library of America, 1993), 514–15; Wright, "Blueprint for Negro Writing," *New Challenge* 2, no. 2 (1937), 53–65, quotes pp. 53, 54, 61. In her somewhat jaundiced biography of Wright, Margaret Walker insists that "Blueprint" appeared under Wright's "signature" but "expressed many ideas and opinions held collectively by members of the South Side Writers' Group." Walker, *Richard Wright, Daemonic Genius: A Portrait of the Man, a Critical Look at His Work* (New York: Warner Books, 1988), 77, 111.

16. Ellison to Wright, 22 April 1940 and 3 November 1941, F. 1314, RWP; Ellison, "The World and the Jug," CE, 164, 167. For instances of Ellison's later denials of Wright's influence and attribution of greater importance to Hemingway and Eliot, see Graham and Singh, *Conversations with Ralph Ellison*, 319–63; Ralph Ellison, introduction to *Shadow and Act*, CE, 49–60; Ralph Ellison, "Remembering Richard Wright,"

CE, 663–79. For a discussion of both Ellison's and Wright's divergences from the formulation of the folk-proletarian relationship outlined in "Blueprint for Negro Writing," see Robin Lucy, "'Flying Home': Ralph Ellison, Richard Wright, and the Black Folk During World War II," *Journal of American Folklore* 120 (2007), 257–83.

17. Ellison, "Change the Joke and Slip the Yoke," *CE*, 111–12; Ellison, "A Very Stern Discipline," (1965), *CE*, 737; Ellison, "Indivisible Man," *CE* 395–96. For the argument that Ellison's approach to myth and ritual was politically regressive, see Ernest Kaiser, "A Critical Look at Ellison's Fiction and at Social and Literary Criticism by and about the Author," *Black World* 20 (December 1970), 53–59, 81–97; and Susan L. Blake, "Ritual and Rationalization: Black Folklore in the Works of Ralph Ellison," *PMLA* 94, no. 1 (1979), 121–36. For an early defense of his method as a means of connecting with white readers, see Lawrence J. Clipper, "Folkloric and Mythic Elements in *Invisible Man*," *CLA Journal* 13 (March 1970), 229–41.

18. Ellison, F. 11, Box 152, REP. See Thomas Wentworth Higginson, *Black Rebellion: A Selection from Travelers and Outlaws* (1889; rpt. New York: Arno, 1969), 215–75, quote p. 225.

19. Ellison, F. 11, Box 152, REP. Ellison's conceptualization of slave revolts as a form of class struggle was clearly influenced by contemporaneous CP historiography, most notably the work of Herbert Aptheker. See *Negro Slave Revolts in the United States, 1526–1860* (New York: International Publishers, 1939).

20. See Hercules Armstrong, "Do They Mean Me?," *New Masses*, 19 July 1938, 6; James P. Johnson and Langston Hughes, "De Organizer: A Blues Opera in One Act," *The Political Plays of Langston Hughes*, ed. Susan Duffy (Carbondale: Southern Illinois University Press, 2000), 177–190, quote p. 183; Donald Ogden Stewart, ed., *Fighting Words* (New York: Harcourt, Brace, 1940), 25–27. Bernard Evslin's proletarian poem, "To Hercules Armstrong," contains the line "For you no Congo drums, no weary blues." The poem was published in a mimeographed pamphlet and issued by "The Young American Writers"; it is filed under "Communism" among Ellison's papers (F. 6, Box 200, REP). *Narodnost* signified both the distinctness of Russian folk culture and the responsibility of the artist to represent folk interests. As an instance of the cultural matrix that the Soviets defined as "national in form, socialist in content," it was connected with traditions of collective resistance and could be articulated with folk cultures elsewhere. See Kate A. Baldwin, *Beyond the Color Line and the Iron Curtain: Reading Encounters between Black and Red, 1922–1963* (Durham, N.C.: Duke University Press, 2002), 208. Ellison saw the Federal Theater production of *John Henry* and determined that even "Paul Robeson's distinct talent couldn't save" the play. "TAC Negro Show," *New Masses*, 27 February 1940, 29–30, quote p. 30. After the war George Pal and United Productions of America produced a nonstereotyped cartoon image of the "steel-drivin' man in *John Henry and the Inky-Poo*, which was awarded an Academy Award nomination for Best Cartoon Short Subject of 1946. Christopher Lehman, "The New Black Animated Images of 1946," *Journal of Popular Film and Television* 29 (summer 2001), 74–82.

21. Wright, "Blueprint for Negro Writing," 56–57; "John Henry" quoted in Lawrence Levine, *Black Culture and Black Consciousness: Afro-American Folk Thought from Slavery*

to Freedom (New York: Oxford University Press, 1977), 438. The definitive account of John Henry as both historical and legendary figure is Scott Reynolds Nelson's *Steel Drivin' Man: John Henry, the Untold Story of an American Legend* (New York: Oxford University Press, 2006). See also Mac Edward Leach, "John Henry," *Folklore and Society: Essays in Honor of Benjamin A. Botkin*, ed. Bruce Jackson (Hatboro, Penna.: Folklore Associates, 1966), 93–106; H. Nigel Thomas, *From Folklore to Fiction: A Study of Folk Heroes and Rituals in the Black American Novel* (Westport, Conn.: Greenwood Press, 1988), 56–60; Norm Cohen, *Long Steel Rail: The Railroad in American Folksong*, 2nd ed. (Urbana: University of Illinois Press, 2000), 61–89; and Richard M. Dorson, "The Career of 'John Henry,'" *Mother Wit from the Laughing Barrel: Readings in the Interpretation of Afro-American Folklore*, ed. Alan Dundes (Jackson: University Press of Mississippi, 1990), 568–77. Books about John Henry to which Ellison would have had access include Louis W. Chappell, *John Henry: A Folk-Lore Study* (1933; rpt. Port Washington, N.Y.: Kennikat Press, 1968); and Roark Bradford's children's book, *John Henry* (New York: Literary Guild, 1931). Both were riddled with racial stereotypes. "Hammer" ("How's your hammer hanging?") also carried sexual innuendoes.

22. Richard Wright, "Joe Louis Uncovers Dynamite," *New Masses*, 8 October 1935. Wright to Ellison, n.d., F. 2, Box 76, REP. Wright's blues poem "King Joe" was produced by Okeh Records with Paul Robeson's vocals and Count Basie's instrumentals. Louis's public image is discussed in Jeffrey T. Sammons, *Beyond the Ring: The Role of Boxing in American Society* (Urbana: University of Illinois Press, 1988), 96–129; and Gerald Early, *The Culture of Bruising: Essays on Prizefighting, Literature, and Modern American Culture* (Hopewell, N.J.: Ecco Press, 1994), 23–32. For more on the links between John Henry and Joe Louis, see Levine, *Black Culture and Black Consciousness*, 420–40. Lawrence Jackson speculates that Ellison authored the unattributed (and highly laudatory) profile of Joe Louis appearing in the *New Masses* on 20 January 1942. "The Birth of the Critic: The Literary Friendship of Ralph Ellison and Richard Wright," *American Literature* 72, no. 2 (2000), 334. Both Henry Armstrong and Joe Louis had friendly relationships with the CP through Ben Davis in the late 1930s. Gerald C. Horne, *Black Liberation/Red Scare: Ben Davis and the Communist Party* (Newark: University of Delaware Press, 1994), 62.

23. Ellison, "Change the Joke and Slip the Yoke," *CE*, 100–112; Hyman to Ellison, 19 July 1942, 24 June 1942, F. 1, Box 51, REP; Ellison, interview with Reed et al., in Graham and Singh, *Conversations with Ralph Ellison*, 347; Stanley Edgar Hyman, *The Armed Vision: A Study in the Methods of Modern Literary Criticism* (New York: Knopf, 1948); Judy Oppenheimer, *Private Demons: The Life of Shirley Jackson* (New York: G. P. Putnam's Sons, 1988), 60, 103–4; Ellison to Hyman, 13 August 1948, F. 1, Box 51, REP. Ellison's famous riposte was originally published in *Partisan Review* alongside Hyman's "The Negro Writer in America: An Exchange," *Partisan Review* 22, no. 2 (1958), 197–211. While he was justifiably miffed about Hyman's misreading of the invisible man as a trickster, Ellison's response exaggerated Hyman's claims about "timeless archetype[s]" and underplayed Hyman's appreciation of the usage of irony by African American writers. Perhaps more than this debate had sparked Ellison's anger; he wrote to Albert Murray soon after the back-and-forth was published, "[Hyman] recently ac-

cused me of having sold out to the movers and shakers of the world" (Ellison to Murray, 28 September 1958, quoted in Rampersad, *RE:B*, 369; this letter is not contained in *Trading Twelves*). Hyman's stated aim in writing *The Armed Vision* was to enable more people to become "capable critics," a project that "menaces . . . vested interests [that] are much bigger game than the priesthood of literary criticism" (9).

24. Hyman to Ellison, 19 July 1945 and 22 August 1945, F. 1, Box 51, REP; Hyman, "Myth, Ritual and Nonsense," *Kenyon Review* 11, no. 3 (summer 1949), 455–75, quotes pp. 463, 471. Hyman theorized the blues as the cultural expression of the Negro lumpenproletariat; Ellison cautioned him to "be careful when applying Marxist concepts to American Negro experience" because of the "fluidity of Negro class lines" (Ellison to Hyman, n.d., Box 6, Stanley Edgar Hyman Papers [hereafter SEHP], Library of Congress). Ellison's close friend Albert Murray, who wrote his master's thesis on the symbolism of fertility and sterility in *The Waste Land* and *The Sun Also Rises*, contributed substantially to the practice of reading backward into *Invisible Man* a dehistoricized and depoliticized notion of myth and ritual. See Murray, *The Hero and the Blues* (Columbia: University of Missouri Press, 1973). The phrase "dedicated and set aside" figures centrally in *Invisible Man*; Ellison's familiar reference to it when writing to Hyman suggests its common usage in their conversations. See chapter 5.

25. See Sir James George Frazer, *The Golden Bough: A Study in Magic and Religion* (1911–13; rpt. New York: Macmillan, 1940), 1 volume abridged, 714; John B. Vickery, *The Literary Impact of The Golden Bough* (Princeton: Princeton University Press, 1973); and Hyman, *The Tangled Bank: Darwin, Marx, Frazer and Freud as Imaginative Writers* (New York: Atheneum, 1974). Through Frazer the Cambridge School could trace their roots back to Henri Hubert and Marcel Mauss's *Sacrifice: Its Nature and Function*, trans. W. D. Hall (Chicago: University of Chicago Press, 1898). For critiques of Hyman and the Cambridge School, see Joseph Fontenrose, *The Ritual Theory of Myth* (Berkeley: University of California Press, 1971); and H. S. Veresnel, "What's Sauce for the Goose Is Sauce for the Gander: Myth and Ritual, Old and New," *Approaches to Greek Myth*, ed. Lowell Edmunds (Baltimore: Johns Hopkins University Press, 1990), 23–90.

26. Jane Ellen Harrison, *Ancient Art and Ritual* (1918; rpt. London: Oxford University Press, 1948), 141; Bronislaw Malinowski, "Myth in Primitive Psychology" (1926; rpt. Westport, Conn.: Negro Universities Press, 1971), 93. See also Bronislaw Malinowski, "Frazer's Position in the Development of Ethnological Theory," *A Scientific Theory of Culture and Other Essays* (Chapel Hill: University of North Carolina Press, 1944), 187–95; Rhys Carpenter, *Folk Tale, Fiction and Saga in the Homeric Epics* (1946; rpt. Berkeley: University of California Press, 1956); Jessie Weston, *From Ritual to Romance* (1920; rpt. New York: Anchor Books, 1957); and Francis Fergusson, *The Idea of a Theater: A Study of Ten Plays: The Art of Drama in Changing Perspective* (Princeton: Princeton University Press, 1949). Ellison was enthusiastic about Fergusson's study, which prominently featured "purpose-passion-perception" and "the concept of tragic rhythm"; he tried to use his influence to get the book published at Random House (Ellison to Hyman, 17 June 1947, F. 1, Box 51, REP).

27. Lord Raglan, *The Hero: A Study in Tradition, Myth and Drama* (1936; rpt. Westport, Conn.: Greenwood Press, 1956); Otto Rank, *The Myth of the Birth of the Hero: A Psychological Interpretation of Mythology* (1914; rpt. New York: Johnson Reprint Corp, 1970); Maude Bodkin, *Archetypal Patterns in Poetry: Psychological Studies of Imagination* (London: Oxford University Press, 1934), 89; Philip Rahv, "The Myth and the Powerhouse," *Partisan Review* 20 (1953), 635–48; Wallace W. Douglas, "The Meanings of 'Myth' in Modern Criticism," *Modern Philology* 50 (1953), 232–42; Harrison, *Ancient Art and Ritual*, 158–59; Jane Ellen Harrison, *Themis: A Study of the Social Origins of Greek Religion, with an Excursus on the Ritual Forms Preserved in Greek Tragedy by Gilbert Murray* (1912; rpt. Cleveland: World Publishing, 1962), 485. Ellison's typed-out excerpts from Gilbert Murray's description of Hercules are in Notes 1942–50, F. 11, Box 152, REP. See also William Troy's essay "Myth, Method, and the Future," 1946, *Selected Essays*, ed. Stanley Edgar Hyman (New Brunswick, N.J.: Rutgers University Press, 1967), which Ellison read at Hyman's suggestion and found useful (Ellison to Hyman, 6 July 1948, F. 1, Box 51, REP).

28. William Empson, *Some Versions of Pastoral* (1935; rpt. Norfolk, Conn.: New Directions, 1950), 3–23; Christopher Caudwell, *Illusion and Reality: A Study of the Sources of Poetry* (1937; rpt. New York: International Publishers, 1970), 41. Ellison would be strongly influenced by Empson's *Seven Types of Ambiguity* (1930; London: Chatto and Windus, 1947), in which Empson defines the seventh and last type as entailing "two opposite meanings defined by the context, so that the total effect is to show a fundamental division in the writer's mind" (192). Ellison would refer frequently to "ambi-invisibility" in the notes and outlines of *Invisible Man*. Both Empson and Caudwell were included in a list of critics supplied by Hyman (Notes 1942–50, F. 5, Box 151, REP).

29. George Thomson, *Aeschylus and Athens: A Study in the Social Origins of Drama* (1940; rpt. New York: Grosset and Dunlap, 1968), iii, 39–40, 93–94, 141–53, 297, 307, 359. In 1950 John Howard Lawson drew upon Thomson's book in his historical materialist defense of the study of myth, praising the study's "dynamic projection of the beginning of class conflict." Lawson, "Myth and Money," *Masses and Mainstream* 3, no. 4 (1950), 72–82. Robert Graves, whose *The White Goddess* is mentioned in Ellison's notes (Notes 1942–50, F. 11, Box 152, REP), treated Hercules as another "pastoral sacred king" who is "bound and beaten by his comrades till he faints, then flayed, blinded, castrated, impaled with a mistletoe stake, and finally hacked into joints on the altar-stone." Graves, *The White Goddess: A Historical Grammar of Poetic Myth* (1948; revised edition, London: Faber and Faber, 1959), 124.

30. Ellison, Notes 1942–50, F. 4, Box 151, F. 10, Box 152, REP; Ellison, "Flamenco," CE, 25. The quotation about Hercules is from Gilbert Murray, *Greek Studies* (Oxford: Clarendon Press, 1946), "Herakles, 'The Best of Men,'" 106–126, quote p. 109. Murray spelled the name "Herakles," the Greek Anglicization (alternately "Heracles"); Ellison used the Latin name, "Hercules." Murray goes on to describe how this "great aboriginal hero . . . unspotted by the world and . . . perform[ing] great deeds, daring and suffering in the service of his village, of Hellas, of Humanity," eventually was

depoliticized and turned into a "Stoic saint" (111, 125). Ellison initially confused different Cambridge School writers, referring to Harrison as the author of *From Ritual to Romance* (Ellison to Hyman, 20 June 1946, F. 1, Box 51, REP).

31. William Sheldon, *Psychology and the Promethean Will: A Constructive Study of the Acute Common Problem of Education, Medicine and Religion* (New York: Harper and Brothers, 1936), 76, 89; Ellison to Wright, 22 April 1940, F. 1314, Box 97, RWP. Other African American texts making use of classical mythology include W. E. B. Du Bois's *The Quest of the Silver Fleece* (1911) and Countee Cullen's *Medea* (1935).

32. André Malraux, "An Interview with André Malraux," *International Literature* 4 (1934), 144–46, quote pp. 145–46; Malraux, "Literature in Two Worlds," *Partisan Review* 2, no. 6 (1935), 14–19, quote pp. 18–19; Malraux, "The Work of Art," *Partisan Review* 2, no. 9 (1935), 33–40. These essays are gathered in a folder marked "Malraux" in Ellison's references files (F. 3, Box 192, REP). Typical of Ellison's later comments about Malraux's fiction is his statement in 1955: "Whenever the heroes of *Man's Fate* regarded their condition during moments of heightened self-consciousness, their thinking was something other than Marxist" ("The Art of Fiction: An Interview," CE, 211).

33. Edward Bland, quoted in "Richard Wright's Blues," CE, 134; Erich Fromm, *Escape from Freedom* (New York: Rinehart, 1941), viii, 36. While making use of Freud in *Illusion and Reality*, Caudwell sharply criticized the subjective and idealist emphasis of psychoanalysis in "Freud: A Study in Bourgeois Psychology," *Studies in a Dying Culture* (1938; rpt. New York: Dodd and Mead, 1958), 158–92. For postwar leftist critiques of Freud, see "Psychoanalysis: A Reactionary Ideology," *Masses and Mainstream* 2, no. 9 (1949), 10–24 (a symposium translated and reprinted from *La Nouvelle Critique*, June 1949); and J. B. Furst, "The Philosophy of Freud," *Masses and Mainstream* 2, no. 12 (1949), 13–26.

34. Hyman, *The Armed Vision*, 205–6; Reuben Osborn, *Freud and Marx: A Dialectical Study* (New York: Equinox Co-Operative Press, 1937), 135, 184, 275; John Strachey, introduction to *Freud and Marx*, 12–13.

35. Harry Slochower, *No Voice Is Wholly Lost: Writers and Thinkers in War and Peace* (New York: Creative Age Press, 1945), 263–77, 309–18, quote pp. 316–17. Ellison thought highly of Slochower's essay "In the Fascist Styx," which appeared in the first issue of *Negro Quarterly* (Ellison to Hyman n.d., Box 6, SEHP; *Negro Quarterly* correspondence F. 6, Box 60, REP). When Slochower was attacked by Eric Bentley in the *Nation* in 1945, Hyman called it a "slimy red-baiting job" (Hyman to Ellison, 22 August 1945, F. 1, Box 51, REP).

36. Ellison, "Beating That Boy," CE, 145–49. The title refers to the practice of talking endlessly about the problems of race and racism.

37. Ibid., 148–50.

38. Ellison to Burke, 23 November 1945, F. 1, Box 38, REP; Ralph Ellison, "The Art of Fiction: An Interview" (1955), CE, 218–19; Graham and Singh, *Conversations with Ralph Ellison*, 363; Michael Denning, *The Cultural Front: The Laboring of American Culture in the Twentieth Century* (London: Verso, 1997), 436. Ellison extensively edited the galleys of *A Grammar of Motives* in 1945 (F. 7, Box 182, REP). For critical discussions that either

efface or sideline the Marxist origins of the Ellison-Burke relationship, see Gregg
Crane, "Ralph Ellison's Constitutional Faith," in Posnock, ed., *The Cambridge Companion to Ralph Ellison* (Cambridge: Cambridge University Press, 2005), 104–20; Beth Eddy, *The Rites of Identity: The Religious Naturalism and Cultural Criticism of Kenneth Burke and Ralph Ellison* (Princeton: Princeton University Press, 2003); Robert O'Meally, "On Burke and Vernacular: Ralph Ellison's Boomerang of History," *History and Memory in African-American Culture*, ed. Genevieve Fabre and Robert O'Meally (New York: Oxford University Press, 1994), 244–60; Robert Genter, "Toward a Theory of Rhetoric: Ralph Ellison, Kenneth Burke, and the Problem of Modernism," *Twentieth-Century Literature* 48, no. 2 (2002), 191–214; and Timothy L. Parrish, "Ralph Ellison, Kenneth Burke, and the Form of Democracy," *Arizona Quarterly* 52 (autumn 1995), 117–48.

39. Denning, *The Cultural Front*, 436; Hyman to Ellison, 19 July 1942, F. 1, Box 51; Ellison to Burke, 23 November 1945 F. 1, Box 38, REP; Burke to Malcolm Cowley, 1 December 1940, in Paul Jay, ed., *The Selected Correspondence of Kenneth Burke and Malcolm Cowley, 1915–1981* (New York: Viking, 1988), 232; Burke to Ellison, 16 December 1945, F. 1, Box 38, REP. Besides Denning, critics who recognize Burke's engagement with Marxism include Hyman, *The Armed Vision*, 347–94; Frank Lentricchia, *Criticism and Social Change* (Chicago: University of Chicago Press, 1983); Robert Wess, *Kenneth Burke: Rhetoric, Subjectivity, Postmodernism* (Cambridge, England: Cambridge University Press, 1996); and Fredric Jameson, "Symbolic Inference: or, Kenneth Burke and Ideological Analysis," *Representing Kenneth Burke: Selected Papers from the English Institute*, ed. Hayden White and Margaret Brose (Baltimore: Johns Hopkins University Press, 1982), 68–91.

40. Burke, "Rugged Portraiture," *New Masses* 11 (April 1934), 46; Burke, "Return after Flight," *New Masses* 18 (February 1936), 26; Burke, "Sour Note on Literary Criticism," *New Republic* 87 (June 1935), 211; Burke to Cowley 3 May 1950, in Jay, *The Selected Correspondence of Kenneth Burke and Malcolm Cowley*, 291. Burke viewed Empson's discussion of the proletarian hero in *Several Versions of Pastoral* as a "profoundly Marxist analysis." *The Philosophy of Literary Form: Studies in Symbolic Action* (Baton Rouge: Louisiana State University Press, 1941), 422–24, quote p. 424.

41. Burke, "My Approach to Communism," *New Masses* 10 (March 1934), 18–20, quote p. 19; Burke, *Permanence and Change: An Anatomy of Purpose* (New York: New Republic, 1935), 212–13; Burke, "Twelve Propositions by Kenneth Burke on the Relationship between Economics and Psychology," *Science & Society* 2 (1938), 242–49, quote p. 248; Burke, *A Grammar of Motives* (New York: Prentice-Hall, 1945), 209–14, quotes pp. 210, 214. Echoing Burke's title, Ellison headed one of his lists of Negro labor leaders with the words, "Twelve Propositions for the Application of Marxism to American Negroes" (Notes 1942–50, F. 9, Box 152, REP).

42. Burke, *The Philosophy of Literary Form*, 201; Burke, *Permanence and Change*, 26–28, 227–28; Burke, "Property as an Absolute," *New Republic*, 1 July 1936, 245–46, quote p. 245. The phrase "trained incapacity" was derived from Thorstein Veblen. See Erin Wais, "'Trained Incapacity': Thorstein Veblen and Kenneth Burke," *KB Journal* 2, no. 1 (2005), online.

43. Burke, *The Philosophy of Literary Form*, 192; Burke, "Twelve Propositions," 243; Burke, "What Is Americanism?," *Partisan Review and Anvil* 3 (1936), 9–11, quote p. 10; Burke, "War and Cultural Life," *American Journal of Sociology* 48 (November 1942), 404–10, quotes pp. 404, 405; Burke, "War and the Collectivistic Nature of Sacrifice," in *A Grammar of Motives*, 394–98, quote p. 398.

44. Burke, "Revolutionary Symbolism in America," 1935, *The Legacy of Kenneth Burke*, ed. Herbert W. Simons and Trevor Melia (Madison: University of Wisconsin Press, 1989), 267–273, quote p. 273; Burke, *The Philosophy of Literary Form*, 46; Burke, "Ideology and Myth," *Accent* 7, no. 4 (1947), 195–205, quotes pp. 204, 205; Burke, *A Rhetoric of Motives* (New York: Prentice-Hall, 1950), 105. In the midst of writing *Invisible Man* Ellison acknowledged that Burke's essay "Ideology and Myth" had "set off a few bells in [his] head" (Ellison to Burke, 25 August 1947, F. 1, Box 39, REP).

45. Burke to Cowley, 3 May 1950, in Jay, *The Selected Correspondence of Kenneth Burke and Malcolm Cowley*, 291; Wess, *Kenneth Burke*, 55–57; Jane Sanders, *Cold War on the Campus: Academic Freedom at the University of Washington* (Seattle: University of Washington Press, 1979), 105–14.

46. Graham and Singh, *Conversations with Ralph Ellison*, 202.

47. Burke, *The Philosophy of Literary Form*, 109, 9, 293, 74; Burke, *Counter-Statement* (1931; rpt. Los Altos: Hermes Press, 1953), 210, 161, 194. Lentricchia asserts that Burke's main contribution to Marxism is that he "took the difficult, sliding notion of ideology, bequeathed to us by *The German Ideology*, out of the areas of intellectual trickery and false consciousness and into the politically productive textual realms of practical consciousness" (*Criticism and Social Change*, 23).

48. Burke, "Ideology and Myth," 201; Burke, *The Philosophy of Literary Form*, 64; Burke, *Permanence and Change*, 148–49.

49. "Bellerophontic letter" refers to the situation of Bellerophon, a hero of Greek mythology who unknowingly delivered a letter that instructed its recipient to kill its bearer, Bellerophon himself.

50. Burke, *The Philosophy of Literary Form*, 20; Burke, *Counter-Statement*, 153, 171.

51. Burke, *The Philosophy of Literary Form*, 77; Fredric Jameson, *The Political Unconscious: Narrative as a Socially Symbolic Act* (Ithaca: Cornell University Press, 1981), 81–82; Lentricchia, *Criticism and Social Change*, 152; Graham and Singh, *Conversations with Ralph Ellison*, 212. While many critics discussing Burkean rhetoric in *Invisible Man* focus on the text's inset speeches, Leon Forrest has appreciated that Ellison's use of equations and clusters, along with, of course, the "purpose-passion-perception" triad, is key to his deployment of Burke's rhetorical theory. See Forrest, "Luminosity from the Lower Frequencies," *Ralph Ellison's Invisible Man: A Casebook*, ed. John F. Callahan (New York: Oxford University Press, 2004), 267–86.

52. Burke, *A Grammar of Motives*, xv–xxiii, 38–41, quote p. 41.

53. Burke, *The Philosophy of Literary Form*, 103; Burke, *Attitudes toward History* (1937; 2nd rev. ed. Los Altos, Calif: Hermes Publications, 1959), 210; Burke, "Twelve Propositions," 244–45; Graham and Singh, *Conversations with Ralph Ellison*, 261. For a discussion of the importance of "Twelve Propositions" in helping Burke map his theory of

dramatism, see Michael Feehan, "Kenneth Burke's Discovery of Dramatism," *Quarterly Journal of Speech* 65 (1979), 405–11.

54. Burke, *A Grammar of Motives*, 402–43, quotes pp. 402, 408; Burke, *Attitudes toward History*, 308–14. In his response to Schlauh, Burke also defended his merging of "categories" and "processes" into "categories of processes" as an enactment of the Hegelian dialectic ("Twelve Propositions," 249).

55. Burke, *The Philosophy of Literary Form*, 109, 76. For a discussion of the admixture of Platonic and Hegelian dialectics in Burke, see Wess, *Kenneth Burke*, 154–56; and Armin Paul Frank, *Kenneth Burke* (New York: Twayne, 1969), 137–38.

56. Burke, *Counter-Statement*, 42; Burke, *The Philosophy of Literary Form*, 202–3, 124; Burke, *A Rhetoric of Motives*, 22.

57. Wess, *Kenneth Burke*, 124; Burke, "Twelve Propositions," 244; Burke, "Without Benefit of Politics," *Nation* 143 (July 1936), 78.

58. Burke, *The Philosophy of Literary Form*, 39–40; Burke, *A Grammar of Motives*, 406.

59. Burke, *Attitudes toward History*, 188–89; Burke, *The Philosophy of Literary Form*, 45–46, 19, 202–3. For depoliticized readings of the "scapegoat process" in Burke, see C. Allen Carter, *Kenneth Burke and the Scapegoat Process* (Norman: University of Oklahoma Press, 1996); and Bernt Ostendorf, "Ralph Waldo Ellison: Anthropology, Modernism, and Jazz," *New Essays on* Invisible Man, ed. Robert O'Meally (Cambridge, England: Cambridge University Press, 1988), 95–121.

60. Burke to Ellison, 16 December 1945, F. 1, Box 38, REP; Orlando Patterson, *Rituals of Blood: Consequences of Slavery in Two American Centuries* (Washington, D.C.: Civitas/Counterpoint, 1998). Patterson discerns a duality in the scapegoated figure of the black American male but attributes it to the "Christian bifocal narrative of sacrifice" (218). Patterson pays extensive tribute to Ellison's "Twentieth-Century Fiction and the Black Mask of Humanity" in his formulation of the concept of the American Dionysus.

61. René Girard, *The Scapegoat*, trans. Yvonne Freccoro (Baltimore: Johns Hopkins University Press, 1986). Girard faults Frazer and the Cambridge School for confusing the scapegoat as "rite" with the scapegoat as "mechanism," as well as for being unaware of the extent to which texts themselves engage in "persecution" (25–30, 119–24). Despite its usefulness in textual analysis, Girard's highly Oedipalized theorization is significantly flawed by its relative inattention to what Burke would call the realm of the "forensic."

62. Ellison to Burke, 23 November 1945, F. 1, Box 38, REP; Burke to Ellison, 16 December 1945, F. 1, Box 38, REP. Burke's essay "Ralph Ellison's Trueblooded Bildungsroman" (1987; in Benston, *Speaking for You*, 349–59), which developed out of a shorter personal letter to Ellison, remains, nor surprisingly, one of the best appreciations of the narrative structure of *Invisible Man*.

63. Ellison, "Twentieth-Century Fiction and the Black Mask of Humanity," CE, 88, 84, 92, 85. Ellison drafted this essay in 1945–46 and anticipated that it would be published in the *Survey Graphic*; it was published in *Confluence* (edited by Henry Kissinger!) in 1953 and republished in *Shadow and Act* in 1964. See Jackson, RE:E, 342–48.

64. Ellison, "A Very Stern Discipline," *CE*, 752–54; Ellison, "Twentieth-Century Fiction," *CE*, 96, 94. For more on Ellison's changing views of Hemingway over the years, see Robert O'Meally, "The Rules of Magic: Hemingway as Ralph Ellison's 'Ancestor,'" in Benston, *Speaking for You*, 245–71. Hemingway was a favorite whipping-post of the left. John Strachey, in *Literature and Dialectical Materialism* (1934; rpt New York: Haskell House, 1974), 42–46, referred to him as a "nihilist."

65. Ellison, "Twentieth-Century Fiction and the Black Mask of Humanity," F. 1, Box 66, REP.

66. Ibid.

67. This postulation of the functional relationship of myth to ritual as an essentially ideological one would persist in Ellison's writing for some time, as he noted in relation to his discussion of D. W. Griffith's white supremacist *The Birth of a Nation*: "Ritual: Keeping Negro in Place; Myth: Negro Inferiority, Bestiality, Cowardliness, Depravity" ("The Shadow and the Act" [1949], F. 6, Box 105, REP).

Chapter Three: Writing from the Left

1. Maryemma Graham and Amritjit Singh, eds., *Conversations with Ralph Ellison* (Jackson: University Press of Mississippi, 1995), 104; Ralph Ellison, "The World and the Jug," *CE*, 161; Ellison, "A Very Stern Discipline" (1965), *CE*, 747. In an interview in 1982 Ellison stated that in 1940, when he showed Wright a story about "some fight that broke out between a chef and a hallboy in a club," Wright replied, "This is *my* stuff." Ellison remarked, "After that I never showed him another piece of fiction" ("A Completion of Personality: A Talk with Ralph Ellison," *CE*, 813). The story in question would have been "Tillman and Tackhead" (Box 165, REP). See also Graham and Singh, *Conversations with Ralph Ellison*, 361–62.

2. For more on the short stories, both titled and untitled, in the Ellison archive, see John F. Callahan's introduction to *Flying Home and Other Stories* (New York: Random House, 1995), ix–xxxviii.

3. Ellison to Babb, 4 July 1943, quoted in Rampersad, *RE:B*, 165–66; Ellison to Wright, 1 February 1948, F. 1314, Box 97, RWP.

4. Ellison, "The Birthmark," *New Masses*, 2 July 1940, 16–17. The story also appeared in the May–June 1945 issue of *Negro Story* magazine, not designated as reprinted from the *New Masses*, under the rubric "Short Stories by or about Negroes for All Americans." In August 1945 Hyman wrote to Ellison that he had noted Ellison's position as an advisory editor to *Negro Story*, which he called "one of the worst magazines I've seen in years." Ellison replied that the editor of the "lousy little mag" was a "little fool" and withdrew his name from the masthead (Hyman to Ellison, 22 August 1945; Ellison to Hyman 16 September 1945, F. 1, Box 51, REP). *Negro Story* was edited largely by African American women; the editor in mid-1945 was Alice C. Browning. See Bill V. Mullen, *Popular Fronts: Chicago and African-American Cultural Politics, 1936–1945* (Urbana: University of Illinois Press, 1999), 106–25.

5. Ellison, "The Birthmark," Box 162, REP. The story was drafted in 1939. Although Rampersad suggests that "The Birthmark" was based on Ellison's encounter at the

NNC in 1940 with a lynching survivor named James McMillian, whose neck bore the marks of a rope (RE:B, 136), it is more likely that McMillian inspired the character of Jerry in "The Initiation" (see below).

6. Ellison, "A Party Down at the Square," *Flying Home*, 3–11, quotes pp. 8, 7, 9, 10, 11. The title of the story was supplied by Callahan (introduction, xxv). As he wrote the story, Ellison evidently had at his elbow an eyewitness account of a lynching, on which he scribbled, "airplane flies over lights" ("Smith was taken . . . ," F. 3, Box 166, REP). He copied into a notebook several other eyewitness accounts of lynchings in 1919–20 (Notes 1942–50, F. 11, Box 152, REP). For a debate over the politics and historical references in the story, see my exchange with Brian Roberts: Barbara Foley, "Reading Redness: Politics and Audience in Ralph Ellison's Early Short Fiction," *Journal of Narrative Theory* 29 (fall 1999), 323–39; Brian Roberts, "Reading Ralph Ellison Synthesizing the CP and the NAACP: Sympathetic Narrative Strategy, Sympathetic Bodies," *Journal of Narrative Theory* 34 (winter 2004), 88–110; Barbara Foley, "Ralph Ellison, Intertextuality, and Biographical Criticism: An Answer to Brian Roberts," *Journal of Narrative Theory* 34 (summer 2004), 229–57; Brian Roberts, "The CPUSA's Line and Atmosphere: Did Ellison and Wright Walk It as They Breathed It as They Wrote?," *Journal of Narrative Theory* 34 (summer 2004), 258–68.

7. The treatment of electricity in "A Party Down at the Square" may have been inspired either by Herndon's description of the electrocution of a fellow worker in *Let Me Live* (1937; rpt. Ann Arbor: University of Michigan Press, 2007), 61–63, or by the rich power-line imagery in Stephen Spender's "The Pylons" (1933) and "The Landscape Near an Aerodrome" (1933). Ellison wrote enthusiastically of Spender in "New Left-Wing American Writers" (see chapter 2). John Strachey, an early influence on Ellison's Marxism, praised "The Pylons" in *Literature and Dialectical Materialism* (1934; rpt. New York: Haskell House, 1974), 33–34.

8. Ellison, "The Black Ball," *Flying Home*, 110–22, quote p. 111.

9. Ibid., 118, 120, 121, 122. The story was originally narrated in the third person ("The Black Ball," Box 162, REP). Different drafts of the story are on different paper (letterhead Ellison acquired in Dayton in 1937–38 and the verso of leaflets advertising a "Folk Songs on the Firing Line" concert in July 1942), indicating that the story was probably begun in the late 1930s but was not finished until at least mid-1942. In the final issue of *Negro Quarterly* 1, no. 4 (1943), 377–79, Henrietta Buckmaster published a review of Philip Van Doren's novel about the abolitionist movement, *Drums of Morning*; the review's title, "The Man with the Branded Hand," alludes to the fiery branding of an antislavery fighter. If the writing of "The Black Ball" was shaped by either the novel or the review, the story was not completed until mid-1943. Ellison continued to use the concert paper for rough drafts through 1943.

10. Ellison, "The Black Ball," Box 162, REP.

11. Ellison, "That I Had the Wings," *Flying Home*, 45–62, quotes pp. 46, 47; Ellison, "That I Had the Wings," F. 1–3, Box 165, REP. For the autobiographical basis of the story in two separate childhood incidents (one relating to the parachuted chicks, the other to a spurred rooster's attack on the young Ellison), see Ellison, "A Completion of Personality," CE, 794; Ellison, "Ralph Ellison: Twenty Years After," in Graham

and Singh, *Conversations with Ralph Ellison*, 209–10. While in the story the chicks meet their demise, in reality they lived through the fall. The fact that Ellison was punished for the rooster incident may inject a personal note into the Promethean theme. Ellison later noted the folk hero status of Kingsberry among Oklahoma's African Americans (Graham and Singh, *Conversations with Ralph Ellison*, 200; CE, 395–96). The other stories in the Buster and Riley series are "Afternoon," "Mr. Toussaint," and "A Coupla Scalped Indians"; all are reprinted in *Flying Home and Other Stories*.

12. Ellison, "That I Had the Wings," *Flying Home*, 51, 53, 54, 61, 62.

13. Ellison, "Editorial Comment," *Negro Quarterly* 1, no. 4 (1942–43), 299. Under the title "If I Had Wings," the story was reprinted in *Negro Story* 1, no. 3 (1944), 3–11. The story was written sometime before 2 April 1943, when Ellison was invited by the editor M. Margaret Anderson to submit it to *Common Ground*, where it appeared in the summer 1943 issue. "Reworked after Anderson's friendly criticism," according to Rampersad (RE:B, 162), the story was evidently finished before the Tuskegee airmen were permitted to take part in combat operations in May 1943. Ellison energetically gathered journalistic materials relating to the airmen in 1942 and 1943; see "Military: African-American Soldiers," F. 11 and 12, Box 203, REP. It is possible that "Ole Bill" signifies William (Bill) Hastie before he resigned in January 1943 as civilian aide to Secretary of Defense William Stimson on the grounds that the military remained entrenched in its segregationist practices.

14. Ellison to Burke, 23 November 1945, F. 7, Box 182, REP. Ellison considerably softened his criticism of Carver by 1976, when he applauded him for having fostered the peanut industry that in turn generated Jimmy Carter (Graham and Singh, *Conversations with Ralph Ellison*, 337). Ellison contemplated a grim sequel to "That I Had the Wings," in which Riley's accidental killing of the chicks and his brutalization by Ole Bill constitute his "conditioning for life. . . . He learns early to repress sensitive emotions." Riley later witnesses through a store window the murder of a black man. The man is ignored by whites and dies (Notes 1942–50, F. 5, Box 151, REP). For more on the skeptical attitude of leftists toward Louis Armstrong, see Steven Tracy, "A Delicate Ear, a Retentive Memory, and the Power to Wield the Fragments," *A Historical Guide to Ralph Ellison*, ed. Steven Tracy (New York: Oxford University Press, 2004), 98–101. "A Coupla Scalped Indians," a 1956 sequel to "That I Had the Wings," treats the theme of circumcision from an apolitical standpoint.

15. Ellison, "Flying Home," in *Flying Home*, 147–73, quote p. 155.

16. Ibid., 161, 171, 172–73; Tracy, "A Delicate Ear," 97–98.

17. This emphasis on Jefferson's vernacular tale as the means to the young airman's arrival home is confirmed by Ellison's own affirmative response to an interviewer's statement in 1971, after the publication of *Invisible Man*, that the "old dirt farmer Jefferson, and not Todd the aviator, is your persona." Ellison replied, "Yes, he's also Thomas Jefferson" (Graham and Singh, *Conversations with Ralph Ellison*, 211). Ellison further connected the phoenix, the vernacular, and American democracy in his celebration of the "pluralistic, melting-pot light of American cultural possibility," which produces "the phoenix's vernacular, but transcendent rising" ("The Little Man at Chehaw Station," 1978, CE, 523). Ellison later reconfigured Jefferson's story

as a conservative parable affirming its hero's following the rules of Heaven ("rules were usually intended to make one think . . . [and to] provide guidance"), thereby "mastering the challenge of one-winged flying, [and] becoming the most skillful one-winged flyer ever to have been grounded by heavenly decision" ("An Extravagance of Laughter," 1985, CE, 620). For readings stressing the myth-folklore-blues connection and Jefferson's role as mentor and healer, see Joseph W. Trimmer, "Ralph Ellison's 'Flying Home,'" *Studies in Short Fiction* 9 (1972), 175–82; Robert O'Meally, "On Burke and Vernacular: Ralph Ellison's Boomerang of History," *History and Memory in African-American Culture*, ed. Genevieve Fabre and Robert O'Meally (New York: Oxford University Press, 1994), 250; and Meili Steele, "Metatheory and the Subject of Democracy in the Work of Ralph Ellison," *New Literary History* 27 (1996), 473–502. Susan Blake offers a sharp critique of Ellison's substitution of myth for folklore in "Ritual and Rationalization: Black Folklore in the Works of Ralph Ellison," *PMLA* 94 (January 1979), 121–36.

18. Ellison, "Flying Home," F. 2 and 3 of 3, Box 163, REP. Ellison would play with the yoke-joke connection in the title to his riposte to Hyman, "Change the Joke and Slip the Yoke" (1958, CE, 100–12).

19. Ellison, "Flying Home," Box 163, REP. Before wine, mead was associated with the Dionysian cult; Ellison's pondering this option for the aviator's name stresses his rebellious, as opposed to merely hubristic, nature. See C. Kerenyi, *Dionysus: Archetypal Image of Indestructible Life*, trans. Ralph Manheim (Princeton: Princeton University Press, 1976), 36–37.

20. Ellison, "Flying Home," F. 1 and 2 of 3, Box 163, REP. Ellison recalled his mother's courageous encounter with the zoo guard in "On Being the Target of Discrimination," CE, 827–29. He paid tribute to his mother's courage, noting that she canvassed against discrimination in housing on behalf of the Socialists and more than once was arrested. Ellison, "That Same Pain, That Same Pleasure: An Interview," 1961, CE, 72.

21. Ellison, "Flying Home, F. 3 of 3, Box 163, REP.

22. Ibid.; Richard M. Dorson, "The Career of 'John Henry,'" *Mother Wit from the Laughing Barrel: Readings in the Interpretation of Afro-American Folklore*, ed. Alan Dundes (Jackson: University Press of Mississippi, 1990), 178–80. In Sterling Brown's "Slim in Hell" (1932), St. Peter gives wings to Slim and invites him to take a tour of hell; Slim reports back that hell is present-day Dixie. Ellison's play upon the name "Dabney Graves" may derive from his reading of Hyman's *Negro Quarterly* review of James Street's *Tap Roots*, a Civil War novel featuring a family of southern abolitionists named Dabney who are wiped out by a Confederate regiment. Dabney *Graves* may be a present-day Confederate, enemy of the John Browns with whom Todd/Mead identifies. See Hyman, "No Roots at All," *Negro Quarterly* 1 (fall 1942), 274–76.

23. Ellison, "Flying Home," F. 3 of 3, Box 163, REP. Hyman and Jackson prompted Ellison in a single afternoon to finish the story, which had been languishing in draft during the summer of 1943, right before he shipped out on the *Sun Yat-Sen* Liberty Ship (Jackson, RE:E, 296).

24. Ellison, "Flying Home," F. 2 of 3, Box 163, REP.

25. Ralph Ellison, "In a Strange Country," in *Flying Home*, 137–46, quotes pp. 143, 139, 142, 144. The story evidently reflects Ellison's own positive wartime experiences among the Welsh in Swansea; he declared in 1968, "I'm a Welsh nationalist" (Graham and Singh, *Conversations with Ralph Ellison*, 157).

26. Ellison, "In a Strange Country," in *Flying Home*, 145–46. The story was reprinted as "Black Yank in Britain" in *Negro Digest* 2, no. 11 (1944), 53–56. Parker, whose name suggests the jazz saxophonist Charlie Parker, was originally named Johnson ("Flying Home," F. 1–3, Box 163, REP). In some details about the Welsh background the story resembles the incomplete tale "A Storm of Blizzard Proportions" (Box 165, REP), as well as the journalistic sketch "The Red Cross at Morriston, Swansea, s.w." (F. 3, Box 165, REP). Ellison saved newspaper clippings featuring the antiracist character of Welsh institutions (Chester Himes 1945–47, Reference File, Box 188, REP). When the sociologist St. Clair Drake was in Cardiff he inquired of Ellison, via the Schomburg librarian Lawrence Reddick, about people whom he should contact (Reddick to Ellison, 14 August 1947, New York Public Library Reference File, Box 92, REP).

27. Ellison, "In a Strange Country," 143. For more on the Battle of Russia, see Benjamin L. Alpers, *Dictators, Democracy, and American Public Culture: Envisioning the Totalitarian Enemy, 1920s–1950s* (Chapel Hill: University of North Carolina Press, 2003), 226–77. The valorization of Robeson here and in "A Hard Time Keeping Up" (*Flying Home*, 97–109), also written in the early 1940s, is at odds with the negative opinions of Robeson as both actor and political figure that Ellison would express from 1945 onward. See the untitled short story fragment featuring Robeson in Notes 1942–50, F. 10, Box 152, REP; and Ellison to Wright, 5 August 1945 and n.d. (1949), F. 1314, Box 97, RWP. That an early draft of "In a Strange Country" was written on the back of the "Folk Songs on the Firing Line" advertisements for the concert sponsored by Wright and Earl Robinson, composer of "Ballad for Americans," suggests that Robeson was on Ellison's mind as he composed "In a Strange Country." *Negro Quarterly* 1, no. 4 (1943) published Jean F. Briere's highly laudatory "To Paul Robeson," which proclaims that the singer's deep voice utters "the sacred hymn of black redemption" (364).

28. Ellison, "Slick Gonna Learn," *Direction* 2 (September 1937), 10–11, 14, 16. Joseph Skerrett proposes that Wright's *Lawd Today* was a model for "Slick Gonna Learn": "The Wright Interpretation: Ralph Ellison and the Anxiety of Influence," *Speaking for You: The Vision of Ralph Ellison*, ed. Kimberly Benston (Washington, D.C.: Howard University Press, 1987), 221.

29. Ellison, "Slick," F. 1 and 2, typescript, Box 159, REP. Lawrence Jackson, in "Ralph Ellison, Sharpies, Rinehart, and Politics," *Massachusetts Review* 40, no. 1 (1999), 78, points out that "Slick" was a common nickname for a hipster or "sharpie." He proposes that Bostic is based on "Harlem's popular radio personality, Joe Bostick." "The Birth of the Critic: The Literary Friendship of Ralph Ellison and Richard Wright," *American Literature* 72, no. 2 (2000), 326.

30. Ellison, 'Slick," "Notes"; "Mister Mac, or, Tale of a Southern Road," Box 159, REP. Ellison considered including the "Mr. Mac" episode, set in Macon County, Alabama,

in "The Initiation" (see below). That he continued to work on the "Slick" novel at least into 1940 is indicated by the presence of a handwritten draft of "A Congress Jim Crow Didn't Attend" among the novel's notes. The novel's setting is confusing, jumping from Alabama to Oklahoma to a city resembling Dayton. In Dayton during the winter of 1937–38 Ellison met the prototype of Slick, an unemployed worker named John Strange, whose wife, Ollie, was in the hospital; the two men went hunting together (Rampersad, RE:B, 102–4). A good deal of the "Slick" manuscript is drafted on the letterhead of a Dayton architect.

31. Ellison, "Slick," typescript, F. 2, Box 159, REP. As in "Flying Home," the reference to the protagonist's activist mother recalls Ellison's own mother.

32. Ibid.

33. Ellison, "February," *Saturday Review of Literature*, 1 January 1955, 25; Ellison, "Slick," F. 2, typescript; "Booker's Reveries"; "Slick and Booker Hunting"; "Notes," Box 159, REP. For more on the appeal of the Spanish Civil War to radical African Americans, see *Black Americans in the Spanish People's War against Fascism*, ed. Joe Brandt (New York: International Publishers, n.d.); Robin Kelley, "'This Ain't Ethiopia, But It'll Do': African Americans and the Spanish Civil War," *Race Rebels: Culture, Politics, and the Black Working Class* (New York: Free Press, 1994), 123–58; and Stacy I. Morgan, *Rethinking Social Realism: African American Art and Literature, 1930–1953* (Athens: University Press of Georgia, 2004), 228–30. Wright wrote several articles for the *Daily Worker* in which he celebrated Angelo Herndon's brother Milton, who was killed in Spain. See Dexter Jeffries, "Richard Wright and the *Daily Worker*: A Native Son's Journalistic Apprenticeship," PH.D. dissertation, City University of New York, 2000.

34. Ellison, "Notes," "Slick," Box 159, REP.

35. Ibid.

36. Ibid.

37. The problem of creating complex Communist protagonists was recognized and discussed in the left press. See Charles Humboldt, "Communists in Novels: I and II," *Masses and Mainstream* 2 (June 1949), 13–31, 2 (July 1949), 44–65. Malraux received a mixed reception among U.S. leftists. *Man's Fate* was the subject of debate in the *New Masses*, 3 July 1934, 43–44, 4 September 1934, 27–30. Harry Slochower altered his opinion of Malraux, finding *Man's Hope* more materialist than either *Man's Fate* or *Days of Wrath*. Slochower, *Three Ways of Modern Man* (New York: International Publishers, 1937), 165–67; Slochower, *No Voice Is Wholly Lost: Writers and Thinkers in War and Peace* (New York: Creative Age Press, 1945), 320–24. Once Malraux abandoned Communist politics, adopted a formalist aesthetic, and was drawn into the postwar French cultural establishment, he would be consistently scored in the left press.

38. Ellison, "The Dream," F. 1 of 3, Box 162, REP.

39. Ibid. In 1971 Ellison commented on the "deliberately ambiguous" appearance of birds in his fiction, sometimes "the furies," sometimes "the doves of peace" (Graham and Singh, *Conversations with Ralph Ellison*, 201). For more on government surveillance of the NNC in the South, see Kenneth O'Reilly, "The Roosevelt Administration and Black America: Federal Surveillance Policy and Civil Rights During the New Deal and World War II Years," *Freedom's Odyssey: African American History Essays from*

Phylon, ed. Alexa Benson Henderson and Janice Sumler-Edmond (Atlanta: Clark Atlanta University Press, 1999), 465–82.

40. Ellison, "The Dream," F. 1 of 3, Box 162, REP.

41. Ibid.

42. Ellison, "The Cars Finally Came to a Stop" (henceforth "The Final Destination"), F. 3, Box 166, REP.

43. Ibid.

44. Ellison, "Paul Character," untitled, n.d., F. 4, Box 166, REP. At the urging of Ferdinand Smith, an NMU official and CP leader, in 1944 the NNC hired a full-time organizer in Alabama by the name of Oscar Bryant. Gerald Horne, *Red Seas: Ferdinand Smith and Radical Black Sailors in the United States and Jamaica* (New York: New York University Press, 2005), 106–7.

45. Ellison, "Paul Character," F. 4, Box 166, REP. For a description of the continual financial difficulties encountered by southern CP organizers, see Hosea Hudson, *Black Worker in the Deep South: A Personal Record* (New York: International Publishers, 1972).

46. Ellison, "Paul Character," F. 4, Box 166, REP.

47. Ellison to Lazenberry, 18 April 1939, quoted in Rampersad, RE:B, 124; Ellison, Notes 1942–50, F. 7, Box 152, REP. A possible historical prototype for Bard is J. Saunders Redding. Ellison jotted, "[Bard] has a certain command of ideas (like Redding) which he has absorbed through his reading. He has never had to prove his mastery of Marxist principles, since the party has opportunistically taken him up so as to have an entering wedge into the college. All this he understands." Redding, whose *No Day of Triumph* ((New York: Harper and Row, 1942) clearly influenced Ellison's portrayal of Negro college life in *Invisible Man* (see chapter 4), was head of the English Department at the State Teachers College in Elizabeth City, North Carolina, from 1938 to 1943 and subsequently professor of English at Hampton University from 1943 to 1966. Richard Wright wrote an approving preface to *No Day of Triumph*, and it was excerpted for the special issue of the *New Masses* (October 1942) focused on the Negro and the war.

48. Ellison, "The Initiation," F. 1–5, Box 164, REP. Another draft characterizes Giles as, alternately, a "blues character" and a "disciplined organizer." Like both the invisible man and Tod Clifton in early drafts of *Invisible Man*, Giles has an affair with a white woman whom he forces to sit under a sun lamp (see chapter 7). Giles could also have been falsely accused of rape by a woman who had fallen in love with him; he would have subsequently "passed in North" (Notes 1942–50, F. 10, Box 152, REP).

49. Ellison, "The Initiation," F. 1–5, Box 164, REP. Ellison considered a still more melodramatic ending: "[Bard] could sacrifice Giles in order to protect boys, who have escaped. Mother survives mob, but kills him for surrendering Giles" (Notes 1942–50, F. 1, Box 151, REP).

50. Familiar with Otto Rank's work on the hero, Ellison may also have read Rank on the double as a "pursuing and torturing conscience." Rank, *The Double: A Psychoanalytic Study*, trans. and ed. Harry Tucker Jr. (Chapel Hill: University of North Carolina Press, 1971), 57.

51. Ellison, Notes 1942–50, F. 11, Box 152, REP.

52. Ellison, "The Art of Fiction: An Interview," CE, 218; introduction to *Invisible Man* (1982), vii, xi. Rampersad estimates that by mid-1945 Ellison had three different novels in mind: the airman novel, one taking place on a college campus and featuring Bard, and the beginnings of *Invisible Man* (RE:B, 194). While it is generally assumed that Ellison never completed either of the first two narratives, it bears noting that Frank Taylor of Random House wrote to him in late 1947 referring to "the novelette." Congratulating Ellison on the positive reception recently greeting the *Horizon* publication of the short story "The Invisible Man" (1947; later to be the Battle Royal chapter of the novel), Taylor noted, "As powerful as it is, in several places, it never achieves the profundity and power of the Invisible Man. The style, of course, is utterly different" (F. 5, Box 65, REP).

53. Graham and Singh, *Conversations with Ralph Ellison*, 380; Ellison, "Gann Wilson," Box 163, REP; Ellison, "The World and the Jug," CE, 187. For more on Ellison's father, Lewis Ellison, see Jackson, RE:E, 1–22; for more on Ellison's desire to go to Spain, see Rampersad, RE:B, 93–95. It bears noting that Ellison in 1964 would castigate as "certain wise men who were then managing the consciences of artists" the Party leaders presumably responsible for Christopher Caudwell's having "throw[n] away his life defending a worthless hill." Caudwell, whom Ellison much admired, joined the International Brigades and was killed within a week of his arrival in Spain.

54. Ellison, "Burr Bullet Head," F. 2, Box 166, REP; Notes 1942–50, F. 10, Box 152, REP. See J. Saunders Redding, *No Day of Triumph*, 119–39. Redding would later expand upon this portrait in his novel *Stranger and Alone: A Novel* (1950; rpt. Harper and Row, 1959), which Ellison reviewed (Ellison, "Collaborator with His Own Enemy," *New York Times Book Review*, 19 February 1950, 4).

55. Ellison, Notes 1942–50, F. 2, Box 151, and F. 11, Box 152, REP.

56. Ellison, Notes 1942–50, F. 11, Box 152, REP.

57. Ellison, Notes 1942–50, F. 6, Box 152, F. 5, Box 151, REP. In an early draft of *Invisible Man*, Ellison developed the theme of the unhappy marriage of two Communists in a short narrative titled "Blues" (alternatively, "Something about Blues") that is narrated by the invisible man after he has gone underground. See chapter 8.

58. Ellison, Notes 1942–50, F. 10, Box 152, REP. Ellison terminates this portrait of his flawed but complex hero with the somewhat murky observation, "Seeks absolutes actually; and in sex practices if not inhibited is act to seek complete eroticism (homo)?"

59. Ellison, "Statement of Plan of Work," "Airman" novel, F. 1, Box 115, REP.

60. Daniel Lang, "A Reporter at Large: Room 11, Stalag 7-B," *New Yorker*, 10 June 1944, 48–59, quote p. 56; Zachary A. Serwer, "Return of a War Prisoner," news release, Army and Navy Committee of the National Jewish Welfare Board, 2 November 1944; Henry Weintraub, "Dear Peggy," 31 October 1944; Ellison to Weintraub, 5 December 1944. All these documents are gathered in F. 1, Box 115, REP.

61. "332nd Flier, Back Home, Tells of Life in German Prison Camp," *Pittsburgh Courier*, 30 June 1945; James E. Smith, "GIs Arrive from Nazi Camps after 3 Months Imprisonment," *Pittsburgh Courier*, 12 May 1945; "Led Guerrillas: Missing Nine Months, Vet Pilot Turns Up," *Pittsburgh Courier*, 30 June 1945. See also Tom O'Connor, "Germany's

Bomb-Flat Areas Are 'Beautiful,'" *PM*, 23 February 1945; "Lieut. Col. James A. Gunn, 3d, Interned Fliers Got Set to Battle Nazis—Rescue Gamble Told," *Sunday News*, 2 September 1944. All these sources are gathered in F. 1, Box 115, REP.

62. Ellison, drafts of "Airman" novel, F. 1, Box 115, REP.

63. Ibid.

Chapter Four: Living Jim Crow

1. Ellison, 1982 introduction to *Invisible Man*, vii; Rampersad, RE:B, 95. Ralph Ellison and Fannie McConnell Buford were not officially married until August 1946. Amelie Bates's family had owned the Waitsfield farm for several generations. John Bates was an amateur boxer; he served as the model for the invisible man in Gordon Parks's 1954 photo-essay of the novel for *Life* magazine. Add Bates was a talented carpenter who made several pieces of furniture for Richard Wright and his family. Keneth Kinnamon and Michel Fabre, eds., *Conversations with Richard Wright* (Jackson: University Press of Mississippi, 1993), 55. Ellison had stayed at the Bates farm previously, in the spring of 1943 (RE:B, 164).

2. Ellison to Hyman, 15 August 1945, Box 6, SEHP; Ellison, letter to Mrs. Hitchcock, Notes 1942–50, F. 4 and F. 3, Box 151; F. 9, Box 152, REP. Ellison moved from Reynal and Hitchcock to Random House in 1946, largely because Frank Taylor, his editor at Reynal and Hitchcock, changed employers. It was at Random House that Ellison began his working relationship of many years with Albert Erskine (Jackson, RE:E, 333–35; Rampersad, RE:B, 210–11).

3. Ellison to Peggy Hitchcock, Notes 1942–50, F. 3, Box 151, and Notes 1942–50, F. 9, Box 152, REP.

4. Ellison, "On Initiation Rites and Power," CE, 537.

5. Ellison's emphasis on universals as the basis for literary communication, drawing heavily upon Burke (and Aristotle), would over the years become increasingly nationalistic and abstract. See, for example, "The Art of Fiction: An Interview" (1955), CE, 212–13; "Society, Morality, and the Novel" (1957), CE, 700–701; 1982 introduction to *Invisible Man*, xx–xxii.

6. Ellison, "Working Notes for *Invisible Man*, CE, 344. "Working Notes" can be dated to the late spring of 1947 because in June Ellison wrote to Hyman that the editors at Random House had considered his novel abstract "quite a piece of writing" (17 June 1947, Box 6, SEHP).

7. Ellison, "Working Notes for *Invisible Man*," CE, 343–49, quotes pp. 342, 343, 349. Although every draft of "Working Notes," of which several are sprinkled throughout Ellison's notes and drafts, contains both the character sketch and the plot summary, the second section of the document was omitted from the version of "Working Notes" published in the first hardcover edition of *The Collected Essays of Ralph Ellison*, ed. John F. Callahan (New York: Modern Library, 1995), 341–45.

8. Ellison, Notes 1942–50, F. 9, Box 152; "Battle Royal 1947–48 and n.d.," Box 162, REP; Ellison, "The Battle Royal," *Horizon* 16 (October 1947), 104–18; Ellison, "The Battle Royal," *'48: Magazine of the Year* 2 (January 1948), 14–15, 20–21, 32. An early version of

the battle royal scene appears in a section titled "Part I—College" (Notes 1942-50,
F. 5, Box 151, REP). Candide is the protagonist of Voltaire's famous novel of that
name (1759), in which the naïve hero is buffeted about as he seeks the best of all
possible worlds; Ellison compared his own hero with Voltaire's. Maryemma Graham
and Amritjit Singh, eds., *Conversations with Ralph Ellison* (Jackson: University Press of
Mississippi, 1995), 206. The novel's prologue appeared as "The Invisible Man: Prologue to a Novel," in *Partisan Review*, January–February 1952, 31–40. Ellison turned
down the opportunity to publish the chapter in *Negro Digest*, where he had previously republished "In a Strange Country" as "Black Yank in Britain." I will henceforth generally refer to the invisible man as "the protagonist," reserving "the narrator" for moments when his retrospective viewpoint is stressed. That Ellison may
have begun work on the battle royal chapter as early as January or February 1945 is
suggested by the fact that, at the top of a manuscript page describing the boys' fight,
there appear the words, "I should like to request a hearing before the board for the
purpose of clearing up several matters pertaining to my draft status" ("Battle Royal,"
Box 142, REP). It was in early 1945 that Ellison was experiencing great anxiety about
the possibility that he would be drafted; by July 1945 the issue was moot. Besides
alluding to the scene in which two black youths are pitted against each other in
Wright's *Black Boy*, the boxing match could draw upon comparable events described
in slave narratives. See Henry Bibb, *Narrative of the Life and Adventures of Henry Bibb,
An American Slave, Written by Himself*, in Gilbert Osofsky, ed., *Puttin' on Ole Massa: The
Slave Narratives of Henry Bibb, Williams Wells Brown, and Solomon Northrup* (New York:
Harper and Row, 1969), 68; and Richard Dorson, *American Negro Folktales* (Green-
wich, Conn.: Fawcett, 1956), 132–35. Olaudah Equiano's *Narrative* is another pos-
sible source. See John Vukomirovich, "Alterity, Community, and a New Intertext for
Ralph Ellison's *Invisible Man*," PH.D. dissertation, Loyola University, 2000, 107–14.
Other possible sources of the fight scene are Len Zinberg's boxing novel, *Walk Hard,
Talk Loud* (1940), which Ellison reviewed for the *New Masses*; and Miguel de Unamuno's *The Tragic Sense of Life*, trans. J. E. Crawford Flitch (1921; rpt. New York: Dover,
1954), 14–15, where man-as-boxer is a metaphor of the human condition. Preoccupied with this "governing ritual," Ellison clipped an article from a newspaper dated
March 1946 about a battle royal in the Bahamas (Notes 1942-50, F. 1, Box 151, REP).
9. Ellison, "Battle Royal," Box 142; Notes 1942-50, F. 5, Box 151, REP. The title "Atlanta
Compromise" was W. E. B. Du Bois's dismissive sobriquet for Washington's address
to the Atlanta Cotton States and International Exposition in 1895. Ellison's more
nuanced treatment of caste in the published text of *Invisible Man* may have derived
from his perusal of John Dollard's influential *Caste and Class in a Southern Town*, 2nd
ed. (1937; Garden City, N.Y.: Doubleday, 1949), which received a mixed review in the
New Masses: Elizabeth Lawson, "Southerntown," *New Masses* 24 (September 1937), 24.
On the libidinal aspects of the battle royal, see Daniel Y. Kim, "Invisible Desires:
Homoerotic Racism and Its Homophobic Critique in Ralph Ellison's *Invisible Man*,"
Novel: A Forum on Fiction 30 (spring 1997), 309–29; and Michael Hardin, "Ralph Elli-
son's Invisible Man: Invisibility, Race, and Homoeroticism from Frederick Douglass
to E. Lynn Harris," *Southern Literary Journal* 37, no. 1 (2004), 96–121.

10. Ellison, Fragments and Partial Drafts, F. 5, Box 151; "Chapel," Box 144, REP. Jackson proposes that the fragment about having been raised in a glass house is associated not with *Invisible Man* but with the unwritten novel about the Tuskegee flyer (*RE:E*, 310–11).

11. Ellison, Notes 1942–50, F. 3, Box 151, F. 8, Box 152, "Emerson," Box 144; "Battle Royal," Box 142, REP. The levee camp story might have drawn upon Wright's "Down by the Riverside" in *Uncle Tom's Children*, or his story "Silt," *New Masses*, 24 August 1937. For more on the Tulsa riot, see Scott Ellsworth, *Death in the Promised Land* (Baton Rouge: Louisiana State University Press, 1982). It also bears noting that Richard Wright passed a portion of his unhappy childhood in Greenwood, Mississippi.

12. Ellison, Notes 1942–50, F. 3, Box 151, REP.

13. Ellison, "The Art of Fiction: An Interview" (1955), CE, 216; Ralph Ellison, "On Initiation Rites and Power: A Lecture at West Point," CE, 532–33. Ellison would go on to compare the boys' torture on the electrified rug with a "practical joke" played on him as an adolescent by a white employer (CE, 539–40). He wrote to Walter Ross, publisher of *'48: The Magazine of the Year*, "[The] aim [of the story] is not naturalism but realism—a realism dilated to deal with the almost surreal state of our everyday American life. Hence it is an irony, not completely of my own creation, that for the boy the kewpi-haired dancer is at once a woman; a symbol of a debased 'white' democracy; an object of fascination comb[in]ing a threat of death with overtones of possible beauty; and, to make the list brief, the embodiment of a most potent sex taboo" (1 March 1948, "Battle Royal 1947–48 and n.d.," Box 162, REP). For readings of the battle royal as the protagonist's entry, however incomplete, into democratic discourse, see Danielle Allen, "Ralph Ellison on the Tragi-Comedy of Citizenship," *Ralph Ellison and the Raft of Hope: A Political Companion to* Invisible Man, ed. Lucas Morel (Lexington: University Press of Kentucky, 2004), 37–57; and John F. Callahan, *In the African-American Grain: The Pursuit of Voice in Twentieth-Century Black Fiction* (Urbana: University of Illinois Press, 1988), 156–60. For the argument that the invisible man's discovered ability to conduct electricity leads him to "enact a powerful blackface critique of existing power structures," see Johnnie Wilcox, "Black Power: Minstrelsy and Electricity in Ralph Ellison's *Invisible Man*," *Callaloo* 30 (fall 2007), 987–1009, quote p. 987. Ellison's early projected treatment of his protagonist's childhood renders problematic such affirmatively ironic interpretations of the novel's opening.

14. Ellison, Notes 1942–50, F. 10, Box 152, REP. For more on the joke about the statue, see Horace Cayton, *Long Old Road* (New York: Trident Press, 1965), 204–5; and Albert Murray, *South to a Very Old Place* (New York: McGraw-Hill, 1971), 123–24. For Ellison's reaction to Park's sociological doctrines, see Jackson, *RE:E*, 141–47. Ellison considered another list of elements for the campus section: "The Dean of Men; Dining Hall; Hospital; President; . . . Women without men; Eva's Escapade; Ely's Crossing; Fires; . . . Cynicism; Suicides; Murders" (Notes 1942–50, F. 7, Box 152, REP). Ely's Crossing was the original name of the Golden Day. For more on the fires at Tuskegee, as well as three murders occurring on the campus in 1931–33, see Frederick D. Patterson, "Administrator and Man," *Robert Russa Moton of Hampton and Tuskegee*,

ed. William Hardin Hughes and Frederick D. Patterson (Chapel Hill: University of North Carolina Press, 1956), 207–8.

15. Ellison, Notes 1942–50, F. 10, Box 152, REP; Graham and Singh, *Conversations with Ralph Ellison*, 232. The name "Bledsoe" may also allude to Julius Bledsoe, the African American opera singer renowned for his performance of "Ol Man River" in Jerome Kern's *Showboat*; he was also notorious for his embarrassing singing of what Alain Locke termed a "mammy interpolation" during a radio program called "The Negro" in 1938, part of the government-sponsored series *Americans All, Immigrants All*. See Barbara Dianne Savage, *Broadcasting Freedom: Radio, War, and the Politics of Race, 1938–1948* (Chapel Hill: University of North Carolina Press, 1999), 40–41.

16. Ellison, "Woodridge," Box 146; Notes 1942–50, F. 5, Box 151, REP. The name Crump may have been intended to invoke the prominent Tennessee Democratic machine politician Edward Hull ("Boss") Crump, who had a significant base in the state's still disenfranchised black population. In *Stranger and Alone* (1950), J. Saunders Redding's satiric novel about Negro college life, a dean is named Bledsoe, and Redding's per-fidious president P. T. Wimbush bears a more than passing resemblance to Ellison's Bledsoe. See Ellison's review of the novel, "Collaborator with His Own Enemy," *New York Times Book Review*, 19 February 1950, 4; and Ellison to Albert Murray, 16 April 1950, in Albert Murray and John F. Callahan, eds., *Trading Twelves: The Selected Letters of Ralph Ellison and Albert Murray* (New York: Modern Library, 2000), 11–13. In the signature of his letter to Emerson, Bledsoe's given name was at first Herbert, not Hebert ("A-Bear"); evidently the novel's bear motif was not yet fully on Ellison's mind (Original typescript, F. 2, Box 147, REP). For more on Ellison's possible use of Redding, see John Vassilovitch, "Ellison's Dr. Bledsoe: Two Literary Sources," *Essays in Literature* 8 (Spring 1981), 109–13.

17. Ellison, "New York," Box 145, REP. Being broke, Ellison rode the rails to get to Tuske-gee his freshman year and was badly roughed up by railroad guards ("bulls"); he would subsequently minimize the significance of this traumatic experience ("An Extravagance of Laughter," CE, 636; "Perspective of Literature," CE, 772–73). See also Lawrence Jackson, "Ralph Ellison's Invented Life: A Meeting with the Ancestry," *A Cambridge Companion to Ralph Ellison*, ed. Ross Posnock (Cambridge, England: Cambridge University Press, 2005), 29–30. Ellison's first short story, "Hymie's Bull," in *Flying Home and Other Stories* (New York: Random House, 1995), 82–88, depicts a violent encounter with a railroad "bull." In his unpublished FWP article on "The Negro and the War" (1940), Ellison notes the indignity experienced in the mid-1930s by the "highest ranking Negro officer in the United States Army," who, after the army in 1931 "began disarming and disbanding its Negro regiments and order-ing their members into labor battalion[s] to serve white troops," was relegated to teaching "classes in military science and tactics" at a southern Negro college where the students trained with guns from which the firing pins had been removed ("The Negro and the War," F. 9, Box 20, REP).

18. Robin D. G. Kelley, *Hammer and Hoe: Alabama Communists During the Great Depression* (Chapel Hill: University of North Carolina Press, 1990), 49–53, quote p. 51. See also James S. Allen, *Organizing in the Depression South* (Minneapolis: MEP, 2001), 76–77.

Harry Haywood, discussing the Reeltown incident, notes that the sheriff was unable to recruit a posse from among the white farmers, who were in substantial sympathy with the sharecroppers. Haywood, *Negro Liberation* (New York: International Press, 1948), 131. It must be noted that invasions of the Tuskegee campus had happened before: in 1923 a mob confronted Moton after he hired Negro doctors and nurses to work in the new Negro Veterans Hospital; his insistence that members of the campus community display no anger riled some faculty members. See Albon L. Holsey, "A Man of Courage," in Hughes and Patterson, *Robert Russa Moton of Hampton and Tuskegee*, 129–32. The campus was clearly vulnerable: many years before, in 1895, Washington was widely believed to have handed over to a mob one Thomas Harris, a Negro lawyer. See Louis R. Harlan, *Booker T. Washington: The Making of a Black Leader, 1856–1901* (New York: New York University Press, 1972), 171–75. Notably, Ellison at one point considered modeling the college president not on Washington but on W. E. B. Du Bois (Notes 1942–50, F. 4, Box 151, REP).

19. Ellison, "Chapel," Box 144, REP. A year before the Reeltown incident, in response to Scottsboro activism and left-led sharecropper organizing in Camp Hill, Alabama, Moton, "hoping to quell black unrest, dispatched representatives to Tallapoosa in a calculated move to turn blacks away from Communism" (Kelley, *Hammer and Hoe*, 42). In his unpublished FWP essay, "The Negro and the War" (1940) Ellison blasted Tuskegee for being "notoriously silent on important issues concerning the Negro; the Herndon and Scottsboro cases are two [glaring] instances. . . . Actual progress has been made in the South below and outside of Tuskegee and the other schools; that type of unity which the Institute was intended to discourage is being achieved not by the educated class but by the sharecroppers and workers" ("The Negro and the War," F. 9, Box 20, REP).

20. The Washington address also contains the famous "throw down your bucket where you are" parable to which the invisible man alludes in his speech. For more on Ellison's college years, 1933–36, see Rampersad, *RE:B*, 52–80.

21. Ellison, Notes 1942–50, F. 4, Box 151, REP.

22. Ellison, "Chapel," Box 144; "Woodridge," Box 146, REP. Woodridge's nightmare about blinding his students suggestively links Negro miseducation with the horrific incident in 1946, much protested by antiracists and discussed in the black and left press, in which North Carolina police gouged out the eyes of the Negro veteran Isaac Woodard, whose surname echoes that of the professor. Ellison mentioned the incident in a letter to Wright (24 August 1946, F. 1314, Box 97, RWP).

23. Ellison, "Woodridge," Box 146, REP; Ellison, Notes 1942–50, F. 8, Box 152, REP; Ellison, introduction to *Shadow and Act*, CE, 57. For more on Ellison's negative experiences with harassment by homosexual administrators at Tuskegee, see Rampersad, *RE:B*, 61–67. In an early draft of the campus section the invisible man states that, in addition to "throw[ing himself] into campus politics[,] . . . sing[ing] in the glee club, becom[ing] a candidate for the debate team, [he] . . . stayed a step beyond the fingers of the dean of men" (Fragments and Partial Drafts, F. 5, Box 151, REP). On the low morale of the faculty at Tuskegee, see Cayton, *Long Old Road*, 189–206. The (in)famous statement by Park was contained in his and Ernest Burgess's *Introduction*

to the Science of Sociology, 3rd revised ed. (1921; Chicago: University of Chicago Press, 1969), 139.

24. Ellison, 1982 introduction to *Invisible Man*, xix; "Woodridge," Box 146, REP. For more on the omitted Woodridge chapter as a critique of heteronormativity, white supremacy, and disciplinarity, see Roderick Ferguson, *Aberrations in Black: Toward a Queer of Color Critique* (Minneapolis: University of Minnesota Press, 2004), 54–58.

25. Ellison," Campus," F. 1, Box 144, REP.

26. Ellison, Notes 1942–50, F. 5, Box 151, REP.

27. Ibid.

28. Ellison, "Working Notes," *CE*, 346.

29. Ellison, Notes 1942–50, F. 10, Box 152, F. 1, Box 151, REP. For contemporaneous sociological commentaries on southern sharecropper life, see Charles S. Johnson, *The Shadow of the Plantation* (Chicago: University of Chicago Press, 1934); and Arthur D. Raper and Ira De A. Reid, *Sharecroppers All* (New York: Russell and Russell, 1941). While there is no evidence that Ellison intended to link Trueblood with the infamous Tuskegee syphilis experiments, Johnson, who based his analysis on the farms in Macon County surrounding Tuskegee, noted the prevalence of the discourse about "bad blood" among local farmers as a result of the experiments (201–7). Regarding the poor health of sharecroppers, Wright wrote in his introduction to St. Clair Drake and Horace Cayton, *Black Metropolis: A Study of Negro Life in a Northern City* (New York: Harcourt, Brace and World, 1945), xxx, "Does the Negro's tremendous fund of repression affect his speech, his walk, his dress, his music, his health? Why are the highest rates of hyper-tension (high blood pressure) to be found among the Negro sharecroppers on the plantations of the pastoral South?"

30. Ellison refers to the same incident in "A Hard Time Keeping Up," a proletarian short story featuring the need for working-class solidarity. "We are all lone wolves," remarks a character regretfully, "each one trying to fight it out alone—like the guy in Birmingham who stood off a whole police force by himself" (*Flying Home*, 104). On the frequent demonstrations in Birmingham, see Kelley, *Hammer and Hoe*, 55–77.

31. Ellison, "Campus," F. 2, Box 144; Notes 1942–50, F. 3, Box 151, REP. For a discussion of the near-absence of systemic Jim Crow violence from Trueblood's version of the blues, see Adam Gussow, "'Fingering the Jagged Grain': Ellison's Wright and the Southern Blues Violence," *boundary 2* 30, no. 2 (2003), 137–55.

32. Ellison, Notes 1942–50, F. 6, Box 152, REP.

33. Ellison, "Prologue," Box 146, REP. In another draft of the passage describing the college, Ellison scrawled, "Waste Land" ("New York," Box 145, REP). For more on Ellison's attempt to inflect Eliot's high modernism for progressive political ends, see William Lyne, "The Signifying Modernist: Ralph Ellison and the Limits of Double Consciousness," *Modern Critical Interpretations: Invisible Man*, ed. Harold Bloom (Philadelphia: Chelsea House, 1999), 179–96. Lyne's thesis applies more fully to the drafts of *Invisible Man* than to the published text.

34. Graham and Singh, *Conversations with Ralph Ellison*, 174; "Golden Day—True Blood," Box 144; Campus, F. 1 and 2, Box 144; Notes 1942–50, F. 6, Box 152, REP.

35. Ellison, "Golden Day—True Blood," Box 144; "Campus," F. 1 Box 144, REP. There is

other fragmentary evidence that Ellison contemplated writing his novel in the third person (Notes 1942–50, F. 3, Box 151, F. 6, Box 152, REP). He considered it a challenge to Henry James, who discouraged first-person narration, to have the protagonist tell his own tale (Graham and Singh, *Conversations with Ralph Ellison*, 263). Ellison commented on Marcher as a prototype for the invisible man himself, who must similarly encounter "a series of ambiguous answers, mis-read the signs and yet persist [until he is] . . . forced to face reality [by] . . . violence" ("Golden Day—True Blood," Box 144, REP). "The Jolly Corner," with its doubling of the wealthy white Spencer Brydon with his ghostly "black man" alter ego, is another possible Jamesian intertext for the Norton-Trueblood encounter.

36. Ellison, "Campus," F. 2, Box 144, REP. In 1941 the *New Masses* ran a photo-essay on American racism titled "Our Way of Life" containing a picture of a tobacco farmer lighting up a cigarette; the caption read, "I bin dyin' for a smoke, Glad you offered, I was afraid to ask. It's funny workin' tobacco and not ownin' a butt" (*New Masses*, 28 January 1941, 15–16, quote p. 15). For psychoanalytic readings paralleling the sharecropper and the millionaire, see Selma Fraiberg, "Two Modern Incest Heroes," *Twentieth-Century Interpretations of* Invisible Man, ed. John Reilly (Englewood Cliffs, N.J.: Prentice-Hall, 1970), 73–79; and Stuart Noble-Goodman, "Mythic Guilt and the Burden of Sin in Ellison's *Invisible Man*," *Midwest Quarterly* 39, no. 4 (1998), 409–32. Ellison's original intention to give greater depth to Norton while at the same time targeting his class function in Trueblood's oppression adds a crucial political dimension to Gillian Johns's deft reading of the episode: "Jim Trueblood and His Critic-Readers: Ralph Ellison's Rhetoric of Dramatic Irony and Tall Humor in the Mid-Century American Literary Public Sphere," *Texas Studies in Literature and Language* 49 (fall 2007), 230–64.

37. Ellison, "Campus," F. 2, F. 1, Box 144, REP. Marcus Klein has proposed that Ellison alludes to Charles Eliot Norton, a friend of Emerson, liberal abolitionist, and post–Civil War supporter of the Freedmen's Bureau. Klein, *After Alienation: American Novels in Mid-Century* (Freeport, N.Y.: Books for Libraries Press, 1964), 136. For more on Charles Eliot Norton, see James Turner, *The Liberal Education of Charles Eliot Norton* (Baltimore: Johns Hopkins University Press, 1999). In the earliest version of the Trueblood episode, the trustee's name is left blank, and he does not ask the invisible man whether he has read Emerson ("Golden Day—True Blood," Box 144, REP).

38. Ellison, "Campus," F. 1, F. 2, Box 144, REP; Charles S. Johnson, *In the Shadow of the Plantation* (Chicago: University of Chicago Press, 1934), 13. A study done in 1935 emphasized the increase in tenancy, the preferential treatment given to landowners by the federal government, and the key ownership role of southern agriculture by northern insurance companies and banks. Charles S. Johnson, Edwin R. Embree, and W. W. Alexander, *The Collapse of Cotton Tenancy: Summary of Field Studies and Statistical Surveys, 1933–35* (Chapel Hill: University of North Carolina Press, 1935). See James S. Allen, *The Negro Question in the United States* (New York: International Publishers, 1936) for the Marxist analysis of the relation of northern capital to the sharecropping economy with which Ellison was familiar.

39. Ellison, "Campus," F. 1, Box 144, REP. A notable exception to the critical tendency to

overlook the anticapitalist critique contained in the Trueblood-Norton interchange is **389** Houston Baker's "To Move without Moving: An Analysis of Creativity and Commerce in Ralph Ellison's Trueblood Episode," *Speaking for You: The Vision of Ralph Ellison*, ed. Kimberly W. Benston (Washington, D.C.: Howard University Press, 1987), 322–48. Baker's useful commentary underestimates the dialectical relationship between the sharecropper and the millionaire, which is emphasized in Ellison's notes and drafts.

40. Ellison, Notes 1942–50, F. 1, Box 151, REP.
41. Ellison, "Campus," F. 2, Box 144. In one version of the toy scene Norton takes the children to the toy store (Notes 1942–50, F. 6, Box 152, REP). The episode of Norton and the toys was based on an anecdote Ellison had heard about "a famous surgeon who, many years before in Alabama, had filled his cars with christmas toys and driven through the farmland of Macon County distributing toys to impoverished share-croppers' children" (preface to the Franklin Library Edition, Box 150, REP).
42. Ellison, "Campus," F. 3, F. 1, Box 144, "Battle Royal," Box 144, REP.
43. Ellison, "Campus," F. 1, Box 144, REP. Ellison also compared the vets with the brutalized but abidingly humane prisoners in Dostoevsky's *House of the Dead* (Notes 1942–50, F. 11, Box 152, REP).
44. Ellison, "Campus," F. 1, F. 2, Box 144; "Golden Day—True Blood," Box 144, REP. For more on Tuskegee's relationship with Rockefeller, see Murray, *South to a Very Old Place*, 107. In his unpublished FWP article on "The Negro and the War" (1940) Ellison emphasized the close connection between Rockefeller and Tuskegee, remarking, "The Rockefellers control the General Education Board which dictates the policies of Negro education. . . . How completely Negro life is controlled directly by large capitalists interest is indicated by the fact that the files of the Rockefeller Foundation in Chicago contain a biographical record of all Negroes who manifest any signs of leadership" ("The Negro and the War," F. 9, Box 20, REP). James K. Vardaman and Theodore G. Bilbo were extreme racist Mississippi politicians. (Vardaman, coincidentally, was editor of the *Greenwood Commonwealth* newspaper.) Ellison discussed the riffing on Rockefeller's sexual prowess in African American folklore in "An Extravagance of Laughter" (1985), CE, 660–61. African Americans were hired into staff positions at the Veterans Hospital starting in 1923, although the top administrative positions went to whites. See Robert J. Norrell, *Reaping the Whirlwind: The Civil Rights Movement in Tuskegee* (New York: Knopf, 1985), 27–30. For more on the relationship between Tuskegee and the Veterans Hospital, see Pete Daniel, "Black Power in the 1920s: The Case of Tuskegee Veterans Hospital," *Journal of Southern History* 36 (August 1970), 368–88.
45. Ellison, "Campus," F. 1, Box 144; "Golden Day—True Blood," Box 144, REP. Verner Mitchell argues that Norton's collapse is occasioned by his perception of the parallels between Trueblood, Jefferson, and himself as violators of black women. "Ellison's *Invisible Man*," *Explicator* 60 (fall 2001), 44–47. At Tuskegee, Cayton was approached by a female student wishing to prostitute herself (*Long Old Road*, 196–98). For a reading of the Golden Day episode as Bakhtinian carnivalesque, see Elliott Butler-Evans, "The Politics of Carnival and Heteroglossia in Toni Morrison's *Song of Solomon* and Ralph Ellison's *Invisible Man*: Dialogic Criticism and African Ameri-

can Literature," *The Ethnic Canon: Histories, Institutions, and Interventions*, ed. David Palumbo-Liu (Minneapolis: University of Minneapolis Press, 1995), 117–39.

46. Ellison, Notes 1942–50, F. 2, Box 151; "Campus," F. 1, Box 144, REP.

47. Ellison, "Vet," Box 146, REP. The vet refers to Engels's essay, "The Part Played by Labor in the Transition from Ape to Man," in Karl Marx and Frederick Engels, *Selected Works*, 3 vols. (Moscow: Progress Publishers, 1970), vol. 3, 66–77.

48. Ellison, "Vet," Box 146, REP.

49. Lewis Mumford, *The Golden Day: A Study in American Culture and Experience* (New York: Boni and Liveright, 1926), 136–58, quote p. 136; Mumford, *Men Must Act* (New York: Harcourt, Brace, 1939), 26. See also Mumford, *Technics and Civilization* (New York: Harcourt, Brace, 1934), 9–59. For commentaries on Ellison's use of Mumford, see Alan Nadel, *Invisible Criticism: Ralph Ellison and the American Canon* (Iowa City: University of Iowa Press, 1988), 85–103; and John S. Wright, *Shadowing Ralph Ellison* (Jackson: University Press of Mississippi, 2006), 131–59.

50. "Suggestions for RE from HF," Notes 1942–50, F. 1, Box 151, REP.

51. Ellison, "Vet," Box 146, REP. For more on "Benito Cereno" as an intertext of the Golden Day episode, see Nadel, *Invisible Criticism*, 104–11.

52. Ellison, "Golden Day—True Blood," Box 144, REP. In an interview in 1961 Ellison recalled "sneak[ing] out to watch [the] . . . farm people's" Founder's Day celebrations on the campus athletic fields ("That Same Pain, That Same Pleasure," CE, 77–78).

53. Ellison, "Golden Day—True Blood," Box 144, REP. Whether or not Ellison was aware of it, the circular dance performed by the farm folk resembles the ring-shout, an African-derived dance central to slave culture. See Sterling Stuckey, *Slave Culture: Nationalist Culture and the Foundations of Black America* (New York: Oxford University Press, 1987).

54. Rampersad, RE:B, 102.

55. Graham and Singh, *Conversations with Ralph Ellison*, 373; Ellison, "The Art of Fiction: An Interview" (1955), CE, 218.

Chapter Five: Becoming Proletarian

1. Ellison, "Working Notes for *Invisible Man*," CE, 345–46; Ellison, "The Little Man at Chehaw Station," CE, 504.

2. Ellison, "Perception," Box 146; Notes 1942–50, F. 2 and 3, Box 151, F. 8, Box 152, REP. In an interview in 1982 Ellison admitted, "I had a hell of a lot more material that didn't get into *Invisible Man*." Maryemma Graham and Amritjit Singh, eds., *Conversations with Ralph Ellison* (Jackson: University Press of Mississippi, 1995), 381.

3. Ralph Ellison, "Harlem Is Nowhere," CE, 320–27, quotes pp. 320, 322, 324, 325; Ralph Ellison, "An Extravagance of Laughter," CE, 619. Wertham had provided psychotherapy to Wright and was involved in the effort to get Ellison exempted from military service. See Rampersad, RE:B, 184, 207–08; and Michel Fabre, *The Unfinished Quest of Richard Wright*, 2nd ed., trans. Isabel Barzun (Urbana: University of Illinois Press, 1993), 236–37, 268.

4. Ellison, Notes 1942–50, F. 5, Box 151, REP.

5. Ellison, "New York Arrival," Box 145, REP. Ellison scribbled "Mantan Moreland" in place of "Stepinfetchit." Both Stepin Fetchit (William Perry) and Moreland were African American comic film actors who often played eye-rolling stereotypical roles. For more on Hoover's role, beginning with the red scare after the First World War, in persecuting black radicals, see Theodore Kornweibel, "Seeing Red": Federal Campaigns against Black Militancy, 1914–1925 (Bloomington: Indiana University Press, 1998). In one draft of the New York section, the invisible man is shown recalling the vet's advice ("Uncle Charles," Box 146, REP); in another ("New York," Box 145, REP), the invisible man's initial subway ride is described in the third person.

6. That Ellison struggled to come up with the "baptism" scene is indicated by a note to himself: "Immediate problem is to allow him to regain consciousness of his immediate past. It must be through a dramatic incident, extremely meaningful. . . . Perhaps it would be . . . effective if he could meet someone like Bledsoe, an encounter which would return the past in all its vividness" (Notes 1942–50, F. 8, Box 152, REP).

7. Ralph Ellison, "Men's House," Box 145, REP.

8. Ibid.; George Thomson, *Aeschylus and Athens: A Study in the Social Origins of Drama* (1940; rpt. New York: Grosset and Dunlap, 1968), 91–119, quote pp. 93–94. That Ellison had Thomson in mind is suggested by his note to himself: "Tribal Men's House" (Notes 1942–50, F. 3, Box 151, REP). He also wrote, "For Y substitute 'Men's House'" (Notes 1942–50, F. 4, Box 151, REP). As more recent work on sexuality in ancient Greek society indicates, Thomson's view of Men's House as a zone protective of heterosexuality was probably inaccurate.

9. Ellison, Notes 1942–50, F. 8 and 9, Box 152, REP.

10. Ellison, Notes 1942–50, F. 9, Box 152, REP.

11. Ellison, F. 6 and 9, Box 152, REP; "Brockaway (Paint Factory)," Box 142, REP. An early draft the paint factory episode is preceded by the heading "Book II," indicating the centrality of the factory experience in defining the next phase of the protagonist's odyssey ("New York," Box 145, REP). Ellison initially designated the code on a can as "SKI-3-69-Y," a notation camouflaging 1, 369 SKY, perhaps an oblique play on the number of lightbulbs that substitute for sunlight in the invisible man's underground den. "Brockaway (Paint Factory)," Box 142, REP. See Rampersad, RE:B, 89, on Ellison's experience working at a paint factory in Astoria, Queens. Ellison at first spelled Brockway "Brockaway" and Lucius "Lucious."

12. Ellison, "Brockaway (Paint Factory)," Box 142, REP.

13. Ibid.; Notes 1942–50, F. 7, Box 152, REP. Ellison jotted a map of the episode's tripartite structure: "Purpose: To hold job until trustees answer his letters. Passion: To remain on the job, do good job of making paint cover and dry. Perception: Deferred when he is not fired as he expects, but is sent in basement to work for Lucious Brockway. New purpose: To remain here by allaying Brockway's fears that he is being groomed for Brockway's job." Ellison further noted, "Symbolic: His unconscious failure to whitewash reality has led to his Northern exile." For more on racism within American craft unions and the CIO's desegregation campaigns, see Herbert R. Northrup, *Organized Labor and the Negro* (New York: Harper and Bros., 1944); and Philip Foner, *Organized Labor and the Black Worker*, 2nd ed. (New York: International Publishers, 1982).

14. Ellison, "Brockaway (Paint Factory)," Box 142, REP; Richard Wright, *Twelve Million Black Voices* (1941; rpt. New York: Thunder's Mouth Press, 1988), 119.

15. Ellison, "Paint Factory," Box 145, REP. In various drafts Brockway subsequently reappears as a nemesis figure. He "wears white suit and white hat, carries cane that he uses like a sword against the IVM, [who thinks], 'And he's probably been watching me all along, knowing me and hating me by both my old and by my Brotherhood name'" ("Sea Cook," "One-Eyed Cook," Box 146, REP).

16. Ellison, "Fragments and Partial Drafts," F. 5, Box 151; Ralph Ellison, "Lostness," Box 145; Ellison, "Fat Man on a Bridge," Box 144, REP.

17. Ellison, Notes 1942–50, F. 3, Box 151; "New York," Box 145, REP.

18. Ellison, "Uncle Charles," "Wheelchair," Box 146, REP.

19. Ellison, "Wheelchair," Box 146, REP. Ellison notes that the woman's name is "Miss Margaret Vevers (or some other Jamesian heroine)," evidently referencing *The Golden Bowl*, in which the tangled relationship between Adam and Maggie Verver, a fabulously wealthy father and his daughter, figures centrally ("Fragments and Partial Drafts," F. 5, Box 150, REP).

20. Ellison, F. 3, Notes 1942–50, Box 151, REP. The obvious Freudian reference is to Dora, Freud's classic account of female hysterical paralysis. See Sigmund Freud, "Fragment of an Analysis of a Case of Hysteria," *Case Histories*, vol. 1. (Harmondsworth, England: Pelican Books, 1977).

21. Ellison associated the woman's treatment of the invisible man with the exploitation of James Wait, the black scapegoat in Conrad's *The Nigger of the "Narcissus"*; he wrote, "Do a section on the psychologically crippled whites who project their neurosis upon Negroes. Remember Conrad" ("Hospital Scene—Working Copy," Box 145, REP).

22. Ellison, "Uncle Charles," Box 146, REP.

23. Remarking in 1971 on his own experiences as a waiter, Ellison struck a humanistic note of his own: "We Negroes are the most ironic observers of the American scene. Those of us who are waiters, maids, nursemaids and cooks are close and concerned observers; and they are not always putting down what they see or fighting the class or race war" (Graham and Singh, *Conversations with Ralph Ellison*, 204). This view contrasts notably not only with "Uncle Charles" but also with the violence-ridden portrait of Negro waiters in the Jim Crow South in Ellison's unpublished short story "Tillman and Tackhead" (Box 165, REP).

24. Ellison, "Uncle Charles." Box 146, REP.

25. Richard Wright, "I Have Seen Black Hands" (1934), *New Masses: An Anthology of the Rebel Thirties*, ed. Joseph North (New York: International Publishers, 1969), 49–51. Uncle Charles's fulfillment of the expectation that all African Americans steal recalls *Black Boy (American Hunger)* (New York: Library of America, 1993), 200. As regards the relationship of invisibility to exploited labor, it is noteworthy that both Charles S. Johnson, in his preface to *The Shadow of the Plantation* (Chicago: University of Chicago Press, 1934), ix, and Wright in his introduction to St. Clair Drake and Horace Cayton, *Black Metropolis: A Study of Negro Life in a Northern City* (New York: Harcourt, Brace and World, 1945), xxxii, cite that same quotation from William

James, which begins, "No more fiendish punishment could be devised, were such a thing physically possible, than that one should be turned loose in society and remain absolutely unnoticed by all the members thereof." The James quotation is from *The Philosophy of William James* (New York: Modern Library, 1925), 128.

26. For a useful catalogue of patriotic images and allusions in the published text, see Floyd R. Horowitz, "Ralph Ellison's Modern Version of Brer Bear and Brer Rabbit in *Invisible Man*," *Twentieth-Century Interpretations of* Invisible Man, ed. John M. Reilly (Englewood Cliffs, N.J.: Prentice-Hall, 1970), 34.

27. Steven Tracy, "A Delicate Ear, a Retentive Memory, and the Power to Weld the Fragments," *A Historical Guide to Ralph Ellison*, ed. Steven Tracy (New York: Oxford University Press, 2004), 104–8, quotes pp. 105, 106; Ellison, "Emerson," Box 144, REP. See also Steven Tracy, "The Devil's Son-in-Law and *Invisible Man*," *MELUS* 15, no. 3 (1988), 47–64. For a sample of Wheatstraw's transgressive lyrics, see Eric J. Sundquist, *Cultural Contexts for Ralph Ellison's* Invisible Man (New York: St. Martin's Press, 1994), 123–24. Paul Garon notes Wheatstraw's emphatic projection of male sexuality: *The Devil's Son-In-Law: The Story of Peetie Wheatstraw and His Songs* (London: Studio Vista, 1971). When a youth, Ellison sat in with his trumpet on a jam session with Wheatstraw.

28. Graham and Singh, *Conversations with Ralph Ellison*, 270. Other possible allusions to blueprints with which Ellison would have been familiar include Roi Ottley's statement, "The Negro stands at the door of a fretful future. What it will be no man can say: there are no blueprints." *"New World A-Coming": Inside Black America* (Cleveland: World Publishing, 1943), 343; Wright's assertion in his introduction to *Black Metropolis*, "The imposed conditions under which Negroes live detail the structure of their lives like an engineer outlining the blue-prints for the production of machines" (xx); and Earl Conrad's judgment, "The pattern of contemporary Jim Crow comes down from slavery almost like a blueprint." *Jim Crow America* (New York: Duell, Sloan and Pierce, 1947), 120. For the argument that Ellison is rejecting Wright's blueprints, see Frederick T. Griffiths, "Copy Wright: What Is an (Invisible) Author?," *New Literary History* 33, no. 2 (2002), 315–34.

29. Ellison, "Emerson," Box 144, REP; Jerry Gafio Watts, *Heroism and the Black Intellectual: Ralph Ellison, Politics, and Afro-American Intellectual Life* (Chapel Hill: University of North Carolina Press, 1994), 108.

30. Ellison, "Emerson," Box 144; Original typescript, F. 3, Box 147; Notes 1942–50, F. 6, Box 152, REP; Leslie Fiedler, "Come Back to the Raft Ag'in, Huck Honey," *Partisan Review* 15 (June 1948), 634–53. Ellison wrote to Hyman in 1947 regarding the "piece on the Negro and homosexuality" in a current issue of *Partisan Review*: "I have been looking for some information on Whitman which will fix the start of his pro-Negro activity as a means of getting into the same theme. The PR essay is in the right direction but still superficial" (15 June 1947, Box 6, SEHP). See also Ellison's reference to Fiedler's essay in "Change the Joke and Slip the Yoke," CE, 104. Regarding the invisible man's possibly overturning the bird cage, Ellison wrote, "If prepared, he might turn over cage of birds in anger, setting them free in the elegant room ("New York," Box 145, REP). That Ellison attached extensive significance to the Robin-as-

scapegoat motif is indicated by his mapping of it as a Burkean pentad: "I found my-self puzzling over the who, what, when, why and where of poor old Robin. . . . Who was Robin, what was his act in what scene, using what agency, for what purpose had be gotten himself tied and hurt and humiliated, as hurt and humiliated as I?" ("At Mary's," F. 2, Box 142, REP). "Pick Poor Robin Clean" was the title of a blues record-ing by Geeshie Wiley and Elvie Thomas (Tracy, "The Power to Weld the Fragments," 108–9). In his essay on Charlie Parker, Ellison would compare the sacrificial figure of "Bird" with "poor Robin" ("On Bird, Bird-Watching, and Jazz," 1962, CE, 256–65).

31. Ellison, "Emerson," Box 144, REP; Sigmund Freud, *Totem and Taboo: Resemblances be-tween the Psychic Lives of Savages and Neurotics*, trans, A. A. Brill (1918; rpt. New York: Random House, 1946), 168, 186. Douglas Steward argues that young Emerson's fail-ure to adhere to the heteronormativity embodied in the incest taboo reveals not his neurosis but his triumph over patriarchal coercion: "The Illusions of Phallic Agency: *Invisible Man, Totem and Taboo*, and the Santa Claus Surprise," *Callaloo* 26, no. 2 (2003), 522–35.

32. Ellison, Notes 1942–50, F. 6, Box 152. In *Lonely Crusade* (1947; rpt. New York: Thun-der's Mouth Press, 1997), Chester Himes evidently shared Ellison's distaste for the parallel between Negroes and homosexuals, denouncing it, through his protagonist, as "stupid and malicious" (36).

33. Ellison, "Emerson," Box 144; Notes 1942–50, F. 8, Box 152, REP. Ellison injected allu-sions to Shakespearean tragedy into an early draft of the Wall Street episode. When young Emerson is about to deliver the blow that will kill the young man's hopes, he murmurs to himself Macbeth's words before murdering Banquo: "If it were done when it is done, / then twere well it were done quickly." The invisible man, well-trained, it seems, by Woodridge, recognizes the quotation's source and then com-pares his situation with that of Hamlet as the bearer of a Bellerophontic letter call-ing upon its reader to put the carrier to death ("Emerson," Box 144, REP).

34. Ellison considered extending the portrayal of Wall Street by having the invisible man undergo a series of interviews with trustees who would "give him elaborate and pompous lectures about [the] school. Describe each. American industrialist types. H. H. Wood" (Notes 1942–50, F. 4, Box 151, REP).

35. Ellison, "Hospital Scene—General," F. 3, Box 145, REP. Ellison titled the folders "Factory Hospital"; "Hospital Scene-General" (1–3); "Hospital and St. Mary's—In Continuity" (1–3)"; "Hospital Scene, Working Copy"; and "Hospital and Escape." He later extracted a composite version of this material and published it as "Out of the Hospital and under the Bar" in 1963. See *Soon One Morning: New Writing by American Negroes, 1940–1962*, ed. Herbert Hill (New York: Knopf, 1963), 242–90. The invisible man's "Mexican revolution" corresponds with the digestive problems that plagued Ellison all his life. A possible source for the hospital episode is Horace Cayton's ex-perience giving blood in a clinic where the sign read, "Blood Makes Good Paint." *Long Old Road* (New York: Trident Press, 1965), 329–38. That Ellison continued to re-think the placement of the hospital episode is indicated in a note to himself written just months before he gave the final draft to his publisher. Apparently still unsure about whether this was the best way to get his protagonist to Mary's, he scribbled

on an envelope postmarked February 1951, "Leaves returns to Mens House and decides to leave and live with Mary. Needed: a more dramatic motive for the move"
("At Mary's," F. 2, Box 142, REP).

36. Ellison, "Hospital Scene—General"; "Hospital—Working Copy," Box 145, REP. The
doctor's list draws together the historic leaders Washington, Douglass, and Du Bois;
the contemporary artists and intellectuals Langston Hughes, James Weldon Johnson, Charles S. Johnson, and most likely Richard Wright and Roland Hayes; the
popular entertainers Mantan Moreland and Bert Williams; the political activists
Lester Granger and A. Philip Randolph; the Communists Eugene Clay Holmes and
Richard B. Moore; and the folk hero John Henry. "Thomas B." probably signifies Bigger Thomas. Ellison jotted, "Game of what's your identity; Heroes and false heroes"
(Notes 1942–50, F. 1, Box 151, REP). This extended list of "heroes and false heroes,"
which conveys a far more complex set of alternative identities than is offered to the
reborn migrant in the 1952 text, may allude to the multiple queries about identity in
the original version of Paul Robeson's "The Ballad for Americans," to each of which
the singer replies, "You know who I am!" See Kevin Jack Hagopian, "'You Know
Who I Am!': Paul Robeson's 'Ballad for Americans' and the Paradox of the Double v
in American Popular Culture," *Paul Robeson: His Life and Legacy*, ed. Joseph Dorinson
and William Pencak (Jefferson, N.C.: McFarland, 2002), 167–79.

37. Ellison, "Hospital and St. Mary's—In Continuity," Box 144; "Hospital Scene—Working Copy," Box 145, REP. The chant about Jack the Rabbit and Jack the Bear is from a
work song appearing in Howard Odum and Guy B. Johnson's *The Negro and His Songs:
A Study of Typical Negro Songs of the South*, quoted in Sundquist, *Cultural Contexts for
Ralph Ellison's* Invisible Man, 120–21. For a discussion of "Jack-the-Bear," see chapter 7.

38. Ellison, "Hospital and Escape," Box 144; "Hospital—General," F. 1, Box 145, REP. The
passage from 1 Corinthians 13 is cited in Ellison's notes several times (Notes 1942–
50, F. 4, Box 151, REP). While the "Cure" resembles electric shock therapy, Ellison
was intentionally vague. He stated in 1971, "I just felt that what I was going to do
would, perhaps carry more power if it weren't spelled out too specifically" (Graham
and Singh, *Conversations with Ralph Ellison*, 196).

39. Ellison, Notes 1942–50, F. 3, Box 151; "Hospital Scene—Working Copy," Box 145, REP.
In *Archetypal Patterns in Poetry: Psychological Studies of Imagination* (London: Oxford
University Press, 1934), which was recommended to Ellison by Hyman, Maude Bod-
kin analyzes the figure of Christ as an archetype of Frazer's hanged god and dis-
cusses the passage from Corinthians as a description of universal rebirth (284–89).
Ellison remarked in 1972 that the novel was "structured on patterns of rebirth [that
are] implicit in tragedy, in the blues, in Christian mythology" (Graham and Singh,
Conversations with Ralph Ellison, 230).

40. For Ellison's later views on Lincoln, see *Juneteenth: A Novel* (New York: Random
House, 1999) and "Tell It Like It Is, Baby," CE, 29–46. See also Brian Reed, "The
Iron and the Flesh: History as Machine in Ellison's *Invisible Man*," *CLA Journal* 37,
no. 3 (1994), 261–73. Douglas Ford suggests that the hospital scene may draw upon
George Schuyler's *Black No More*, which "depicts racial assimilation occurring

through a form of electrocution." "Crossroads and Cross-Currents in *Invisible Man*," *Modern Fiction Studies* 45, no. 4 (1999), 892.

41. Ellison, "Hospital and St. Mary's—In Sequence," F. 1, Box 144; "Hospital Scene—General," F. 3, Box 145, REP.

42. See Leon Trotsky, *The Permanent Revolution: Results and Prospects* (1931; rpt. New York: Merit Press, 1969); J. V. Stalin, "The October Revolution and the Tactics of the Russian Communists," *Works*, 13 vols. (Moscow: Foreign Languages Publishing House), vol. 4, available on Marxists.org. While both Trotskyists and Stalinists invoked Lenin in support of their theses, Lenin's writings reveal that soon after the Bolshevik Revolution he rapidly relinquished his earlier skepticism about building socialism in one country. See V. I. Lenin, "Our Foreign and Domestic Position and Party Tasks, Speech Delivered to the Moscow Gubernia Conference of the R.C.P.(B.), November 21, 1920," *Collected Works*, 41 vols. (Moscow: Progress Publishers, 1966), vol. 31, 410–14. This debate had further implications for the "Negro question" in the United States: the Trotskyists believed that the Negro producing masses should be granted the right of self-determination (in a nongeographical sense) but organized only around proletarian demands; the Stalinists called for both multiracial proletarian organizing and geographical self-determination in the Black Belt in order to move toward socialism and at the same time compensate for the lag embodied in the South. The opposed positions on the "Negro question" are exemplified in, respectively, Max Shachtman, *Race and Revolution*, ed. Christopher Phelps (London: Verso, 2003); and James. S. Allen, *The Negro Question in the United States* (New York: International Publishers, 1936). See also C. L. R. James, *C. L. R. James on the "Negro Question,"* ed. Scott McLemee (Jackson: University Press of Mississippi, 1996). The draft containing references to the socialist doctor and to "socialism in one country" is dated 1949, indicating that Ellison considered retaining this political allusion for some time.

43. Ellison, "Hospital Scene—General," F. 3, Box 144, REP. The portrait of the leftist doctor suggests Arthur Koestler's derogatory portrait of the typical Communist in *The Yogi and the Commissar* (New York: Macmillan, 1945), 8, where the commissar's subconscious is said to have been "dealt with not on the analyst's sofa but on the surgeon's table by an amputating knife." Ellison was evidently familiar with Koestler's novel, having clipped and saved F. O. Matthiessen's *New York Times* review (27 May 1945; "Arthur Koestler," Box 190, REP). Maureen E. Curtin makes explicit the role of the hospital scene in shifting the text's critique away from explicitly hierarchical forms of domination and toward "the [Brotherhood's] project to discipline black bodies through the cultivation of objectivity": "Materializing Invisibility as X-Ray Technology: Skin Matters in Ralph Ellison's *Invisible Man*," *LIT: Literature Interpretation Theory* 9 (April 1999), 281–97, quote p. 282.

44. Ellison, "Hospital Scene—General," F. 3, Box 145; "Hospital and St. Mary's," F. 1, Box 144; "At Mary's," F. 2, Box 142; "Hospital Scene—Working Copy," F. 145, REP. In a fragment where Ellison considers moving directly from the hospital scene to the eviction—"cut[ting] out Mary, LeRoy and Cleo"—he jotted, "So I was hit on the head by a machine but I was tougher than John Henry, because I lived through it. I layed down but didn't die" (Notes 1942–50, F. 1, Box 151, REP).

45. Ellison, "At Mary's," F 2, Box 142; "Hospital Scene—General," F. 3, Box 145, REP. The invisible man is evidently unaware that there are no penguins in the Arctic. For more on the relationship between the homosexual in the alley and the "single white figure" of the invisible man's antagonists, see Daniel Y. Kim, *Writing Manhood in Black and Yellow: Ralph Ellison, Frank Chin, and the Literary Politics of Identity* (Stanford: Stanford University Press, 2005), 62–65.

46. Ellison, "Hospital Scene—General," F. 1, 2, and 3, Box 145; "Hospital and Escape," Box 144, REP.

47. Ellison, "Hospital and St. Mary's—In Continuity, F. 2, Box 144; "Blind Man," Box 142; "Cleo and Mt. Morris," Box 144; "Hospital and Escape," Box 144, REP.

48. Ellison, "Out of the Hospital and under the Bar," 242–90, quote p. 242; "Hospital Scene—General," F. 3, Box 145; REP. Readers familiar with the 1963 story will note that Ellison eliminated the more grotesque features originally attributed to Mary. On several occasions subsequently Ellison expressed regret that he had excised the fuller depiction of Mary—whom he viewed as an embodiment of the folk—from the novel.

49. For more on Ellington's "Jack-the-Bear," see Tracy, "A Delicate Ear," 88–90. Ellison routinely denied that Wright's novella inspired his novel; this excised episode, however, shows the unmistakable influence of Wright (Ellison to Hyman, 29 May 1970, Box 6, SEHP; Graham and Singh, *Conversations with Ralph Ellison*, 211). Ellison noted that the guards are "symbolically regressive and would keep him at this stage of his development" (Notes 1942–50, F. 3, Box 151, REP).

50. Ellison, Notes 1942–50, F. 4, Box 151; "Blind Man," Box 142, REP. "Apotropaic" signals a talismanic quality.

51. Ellison, Notes 1942–50, F. 5, Box 151, REP. He jotted, "The theme of treason must return at all pivotal points, thus he must meet man who reminds him of his grandfather soon after he comes to old Mary's. A Crucial encounter. 'Times flying, souls dying, the coming of the Lord draweth nigh'" (Notes 1942–50, F. 8, Box 152). In Harlem during the late 1940s Ellison would often encounter on the street the blind blues pioneer W. C. Handy (Jackson, RE:E, 388).

52. Stuart Noble-Goodman, "Mythic Guilt and the Burden of Sin in Ellison's *Invisible Man*," *Midwest Quarterly* 39, no. 4 (1998), 409–32. Some important texts in the scholarship on the novel's representation of women are Anne Folwell Stanford, "He Speaks for Whom? Inscription and Reinscription of Women in *Invisible Man* and *The Salt Eaters*," *The Critical Response to Ralph Ellison*, ed. Robert J. Butler (Westport, Conn.: Greenwood Press, 2000), 115–26; Claudia Tate, "Notes on the Invisible Women in Ralph Ellison's *Invisible Man*," *Speaking for You: The Vision of Ralph Ellison*, ed. Kimberly W. Benston (Washington, D.C.: Howard University Press, 1987), 163–72; Shelly Eversly, "Female Iconography in *Invisible Man*, *The Cambridge Companion to Ralph Ellison*, ed. Ross Posnock (Cambridge: Cambridge University Press, 2005), 172–87; James S. Smethurst, "'Something Warmly, Infuriatingly Feminine': Gender, Sexuality, and the Work of Ralph Ellison," in Tracy, *A Historical Guide to Ralph Ellison*, 115–42. Ellison remarked in an interview in 1971, "The early women in my fiction [stand] for established values rather than as, in Freudian terms, castrators. I would

say that they were 'circumcisors'" (Graham and Singh, *Conversations with Ralph Ellison*, 196–97).

53. Ellison, Notes 1942–50, F. 5, Box 151; "At Mary's," F. 2, Box 142, REP; Ellison, "Did You Ever Dream Lucky?," *New World Writing* 5 (April 1954), 134–45.

54. Ellison, "At Mary's," F. 2, Box 142; Notes 1942–50, F. 4 and 3, Box 151, REP. Ellison noted, "Old Mary might tell experiences of working for white family in which husband was concerned with same problems against which IVM is struggling. A 'mirroring' technique" (Notes 1942–50, F. 2, Box 151, REP). It bears noting that, as a worker in Harlem Hospital, Mary Rambo would have come into contact there with Communist organizers. See Gerald Horne, *Black Liberation / Red Scare* (Newark: University of Delaware Press, 1994), 156–57; Mark Naison, *Communists in Harlem During the Depression* (1983; rpt. Urbana: University of Illinois Press, 2005), 78–79.

55. Ellison, "At Mary's," F. 2, Box 142; Notes 1942–50 F. 4, Box 151, F. 6, Box 152; "Cleo and Mt. Morris Park," Box 144, REP. In New York in the era of the New Deal, 29 percent of African American families had at least one lodger, as opposed to 6 percent of white families. See Cheryl Lynn Greenberg, *"Or Does It Explode?": Black Harlem in the Great Depression* (New York: Oxford University Press, 1991), 191.

56. Ellison, "LeRoy's Journal," Box 145; Notes 1942–50, F. 9, Box 152, REP. Ellison's own childhood in Oklahoma brought him into contact with Native Americans, as well as what he termed the "Indian-Negro confusion" of blended groups ("Hidden Name and Complex Fate," *CE*, 201–2).

57. Ellison, "At Mary's," F. 2, Box 142; Notes 1942–50, F. 3, Box 151, REP. One draft includes a twelve-page conversation, apparently among women at a hair parlor, about the Harlem uprising in 1935. "Didn't we get jobs on 125th Street after the last riot[?]" asks one woman. "We need to have some more riots. We ought to have one every six months to keep things straightened out" ("At Mary's," F. 2, Box 142, REP). That Ellison envisioned Mary's boarders as a means of getting at political issues is indicated by his note, "Through Mrs. Garfield's comments about her husband's fortunes we might touch on development of Negroes as craftsman, specialist, industrial workers etc. Unionism" (Notes 1942–50, F. 4, Box 151). Regarding Mr. Portwood's discussion of leadership, Ellison observed, "This is actually a description of system of checks and balances applied to theme of Negro leader" (Notes 1942–50, F. 5, Box 151, REP).

58. Ellison, "At Mary's," F. 2, Box 142; "Cleo and Mt. Morris Park," Box 144, REP. Ellison varied the spelling of LeRoy and Leroy; the earliest handwritten versions refer to "LeRoy," which emphasizes his identity as "the king" (Notes 1942–50, F. 9, Box 152 REP). For the sake of consistency I use only "LeRoy," amending Ellison's spelling as needed, including in the title of the folder he marked "Leroy's Journal." Although LeRoy's orphan status aligns him with Raglan's hero, Ellison considered the possibility that LeRoy is Mary's son, and even that the vet might be his father (Notes 1942–50, F. 8 and 11, Box 152, REP). Ellison contemplated other versions of LeRoy's death, including his having fallen off the boat accidentally and his having died trying to save Treadwell from drowning, which would make Treadwell feel responsible for his death ("At Mary's," F. 2, Box 142; Notes 1942–50, F. 3, Box 151, REP). In the

earliest draft Treadwell suspects that LeRoy was murdered because of "the union business," but he is not sure (F. 11, Box 152, REP).

59. Ellison, Notes 1942–50, F. 11, Box 152; "At Mary's," F. 2, Box 142, REP. In his influential *The Mass Psychology of Fascism*, 3rd ed., trans. Vincent P. Carfagno (1942; rpt. New York: Farrar, Straus, 1970), 27, Reich wrote, "The family is the authoritarian state in miniature, to which the child must learn to adapt himself as a preparation for the general social adjustment required of him later." Ellison's notes refer to Reich's book (Notes 1942–50, F. 10, Box 152, REP). Treadwell's portrayal recalls "Beating That Boy," where Ellison asserts, "It is practically impossible for the white American to think of sex, of economics, his children or womenfolk, or of sweeping socio-political changes, without summoning into consciousness fear-flecked images of black men."

60. Ellison, "At Mary's," F. 2, Box 142, REP. Ellison noted, "Treadwell looks like a red-necked cracker, except he is one who has been somehow transformed. He combines the cracker with Norton traits. It is this which confuses the folks at old Mary's" (Notes 1942–50, F. 1, Box 151, REP). Ellison, who was in Le Havre during the war, wrote to Fanny Buford on 10 March 1945 of the "stupidity and chauvinism" of Americans in France (quoted in Rampersad, *RE:B*, 186).

61. Ellison, "At Mary's," F. 2, Box 142; "Cleo and Mt. Morris Park," Box 144; "LeRoy's Journal," Box 145, REP. Treadwell also speaks of "dedication to a sacred purpose."

62. Lord Raglan, *The Hero: A Study in Tradition, Myth and Drama* (1936; rpt. Westport, Conn.: Greenwood Press, 1956); Gilbert Murray, in Jane Ellen Harrison, *Themis: A Study of the Social Origins of Greek Religion, with an Excursus on the Ritual Forms of Greek Tragedy by Gilbert Murray* (1912; rpt. Cleveland: World Publishing, 1962), 343; James Frazer, *The Golden Bough: A Study in Magic and Religion*, abridged version (New York: Macmillan, 1940), 362–79.

63. Thomson, *Aeschylus and Athens*, 40; Harrison, *Themis*, 485; Jane Ellen Harrison, *Ancient Art and Ritual* (1918; rpt. London: Oxford University Press, 1948), 45–46; Frazer, *The Golden Bough*, 714; Jane Ellen Harrison, *Prolegomena to the Study of Greek Religion*, 3rd ed. (New York: Meridian Books, 1955), 261. For more on totemic consumption, see Frazer, *The Golden Bough*, 505–18, 689–93; and Rhys Carpenter, *Folk Tale, Fiction and Saga in the Homeric Epics* (1946; rpt. Berkeley: University of California Press, 1956). Ellison's naming one draft of the rooming house section "Hospital and St. Mary's" underlines Mary's associations with the mother of Christ. Jessie Weston, in *From Ritual to Romance* (1920; rpt. New York: Anchor Books, 1957), 9—which T. S. Eliot acknowledged as his principal source of the fisher king myth in *The Waste Land*— repeated the "le roi est mort" ritual pronouncement from Frazer. Bodkin stressed the continuity between the Christ story and other *Golden Bough* myths (*Archetypal Patterns in Poetry*, 284–89). For a useful comparison of Raglan's study with Otto Rank's *The Myth of the Birth of the Hero* and Alan Dundes's *The Hero Pattern and the Life of Jesus*, see Robert A. Segal, ed., *In Quest of the Hero* (Princeton: Princeton University Press, 1990).

64. Ellison, Notes 1942–50, F. 8, Box 152; F. 4, Box 151; F. 10 Box 152; F. 3 Box 151, REP; Francis Fergusson, *The Idea of a Theater: A Study of Ten Plays: The Art of Drama in Chang-*

ing Perspective (Princeton: Princeton University Press, 1949), especially 13–41; Murray, in Harrison, *Themis*, 343–44. Ellison jotted, "LeRoy must do something for everyone at Mary's. For Mary he might be kind of son. For Cleo a lover, for Sam a younger version of himself. For Mrs. Garfield a shrewd man who has helped her collect insurance, etc." (Notes 1942–50, F. 4, Box 151, REP). The terms *pharmakos* and *sparagmos* denote somewhat different aspects of the sacrificed or dismembered scapegoat or its totemic surrogate; the latter is more likely to be used only in relation to the animal being sacrificed. Ellison tended to use the terms interchangeably in his notes.

65. Ellison wrote, "LeRoy's loneliness drives him to sea, into the destructive element; for he realizes the isolation implicit in his role of the dedicated" (Notes 1942–50, F. 3, Box 151). Ellison also viewed immersion in the "destructive element" as a metaphor for artistic creation (1982 introduction to *Invisible Man*, xviii); in a draft of the preface published in 1980, containing a longer version of the invisible man's "I am an invisible man" address, Ellison adds of his hero, "He was my own destructive element" (preface to the Franklin Library Edition, Box 150, REP). For a discussion of the varying roles of scapegoats in Conrad's fiction, see Andrew Mozina, *Joseph Conrad and the Art of Sacrifice: The Evolution of the Scapegoat Theme in Joseph Conrad's Fiction* (New York: Routledge, 2001). The *Moby-Dick* allusion may also illuminate the invisible man's rescue from the hospital machine by Mary: he is a modern Ishmael, she a version of the cruising Rachel, searching for one son lost at sea and finding another. Ellison may also have been riffing on Joyce's *Finnegan's Wake* in his representation of Mary's dinner, as well as on Coleridge's "The Rime of the Ancient Mariner" in his portrayal of the guilt-burdened Treadwell.

66. Ellison, "At Mary's," F. 2, Box 142; "Cleo and Mt. Morris Park," Box 144, REP. Speculating on an alternate sexual history for his protagonist, Ellison jotted, "IVM is a black male virgin. Scenes of first affair with woman. Girl in diner" (F. 10, Box 152, REP). One note suggests Ellison's uneasiness about creating Cleo: "What if after failing to satisfy her, he turns against her and gives [an] insincere lecture about danger of doing what she has done? What if in this lecture he says essentially those things said about Negro folk by those Negroes who do not understand them and who dislike the reality for which they stand? . . . that they are lazy, trouble making, loud, disorderly, crude, loose moraled, unclean smelly." Ellison interjected the parenthetical comment, "Now its coming close to home. I feel my composure going. I want to scream. I can no longer strive to achieve 'objectivity,' to present those times and those selves with the proper literary effects" (Notes 1942–50, F. 6, Box 152, REP).

67. Ellison, Notes 1942–50, F. 6, Box 152; "Cleo and Mt. Morris Park," Box 144, REP. Cleo's presence may be illuminated by the rules of Torah reading, namely, that LeRoy is in another symbolic register a kohen, or Jewish high priest descended from Moses's brother Aaron, who, "because he serves in the Bet Mikdash . . . [and has been] dedicated and set aside," must abstain from contact with a prostitute or dishonored woman. See website of Bet Midrash Virtuali; also Leviticus 21:6–7. Regarding Cleo's possible political role, Ellison speculated, "After meeting Jack and deciding to leave Mary's, the invisible man dreams of leaving Cleo: he is on stilts on

Harlem street, she calls upon him to 'come down from there.' Afterwards, he sleeps *like 'a rock or a man that was dead'* (L. Hughes)" (Notes 1942–50, F. 9, Box 152, REP). The allusion here is to Hughes's poem "The Weary Blues." "Delphinia" might further associate Cleo with LeRoy insofar as he was murdered at sea during a storm. Evidently alert to the gendered implications of the worship of Apollo at Delphi, Ellison remarked that this worship marked "the change from a matriarchal to a patriarchal society" (Graham and Singh, *Conversations with Ralph Ellison*, 211).

68. Ellison, Notes 1942–50, F. 5 and 4, Box 151, REP.

69. Ellison, Notes 1942–50, F. 2, Box 151, REP; Gerald Horne, *Red Seas: Ferdinand Smith and Radical Black Sailors in the United States and Jamaica* (New York: New York University Press, 2005), 88; Herndon, *Let Me Live* (New York: Random House, 1937), 119–22; James S. Allen, *Organizing in the Depression South: A Communist's Memoir* (Minneapolis: MEP, 2001), 89–90; Ellison, "National Negro Congress," Box 91, REP; Earl Conrad, *Jim Crow America*, 168; Martha Biondi, *To Stand and Fight: The Struggle for Civil Rights in Postwar New York City* (Cambridge, Mass.: Harvard University Press, 2003), 8. Mulzac's memoir, *A Star to Steer By*, was published by the CP-sponsored International Publishers in 1963. Ellison and Herndon published in *Negro Quarterly* 1, no. 4 (1943), 330–44, Noah Landau's "The Negro Seaman," which traced the history of Negro sailors' support for slave rebellions, noting the role of seamen in arranging Frederick Douglass's escape from slavery. See also William S. Swift, "The Negro in the Offshore Maritime Industry," *Negro Employment in the Maritime Industries*, ed. Lester Rubin, William S. Swift, and Herbert R. Northrup (Philadelphia: Wharton School, 1974), 78–81; Richard O. Boyer, *The Dark Ship* (Boston: Little, Brown, 1947); Beth McHenry and Frederick N. Myers's proletarian novel *Home Is the Sailor: The Story of an American Seaman* (New York: International Press, 1948). In a lecture in 1969 Ellison recalled the Negro cultural traits of white crewmen (CE, 532). Not all sailors absorbed the outlook of the NMU, however. Wright recorded in his journal on 7 January 1945 that he had just spoken with Ellison, who had "heard from the Maritime Union that many of the ships have had racial trouble on the high seas; that the Negro and white crews have fought; that on some instances the naval gun crews have had to threaten the whites and blacks with their guns to keep them from rioting while carrying cargoes to the war zones! . . . A white man and a Negro got into an argument; the white man told the Negro: I'll grab you about your fucking goddam neck and leap into the sea with you, you black bastard, though I can't swim a single fucking lick! I'll get a half-nelson on your black neck and won't turn loose till we both reach the bottom of the sea!" (F. 1860, Box 117, RWP).

70. Horne, *Red Seas*, 86–87, 195–200; Browder quoted in Philip Selznick, *The RAND Corporation: The Organizational Weapon: A Study of Bolshevik Strategy and Tactics* (New York: McGraw-Hill, 1952), 185. For more on the postwar purging of leftists from the maritime unions, see David Caute, *The Great Fear: The Anti-Communist Purge under Truman and Eisenhower* (New York: Simon and Schuster, 1978), 392–400. According to Ellen Schrecker, *Many Are the Crimes: McCarthyism in America* (Boston: Little, Brown, 1998), 269, "Between 50 and 70 percent of the sailors and longshoremen who were dismissed under the port-security program were either blacks or foreigners."

71. Ellison, "The Booker T.," *New Republic*, 18 February 1946, 262; John Beecher, *All Brave Sailors: The Story of the S.S. Booker T. Washington* (New York: L. B. Fischer, 1945). In one draft Treadwell states that LeRoy was killed by a faction working "to split the union" ("LeRoy's Journal," Box 145, REP). Ellison recalled that during his FWP days he "was in on the agitation which led to the creation of the National Maritime Union, when broken bottles and bricks and every damn thing else were being thrown down on South Street" (Graham and Singh, *Conversations with Ralph Ellison*, 199).

72. Ellison, "LeRoy's Journal," Box 145; Notes 1942–50, F. 6, Box 152, REP. Notes to Ellison's handwritten first draft of the journal read, "Techniques and personality: Keep this stuff to them. Let LeRoy write of human condition most time, not just of Negro position: Leadership; Social Responsibility; Treason; Absurd nature of human life; snipes at shallow philosophy; his own problems. Don't let him run away with anything" (Notes 1942–50, F. 9, Box 152, REP). Ellison contemplated adding to the list "a book on flood control and 'Some of My Best Friends Are Niggers,' by Oglethorpe P. Longstreet" (Notes 1942–50, F. 6, Box 152, REP). The "book on mathematics" is probably Scott Buchanan's *Poetry and Mathematics*, which Ellison read at the suggestion of Hyman, who admired Buchanan's "treatment of imaginative literature in terms of the metaphors of mathematics." *The Armed Vision: A Study in the Methods of Modern Literary Criticism* (New York: Knopf, 1948), 380 n.

73. Ellison, "LeRoy's Journal," Box 145; "Brotherhood, Arena Speech," Box 143, REP. For more on doubling in *Invisible Man*, see Leon Forrest, "Luminosity from the Lower Frequencies," *Ralph Ellison's* Invisible Man: *A Casebook*, ed. John F. Callahan (New York: Oxford University Press, 2004), 267–86. The reference to Munich reminds us that Norton's daughter died after collapsing at an embassy party in Munich; the multimillionaire trustee has "sowed corruption," it would seem, in both the Jim Crow South and Nazi Germany. Ellison entertained the possibility that the invisible man would get a job "working for mistress of Ambassador millionaire, as chauffeur. He believes that if he is successful in having relationships with woman he can make money on the stock market. . . . At same time he is active politically. Learns, by opening briefcase[,] that Munich has been prepared by ambassadors, wants to act but is stopped by realization that no one would believe him—even in the part. Portrait of ambassador's sex life, the woman problem" (Notes 1942–50, F. 2, Box 151, REP).

74. Ellison, "LeRoy's Journal," Box 145, REP; Office memorandum, 30 June 1958, FBI file, Ralph Waldo Ellison. LeRoy's critical comments on Douglass suggest Ellison's familiarity with Benjamin Quarles's laudatory but distinctly nonhagiographical biography, *Frederick Douglass* (Washington, D.C.: Associated Publishers, 1948), in which Quarles opined that Douglass was "broad rather than deep" (ix).

75. Ellison, "LeRoy's Journal," Box 145; Notes 1942–50, F. 11, Box 152, REP.

76. Ellison, "LeRoy's Journal," Box 145; Notes 1942–50, F. 2, Box 151, REP. In an attempt to combat attacks by the House Un-American Activities Committee on radical influences in the media, the NMU, along with the People's Radio Foundation, applied for a radio license in 1946; both organizations were turned down the next year. See Elizabeth Fones-Wolf, *Waves of Opposition: Labor and the Struggle for Democratic Radio* (Urbana: University of Illinois Press, 2006), 125–61.

78. It bears noting that the final word of Wright's autobiography is "human": "I would send other words to tell, to march, to fight, to create a sense of the hunger for life that gnaws in us all, to keep alive in our hearts a sense of the inexpressibly human." *Black Boy (American Hunger): A Record of Childhood and Youth* (New York: Library of America, 1993), 384. The phrase "more human" would recur in Ellison's writings after *Invisible Man*, reinflected to convey nationalism rather than working-class radicalism. He referred to the pioneering Oklahoma environment of his childhood, for instance, as "more fluid" and "more human" than other parts of the country ("That Same Pain, That Same Pleasure," 1961, CE, 65).

79. Ellison to Murray, 24 July 1953, in Albert Murray and John F. Callahan, eds., *Trading Twelves: The Selected Letters of Ralph Ellison and Albert Murray* (New York: Modern Library, 2000), 54–56. The phrase "dedicated and set aside" appears in *Juneteenth* in relation to the sacrificial character of Bliss/Sunraider; clearly it continued to carry a powerful charge for Ellison long after LeRoy's demise.

80. Ellison, Notes 1942–50, F. 1, Box 151, REP. The memo is initialed "HF"; Jackson notes Ford's role in the revision process (RE:E, 414–16). Ellison apparently considered various options before eliminating LeRoy. One was that, if LeRoy were actually Mary's son, this would mean "Treadwell out; unions out of LeRoy's story" (Notes 1942–50, F. 8, Box 152, REP).

81. Ellison, "Emerson," Box 144, REP.

Chapter Six: Finding Brotherhood

1. For Ellison's routine denials that the Brotherhood is the CP, see Maryemma Graham and Amritjit Singh, eds., *Conversations with Ralph Ellison* (Jackson: University Press of Mississippi, 1995), 73, 221, 542. Although the term *brotherhood* has a long history in union nomenclature, especially in the 1930s and 1940s it bore leftist associations. The NMU referred to the "brotherhood-of-the-sea." Gerald Horne, *Red Seas: Ferdinand Smith and Radical Black Sailors in the United States and Jamaica* (New York: New York University Press, 2005), 88. The Communist (and later blacklisted) screenwriter Ring Lardner Jr. worked on the antiracist animated short film titled *Brotherhood of Man* in 1946. Christopher P. Lehman, "The New Black Animated Images of 1946," *Journal of Popular Film and Television* 29 (summer 2001), 74–82.

2. Ellison, letter to Peggy Hitchcock, n.d., Notes 1942–50, F. 3, Box 151; F. 9, Box 152, REP. Although in the 1952 text "brotherhood" is spelled with a lowercase *b*, in early drafts Ellison referred to the "Brotherhood." As in the case of LeRoy/Leroy, I shall adhere to the original spelling in my allusions to the organization.

3. Ellison, Notes 1942–50, F. 3, Box 151, REP; Ellison, "Working Notes *for Invisible Man*," CE, 347.

4. While a very early draft designates the invisible man's arrival at Mary's as the beginning of "Book III, Perception," most others begin "Book III, Political Life," with the eviction episode (chapter 13 in the published text). See Ellison, "Brotherhood," F. 1, Box 142; "Perception," Box 146, REP.

5. For a typical instance of the vernacular reading of the yam scene, see Marc C. Conner, "The Litany of Things: Sacrament and History in *Invisible Man*," in *Ralph Ellison and the Raft of Hope: A Political Companion to* Invisible Man, ed. Lucas Morel (Lexington: University Press of Kentucky, 2004), 171–92. For a critique of the "objectification of culture" embodied in the scene, see Christopher Shannon, *A World Made Safe for Differences: Cold War Intellectuals and the Politics of Identity* (Lanham, Md.: Rowman and Littlefield, 2001), 56. See also Jerry Watts's critique of Ellison's "folk pastoralism" in *Heroism and the Black Intellectual: Ralph Ellison, Politics, and Afro-American Intellectual Life* (Chapel Hill: University of North Carolina Press, 1994), 101–4. Besides echoing Genesis ("I am what I am"), the invisible man's proclamation can be traced to Joyce's "I am yam" in *Finnegan's Wake*. Robert N. List, *Dedalus in Harlem: The Joyce-Ellison Connection* (Washington, D.C.: University Press of America, 1982), 105. Paul Robeson's "now you know who I am" in Earl Robinson's "Ballad for Americans" (Lyrics Playground website) is another possible source.

6. Ellison, Notes 1942–50, F. 2, Box 151, REP.

7. Ellison, "Brotherhood," F. 1, Box 142; Notes 1942–50, F. 2, Box 151, REP.

8. Richard Wright, *Twelve Million Black Voices* (1941; rpt. New York: Thunder's Mouth Press, 1988), 144; Ellison, "Eviction," Box 144, REP. Evictions figure centrally as turning points in several texts set in the Depression: Langston Hughes's "Angelo Herndon Jones: A One-Act Play of Negro Life," *The Political Plays of Langston Hughes*, ed. Susan Duffy (Carbondale: Southern Illinois University Press, 2000), 147–62; Ted Ward's *Big White Fog* (Alexandria, Va.: Alexander Street Press, 2004); Horace Cayton's *Long Old Road* (New York: Trident Press, 1965), 178–81; and Lloyd Brown's *Iron City* (1951; rpt. Boston: Northeastern University Press, 1994), 52–61. For more on Communists and the antieviction movement, see Mark Naison, *Communists in Harlem During the Depression* (New York: Grove Press, 1983); Gerald Horne, *Black Liberation/Red Scare: Ben Davis and the Communist Party* (Newark: University of Delaware Press, 1994); Arna Bontemps and Jack Conroy, *They Seek a City* (Garden City, N.Y.: Doubleday, Doran, 1945), 159–61; and St. Clair Drake and Horace Cayton, *Black Metropolis: A Study of Negro Life in a Northern City* (New York: Harcourt, Brace and World, 1945), 86–89.

9. Ellison, "Eviction," Box 144; REP. Lenin drew the title *What Is to Be Done?* from a revolutionary novel (1863) by the pro-*narodnik* writer Nikolai Chernyshevsky; in its proposition that the Russian peasant commune contains the possible basis for socialist construction, the novel draws an implicit parallel between Russian peasants and African Americans in the South. This parallel was developed in Lenin's writings on the peasant question and was invoked by American theorists of "the Negro question." See Vladimir Lenin, *Collected Works*, 44 vols. (Moscow: Foreign Language Publishing House, 1960–70), vol. 40; James S. Allen, *The Negro Question in the United States* (New York: International Publishers, 1936), 169–203; and Harry Haywood, *Negro Liberation* (New York: International Publishers, 1948), 116–35.

10. Ellison, "Eviction," Box 144, REP. For more on the Harlem riot of 1943, see chapter 7. In the early drafts and outlines contained in the folder marked "New York Arrival," Ellison notes that the invisible man comes north in the "early years of the Depres-

sion" (Box 145, REP). Aware of the problems posed by his divergent time frames, Ellison played around with the dates associated with the Provos. In the 1952 text Primus Provo is eighty-seven; in an earlier version he is seventy-five ("Eviction," Box 144; "Brotherhood," F. 1, Box 142, REP). Four possibilities emerge. (1) If the eviction scene takes place around 1933, as is suggested by the allusions to Clifford James and R. R. Moton, and Primus Provo is eighty-seven, he would have been born in approximately 1846 and is plausibly the man who is referred to as "my negro Primus Provo" in the letter of manumission signed in 1859 by John Samuels of Macon, which the invisible man sees among the possessions set out on the curb. (2) If the scene takes place sometime after Pearl Harbor (accounting for the soldier in uniform) — say, 1942 — then the eighty-seven-year-old Primus Provo would have been born around 1855, still plausibly the "my negro" referred to in the letter, although one might expect Samuels to have noted that he was manumitting a child. (3) If the evicted man is seventy-five and the eviction takes place around 1942, then the Primus Provo referred to in the letter could not be the evicted man and would probably be his father. (4) If the eviction takes place in around 1932 and the evicted man is seventy-five, he would have been born around 1855 and would have been a child when freed in 1859. Ellison's decision to make the evicted man eighty-seven and to imply that he is the Primus Provo referred to in the letter of manumission indicates that he wished the published text to convey the impression that the eviction occurs in the early 1930s, and not during wartime. For various attempts to work out Ellison's time frame, see Marc Singer, "'A Slightly Different Sense of Time': Palimpsestic Time in *Invisible Man*," *Twentieth-Century Literature* 49 (fall 2003), 388–420; Christopher Powers, "Ambivalent Freedom: The Politics of Style in the Writings of James Joyce and Ralph Ellison," PH.D. dissertation, Johns Hopkins University, 2003; and Christopher Z. Hobson, "*Invisible Man* and African American Radicalism in World War II," *African American Review* 39, no. 3 (2005), 355–76. Hobson proposes that the Harlem section of the novel takes place over some sixteen months, most likely in 1933–34. He points out, however, that "references to Joe Louis, government production, and riots in Harlem (1935 and 1943) stretch the implicit time scheme into the next decade" (371, n. 7). Lawrence Jackson remarks that Ellison's Colonial-era research for the FWP led him to discover that "a Negro man, curiously called Primus, . . . had worked in the [printing trade] and lived in Boston and Portsmouth until he was past ninety" (RE:E, 213).

11. Ellison, Notes 1942–50, F. 2, Box 151, F. 9, Box 152, "Brotherhood," F. 1, Box 142, REP.
12. Wright, *Twelve Million Black Voices*, 144.
13. Pancho Savery, "'Not like an arrow, but a boomerang': Ellison's Existential Blues," *Approaches to Teaching Ralph Ellison's* Invisible Man, ed. Susan Resnick Parr and Pancho Savery (New York: Modern Language Association, 1989), 65–74, quote p. 72.
14. Ellison, "Priest Scene," Box 146, REP.
15. Ellison, "Perception," F. 1; "Priest Scene," Box 146, REP. In one version the deck of cards is a trick deck, consisting only of "Jokers and Aces of Spades."
16. "Allegretto . . . Moderato" are terms designating musical speed; "Allia Gallia" is a corrupted version of the opening of Julius Caesar's *Gallic Wars*; "Ultima Thule" was

the mythic land beyond the limits of known exploration in ancient and medieval times. Father Divine, who proclaimed himself to be God, was a cult leader based in Harlem during the Depression era; he was pro-capitalist but opposed to inequality based on race and gender. Although the CP was in loose alliance with him during the 1930s, many Party members questioned the connection; Father Divine was suspected of living far more comfortably than most of his ascetic followers. See Robert Weisbrot, *Father Divine and the Struggle for Racial Equality* (Urbana: University of Illinois Press, 1983); and Jill Watts, *God, Harlem, U.S.A.* (Los Angeles: University of California Press, 1992). For Father Divine's speech, titled "Man's Exigency Is God's Opportunity," see the website Libertynet.

17. Ellison, "Priest Scene," Box 146; "Suggestions for RE from HF," Notes 1942–50, F. 1, Box 151, REP. An early option was to place the priest scene between "Wheelchair" and the version of "Uncle Charles" featuring Charles Dupré, the waiter at Men's House (Notes 1942–50, F. 9, Box 152, REP). Another note associates the priest scene with "life behind the naturalistic curtain" and places it even before the "Wheelchair" episode (Notes 1942–50, F. 8, Box 152, REP). Still another possibility was to situate the priest scene late in the "Brotherhood" section, when the protagonist is speaking with Barrelhouse upon returning to Harlem (Notes 1942–50, F 5, Box 151, REP).

18. Ellison, "Perception," F. 1, Box 146, REP.

19. Ibid.

20. Ibid.; Fragments and Partial Drafts, F. 3, Box 151, REP.

21. The term *dozens* refers to a verbal contest, usually among or between men, routinely involving signifying on "Yo Momma" or other female relatives. For a description of a 1930s Harlem torchlight parade, see Richard Wright, "Torchlight March Called August 7 by Harlem Group," *Daily Worker*, 27 July 1937. The McGee and Martinsville Seven cases both involved false charges of black male sexual assault of white women. See Gerald Horne, *Communist Front? The Civil Rights Congress*, and Eric W. Rise, *The Martinsville Seven: Race, Rape, and Capital Punishment* (Charlottesville: University of Virginia Press, 1995).

22. Ellison, "Perception," F. 1, Box 146; Ellison, "Brotherhood, Cthonian", Box 143, REP. (Ellison initially misspelled Chthonian as "Cthonian.") The unnamed feminist's interest in domestic workers relates to the so-called "slave markets" in the Bronx and Brooklyn, where women, mostly African American, sought daily and weekly household employment. See Ella Baker and Marvel Cooke, "The Bronx Slave Market," *Crisis* 11 (November 1935): 330–31, 342. Carl Offord treated this subject in *The White Face* (New York: McBride, 1943), as did Wright in his unpublished *Black Hope*. Fanny Ellison (then Buford) gathered information for Wright on the topic (Wright to Ellison, 3 February 1940, F. 1, Box 76, REP; Ellison to Wright, 14 April 1940, F. 1314, Box 97, RWP).

23. Ellison, Notes 1942–50, F. 11, Box 152, REP. In a close reading of the manuscript, Shirley Jackson queried Ellison, "Douglass for Washington?"; evidently she recognized that Douglass would have been a more appropriate choice ("Shirley Hyman's Notes," Notes 1942–50, F. 6, Box 152, REP). That the Depression-era and wartime CP held up Douglass as its principal black historical hero and model for present

leadership is abundantly illustrated. Earl Browder called James Ford "the Frederick Douglass of our time." Harry Haywood, *Black Bolshevik: The Autobiography of an Afro-American Communist* (Chicago: Liberator Press, 1978), 492. Ford himself wrote that Washington, Lincoln, and Douglass were the "three great heroes of American democracy." *The Negro and the Democratic Front* (New York: International Publishers, 1938), 136. Earl Conrad noted that Douglass's *Life and Times* was a "primer" on "the Negro question" for whites and blacks alike. "Everyone wants to be FD," he wrote. *Jim Crow America* (New York: Duell, Sloan, and Pearce, 1947), 57, 191. An Abraham Lincoln Brigade unit dubbed itself the Frederick Douglass Machine Gun Company; a CP-led Harlem mass cultural organization was named the Frederick Douglass Historical and Cultural League.

24. Ellison, original typescript, F. 4, Box 147, REP.

25. Ibid. See Arthur Schlesinger, "The U.S. Communist Party," *Life* 29 (July 1946), 84–85; Schlesinger, *The Vital Center: The Politics of Freedom* (Boston: Houghton Mifflin, 1949), 121. See also Herbert Aptheker, "The Schlesinger Fraud," *Masses and Mainstream* 2 (October 1949), 23–35. Damon's comment was quoted by one Timothy Holmes (a.k.a. George Hewitt), a former Party member turned government agent, to Frederick Woltman, a *World-Telegram* reporter renowned for his anti-Communism, who subsequently wrote a series of articles titled "Reds in U.S. Exploit Woes of the Negro," *New York World-Telegram*, 22 March 1944, 1, 17, 21; 23 March 1944, 9, 24; 24 March 1944, 14. Whatever his differences and criticisms, Herndon never publicly criticized the Party or repudiated *Let Me Live*. For an account of the connections between Damon, Herndon, Woltman, and Schlesinger, see Barbara Foley, "The Rhetoric of Anticommunism in *Invisible Man*," *College English* 59 (September 1997), 530–47.

26. The CP's commitment to fighting white chauvinism, embodied in the early 1930s in the Harlem Party "trial" of a racist member, August Yokinen, impressed African Americans (Naison, *Communists in Harlem During the Depression*, 47–49). In the late 1940s, however, there occurred an internal Party struggle against white chauvinism that, in the eyes of some members, both African American and white, became obsessive. See Haywood, *Black Bolshevik*, 586–604; Pettis Perry, "Destroy the Virus of White Chauvinism," *Political Affairs* 28 (June 1949), 1–13; Lloyd Brown, "Words and White Chauvinism," *Masses and Mainstream* 3 (February 1950), 3–11. Gerald Horne concludes that the CP, while perhaps "overly zealous" as regards eradicating internal racism, was "miles ahead of other U.S. institutions in fighting racism" and "could only impress blacks, who were more accustomed to zeal in avoiding this fight" (*Black Liberation / Red Scare*, 204).

27. Ellison, Original typescript, F. 4, Box 147, REP. For a discussion and extensive illustration of the practice of name changing in the CP, see Jeffrey B. Perry, "Pseudonyms: A Reference Aid for Studying American Communist History," *American Communist History* 3, no. 1 (2004), 55–126. Ellison also changed the color of the liquid with which the invisible man's recruitment is toasted. In the original typescript it is a white liquid, presumably absinthe; in the published text it is a "clear" liquid, suggesting vodka, a drink associating the Brotherhood with Russia. See Russell Fischer, "*Invisible Man* as History," *CLA Journal* 17 (1974), 338–67. Shirley Jackson, in

her laundry list of suggestions to Ellison, queried the whiteness of the liquid (Notes 1942–50, F. 6, Box 152, REP).

28. Ellison, "Brotherhood, Louise," Box 143, REP. Copying out Othello's speech greeting Desdemona, Ellison underlined the words, "If I were now to die, / twere now to be most happy" (Notes 1942–50, F. 6, Box 152, REP).

29. Ellison, "Brotherhood, Louise," Box 143, REP. Ellison considered the possibility that the invisible man might "tell L. some revolting story which frightens her off. Substitute story of castration for that of aunt. Rejection." In a handwritten draft the invisible man tells of his having witnessed the chasing down and killing of one Luke Goldsmith ("Brotherhood, Louise," Box 143, REP). The story about the laundress and the coal oil would appear in *Juneteenth* (218–20). While he was separated from his first wife, Rose Poindexter, Ellison had a brief but intense affair with the white Communist writer Sanora Babb; it is possible that Louise embodies some of her traits. See Rampersad, RE:B, 147–51.

30. J. Saunders Redding, *On Being Negro in America* (Indianapolis: Charter Books, 1951), especially 51–90. Redding's portrait of the left here contrasts dramatically with the generally favorable representation in *No Day of Triumph*. Exploitive black-white sexual relationships are a central theme of Himes's *Lonely Crusade*. In an interview in 1955 Ellison declared that the invisible man "would have been incapable of a love affair; it would have been inconsistent with his personality" ("The Art of Fiction: An Interview," 1955, CE, 221).

31. Ellison, "Brotherhood, Louise," Box 143, REP; Ellison to Hyman, 27 October 1949, Box 6, SEHP. The passage also makes reference to the date 1 April 1981, which may refer to the congressional hearings about the revived Ku Klux Klan in the spring of that year. While the designation of April Fool's Day may comment on the hearings' hypocrisy, the date may allude to the post–Civil War promises betrayed during Reconstruction. It bears noting that 1871 was also the year of the Paris Commune. The passage is a full-to-overflowing cornucopia of literary and historical references, patently emulating *Finnegan's Wake*. Ellison was probably wise to leave it out of the published text.

32. Jane Harrison, *Prolegomena to the Study of Greek Religion*, 3rd ed. (1903; rpt. Cambridge: Cambridge University Press, 1922), 260. For a useful analysis of Harrison's treatment of the chthonian deities, as well as of the alterations in her analysis between *Prolegomena* and *Themis*, see Park McGinty, *Interpretation and Dionysos: Method in the Study of a God* (The Hague: Mouton, 1978), 71–103. Robert Butler reads *Invisible Man* as an extended re-allegorization of Dante's *Inferno*, with Jack, predictably, inhabiting the innermost circle of hell. "Dante's Inferno and Ellison's *Invisible Man*: A Study in Literary Continuity," *The Critical Response to Ralph Ellison*, ed. Robert Butler (Westport, Conn.: Greenwood Press, 2000), 95–105. For more on Sybil and the connection with Eliot's poem, see chapter 7.

33. Ellison, "Brotherhood," F. 2, Box 143, F. 1, Box 142, REP. See Harrison, *Prolegomena*, chapter 6, "The Making of a Goddess," 257–321. Ellison's notes contain a passage copied from Robert Graves's *The White Goddess* (Notes 1942–50, F. 11, Box 152, REP). In his biography of Frederick Douglass, Benjamin Quarles pointed out that Doug-

lass considered the title "The Brotherhood" for his new abolitionist journal but rejected it because it "implied the exclusion of the sisterhood." *Frederick Douglass* (Washington, D.C.: Associated Publishers, 1948), 84. The journal ended up being titled *North Star*.

34. Ellison, "Perception," F. 2, Box 146, REP; "Money Changers," Box 145, REP.

35. Ellison, "Brotherhood," F. 1, Box 142, REP.

36. Ibid.

37. Ellison, "Brotherhood, Arena Speech," Box 143; Notes 1942–50, F. 11, Box 152, REP. Gerald Early identifies the blinded African American prizefighter as Sam Langford: *The Culture of Bruising: Essays on Prizefighting, Literature, and Modern American Culture* (Hopewell, N.J.: Ecco Press, 1994), 20. As Joseph Ramsey points out, however, Ellison makes it clear that the fighter was "so dark and battered that he might have been of any nationality." "Red Pulp: Radicalism and Repression in U.S. Mid-Twentieth-Century 'Genre Fiction,'" PH.D. dissertation, Tufts University 2007, 334.

38. Ellison, "Brotherhood, Arena Speech," Box 143; Notes 1942–50, F. 11, Box 152; "Brotherhood," F. 2, Box 143; "Perception," F. 2, Box 146, REP. The invisible man's childhood memory of the bulldog called Master is originally recalled without prompting the comparison of Jack with a "toy bull terrier" (338) ("Perception," F. 2, Box 146, REP).

39. Ellison, "Brotherhood, Arena Speech," Box 143; "Perception," F. 2, Box 146, REP. The invisible man's argument by parable suggestively recalls the story of the two donkeys that combine their efforts in the Rev. Owen Whitfield's speech at the NNC in 1940 (see chapter 1). For more on the frequent prayer invocations at CP rallies and meetings, see Robin D. G. Kelley, *Hammer and Hoe: Alabama Communists During the Great Depression* (Chapel Hill: University of North Carolina Press, 1990).

40. Ellison, "Brotherhood, Arena Speech," Box 143; Ellison, "Miscellaneous Scenes," Box 145, REP.

41. Ellison, "Perception," F. 2, Box 146; "Brotherhood, Arena Speech," Box 143, REP. A number of critics acknowledge the powerful sense of unity at the arena rally but disconnect this from leftist politics. See, for example, Gregory Stephens, *On Racial Frontiers: The New Culture of Frederick Douglass, Ralph Ellison, and Bob Marley* (Cambridge: Cambridge University Press, 1999), 131.

42. Ellison, Fragments and Partial Drafts, F. 1, Box 151; "Brotherhood, Arena Speech," Box 143; "Brotherhood," F. 2, Box 143, REP. Kerry McSweeney argues that while the arena speech "is given high marks by commentators because it comes from the heart rather than the head — is emotional rather than scientific," it is manipulative and "inauthentically personal." Invisible Man*: Race and Identity* (New York: Twayne, 1988), 99.

43. Ellison, Original typescript, F. 4, Box 147; "Perception," F. 2, Box 146, REP.

44. Ellison, Fragments and Partial Drafts, F. 5, Box 151, REP.

45. Langston Hughes, "Good Morning, Revolution!," *Collected Poems of Langston Hughes*, ed. Arnold Rampersad (New York: Knopf, 1995). Ellison copied out in his notes a long passage from Malraux's novel (Notes 1942–50, F. 9, Box 152, REP). The final scene of *Days of Wrath* depicts a mass antifascist rally similar in tone to the arena rally in *Invisible Man*. See André Malraux, *Days of Wrath*, trans. Haakon M. Chevalier

(New York: Random House 1936). *Days of Wrath* was one of the books given to Elli-son by Hughes the day after Ellison arrived in Harlem (Rampersad, RE:B, 83). If the speech takes place in the early to mid-1930s, as is suggested by other chronological schemes operating in the novel, the seventy-nine years would refer, implausibly, to sometime in the mid-1850s.

46. Ellison, Miscellaneous Scenes, Box 154; Notes 1942–50, F. 3, Box 151; "Brotherhood," F. 5, Box 143, REP.

47. Ellison, "Brotherhood," F. 1, Box 142; F. 3 and 5, Box 143, REP.

48. Ellison, "Brotherhood," F. 3, Box 143, REP. Ellison would almost certainly have known that Wright, when working at the *Daily Worker* in the late 1930s, made only eighty dollars per month. Hazel Rowley, *Richard Wright: The Life and Times* (New York: Henry Holt, 2001), 127. The grandfather's statement about Saul and Paul refers to the conversion of Saul to Christianity after having a vision of Christ while on the road to Damascus. As Saul he was a persecutor of Christians; as Paul he was the preeminent proselytizer of early Christianity. See Acts 9:1–31.

49. Ellison, "Brotherhood," F. 3, Box 143, REP.

50. Thomson stressed the centrality of name changing to initiation ceremonies—at which grandfathers would be present—in the Men's House of the ancient Greek clans and tribes. George Thomson, *Aeschylus and Athens: A Study in the Social Origins of Drama* (1940; rpt. New York: Grosset and Dunlap, 1968), 91–119. The allusions here are to Douglass's third and last autobiography, *The Life and Times of Frederick Doug-lass*, in which he revealed the network that had enabled him to escape from slavery; in the two earlier versions, published before the Civil War, he could not reveal this information. Ellison was intimately acquainted with *The Life and Times*, having writ-ten an unpublished review essay of the 1942 edition issued by the Negro Publica-tion Society of America, along with Henrietta Buckmaster's *Let My People Go* (Notes 1942–50, F. 11, Box 152, REP).

51. Ellison, "Brotherhood," F. 1, Box 143, REP.

52. Ibid.

53. Ibid.; F. 3, Box 143, REP.

54. Ellison, "Brotherhood," F. 1, Box 142, REP. In a note on the interview episode Ellison wrote, "Freedom the consciousness of necessity / Possibility, the consciousness[,] the awareness of the possibility of freedom" below the phrase "first figure of im-portance to emerge during Depression" (Notes 1942–50, F. 1, Box 151, REP). Perhaps he associated this scene in the novel with the growing importance of a particular Depression-era CP organizer in Harlem.

55. In his analogies with natural processes the invisible man is playing around with concepts developed by Engels in *Anti-Duhring: Herr Eugen Duhring's Revolution in Sci-ence*, trans. Emile Burns (New York: International Publishers, 1939), and *Dialectics of Nature*, trans. Clemens Dutt (New York: International Publishers, 1940). For an analysis of the photographic lens trope in relation to different gradations of sight and blindness in *Invisible Man*, see Sara Blair, "Ellison, Photography, and the Origins of Invisibility," *The Cambridge Companion to Ralph Ellison*, ed. Ross Posnock (Cam-bridge: Cambridge University Press, 2005), 56–81.

56. Ralph Ellison, "Hattie and Julius Franklin," Box 144, REP. On featuring interracial groups of people on CP posters, see James A. Miller, Susan D. Pennypacker, and Eve Rosenhaft, "Mother Ada Wright and the International Campaign to Free the Scottsboro Boys," *American Historical Review* 106 (April 2001): 387-430, quote 410.

57. Ellison, "Brotherhood," F. 1, Box 143, REP.

58. Ellison, Notes 1942-50, F. 6, Box 152; "Brotherhood," F. 3, Box 144, REP. The Knopf editor Harry Ford, who also had urged the elimination of LeRoy, opined that the "Brotherhood chiefs' self delusion is well established elsewhere, and there's no other intrinsic merit in the scene with the Franklins" ("Suggestions for RE from HF," Notes 1942-50, F. 1, Box 151, REP). Ford's assessment of the episode's lack of "intrinsic merit" speaks volumes about the attitudes guiding his editorial suggestions. For more on the "Don't Buy Where You Can't Work" campaigns, see Cheryl Lynn Greenberg, *"Or Does It Explode?": Black Harlem in the Great Depression* (New York: Oxford University Press, 1991), 45-92. There is no basis for thinking that either Julius or Hattie Franklin had a historical prototype. It bears noting, however, that a graphic in a special issue of *New Masses* devoted to the Negro during wartime depicted an "Honor Roll of Negro War Heroes." Cited first was Dorie Miller, renowned for manning a machine gun and saving his fellow sailors during the attack on Pearl Harbor; cited third was one Julius Franklin ("Eyes on the South," *New Masses*, 27 October 1942, 6).

59. Ellison, "Brotherhood, Fired Tenement," Box 143, REP. Housing concerns figured prominently in the 233 articles Wright wrote for the *Daily Worker* in 1937. See Dexter Jeffries, "Richard Wright and the *Daily Worker*: A Native Son's Journalistic Apprenticeship," PH.D. dissertation, City University of New York, 2000. In the fall of 1942 the CP helped to organize a dramatic rent strike at a tenement on 128th Street nicknamed "House of Horrors." See *Daily Worker*, 6, 8, 9, 10, 14, 21 October 1942. According to an FBI report in 1943, NMU members were involved in helping to organize rent strikes in Harlem (Horne, *Red Seas*, 103).

60. Ellison, "Brotherhood, Fired Tenement," Box 143, REP; Wright, *Twelve Million Black Voices*, 144. In another version it is Cleo the invisible man thinks he sees going into the building. His eavesdropping recalls Ellison's experience as an FWP interviewer overhearing people talking in Harlem apartments. See "The Little Man at Chehaw Station" (CE, 519-23). The term *Ofay* is a derogatory term for white people; its origin is uncertain, but it may be a pig latin version of "foe." As the cold war heated up, one of the questions routinely asked by FBI investigators attempting to determine whether or not a given white person was a Communist was, "Have you ever had Negroes in your home?" See Robert Justin Goldstein, *Political Repression in Modern America: From 1870 to the Present* (Cambridge, Mass.: Schenkman, 1978), 303.

61. "Brotherhood, Fired Tenement," Box 143; Notes 1942-50, F. 3, Box 151; Miscellaneous Scenes, Box 145, REP.

62. Ellison, "Brotherhood, Bear in Window," Box 143, "Brotherhood," F. 5, Box 143, REP.

63. Ellison, "Brotherhood, Bear in Window," Box 143, REP. For more on "Jack the Bear," see Floyd R. Horowitz, "Ralph Ellison's Modern Version of Brer Bear and Brer Rabbit in *Invisible Man*," in Butler, *The Critical Response to* Invisible Man, 45-49; and

Charles Scruggs, *Sweet Home: Invisible Cities in the Afro-American Novel* (Baltimore: Johns Hopkins University Press, 1993), 127–27. Ellison and Murray engaged in extensive joking about "bearology" in their correspondence, where the term *bear* seems to have signified not just the folk figure but everything from a "bear" of a manuscript to a sexually aroused woman. See Albert Murray and John F. Callahan, eds., *Trading Twelves: The Selected Letters of Ralph Ellison and Albert Murray* (New York: Random House, 2001), 22, 28, 32–34, 37, 50.

64. Rhys Carpenter, *Folk Tale, Fiction and Saga in the Homeric Epics* (1946; rpt. Berkeley: University of California Press, 1956), 156; Ellison, Notes 1942–50, F. 10, Box 152, REP.

Chapter Seven: Recognizing Necessity

1. Ellison, Notes 1942–50, F. 8, Box 152, REP; Ellison, "Working Notes, CE, 349.

2. Ellison, "Working Notes," CE, 348; Ellison, "Brotherhood," F. 5, Box 143, REP; Notes 1942–50, F. 8 and 6, Box 152; F. 5, Box 151, REP.

3. Ellison, "Prologue," Box 146, REP. While one version of the skin-lightening and hair-conking passage is situated in the folder titled "Prologue," it is in a different typeface from the surrounding text and is accompanied by the notation, "Dear Frank, This section (or scene from a section) comes in the third book of the novel." ("Frank" would have been Frank Taylor, one of Ellison's editors.) Ellison contemplated including the passage during the invisible man's stay at Men's House after the paint factory explosion, while he pursues a post-Brotherhood career "among the liberals," and while he is on vacation from the Brotherhood. See "Brotherhood," F. 5, Box 144; Notes 1942–50 F. 5, Box 151; F. 6, Box 152, REP.

4. Ellison, "Bar Scene," Downtown," Box 142, REP. In one variant the second worker says, "The sure sign of a decadent society."

5. Ibid. "Bojangles" was William "Bojangles" Robinson (1878–1949), an African American vaudeville entertainer, dancer, and movie actor. While "Bojangles" Robinson is memorable primarily for his vaudeville expertise and accession to racial stereotypes, he reportedly "jumped from his seat and mounted the stage of cheer on the embattled black community" during a performance in New York City of Paul Peters's and George Sklar's leftist play *Stevedore*. See James A. Miller, *Remembering Scottsboro: The Legacy of an Infamous Trial* (Princeton: Princeton University Press, 2009), 109.

6. For different locations of the passage, see "Prologue," Box 146, and "Bar Scene, Downtown," Box 142, REP.

7. Ellison, Notes 1942–60, F. 6, Box 152; "Brotherhood," F. 5, Box 143, REP. J. Saunders Redding's portrayal of the unnamed Negro college president in *No Day of Triumph* (New York: Harper and Row, 1942), 138, includes a reference to his pro-Hitler sentiments: "There's a lot of propaganda about this totalitarian business. . . . All the Italians and eighty-five million Germans can't be all that wrong."

8. Ellison, Notes 1942–50, F. 6, Box 152; "Brotherhood," F. 4, Box 143, REP. Clinton Brewer, who had been imprisoned for murder in 1923 at the age of eighteen, was the talented composer of "Stampede in G Minor," of which Count Basie made a recording. Wright's intercession in March 1941 played a key role in Brewer's release in May;

he committed another murder in July 1941. He was saved from execution by the testimony of Wright's friend, the psychiatrist Frederic Wertham, later the director of the LaFargue Clinic, who authored *Dark Legend* (1941), a study of matricide. See Michel Fabre, *The Unfinished Quest of Richard Wright*, 2nd ed. (Urbana: University of Illinois Press, 1993), 236–37. Wright kept in his files an article on the Brewer-Wright debacle clipped from the *New York Amsterdam News* of 11 October 1941 titled "Dick Wright's Bigger Thomas Comes to Life" (F. 1806, Box 113, RWP). In 1962 Ellison referred to the case without mentioning Wright's involvement ("The World and the Jug," CE, 187). Ellison evidently helped Wright, who was out of the country in the spring of 1941, with the Brewer case, writing to him on 12 April, "Nothing has turned up on the Brewer thing" (F. 1314, Box 97, RWP). The Wright-Brewer case uncannily resembles the relationship between the novelist Norman Mailer and the prisoner and writer Jack Abbott, author of *In the Belly of the Beast* (1981): Mailer helped secure Abbott's parole in 1981, and Abbott killed again six weeks after his release.

9. Ellison, Notes 1942–50, F. 1, Box 152; F. 5, Box 151; F. 9, F. 6, Box 152; "Brotherhood," F. 2, Box 143, REP.

10. In his autobiography Horace Cayton tells of an encounter with Nancy Cunard, the wealthy left-wing antiracist and feminist, in which her robe slips open, revealing her "long tapering legs" and "prominent breasts." *Long Old Road* (New York: Trident Press, 1965), 217. For a discussion of the role played by CP theory and practice regarding the "woman question" in the founding of the modern feminist movement, see Kate Weigand, *Red Feminism: American Communism and the Making of Women's Liberation* (Baltimore: Johns Hopkins University Press, 2001). See also "Red Feminism: A Symposium," *Science and Society* 66 (winter 2002-3), 498–535.

11. Ellison, "Brotherhood," F. 2, Box 143; Ellison, "Sybil" and "Red Robe," Box 146, REP. The invisible man's views here do not diverge far from his creator's. He described to Wright his experience of being "the only man present" in a discussion of sexuality in *Native Son* with a group of "female government employees" whom he referred to as "nice, if insipid bitches"; he also shared with Wright his assessment that women "never stray far from biological reality—even when they cloak themselves with intellectual sheep's clothing" (22 April 1940 and 11 May 1940, F. 1314, Box 97, RWP).

12. Ellison, "Brotherhood," F. 4, Box 143; Notes 1942–50, F. 5, Box 151, REP.

13. Ellison, Notes 1942–50, F. 5, Box 151; Brotherhood," F. 2, Box 143; "Sybil," Box 146; Original typescript, F. 5, Box 147, REP. Ellison originally spelled "Sybil" as "Sibyl." For the argument that the sex scene between the invisible man and Sybil entails not a display but a refusal of phallic power, see Douglas Steward, "The Illusions of Phallic Agency: *Invisible Man, Totem and Taboo,* and the Santa Claus Surprise," *Callaloo* 26, no. 2 (2003), 522–35.

14. Ellison, "Working Notes," CE, 348. Ellison's emphasis on Othello's racial self-doubt may have been influenced by the reading of Shakespeare's tragedy by John Middleton Murry, whose *Shakespeare* (London: Jonathan Cape, 1936) is cited in Ellison's reading notes (Notes 1942–50, F. 4, Box 151, REP). Murry views Othello as "a man who loves entirely yet cannot quite believe that he is entirely loved" (311–21, quote p. 316).

15. Ellison, "Brotherhood," F. 2, Box 143; Notes 1942–50, F. 5, Box 151, REP. In his re-

view of *Invisible Man* Saul Bellow commented that the invisible man's "love affair with a white woman is all too brief." "Man Underground," *Commentary* 13 (June 1952), 608–10, quote p. 610. This assertion suggests that Bellow may have read the novel in manuscript but did not reread the final version when he was asked to review it; however, in a letter to me (6 October 1995) Bellow denied that he had even been acquainted with Ellison prior to the publication of *Invisible Man*. He wrote, "I reviewed it more than 40 years ago, well before Ellison and I became friends. My memory, however, is fairly reliable and I am able to tell you that I did not read his manuscript—nor was I one of those people whom Ellison consulted. Stanley Edgar Hyman was one of them and I think that Kenneth Burke was another. Ralph did speak quite often of a love affair but I'm sure my recollection of this is inexact, and inexactitude is apt to lead to gossip." Bellow's memory was faulty on at least some counts, however, since Ellison's casual statement to Albert Murray in January 1951, "I was talking with Bellow," indicates that the two men knew one another personally before the novel was published over a year later. Ellison to Murray, 8 January 1951, in Albert Murray and John F. Callahan, eds., *Trading Twelves: The Selected Letters of Ralph Ellison and Albert Murray* (New York: Random House, 2001), 25.

16. Ellison, Notes 1942–50, F. 1 and 2, Box 151, REP.

17. Ellison, Notes 1942–50, F. 2 and 5, Box 151; F. 6, Box 152, REP.

18. Ellison, Notes 1942–50, F. 8, Box 152, REP.

19. Ellison, "Brotherhood, Bear in Window," Box 143; "Brotherhood," F. 3, Box 143, REP; Keith Byerman, *Fingering the Jagged Grain: Tradition and Form in Recent Black Fiction* (Athens: University of Georgia Press, 1985), 11–40, quote p. 12.

20. Ellison, "Brotherhood," F. 3, Box 143, REP. Given the negative associations with the Dickensian names Thrilkild and Wrestrum, it is odd that Elmo, this character's original name, was historically the patron saint of sailors. St. Elmo's fire, the gathering of an intense electrical charge on a ship's mast, was routinely viewed as an omen of good luck.

21. Ellison, "Brotherhood," F. 3, Box 143; Notes 1942–50, F. 5, Box 151, REP; Ellison, "Remembering Richard Wright," *CE*, 673. The historical prototype of Wright's Nealson is probably Harry Haywood. Another parallel with Wright consists in Ellison's early characterization of the Harlem Brotherhood as hostile to the invisible man because of his superior education. See Constance Webb, *Richard Wright: A Biography* (New York: G. P. Putnam's Sons, 1968), 145. In his reply to Irving Howe in 1964 Ellison emphasized the hostility of whites toward Wright, noting, "[Wright] feared I would allow myself to be used against him by political manipulators who were not Negro and who envied and hated him" ("The World and the Jug," *CE*, 185).

22. Ellison, "Brotherhood," F. 2, Box 143; Notes 1942–50, F. 2. Box 143, REP. Possible historical prototypes for Wrestrum include Haywood, Abner Berry, Theodore Bassett, and James Ford, all prominent African American Communists whom Ellison and Wright both disliked.

23. Ellison, "Brotherhood," F. 5, Box 143, REP; Ellison to Murray, 8 January 1952, *Trading Twelves*, 25. For an aporetic reading of Ellison's "plunging" metaphor, see Jim Neighbors, "Plunging outside History: Naming and Self-Possession in *Invisible Man*," *Afri-*

can American Review 36, no. 2 (2002), 227–43. Kimberly Lamm, "Visuality and Black Masculinity in Ralph Ellison's *Invisible Man* and Romare Bearden's Photomontages," *Callaloo* 26, no. 3 (2003), 813–35, argues that Clifton's "plunge outside history" warrants a "psychoanalytically-inflected reading of *Invisible Man*."

24. Ellison remarked in 1974, "[Clifton] turn[s] against that part of himself [strong hope and investment in the Brotherhood] and tries to kill it off." Maryemma Graham and Amritjit Singh, eds., *Conversations with Ralph Ellison* (Jackson: University Press of Mississippi, 1995), 270.

25. Ellison, Notes 1942–50, F. 9, Box 152, F. 4, Box 151; "Brotherhood," F. 4 and 5, Box 143, REP. One possible historical source of Clifton is Philip Arundel, a young "lieutenant" of the Harlem black nationalist Sufi Abdul Hamid, who defected and joined the Young Communist League, where he was a popular leader. See Claude McKay, *Harlem: Negro Metropolis* (1940; rpt New York: Harcourt, Brace Jovanovich, 1968), 206. Another is Howard "Stretch" Johnson, a former Cotton Club dancer who became a YCL leader in the late 1930s. The Harlem branch of the YCL had some 250 members in 1939. See Gerald Horne, *Black Liberation/Red Scare: Ben Davis and the Communist Party* (Newark: University of Delaware Press, 1994), 58. For the argument that Clifton's physical portrayal is homoerotic, see Michael Hardin, "Ralph Ellison's *Invisible Man*: Invisibility, Race and Homoeroticism from Frederick Douglass to E. Lynn Harris," *Southern Literary Journal* 37, no. 1 (2004), 96–121.

26. Ellison, "Brotherhood," F. 5, Box 143, REP.

27. Ellison, "Brotherhood," F. 4 and 3, Box 143; Ellison, "Brotherhood, Tod Clifton," Box 143, REP. Ellison jotted in his notes to the chapter a quotation from Malraux's *Man's Fate*: "The corruption of history is a farce of marionettes" ("Brotherhood, Tod Clifton," Box 143, REP). The words of Clifton's chant closely resemble Andy Razaf's lyrics to "Sambo's Syncopated Russian Dance": "Both Lenin and Trotsky / They do the Kazotsky / To Sambo's syncopated Russian dance. / . . . Once they were about to shoot him / Where the Volga flows, / Now the Soviets salute him, / Ev'rywhere he goes." Quoted in Barry Singer, *Black and Blue: The Life and Lyrics of Andy Razaf* (New York: Schirmer, 1992), 239. Razaf's lyrics, while somewhat surreal, seem more pro-Soviet than not. W. T. Lhamon Jr. implausibly argues that the Sambo dolls possess a "subversive" quality that the invisible man misses. *Deliberate Speed: The Origins of a Cultural Style in the American 1950s* (Cambridge, Mass.: Harvard University Press, 2002), 54–56.

28. Ellison, "Brotherhood," F. 5 and 4, Box 143, REP.

29. Ellison, "Brotherhood," F. 4, 2, and 5, Box 143, REP; Ellison to Hyman, 27 October 1949, Box 6, SEHP. This draft conversation belies Ellison's later remark that Clifton cannot share with the protagonist his view that the Brotherhood has engaged in a "sell-out" because the latter is a "naïve, figurehead leader . . . too full of illusions to face up to the Machiavellian nature of political reality." Ellison to John Lucas, 29 July 1969, quoted in John F. Callahan, *Ralph Ellison's* Invisible Man: *A Casebook* (New York: Oxford University Press, 2004), 50.

30. For more on Clifton's Christ-like aura, see Alan Nadel, *Invisible Criticism: Ralph Ellison and the American Canon* (Iowa City: University of Iowa Press, 1988), 63–84.

31. Ralph Ellison, "The Little Man at Chehaw Station," CE, 509.

32. Ellison, "Brotherhood," F. 3, Box 143, REP. In an interview in 1955 Ellison responded to a query about whether or not Ras was based on Marcus Garvey. He said that he had fleshed out Ras one evening in 1950, after an interchange with "some white liberals": "[They] thought the best way to be friendly was to tell [my wife and me] what it was like to be a Negro. . . . I had already sketched Ras, but the passion of his statement came out after I went upstairs that night feeling that we needed to have this thing out once and for all" ("The Art of Fiction: An Interview," 1955, CE, 222).

33. Robert A. Hill, compiler and editor, The FBI's RACON: Racial Conditions in the United States During World War II (Boston: Northeastern University Press, 1995), 6, 32, quote p. 193; John Roy Carlson, Under Cover: My Four Years in the Nazi Underworld of America (New York: E. P. Dutton, 1943), 155. Critical commentary on Ras has tended to emphasize the Rastafarian and Ethiopianist connection implied in his name and to bypass his basis in Harlem fascists. See, for example, Robert E. Fleming, "Ellison's Black Archetypes: The Founder, Bledsoe, Ras, and Rinehart," CLA Journal 32 (June 1989), 426–32; Wilson J. Moses, "Invisible Man and the American Way of Intellectual History," Approaches to Teaching Ralph Ellison's Invisible Man, ed. Susan Resnick Parr and Pancho Savery (New York: Modern Language Association, 1989), 58–64; and D. J. Kehl, "Ellison's Invisible Man and the Rastafarians," Notes on Contemporary Literature 13 (September 1983), 9–11.

34. Roi Ottley, "New World A-Coming": Inside Black America (Cleveland: World Publishing Company, 1943), 118; Hill, The FBI's RACON, 193. Claude McKay defended Hamid against the charge of anti-Semitism in Harlem: Negro Metropolis, 198–200. See also Gerald Horne, Race War: White Supremacy and the Japanese Attack on the British Empire (New York: New York University Press, 2004), especially "War/Race," 105–27; and Paul Gilroy, Against Race: Imagining Political Culture beyond the Color Line (Cambridge, Mass.: Belknap Press of Harvard University Press, 2000), especially "Black Fascists," 231–37. The HUAC chair Martin Dies attempted to prosecute Carlson for impersonating a Nazi during his research for Under Cover. See William Gellerman, Martin Dies (New York: John Day, 1944), 273–74.

35. Ellison to Hughes, 30 January 1939, Box 54, Hughes Papers, Beinecke Library, Yale University; Ottley, "New World A-Coming," 117; Carl Ruthen Offord, The White Face (New York: McBride, 1943). Wright's unpublished novel, which toward the end features fascist organizing in Harlem, was intended as "a foreshortened, dramatic picture . . . of woman from feudalism to fascism" (Black Hope, F. 292, Box 18, RWP).

36. Thomas Schaub, American Fiction in the Cold War (Madison: University of Wisconsin Press, 1991), 112. In a letter written in 1969 Ellison remarked that in their final encounter the invisible man silences rather than kills Ras because he is in fact "yearning for a reconciliation both with reality and with Ras" (Ellison to John Lucas, 29 July 1969, quoted in Callahan, Ralph Ellison's Invisible Man, 51).

37. Ellison, Original typescript, F. 6, Box 147, REP.

38. The narrator's comment about the "laboratory experiment" could refer to Wright's analogy between novel writing and laboratory science in "How Bigger Was Born." For an instance of the argument that the hipsters signal an understanding of

history-as-boomerang that is beyond the Brotherhood's rigid abstractions, see Robert O'Meally, "The Rules of Magic: Hemingway as Ellison's 'Ancestor,'" in Callahan, *Ralph Ellison's* Invisible Man, 179–82. For a critique of Ellison's zoot-suiters as metaphysical and ahistorical creatures detached from the riots of 1943, see Charles Scruggs, *Sweet Home: Invisible Cities in the Afro-American Novel* (Baltimore: Johns Hopkins University Press, 1993), 130–31.

39. Ellison, "Brotherhood," F. 3, Box 143; Notes 1942–50, F. 2, Box 151, REP. Ellison's portrayal of history as a gambler may have drawn from Dostoevsky's story of that name, which is referenced in his notes (Notes 1942–50, F. 10, Box 152, REP).

40. Ellison, Notes 1942–50, F. 6, Box 152, REP.

41. James Frazer, *Man, God and Immortality: Thoughts on Human Progress* (Princeton: Princeton University Press, 1973), 30.

42. Ralph Ellison, "Rhinehart," Box 146, REP; Ellison, "The Art of Fiction: An Interview," CE, 223. Ellison variously spelled the name "Rhinehart" and "Rinehart"; it is possible that in the latter spelling he was signifying on Count Basie's "Harvard Blues" or on the name of the Rinehart publishing company, which Hyman held in low repute (Hyman to Ellison, 19 July 1942, Box 6, SEHP). Although in 1955 he would indicate a kinship between Rinehart and Melville's *Confidence Man* (CE, 223), Ellison observed to Hyman in 1949 that he had not read Melville's novel before Rinehart took shape (Ellison to Hyman, 21 February 1949, Box 6, SEHP). For instances of the Rinehart workshop, see Herman Beavers, "Documenting Turbulence: The Dialectics of Chaos in *Invisible Man*," *Ralph Ellison and the Raft of Hope: A Political Companion to* Invisible Man, ed. Lucas Morel (Lexington: University Press of Kentucky, 2004), 193–217; and Hsuan Hsu, "Regarding Mimicry: Race and Visual Ethics in *Invisible Man*," *Arizona Quarterly* 59, no. 2 (2003), 107–40.

43. Ellison, "The Art of Fiction: An Interview," CE, 223; Original typescript, F. 6, Box 147; Fragments and Partial Drafts, 1951, n.d., Box 150, REP. The draft in which Ellison mentions the "wealthy broker [and] reactionary writer on politics" was retyped in July 1951, so apparently he considered keeping this mention until late in the novel's composition. For a critique of the view of Rinehart as trickster hero, see Robert E. Washington, *The Ideologies of African American Literature: From the Harlem Renaissance to the Black Nationalist Revolt: A Sociology of Literature Perspective* (Lanham, Md.: Rowman and Littlefield, 2001), 213–16.

44. Ellison, Notes 1942–50, F. 10, Box 152, REP. In the published novel one of Rinehart's lovers refers to him as "Bliss" (494). Ellison said the initials B. P. stood for Bliss Proteus in his essay "Change the Joke and Slip the Yoke" (1958, CE, 110). For more on the re-creation of Rinehart as Sunraider, see Barry Shank, "Bliss, or Blackface Sentiment," *boundary* 2 30, no. 2 (2002), 47–64.

45. Gerald Horne, *The Color of Fascism: Lawrence Dennis, Racial Passing, and the Rise of Right-Wing Extremism in the United States* (New York: New York University Press, 2006), 13. In the mid-1940s the press dwelled on Dennis's swarthy complexion and tightly curled hair, but major news sources did not openly declare him to be a Negro. Horne speculates that Dennis's racial background remained officially unrevealed because so many prominent American financiers and politicians had been gulled by Dennis

that this revelation would have been too embarrassing. In *Hitler's Black Victims: The Historical Experiences of Afro-Germans, European Blacks, Africans, and African Americans in the Nazi Era* (New York: Routledge, 2003), 122, Clarence Lusane writes that Dennis was known as "the mulatto boy evangelist." Rinehart also resembles various preachers active in Harlem described by Arthur Huff Fauset in *Black Gods of the Metropolis: Negro Religious Cults of the Urban North* (Philadelphia: University of Pennsylvania Press, 1944). A comparison with Adam Clayton Powell Jr. is not entirely inappropriate. In a *New Masses* profile Richard O. Boyer wrote, "[Powell] has half a dozen jobs and half a dozen roles, ranging from insurance executive to spiritual adviser, and he slips out of one and into another with an amazing fluidity" ("Councilman Powell of Harlem," *New Masses*, 3 November 1942, 16). Ellison's notes contain a card advertising a sermon by one Rev. J. H. Tompkins titled "Behold the Invisible" (Notes 1942–50, F. 3, Box 151, REP). See also St. Clair Drake and Horace Cayton, *Black Metropolis: A Study of Negro Life in a Northern City* (New York: Harcourt, Brace and World, 1945), 412–29.

46. Ellison, Notes 1942–50, F. 10, Box 152, REP. The CP leader A. B. Magil sharply attacked Dennis as a fascist parading as an antifascist at the American Writers Congress of 1939. "Front-Line Trenches," *Fighting Words*, ed. Donald Ogden Stewart (New York: Harcourt, Brace, 1940), 144. Kenneth Burke and Joseph Freeman were the other speakers in the session.

47. Ellison, "A Lament for Tod Clifton," F. 8, Box 164, REP. This passage was not included in the anthology *Black Hands on a White Face: A Time-Piece of Experiences in a Black and White America: An Anthology*, ed. Whit Burnett (New York: Dodd, Mead, 1971), which instead featured as its Ellison contribution "The Power Line Tapped," an excerpt from the prologue (229–41). Story magazine editor Burnett—along with his first wife, Martha Foley—had published various left-leaning writers but kept the lid on their radicalism. In publishing Wright's "Bright and Morning Star," for instance, he "advised Wright to cut all reference in the story to the Scottsboro trial and the International Labor Defense" (Miller, *Remembering Scottsboro*, 154).

48. Ellison, "Brotherhood, Tod Clifton," Box 143, REP.

49. Ibid.; Dexter Jeffries, "Richard Wright and the *Daily Worker*: A Native Son's Journalistic Apprenticeship," PH.D. dissertation, City University of New York, 2000. For more on campaigns against police brutality led by the CP during the wartime years, see Hill, *The FBI's RACON*, 178–79; Horne, *Black Liberation/Red Scare*, 175–77. After the war police lynchings were a principal focus of an antiracist petition submitted to the United Nations. See William L. Patterson, ed., *We Charge Genocide: The Historic Petition to the United Nations for Relief from a Crime of the United States Government against the Negro People* (New York: International Publishers, 1951). See also Benjamin J. Davis's account of the postwar "crusade against lynching" in *Communist Councilman from Harlem: Autobiographical Notes Written in a Federal Penitentiary* (New York: International Publishers, 1969), 165–70. For an instance of the critical commentaries that occlude the Communist ambience of the funeral, see Lucas Morel's celebration of it as a "cultural melting pot" in which "Negro Americans can lead Americans of

all races into a unity of purpose": "Ralph Ellison's Democratic Individualism," in Morel, *Ralph Ellison and the Raft of Hope*, 63).

50. Ellison, Notes 1942–50, F. 1, Box 151; F. 6, Box 152, REP; Arthur Koestler, *Darkness at Noon*, trans. Daphne Hardy (New York: Macmillan, 1941). A passage about blindness from Koestler's novel serves as the epigraph to George S. Counts's and Nucia Lodge's anti-Soviet polemic, *The Country of the Blind: The Soviet System and Mind Control* (Westport, Conn.: Greenwood Press, 1949). Typical products of the eye scene industry include Kimberly W. Benston, "Controlling the Dialectical Deacon: The Critique of Historicism in *Invisible Man*," *Delta* 18 (1984), 89–103; and T. V. Reed, *Fifteen Jugglers, Five Believers: Literary Politics and the Poetics of American Social Movements* (Berkeley: University of California Press, 1992), 58–86. It is noteworthy that while most of the novel's original reviewers congratulated Ellison for his highly critical representation of the left, a few, even while agreeing with its substance, found the text's portrayal of the Brotherhood excessively cartoonish. See, for example, Bellow, "Man Underground"; Richard Chase, "A Novel Is a Novel," *Kenyon Review* 14 (autumn 1952), 678–84; and William Barrett, "Black and Blue," *American Mercury* 74 (June 1952), 100–104.

51. Ellison, Notes 1942–40, F. 4 and 5, Box 151; Original typescript, F. 4, Box 147; "Brotherhood," F. 2, Box 143, REP.

52. Ellison, "Brotherhood," F. 3 and 6, Box 143, REP.

53. Ellison, "Brotherhood," F. 6, Box 143, REP. While the Cyclopean brother does not need a historical referent, it bears noting that in May 1949 in Birmingham, Alabama, the leader of the pro-Communist Mine, Mill and Smelter Workers Union lost an eye when he and several other unionists were brutally beaten in a raid of their local by anti-Communist miners. See Richard Fried, *Nightmare in Red: The McCarthy Era in Perspective* (New York: Oxford University Press, 1990), 96.

54. Ellison, "Brotherhood," F. 3, Box 143; Elizabeth Bentley, *Out of Bondage: The Story of Elizabeth Bentley* (New York: Devin-Adair, 1951), 94–95. Bentley resolved her moral dilemma about handing in former friends by proposing, "These old friends of mine had become, in the hands of the Communist movement, no longer individuals but robots; they were chained in an intellectual and moral slavery that was far worse than any prison" (281). Jacob Golos is designated one of the "Russian-born . . . mystery men" running the CPUSA by another former Communist who became an FBI informant, Louis Budenz. Other possible prototypes for Jack among Budenz's robotic portrayals are Alexander Bittleman, Alexander Trachenberg, and J. V. Peters, one of whose Party names was Jack Roberts. Louis Budenz, *This Is My Story* (New York: McGraw-Hill, 1947), 238–42, 29, 38–41, 238–42, 247. President Truman called the Smith Act defendants "traitors" during their trial in 1949.

55. Ellison, Original typescript, F. 6, Box 147, REP. Daniel Kim argues that the "single white figure" embodies the predatory homosexual desire for black men ascribed to the novel's white male characters." *Writing Manhood in Black and Yellow: Ralph Ellison, Frank Chin, and the Literary Politics of Identity* (Stanford: Stanford University Press, 2005), 62.

56. Ellison, "Brotherhood," F. 2, Box 143; Notes 1942–50, F. 4, Box 151, and F. 152, Box 6; Miscellaneous Scenes, Box 145, REP. The closest the invisible man gets to seeking out an alternative to the Brotherhood in the 1952 text is briefly to ponder "organizing a splinter movement," which he immediately dismisses (510–11). The nightmare about the baseballs relates provocatively to a similar scene in John Sanford's *The People from Heaven* (1943; rpt. Urbana: University of Illinois Press, 1995), 78.

57. Ellison "Revenge in Mt. Morris Park," Box 146; "Brotherhood," F. 5, Box 143, REP.

58. Ellison, "Cleo and Mt. Morris Park," Box 144, REP. "Ella" most likely refers to Ella Fitzgerald. "Betty" probably refers to Betty Carter, although if it does, Cleo's allusion takes her beyond 1943 (the date of the Harlem Riot soon to be portrayed in the novel), since Carter was born in 1929 and first sang with Charlie Parker in Detroit when she was sixteen (in 1945). She toured with Lionel Hampton in the late 1940s, at which time she was given the nickname "Betty Bebop." Carter was just developing her reputation when Ellison wrote this passage, presumably in the late 1940s.

59. For more on images of Louis during the Depression and the war, see Jeffrey T. Sammons, *Beyond the Ring: The Role of Boxing in American Society* (Urbana: University of Illinois Press, 1988), 96–129; and Gerald Early, *The Culture of Bruising: Essays on Prizefighting, Literature, and Modern American Culture* (Hopewell, N.J.: Ecco Press, 1994), 23–32. For more on Ellison and Wright in relation to *The Negro Soldier*, see chapter 2.

60. While Rampersad accurately points out that no reason is ever given for the Brotherhood's purported desire to see Harlem go up in flames (RE:B, 255), many commentators reproduce without question the narrator's accusation of murder. See, for example, Nicole A. Waligora-Davis, "Riotous Discontent: Ralph Ellison's 'Birth of a Nation,'" *Modern Fiction Studies* 50, no. 2 (2004), 385–410; and A. Timothy Spaulding, "Embracing Chaos in Narrative Form: The Bebop Aesthetic in Ralph Ellison's *Invisible Man*," *Callaloo* 27, no. 2 (2004), 481–501. Thomas S. Engeman even proclaims that the Brotherhood caused the riot "to checkmate American foreign policy," evidently confusing the years of the Nonaggression Pact with those of the Grand Alliance and perhaps even the cold war ("*Invisible Man* and *Juneteenth*: Ralph Ellison's Literary Pursuit of Racial Justice," in Morel, *Ralph Ellison and the Raft of Hope*, 97). For more on Sybil as analogue to the *Odyssey*'s Sibyl, see Scruggs, *Sweet Home*, 125–27; and Christopher A. Shinn, "Masquerade, Magic, and Carnival in Ralph Ellison's *Invisible Man*," *African American Review* 36, no. 2 (2002), 243–63. The *Odyssey* as intertext of *Invisible Man* is explored at length in Patrice D. Rankin, *Ulysses in Black: Ralph Ellison, Classicism, and African American Literature* (Madison: University of Wisconsin Press, 2006). Ellison wrote of his protagonist during the riot, "Ulysses strives constantly to return home" (Notes 1942–50, F. 8, Box 152, REP).

61. Ellison, Notes 1942–50, F. 11, Box 152; "Brotherhood," F. 3, Box 143; REP. In "Harlem Is Nowhere" (1948) Ellison described the Harlem riots of 1935 and 1943 as "spontaneous outbreaks" resulting in large part from the profound disorientation of Harlem's typical "peasant" migrant, who "lack[ed] a clear explanation of his predicament—the religious ones being inadequate, and those offered by political and labor leaders obviously incomplete and opportunistic" (CE, 326, 325). This assessment, while cynical, was hardly tantamount to an accusation of murder. The tan-

gency between this essay and the early drafts of the riot episode, as well as the inclusion of the riot in "Working Notes," suggest that Ellison reworked the riot episode over several years.

62. The congressman may allude to Frank Hague, mayor of Jersey City, a "notoriously red-baiting machine politician whose perfect track record in backing Roosevelt's war policy won him the CP's change of heart" but who was "widely mocked in the press." Benjamin L. Alpers, *Dictators, Democracy, and American Public Culture: Envisioning the Totalitarian Enemy, 1920s–1950s* (Chapel Hill: University of North Carolina Press, 2003), 223.

63. Ellison, Miscellaneous Scenes, Box, 145; "Brotherhood," F. 5 and 2, Box 143, REP.

64. Ellison, "Eyewitness Story of Riot: False Rumors Spurred Mob," *New York Post*, 1 August 1943; Ellison, "Harlem 24 Hours After—Peace and Quiet Reign," *New York Post*, 3 August 1943; Ellison, Notes 1942–50, F. 4 and F. 1, Box 151; F. 8, Box 152, REP. In 1963 Ellison himself granted that the riot of 1943 is referenced in *Invisible Man* (Graham and Singh, *Conversations with Ralph Ellison*, 80–81). The rumors of Bandy's death proved false: he was wounded but not killed. An early draft passage depicts the shooting of Scofield as the cause of the riot (Notes 1942–50, F. 8, Box 152, REP). In another draft Ellison scribbled "the very rich ones" next to a description of the machine gun–wielding National Guardsmen ("Brotherhood," F. 5, Box 143, REP).

65. "Get the KKK," editorial, *New Masses*, 10 March 1942, 3; Reverend Ben Richardson, "Can it Happen in Harlem Again?," *New Masses*, 17 August 1943, 14–16; Carl Ruthen Offord, "America's Ghettos," *New Masses*, 21 September 1943, 11–12. For a discussion of white supremacist organizing of wartime strikes, see George Lipsitz, *Rainbow at Midnight: Labor and Culture in the 1940s* (Urbana: University of Illinois Press, 1994), 69–95. For more on the Harlem riot, see Harold Orlansky, *The Harlem Riot: A Study in Mass Frustration* (New York: Social Analysis, 1943); and Dominic J. Capeci, *The Harlem Riot of 1943* (Philadelphia: Temple University Press, 1977). That Ellison retained a selective concern with verisimilitude is shown in his timing how long it would take the invisible man to walk some twenty-nine blocks by clocking the trip himself (Notes 1942–50, F. 4, Box 151, REP). See Barbara Foley, *Telling the Truth: The Theory and Practice of Documentary Fiction* (Ithaca: Cornell University Press, 1986) for a discussion of the relationship between factual and fictional assertions in works of literature.

66. La Guardia quoted in Capeci, *The Harlem Riot of 1943*, 83; Ellison, "Eyewitness Story of Riot"; Richard Wright, *Twelve Million Black Voices* (1941; rpt. New York: Thunder's Mouth Press, 1988), 145; Mike Gold, "Change the World!," *Daily Worker*, 6 August 1943; Ellison, "Harlem Is Nowhere," CE, 326; For the debate over the causes of the riot, see Adam Clayton Powell Sr., *Riots and Ruins* (New York: Richard R. Smith, 1945); and Nat Brandt, *Harlem at War: The Black Experience in World War II* (Syracuse: Syracuse University Press, 1996), 183–206.

67. John F. Neville, *The Press, the Rosenbergs, and the Cold War* (Westport, Conn.: Praeger, 1995), 36.

68. The journal which more than any other specialized in accusing the CP of manipulating African American oppression for its own ends was the *Crisis*, which by 1949 was programmatically anti-Communist (and anticommunist). See also Wilson Record,

The Negro and the Communist Party (Chapel Hill: University of North Carolina Press, 1951); and William A. Nolan, *Communism versus the Negro* (Chicago: Henry Regnery, 1951). Nolan purports to "convict the Communist party through the medium of its own dialectical deceits" (vii). For a critique of Record's scholarship, see Gerald Horne, *Black and Red: W. E. B. Du Bois and the Afro-American Response to the Cold War 1944–1963* (Albany: State University of New York Press, 1986), 292–95.

69. Ellison, Notes 1942–50, F. 4, Box 151, REP; see chapters 4 and 6.

70. Ellison, Notes 1942–50, F. 4, Box 151, REP. The implied parallel between Brother Jack and Faulkner's proto-storm trooper Percy Grimm clearly articulates the logic of the "two totalitarianisms" thesis. Anne Anlin Cheng, in an anti-identitarian reading that ends up celebrating the invisible man's final acceptance of division and dismemberment, goes so far as to proclaim the castration nightmare a "quite radical" epistemological and psychological triumph, a manifestation of individualist "resistance against group consolidations." "Ralph Ellison and the Politics of Melancholia," *The Cambridge Companion to Ralph Ellison*, ed. Ross Posnock (Cambridge, England: Cambridge University Press, 2005), 121–36, quote p. 135.

71. Graham and Singh, *Conversations with Ralph Ellison*, 259–60; Ellison, Notes 1942–50, F. 6 and 9, Box 152; Original typescript, F. 6, Box 147, REP. Ellison followed the Hiss-Chambers testimony carefully, preserving an extensive set of newspaper clippings ("Chambers, Whittaker, and Alger Hiss," Box 182, REP).

72. See Ralph de Toledano, *Seeds of Treason: The True Story of the Chambers-Hiss Tragedy* (Boston: Western Islands, 1962), 169–86. The issue of recognizing handwriting also figured significantly in the espionage (1949) and conspiracy (1950) trials of the American Communist Judith Coplon. See Ellen Schrecker, "Before the Rosenbergs: Espionage Scenarios in the Early Cold War," *Secret Agents: The Rosenberg Case, McCarthyism, and Fifties America*, ed. Marjorie Garber and Rebecca L. Walkowitz (New York: Routledge, 1995), 127–41.

Chapter Eight: Beginning and Ending

1. For a discussion of the echo of Hemingway's "A Clean, Well-Lighted Place" in the epilogue, see Robert O'Meally, "The Rules of Magic: Hemingway as Ellison's 'Ancestor,'" *Speaking for You: The Vision of Ralph Ellison*, ed. Kimberly W. Benston (Washington, D.C.: Howard University Press, 1987), 255–56. While critics of the novel are divided over whether the invisible man will actually emerge, only once—in his exchange with Irving Howe—did Ellison suggest that the invisible man's claim to a world of "infinite possibilities" should be taken ironically ("The World and the Jug," CE, 157). All of Ellison's other comments after 1952 assert that the protagonist not simply plans to emerge, but, by publishing his memoir, has already done so. See Maryemma Graham and Amritjit Singh, eds., *Conversations with Ralph Ellison* (Jackson: University Press of Mississippi, 1995), 203, 220, 231; Ellison, "Change the Joke and Slip the Yoke," CE, 111; Ellison, "The Art of Fiction: An Interview," CE, 218–19.

2. James Baldwin, "Everybody's Protest Novel" (1949), *The Norton Anthology of African-American Literature*, 2nd ed., ed. Henry Louis Gates Jr. et al. (New York: Norton,

2004), 1699; Arthur Schlesinger Jr., *The Vital Center: The Politics of Freedom* (Boston: Houghton Mifflin, 1949), 57; Hannah Arendt, *The Origins of Totalitarianism*, revised ed. (1951; San Diego: Harcourt Brace Jovanovich, 1979), 473; Lionel Trilling, *The Liberal Imagination: Essays on Literature and Society* (New York: Viking, 1950), 9, 11. To posit that Trilling aided in the cultural conditioning of an anticommunist audience is not to argue that Ellison and Trilling were in agreement on many issues. For their divergences, see John S. Wright, *Shadowing Ralph Ellison* (Jackson: University Press of Mississippi, 2006), 161–93. Willie McGee was a black Mississippian accused of raping a white woman with whom he was having a consensual sexual relationship. He was the object of a concerted CP defense campaign, including a brigade of white women going door to door in Mississippi to garner support for him, that was undertaken simultaneously with the second wave of Smith Act trials. See Gerald Horne, *Communist Front? The Civil Rights Congress, 1946–1956* (Rutherford, N.J.: Fairleigh Dickinson University Press, 1988), 87–97; Jessica Mitford, *A Fine Old Conflict* (New York: Knopf, 1971).

3. For discussions of the spiral theory of history in the Marxist tradition, see Frederick Engels's 1840 letter to the *Telegraph fur Deutschland*, available on Marxists.org; and Vladimir Lenin, "Summary of Dialectics," *Collected Works*, 44 vols. (Moscow: Foreign Language Publishing House, 1960–70), vol. 38, 221–22, and "On the Question of Dialectics," *Collected Works*, vol. 38, 359. Ellison's explanation in 1972 of the boomerang metaphor is not illuminating: "I described [history] as a parabola because a boomerang moves in a parabola. It goes and comes. It is never the same thing. There is implicit in the image the old idea that those who do not learn from history are doomed to repeat its mistakes, history comes back and hits you. But you really cannot break down a symbol rationally. It allows you to say things that cannot really be said" (Graham and Singh, *Conversations with Ralph Ellison*, 231). His confusing metaphors have not prevented critics from using them to characterize the Brotherhood's view of history as at once teleological and mechanical, cyclical and linear. See, for example, Marc Singer, "'A Slightly Different Sense of Time': Palimpsestic Time in *Invisible Man*," *Twentieth-Century Literature* 49, no. 3 (2003), 388–420.

4. For the argument that the voices heard in the epilogue and in the 1982 preface are virtually identical, and that the preface thus functions as a "concluding sequel" to the novel, see Steven Marx, "Beyond Hibernation: Ralph Ellison's 1982 Version of *Invisible Man*," *Black American Literature Forum* 23 (winter 1989), 701–21, quote p. 708. See also Myles Weber, *Consuming Silences: How We Read Authors Who DON'T Publish* (Athens: University or Georgia Press, 2005), 117–31 and H. William Rice, *Ralph Ellison and the Politics of the Novel* (Lanham, Md.: Lexington Books, 2003).

5. For a discussion of the prologue and epilogue in the context of the authenticating apparatus inherited from the genre of the slave narrative, see Robert B. Stepto, "Literacy and Hibernation: Ralph Ellison's *Invisible Man*," in Benston, *Speaking for You*, 360–85. Ellison's use of a prologue and epilogue may have been influenced by Gilbert Murray's discussion the role played in Greek tragedies by such framing devices, which enable the Chorus to speak directly to the audience and invoke the presence of the "rerisen god." See Jane E. Harrison, *Themis: A Study of the Social Ori-*

gins of Greek Religion, with an Excursus on the Ritual Forms Preserved in Greek Tragedy by Gilbert Murray (1912; rpt. Cleveland: World Publishing, 1962), 359–63, quote p. 363. For an analysis of the epilogue's movement from an implied reader who is black to one who is presumably raceless, see Michel Fabre, "The Narrator/Narratee Relationship in *Invisible Man*," *Callaloo* 8 (fall 1985), 535–43. Ellison remarked in a seminar in Salzburg in 1954 that the novel was addressed primarily to black readers: "There are lots of little things, sayings and folklore, that whites can't really understand." Quoted in Robert O'Meally, introduction to *New Essays on* Invisible Man, ed. Robert O'Meally (Cambridge, England: Cambridge University Press, 1988), 22, n. 28. See also Ralph Ellison, "Some Questions and Some Answers," 1958, *CE*, 296. For an analysis of Ellison's rhetoric of consensus in the prologue and epilogue, see Robert Bataille, "Ellison's *Invisible Man*: The Old Rhetoric and the New," *Black American Literature Forum* 12, no. 2 (1978), 43–45. See also Valerie Smith's argument that in the prologue and the epilogue Ellison "loads the dice" in his protagonist's favor." "The Meaning of Narration," in O'Meally, *New Essays on* Invisible Man, 25–53, quote p. 52.

6. In commentaries after the novel's publication Ellison gave widely varying accounts of the composition of the prologue and epilogue, sometimes indicating that they were formed in his mind from the start, sometimes stating that, although "I am an invisible man" came to him in 1945, the rest of the prologue and the entire epilogue were written late in the novel's creation. See the 1982 introduction to *Invisible Man*, xxiii; Graham and Singh, *Conversations with Ralph Ellison*, 263; Ellison, "The Art of Fiction: An Interview," *CE*, 220.

7. Richard Wright, "How Bigger Was Born," *Native Son* (1940; reprinted and revised, New York: Library of America, 1993), 540; Ellison, "Prologue," Box 146, REP; Feodor Dostoevsky, *Notes from Underground, The Short Novels of Dostoevsky*, trans. Constance Garnett (New York: Dial Press, 1945), 132; Wright, "The Man Who Lived Underground," *Eight Men* (New York: Thunder's Mouth Press, 1987), 27–92. Ellison later denied that Wright's novella significantly influenced his portrayal of his basement-dwelling protagonist, claiming the preponderant influence of Dostoevsky (1982 introduction to *Invisible Man*, xix; Ellison to Hyman, 29 May 1970, Box 6, SEHP; Ellison, "On Initiation Rites and Power," *CE*, 541). For more on the influence of Dostoevsky, see Joseph Frank, "Ralph Ellison and a Literary 'Ancestor': Dostoevski," *Modern Critical Interpretations of* Invisible Man, ed. Harold Bloom (Philadelphia: Chelsea House, 1999), 45–60. For a discussion of the homage paid in the published opening to H. G. Wells's *The Invisible Man*, see Michael Hardin, "Ralph Ellison's Invisible Man: Invisibility, Race, and Homoeroticism from Frederick Douglass to E. Lynn Harris," *Southern Literary Journal* 37, no. 1 (2004), 96–121. Also invoked in the prologue and epilogue is Miguel de Unamuno's *The Tragic Sense of Life*, where the philosopher proclaims that he is "no stranger to other men, being made of flesh and bone"; that he is suspended between yes and no; and that "progress" is a "disease." *The Tragic Sense of Life*, trans. J. E. Crawford Fitch (1921; rpt. New York: Dover, 1954), 1, 13–14, 19.

8. Ellison, "Prologue," Box 146, REP; Richard Wright, *Lawd Today* (1963; rpt. Boston: Northeastern University Press, 1993). Although *Lawd Today* was not published until after Wright's death, it was written in the late 1930s and would have been available

for Ellison to read in manuscript. Gwendolyn Brooks's "The Sundays of Satin-Legs
Smith" (1945) similarly satirizes the dress of an alienated would-be "sharpie."

9. Ellison, "Prologue," Box 146, REP.

10. Ibid.; Ellison, "Men's House," Box 145, REP.

11. Ellison, "Prologue," Box 146, REP.

12. Ibid. The harsh racialization of invisibility in these early drafts of the novel's open-ing calls into question critical discussions of the presumed benefits of living behind the veil. See, for example, Pierre A. Walker's statement that the novel displays invisi-bility to be "both a good in itself and . . . a way of transcending the constraints im-posed by being invisible." "Theoretical Dimensions of *Invisible Man*," *Literary Influence and African-American Writers: Collected Essays*, ed. Tracy Mishkin (New York: Garland, 1996), 245–68, quote 250.

13. Ellison, "Prologue," Box 147; "Fragments and Partial Drafts," F. 1, Box 150; Origi-nal typescript, F. 6, Box 147, REP. Steven Tracy points out that "criticism from the Left berated Armstrong for gleefully reaping the benefits of the capitalist system by abandoning his New Orleans roots for commercial appeal and not retaining his artistic integrity." "The Power to Weld the Fragments," *A Historical Guide to Ralph Ellison*, ed. Steven C. Tracy (Oxford: Oxford University Press, 2004), 99. On Arm-strong's role as a goodwill ambassador for the State Department in the mid-1950s, see Penny Von Eschen, *Race against Empire: Black Americans and Anticolonialism 1937–1957* (Ithaca: Cornell University Press, 1997), 177–80. For more on Bolden, an early jazz pioneer who left no recordings but enjoys a nearly mythical reputation, see Don Marquis, *In Search of Buddy Bolden: First Man of Jazz* (Baton Rouge: Louisiana State University Press, 1978). In the early twentieth century Bolden performed for inte-grated working-class audiences; New Orleans's Union Sons Hall, one of his venues, became known as "Funky Butt Hall" (68). See also Sam Yaffe, *Fascinating Rhythm: Reading Jazz in American Writing* (Princeton: Princeton University Press, 2006), 61–98. Lawrence Jackson proposes that Ellison substituted Armstrong for Bolden on the advice of his editor Albert Erskine (RE:E, 426).

14. Ellison, "Prologue," Box 147, REP; Ellison, "Let Us Consider the Harlem Crime Wave," F. 3, Box 101, REP. In this seething commentary, apparently written before the riot in August 1943, Ellison repeatedly terms the living standards imposed upon Harlemites a "crime," a "treason against the State" that is "their own making—they who own and rule the land—not ours."

15. Ellison, "Prologue," Box 147, REP. The invisible man originally identifies his antago-nist as "Consolidated Edison," not Monopolated Light and Power. The theft of elec-tricity was common in low-income New York neighborhoods in the 1930s and 1940s. See Cheryl Lynn Greenberg, *Or Does It Explode? Black Harlem in the Great Depression* (Chapel Hill: University of North Carolina Press, 1991), 175–78. Ellison himself en-gaged in the practice of siphoning off electrical power (Jackson, RE:E, 280–81). He clipped and saved a newspaper article dated July 1948 about an entire hobo jungle living off tapped power lines (Notes 1942–50, F. 1, Box 151, REP). Roi Ottley and William Weatherby reported that in Depression-era New York over ten thousand Negroes lived in barely converted basements that were termed "dungeons." *The*

Negro in New York (New York: New York Public Library, 1967), 266–67. John S. Wright notes that in his specification of filament bulbs the narrator glancingly alludes to the Negro inventor and electrical engineer Lewis Latimer, the "black Edison," who patented the filament bulb in 1881 and superintended the electrification of several large cities, including New York. *Shadowing Ralph Ellison* (Jackson: University Press of Mississippi, 2006), 158–59.

16. Ellison, Original typescript, F. 1, Box 147, REP; Douglas Ford, "Crossroads and Cross-Currents in *Invisible Man*," *Modern Fiction Studies* 45, no. 4 (1999), 887–904, quote p. 897.

17. Ralph Ellison, "At Mary's," F. 1, Box 142, REP. Russell may reflect an element of Ellison's own experience. Ellison told Sanora Babb—with whom he had an affair while separated from his first wife, the African American Communist singer and dancer Rose Poindexter—that he viewed Rose as a "symbol" (Ellison to Babb, 7 February 1942, quoted in Rampersad, RE:B, 150).

18. Ellison, "Prologue," Box 147, REP. At one point Ellison designated as chapter 25 what we know as the epilogue (Fragments and Partial Drafts, F. 1, Box 150, REP).

19. Ellison, Notes 1942–50, F. 9, Box 152, REP.

20. Ellison, Original typescript, F. 6, Box 147; Miscellaneous Scenes, Box 145, REP.

21. Ellison, Original typescript, F. 6, Box 147; Fragments and Partial Drafts, F. 3, Box 151, REP.

22. It has been argued that the three different stages of the invisible man's meditation describe an important psychological and political progression; these stages are not discernible in the early drafts. See Fabre, "The Narrator/Narratee Relationship in *Invisible Man*"; Joseph W. Trimmer, "The Grandfather's Riddle in Ralph Ellison's *Invisible Man*," *Black American Literature Forum* 12, no. 2 (1978), 46–50; and Christopher Z. Hobson, "*Invisible Man* and African American Radicalism in World War II," *African American Review* 39, no. 3 (2005), 355–76. In a sharp critique of the elevation of the grandfather in the epilogue, Donald Gibson notes that the old man "advocates a . . . war so private and subjective that the enemy does not even recognize that he is at war." *The Politics of Literary Expression: A Study of Major Black Writers* (Westport, Conn.: Greenwood Press, 1981), 66. For a defense of "affirming the principle" from Gibson's critique, see Meili Steele, "Metatheory and the Subject of Democracy in the World of Ralph Ellison," *New Literary History* 27, no. 3 (1996), 473–502. Steele's essay is an instance of the blending of antifoundationalist epistemology with foundationalist liberal pluralism that undergirds much contemporary commentary on Ellison.

23. Ellison, Original typescript, F. 6, Box 147, REP.

24. Ellison, Fragments and Partial Drafts, 1951 and n.d., Box 150; Original typescript, F. 6, Box 147; "Manhole," Box 145; Notes 1942–50, F. 6, Box 152, REP.

25. Ellison, Fragments and Partial Drafts, 1951 and n.d., Box 150, REP. At first only Lenin and Napoleon are mentioned; participants in the Grand Alliance are latecomers to the list. For more on the rhetoric of cold war liberalism, see Christopher Lasch, *The Agony of the American Left* (New York: Knopf, 1969); Mary Sperling McAuliffe, *Crisis on the Left: Cold War Politics and American Liberals, 1947–1954* (Amherst: University of Massachusetts Press, 1978); and Job L. Dittberner, *The End of Ideology and American*

Social Thought: 1930–1960 (Ann Arbor: University of Michigan Research Press, 1979). For a defense of cold war liberalism, see Guenter Lewy, *The Cause That Failed: Communism in American Political Life* (New York: Oxford University Press, 1990).

26. Ralph Ellison, "That Same Pain, That Same Pleasure," 1961, CE, 80. Christopher Shannon faults the epilogue for "celebrat[ing] an American pluralism completely at odds with the reality presented in the novel." *A World Made Safe for Differences: Cold War Intellectuals and the Politics of Identity* (Lanham, Md.: Rowman and Littlefield, 2001), 53. Julia Eichelberger, by contrast, reads the novel as a "hymn to democracy" and the epilogue as a "celebration of heteroglossia." *Prophets of Recognition: Ideology and the Individual in Novels of Ralph Ellison, Toni Morrison, Saul Bellow, and Eudora Welty* (Baton Rouge: Louisiana State University Press, 1999), 25, 55. In his original formulation of ambiguity as division in the mind, Ellison drew upon William Empson's *Seven Types of Ambiguity*, 2nd ed. (1930; rpt. London: Chatto and Windus, 1947).

27. Ellison, "The Art of Fiction: An Interview," 1955, CE, 223–24. For a contemporaneous discussion of the importance of desegregation to the international image of the United States during the early cold war, see Lee Nichols, *Breakthrough on the Color Front* (New York: Random House, 1954).

28. See Ellison, "Norton in the Subway," Box 145, REP. The passage was originally located midway through the "Brotherhood" section of the novel. In their correspondence Ellison and Wright routinely used the phrase "the boys" to refer to CP members. For more on the exclusion of Communists from the category of "real Americans" in cold war discourse, see Joel Kovel, *Red-Hunting in the Promised Land: Anticommunism and the Making of America* (New York: Basic Books, 1994).

29. Ellison, "The World and the Jug," CE, 161–62; Simone de Beauvoir, *The Ethics of Ambiguity*, trans. Bernard Frechtman (New York: Philosophical Library, 1948). Ellison cited Beauvoir in his notes to *Invisible Man* (Notes 1942–50, F. 2, Box 151, REP). Jerry Watts criticizes at length the existentialist notion of freedom in *Invisible Man: Heroism and the Black Intellectual: Ralph Ellison, Politics, and Afro-American Intellectual Life* (Chapel Hill: University of North Carolina Press, 1994). For more on the New Critics' enshrinement of ambiguity and paradox, see Alexander Karanikas, *Tillers of a Myth: Southern Agrarians as Social and Literary Critics* (Madison: University of Wisconsin Press, 1966); and Tobin Siebers, *Cold War Criticism and the Politics of Skepticism* (New York: Oxford University Press, 1993). For a critique of the invisible man's yes/no as pseudo-dialectic, see Timothy Brennan, "Ellison and Ellison: The Solipsism of *Invisible Man*," *CLA Journal* 25 (December 1981), 162–81. Ellison became involved in the activities of the CIA-backed Congress for Cultural Freedom starting in 1956 (Rampersad, *RE:B*, 330–31).

30. For recent commentaries on *Invisible Man* that in various ways affirm the connection between liberal pluralist politics and antifoundational epistemology, see the following essays in Lucas Morel, ed., *Ralph Ellison and the Raft of Hope: A Political Companion to* Invisible Man (Lexington: University Press of Kentucky, 2004); James Seaton, "Affirming the Principle," 22–36; Danielle Allen, "Ralph Ellison on the Tragi-Comedy of Citizenship," 37–57; and Lucas Morel, "Ralph Ellison's Democratic Individualism," 58–90. For recent skeptical readings of the politics of the epilogue, see Kenneth

Warren's commentary on the "cultural turn in black politics" in *So Black and Blue: Ralph Ellison and the Occasion of Criticism* (Chicago: University of Chicago Press, 2003), 25–41; and Roderick Ferguson's discussion of the rhetoric of diversity in *Aberrations in Black: Toward a Queer Color Critique* (Minneapolis: University of Minnesota Press, 2004), 54–81.

31. Notably some early readers of the novel remarked that its treatment of the "Communist Party, or the Brotherhood" enables the white reader to think, "Ah, they're the guilty ones. They're the ones who mistreat him, not us." Ellison replied that the novel was "not an attack on white society" ("The Art of Fiction: An Interview," 1955, *CE*, 221). Addison Gayle argued in 1976 that the novel's claim to universality is spurious because all the white characters are so negatively portrayed that none of them is "free to experience the immense possibilities of life." *The Way of the New World: The Black Novel in America* (Garden City, N.Y.: Doubleday, 1976), 256–57. For the argument that Ellison's address to "you" in the epilogue queries the racism accompanying many white readers' embrace of an "abstract, coherent selfhood," see Lesley Larkin, "Postwar Liberalism, Close Reading, and 'You': Ralph Ellison's *Invisible Man*," *LIT: Literature Interpretation Theory* 19 (July–September 2008), 268–304, quote p. 295.

32. T. S. Eliot, *Four Quartets* (New York: Harcourt, Brace and World, 1943), 58; Paul Robeson, "American Negroes in the War" (1943), *Paul Robeson Speaks: Writings, Speeches, Interviews, 1918–1974*, ed. Philip S. Foner (New York: Citadel Press, 1978), 147.

33. Earl Robinson, "Ballad for Americans," available on the Lyrics Playground website; Barbara Dianne Savage, *Broadcasting Freedom: Radio, War, and the Politics of Race, 1938–1948* (Chapel Hill: University of North Carolina Press, 1999), 76; *Native Land* epilogue quoted in William Alexander, *Film on the Left: American Documentary Film from 1931 to 1942* (Princeton: Princeton University Press, 1981), 239. For a defense of "Ballad for Americans" against the charge of sentimental patriotism, see Michael Denning, *The Cultural Front: The Laboring of American Culture in the Twentieth Century* (London: Verso, 1997), 115–18, 128–32. At the American Writers Congress in 1939 there was a forum about using the airwaves on behalf of progressive politics. "Aerial Assault," *Fighting Words*, ed. Donald Ogden Stewart (New York: Harcourt, Brace, 1940), 79–105.

34. Earl Robinson, "Ballad for Americans."

35. William O. Douglas, address, National Book Award, 27 January 1953, Special Collections, Butler Library, Columbia University; Savage, *Broadcasting Freedom*, 106–53; Ellison to Murray, 9 April 1953, in Albert Murray and John F. Callahan, eds., *Trading Twelves: The Selected Letters of Ralph Ellison and Albert Murray* (New York: Random House, 2001), 45. MacLeish, writing to Pearl Buck earlier that month about "Communists in teaching," expressed disapproval of some of the extreme tactics of "Senator McCarthy" but noted, "No man who accepts a prior loyalty to any authority other than his own conscience, his own judgment of the truth, should be permitted to teach in a free society." He boasted, "I was, I think I can say without immodesty, one of the first American writers to attack the Marxists." *Letters of Archibald MacLeish*, ed. R. H. Winnick (Boston: Houghton Mifflin, 1983), 363–65.

selected bibliography

Bibliographical Note

This bibliography contains a complete listing of all writings by Ralph Ellison relevant to the composition of *Invisible Man*. It also contains a compilation of all the book-length studies of Ellison's oeuvre cited in this study. Individual journal articles, book chapters, and anthologized essays are referenced in the text and endnotes; their authors are listed in the index. A full listing of the hundreds of contributions to Ellison scholarship is available online at the MLA International Bibliography.

Library and Manuscript Collections

Interview with Abner Berry. Oral History of the American Left, Tamiment Library, New York University, New York City.

Interview with Howard "Stretch" Johnson. Oral History of the American Left, Tamiment Library, New York University, New York City.

Josie Craig Berry Papers. Special Collections, University of Oklahoma Library, Tulsa, Okla.

"The Negro in New York," Federal Writers Project. Schomburg Center for Research in Black Culture, New York City.

Ralph Ellison Papers. Manuscript Collection, Library of Congress, Washington, D.C.

Richard B. Moore Papers. Schomburg Center for Research in Black Culture, New York City.

Richard Wright Papers. James Weldon Johnson Collection. Beinecke Library, Yale University, New Haven, Conn.

Stanley Edgar Hyman Papers. Manuscript Collective, Library of Congress, Washington, D.C.

Ellison's Uncollected Published Essays, Reviews, and Short Stories, Listed by Date

"Creative and Cultural Lag." *New Challenge: A Literary Quarterly* 2, no. 2 (1937): 90–91.

"Slick Gonna Learn." *Direction* 2 (September 1937): 10–11, 14, 16.

"Practical Mystic." *New Masses*, 16 August 1938: 25–26.

"Anti-Semitism among Negroes." *Jewish People's Voice*, 3 April 1939: 3, 8.

"Judge Lynch in New York." *New Masses*, 15 August 1939: 15-16.

"Ruling-Class Southerner." *New Masses*, 5 December 1939: 27.

"Javanese Folklore." *New Masses*, 26 December 1939: 25-26.

"Camp Lost Colony." *New Masses*, 6 February 1940: 18-19.

"The 'Good Life.'" *New Masses*, 20 February 1940: 27.

"TAC Negro Show," *New Masses*, 27 February 1940: 29-30.

"Hunters and Pioneers." *New Masses*, 19 March 1940: 26.

"Anti-War Novel." *New Masses*, 18 June 1940: 29-30.

"The Birthmark." *New Masses*, 2 July 1940: 16-17.

"Stormy Weather." *New Masses*, 24 September 1940: 20-21.

"Big White Fog." *New Masses*, 12 November 1940: 22-23.

"Argosy across the USA." *New Masses*, 26 November 1940: 24.

"Negro Prize Fighter." *New Masses*, 17 December 1940: 26-27.

"Philippine Report." *Direction* 4 (summer 1941): 13.

"Richard Wright and Recent Negro Fiction." *Direction* 4 (summer 1941): 12-13.

"Recent Negro Fiction." *New Masses*, 5 August 1941: 22-26.

"The Great Migration." *New Masses*, 2 December 1941: 23-24.

David Wilson [Ralph Ellison], "Treasury of Negro Literature." *Sunday Worker*, 8 March 1942: 6.

"Statement of Policy." Editorial, *Negro Quarterly* 1, no. 1 (spring 1942): 3-4.

"Transition." *Negro Quarterly* 1, no. 1 (spring 1942): 87, 91, 92.

"Native Land." *New Masses*, 2 June 1942: 29.

"Editorial Comment." *Negro Quarterly* 1, no. 2 (summer 1942): i-iv.

"Editorial Comment." *Negro Quarterly* 1, no. 3 (fall 1942): 195-96, 240.

"Editorial Comment." *Negro Quarterly* 1, no. 4 (winter-spring 1943): 295-302.

"Eyewitness Story of Riot: False Rumors Spurred Mob," *New York Post*, 1 August 1943.

"Harlem 24 Hours After—Peace and Quiet Reign," *New York Post*, 3 August 1943.

"New World A-Coming," *Tomorrow* 3 (September 1943): 68.

"The Booker T." *New Republic* 114 (1946): 261-62.

"The Battle Royal." *Horizon* 16 (October 1947): 104-18.

"The Battle Royal." *'48: Magazine of the Year* 2 (January 1948): 14-15, 20-21, 32.

"Collaborator with His Own Enemy." *New York Times Book Review*, 19 February 1950: 4.

"The Invisible Man: Prologue to a Novel." *Partisan Review*, January–February 1952: 31-40.

"Did You Ever Dream Lucky?" *New World Writing* 5 (April 1954): 134-45.

"Beware of the Snake Who Dresses Like a Man." *People's Daily World*, 17 November 1954: 5.

"February." *Saturday Review of Literature*, 1 January 1955: 25.

"Out of the Hospital and under the Bar." *Soon One Morning: New Writing by American Negroes, 1940–1962*, ed. Herbert Hill, 242-90. New York: Knopf, 1963.

"The Power Line Tapped" (prologue to *Invisible Man*). *Black Hands on a White Face: A Time-Piece of Experiences in a Black and White America: An Anthology*, 229-41. Ed. Whit Burnett. New York: Dodd, Mead, 1971.

Essay Collections, Interviews, Published Letters,
and Published Fiction by Ellison

The Collected Essays of Ralph Ellison, rev. edn. Ed. John F. Callahan. New York: Modern
Library, 2003.

Conversations with Ralph Ellison. Ed. Maryemma Graham and Amrijit Singh. Jackson: University Press of Mississippi, 1995.

Flying Home and Other Stories. Ed. John F. Callahan. New York: Random House, 1996.

Invisible Man. 1952; rpt. with an introduction. New York: Random House, 1982.

Juneteenth: A Novel. Ed. John F. Callahan. New York: Random House, 1999.

Trading Twelves: The Selected Letters of Ralph Ellison and Albert Murray. Ed. Albert Murray and
John F. Callahan. New York: Modern Library, 2000.

Volumes of Critical Commentary, Theses,
and Book-Length Studies of Ellison

Benston, Kimberly, ed. *Speaking for You: The Vision of Ralph Ellison*. Washington, D.C.:
Howard University Press, 1987.

Bloom, Harold, ed. *Modern Critical Interpretations*: Invisible Man. Philadelphia: Chelsea
House, 1999.

Butler, Robert J., ed. *The Critical Response to Ralph Ellison*. Westport, Conn.: Greenwood
Press, 2000.

Callahan, John F., ed. *Ralph Ellison's* Invisible Man: *A Casebook*. New York: Oxford University Press, 2004.

Jackson, Lawrence. *Ralph Ellison: Emergence of Genius*. New York: John Wiley, 2002.

Jeffries, Dexter. "Richard Wright and the *Daily Worker*: A Native Son's Journalistic Apprenticeship." PH.D. dissertation, City University of New York, 2000.

Kim, Daniel Y. *Writing Manhood in Black and Yellow: Ralph Ellison, Frank Chin, and the Literary
Politics of Identity*. Stanford: Stanford University Press, 2005.

List, Robert N. *Dedalus in Harlem: The Joyce-Ellison Connection*. Washington, D.C.: University Press of America, 1982.

McSweeney, Kerry. Invisible Man: *Race and Identity*. New York: Twayne, 1988.

Morel, Lucas. *Ralph Ellison and the Raft of Hope: A Political Companion to* Invisible Man.
Lexington: University Press of Kentucky, 2004.

Nadel, Alan. *Invisible Criticism: Ralph Ellison and the American Canon*. Iowa City: University
of Iowa Press, 1988.

O'Meally, Robert. *The Craft of Ralph Ellison*. Cambridge, Mass.: Harvard University Press,
1980.

Parr, Susan Resnick, and Pancho Savery. *Approaches to Teaching Ralph Ellison's* Invisible
Man. New York: Modern Language Association, 1989.

Porter, Horace A. *Jazz Country: Ralph Ellison in America*. Iowa City: University of Iowa
Press, 2001.

Posnock, Ross. *The Cambridge Companion to Ralph Ellison*. Cambridge, England: Cambridge University Press, 2005.

Powers, Christopher. "Ambivalent Freedom: The Politics of Style in the Writings of James Joyce and Ralph Ellison." PH.D. dissertation, Johns Hopkins University, 2003.

Rampersad, Arnold. *Ralph Ellison: A Biography*. New York: Knopf, 2007.

Rankin, Patrice D. *Ulysses in Black: Ralph Ellison, Classicism, and African American Literature*. Madison: University of Wisconsin Press, 2006.

Reavis, Dick Johnson. "Defamatory Man: Ralph Ellison and the Communist Party." M.A. Thesis, University of Texas, Arlington, 1998.

Reilly, John, ed. *Twentieth-Century Interpretations of* Invisible Man. Englewood Cliffs, N.J.: Prentice-Hall, 1970.

Rice, H. William. *Ralph Ellison and the Politics of the Novel*. Lanham, Md: Lexington Books, 2003.

Sundquist, Eric J., ed. *Cultural Contexts for* Invisible Man. Boston: Bedford Books, 1995.

Thomas, P. L. *Reading, Learning, Teaching Ralph Ellison*. New York: Peter Lang, 2008.

Tracy, Steven C. *A Historical Guide to Ralph Ellison*. Oxford: Oxford University Press, 2004.

Warren, Kenneth. *So Black and Blue: Ralph Ellison and the Occasion of Criticism*. Chicago: University of Chicago Press, 2003.

Watts, Jerry Gafio. *Heroism and the Black Intellectual: Ralph Ellison, Politics, and Afro-American Intellectual Life*. Chapel Hill: University of North Carolina Press, 1994.

Wright, John S. *Shadowing Ralph Ellison*. Jackson: University Press of Mississippi, 2006.

index

Made in the USA
Monee, IL
06 November 2024

Barbara Foley is Professor II in the English
Department at Rutgers, the State University
of New Jersey, Newark. She is the author of
*Spectres of 1919: Class and Nation in the Making of
the New Negro* (2003), *Radical Representations:
Politics and Form in U.S. Proletarian Fiction, 1929–
1941* (1993), and *Telling the Truth: The Theory and
Practice of Documentary Fiction* (1986).

Library of Congress Cataloging-in-Publication Data
Foley, Barbara, 1948–
Wrestling with the left : the making of Ralph Ellison's
Invisible man / Barbara Foley.
p. cm.
Includes bibliographical references and index.
ISBN 978-0-8223-4817-7 (cloth : alk. paper)
ISBN 978-0-8223-4829-0 (pbk. : alk. paper)
1. Ellison, Ralph. Invisible man. 2. Ellison, Ralph—
Political and social views. I. Title.
PS3555.L6251534 2010
813'.54—dc22
2010005246